# DATE DUE

| | | | |
|---|---|---|---|
| | | | |
| | | | |
| | | | |
| | | | |
| | | | |
| | | | |
| | | | |
| | | | |
| | | | |
| | | | |
| | | | |
| | | | |
| | | | |
| | | | |
| | | | |
| | | | |
| | | | |
| | | | |
| | | | |

DEMCO 38-296

OXFORD GUIDES TO CHAUCER

*The Shorter Poems*

*Oxford Guides to Chaucer*

# The
# Shorter Poems

A. J. MINNIS
with V.J. SCATTERGOOD
and J.J. SMITH

CLARENDON PRESS · OXFORD

1995

*ess, Walton Street, Oxford* OX2 6DP

*ford New York*
*kland Bangkok Bombay*
*Town Dar es Salaam Delhi*
*ng Kong Istanbul Karachi*
Kuala Lumpur *Madras Madrid Melbourne*
*Mexico City Nairobi Paris Singapore*
*Taipei Tokyo Toronto*
*and associated companies in*
*Berlin Ibadan*

*Oxford is a trade mark of Oxford University Press*

*Published in the United States*
*by Oxford University Press Inc., New York*

© *A. J. Minnis, V. J. Scattergood, J. J. Smith* 1995

*British Library Cataloguing in Publication Data*
*Data available*

*Library of Congress Cataloging in Publication Data*
*Minnis, A. J. (Alastair J.)*
*The shorter poems / A. J. Minnis.*
*(Oxford guides to Chaucer)*
*Includes bibliographical references (p. ) and index.*
*1. Chaucer, Geoffrey, d. 1400—Criticism and interpretation*
*I. Title. II. Series.*
*PR1924.M47 1995 821'.1—dc20 94–25135*
*ISBN 0–19–811193–2*

1 3 5 7 9 10 8 6 4 2

*Set by Hope Services (Abingdon) Ltd.*
*Printed in Great Britain*
*on acid-free paper by*
*Bookcraft Ltd,*
*Midsomer Norton, Avon*

*for Florence*
*once more*

# FOREWORD

THE idea for a series of guides to Chaucer originated in a sense that medieval studies in general and Chaucerian studies in particular had advanced to a point where a reappraisal of his poetry was both possible and necessary. The three volumes are devoted to the shorter poetry, *Troilus and Criseyde*, and the *Canterbury Tales*. We see these books as fulfilling a role comparable to the introduction to a good edition, but at greater length than would be possible there. The kind of line-by-line expository material that the notes to an edition would contain is included only where such matters are of wider importance for an understanding of the whole text or where recent scholarship has made significant advances. We hope to provide readers of Chaucer with essential and up-to-date information, with the emphasis falling on how the interpretation of that information advances our understanding of his work; we have therefore gone beyond summarizing what is best known to suggest new critical readings.

The original plan for the series was designed to provide some degree of consistency in the outline of the volumes, but it was part of the project from the start that there should be plenty of room for each author's individuality. We hope that our sense of common interests and concerns in our interpretation of Chaucer's poetry will provide a deeper critical consistency below the diversity. Such a paradox would, after all, be true to the nature of our subject.

Helen Cooper
A. J. Minnis
Barry Windeatt

# ACKNOWLEDGEMENTS

WARM thanks are due to Helen Cooper of University College, Oxford, who read each and every part (some in several drafts) of this book. The final version is a lot better for her wonderfully astute and constructive remarks. Professor John Burrow (University of Bristol), Professor Felicity Riddy (University of York), and Dr Ruth Evans (University of Wales–Cardiff) commented sagaciously on particular sections. And by happy coincidence my York colleague Nicholas Havely was working on an edition of the *House of Fame* at the same time as I was writing my chapter on that text; we enjoyed a fruitful exchange of ideas. I have also been fortunate in my graduate students. To Paul Bernhardt I owe valuable discussion of notions (both medieval and modern) of play and game, and Rosalynn Voaden has done much to raise my gender–consciousness.

Two Chaucerians generously supplied me with typescript copies of their books at press: many thanks to Sheila Delany for *The Naked Text: Chaucer's 'Legend of Good Women'* and Marilynn Desmond for *Reading Dido: Gender, Textuality and the Medieval 'Aeneid'*. Professor Bruno Roy (University of Montréal) provided extracts from the forthcoming edition, prepared in association with F. Guichard Tesson, of Evrart de Conty's remarkable Old French commentary on the *Echecs amoureux*. Unfortunately, the final versions of Christopher Baswell's *Virgil in Medieval England: Figuring the 'Aeneid' from the Twelfth Century to Chaucer* and Florence Percival's *Chaucer's Legendary Good Women* arrived too late to be taken into account. Both are being published by Cambridge University Press, and both are warmly recommended.

Extracts from *An Arundel Tomb* have been taken from *Collected Poems* by Philip Larkin, copyright © 1988, 1989 by the Estate of Philip Larkin, and reprinted by permission of Faber and Faber Ltd. and Farrar, Straus & Giroux, Inc. (New York).

My greatest debt of all is indicated by the dedication.

Alastair Minnis

# CONTENTS

# ABBREVIATIONS

| | |
|---|---|
| *AHDLMA* | *Archives d'histoire doctrinale et littéraire du moyen âge* |
| *AnM* | *Annuale Medievale* |
| CCSL | Corpus christianorum, series latina |
| *ChR* | *Chaucer Review* |
| CSEL | Corpus scriptorum ecclesiasticorum latinorum |
| EETS ES | Early English Text Society, Extra Series |
| EETS OS | Early English Text Society, Original Series |
| *ELH* | *English Literary History* |
| *JEGP* | *Journal of English and Germanic Philology* |
| *JMRS* | *Journal of Medieval and Renaissance Studies* |
| *MÆ* | *Medium Ævum* |
| *MED* | *Middle English Dictionary* |
| *MLN* | *Modern Language Notes* |
| *MLR* | *Modern Language Review* |
| *MP* | *Modern Philology* |
| *MS* | *Mediaeval Studies* |
| *NM* | *Neuphilogische Mitteilungen* |
| *OGC* | *Oxford Guides to Chaucer* |
| *PBA* | *Proceedings of the British Academy* |
| *PL* | *Patrologia latina*, ed. J.-P. Migne (Paris, 1844–64) |
| *PMLA* | *Publications of the Modern Language Association of America* |
| *RES* | *Review of English Studies* |
| *RTAM* | *Recherches de théologie ancienne et médiévale* |
| *SAC* | *Studies in the Age of Chaucer* |
| SATF | Société des Anciens Textes Français |
| *SP* | *Studies in Philology* |
| STS | Scottish Text Society |
| *TLS* | *Times Literary Supplement* |
| *UTQ* | *University of Toronto Quarterly* |
| *YES* | *Yearbook of English Studies* |

*Abbreviated titles of poems*

| | |
|---|---|
| BD | *The Book of the Duchess* |
| CT | *The Canterbury Tales* |
| LGW | *The Legend of Good Women* |
| HF | *The House of Fame* |
| PF | *The Parliament of Fowls* |
| T&C | *Troilus and Criseyde* |

# INTRODUCTION

The objective of this book is to give an up-to-date summary of what is known about Chaucer's Shorter Poems, to offer new ideas and interpretations, and to stimulate debate about the cultural significance of those texts, both in Chaucer's day and in our own.

Above all else, it is concerned to offer different ways of reading Chaucer, and to consider the ideological implications of various readings. Therefore it is deliberately and frankly pluralistic, interweaving the views of critics who wrote over fifty years ago with those which were published in the summer of 1993 (our general cut-off point), scholarship on dates and sources with contemporary theoretical approaches, literary history of a traditional kind with historicist procedures which have gained currency recently, and also medieval hermeneutics with modern. It is hoped that the result will appeal to a wide range of readers and will encourage readers to widen their range.

Of course, much of today's critical theory is in the process of radical transformation. But the notion that one day we will get back to where we started (as if there could be consensus about *that*) and rediscover some monolithic critical bedrock underneath all the fashionable flux is a mind-numbing illusion. Current and future revisionisms can be understood only with knowledge of what is being revised. Granted that the sands are shifting, Chaucer criticism must shift with them or be trapped within an ideological time-warp which will deny the present cultural significance of his fictions and marginalize medieval literature within today's disenchanted groves of academe. Process is all.

That said, I want to add that we—and here I am speaking for all the contributors to this volume—have operated on the assumption that if an idea is worthwhile, it is worth explaining plainly (though complex effects can sometimes require complex expression). The mandarin language of some recent criticism may be understood as a device to empower innovative methods, to proclaim the professionalism and pedagogic value of readings which are going against some establishment or other. But the political wisdom of such moves can be questioned, inasmuch as they may play into the hands of hostile witnesses who shout loudly that the emperor has no clothes (quite missing the point that they are dealing with difference rather than absence). Besides, since the intended audience of this book includes first-time readers of Chaucer, we have opted for clarity rather than 'professionally correct' difficulty, while maintaining our conviction that introducing Chaucer must entail the self-conscious introduction of various methods of reading Chaucer.

## Notes on Terminology

In accordance with this agenda, the following working definitions are offered of some of the terms which appear in this book. Other terms will be explained on their first occurrence.

'Character' has generally been avoided, because it may be misleading. In the past it has often involved the imposition of the notion of autonomous, originating, and fixed (though capable of 'developing') personalities upon literary phenomena which in the first instance are better understood as linguistic, rhetorical, and textual constructs. The fact that we are dealing with creatures who 'live' only in the words of the text is evidenced by a passage in a poem which the young Geoffrey Chaucer knew intimately, Guillaume de Machaut's *Jugement dou roy de Behaingne*. Here the personification Reason claims that she knows that a lovelorn knight has spoken well (*bien parlé*) because she has 'found it written out above' (*en escript l'ai ci dessus trouvé*, 1782). This figure is very aware that the knight and 'she' are participating in a text. (As a matter of stylistic convenience, and to avoid convolutions which might compromise clarity, in the following chapters the personal pronouns 'he' and 'she' are used in relation to such non-persons.)

The term 'persona' has been adopted because it presupposes a theory of *speaking voices*, of constructs which feature in texts only inasmuch as 'they' have something to say. The distinction between textual speech *in propria persona* (involving the voice of the author) and *in personal aliorum* (involving the voices of other constructs) is found in a wide range of medieval commentaries on texts both sacred and profane, and was used to good effect in the early fifteenth century *querelle* over the meaning of the *Roman de la Rose*, wherein Jean de Meun's defenders argued that certain offensive statements in the poem are made by *personae of* whom the author himself did not approve, Jean being responsible only for what he says *in propria persona*. (It should be recognized, of course, that this Jean-figure is 'himself' a textual construct.) Chaucer's fictions reveal him to have been acutely aware of the literary possibilities for assigning, devolving—and indeed of disavowing—responsibility for speech-acts. More generally, the term 'persona' may serve as a reminder that Chaucer's poetic is rhetorical (addressed to specific audiences) and oral (conceived of in performance terms). Very revealingly, Chaucer's Troilus, alone without any company and disputing with himself about destiny and free will, can break off for a moment to reassure his creator's audience that he will not bore them rigid: 'now herkene, for I wol nat tarie' (*Troilus and Criseyde*, iv. 1029). (To say that he is speaking 'out of character' here should raise the issue of whether in the first place he had a 'character'—in the sense defined above—to speak in.) Moreover, that poetic is governed by a semiotics which regards the spoken word as primal, written language being the record of sounds. Chaucer paid his sophisticated tribute to that medieval truth in the *House of Fame*.

'Subjects' and 'subjectivities' are used in the post-structuralist senses of the terms which owe much to the psychoanalytic theories of Jacques Lacan. As appropriated by recent criticism, the basic idea is that 'the subject' (*sujet*) is a construct—the product of, for example, language or ideology or social factors—and divided against itself, rather than something which is unified, self-determining, autonomous, and originary. This approach aligns itself against a 'humanist ideology', which it regards as dependent on assumptions about the primacy of the autonomous and unified individual (it has to be said that such discussions can simplify complicated intellectual positions into soft targets). Hence Philip Rice and Patricia Waugh declare that the idea of 'a sovereign self, whose essential core of being transcends the outward signs of environmental and social conditioning', has been disrupted by post-structuralism, which holds that 'the subject, and that sense of unique subjectivity itself, is constructed in language and discourse; and rather than being fixed and unified, the subject is split, unstable and fragmented' (p. 119). 'The subject', and by extension the subjectivities which are presented in literature, may consequently be regarded as 'sites' rather than centres or real presences. In other words (the words being Jeremy Hawthorn's), 'the subject is where things happen, or that to which things happen, rather than that which makes things happen: extra-individual forces use the subject to exert their sway, the subject does not use them' (p. 181). My readings of Chaucer's Shorter Poems often seek to disclose subjects which are determined by an array of social and cultural forces and to identify points of convergence at which the faultlines between—and indeed within—the pressing ideologies are revealed.

'Discourses' are not the discrete utterances of alleged individuals, but rather systems of language use, with characterizing vocabularies and idioms, which function antagonistically, defining themselves in relation to other discourses. They depend crucially on where and against what they operate, on the priorities and values they assume, and on the position which their speakers occupy within a given hierarchy, whether political, social, professional, religious, intellectual, gender-based, ethnic, or whatever. As Diane Macdonell puts it, 'A discourse, as a particular area of language use, may be identified by the institutions to which it relates and by the position from which it comes and which marks it out for the speaker.' This method of identification will certainly help us to explore the discourses of 'courtly love', of normative masculine and feminine behaviour, of fashionable entertainment, and the like. 'That position does not exist by itself', continues Macdonell; 'Indeed, it may be understood as a standpoint taken up by the discourse through its relation to another, ultimately an opposing, discourse' (pp. 1–3). Such an understanding is invaluable for, for example, a reading of the *Legend of Good Women*, wherein Chaucer places a discourse of male infidelity in opposition to the culturally dominant discourse of female frailty.

'Intertextuality' is used in the sense given currency by Julia Kristeva. 'Intertextual' reading pays attention to the various ways in which a text is connected to other texts, whether by explicit citation or subtle allusion, or by the assimilation and/or rejection of the formal and substantive features of an earlier text, or more generally by shared participation in a common stock of literary conventions and rhetorical procedures. Chaucerian intertextuality is remarkably varied, ranging from the near-pastiche of Old French poems in the *Book of the Duchess* through the revaluation (or is it devaluation?) of Virgilian narrative in the *House of Fame* and the subtextual affirmation of difference from Macrobius and Alan of Lille in the *Parliament of Fowls* to the gyno / gamocentric editorializings of the *Legend of Good Women*.

Finally, a few words on 'New Historicism', 'dissident reading', and 'gender criticism'. 'Gender' is used to designate the social construction of 'what men and women are like' rather than biological sex, though it should be noted that the term 'biological sex' is itself controversial, and hence so is this distinction (cf. p. 70 below). 'New Historicism' is, or has been, a convenient label for what is actually a range of diverse, though sometimes interweaving, preoccupations, all of which entail a materialist view of culture. While I have considerable reservations about some of its typical assumptions and manœuvres, I certainly share Stephen Greenblatt's professed concern for 'the larger networks of meaning in which both the author and his works participate', on the one hand, and on the other, his reluctance to have literature 'absorbed entirely into an ideological superstructure' (pp. 4–5). Hence my readings of Chaucer's love-visions within an anthropology of courtly didacticism and play and as inscriptions of aristocratic ideals of conduct and processes of cultural fashioning. Understanding Chaucer's poetry entails understanding something of the 'cultural poetics' within which it took on its meanings, though we should be aware of the 'impossibility of fully reconstructing and reentering' any past culture, 'of leaving behind one's own situation' (to adopt more expressions from Greenblatt).

One of the main aspects of New Historicism (in certain versions) which has been resisted here is the insistence that any potential for subversion is 'inevitably defeated or co-opted by the dominant institution', to borrow a phrase from Lynda E. Boose (p. 741). Walter Cohen has rightly protested that this produces if not 'something like a totalitarian model, then at least . . . a sense of the almost inevitable defeat of the poor, the innocent, and the oppressed . . . unless one is an aristocrat, there is nothing to be done' (pp. 35, 36). In critical terms this means that, for example, the subversive power of Shakespearean drama ends up being subordinated to some authoritarian cultural agenda, the bard himself becoming a sort of apologist for state orthodoxies. By the same token, Chaucer is revealed as occupying the position of sophisticated princepleaser: a reading which in general has indubitable purchase for the Shorter Poems (granted the risk of reductivism), but which becomes problematic when he arouses suspicions of subversion—of (for instance) aristocratic mores, traditional misogyny, indeed of authoritarian literary theory. One way of responding to this would be to say that criticism requires a new version of historicism, as when Alan Sinfield turns to Raymond Williams for support for the view that 'cultural materialism' should seek 'to discern the scope for dissident politics of class, gender, and sexual orientation, both within texts and in their roles in cultures' (pp. 9–10). Such 'dissident reading' has encouraged my own identifications of certain prospects of dissidence in Chaucerian fiction.

Moreover, a cultural poetics which supposes that whatever is subversive in culture inevitably suffers defeat may well find it difficult to assign sufficient value to the roles played by women in history or to the roles played by female subjectivities (as constructed by both male and female writers) in texts. Not that this hermeneutic strategy is uniquely disempowering for women: other strategies function in a similar way. As Elaine Showalter has shrewdly remarked, 'The experience of women can easily disappear, become mute, invalid and invisible, lost in the diagrams of the structuralist or the class conflict of the Marxists' (p. 271).

The converse, however, can also be true: literary formalism and class conflict (along with a host of other political, social, and aesthetic considerations) can be lost in the exclusive pursuit of a feminist agenda. Feminist and gender criticisms are capable of creating discourses quite as totalizing as those of New Historicism, structuralism, or Marxism. My own preference—for, given the different premises involved here, all one can do is establish a preference—is for a historicized gender criticism which attempts to respect the room for dissent which the culture of Chaucer's day allowed, in so far as that can be recuperated by recourse to such evidence as is available to us.

## Bibliographical Note

In uniformity with the other Oxford Guides to Chaucer, quotations from the texts of the Shorter Poems and of Chaucer's other works are from the *Riverside Chaucer*. In addition, I have drawn on other editions, listed below; the editions of single poems are especially recommended as valuable study aids.

The Bibliography printed at the end of this volume lists the publications which we have used in preparing it. Each section of each chapter is followed by its own brief annotated bibliography, which follows the order and sequence of the preceding discussion. When an item is cited for the first time, a complete reference is given. Thereafter an abbreviated form is used, with the author's surname and short title. The full reference may easily be obtained by consulting the Bibliography.

### EDITIONS

Benson, Larry D. (general ed.), *The Riverside Chaucer* (Boston, 1987; Oxford, 1988 (paperback)).

Brewer, D. S. (ed.), *Chaucer, 'The Parlement of Foulys'* (Manchester, 1960; repr. 1972).

Donaldson, E. T. (ed.), *Chaucer's Poetry: An Anthology for the Modern Reader*, 2nd edn. (New York, 1975).

Fisher, John H. (ed.), *The Complete Poetry and Prose of Geoffrey Chaucer* (New York, 1977).

Havely, N. R. (ed.), *Chaucer, 'The House of Fame'*, Durham and St Andrews Medieval Texts (Durham, 1994).

Kane, George, and Cowen, Janet (eds.), *Chaucer, 'Legend of Good Women'* (East Lansing, Mich., 1994).

Pace, George B., and David, Alfred (eds.), *A Variorum Edition of the Works of Geoffrey Chaucer*, vol. v: *The Minor Poems* (Norman, Okla., 1982).

Phillips, Helen (ed.), *Chaucer, 'The Book of the Duchess'*, Durham and St Andrews Medieval Texts, rev. repr. (Durham, 1984).

Robinson, F. N. (ed.), *The Works of Geoffrey Chaucer*, 2nd edn. (Boston and Oxford, 1957).

Skeat, W. W. (ed.), *The Works of Geoffrey Chaucer* (7 vols., Oxford, 1894–1900).

### FACSIMILE EDITIONS

*Bodleian Library, MS Fairfax 16*, with an introduction by John Norton Smith (London, 1979).

*Cambridge University MS Gg.4.27*, with an introduction by M. B. Parkes and R. Beadle (Cambridge, 1979–81).

*The Findern Manuscript. Cambridge University Library MS Ff.1.6*, with an introduction by Richard Beadle and A. E. B. Owen (London, 1977).

*Manuscript Bodley 638. Bodleian Library, Oxford University*, with an introduction by Pamela Robinson. The Variorum Chaucer: Facsimile Series of the Works of Geoffrey Chaucer, vol. 2 (Norman, Okla., 1982).

*Manuscript Pepys 2006. Magdalene College, Cambridge*, with an introduction by A. S. G. Edwards. The Variorum Chaucer: Facsimile Series of the Works of Geoffrey Chaucer, vol. 6 (Norman, Okla., 1985).

*Manuscript Tanner 346. Bodleian Library, Oxford University*, with an introduction by Pamela Robinson. The Variorum Chaucer: Facsimile Series of the Works of Geoffrey Chaucer, vol. 1 (Norman, Okla., 1980).

*Manuscript Trinity R.3.19. Trinity College, Cambridge University*, with an introduction by Bradford Y. Fletcher. The Variorum Chaucer: Facsimile Series of the Works of Geoffrey Chaucer, vol. 5 (Norman, Okla., 1987).

Machaut's *Jugement* is quoted from the edition by James I. Wimsatt and William W. Kibler, *Guillaume de Machaut, 'Le Jugement du roy de Behaigne' and 'Remede de Fortune'* (Athens, Ga., and London, 1988). On medieval *persona* theory see A. J. Minnis, 'Theorizing the Rose: Commentary Tradition in the *Querelle de la Rose*', in Piero Boitani and Anna Torti (eds.), *Poetics: Theory and Practice in Medieval English Literature* (Cambridge, 1991), pp. 13–36. A cogent discussion of the Chaucerian I-persona is offered by David Lawton, *Chaucer's Narrators* (Cambridge, 1985), esp. pp. 36–75.

P. Rice and P. Waugh, *Modern Literary Theory. A Reader* (London and New York, 1989). Jeremy Hawthorn, *A Concise Glossary of Contemporary Literary Theory* (London and New York, 1992). See further the lucid study by J. Henriques, W. Hollway, C. Urwin, C. Venn, and V. Walkerdike, *Changing the Subject: Psychology, Social Regulation and Subjectivity* (London and New York, 1984), esp. pp. 203–63. On the *sujet* in Chaucerian fiction see especially the nuanced application of Lacanian ideas in Lee Patterson, *Chaucer and the Subject of History* (London, 1991). Moreover, H. Marshall Leicester has argued that the Canterbury tale-tellers cannot be 'treated as preestablished, determinate, and self-certain entities, even when they appear to want to treat themselves that way': *The Disenchanted Self. Representing the Subject in the 'Canterbury Tales'* (Berkeley and Los Angeles, 1990), pp. 14–15.

Diane Macdonell, *Theories of Discourse: An Introduction* (Oxford, 1986), pp. 1–3.

Stephen Greenblatt, *Renaissance Self-Fashioning. From More to Shakespeare* (Chicago and London, 1980). Lynda E. Boose, 'The Family in Shakespeare Studies; or—Studies in the Family of Shakespeareans; or—The Politics of Politics', *Renaissance Quarterly*, 40 (1987), 707–42. Walter Cohen, 'Political Criticism of Shakespeare', in Jean E. Howard and Marion F. O'Connor (eds.), *Shakespeare Reproduced: The Text in History and Ideology* (New York and London, 1987), pp. 18–46. Alan Sinfield, *Faultlines. Cultural Materialism and the Politics of Dissident Reading* (Oxford, 1992). In the brand of cultural materialism characteristic of New Historicism the influence of latter-day Marxism may be perceived, particularly that promulgated by Louis Althusser, who holds that works of art, far from being wholly determined by socio-economic forces, have a 'relative autonomy' and are 'overdetermined' in the sense that they are determined by a matrix of many factors. Cf. K. M. Newton (ed.), *Twentieth-Century Literary Theory. A Reader* (Basingstoke and London, 1988). p. 241.

See further the important critique of New Historicism by Marguerite Waller, 'The Empire's New Clothes: Refashioning the Renaissance', in Sheila Fisher and Janet E. Halley (eds.), *Seeking the Woman in Late Medieval and Renaissance Writings. Essays in Feminist Contextual Criticism* (Knoxville, Tenn., 1989), pp. 160–83. 'Their own discursive practices bespeak a desire for, an investment or belief in, the epistemology of authority', she claims (p. 161). 'Class- and gender-centered historiographies no less than deconstruction (and often with its help) are showing that the kind of knowledge for which new historicism seems to be nostalgic depends upon exclusivity, the privileged position of one class, race, or gender' (pp. 163–4).

Elaine Showalter, 'Towards a Feminist Poetics', in Newton (ed.), *Twentieth-Century Literary Theory*, pp. 268–72.

# Chaucer's Shorter Poems:
# Social and Cultural Contexts

*The Poet and the Princes*

Our first clear sighting of the historical Chaucer is in the late 1350s, when he appears as a retainer, probably a page, of Elizabeth de Burgh, Countess of Ulster and wife of Lionel, son of King Edward III. Lionel was involved in the English invasion of France in September 1359; at one point in this campaign Chaucer was captured, but soon ransomed. During the peace negotiations at Calais in October 1360, the prince paid him for carrying letters from there to England, which may mark the beginning of his career as international courier and diplomat. When he reappears from the mists of the period 1360–6, Chaucer may well be going about the royal family's business: he is named as the recipient of a safe conduct through Navarre. In 1366 his father, a prosperous London wine merchant, died. And by 12 September of the same year he had married a certain 'Philippa', usually identified as Philippa de Roet, whose family (or at least father) had come to England from Hainault with Edward's Queen Philippa.

In 1367 Chaucer is first referred to as a squire to the king's chamber. Two further references back this up, but it has been suggested (by Richard Firth Green) that in fact he was only a squire of the household or *familia*, a more lowly position. Whatever the truth of the matter, there is no doubt that Chaucer did the king some service at home and abroad. His subsequent foreign travel is cursorily documented: 'overseas' (mission and destination unspecified) in 1368; on campaign in France with John of Gaunt in 1369; 'on the king's service overseas', probably in Flanders, in 1370; to northern Italy on a trade (and perhaps also military) mission in 1372–3; 'on the king's secret business', presumably overseas, in 1376; to France and Flanders on several occasions in 1377; to Italy again, this time Lombardy, in 1378; to Calais in 1387.

On 8 June 1374 Chaucer was appointed Controller of the Wool Custom and Subsidy, and on 20 April 1382 to the less important controllership of the Petty Custom, which involved import and export duties on wine and other merchandise. Much depended on the collection of the wool tax, for this was the main source of royal income in peacetime. Chaucer carried out this task until December 1386—an exceptionally long tenure. From this period comes a curious record, whereby a certain

Cecilia Chaumpaigne, daughter of a London baker, released Chaucer from all legal actions in respect of her 'rape'. Chaucer scholars have wondered whether this term could mean abduction rather than physical rape; the latest study is inconclusive, but indicates that the phrase 'de raptu meo' was as inflammatory in Chaucer's day as it has proved to be in ours. The circumstances are far from clear, and are likely to remain so. What is perfectly clear is the high rank of Chaucer's witnesses: they included Sir William Beauchamp, chamberlain of the king's household from 1378 until 1380/1, Sir William Neville, who became Admiral of the North in 1372, and Sir John Clanvowe (1341–91), one of Richard II's chamber knights. The appearance of Clanvowe's name is of special interest to literary and intellectual historians, for he seems to have been the author of a poem, *The Book of Cupid*, which is full of echoes of Chaucer's verse; and he was one of the group of 'Lollard knights' whose piety may have been influenced by some of the views of John Wyclif—who, it should be remembered, for long enjoyed Gaunt's patronage and protection. Chaucer's eminent social standing and his enjoyment of considerable political power are manifest.

In the late 1380s Chaucer seems to have gradually moved to live in Kent, probably Greenwich, making the final break with his home in Aldgate in 1386. In 1385 he had been included in a commission of peace for Kent; in 1386 he was elected as one of the two 'knights of the shire' (i.e. members of the House of Commons) who represented Kent in Richard II's experimental parliament. Three years later came his most prestigious and demanding appointment: he became King Richard's Clerk of the Works, with responsibility for the accounts relating to building and maintenance. During the two years in which he held this position he oversaw 'works' at Westminster Palace and seven of Richard's favourite manors. (A new profession of 'civil servant' was emerging, as secular bureaucrats took over the administration of government from the clerics who had previously performed this function.) Chaucer's final appointment under Richard was to the administrative position of deputy forester at North Petherton in Somerset, a typical reward for good service. The deposition of Richard and the accession of Henry IV seem to have made little difference to Chaucer's fortunes: he was, after all, a long-standing servant of the house of Lancaster, and the new king was the son of John of Gaunt and his first duchess, Blanche; the fact that Chaucer had commemorated her in verse, in the *Book of the Duchess*, would certainly not have been to his disadvantage. As king, Henry renewed various grants which Richard had given Chaucer, and even added an extra annuity. In December 1399 Chaucer leased a house near Westminster Abbey. After June 1400 the records of payments of his royal grants cease; according to a sixteenth-century tradition he died on 25 October of that year. Chaucer's burial in Westminster Abbey was for reasons quite unconnected with his poetry, though his tomb (not erected until 1556) marked the beginnings of Poet's Corner. Doubtless he would have relished the irony.

Indeed, none of the rewards that Chaucer received during his career can be proved to have been in recognition of his poetry. It is not even clear if the courts of Edward III and Richard II provided stimulating milieux in which the types of poetry he practised were encouraged; some recent criticism has come close to espousing the theory of lonely, independent genius, or has seen Chaucer as a member of a small coterie of intellectuals. Some of them were courtiers, but that (the argument runs) was not the determinant of their cultural sophistication. To summarize such evidence as does exist, the court of Edward III seems to have been the better place for an ambitious poet. The king and his circle were familiar with a wide range of figures from *chansons de geste* and romances, as well as devotional and encyclopaedic works, to judge from surviving lists of books and *objets d'art*. Edward's queen, Philippa, daughter of William III, count of Hainault, brought the sophisticated cultural tastes of her family to England, and was regarded as an appropriate recipient and addressee of poems. Thus Jean Froissart (*c.*1337–after 1404), on his arrival in England, was, on his own testimony, well rewarded for the history (probably in verse, now lost) which he presented to Queen Philippa; he served as her secretary until she died in 1361. In his chronicles Froissart celebrated the 'splendid and honourable court', presided over by a 'king feared by three kingdoms' and a 'noble queen' whom he served 'with beautiful ditties and treatises of love'. However, in those same chronicles Chaucer is mentioned only as a diplomat.

Another figure who received some employment in Edward's court was Jean de la Mote, a major figure in the development of the French poetic *formes fixes* (ballade, rondeau, virelay, chant royal, and lay). It was Philippa, rather than any other offspring, to whom Jean addressed his lament on the death of William III of Hainault, *Li Regret Guillaume*. When Jean was taken to task by Philippe de Vitry for having become 'a serf of King Arthur' (presumably Edward III) in 'Albion cursed by God', he spiritedly responded that he served 'well against evil . . . in Albion'. Indeed, he declares, elsewhere he 'never had inspiration or flight', and so he in no way belongs to Gaul (trans. Wimsatt, pp. 52–5). This can only be taken to mean that his creativity was encouraged in Edward's court. Although there is no evidence that Jean de le Mote was still alive when Chaucer entered Edward's court in the late 1350s, it seems reasonable to assume that at least some of his poetry had survived in that milieu. Edward's uncle, Henry of Lancaster, wrote a book on the laws of war, which has not survived, and a penitential treatise, *Le Livre de seyntz medicines* (1354), which has. He was the father of the duchess Blanche.

Of even more obvious significance is the presence at Edward's court (and later Richard II's) of a French poet on whom Chaucer himself lavished the greatest praise: Oton de Graunson (*c.*1340–97) is described as the 'flour of hem that make in Fraunce' at the end of *The Complaint of Venus*, which is an adaptation of three ballades by the French knight-poet. He was a retainer of John of Gaunt's, and his name, like Chaucer's, often appears in Gaunt's register—and on two occasions they appear together in records of gifts. There seems no reason to doubt that they knew each other personally. The general picture, then, is one of cultural interest and interchange. James Sherborne is summing up a prevailing view when he declares: 'My impression is that until at least 1360 the court of Edward III was probably more fun than that of his grandson' (p. 25).

That remark, however, is part and parcel of a recent scholarly assault—of massive proportions—on the idea, as put forward so eloquently by Gervase Mathew, that there was an identifiable 'court culture' in the age of Richard II, presided over by a royal patron of the arts who encouraged the literary development of the English language. Of special significance for literary scholars was the demonstration that the so-called *Troilus* frontispiece (in Cambridge, Corpus Christi College MS 61), which appears to show Chaucer reading a poem to a court audience which might include the king himself, is dependent on two iconographic traditions which have nothing to do with the depiction of actual court practice: the upper scene seems to be based on 'procession' pictures; the lower and main scene, on quite standard 'preaching' or 'teaching' pictures. Perhaps the high point of such scholarly scepticism was reached in a series of ten papers delivered at the Colston Research Society Symposium held at Bristol University in the spring of 1981, and subsequently edited by V. J. Scattergood and J. W. Sherborne as *English Court Culture in the Later Middle Ages* (1983). The papers do their utmost to call that title in question. Typical is the remark of Sherborne that it is 'hard to fashion a portrait of Richard as a significant cultural force, let alone a cultural leader' (p. 21). And Jonathan Alexander argues that 'No English king, not even Henry VI, seems to have had the interest in books and learning of Charles V [of France]'. 'The foreign artists of works of art that come to England', he continues, 'come to fill a vacuum' (pp. 161, 162).

This is fair comment. And yet, further investigation reveals that very often we are dealing with matters of emphasis, with plenty of room being left for dissent and downright contradiction. 'Even if the overall effect of these essays is a little too sceptical, they cannot fail to be salutary,' remarks John Burrow in his introduction to the Colston volume (pl. x). They have had their salutary effect; now we may recognize that, in some respects at least, they were too sceptical. Mathew's book is indeed full of overstatements and unsupportable generalizations, which can rightly be left behind. But his holistic approach to the issue of Ricardian aesthetics (which involves political and social analysis) has much to commend it, and it is time that his notion of an 'international court culture' was reclaimed and modified to serve as a useful instrument of scholarship.

A useful introduction to Chaucer's life and career is afforded by the essay by M. M. Crow and V. E. Leland in the *Riverside Chaucer*, pp. xi–xxii. The fundamental sources have been edited by M. M. Crow and C. C. Olson, *Chaucer Life-Records* (Oxford, 1966). See also the biographies of Chaucer by George Kane, *Chaucer* (Oxford, 1984), and Donald R. Howard, *Chaucer and the Medieval World* (London, 1987). John Gardner, *The Life and Times of Chaucer* (New York, 1977), is a mixture of truth (as currently understood), half-truth, and novelistic invention. Particularly recommended is the latest Chaucer biography, by Derek Pearsall, *The Life of Geoffrey Chaucer* (Oxford and Cambridge, Mass., 1992), which contains excellent summaries of the latest scholarship and bibliography, in addition to much fresh insight. See further Donald R. Howard, 'Chaucer the Man', *PMCA* 80 (1965), 337–43, and Lister M. Matheson, 'Chaucer's Ancestry: Historical and Philological Reassessments', *ChR* 25 (1991), 171–89. The latest treatment of the Chaucer 'rape' case is by Christopher Cannon, '*Raptus* in the Chaumpaigne Release and a Newly Discovered Document concerning the Life of Geoffrey Chaucer', *Speculum*, 68 (1993), 74–94.

Richard Firth Green, *Poets and Princepleasers: Literature and the English Court in the Late Middle Ages* (Toronto, 1980), p. 68.

*The Book of Cupid*, attributed to Sir John Clanvowe, has been edited by V. J. Scattergood in *The Works of Sir John Clanvowe* (Cambridge, 1975). For the arguments in favour of Clanvowe's authorship see V. J. Scattergood, 'The Authorship of *The Boke of Cupide*', *Anglia* 82 (1964), 37–49. On Clanvowe and the other 'Lollard Knights' see pp. 19–20 below.

On cultural patronage at the court of Edward III see especially Juliet Vale, *Edward III and Chivalry: Chivalric Society and its Context, 1270–1350* (Woodbridge, 1983), pp. 42–56. The Froissart remarks are cited from Derek S. Brewer, *Chaucer*, 3rd edn. (London, 1973), p. 9. Froissart describes his gift to the Queen at *Chroniques*, ed. S. Luce and G. Raynaud (Paris, 1869–99), i. 120. Some of the king's attitudes towards Scotland seem to be reflected in Froissart's verse romance *Meliador*, on which see A. H. Diverres, 'Froissart's *Meliador* and Edward III's Policy towards Scotland', in *Mélanges offerts à Rita Lejeune* (Gembloux, 1969), ii. 1399–409.

The exchange between la Mote and de Vitry is quoted from James I. Wimsatt, *Chaucer and the Poetry of 'Ch'* (Cambridge, 1982). But see further the important article by F. N. M. Diekstra, 'The Poetic Exchange between Philippe de Vitry and Jean de la Mote: A New Edition', *Neophilologus*, 70 (1986), 504–19. On Graunson see Haldeen Braddy, *Chaucer and the French Poet Graunson* (Port Washington, NY, 1968), though this study should be used with caution. The most substantial and thorough discussion of Chaucer in relation to his French contemporaries (including those connected with the English court) is James I. Wimsatt's splendid monograph *Chaucer and his French Contemporaries* (Toronto, 1991).

Gervase Mathew, *The Court of Richard II* (London, 1968). On the *Troilus* frontispiece see Derek Pearsall, 'The *Troilus* Frontispiece and Chaucer's Audience', *YES* 7 (1977), 68–74; *Troilus and Criseyde, A Facsimile of Corpus Christi College Cambridge MS 61*, with

introductions by M. B. Parkes and E. Salter (Cambridge, 1978), pp 15–23. The iconographic precedents mentioned above do not, it should be emphasized, rule out the possibility that the frontispiece does indeed represent actual conditions in which poetry
was enjoyed: of course, artists followed models, but this does not mean that the scene
depicted was of their own invention rather than being an attempt to represent life, in
however idealized a form.

V. J. Scattergood and J. W. Sherborne (eds.), *English Court Culture in the Later Middle
Ages* (London, 1983). With John Burrow's remark compare the views of Michael
Bennett, who comments that the Colston scholars 'came close to staging a second deposition of the king'; this movement has 'gone rather too far', he suggests; 'we need royalty to account for some of the literary evidence'. 'The Court of Richard II and the
Promotion of Literature', in Barbara A. Hanawalt (ed.), *Chaucer's England. Literature
in Historical Context*, Medieval Studies at Minnesota, 4 (Minneapolis, 1992), p. 4.


## An International Court Culture

It is significant that, of all the papers delivered at the Colston symposium,
the one which took the most positive line on the topic of court culture
had as its subject the large part which music and song played in the life
of aristocratic households. True, given that here the determining influences were French, we cannot speak of a distinctive Ricardian or English
tradition. But the cultural significance of that distinction is questionable,
given that at this time the 'international court culture' (to recuperate
Mathew's phrase) was predominantly French in style and often in language; to be able to read and speak the right kind of French was to be
noble and 'of the court' (or at least 'courtly').

One may recall Froissart's well-known account of King Richard's reaction to his present of a 'fayre boke, well enlumyned', which contained 'all
the matters of amours and moralytees that in four and twentie yeres
before I hadde made and compyled' (trans. Bourchier, vi. 130):

Than the kynge desyred to se my booke that I had brought for hym: so he sawe
it in his chambre, for I had layde it there redy on his bedde. Whanne the kynge
opened it, it pleased hym well, for it was fayre enlumyned and written, and covered with crymson velvet, with ten botons of sylver and gylte, and roses of golde
in the myddes, with two great claspes gylte, rychely wrought. Than the kyng
demaunded me wherof it treated, and I shewed hym howe it treated of maters
of love; whereof the kynge was gladde and loked in it, and reed it in many places,
*for he coulde speke and rede Frenche very well*; and he tooke it to a knyght of hys
chambre, named syr Rycharde Creadon, to beare it into his secrete chambre. (vi.
147; my italics)

Sir John Montagu, Earl of Salisbury between 1397 and 1400 and Knight
of the Garter, composed 'balades et chançons / Rondeaulx et lais', and
Chaucer's friend John Gower (?1330–1408) wrote extensively in French
(*Mirour de l'Homme, Cinkante Ballades, Traitie pour Essampler les Amantz*

*Marietz*). At least some of the songs and lecherous lays which Chaucer ashamedly acknowledges in his controversial *Retracciouns* were almost certainly in French, and even if the French poems of the mysterious 'Ch' in University of Pennsylvania MS French 15 are not by Chaucer, they are at least representative of the types of poem he would have written in that language. And when Eustache Deschamps (*c.*1346–*c.*1406) came to praise Chaucer, he singled out his successful transmission of French texts and literary fashions into English: 'Grant translateur, noble Gieffroy Chaucier'.

It is also noteworthy that that dedicated follower of fashion, Chaucer's Prioress, should pride herself on her French—though the far more sophisticated poet notes that this was

> After the scole of Stratford atte Bowe,
> For Frenssh of Parys was to hire unknowe.
> 
> (*CT*, General Prologue, I(A) 125–6)

Here we have what might be described as the chain-store equivalent of the designer model. To put it another way, the 'true blues' apparently did, and certainly were expected to, enjoy things French, and those with social aspirations were obliged to share such tastes. Hence the Prioress's manners are, quite literally, straight out of the *Roman de la Rose*, which was, among many other things, a 'courtesy book' which described elegant prestige behaviour. All this testifies to the status which France's language and literature continued to enjoy in an age which is supposed to have seen 'the triumph of English'.

Courtly poems other than Chaucer's have a similar tale to tell. Sir John Clanvowe's *Book of Cupid*, 'perhaps the earliest and one of the best poems to show the influence of Chaucer' (as V. J. Scattergood puts it, p. 9), nevertheless has affinities with French poems by Jean de Condé (*c.*1275/80–1345) and Deschamps, and, more conclusively, it marks the first appearance in English of a stanza form which was used by Deschamps, Froissart, and Alain Chartier (*c.*1390–*c.*1440), a quintain of usually decasyllabic lines which rhyme *aabba*. Then there is the rich evidence afforded by Charles d'Orléans (1391–1465), nephew of one French king (Charles VI) and father of another (Louis XII), who was captured at Agincourt (1415) and spent the next twenty-five years of his life living in exile in England, being moved from noble household to noble household—one of his hosts being, rather intriguingly, the Duke of Suffolk, husband of Chaucer's granddaughter Alice. Charles's English poems were, some have argued, influenced by Chaucer and Gower, but the French poems he wrote in England, mainly ballades, are reminiscent (particularly in their use of *rime assonante*) of Graunson, Deschamps,

Guillaume de Machaut (*c*.1300–77), and Jean de Garencières (1370?–1415), while his allegorical strategies resemble those of Machaut and Chartier.

Then again, John Lydgate's *Complaynt of a Loveres Lyfe* and *The Temple of Glas* (both written probably before *c*.1412), although inspired by Chaucer's *Book of the Duchess* and *House of Fame* respectively, remain very much within the boundaries of the allegorical landscape of Guillaume de Lorris's part of the *Roman de la Rose* and the emotional and artistic range of 'the school of Machaut'. In particular, the *Complaynt of a Loveres Lyfe* has been supposed to reveal the influence of Froissart's *Dit du Bleu Chevalier* and Machaut's *Dit dou Vergier*. Indeed, it could even be said that these Lydgate poems are much more in the spirit of the French allegories of love than are the corresponding Chaucer poems, for while Chaucer assimilated the elaborate expressiveness characteristic of the *formes fixes* to the larger concerns of narrative, Lydgate's frame stories are modest show-cases for individually impressive, and detachable, lyric protestations. The 'Chaucer tradition', then, led those who followed it to France rather than Italy, a fact which should make us more sensitive to Chaucer's own debts to French tradition. There is thus no justification whatever for branding the writers who followed in Chaucer's footsteps as narrow-minded conservatives who were sadly unaware that the Renaissance, for which an Italianate Chaucer was the unique literary forerunner, was just around the corner.

In sum, the continuing vitality of French poetic fashions in the age of Chaucer and far beyond is at once indubitable and impressive. After a period in which the Italian influence on Chaucer has been stressed, some of the most recent Chaucer scholarship is moving towards reappraisal and reiteration of his debt to French traditions, including Old French court poetry. This is rightly encouraging the rehabilitation of 'the international court culture' as a useful perspective from which to view at least some of Chaucer's poems. There is no reason to doubt that many of King Richard's courtiers, and indeed the king himself, participated in that culture—in other words, they may be regarded as 'consumers' of it (this will be a crucial notion throughout the following discussion). Instead of blaming the king and his familiars for doing little to encourage a distinctively English culture, we may with equal justice affirm the utterly fashionable involvement of creative artists and courtly consumers with the dominant cultural forms of the day. And in these tastes, Richard and Ricardians were no different from their immediate predecessors or successors.

Of course, the English language was gaining in status. Indeed, it could be said that Froissart's complimentary reference to Richard II's French is comprehensible only if the king did not have French as his first language, or at least was not expected to have fluent French. Certainly the king allowed his Cheshire retainers to address him familiarly 'in materna lingua', to the horror of the Kenilworth chronicler. His uncle Thomas of Woodstock owned an English (Wycliffite) Bible, and wrote his alleged confession of treason in English. According to the Lollards, John of Gaunt championed the cause of the English Bible, while Queen Anne of Bohemia had a copy of the Gospels, accompanied by a commentary, in English. (But can those claims be believed? Far more plausible is John Wyclif's remark that the Queen owned Scripture in Czech, German, and Latin.) At any rate, it would seem that English was gradually replacing French as the medium through which Latin was taught. And a preference for English, at least in some contexts, is quite comprehensible as a reflex of the nationalism which the Hundred Years War with France fostered. Indeed, 'a more aggressively nationalistic ethos' can be discerned as far back as the late 1360s, at the court of Edward III, as Michael Bennett has noted (p. 7).

'That Chaucer was writing in English by 1370 is indeed inexplicable if we suppose the court was French speaking', asserts Thorlac Turville-Petre (p. 100), a view I would certainly endorse (with the caveat that the question is best posed in terms of the relative frequency of the three available languages, Latin, French, and English, rather than as a competition between two or more of them). We can hardly prove court interest in English writing from Chaucer's having written in English, since that would smack of circularity. However, granted that Chaucer's first and most significant audience included some of the most influential people in the land (about which more later), it would seem to follow that his use of English was consistent with their tastes and expectations. Certainly he would not have written in a language which was unfamiliar or distasteful to them. Michael Bennett has suggested that, in the sophisticated literary language forged by Chaucer and Gower (and indeed by the *Gawain* poet), 'it is tempting to see the sort of assurance that could only come from the highest sponsorship' (p. 8). If this is accepted, then that 'sponsorship' must be taken as involving the promotion of English.

There is some evidence, then, that during Chaucer's lifetime it was becoming fashionable to write in English—or at least to make French matter and models available in English. It is probably misleading to speak in oppositional terms of French and English as literary languages, because very often (as our discussion above certainly indicates) French literary concerns were being carried over into English. In this sense, Chaucer's use of English can be seen—to borrow a phrase from Elizabeth Salter— as a triumph of internationalism.

The opening allusion is to the article by Nigel Wilkins, 'Music and Poetry at Court: England and France in the Late Middle Ages', in Scattergood and Sherborne (eds.), *English Court Culture*, pp. 183–204. See further N. Wilkins, *Music in the Age of Chaucer* (Cambridge, 1979); *idem*, *Chaucer Songs* (Cambridge, 1980); *idem*, *'En Regardant Vers le Païs de France*: The Ballade and the Rondeau, a Cross-Channel History', in W. M. Ormrod (ed.), *England in the Fourteenth Century: Proceedings of the 1985 Harlaxton Symposium* (Woodbridge, 1986), pp. 298–323.

The passage from Froissart's *Chroniques* is quoted in the translation made by Sir John Bourchier, second Lord Berners, between 1523 and 1525: *Chroniques*, trans. Sir John Bourchier, with an Introduction by W. P. Ker, Tudor Translations xxvii–xxxii (London, 1901–3). Cf. the recent translation by G. Brereton (Harmondsworth, rev. edn., 1978), pp. 403, 408. The statement about Montagu comes from Jean Creton's *Metrical History of the Deposition of King Richard II*, ed. J. Webb, *Archaeologia*, 20 (1824), 297. On University of Pennsylvania MS French 15 see Wimsatt, *Chaucer and the Poems of 'Ch'*. For the text, along with an English translation, of the Deschamps ballade ('O Socratès plains de philosophie') see Derek Brewer (ed.), *Chaucer: The Critical Heritage* (London, 1978), i. 40–2.

Clanvowe, *Works*, ed. Scattergood. Wimsatt, *Chaucer and his French Contemporaries*. John Fox, *The Lyric Poetry of Charles d'Orléans* (Oxford, 1969), pp. 132–7; Charles d'Orléans, *French Chansons*, ed. Sarah Spence (New York and London, 1986), p. xxiii. According to James Wimsatt, Froissart's *Dit dou Bleu Chevalier* was influenced by Chaucer's *Book of the Duchess* rather than the other way around: *Chaucer and the French Love Poets* (Chapel Hill, NC, 1968), pp. 129–33. However, this view has been challenged convincingly by Susan Crane, 'Froissart's *Dit dou Bleu Chevalier* as a Source for Chaucer's *Book of the Duchess*', *MÆ* 61 (1992), 59–74.

On Anne of Bohemia's ownership of Scripture see especially Anne Hudson, *The Premature Reformation: Wycliffite Texts and Lollard History* (Oxford, 1988), pp. 30 n. 127, 248, 417. Professor Hudson is inclined to dismiss the story about Anne's English Gospels as a Lollard fabrication.

M. Bennett, 'Promotion of Literature'. Thorlac Turville-Petre, review of Vale, *Edward III and Chivalry*, and Scattergood and Sherborne (eds.), *English Court Culture*, in *Nottingham Medieval Studies*, 27 (1983), 92–101. Elizabeth Salter, 'Chaucer and Internationalism', *SAC* 2 (1980), 71–9; see further her book, *Fourteenth-Century English Poetry: Contexts and Readings* (Oxford, 1983), pp. 19–51.

On the late medieval status of English in general see N. F. Blake (ed.), *The Cambridge History of the English Language*, vol. 2: *1066–1476* (Cambridge, 1992), pp. 5–9, 423–32; also the relevant discussion and references in this book's appendix on 'Chaucer's Language'. Of particular importance is the growing use of English in the teaching of Latin. John Trevisa's famous accreditation of the Oxford schoolmaster John of Cornwall as having substituted English for French as the medium for teaching Latin *c.*1350 requires full reconsideration in the light of the materials recently presented by Tony Hunt, *Teaching and Learning Latin in Thirteenth-Century England* (Cambridge, 1991). John was certainly not the first to use English extensively in this way: English glosses appear alongside French in texts from the eleventh century onwards. Perhaps the point was rather that he made *exclusive* use of English in his teaching of Latin? Moreover, Hunt's work supports the hypothesis that in the thirteenth century Anglo-Norman was an 'acquired language' rather than a true vernacular. As a language of culture and administration it prospered in that century and beyond, but as a means of acquiring Latin it itself had to be acquired first, or along with the Latin. Hence 'we have to deal both with the practice of applying the concepts of Latin grammar to French . . . and with the custom of explaining the rules of Latin by reference to the usage of French' (i. 13). And English was always there, as a constant point of reference and source of vernacular equivalents for the Latin, and *de facto* for the Anglo-Norman as well. On the Middle English grammars of Latin see David Thomson (ed.), *An Edition of the Middle English Grammatical Texts* (New York and London, 1984); C. R. Bland, *The Teaching of Grammar in Late Medieval England: An Edition, with Commentary, of Oxford, Lincoln College MS Lat. 130* (East Lansing, Mich., 1992).

## Courtly Consumption and Social Formation

The only clear example of a royal commission of a poem in the age of Richard II is the king's request that John Gower write 'Som newe thing' for him to read (*Confessio Amantis*, Prol. 51\*). Gower duly produced an anthology of stories of love and political lore, designated as 'A bok for king Richardes sake' (Prol. 24\*). Mathew imagined Geoffrey Chaucer as performing several of his poems at court and being rewarded for them, but there is no firm evidence for this, and the scepticism expressed in the Colston Symposium proceedings volume is perfectly understandable in this case.

However, it should be noted that Chaucer and Gower (particularly Chaucer) were on good, perhaps in some cases intimate, terms with some of the most powerful men (and women?—more on that later) in the country, including people who were very influential at court. In particular, there seems to have been a receptive company of courtiers who shared an interest in poetry and a highly personal and earnest piety. The chroniclers Knighton and Walsingham give lists of knights who were either Lollards or supporters of Lollards; when the evidence is sifted, a loose group of seven figures is revealed: Sir Richard Sturry, Sir Lewis Clifford, Sir William Neville, Sir John Clanvowe, Sir Thomas Latimer, Sir John Montagu, and Sir John Cheyne. The evidence that certain of the named individuals were actually heterodox is slim, and in any case there were particular brands of English piety which had superficial resemblances to Lollardy, or indeed may have been influenced by some but not all of the major aspects of Wycliffite thinking, thereby rendering facile labelling impossible. At the very least, there is no reason to doubt the genuine interest of some courtiers in profound theological matters or their ability to grasp and discuss issues of that kind, even though they lacked the tools of the scholastic trade. Bishop Reginald Pecock, who in the 1450s sought single-handedly to provide a vernacular corpus of philosophical and theological works which would counteract the Lollard one, confidently asserted that he had found gentlemen of the laity who could 'conceive, vndirstonde, reporte and comune' the highest matters which he had written about, even though they knew few of the proper 'termes or wordis'. Indeed, he continues, certain 'ful hiȝe

and woþi maters in her dignyte touching booþ god hise benefetis and
his lawis' are easier to understand than less dignified matters such as
points of English law or business procedure (ed. Greet, pp. 20–1).
William Langland regarded this same phenomenon quite differently,
attacking those great nobles who presume to talk at table of Christ and
his powers (*Piers Plowman*, B x. 103–10).

Secular poetry and religious piety were quite compatible, even com-
plementary, interests in the Ricardian period; a more censorious age was
to follow, of Lollard hunting and suspicion of vernacular writings.
Clanvowe was apparently the author of a poem (*The Book of Cupid*,
already mentioned above) which contains echoes of at least two and possibly three of Chaucer's poems, and Clanvowe and Neville were involved
with the puzzling Chaucer 'rape' case. It was Lewis Clifford who brought
Deschamps' poem in praise of Chaucer from France; Clifford is himself
mentioned in it. Elsewhere Deschamps gives him the epithet 'amorous',
which we may take to mean that he could speak well of love, was well
versed in the fashions of *fin' amors*. (The chronicler Thomas Walsingham
criticized Richard's courtiers as being knights of Venus rather than of
Bellona, of the bedchamber rather than the battlefield.) Clifford's son-in-
law, Sir Philip de la Vache, seems to have been the addressee of
Chaucer's ballade *Truth* (or at least one version thereof). The (now lost)
French poems of John Montagu were highly regarded by no less a literary judge than Christine de Pizan. Richard Sturry played a major part in
arranging the audience at which Froissart presented Richard II with his
book 'of love'. As K. B. McFarlane says, 'the literacy of the group was
exceptional' (p. 185), and if we are looking for a court audience which
could have appreciated, and may have encouraged, Chaucer's art, surely
this could be it or at least part of it. While James Sherborne is absolutely
right to caution us against building on the shared interests of royal familiars the hypothesis that 'proximity to the king or interaction within his
court noticeably promoted them or gave them a common stamp of a particular kind' (p. 23), that 'stamp' is so 'common' and so distinctive, and
fits in so well with such other pieces of evidence as we do possess, that
it would be perverse to suppose that the court membership which those
figures shared was, as far as their acquisition and development of literary
culture were concerned, an irrelevance or the merest coincidence. V. J.
Scattergood is, to my mind, more judicious, if a trifle over-cautious, when
he concludes that 'in and around the court of Richard II' the 'circumstances for the production and dissemination of literature were obviously
not unfavourable' (p. 41). The evidence for courtly 'consumption' of literature should be given its full due.

It may be objected that many of the knights we have just mentioned were non-aristocratic courtiers, whose tastes and accomplishments can hardly be taken as representative of those of the English nobility. Scattergood has suggested that while the poetry of Gower and Chaucer does indeed seem on occasion to have 'an aristocratic courtly audience in mind', 'its more significant readers appear to have been career diplomats, civil servants, officials and administrators who were attached to the court and the government'—in other words, very much the outer court circle rather than the inner one (p. 38). And he proposes a distinction between the more modern literary tastes of these 'new men' and the old-fashioned tastes of noble families who, knowing little or nothing of Machaut and Deschamps, relied 'almost exclusively on romances' for their entertainment (p. 40). This point is well taken, but the contrast should not be made too sharply (as Scattergood acknowledges). Isabella, Duchess of York in Chaucer's lifetime (and sister-in-law of John of Gaunt), owned poems by Machaut as well as a *Lancelot*. Then again, while it is certainly true that Clanvowe, Sturry, Clifford, and Cheyne came from the lesser gentry (as indeed did John Gower), against this may be cited the fact that Montagu and Neville came from important noble families. More importantly from our point of view, no less than five of the courtiers we have discussed above, namely Clanvowe, Clifford, Neville, Sturry, and de la Vache, were chamber knights—and this, surely, takes us to the very centre of the court, into the *camera regis*.

But how close actually were they to King Richard? 'It is uncertain', warns Sherborne, 'how much this grouping of men owed to the king himself, for most of them had previously been servants or associates of the Black Prince or of Princess Joan' (p. 23). But past association need not rule out present affinity. Hence Christopher Given-Wilson can say that Sturry, 'clearly a favourite of the old king's', was a 'trusted diplomat and councillor' of Richard's 'until his death in 1395' (p. 148). And Given-Wilson places Clanvowe among the chamber knights of the 1380s who were 'clearly men of the king's own choice' (p. 162). The researches of Given-Wilson and J. A. Tuck have emphasized the close friendships which existed between Edward III and Richard II and their chamber knights; in the light of this work Sherborne is obliged to admit that 'these men were not second-class courtiers' (p. 17 n. 21). Here it is perhaps worth recalling that the relatively lowly origins of another chamber knight, Sir Simon Burley, did not prevent him from becoming the young king's tutor—one can hardly get closer to the king than that. Surely the issue of intimacy is the important point here: no matter what their origins or previous loyalties had been, the knights of the chamber were Richard's familiars, men trusted on important diplomatic business and rewarded with well-paid posts, and it seems reasonable to assume that some of their intellectual tastes and interests were shared by—perhaps they may even have been influenced by—the king.

Granted, then, that the chamber knights were close to the king, the other part of the question presents itself: how close were they to Chaucer? Within the elaborate hierarchy of the king's affinity the chamber knights were near the top, and the squires of the king's household, including Chaucer, near the bottom. This assumes that Green is right in identifying the poet as one of those *armigeri familia regis* who, according to Given-Wilson, almost certainly came to the court on rotation. He had been (as some scholars still think) an *armigeri camere regis*, one of the twenty or so squires of the chamber who attended personally on the king, that would put him in the social group immediately under that of the chamber knights, and make his various confidential services for royalty more comprehensible. Lee Patterson, who follows the Green hypothesis, speaks of a substantial gap in status and power between the poet and his high-ranking acquaintances. For him Chaucer is very much a man on the margins—a good place for a poet to be, certainly, but a difficult place to seek information concerning the specific audience or audiences he had in mind when he composed his early poems. 'Every assertion' about the poet's social location 'requires a qualification', declares Patterson.

He is the son of a rich merchant, but one educated in noble households; a king's squire, but one who fulfilled the duties of a clerical administrator; a modest servant of the Crown, but one who numbered among his friends some of the king's closest associates. . . . what the evidence reveals is a Chaucer on the boundary between distinctive social formations. Not bourgeois, not noble, not clerical, he nevertheless participates in all three of these communities. (p. 39)

This analysis allows ample space for contact and communication between Chaucer and 'some of the kings's closest associates', though that is not the point which Patterson is concerned to make here, of course. Paul Strohm does make it, suggesting that Chaucer's 'realization of himself as a social being occurred primarily within the supple bounds of the king's affinity'. The affinity's flexible social circumstances, he believes, encouraged 'horizontal' ties based on common interest, which often ran across the 'vertical' ties associated with the more hierarchical formations (p. 46). And on this horizontal axis may be sought the audience of Chaucer's courtly poetry.

Problems arise, however, when Patterson tries to place Chaucer's high-ranking contacts also on the margins. The fact that men like Clifford, de la Vache, and Clanvowe were friends of the poet, he claims, 'says far more about their alienation from the world of power and honour in which they habitually operated than it does about Chaucer's affiliations with that world' (p. 39). He cites McFarlane's demonstration of the unorthodox religious beliefs of the 'Lollard knights', adding that Clanvowe (in his devotional treatise *The Two Ways*) made explicit his critique of the honour world of chivalry. All this is highly problematic. For a start, Gaunt had patronized and protected Wyclif for a long time (as we have already noted), dropping him only when his controversial views on the eucharist turned him into a serious political liability. So, until around 1382 (when Wyclif, having had two propositions on the eucharist condemned at Oxford, rejected Gaunt's advice to be discreet), an interest in the schoolman's opinions did not put anyone beyond the pale. Then there is the major matter of what exactly constitutes Lollard belief. Clanvowe and Neville (who, as noted above, had supported Chaucer in his rape case) died near Constantinople in October 1391, either on pilgrimage or on crusade. Either venture would have been frowned upon by many Lollards, who were vociferously opposed to pilgrimages and often criticized crusades. Not that one had to be a Lollard to criticize crusading: John Gower did so in his book for King Richard's sake, the *Confessio Amantis* (iii. 2485 ff.). And Clanvowe's criticism of earthly glory is hardly surprising in view of the genre within which he is writing and the clerkly attitudes it necessitates (cf. p. 212 below). Chaucer's friends, then, were not as unusual as Patterson makes out, and the poet's connections with them can hardly be taken as evidence that he himself occupied an anomalous situation.

Chaucer's poetry may even have helped those friendships develop. Clanvowe's *Book of Cupid* displays the influence of two, and maybe three, of his works, which surely is evidence of the level of respect in which Chaucer was held by at least some members of the *camera regis*. The French poetry of another chamber knight, Sir John Montagu, was 'probably written . . . for a circle more socially elevated and more focused on the Continent than Chaucer's own', according to Strohm (p. 42). But Chaucer was, or became, more aware than any other Englishman of his day of the latest literary developments on the Continent, and his subtle variations on the typical themes of the *dits amoreux* in the *Book of the Duchess*, the *Parliament of Fowls*, and the prologue to the *Legend of Good Women* would have needed people like Montagu to appreciate them. George Kane has described the *Book of the Duchess* as a 'sensational' poem for its time, 'polite literature as sophisticated as its French progenitors, not admonitory or rustic or provincial' (p. 24). Throughout this work, he continues, Chaucer is writing as a self-styled 'rival' to the well-connected and much-patronized French poets, ostentatiously reproducing in English 'actual *identifiable* effects' (italics mine) from their *dits*. No doubt Montagu could have identified them, and perhaps Isabella of York as well. There is no reason, then, to suppose that Chaucer wrote exclusively or even mainly for his social equals, though one may speculate that such 'new men' would have been more likely to follow court fashions assiduously, thereby displaying their talents and good taste and (of course) increasing their chances of preferment in the process.

Indeed, as Strohm recognizes (*Social Chaucer*, pp. 50–1), Chaucer's life and work conformed in some ways to the typical career of the 'court poet', most obviously in his 'advice to princes' writings, the most prominent of which are *Lak of Stedfastness* (on which see pp. 489–92 below) and the *Tale of Melibee*. The *Knight's Tale* indicates Chaucer's interest in types of kingship (the tyrant Creon being set in opposition to the ideal philosopher-ruler Theseus), and some have detected a similar concern in his depiction of the God of Love's absolutist tendencies in the prologues to the *Legend of Good Women*. Moreover, the *De consolatione philosophiae* of the philosopher and statesman Boethius (*c.*480–*c.*524), which Chaucer rendered into literal English prose, was in several of its French translations a favourite text in court circles. Jean de Meun's version, a primary source of Chaucer's own, was addressed to King Philippe le Bel. The *Boece* lacks such a dedicatory preface (at least in the form in which it has come down to us), which is one of the most remarkable things about the work, for it would have made an appropriate gift (just the kind of thing they expected to receive) for some high-ranking aristocrat like Gaunt, perhaps even for the king himself. Then there is the fact that Thomas Usk included in his *Testament of Love* (1385–6?) an elaborate praise of Chaucer, having drawn on his *Boece* as a major source and echoed the *House of Fame*. Given that this work was written to curry favour with the royal faction, Usk would not have afforded Chaucer such an elevated position unless he was convinced that his name was one to conjure with. Moreover, Usk's belief that his prose treatise (an allegorical work requiring no little intelligence to decode) might help to deflect his punishment is, for our purposes, probably more significant than its actual failure to save him from the executioner, that failure reflecting the decline of Richard II's power in 1388.

A minimalism similar to that which pervades some recent assessments of the significance of poetry in general, and Chaucer's in particular, within English court circles, is also apparent in current views of the cultural import of Chaucer's marriage. Philippa de Roet, Patterson says, brought him only a modest annuity, was not landed, and as a foreigner did not have much standing among the English nobility. Against that may be set the following points: she was a *domicella reginae* of Queen Philippa of Hainault (and therefore the best sort of foreigner, so to speak), subsequently in the service of Gaunt's second wife, Constance of Castile, and apparently the sister of the woman who became Gaunt's mistress and eventually his third wife. Such contacts make it the less surprising that Chaucer should have thought of directing a copy of his *Legend of Good Women* to Richard II's queen (cf. pp. 327–9 below). Philippa may not have brought the poet much wealth, but she may have helped to bring his poems into the homes of high-ranking women.

However, Richard Green has urged that the number of women in royal households was far less than one might easily infer from the appeals to them in courtly literature, and noted the separateness of the respective households of kings and queens. If we think of Chaucer as reading aloud his poems 'after supper in the king's chamber or hall . . . we must think of him reading to an audience which was primarily, if not exclusively, male' (p. 149). Yet Green also emphasizes that 'Though the number of women at Richard II's court was probably proportionately very small, it was undoubtedly larger than at earlier periods' (p. 151), this being perhaps a general European trend. In other words, though the numbers of women were small their presence was highly significant, requiring some sort of literary attention and address, and therefore the notion of Chaucer reading to a mixed audience should not be dismissed out of hand as a literary fiction. One rather unfortunate, and no doubt quite unintentional, effect of Green's admirable study has been to discourage discussion (particularly among male critics) of the female audience which may plausibly be allowed to Chaucer. Strohm and Patterson steer well clear of the problem in their recent New Historicist discussions of literature and the Ricardian court, though (for example) Strohm's warning against confusing the audience *implied* by Chaucer's poetry (which contains many women readers and listeners) with his *actual* audience functions to reinforce the more negative part of Green's analysis. We need more work on those 'separate' households of queens and aristocratic women, with special reference to their consumption of literature. For the nonce, suffice it to note that women from that privileged social group certainly did not need men to read vernacular poetry to them or to enable them to engage in *ad hoc* literary debates (cf. pp. 293–9, 444–52 below).

And there is a strong possibility that at least one of the textual communities to which Chaucer directed his *Legend of Good Women* included aristocratic women such as Philippa of Lancaster, the daughter of Gaunt and Blanche, whom the poet's wife may have known well. Possibly she also knew to some extent Isabella, Duchess of York (the wife of Gaunt's brother Edmund and the sister of his second wife), who owned poems by Machaut, as we have already noted. Intriguingly, Isabella's son Edward, to whom she willed her Machaut along with her *Lancelot*, quoted the prologue to Chaucer's *Legend of Good Women* in the hunting treatise *The*

*Master of Game* which he produced between 1406 and 1413. While it is impossible to prove that such women were aware of some of Chaucer's poems, it would be stretching scepticism too far to suppose that they were completely ignorant of all of them.

John Gower, *The English Works*, ed. G. C. Macaulay, EETS ES 81–2 (Oxford, 1900–1). All subsequent Gower citations are from this edition. Mathew, *Court of Richard II*.

On the 'Lollard Knights' see especially K. B. McFarlane, *Lancastrian Kings and Lollard Knights* (Oxford, 1972), pp. 139–232; Hudson, *Premature Reformation*, pp. 63, 90, 110–19, 216–17, 368, 421–3, 430, 516; J. A. Tuck, 'Carthusian Monks and Lollard Knights: Religious Attitudes at the Court of Richard II', *SAC, Proceedings*, 1 (1984), 149–61.

Reginald Pecock, *The Reule of Crysten Religioun*, ed. W. C. Greet, EETS OS 171 (London, 1927). What a learned layman could achieve is well illustrated by an enormous encyclopaedic project, the *Omne Bonum*, which was pursued by Jacobus Palmer, a London bureaucrat, who died in 1375. He was also the scribe of a manuscript containing William of Nottingham's *Unus ex quatuor* (a treatise which demonstrates the harmony of the four gospels). See Penn R. Szittya, *The Antifraternal Tradition in Medieval Literature* (Princeton, NJ, 1986), pp. 67–81. William Langland, *The Vision of Piers Plowman: A Complete Edition of the B-Text*, ed. A. V. C. Schmidt (London and New York, 1978). All subsequent Langland citations are from this edition.

For the Deschamps poem in praise of Chaucer see the reference above, p. 18. Clifford is called 'l'amoureux-Cliffort' in Eustache Deschamps, *Oeuvres complètes*, ed. Marquis de Queux de Saint-Hilaire and G. Raynaud, SATF (Paris, 1878–1903), iii. 375–6. On the Deschamps–Chaucer link see G. L. Kittredge, 'Chaucer and Some of his Friends', *MP* 1 (1903), 1–18; Laura Kendrick, 'Rhetoric and the Rise of Public Poetry: The Career of Eustache Deschamps', *SP* 80 (1983), 1–13. The importance and continuity of French culture in English court circles is affirmed by Rossell Hope Robbins, 'Geoffroi Chaucier, Poète Français, Father of English Poetry', *ChR* 13 (1978), 93–115. The citation of Walsingham, monk of St Albans (c.1345–1422), is from the *Historia Anglicana*, ed. H. T. Riley (London, 1863–64), ii. 156; cf. M. Bennett, 'Promotion of Literature', p. 9. On Walsingham's other works, which include a collection of 'lives' of the major Latin poets, a moralized *Metamorphosis* (the *Arcana deorum*), and an expanded version of the *Ephemeris belli Troiani* attributed to Dictys Cretensis (the *Dites ditatus*), see A. G. Rigg, *A History of Anglo-Latin Literature, 1066–1422* (Cambridge, 1992), pp. 297–8. On Montagu's poetry see McFarlane, *Lancastrian Kings*, p. 182. Froissart describes Sturry as 'an auncyent knyght, whome I knewe in kynge Edwardes dayes'; trans. Bourchier, vi. 140; cf. pp. 141–7, on how Sturry confided in him and subsequently helped to bring about his audience with the king.

James Sherborne, 'Aspects of English Court Culture in the Later Fourteenth Century', in Scattergood and Sherborne (eds.), *English Court Culture*, pp. 1–27. V. J. Scattergood, 'Literary Culture at the Court of Richard II', *ibid.* 29–43. Isabella of York left to her son Edward two books, 'marchart et launcelot'; cited by K. B. McFarlane, *The Nobility of Later Medieval England* (Oxford, 1973), p. 236 n. 5. To Sir Lewis Clifford she bequeathed her 'livre de vicez et vertuz' (cf. p. 30 below). On the 'new men' see especially Anne Middleton, 'Chaucer's "New Men" and the Good of Literature in the *Canterbury Tales*', in Edward W. Said (ed.), *Literature and Society*, Selected Papers from the English Institute, NS 3 (Baltimore and London, 1980), pp. 15–56. On Chaucer and the king's affinity see especially Paul Strohm, *Social Chaucer* (Cambridge, Mass., and London, 1989), pp. 24–46.

Christopher Given-Wilson, *The Royal Household and the King's Affinity. Service, Politics and Finance in England, 1360–1413* (New Haven, Conn., and London, 1986). J. A. Tuck, 'The Baronial Opposition to Richard II, 1377–89' (Ph.D. diss., University of Cambridge, 1966); *idem, Richard II and the English Nobility* (London, 1973).

Patterson, *Subject of History.* Strohm, *Social Chaucer.* Kane, *Chaucer.* The bibliography on Chaucer's audience is vast. In addition the references given above see especially Pearsall, *Life of Chaucer,* pp. 178–85; Dieter Mehl, 'Chaucer's Audience', *Leeds Studies in English,* NS 10 (1978), 58–73; Anne Middleton, 'The Idea of Public Poetry in the Reign of Richard II', *Speculum,* 53 (1978), 94–114; Richard Firth Green, 'The *Familia Regis* and the *Familia Cupidinis*', in Scattergood and Sherborne (eds.), *English Court Culture,* pp. 87–108; also the discussion by Strohm, R. F. Green, R. T. Lenaghan, and Patricia J. Eberle in *ChR* 18 (1983), 136–81.

For recent scholarship on the *Boece* see A. J. Minnis (ed.), *Chaucer's 'Boece' and the Medieval Tradition of Boethius* (Cambridge, 1993). On Usk see especially Paul Strohm, 'Politics and Poetics: Usk and Chaucer in the 1380s', in Lee Patterson (ed.), *Literary Practice and Social Change in Britain, 1380–1530* (Berkeley and Los Angeles, 1990), pp. 83–112. The dating of the *Testament* is discussed on p. 97.

The tenuousness of the link between Philippa Chaucer and Sir Paon de Roet is rightly emphasized by Pearsall, *Life of Chaucer,* pp. 49–51. It should be noted also that what seems to be the earlier version of the prologue to the *Legend* is usually dated between 1386 and 1388, while Chaucer's wife died in 1387; moreover, their respective careers and duties meant that they had to live apart for long periods.

Richard Firth Green, 'Women in Chaucer's Audience', *ChR* 18 (1983), 146–54. A more positive line is taken by Michael Bennett, 'Promotion of Literature', who states that 'Ladies certainly figured prominently in court circles, and it is significant that his [i.e. Richard's] improvements at Eltham and Clarendon included dancing rooms'. 'The extension and renovation of the palaces at Eltham, King's Langley, and Sheen in the mid-1380s must testify to Richard's interest in providing a congenial setting for courtly dalliance' (p. 9). On the sparse evidence for female readership of Chaucer which may be gleaned from the manuscripts of his works, see Carol M. Meale, '"... alle the bokes that I haue of latyn, englisch, and frensch": Laywomen and their Books in Late-Medieval England', in C. M. Meale (ed.), *Women and Literature in Britain 1150–1500* (Cambridge, 1993), p. 142.

For the *LGW* quotation in Edward of York's *Master of Game* see p. 327 below. The meaning of the term 'textual community' is defined on p. 305.

## Princepleasing and the Poetics of Reticence

Another means of negotiating the position that, whatever the poet's social position may have been, his poems would have been welcome in the *camera regis,* takes the form of a demonstration that he wrote about matters in which the king was interested. The contents of Oxford, Bodleian Library MS Bodley 581, a compilation of texts apparently made for Richard II, are highly revealing. (The book may even have been commissioned by him, as Mathew assumes, but that is a dubious inference.) Richard is complimented in the most effusive terms at the beginning of the first item in this manuscript, *De quadripartita regis specie* (a treatise in the 'advice to princes' genre). The *Liber judiciorum,* a geomantic work which occupies fols. 9ᵛ–7ʳ, has a colophon which declares that it was prepared for the 'consolation' of the most noble king in 1391 (beside this statement is what seems to be a portrait of Richard II). A collection of astrological diagrams, which occupies fols. 87ᵛ–89ᵛ, bears the title *Rosarium Regis Ricardi*. The other texts found therein are a dream-vision treatise, the *Somniale Danielis*, which deals briefly with the causes, effects, and interpretations of different kinds of dreams; the *Phisionomia Aristotelis*, which explains how one can discover the character of a man from his features; a second geomantic tract; and a planetary table.

Taken as a whole, this book designed to please a prince is a veritable index of major literary and intellectual tastes in Ricardian England. Its concerns are clearly reflected in much literature of the time, and most of all in Chaucer's works. His mastery and manipulation of the dream-vision form will be demonstrated below; much dream-lore is retailed by Gower and William Langland also. The prophet Daniel, who gives his name but nothing else to the treatise mentioned above, was often cited as an authority on dreams—for example, by Langland in *Piers Plowman* (B vii. 150–1) and Gower in the *Confessio Amantis* (Prol. 590–880, i. 2859–953, and vi. 1405). It is worth adding that Richard's tutor Sir Simon Burley owned a copy of the *Somniale Danielis* (in French); another copy belonged to the king's uncle, Thomas of Woodstock, Duke of Gloucester. Chaucer had much to say on the problems relating to stellar influence and predestination. His interest in the more technical aspects of astronomy and astrology is evident from many passages in his poems, as well as the *Treatise on the Astrolabe* (along with the *Equatorie of the Planetis*, if that may be accepted as Chaucer's work); and the depth of his expertise has been established beyond all doubt by John D. North's recent study. A passage in the *Knight's Tale* evinces some knowledge of the closely associated pseudo-science of geomancy. Chaucer's excursions into the 'Advice to Princes' mode have already been noted. Moreover, the seventh book of Gower's *Confessio Amantis* consists of a *de regimine principum* which is in part indebted to the main source of the *De quadripartita regis specie*: namely, the pseudo-Aristotelian *Secretum secretorum*. Gower had presumed to instruct King Richard in his duties in the sixth book of an earlier poem, the Latin *Vox clamantis*.

In other words, if one takes the contents of MS Bodley 581 in conjunction with Richard's interest in love-poetry, as illustrated by the king's warm reaction to Froissart's presentation volume (it being unclear from *Confessio Amantis*, Prol. 24–92*, if Richard's request that Gower should write 'Som newe thing' for him to read was a specific request for a love-poem), Chaucer and Gower seem to have been writing the kinds of things which he wanted to read. Of course, it could be objected that there is nothing particularly personal in these allegedly regal tastes—though one may feel that Richard had special reasons for wanting to know what the future would bring and how he could identify his true friends. Indeed, French kings and nobles were interested in exactly the same subjects. But this is simply to say, yet again, that Richard was a prince of his time. And a prince who was pleased to be linked with a great poet of antiquity in his tomb inscription, if we may assume that he himself had chosen it: 'Prudent and pure, Richard II, lawfully king, conquered by fate . . . Tall in stature, he was prudent in mind like Homer (*animo prudens ut Omerus*). He favoured the Church, and aided the nobles . . .' (the original Latin is in rather clumsy leonine hexameters).

The minimal conclusion which can be drawn from all this is that, as courtly consumers, the king and his intimates were definitely not out of step with the literary culture of their day; to speculate that Richard actively encouraged it may be rash, but is by no means a ridiculous supposition. While there is no hard evidence that any of his personal attitudes directly influenced a word that Chaucer, Gower, Clanvowe, or Montagu wrote, it is apparent (in the case of the first three here named) that much of their poetry was in keeping with the predilections of King Richard and Queen Anne, and/or those of their courtiers, in so far as we can infer these from the scraps of evidence which we have. It is most unfortunate that the records of Richard's personal expenditure, the chamber accounts, do not survive. As Richard Green and Michael Bennett have emphasized, those would have given the details of the king's gifts and rewards to those who had pleased or entertained him, hence revealing *inter alia* the nature and extent of any royal interest in literature.

At this point what may be called the 'symptomatic' argument should be considered; namely, that what has survived is to be regarded as indicative of much that may well have existed but has been irretrievably lost. This argument is especially appropriate, given that the later ruling dynasty had a considerable vested interest in obscuring and indeed destroying the achievements of Richard II and his affinity. Artefacts associated with the deposed king would have had even less chance of survival than usual; the same could be said about certain items belonging to knights who were suspected of Lollardy. Following Michael Bennett, one can point to Gower's suppression of his original prologue to the *Confessio Amantis*, the effacement of Richard's portrait in MS Bodley 581, and the destruction by Bolingbroke of the white hart and hind which Thomas Holland, Duke of Surrey, had set on the gates of Warwick Castle. In short, suspecting that the evidence has been suppressed or at least tampered with, we are obliged to make the best we can of the little we have, with no way of knowing whether it is representative or exceptional. One may ruefully recall the passage in Chaucer's *House of Fame* wherein a company which requests the 'good renoun' which their works deserve suffers a curt dismissal by a goddess who is no respecter of intrinsic merit:

> 'I werne yow hit, quod she [Fame] anon;
> Ye gete of me good fame non,
> Be God, and therefore goo your wey.'
> 'Allas,' quod they, 'and welaway!
> Telle us what may your cause be.'
> 'For me lyst hyt noght,' quod she . . .                    (1559–64)

Fame is fickle, artistic works are fragile, and history is in the hands of the victor.

What, then, of Chaucer's own allusions to the great and powerful? How do they help us to locate his work? The most substantial reference is found in the *Book of the Duchess*, an elegy for 'goode faire White' (948), Duchess Blanche of Lancaster, John of Gaunt's first wife. The ending of this poem puns on 'long castel' (meaning 'Lancaster') and 'ryche hil' (one of Gaunt's titles was Earl of Richmond), while the 'walles white' allude to Blanche herself (1318–20). There is no reason to doubt that Blanche's death occasioned this poem, and it is highly unlikely that the Gaunt household would have been unaware or unappreciative of it. Moreover, one of the versions of the prologue to the *Legend of Good Women* alludes to Queen Anne of Bohemia, who is to receive a copy; and this poem, along with the *Parliament of Fowls*, which was probably written in celebration of some St Valentine's Day, seems designed to be read aloud in mixed and/or single-sex gatherings of aristocrats, on occasions whether grand or modest we cannot tell. St Valentine's Day is also lauded in the *Legend* and the *Complaint of Mars*. The scribe John Shirley associated the *Complaint of Mars* and the *Complaint of Venus* with Isabella of York and John Holland, Duke of Exeter. Rather than alluding to an adulterous affair, however, Shirley's cryptic comment may refer to a courtly 'disguising' or 'mumming' at which one or both of the poems were recited by those aristocrats. Unfortunately, corroborative evidence is lacking in the complaints themselves, and we know from other cases that Shirley's claims can be far off the mark. We are on safer ground in detecting a punning allusion to Sir Philip de la Vache in one copy of the envoy to Chaucer's moral ballade *Truth*: this de la Vache was the son-in-law and heir of the 'Lollard knight' Sir Lewis Clifford. Isabella of York left Clifford her book 'of vices and virtues' in her will. Finally, to move beyond the age of Richard II, Chaucer's *Complaint to his Purse* is often regarded as a plea, or at least a reminder, to Henry IV, which (the argument continues) perhaps brought about the desired payment; but this is sheer conjecture (cf. pp. 510–11 below).

Such allusions and inferences—others will be considered in the chapters that follow—have rightly excited many Chaucerians; yet they appear insubstantial in the light of what is known of the courtly contexts and connections of the Old French princepleasers who exerted such an influence on the young Chaucer. Machaut's first patron was Jean of Luxembourg, King of Bohemia, whose sagacity is praised in the *Jugement dou Roy de Behaingne*. The beloved lady in Machaut's *Remede de Fortune* is based on Jean's daughter Bonne, while the lover who is forced to part with his beloved in the *Dit de la fonteinne amoureuse* is apparently modelled on one of Bonne's sons, the Duke of Berry: Machaut identifies both the Duke and himself in an anagram near the beginning of that poem. Moreover, he composed two long poems for Charles, King of Navarre, and his sixth *complainte* is written on behalf of Peter of Cyprus to Margaret of Flanders. Froissart too moved in the orbit of the highest nobility: in his *Temple d'Honneur* he declares that he has met no less than ten kings and also an emperor at Rome. Froissart's *Prison amoureuse* and *Dit dou Bleu Chevalier* honour one of his patrons, Wenceslas of Brabant, Bonne's brother and a poet in his own right: eighty of his poems are inserted in Froissart's *Meliador*. Similarly, Deschamps alleged his intimacy with the French royal family, especially Charles VI and Louis of Orléans. Here aristocratic approval and involvement affirm the high quality and prestige of the poetry.

But such was not Chaucer's style; when he dropped names, they were of writers rather than of royalty. One might even say that Chaucer's own personality (in so far as one can speculate about that) has muddied the waters. It is one of the great paradoxes of literary history that someone who has a convincing claim to the title of 'the father of our English poets' (as George Puttenham called him) should have been so reticent about affirming his status as a poet and the merits of his art. The contrast with Machaut's sense of poetic identity is instructive. Here was an accomplished princepleaser who confidently displayed his expertise in the art of courtly love whilst urbanely complimenting his patrons on their refinement and sagacity. According to Machaut's poetic, no one could write adequately of love without having actually experienced all its noble (and ennobling) passion and pain. The *Book of the Duchess* opens with an instantly recognizable (to connoisseurs of French courtly poetry) portrait of the unrequited and sleepless courtly lover, his horizons bounded by the text and gloss of the *Roman de la Rose*. Yet it is this figure's *lack* of experience rather than his expertise which is his distinguishing characteristic. And in subsequent poems that persona was to develop into a bookish, detached observer who disclaims personal knowledge of love ('I knowe nat Love in dede', *Parliament of Fowls*, 8), and declares that he writes of the subject without personal feeling: 'of no sentement I this endite'; 'I speeke of love unfelyngly' (*Troilus and Criseyde*, ii. 13, 19–21).

The difference between this and Machaut's self-image, or indeed Giovanni Boccaccio's similar poet-portrait in *Il Filostrato* (the primary source of *Troilus and Criseyde*), could hardly be greater. When Chaucer discovered the Italian poets, he became aware (to what extent is not clear) of Dante's grand claims for himself as vatic poet and for his illustrious vernacular; he certainly knew about Petrarch's coronation as poet laureate. Yet, with the exception of the ending of *Troilus* (the most Italianate of all his works), where he places his 'litel bok' in deferential but definite proximity to 'Virgile, Ovide, Omer, Lucan, and Stace' (v. 1786–92), his reaction to all this was to work harder at turning self-deprecation into a fine art. The nadir (or is it the peak?) of this process must surely be the moment in the *Canterbury Tales* in which an ineffectual elvish figure who perpetually stares at the ground, avoiding human contact (viii. 696, 703–4), recites the worst poem of all, the drasty rhymes of *Sir Thopas*. Yet this poem is a superb parody, and the fact that Chaucer here, in the most ambitious and original of all his literary works, chose (at least initially, for the *Melibee* follows) to make his personal mark with a parody speaks volumes in itself. It certainly seems reasonable to assume that someone like this is unlikely to have made the most, at least in his writings, of whatever connections he may have had or expressions of royal favour or interest he may have received.

The contrast with Gower's proud account of how Richard II invited him onto the royal barge to talk, 'amonges othre thinges', about his poetry is obvious. However, Chaucer was not alone in such reticence. At the end of Clanvowe's *Book of Cupid* all the birds decide to hold a parliament to debate the respective merits of the cuckoo and the nightingale, the venue being the green in front of Queen Anne's window at Woodstock Manor (she was there with Richard in 1389 and almost certainly at other times as well):

> And this shal be, withouten any nay,
> The morwe of Seynt Valentynes day,
> Vnder the maple that is feire and grene,
> Before the chambre wyndow of the Quene
> At Wodestok, vpon the grene lay.                    (281–5)

From this modest reference, and from the way in which the narrator is presented as a somewhat naïve figure (cf. p. 291 below) inasmuch as he defends the over-optimistic nightingale against the worldly-wise and cynical cuckoo, one could never have inferred that this poem's author was 'an intimate and trusted member of Richard's "court party"', as Scattergood calls him (p. 26). But that is precisely what he was. Can this be taken as evidence of a general Ricardian court style in literature, a poetics of reticence? (Gower being in the outer circle, could be regarded as therefore less susceptible to the charms of designer understatement.) It might be said that there is something quintessentially English about this polite self-effacement—the contrast with French ostentation being marked—but I have no wish to lapse into vacuous generalizations about national stereotypes. Besides, Clanvowe could simply have learned such literary manners from Chaucer.

Whatever its causes, the reticence in Chaucer—and Clanvowe—is certainly marked, and therefore one should not dismiss lightly the hypothesis that Chaucer's few and restrained allusions to court personages may be the mere tip of an iceberg. This, of course, cannot be proved or disproved. But the idea tantalizes. While it is impossible to say how much 'fun' it was for a poet at the court of Richard II (in whatever circle), it would seem that reports of the dearth of literary culture there have been greatly exaggerated.

On Bodley 581 see Mathew, *Court of Richard II*, pp. 40 1; Jean-Philippe Genet (ed.), *Four English Political Tracts of the Later Middle Ages*, Camden Fourth Series, 18 (London, 1977), pp. 22–30 (followed by an edition of the *De quadripartita regis specie*, pp. 31–9). On Gower's interest in the prophet Daniel see Russell A. Peck, 'John Gower and the Book of Daniel', in R. F. Yeager (ed.), *John Gower: Recent Readings* (Kalamazoo, Mich., 1989), pp. 159–87. John D. North, *Chaucer's Universe* (Oxford, 1988).
The tomb epitaph's comparison of Richard II with Homer is made much of by M. Bennett, 'Promotion of Literature', p. 16, who speculates that maybe 'the king regarded himself as a man who, like Homer, understood the past and foresaw the future, drawing on the traditions of his people, securing their transmission, and shaping them for visionary ends. If the king felt that he had played some role in the promotion of English literature . . . the identification with Homer would be the more apt. Richard II, after all, presided over a court in which a remarkable cluster of poets found inspiration, and his sponsorship beginning in the mid-1380s might well have been crucial in firmly establishing the status of English as a language of high literary endeavor. If the deposition and death of Richard II were responsible for the final break-up of the remarkable coterie of courtiers that had been the primary audience for Chaucer's verse, and for the ending of that eccentric flow of patronage that was probably the frame for the finest works in the alliterative revival, it would explain a great deal about the sudden ending of England's first "golden age" of literature and about the patterns of literary activity and sponsorship in the fifteenth century. The Lancastrian kings should perhaps be seen as maintaining, in a less eclectic and generous spirit, a tradition of royal patronage first properly established in the reign of Richard II.' There are many problems with this analysis, the fundamental one being that it seems to have constructed a large claim from very slim evidence. Then again, Bennett's view of Homer is quite anachronistic. In Chaucer's day he was often regarded as a propagandist for the Greeks

(in the *House of Fame* 'oon' says that he was a maker of lies; cf. pp. 230–1 below), whereas the British saw themselves as the descendants of the Trojans. Cf. particularly the wish of Nicholas Brembre, several times Lord Mayor of London, to rename London as 'New Troy'; he had hoped—with the help of the king—to become 'Duke of Troy' (Windeatt, *OGC: T&C*, p. 8). It may be wondered, therefore, if the featuring of the name 'Omerus' in the epitaph was due to the requirements of rhyme and metre rather than those of ideology.

Green, *Poets and Princepleasers*, pp. 5–6; M. Bennett, 'Promotion of Literature', 14–15. On the destruction of objects associated with the king see Bennett, pp. 15–16. Information regarding the various biases at work in chroniclers' accounts of Richard may be gleaned from Antonia Grandsen, *Historical Writing in England*, ii: *c.1307 to the Early Sixteenth Century* (London and Henley, 1982), 157–93; and John Taylor, *English Historical Literature in the Fourteenth Century* (Oxford, 1987), pp. 175–94.

John of Gaunt had connections with two Anglo-Latin writers. Richard Maidstone, his confessor, composed a 548-line Latin poem on London's welcome for Richard II in August 1392; he also prepared a verse translation, in English, of the penitential Psalms (cf. EETS OS 155 (London, 1917), pp. xvi–xvii, 103–4). Walter of Peterborough wrote a 670-line Latin poem, mainly in single-sound elegiacs, on the English expedition to Spain and the battle of Najera in 1367, which was led by the Black Prince and John of Gaunt. Its prologue, addressed to Gaunt's treasurer, John Marton, praises both these princes. Walter also produced a Christian allegorization of Ovid's *Metamorphoses* for Gaunt ('duce pro nostro'), and wrote a 5,000-line Latin poem for the Black Prince at the Battle of Poitiers in 1356 (he claims to have been the prince's poet on that occasion). Neither of these last two works has survived. See Rigg, *History of Anglo-Latin Literature*, pp. 276–8, 285–6.

On the controversy surrounding Shirley's comment on the complaints of Mars and Venus see especially John Norton Smith, *Geoffrey Chaucer* (London, 1974), pp. 24–5; also the brief discussion and the references in the *Riverside Chaucer*, p. 1079.

For Puttenham's statement see G. Gregory Smith (ed.), *Elizabethan Critical Essays* (London, 1904), ii. 17. On Machaut's self-construction in his poetry see especially Kevin Brownlee, *Poetic Identity in Guillaume de Machaut* (Madison, Wis., 1984).

Clanvowe, *Works*, ed. Scattergood. It should be added that there may well have been good political reasons for at least some manifestations of Chaucer's reticence. Strohm, 'Politics and Poetics', suggests that he probably realized as early as 1384–5 that the wind was blowing against the royal party (pp. 91–2); if indeed he was seeking to 'curtail his royal commitments' (p. 93), he would certainly not have been trumpeting his royalist links in poetry. Cf. Pearsall, *Life of Chaucer*, pp. 208–9.

M. Bennett, 'Promotion of Literature', declares that there are grounds for supposing that Richard II played a more positive role in the promotion of English letters than has been recently allowed. He talks of a major literary 'breakthrough in the mid-1380s, the very time when it becomes meaningful to talk about the impact of the king's personality and the role of the court' (p. 11). Furthermore, 'In the 1390s litterateurs like Jean Froissart, Eustace Deschamps, Oton de Grandson, Philippe de Mézières, Christine de Pisan, and Jean Creton did not share the contempt for the English court evident in some modern scholarship' (p. 10). 'When it comes to setting the conditions for the sudden scaling of the heights of vernacular eloquence, the gentry and the bourgeoisie seem unlikely heroes', given that social contexts imposed definite ceilings on literary quality (p. 4). Although the literary culture under discussion 'is wholly conceivable on the fringes of rather than within the court itself', he continues, 'it is a little perverse to come so close to the royal court, and then to remain so obdurately on its threshold' (p. 7). Cf. to some extent Salter, 'Chaucer and Internationalism', who argues that the wish to challenge the insubstantial documentation of older accounts of Chaucer as court poet, 'with patrons among the innermost circles of the English royal family', should not lead us so far in the opposite direction 'as to exclude the possibility that those innermost circles were, in fact, influential upon the development of his literary as well as his professional activities'. 'It is difficult to believe that Richard knew little of Chaucer's poetry, and cared less' (pp. 79–80).

# Chaucer and the Love-Vision Form

The literary form which dominates Chaucer's Shorter Poems is that of the dream-vision: the *Book of the Duchess, House of Fame*, and *Parliament of Fowls* and the prologue to the *Legend of Good Women* all feature narrators who experience highly significant slumber. The main subject treated within the dream framework is love, though in the *House of Fame* as we now have it love-tidings are promised but not actually reported. It is appropriate, therefore, to provide a general discussion of these matters at the outset, before proceeding to consider the individual poems.

## *'Sweven in ryme': The Art of Dreaming*

The love-vision form enjoyed a quite exceptional vogue in the late medieval period, appearing in many guises and in several European languages. Of all the vernacular genres which flourished then, it was probably the most consummately ambiguous and contested, capable of either elevation through citation of biblical visions or denigration by reference to scientific and medical warnings against taking dream phenomena too seriously or with the wrong kind of seriousness. Chaucer's visions of love, like the dream-books which his narrators read before embarking on their own dreams, were of course not reports of actual visions, but rather literary inventions which drew their terms of reference from dream theory. It is necessary, then, to understand something of the theory in order to better grasp the significance of the texts and to locate the site on which old fact joined forces with new fiction.

Before recounting his dream of the Man in Black, the narrator of the *Book of the Duchess* refers to two great experts in the art of dream divination: namely, Joseph, who explained the dreams of Pharaoh (Genesis 41), and Macrobius (*fl.* 400), who wrote a commentary on the *Somnium Scipionis* of Marcus Tullius Cicero (106–43 BC). A little later we are told that the room in which the dreamer first finds himself is decorated with scenes from the *Roman de la Rose*. Begun by Guillaume de Lorris, who wrote the first 4,058 lines between 1230 and his death in 1237, this poem was completed by Jean de Meun, a university-trained scholar based in Paris, who added 17,722 lines between *c.*1269 and 1278. Their account of how an ardent lover rejects the advice of Reason in order to woo and eventually win his lady, who is imaged as a rose, was the most widely read and influential of all the vernacular love-visions. Indeed, Chaucer's reference to Macrobius's commentary on the *Somnium Scipionis*—

> . . . Macrobeus
> (He that wrot al th'avysyoun
> That he mette, kyng Scipioun,        *that King Scipio dreamed*
> The noble man, the Affrikan—
> Suche marvayles fortuned than)        (284–8)

—may well have come from the beginning of the *Roman*, where Guillaume de Lorris speaks of Macrobius 'who did not take dreams as trifles, for he wrote of the vision which came to King Scipio' (7–10; trans. Dahlberg, p. 31). In fact, Scipio was not a king. Guillaume seems to have led Chaucer into making this mistake—or is it a medievalization (as when Orpheus becomes King Orfeo in the Middle English romance *Sir Orfeo*)? At any rate, the Middle English text does add one detail which is not in the *Roman*, in giving Scipio his cognomen 'the Affrikan'. And by the time Chaucer wrote the *Parliament of Fowls* he certainly had studied the *Somnium Scipionis*—and, by implication, Macrobius—in some detail, for that poem begins with a summary of this seminal dream-vision (cf. pp. 266–71).

Macrobius distinguishes between five main types of dreams (*In Somnium Scipionis*, i. 3; trans. Stahl, pp. 87–92). These are the enigmatic dream (*somnium*), the prophetic vision (*visio*; cf. Chaucer's 'avision', *BD* 285, *HF* 7), the oracular dream (*oraculum*; cf. 'oracle', *HF* 11), the nightmare (*insomnium*), and the apparition (*visum*, *phantasma* in Greek; cf. Chaucer's 'fantome', *HF* 11). The last two, declares Macrobius, are not worth interpreting since they have no prophetic significance. The apparition occurs when one is half-asleep, between wakefulness and slumber; in which condition a man, supposing he is fully awake, may imagine spectres rushing at him or an incubus pressing upon him. Nightmares are caused by some sort of distress, whether mental (as when the lover dreams of having his mistress or of losing her) or physical (caused, for example, by an excess of food or drink), or by anxiety about the future, as when a man dreams that he is gaining or losing some important position. Virgil, Macrobius continues, holds nightmares to be deceitful; thus, the poet has the love-stricken Dido say to her sister Anna, 'what dreams (*insomnia*) thrill me with fears?' (*Aeneid*, iv. 9). The concerns of love 'are always accompanied by nightmares'. The other three types of dream, however, are of assistance in foretelling the future. In the *oraculum* a pious or revered individual, or even a god, appears to reveal to the dreamer what will or will not transpire, and what should or should not be done about it. As Chaucer puts it, in these cases

> . . . the soule of propre kynde     *of its individual nature*
> Be so parfit, as men fynde,
> That yt forwot that ys to come     *knows in advance*
>
> (43–5)

These dreams have one major distinguishing characteristic: they actually come true. The enigmatic dream, however, is the type which 'conceals with strange shapes and veils with ambiguity the true meaning of the information being offered, and requires an interpretation for its understanding'. There are five types of this dream, according to Macrobius: the personal, alien, social, public, and universal. The personal *somnium* occurs 'when one dreams that he himself is doing or experiencing something; alien, when he dreams this about someone else; social, when his dream involves others and himself; public, when he dreams that some misfortune or benefit has befallen the city' or some other public site; 'universal, when he dreams that some change has taken place in the sun, moon, planets, sky, or regions of the earth'.

However, a given dream can partake of several of these types; thus Scipio's dream 'embraces the three reliable types mentioned above, and also has to do with all five varieties of the enigmatic dream' (trans. Stahl, p. 90). Following this lead, we could classify the adventures of Chaucer's dreamers as follows. The Man in Black in the *Book of the Duchess* is a revered individual of the type expected in a true dream or *oraculum*; one could say the same about Alceste and the God of Love in the prologue to the *Legend of Good Women*. The *Parliament of Fowls* is briefly honoured with the presence of Scipio Africanus the Elder, straight from Cicero's *Somnium Scipionis*, and subsequently Dame Nature holds sway. In the *House of Fame*, however, a man of great authority is heralded but does not actually appear in the poem as we have it. However, none of these figures makes a clear and definite pronouncement about the future; no interpretation of the dream in question is offered directly within the poem itself, that activity being left to the audience, though the basic meaning is obvious enough. The Chaucerian self-construction, however, refuses to discuss what he has dreamed, limiting himself to declaring that it is a 'queynt . . . sweven' (*BD* 1330) or a 'wonderful . . . drem' (*HF* 62). Indeed, the dream of the Man in Black is said to be so 'curious' (as well as 'swete') a 'sweven' that no man had the intelligence to interpret it correctly, not even those two renowned authorities, Joseph and Macrobius.

It would seem, then, that the fictional dreams of Chaucer's Shorter Poems to some extent mimic the scientific category of the enigmatic dream. Moreover, they can be said to partake of several of its five varieties—without of course being actually divinely inspired, genuinely prophetic of future events. All of them are personal in that the I-personae are dreaming about themselves; alien, in that they are dreaming about the doings of others (the Man in Black in the *Book of the Duchess*; the eagle, Lady Fame, etc. in the *House of Fame*; the inhabitants of the *locus amœnus* and the various birds in the *Parliament*; the God of Love and Alceste in the prologue to the *Legend*); social, in that they themselves are involved, in various ways and to different extents, with those other people and creatures. The various companies of suppliants to Lady Fame, as described in the third book of the poem which bears her name, lend it a public dimension; in the *Parliament* the different levels of society are represented by the various species of birds, while the *Legend* could be called a public poem inasmuch as it considers the fates of high-ranking women at the hands of mendacious menfolk. The *House of Fame* and the *Parliament* both contain visions of the workings of the universe, thereby having a universal aspect.

A major technical difference, however, which separates the dream-poems under discussion from the dreams analysed thus by Macrobius, is that they are encoding present or past events and ideas rather than prophesying future ones: they lack that essential characteristics of the significant dream, the foretelling of some future event. In this way they contrast with, say, the dream of Chauntecleer, which features the frightening image of a hound-like creature, yellowish-red in colour and tipped with black. That does turn out to be a true indicator of his future capture by a fox: but according to his wife, he has merely suffered from a nightmare caused by a bodily imbalance. He is too choleric and melancholic, she declares, which explains why he has dreamt of something red and black in colour; a laxative will soon put matters right (*Nun's Priest's Tale*, VII. 2923–69). Are the dreams of Chaucer's personae therefore to be classified as examples of the *insomnium*, mere reflexes of some physical or mental disturbance such as love, over-indulgence, and the like? Given that they are specified as love-visions, are they to be put on a par with the fearsome *insomnia* of Dido? On the face of it, that would certainly diminish their status, even trivialize them—or at best reduce them to illustrations of behaviour which should be avoided. But there were other systems for describing and interpreting dreams apart from the Neoplatonic grid of Macrobius. In order to make this clear, we will have to widen the discussion.

Aristotle was a lot more sceptical about dreams than Plato had been. Man cannot think without images (*phantasmata, imagines*), he believed; the mental faculty which produces them, the imagination, is essential for the processes of human thought. However, it can deceive the mind, as when it tells us that the sun is only a foot in diameter. It is crucial, therefore, that the imagination be controlled by the reason. Unfortunately, on occasion this control is not exercised, as when someone is gripped by some powerful emotion (such as anger or desire), hindered by some physical disease or impediment—or asleep. In dreams, owing to the inactivity of the sense and the intellect, the imagination becomes particularly vivid (*De somniis*, iii; 460$^b$–1$^a$). When its phantasms seem to refer to future events, are they to be regarded as prophetic? This is not incredible, says Aristotle, but highly unlikely (*De divinatione per somnum*, i). Do any dreams, then, have a divine origin? The very idea is absurd, pronounces Aristotle, because in addition to its irrationality, one observes that dreams do not come to the best and wisest, but to commonplace persons, all sorts of men (462$^b$). He proceeds to suggest a rational explanation for such phenomena, concluding that most prophetic dreams are to be classed as mere coincidences (463$^{a–b}$).

By contrast, Plato believed that divine powers can use the human imagination as a means of communicating with the human mind through the implanting of visions. In *Republic* IX he argues that if a man manages to quieten the parts of his mind which are likely to produce hallucinations, he can in sleep receive divine emanations: 'then he attains truth most nearly, and is least likely to be the sport of fantastic and lawless visions' (571$^d$–72$^b$; trans. Jowett, ii. 442). In the *Timaeus* a vision of this sort is conceived of as a kind of disorder or madness: 'God has given the art of divination not to the wisdom, but to the foolishness of man. No man, when in his wits, attains prophetic truth and inspiration.' While he continues to be demented, 'he cannot judge of the visions which he sees or the words which he utters'; this can be done only after he recovers his wits (72$^a$; trans. Jowett, iii. 759). This doctrine was, quite clearly, regarded by Aristotle as subversive; hence his remark that so-called prophetic dreams come not to 'the best and wisest of men'. But for Plato the expert in dialectic was not the highest type of the man of vision.

Christian philosophers sought to negotiate positions which accommodated elements of both Platonic enthusiasm and Aristotelian scepticism. The importance of dreams and visions in Hebrew literature made it an easy step to the belief that God communicates truth to man in terms of imagination. Hence Augustine, in his *De Genesi ad Litteram*, refers to divine influence on the imagination when speaking of 'spiritual' vision, this being a sort of mean between the extremes of 'corporeal' vision and 'intellectual' vision. 'Corporeal' vision refers to normal sight; it can be deceptive, as when a navigator thinks that the stars are moving. 'Intellectual' vision occurs when God is seen in his own nature, as the rational and intellectual part of man is able to conceive of him. This never errs; it is beyond all likeness and every image. 'Spiritual' vision combines aspects of both these types, given that here one sees not a body but an image of a body, thus falling 'between that which is truly a body and that which is neither body nor the likeness of body' (xi. 24. 50; trans. in Bundy, p. 171).

This categorization was highly popular in medieval exegesis. It was summarized, in simplified form, in the Apocalypse prologue attributed to the twelfth-century theologian Gilbert of Poitiers, which was incorporated into the 'Paris Bible' as one of the standard set of prefaces. In this account of the *triplex genus visionum* the *visio spiritualis seu imaginaria* is said to occur when, either sleeping or awake, we see a likeness of something which betokens other things, as when the sleeping Pharaoh dreamed of ears of corn growing (Genesis 41: 5) or the awake Moses beheld the bush burning but not being consumed (Exodus 3: 2). This type corresponds fairly closely to the *oraculum*, or enigmatic dream, as defined by Macrobius. By contrast, in *visio intellectualis*, due to the revelation of the Holy Spirit, the human mind understands the truth of spiritual mysteries to the extent that it is capable of so doing. The obvious example of this occurred, as many medieval transmitters of Augustine's doctrine note, when St Paul was taken up (*raptus*) into the third heaven (2 Corinthians 12: 2-4). But Gilbert, rather surprisingly, declares that this happened in St John's Apocalypse also, on the grounds that the saint not only saw the images but also understood their significance. Not everyone agreed with him—after all, Augustine himself had classified the Apocalypse as a spiritual vision. However, Gilbert's desire to elevate the text which constituted the most extensive piece of visionary writing in the Bible is quite understandable. But who, then, was the most outstanding prophet? The twelfth-century standard gloss on the Bible, the *Glossa ordinaria*, names David, 'because he prophesied most clearly about Christ without any imaginary vision'. St Thomas Aquinas, however, opted for Moses for several reasons, including that the sight of understanding was most eminent in him and the sight of imagination existed in him most perfectly. These accounts make clear the considerable room for confusion within a given system of classification of visions and/or dreams, due to the inherent conflicts between the heterogeneous ideas which Christian thinkers were trying to yoke together.

The veracity of the above-mentioned scriptural visions was, of course, unimpeachable, but the rarity—and pastness—of such occurrences was generally emphasized, along with the supposition that later visionary experience had to be treated with the utmost caution, due to the possible unreliability of some dreamers, the natural potential which dream imagery had to mislead, and the fact that not only God but also the Devil could influence men through their imaginations. Thomas Aquinas admitted that moral goodness is not necessary for prophecy, for this gift can be bestowed on a sinner (like Balaam, for instance; cf. Numbers 22). Far more worrying is the fact that the Devil, who strives to darken man's reason, can lead men to sin by stimulating the imagination and the sense appetite (*Summa theologiae*, 1a 2ae, q. 80, art. 2). Aquinas gives the example of enticement to sexual sin, expanding Aristotle's statement in *De somniis* (ii. 460ᵇ) that 'even the faintest resemblance attracts the lover to the beloved' to include the doctrine that the Devil can stir up passions in the sense appetite to make one even more acutely aware of the imagined reality—hence even a 'faint resemblance' can produce a considerable temptation (trans. Fearon, pp. 223, 225). Imagination, then, plays a major part in much prophecy, but Aquinas apparently regarded it as a mixed blessing. He fully accepts, however, that not all prophecy is supernatural: it can be natural, deriving from the power of created causes, as when, for example, the imagination is influenced by heavenly bodies 'in which there pre-exist some signs of certain heavenly events' (trans. McGlynn, p. 119).

It was the natural causes of dreams, including those supposed to signify future events, which were emphasized in the brief treatise *De somniis* by the 'Latin Averroist' Boethius of Dacia, a major figure within the Arts Faculty at the University of Paris in the early 1270s. Some of our dreams have no connection whatever with future events, he argues, but are matters of coincidence: 'the event would have happened even if there had been no appearance similar to it in a dream' (trans. Wippel, p. 71). Dreams can be caused not by external but by internal forces, from the body or from the soul. Bodily causes include the motions and combinations of fumes and vapours and the various rates at which they rise. Thus, black and earthly vapours may cause someone to dream of flames and fires or of black monks (i.e. Benedictines), 'and certain foolish ones, having awakened, swear that they have seen devils while they were asleep' (p. 75). On the other hand, the power of imagination may be moved by clear vapours, so that sleepers 'dream that they are seeing brilliant places and angels singing and dancing. And when they have awakened they swear that they were carried away (*raptos*) and have in truth seen angels. And they are deceived because they are ignorant of the causes of things.' Illness may produce similar effects. But, none the less, Boethius adds hastily, 'I do not deny that by divine will an angel or a devil can in truth appear to a person who is sleeping or to one who is ill.' Soon he moves to discuss dreams produced in us from the side of the soul. Clearly influenced by the second chapter of Aristotle's *De somniis*, he notes that 'when a sleeper is subject to a strong passion of fear or of love, his imaginative power forms images which correspond to these passions such as a phantasm of an enemy or of his beloved' (pp. 76–7). The extent to which

Boethius strives to arrive at a scientific explanation of dreams in terms of their causes is remarkable, but he was too naturalistic for some. The thirty-third article on the list of propositions condemned at Paris by Bishop Stephen Tempier in 1277, 'That raptures and visions do not take place except through nature', seems to refer to this treatise. Obviously Boethius's protestation that he does not deny that the divine will can act on the imagination, as quoted above, was too little and too late.

Given the suspicion of imagination which runs through these accounts, it is little wonder that we have no fully articulated theory of *literary* dream-vision—that is, a theory to describe and justify the fictions which were stimulated by the facts of visionary experience as recorded in the Bible and other works of unimpeachable authority. This is most evident in the *Roman de la Rose*. Far from providing a self-justifying genre theory, this poem actually appears to undermine that human faculty which, according to medieval psychological analyses, was its very source and mechanism. In particular, Jean de Meun evinces unease about the reliability of the human powers of eyesight and imagination, and displays a disposition to seek natural causes for unusual phenomena, reminders that he lived and wrote in that Parisian intellectual milieu which could produce a thinker like his contemporary Boethius of Dacia. Jean has his Dame Nature remark that many people are so deceived by their dreams that they suffer extreme forms of sleep-walking, getting up and ready for work, and seizing their tools, even going considerable distances on horse-back. 'Then, when their common senses awake, they are completely amazed, and marvel'—and tell others 'that devils have taken them from their houses and brought them there. But they themselves brought themselves' (18,319–26; trans. Dahlberg, p. 304). Sometimes sickness acting on the imagination can cause such extraordinary events or an excess of melancholy or fear. Then again, certain contemplatives 'cause the appearance in their thought of the things on which they have pondered, only they believe that they see them quite clearly and outside themselves. But what they see is only a trifling lie' (18,357–63; pp. 304–5). Such a one, Nature declares with heavy irony, has experiences similar to Scipio's, seeing 'hell and paradise, heaven, air, sea, and earth, and all that one may seek there' (18,368–70). Alternatively, he may dream of people enjoying themselves in their rooms or out hunting, of 'wars and tournaments, balls and carols, and viols and citoles', of various smells or tastes, or indeed of feeling his beloved in his arms, even though in reality she is not there (18,376–88). Those 'who burn with love for one another' dream at night 'of the beloved things that they have asked for so much by day' or about possible impediments to their passion, just as those who are in a state of deadly hatred dream of anger and battles, or prisoners dream of their release or indeed their execution, depending on how hopeful they are (18,396–418).

A similar list of examples is provided by Chaucer in the *Parliament of Fowls*:

> The wery huntere, slepynge in his bed,
> To wode ayeyn his mynde goth anon;
> The juge dremeth how his plees been sped;            *cases*
> The cartere dremeth how his cart is gon;
> The riche, of gold; the knyght fyght with his fon;      *foe*
> The syke met he drynketh of the tonne;   *sick person dreams, cask*
> The lovere met he hath his lady wonne.         (99–105)

Both Jean and Chaucer are following a Claudian passage (*De IV consulato honorii*, 3–10) which was given wide currency by its inclusion in the grammar school anthology known as the *Liber Catonianus*, this title being due to the fact that it includes the *Distichs* of Pseudo-Cato. However, while the words may be Claudian's, the sceptical spirit behind them is very much that of the second book of *De somniis* (460ᵇ); they may be read as an amplification of Aristotle's statement that, when excited by emotions, we are easily deceived in respect of the operations of sense perception: for example, the coward when moved by fear, the amorous person by amorous desire; so that the former thinks he sees his enemies approaching and the latter that he sees the object of his desire.

Jean's failure to provide a literary theory of dream-vision was to some extent remedied by the first formal commentary to be written on a poem originally composed in French, the anonymous *Echecs amoureux* ('Chess of Love'), which was cast in the mould of the *Roman* sometime between 1370 and 1380. The commentator has recently been identified as Evrart de Conty (*c*.1330–1405), physician to Charles V and also to Blanche of Navarre, widow of Philippe VI. Writing during the 1390s, Evrart offered several justifications for the writing of fiction, one of them being the objective of speaking more safely and blamelessly. Plato, unlike Aristotle, made use of fiction, as when he composed the myth of Er, imagining how a knight who had been killed in battle returned to pronounce on the state of the soul after death. This method, however, did not appeal to certain people, who felt that he should have spoken openly on the subject. This ignorant reaction explains why, in his *Somnium Scipionis*, Cicero did not follow Plato's example, but instead used 'the mode of a dream', thereby avoiding all unreasonable objections. All this is based on Macrobius, *In Somnium Scipionis*, i. 1–2. Evrart saw, more clearly than many other readers of Macrobius, that Cicero was writing fiction (fiction which contained truth, to be sure; a veritable *narratio fabulosa*) rather than reporting an actual vision. He adds that the dream form 'sometimes excuses the person who speaks of many things that would be considered badly said' if they were taken as actually having happened or in a literal way. For the dreamer can always excuse himself on the grounds that he himself cannot be held responsible for what he dreamt about, declaring that 'it seemed that way to him while he slept and that it was imposed on him in a dream'.

Another *maniere de faindre*, continues Evrart, is the form of 'imaginary vision' (*ymaginaire vision*). This method was employed by Boethius in *De consolatione philosophiae*, when he wished to speak of the great misery into which Fortune had cast him. 'And he did this to avoid all presumption'— presumably meaning that by using the figure of Philosophy, he avoided setting himself up as a great authority on such high matters as divine providence and foreknowledge. This method is also used in the *Echecs amoureux*, Evrart continues. For the poet wished to imagine (*presendre*) that this vision of Nature and the things which later followed from it were neither a dream—presumably he means a real dream that the poet had actually experienced—nor a vision as real as those corporeal sights which are to be taken at face value. Thus, his vision was an 'imagined thing', a fiction. Imaginary vision, then, has moved from being a divine gift of significant imagery which with correct interpretation can yield accurate information about future events, an oracle which comes willy-nilly to the human recipient (as in the Augustinian theory of the *triplex genus visionum*), to something made up, quite voluntary, within human control, and not necessarily having anything to do with the future—an act of deliberate literary creation.

The poets who engaged in deliberate literary creation of dream-visions in the European vernaculars inherited the doctrines, often confused and conflicting as they were, which have been outlined above. And they made intriguing, sometimes quite extraordinary, use of them. In particular, they were able to exploit what Steven Kruger has called the 'doubleness' or 'middleness' of many dreams; the problem of their origin (divine or natural?), and hence of their truth, put them in 'a middle position', where they were 'involved in both the true and the false, exploring relations between divinity and the mundane, between mind and body' (p. 52). Such dreams, Kruger argues, 'are able to navigate that middle realm where connections between the corporeal and incorporeal are forged, where the relationship between the ideal and the physical is defined. Dreams can thus explore a wide range of human and universal experience, from the most exalted to the most debased' (p. 34). For the poets, here were means of invoking authority (both biblical and philosophical) whilst exploiting experience, of implying the existence of impersonal truth whilst offering conspicuous fiction; of at once claiming individual prestige and professing decorous modesty, of making large—indeed, sometimes controversial and *risqué*—claims which were accompanied by disclaimers of personal responsibility for what had been said within the dream framework. For people cannot help what they dream; the Franciscan theologian Richard of Middleton was expressing a common view when he answered in the negative the question of whether man naturally has the use of his free will in dreams.

Many of these strategies may be illustrated by the end of the *visio* of William Langland's *Piers Plowman* (B vii. 145–67). The narrator has often wondered about the meaning of his dreaming, but, he adds quite disingenuously, he has no real taste for dream interpretation, for he knows that it often fails.

> Cato and canonistres counseillen us to leve
> To sette sadnesse in songewarie—for *sompnia ne cures*.     (150–1)

Immediately after this warning, however, he proceeds to cite Daniel's interpretation of the dreams of King Nebuchadnezzar (Daniel 2: 36 ff.) and Jacob's explanation of the marvellous dream of his son Joseph (Genesis 37: 10 ff.). Clearly, *some* dreams are to be taken very seriously, and can yield profound truths. The narrator's own dreams therefore deserve further consideration. His citation of (Pseudo-)Cato refers to a famous passage from the *Distichs*, ii. 3: 'Sompnia ne cures, nam mens humana quod optat, dum vigilat, sperat' ('Take no account of dreams, for while asleep the human mind sees what it hopes and wishes for'). A proverb apparently derived from this was in circulation in Chaucer's day: 'Sompnia ne cures, nam fallunt sompnia plures' ('Take no account of dreams, for dreams deceive many'). The opinion of 'Catoun' is one of the many pieces of dream lore which Dame Pertelote inflicts on her husband:

> Lo Catoun, which that was so wys a man,
> Seyde he nat thus, 'Ne do no fors of dremes'?
> > (*Nun's Priest's Tale*, VII. 2940–1)

Chauntecleer grumpily retorts that he can prove the contrary from authorities greater than Cato.

But in the Langland quotation the pagan philosopher is backed up by the canon lawyers ('canonistres') of the Christian Church. One of the passages which he may have had in mind was Gratian's condemnation of several methods of foretelling the future, including astrological and calendrical methods, as well as prognosis by dreams. One dream-interpretation handbook in particular, the *Somniale Danielis*, is singled out for special criticism in Gratian's attack on 'dreambooks written down and entitled with the false name of Daniel', the point being that Daniel's name is being used falsely, to lend authority to a text which has none. People who consult such works are regressing into paganism, declares the canon lawyer (*Decretum*, ii. 26, q. 7, ch. 16; trans. Kruger, p. 13). Similarly, in the *Policraticus* (or 'Frivolities of Courtiers and Footprints of Philosophers'), which in 1159 John of Salisbury dedicated to chancellor Thomas Beckett, the *Somniale Danielis* is named once again, and condemned as 'apparently lacking in the weight which truth carries'. The whole tradition of the activity of dream interpretation 'is foolish', John continues, 'and the circulating manual of dream interpretation passes brazenly from hand to hand of the curious' (ii. 17; trans. Pike, p. 84).

Those curious neo-pagans included King Richard II (a version of the *Somniale* being included in MS Bodley 581), Richard's tutor Sir Simon Burley, and Thomas of Woodstock, Duke of Gloucester (cf. p. 28 above). The practice of investigating the meaning of dreams seems to have remained a fashionable pastime among the powerful, despite all the warnings—indeed, the warnings may have added a certain *frisson*. It is impossible to refrain from pointing out the irony that the *Somniale* does not seem to have enhanced the powers of foresight of any of those men. Richard's fate is well known, Burley was executed by the Merciless Parliament, and Woodstock died in suspicious circumstances, perhaps murdered. *Sompnia ne cures* . . .

One of John of Salisbury's main objections to the *Somniale* was that it did not respect the ambiguous nature of certain dreams. 'If ambiguous language is used which lends itself to many interpretations', then the person who 'stubbornly makes some particular decision without taking into consideration these meanings' must surely be regarded as 'quite ignorant'. 'Careful discrimination is to be made amid all this multiplicity of meanings,' John continues, lest one should fall into error. The *Somniale*, however, simply 'allows but one meaning to one thing' (*Policraticus* ii. 17; p. 84). To expand John's point with some sample interpretations from the *Somniale*: dreaming of birds and fighting with them foretells strife; of reading books or of hearing them being read, a time of happiness or the announcement of good tidings. Seeing a dead man means future pleasure, whereas kissing him signifies vital life, and talking with him, some kind of profit or benefit. A black horse intimates anxiety; a white horse, goodness. Dreaming of sleeping with one's sister invariably signifies an injury or loss; with one's mother, security; with a virgin, anxiety! Apparently each and every instance of any one of these significant dreams has one and the same meaning; every person who, say, dreams about books can look forward to something pleasant. These reductive prognoses are far from discriminating; they have failed to take to heart the warning of

Macrobius that 'all portents and dreams conform to the rule that their announcements, threats or warnings of imminent adversity are always ambiguous' (*In Somn. Scip.*, i. 7. 1; trans. Stahl, p. 118).

The ambiguity of much dream imagery, along with the ambiguity concerning the origin of certain dreams, was skilfully elaborated by many of the creators of dream-vision literature. For example, Jean's part of the *Roman de la Rose* can be read as the knowing presentation of a passion-induced fancy, a product of that overthrow of rational judgement which commonly occurs during sleep. And yet the entire *Roman* stands as a work which contains 'the whole art of love', as Guillaume de Lorris says (38). And it certainly was received, for better or worse as it were, as a medieval *Ars amatoria* in the *querelle de la Rose* of the early fifteenth century (cf. pp. 391, 430 below).

Despite the indubitable value of much of the poem's doctrine, a large question mark hangs over it: the dreamer, as a lover, may not be a reliable teacher; he is not the best kind of person to have received a truthful dream. In Plato's *Phaedrus* the power of vision, insight, or intuition is described in terms of the madness of the lover: it is the state attainable only by souls of the highest type, those of the philosopher or artist or some musical and loving nature. They alone have the highest insight, because they alone can remember in sufficient measure something of the external beauty of that real world in which their souls pre-existed before being imprisoned in the flesh. In this theory 'the prophet, the poet and the lover are as closely bound together in the bonds of imagination as ever Shakespeare's lunatic, lover, and poet', as. M. W. Bundy nicely puts it (p. 55). But the *Phaedrus* was a closed book to authors of love-visions like Jean de Meun and Chaucer. Philosophers of their day invariably took the strong moral line against lovers' dreams which is represented by the passage from Aquinas quoted above. Similarly, in the *Livre de Divinacions* which Nicole Oresme wrote between 1361 and 1365, genuine prophetic visions are said to 'come to men of sober and peaceful life, whose souls are like clear and shining mirrors, clean from all worldly thoughts'. On the other hand, Nicole continues, 'concupiscence and melancholy prevent prophecy' (trans. Coopland, pp. 92–3).

No one could have laid such a charge against Dante, because in the *Comedy* his lady Beatrice is safely dead. In this, the medieval vision-poem *par excellence*, the narrator experiences a rapture which is described in terms evocative of St Paul's elevation to the third heaven (cf. pp. 161–2 below). But Dante draws back from an unequivocal statement that he is describing a *visio spiritualis* of the highest kind, which involves understanding rather than mere imagination; indeed, the poem ends by emphasizing that the I-persona's human mind was incapable of receiving (just as now it is incapable of communicating) his heavenly vision, his high fantasy ('alta fantasia') having reach its limit. More than literary decorum restrained Dante and his contemporaries from claiming something which implied a superlative gift of divine grace. Some ambivalence *had* to remain.

Thus, Dante's medieval commentators could debate if the vision described in the *Comedy* had really happened to its author or if it was fictional. And Chaucer's *House of Fame*, a poem clearly written with the *Comedy* in mind, opens with a narrator who is frankly confused by all the technical jargon traditionally used to classify dreams and by the varying explanations of their causes—good luck, he declares, to the great clerks who deal with this puzzling matter! (1–65). This echoes the end of the excursus on dreams by Jean de Meun's Nature, where she declares that she does not want to say any more about dreams, 'about whether they are true or lies, whether one should distinguish among them or if they should all be despised, about why some are more horrible, others more beautiful and peaceful, according to their appearances in different dispositions . . . or about whether God sends revelations through such visions or the malign spirits do so, to put people in danger' (18,499–512; trans. Dahlberg, pp. 306–7). Also, like Langland's narrator at the end of his *Visio*, the Chaucer-persona modestly admits his inability to solve such difficult matters which, of course, leaves his literary vision open to interpretation, and the possibility that it may well contain profound truth is also left very much open. Strategic profession of inadequacy actually valorizes a dream-poem. And as part of that process the audience is alerted to the work's richness, its very obscurity and difficulty challenging the reader, making demands on his (for 'his' it usually was) interpretative abilities, inviting him to play Joseph to Pharaoh, Daniel to Nebuchadnezzar (cf. Daniel 2). Thus the responsibility for the determination of the text's meaning is, rather flatteringly, transferred to the textual community.

Which brings us to consider Chaucer's specific ambiguities. Lines 99–105 of the *Parliament* (the passage derived from Claudian, as quoted above, p. 44) have been used to identify the narrator's dream as a *somnium animale*, produced by mental activity or disturbance (cf. *Riverside Chaucer*, p. 996). Here a distinction is being applied that was expressed well by the medieval physician Petrus de Abano, who contrasted this type of dream with the *somnium naturale*, which is of physical rather than mental origin (being caused by some bodily imbalance), and also with the *somnium coeleste* (of divine origin; cf. the Macrobian *oraculum*). Petrus's threefold division seems to be an adaptation of the Augustinian theory of the *triplex genus visionum*, as carried out by doctors who had as their main concern earth-bound dreams which were symptomatic of medical conditions.

But the motivation which Chaucer's text invokes is more complicated than that normally associated with the *somnium animale*. Immediately after raising the possibility that it was his reading of Scipio Africanus the Elder which caused his dream (106–12), the narrator of the *Parliament* declares his preference for the view that it was divinely inspired—in this case by a pagan deity, Venus Cytherea, who 'madest me this sweven for to mete' (113–5). Elsewhere Chaucer similarly fictionalizes the belief that God can inspire significative dreams by attributing this power to some deity from classical mythology, as when he has Troilus declare that his dream about Criseyde was due to the agency of 'the blysful goddes, thorugh here grete myght' (v. 1250–1); earlier in the same book Pandarus attributes to Trojan 'prestes of the temple' the doctrine that 'dremes ben the revelaciouns / Of goddes', though at that point he adds that they may also be infernal illusions or the result of some medical condition (365–71). Returning to the *Parliament*, it is important to note that in the passage under discussion the narrator proceeds to identify Venus as a planet-god (the combination of planetary and mythological aspects of the pantheon being a common feature of late medieval mythography). This 'blysful lady swete' is something *seen* in the sky ('I sey the north-north-west'), not some remote, hidden agency of the deity. Here the clear implication is that astrological influence—a natural cause once again—is the determining factor. In the commentary on the Book of Wisdom which the English Dominican Robert Holcot produced in the mid-1330s (a work which seems to have been a major source of the Nun's Priest's dream theories) the influence of heavenly bodies is included in a list of causes of dreams. For example, the stars can cause men to dream of war and of the fertility or sterility of the earth. In the case of the *Parliament*, it may be noted that dreams about love are to be expected when Venus is in the ascendant. However, late medieval clerics could also suggest that the pagan gods constituted the idolatrous deification of natural impulses. A euhemeristic reading of the *Parliament*'s Venus Cytherea would see her in terms of human desire, or at least (given the bookish detachment of Chaucer's narrator) the wish to read about other people's desire. Which brings us back to the *somnium animale* theory. The circularity is complete, the ambiguity consummate.

The planet-god Venus, however interpreted, could also be said to underlie the dream in the *House of Fame*, in so far (perhaps not very far: see below, pp. 208–10) as that work can be regarded as a love-poem in the making. But Chaucer prefers to refer the initiative to the very top, so to speak, to Jupiter himself. As the loquacious eagle explains, Jupiter has taken upon himself the responsibility of rewarding the poet for long service to Cupid and Venus, by sending his messenger to conduct 'Geffrey' to a place where he will find plenty to write about. It could be inferred— though Chaucer does not go as far as to actually suggest it—that Jupiter therefore must have inspired the dream. However, the waters are muddied further by the invocation with which the third book begins, where the narrator requests the guidance of Apollo, 'God of science and of lyght' (1091), without any suggestion whatever that that deity may have been in any way responsible for Geffrey's dreaming as such; it seems more obvious to read that passage rather as a dispelling (however temporary) of the fiction of dreaming, as the poet makes a statement about the nature of his own art. Not that it can be taken that simply for very long—for the tone soon moves from the sublime (or was it the mock-sublime?) to the ridiculous (cf. pp. 176–80 below).

It is possible to approach the *Legend of Good Women* in a similar manner, although there the detail is less telling. The narrator's delight in flowers quite naturally leads to dream of the flower-lady Alceste and of those who follow the flower and the leaf respectively (cf. pp. 327–9, 349 50 below). However, the fact that the God of Love appears to him along with Alceste could be taken as indicating that that particular deity was the primary cause of the dream. Duly demythologized, the God of Love becomes those human emotions which underlie the poem, governing the lives, loves, and deaths of the women who fill its pages.

But the *Book of the Duchess* is rather different. There Chaucer seems to be making reference to at least three types of dream: the *somnium coeleste*, the *somnium animale*, and the *somnium naturale*. The first of these categories clearly includes Alcione's dream of her dead husband, a vision of divine origin, or *oraculum*, if ever there was one. Juno, the queen's special goddess ('hir goddesse', 109), enlists the aid of the god of sleep in revealing the grim truth about the death of Ceyx. Chaucer does not go so far as to claim a similar pedigree for his narrator's dream of the Man in Black, not even by invoking gods who are fictional and hence safe to describe as sources of inspiration. But the statement that this 'ynly swete', 'wonderful' dream would defeat the interpretative powers even of Joseph and Macrobius (275–89) certainly claims for it a status far in excess of anything which Chaucer proposed for any of his subsequent *swevenes in ryme*. On the other hand, the poem affords sufficient evidence for the view that the Chaucerian I-persona's reading of a dream-book has caused his own dream, a strategy that he was to repeat in the *Parliament*. The Ovidian tale of ancient love and loss, featuring a sorrowing wife mourning her dead husband, can be seen as instigating the dreamer's vision of a more recent bereavement, wherein a sorrowing husband (though not specifically identified as such) mourns his dead wife. This inversion is mild compared with some of the stark reversals of value found in certain standard dream divinations, as when the *Somniale Danielis* claims, for example, that dreams about the dead foretell pleasure (cf. p. 47 above). All this falls within the category of the *somnium animale*.

Chaucer's appeal to stock characteristics of the *somnium naturale*, however, is what really separates this, his first dream-poem, from the ones he went on to write. In the encyclopaedic *De proprietatibus rerum* which Bartholomew the Englishman wrote around 1230, the bodily humours are identified as the causes of certain dreams (vi. 27). Thus, the melancholic person will dream of sorrow. Furthermore, the black vapours produced by *melancholia* cause dreams of black things, as when one sees black monks or devils, as Boethius of Dacia noted. Similarly, a surfeit of melancholy has caused Chauntecleer to dream of the black parts of the monster which, on Dame Pertelote's analysis, his imagination has created. She elaborates the point thus:

> the humour of malencholie
> Causeth ful many a man in sleep to crie
> For feere of blake beres, or boles blake,    *bears, bulls*
> Or elles blake develes wole hem take.    (VII. 2933–6)

At the very beginning of the *Book of the Duchess* we learn that the dreamer is beset by melancholy and fear of death:

> thus melancolye
> And drede I have for to dye . . .    (23–4)

The sleeplessness and heaviness which are symptoms of his eight-year 'sicknesse' have slain his vital spirits, causing all kinds of fantasies to prey on his mind (25–9). Little wonder, then, that this figure should dream of death—and of something black; of a Man in Black whose bereavement has turned him into the very embodiment of sorrow: 'y am sorwe, and sorwe ys y' (597). On this view, the dream is very much the dreamer's, the manifestation of his own physical condition. Yet, the Man in Black is at the very centre of the text—indeed, is *the* centre thereof—and so it is his condition which is marked out as important. Is this a case of suffering transferred—the Man in Black being the projection of the dreamer's suffering? Or suffering deferred? Deferral I believe it to be, the dreamer deferring to the dreamed, instantly recognizing the superiority of the suffering of the Man in Black, and sympathizing with it as he facilitates its full expression.

Thanks in large measure to Aristotelian scepticism, which encouraged systematic analysis of the natural causes of things, dream phenomena could be considered as signs with their own earthly and empirical significance. The fact that dreams may have natural causes does not, *pace* the Macrobian evaluative grid with which we began, trivialize them. Rather it ensures that they are taken with the right kind of seriousness, as when they are considered as symptoms which may be medically diagnosed and a remedy recommended. But what possible remedy can be offered for the *melancholia* which seems to pervade the *Book of the Duchess*? And where exactly is that *melancholia* located, in the psyche of the dreamer or of the Man in Black? One of the poem's most striking features is that it admits both ways of reading its own genesis, though surely it is significant that, while the poem begins with the dreamer's suffering, it certainly does not end there, since the Man in Black's superior suffering comes to fill the work's psychic space. In terms of dream psychology, the Man in Black is a creature of the dreamer's making, one of the 'fantasies' which fill his troubled 'hede' (28). In terms of the poem's emotional logic, it is the Man in Black who is in control, with the dreamer serving as *his* creature—the emphasis falling on service of an utterly honourable kind.

This argument will be taken further in our subsequent consideration of the nature of the remedy, the form of the consolation, which is offered by the *Book of the Duchess*. Suffice it to say here that the complexity of these interpretative issues may be taken as manifesting the challenge and stimulus which medieval notions about dreams presented to those poets who sought to turn dreaming into a fine art.

Macrobius, *Commentarium in Somnium Scipionis*, trans. William Stahl (New York, 1952; repr. 1990). For the Latin text see Macrobius, *Opera*, ed. J. Willis, Bibliotheca scriptorum Graecorum et Romanorum Teubneriana (Leipzig, 1963).

*Roman de la Rose*, ed. Ernest Langlois (Paris, 1914–24); trans. Charles Dahlberg (Princeton, NJ, 1971). On Guillaume de Lorris, Macrobius, and dream theory see the important treatment by David F. Hult, *Self-Fulfilling Prophecies: Readership and Authority in the First 'Roman de la Rose'* (Cambridge, 1986), pp. 114–37; also Sylvia Huot, *The 'Romance of the Rose' and its Medieval Readers* (Cambridge, 1993), pp. 18–21.

Plato, *Dialogues*, trans. B. Jowett, 4th edn. (Oxford, 1953). There are many translations of Aristotle's *De somniis* and *De divinatione per somnium*; see e.g. Aristotle, *Basic Works*, trans. R. McKeon (New York, 1941), pp. 618–25, 626–30. See further the well-annotated editions by David Gallop, *Aristotle on Sleep and Dreams* (Peterborough, Canada, 1990).

Steven Kruger, *Dreaming in the Middle Ages* (Cambridge, 1992). M. W. Bundy, *The Theory of Imagination in Classical and Medieval Thought* (Urbana, Ill., 1927). On the different attitudes to dreams which were held by Plato and Aristotle see especially Bundy, pp. 50–8, 75–81, and Kruger, pp. 26–34, 83–122. For medieval theories of imagination and its literary implications see Mary Carruthers, *The Book of Memory. A Study of Memory in Medieval Culture* (Cambridge, 1990), esp. pp. 1–4, 51–4, 58–9, 197, 229; E. Ruth Harvey, *The Inward Wits: Psychological Theory in the Middle Ages and the Renaissance*, Warburg Institute Surveys, 6 (London, 1975); and Douglas Kelly,

*Medieval Imagination. Rhetoric and the Poetry of Courtly Love* (Madison, Wis., 1978). Kelly discusses the *Roman de la Rose*, Machaut, Froissart, Charles d'Orléans, and René d'Anjou. There is also an abundance of relevant material in Janet Coleman, *Ancient and Medieval Memories: Studies in the Reconstruction of the Past* (Cambridge, 1992). Much scholarship on *imaginatio* and *vis imaginativa* has been prompted by the enigmatic figure Ymaginatif in Langland's *Piers Plowman*; see A. J. Minnis, 'Langland's Ymaginatif and Late-Medieval Theories of Imagination', *Comparative Criticism*, 3 (1981), 71–103, and Ernest Kaulbach, *Imaginative Prophecy in the B-Text of 'Piers Plowman'*, Piers Plowman Studies, 8 (Cambridge, 1993).

For Augustine's distinction between the various kinds of vision in *De Genesi ad Litteram*, xii. 7. 16, see CSEL xxviii, sect. 3, pt. i, p. 186. It is translated and discussed by Bundy, *Theory of Imagination*, p. 171, and Kruger, *Dreaming*, p. 37; see also Minnis, 'Langland's Ymaginatif', for Gilbert of Poitiers. On David as the most outstanding prophet see A. J. Minnis and A. B. Scott (eds.), *Medieval Literary Theory and Criticism, c.1100–c.1375: The Commentary Tradition*, rev. edn. (Oxford, 1988), p. 271.

The Aquinas texts cited are as follows. *De veritate*, q. xii, art. 3 ('Is prophecy natural?'); q. xii, art. 5 ('Is moral goodness required for prophecy?'); q. xii, art. 14 ('Was Moses more outstanding than other prophets?'); all translated by J. V. McGlynn, *St Thomas Aquinas: The Disputed Questions on Truth*, vol. 2 (Chicago, 1963), pp. 114–24, 128–30, 176–9. St Thomas Aquinas, *Summa theologiae*, Blackfriars edn. (London and New York, 1964–76), vol. 25, ed. and trans. John Feardon, pp. 128–80.

Boethius of Dacia, *On the Supreme Good, On the Eternity of the World, On Dreams*, trans. John F. Wippel, Medieval Sources in Translation, 30 (Toronto, 1987). For the Latin text see N. G. Green-Pedersen, *Boethii Daci Opera. Opuscula De aeternitate mundi, De summo bono, De somniis*, Corpus Philosophorum Danicorum Medii Aevi, 6/2 (Copenhagen, 1976). On the 1277 condemnations see especially J. Wippel, 'The Condemnations of 1270 and 1277 at Paris', *JMRS* 7 (1977), 169–201; R. Hissette, *Enquête sur les 219 articles condamnés à Paris le 7 mars 1277* (Louvain and Paris, 1977), and 'Étienne Tempier et ses condemnations', *RTAM* 47 (1980), 213–70. Nowadays they are often regarded as a backlash against the new, often dangerous ideas which had come to the West through the recently recovered *libri naturales* of Aristotle, which were accompanied by the extensive commentaries of Arab scholars who, as Muslims, were regarded as untrustworthy by Christians, despite their great learning.

On Evrart de Conty see F. Guichard Tesson, 'Evrart de Conty, auteur de la "Glose des Eschecs amoureux"', *Le Moyen français*, 8–9 (1981), 111–48. The French text has been edited by Tesson and Bruno Roy, *Le Livre des Eschez amoureux moralisés. Edition critique* (Montreal and Paris, 1994). I have drawn on the translation by Joan Morton Jones, to which I have made some alterations: 'The Chess of Love [Old French Text with Translation and Commentary]' (Ph.D. diss., University of Nebraska, 1968).

Richard of Middleton, Primi quodlibeti, art. 5, q. 2, in *Quodlibeta* (Brescia, 1591), pp. 23–5.

*Disticha Catonis*, ed. Marcus Boas (Amsterdam, 1952). This has been translated by W. J. Chase, *The Distichs of Cato: A Famous Medieval Textbook*, University of Wisconsin Studies in the Social Sciences and History, 8 (Madison, Wis., 1992). The 'Sompnia ne cures, nam fallunt sompnia plures' proverb is recorded by Hans Walther, *Proverbia sententiaeque latinitatis medii aevi: Lateinische Spichwörter und Sentenzen des Mittelalters in alphabetischer Anordnung*, 5 (Göttingen, 1967), p. 72 (no. 30,026). John of Salisbury, *Frivolities of Courtiers and Footprints of the Philosophers. Being a translation of the First, Second and Third Books of the 'Policraticus' of John of Salisbury*, trans. Joseph B. Pike (Minneapolis and London, 1938). The Latin text has been edited by C. C. J. Webb (Oxford, 1909).

For the *Somniale Danielis* see L. T. Martin (ed.), *Somniale Danielis: An Edition of a*

*Medieval Latin Dream Interpretation Handbook* (Frankfurt, 1981); Steven R. Fischer, *The Complete Medieval Dreambook: A Multilingual, Alphabetical 'Somnia Danielis' Collation* (Bern and Frankfurt, 1982).

Plato, *Phaedrus*, tr. Jowett, iii. 133–89. G. W. Coopland, *Nicole Oresme and the Astrologers. A Study of his 'Livre de Divinacions'* (Liverpool, 1952). Oresme's work seems to have been known to Deschamps and Philippe de Mézières. For Petrus de Abano see W. C. Curry, *Chaucer and the Medieval Sciences*, rev. edn. (London, 1960), pp. 207–8. On Holcot as a source of the Nun's Priest's dream doctrine see R. A. Pratt, 'Some Latin Sources of the Nonnes Preest on Dreams', *Speculum*, 52 (1977), 538–70.

*On the Properties of Things. John Trevisa's translation of Bartholomaeus Anglicus, 'De Proprietatibus Rerum'*, ed. M. C. Seymour *et al.* (Oxford, 1975).

Dream interpretation was included among the illicit means of attempting to predict the future condemned by Bradwardine in his *Sermo Epinicius*, preached before Edward III and his lords. See H. A. Oberman and J. A. Weisheipl, 'The *Sermo Epinicius* ascribed to Thomas Bradwardine (1346); *AHDCMA* 25 (1958), 295–329. It is God alone, Bradwardine declares, and not any secondary cause such as the stars, fate, or fortune, who must be thanked for the victory. In similar vein, in his *Livre de Divinacions* Oresme condemns 'greed of knowing the future' (p. 95), and warns kings and princes of the dangers of attempting to search out 'hidden matters or the hazards and fortunes of the future, whether by astrology, geomancy, nigromancy, or by any other such arts, if they can correctly be called arts' (p. 51).

On medieval dream literature, in addition to the above, see Piero Boitani, 'Old Books Brought to Life in Dreams: The *Book of the Duchess*, the *House of Fame*, the *Parliament of Fowls*', in Piero Boitani and Jill Mann (eds.), *The Cambridge Chaucer Companion* (Cambridge, 1986), pp. 39–57; Carolly Erickson, *The Medieval Vision: Essays in History and Perception* (New York, 1976); Constance B. Hieatt, *The Realism of Dream-Visions: The Poetic Exploitation of the Dream-Experience in Chaucer and his Contemporaries* (The Hague and Paris, 1967); Kathryn L. Lynch, *The High Medieval Dream Vision: Poetry, Philosophy and Literary Form* (Stanford, Calif., 1988); Jacqueline T. Miller, 'Dream Visions of *Auctorite*', in her *Poetic License: Authority and Authorship in Medieval and Renaissance Contexts* (New York and Oxford, 1986), pp. 34–72; A. C. Spearing, *Medieval Dream-Poetry* (Cambridge, 1976), esp. pp. 55–62.

## Fin' amors *and the Engendering of Emotion*

'Courtly love', the elaborate code of 'designer emotion' practised by the Man in Black in pursuit of 'faire White', by the three aristocratic eagles who all love the same formel in the *Parliament of Fowls*, and (most elaborately of all in Chaucer) by Troilus as he loves, wins, and loses Criseyde, is the forerunner of romantic love and 'courtship' as generally understood today. It has been democratized and diluted, to be sure; many of its large rhetorical gestures pruned, its trials and tribulations made accessible to mass audiences. But 'falling in love' nowadays is very much like it used to be, at least in literature. (The extent to which literature has influenced cultural practice in this regard is a moot point.) Mills and Boon novels in the United Kingdom and Harlequin novels in North America are the direct descendants of texts like the *Book of the Duchess*. The survival of *fin' amors* has been remarkable.

According to the usual (reductive but firmly rooted) narrative, it all began, or at least assumed its definitive shape, in southern France in the early twelfth century. Then the phenomenon was called *fin' amors* (cf. Chaucer's term 'fyn lovynge' in the *Legend of Good Women*, F Prol. 544). The first use—or at least the first significant use—of the term *amour courtois* seems to have been as recent as 1883, in an article by Gaston Paris on what he regarded as the first poem to feature this new kind of love in northern France, Chrétien de Troyes' *Chevalier de la charrette* (*c*.1172). Chrétien tells us that he was writing under the influence of Marie, Countess of Champagne (daughter of Louis VII of France and Eleanor of Aquitaine), who provided him with both the material and the manner of treatment. Paris's account set the trend for describing 'courtly love' as illicit, furtive, and extramarital. The male position is one of ostentatious inferiority; even the bravest of warriors trembles in the presence of his lady, living in a state of constant anxiety lest he should displease her, however inadvertently. The female's position is of aloof detachment; she deliberately acts in a capricious and haughty manner, imposing all kinds of tests on her long-suffering suitor, expecting performances of the most impeccable, perhaps even superhuman, kind. Thus, Chrétien's Guinevere is furious because Lancelot hesitated just for a moment before enduring the demeaning cart-ride which brings him to her assistance. Love can thus become a spur to valiant deeds. Above all else, love is an art with its own rules.

For C. S. Lewis, the rule-book was the *De amore* of Andreas Capellanus, a rather mysterious figure who claims, *inter alia*, to be reporting adjudications on matters of love by Marie, Countess of Champagne, and Queen Eleanor. In this Latin prose treatise (which may date from the period 1181–7, and seems to have some relationship, however indirect, with ideas found in Chrétien's *Chevalier de la charrette*) the various symptoms and strategies of love are described in elaborate detail, and the extraordinary claim is made that love cannot exist within marriage. Lewis, following Violet Paget, accounts for such sentiments with reference to feudal conditions in which there was an enormous preponderance of men over women. Only the most senior and powerful males were allowed the luxury of marriage; the rest of noble mankind (younger sons, subalterns without fortunes, and so forth) could only adore the wives of their betters from afar. Apart from this, Lewis adds, there were two factors which 'prevented the men of that age from connecting their ideal of romantic love with marriage'. First of all, marriage had nothing to do with love, since all matches were dictated by sociopolitical interest: 'Any idealization of sexual love, in a society where marriage is purely utilitarian, must begin by being an idealization of adultery' (p. 13). Secondly, Christian distrust of passionate love and its grudging allowance of only a functional, procreative sexuality to married couples ensured that love and marriage were at odds. This explains why Ovid's *Ars amatoria* was so fundamentally misunderstood in the later Middle Ages, the advice offered by this mock-reverential handbook on the nice conduct of illicit loves being recommended seriously by a culture which had missed the joke.

No aspect of this theory has remained unchallenged. The sociological analysis on which it rests has been proved to be reductive and partial. For instance, several historians, most notably John F. Benton, have asserted that there is no evidence for actual courts of love at the court of Champagne within which courtly love could flourish, and have generally challenged Andreas's credibility as a reliable witness. D. W. Robertson attacked on a different front, reading *De amore* as an ironical work which, far from praising courtly love, actually condemns it. (The fact that Robertson can make such a strong argument is ample testimony to the ambivalence of the text. Various other types of ironical reading have been put forward, but the meaning and significance of what Andreas wrote remain elusive. What does seem to be certain is that *De amore* was little read in the country of its origin, France, and also in England, and that those who did read it were mainly clerics.) More fundamentally, courtly love and marriage are regarded as perfectly compatible in much literature of the later Middle Ages. For a start, while some troubadour poems are indeed addressed to married women, in the great majority of cases there is no clear indication of the lady's conjugal status. Moreover, in the poetry of northern France those aspects of courtly love which militate against Christian ethics are mitigated, or indeed problematized (as in Chrétien), and when courtly love crosses the channel, it appears in all shapes and forms in English texts. It is better, then, to think in terms of a series of formulas which are capable of wide application and adaptation, which can figure in many kinds of context—in describing romantic love which exists in adultery, in marriage, or without either. Chaucer's term 'fyn lovynge' occurs in the context of extravagant praise of Alceste, the best of all wives, and most of the heroines of the *Legend of Good Women* are either married or determined to be married (cf. pp. 412–21 below). And Ovid, *pace* Lewis, was in some medieval contexts regarded as an advocate of married love, his *Heroides* (the text that Chaucer was trying to surpass in the *Legend*) being read as recommending Penelope's licit love and condemning Medea's mad passion and Phyllis's foolishness.

In the *Book of the Duchess* the affections of the Man in Black and his white lady are described in terms of pure *fin' amors*. John of Gaunt (or, his retainers on his behalf) would certainly not have taken kindly to his feelings for his dead wife being sullied by association with literary conventions which bore the stigma of adultery. The fact that Chaucer felt free to use those conventions may be taken as evidence that the problem simply did not exist. The eventual marriage of Gaunt and Blanche is not mentioned: the ring which White gives the Man in Black at lines 1273–4 is probably meant to be understood simply as a love-token (as is indicated by its description as the 'firste thyng' she gave him—hardly an appropriate way of referring to a wedding ring). The few lines which praise their many happy years together (1287–97) do not specify marital union. Why does Chaucer avoid such a mention? Various answers are possible. The simplest is that much more than that is absent from the narrative, including the details of Blanche's death; there is no justification, therefore, for privileging one omission over another. Alternatively, it could be said, with much truth, that the discourse of courtly love traditionally centres on pursuit rather than possession, on the courtship process rather than on its consummation, whether in sex or marriage or both. But sexual consummation eventually occurs in *Troilus and Criseyde*, one might object; and in many other medieval romances courtly love does end in contented marriage (as, for example, in the *Knight's Tale* and the *Franklin's Tale*). It is more likely, then, that Chaucer's choice of parameters was governed by a desire to present the love of Gaunt and Blanche in all the joy and wonder of its first bloom: the older and sadder Man in Black looks back nostalgically at the best years of his life, when he was young and in love. What came later pales into insignificance for the moment of the poem.

The omission of marriage also creates ample space for indication of the rational basis on which the relationship rests. Here we may detect the influence of yet another tradition which contributed to the matrix of romantic love, the ideal of male friendship. In an interesting study which has not received the attention it deserves, Erik Kooper has suggested that Chaucer is being innovative in assimilating some of the values of *amicitia* to *conjugalis affectio*. But the influence seems to have been of much longer duration, going back far beyond Chaucer, and of greater cultural penetration. However much Ovid may have influenced the formulation and development of 'fyn lovynge', at least some of its roots are in Cicero, who in *De amicitia* extols the virtues of the love of another for the other's sake. Thus the emotion 'finds its expression in giving and serving, not in getting', as Gervase Mathew puts it; this love is 'frustrated not when it fails to get but when it ceases to give' (p. 134). As transferred to heterosexual relations (as, for example, in medieval marriage sermons), this originally all-male code of practice produces an emphasis on reciprocity of affection, mutual need, and above all else a relationship grounded on reason rather than mere physical passion.

In his *De spirituali amicitia* (*c.*1150) the English Cistercian monk Aelred of Rievaulx distinguishes between love from reason alone (as when we love our enemies because God has commanded us to) and love from affection alone (because of bodily qualities, such as beauty, eloquence, and the like), concluding that the best form of love is the one which results from both these motivations. This occurs when 'he, whom reason urges should be loved because of the excellence of his virtue, steals into the soul of another by the mildness of his character and the charm of a praiseworthy life. In this way reason unites with affection so that the love is pure because of reason and sweet because of affection' (iii. 2–3; trans. Laker, pp. 91–2). If the 'he' (Aelred is writing for his fellow monks) were changed to 'she', that passage could appropriately be applied to 'faire White'. It should be noted, of course, that in the Man in Black's case it is the woman's beauty which first strikes him rather than her reason— but then, that is what we would expect (the argument could run), given that, as he himself admits, he was then very impressionable (a *tabula rasa* awaiting the inscriptions of experience), living in his 'firste youthe' in 'ydelnesse' (779–97). Naturally, a young man with 'varyinge' thought would be most susceptible to pleasing sense perceptions. But 'White' takes him, in all his youth, in her 'wise governaunce' (1285–6), the over-all description affirming (as already noted) her superlative moral qualities (cf. p. 88 below). She is not only the 'fairest' but also the 'beste', a woman in the mould of those virtuous wives of antiquity, the 'good' Penelope and the 'noble' and 'trewe' Lucrece (1079–87). Only the latter is identi-fied as a 'wyf' here, the term having the technical sense of 'married woman', but the reputation of both figures as illustrative of *bona matri-monii* was widespread, and the clear implication is that White is also 'good wife' material.

Further proof of White's rationality is provided by her refusal to behave in a way which certain haughty heroines seemed to relish: send-ing their suppliants out on perilous expeditions to prove that they are worthy of their love. The places mentioned are real enough (Wallachia, Prussia, Tartary, Turkey), all beset by wars and crusading campaigns in Chaucer's time. But the imperious behaviour avoided by White in any case smacks of literary fiction, and there is probably a touch of gentle mockery of this aspect of romance convention in the Man in Black's remark that his lady 'ne used no suche knakkes [i.e. tricks] smale' (1033), journeys of the kind here envisaged hardly being small affairs in terms of distance and danger! Fair White is obviously no sister of Guinevere; she takes no delight in exercising her power in a capricious way, and dis-plays just the right amount of *hauteur* to assay her lover's seriousness and assert that she will not be won lightly: as Chaucer was to say on another occasion, 'By proces and by goode servyse / He gat hire love, and in no sodeyn wyse' (*Troilus and Criseyde*, ii. 678–9). Thus, in the relationship of the Black Knight and 'faire White' reason unites with affection.

It remains for us to consider the implications of the conventions of courtly love for the construction of gender (the term 'gender' here being taken, as is common in gender criticism, to refer to social constructs rather than biological sex). Recently there has been considerable interest in the so-called feminized hero, the basic point being that *fin' amors* places the male in the position of subservience, dependence, and suffering which is traditionally occupied by the female. Within these parameters emotional excess is perfectly acceptable, even admirable, in a man (*pace* what the moralizers of Chaucer's day and of our own would say); a sign not of weakness but of generous nobility and aristocratic sensitivity. This produces a somewhat schizoid hero who is a lion on the battlefield and a lamb in the bedchamber. That this was not simply a literary fiction but a code of fashionable conduct which actual knights sought to follow is made abundantly clear by a sermon which Thomas Bradwardine—the 'Bisshop Bradwardyn' referred to as an authority on fate and predestination in the *Nun's Priest's Tale* (VII. 3242)—preached before Edward III and his lords on the occasion of the English victories at Crécy and in Scotland. Bradwardine is a hostile witness, of course (his objective being to prove that God, and God alone, should be thanked for the English successes), but the object of his scorn is clearly identifiable.

[T]hey [some of the English soldiers] seem to emulate antique pagans worshipping Hymen or Cupid, the god of carnal love. Soldiering in Venus, associating themselves with the retinue of Aphrodite, they think the vigour of their audacity to be probity, victory, or triumph. But they say that no-one can be vigorous unless he is amorous, or loves amorously, that no-one can fight strenuously to excess unless he loves to excess. . . . They labour strenuously in arms to make for themselves a name like the name of the greatest on earth . . . And why do they wish such a name? That they may be loved by foolish women. (trans. in Robertson, p. 6)

One 'antique pagan' whose behaviour might have incensed Bradwardine is Chaucer's Troilus, whose distress in unrequited love and subsequent vulnerability in the presence of his lady have few parallels in the history of courtly love literature. Despite this, as he returns from the battlefield, Troilus displays the conventional attributes of manhood to such good advantage that 'It was an heven upon hym for to see' (ii. 631–44). Criseyde is certainly impressed—'Who yaf me drynke?' (651). His 'manhod and his pyne' make love grow within Criseyde (ii. 676), and when he is obliged to lead her out from Troy to the enemy camp, he conceals his emotions well: he 'gan his wo ful manly for to hide' (v. 30). Similarly, the Man in Black, on realizing that someone is witnessing his lamentation, exercises a self-control which is as admirable as it is extra-ordinary (a point to which we will return; cf. pp. 106–10 below). And in the *Parliament of Fowls*, despite all the 'payne' which the three tercel eagles profess in their love for the one and only formel, when the sug-gestion is made that they should fight for her, they are 'Al redy!' (540). There is, then, nothing necessarily effeminate about the feminized hero, as Jill Mann rightly emphasizes. But here we should pause for a moment to reflect that in the case of such male *sujets* the 'feminine' is tacitly being rewritten; when they occupy this subject position, it is very different from when fictive females occupy it: qualities generally deemed to be dis-abling and disempowering in a woman are being taken as admirable in a man. Some versions of textual feminization *do* carry a considerable neg-ative charge, however, a matter which will be addressed below, mainly in the chapter on the *Legend of Good Women*.

But here our subject is the textual construction and manipulation of suffering. Women are often characterized through their suffering, as when the abandoned women in, for example, Ovid's *Heroides* and Chaucer's *Legend of Good Women* lament their missing menfolk. In the *Book of the Duchess* it is the Man in Black who laments absence—yet there is no way in which the presence of White could be restored, at least in this life. The suffering of legions of courtly lovers is mitigated by hope, the possibility that the longed-for lady will show some 'grace' and favour to the suitor if only he suffers exquisitely enough, thus manifesting the extent of his adoration. Here, no matter what the depth or duration of supposedly 'feminized male' emotion, the response will and can never come. Death, however, absolves White from complicity in this. Or, alter-natively, one might say that Chaucer's text absolves her, for in this poem her death functions within a strategy that serves the interests of the male protagonists.

And that raises the question: what has the woman to do with all this male suffering anyway? It could be argued that the poets and their patrons are mainly concerned with the desire and ambitions of males, the beloved being reduced to a site for their courtly self-fashioning. Maud Ellmann's approach to this matter, after Jacques Lacan's essay on woman's *jouissance*, takes the *Book of the Duchess* as 'a scene of dialogue forever vexed by the absent object of desire' (p. 100). The gulf between the beholder and the beheld, the imploring lover and the aloof beloved, has widened into the chasm between the living and the dead, between all that makes life worth living and the eternal other, which is absent always from those who remain in this world. 'Blanche', argues Ellmann, 'is the name that Chaucer chose to speak of "woman", or rather of the vagrant gap where woman does not appear, does not *take place*. Blanche is dead. And *The Book of the Duchess* is the tomb in which she lies encrypted' (p. 100). White, Chaucer tells us, loves her own name (1018). This means that she

must love her namelessness, her own blancheur: it is as if the name must be erased in the perfection of its own propriety. But is it not through whiting out the name of woman that patrilineal properties must always institute themselves? Namelessness enables women to circulate between the names and properties of men. Blanche herself, as her name implies, has no intrinsic properties: she represents the currency through which names, places and properties are realigned. (p. 105)

The main problem with this is that the imagery of whiteness is being given a value which it indubitably did not have in late medieval semiotics in general and, I believe, in the *Book of the Duchess* in particular. A more historicized reading is intimated by James Wimsatt's argument that Blanche has been apotheosized by means of imagery traditionally associated with the Virgin Mary, of shining, flawless brightness. Thus White's neck is likened to a tower of ivory (946; cf. Song of Songs 7: 4, a common epithet applied to the Virgin). She is a bright torch from which every man may take light (962–5), though her own brightness is not thereby diminished. A few lines later (985) she is likened to a mirror. All this is reminiscent of the depiction of wisdom in Wisdom 7: 26–7, 'she is the brightness of eternal light, and the unspotted mirror of God's majesty, and the image of his goodness. . . . remaining in herself the same, she reneweth all things.' Imagery of this kind was frequently applied to Mary, generally regarded by exegetes as the *illuminatrix* who carried the never-fading light into the world. And of course the symbol of the phoenix which Chaucer introduces at lines 981–4 was used to represent not only Christ but also the Virgin. This is not, of course, to suggest that White is, in some allegorical sense, to be perceived as a type of Mary. Rather, a religious discourse is being used to construct her secular subjectivity. The images and idioms we have described here had a distinguished pedigree because of their association with the Virgin, and as related to White may be seen as part and parcel of a strategy of valorization of a lesser but much-loved creature, a more earthly woman who partook of some of the qualities which the Queen of Heaven possesses in abundance. As constituted by this discourse, fair White intimates everything that is fair and bright, all light and loveliness, whereas the blackness of the bereaved knight oppositionally symbolizes 'absence, darkness, death, things which are not' (to borrow a phrase from Donne's 'Nocturnal upon St Lucy's Day').

But let us return to Ellmann. Her analysis presents Blanche, one of the greatest heiresses of Chaucer's day, as the victim of a 'traffic in women' (to bring in Gayle Rubin's phrase), that 'political economy' of sex whereby female lives are converted into marriage alliances which serve male interests and secure patrilineal transmission of wealth and power within the dominant social group. Defenceless in death, the blanching of all that made her a historical individual continues, with the poet participating in the process. And that is the direction in which Elaine Tuttle Hansen extends Ellmann's reading, in her discussion of feminization in the *Book of the Duchess*. Despite the homosocial alliance between dreamer and black knight, she argues, there is a definite friction between them; they are, in a sense, fighting over White's body, just as the Abbot of St Albans and the Bishop of Lincoln had (according to the historical record) competed over the right to say high mass over Blanche's body. 'Blanche refigured as White', Hansen claims, functions as 'a sign of the male lover's comprehension, his higher experience, his finer appreciation; the idea of the perfect woman is a site not only of conversation but also of competition between the two men, where the lover articulates his authority over the writer' (p. 80). In the face of this charge, the positive notion that the black knight and the poet have 'both masculine and feminine attributes and roles' seems to pale into insignificance. 'Woman, in the form of the female character, is brought to represent life precisely in order to be killed off, silenced, displaced, ignored, again and again' (p. 84). Having at long last reached the definitive declaration that White 'ys ded', the two men part, having nothing more to say, and go their separate ways. Gaunt has another rich heiress to marry; the poet has other poems to write, a successful career to make.

One possible response to this would be to say: but surely White may be perceived as directing masculine thought and feeling even from beyond the grave? Which would be to provoke the counter-argument that the way in which the I-persona and the Man in Black think about White as representative of woman as Other functions mainly to confirm their presuppositions and prejudices about correct male conduct. She is therefore serving their purposes, not her own. In a phallocentric world, men control most if not all of the empowering discourses, and woman is inevitably subject to masculine thought and feeling.

That proposition brings us to what for many is the crux of the matter: to what extent, if at all, can courtly love be seen, whether in historical terms or from the perspective of gender criticism, as an agent of sexual/textual liberation? During the first half of this century the view persisted that courtly love was a reflex of an ancient Germanic respect for women (a surviving vestige of a matriarchal ethos), which actually worked to improve the status of women in medieval society. For example, Karl Vossler suggested that, the Gothic spirit of chivalry having been transplanted to Provence, there warriors were tamed by the power of women, which came to rival that of the Church, the result being a considerable refinement of attitudes and behaviour among the ruling classes. More recently, Robert Miller has spoken of the 'civilizing influence' of courtly love: 'In this quaint way, the western world was delivered from the Dark Ages' (pp. 335–6). Charles Camproux is similarly convinced of a 'will toward the emancipation of women' (p. 101), while Diane Bornstein believes that courtly love 'celebrated woman as an ennobling spiritual and moral force, thus expressing a new feminism that contradicted both the antifeminism of the ecclesiastical establishment and the sexual attitudes endorsed by the church' (p. 669). Against this, it could be argued that the cruelty (however short-term in practice) of the courtly lady proved what misogynists had been saying for centuries—that women were alluring, dangerous creatures, who entrapped men with their wiles and then tormented them. Thus men were reduced to weak servants in a way quite contrary to the decorums of reason and rank—so much for the 'feminized hero', as seen from the high moral ground occupied by, for example, Thomas Walsingham, who complained that Richard II's courtiers were knights of Venus rather than of Bellona (cf. p. 20 above). Or by 'Bisshop Bradwardyn', who assured Edward III's soldiers that devotion to women was enervating rather than invigorating. Of course, this is utterly predictable clerkly comment on women. But what if aristocratic males, far from opposing the 'ecclesiastical establishment', were ultimately on the same side as the clerics, using a discourse which was different but equally disempowering?

That is the view recently articulated by R. Howard Bloch, who sees courtly love as an instrument of misogyny or a force in parallel with it. 'As long as woman was property to be disposed of', he argues, 'she was deprecated in accord with received misogynistic notions of the feminine as the root of all evil; but as soon as woman became capable of disposing—and, more specifically, of disposing of property—she was idealized in the terms of courtly love' (p. 196). It is no accident that *fin' amors* came into its own in the south of France, he believes, for there the heiresses and dowagers had most power and hence posed the greatest threat. Moreover, this was where Robert d'Arbrissel, regarded by Bloch as a genuine champion of women, had founded the monastery of Fontevrault, a mixed house with which many of the most culturally influential women of the age, including Eleanor of Aquitaine and Marie of Champagne, had an association. A religious discourse which was generated by economically powerful women was hijacked by worried noblemen (led by William IX, Duke of Aquitaine, 'the first troubadour'), who sought to regain the initiative by secularizing that discourse and reducing the women to passive objects of their adoration. Then again, the developing theology of marriage placed an emphasis on mutual consent, which meant that (in theory at least) the woman had the power of acceptance or refusal. Courtly love respected and reflected that power, but sought to limit it. The fear of women playing a role in history thus expressed itself in an elevation above the temporal which was carried out by the idealization of the feminine that courtliness comprised. Woman was rendered unworthy of all worldly involvement as the emphasis was placed on her supreme worth in areas which were sociopolitically insignificant. Bloch sums up as follows:

Although the discourse of courtliness, which places the woman on a pedestal and worships her as the controlling *domna*, seems to empower women along with an enabling femininity, it is yet another ruse of sexual usurpation thoroughly analogous to that developed in the early centuries of our era by the fathers of the church. No less than the discourse of [clerkly] misogyny does that of courtly love reduce woman to the status of a category. . . . Misogyny and courtly love are co-conspiring abstractions of the feminine whose function was from the start, and continues to be, the diversion of women from history by the annihilation of the identity of individual women, hidden behind the requirement of discretion and the anonymity of the *domna*, and thus the transformation of woman into an ideal. Courtliness is, at bottom, a competing mode of coercion that will, alongside misogyny, continue to hide its disenfranchising effects behind the seductions of courtesy, and thus to dominate the discourse of lovers in the West. (pp. 196–7)

There is much here of apparent relevance to the *Book of the Duchess*. Let us explore some possibilities, before offering a critique of the approach. Armed with Bloch's thesis, one could go beyond Ellmann and Hansen to see it as the quintessentially misogynistic courtly poem, a work which dehistoricizes Blanche, the route through whom much power and wealth came to John of Gaunt, in the very act of celebrating her beauty and her delimitingly feminine virtue. That is to say, her virtue is rigidly confined to an area within which female honour can function without interfering with the exercise of political power and the transmission of property; her greatest achievement is as a sort of 'finishing school' for the man who will sire the future king of England (not that Chaucer could have predicted that, of course). In particular, the power of woman's word is illustrated by the only word with which White is credited in the entire poem: 'Nay' (1243). This is allegedly uttered when she first refuses the Man in Black, exercising her right to choose, to accept or reject the man who seeks to court her. When she uses it, she has some real power; as soon as she stops saying 'No', that power ceases. Similarly, in the *Parliament of Fowls* the formel eagle, representative of aristocratic women, has her 'choys al fre' (649). But the power of these females is at best partial; they seem to have the right of 'respit' or deferral rather than of utter refusal. A year hence, and they must accept the inevitable.

But there are many problems with Bloch's thesis, particularly its total-izing determination to find only a few interrelated causes, all aspects of a male conspiracy, for what seems to have been a historical phenomenon of extraordinary complexity and ambivalence. Moreover, his postulation of medieval religious discourse as offering considerable scope for female empowerment will appear quite implausible to anyone who is aware of, for example, the institutional suspicion with which the Church regarded its women visionaries (even including one as aristocratic as St Bridget), or its blanket refusal to take seriously the idea that women could be taught speculative theology, let alone be considered as teachers or priests. And surely if the aristocratic males of Aquitaine had been worried by uppity women, they would have found more straightforward and direct ways of reasserting the *status quo* than creating a discourse which worked with such subtlety and stealth to effect its suppression. Literary critics may believe that the pen is mightier than the sword, but the rest of the world seems to function on the assumption that poetry makes nothing happen (to borrow W. H. Auden's phrase).

Courtly love, Bloch says, is perhaps the best example of 'Doormat-Pedestal' tactics, which seek to elevate woman in order to debase her. But does the elevation of woman inevitably result in her debasement—or, bet-ter, in exactly the same degree or kind of debasement? Doubtless any essentializing statement of the 'Woman is . . .' type is misogynistic in Bloch's broad definition of the term, but there may be degrees of misogyny, and (even more importantly) certain kinds of misogyny may be more elastic than others. Surely at least *some* women would have pre-ferred praise (however stereotyping it may have been) to condemnation as inveterately sluttish creatures who lead men astray. The latter admit-ted of little negotiation; the former, however, in some cases and in some circumstances, may have held out possibilities for collusion and redirec-tion (a time-honoured strategy for survival at worst and manipulation at best). For example, in her *Livre de la Cité des Dames* (1405) Christine de Pizan appropriates 'woman on pedestal' discourse in her brilliant counter-attack against 'woman as doormat' discourse. I, for one, do not want to be boxed into an interpretative situation in which Christine becomes a gender-alienated woman who is 'reading as a man' and generally collab-orating with the patriarchical establishment in the subtle suppression of women through sublimating praise. For this would be to ignore the his-torical moment of what Christine was doing, and misread its cultural sig-nificance within that moment. And that, in my view, points to the fundamental flaw in Bloch's analysis. For all its protests against the way in which courtly love functioned to divert 'women from history through an annihilation of the identity of individual women' (p. 197), the method here practised seems itself to be annihilating specific historical circumstances.

A comprehensive historical location of *fin' amors* must accommodate the fact that it was often regarded as being dangerously transgressive of ethical and religious norms. That much should be obvious from the reactions of Walsingham and Bradwardine which were quoted above. (There is also the suggestion in those statements that such amatory behaviour may impair military efficiency, but here clerics are talking, rather than professional soldiers: then, as now, assumptions about female approval, including the promise or possibility of sexual reward, for manly prowess in battle may have functioned to boost morale.) Their message is clear: devotion to Cupid threatens the worship of Christ; the cult of Venus subverts the cult of the Virgin. A similar thrust may be discerned in Stephen Tempier's inclusion in the 1277 Paris condemnations of Andreas Capellanus's *De amore*. This book is named in Tempier's prefatory remarks (complete with its *incipit* and *explicit*, so there can be no mistaking its identity), and is grouped among works on geomancy and divination, all of which, the Bishop declares, are contrary to orthodox faith and good morals. Moreover, some of the condemned propositions themselves could be taken as referring to ideas in the *De amore*, on a partial and reductive reading of what Andreas actually says: for example, that extramarital sex is not necessarily sinful, that continence (by which one abstains from sexual pleasures) is not essentially a virtue, and that the will is not free to counter the urgings of desire. Tempier seems to have been worried by the prospect of sexuality being elevated beyond the confining boundaries of marriage and, more generally, beyond the inferior place assigned to it within the hierarchy of ethical and intellectual values. And Chaucer, it must be added, would hardly have classified all of his four major dream-vision poems as 'enditynges of worldly vanitees' or placed them in the company of 'many a leccherous lay' and those Canterbury Tales which lead into sin (to quote the *Retracciouns*) if he had regarded them as the morally conventional works which certain types of modern criticism have laboured to turn them into. What made such poems transgressive, it may be inferred, was (*inter alia*) their advocacy of *fin' amors* and textualization of 'the feminine', as constructed in Chaucer's day, in many of its aspects, ranging from exclusively secular celebration of a dear, dead woman to the creation of Cupid's female saints, and of course including the strategies of 'feminization' in all their complexity and ambivalence. This argument takes us rather far away from the patriarchal conspiracy postulated by Bloch.

Moreover, in the case of the *Book of the Duchess* there are many specific historical circumstances which, fortunately, we have the means of investigating, including the formulas of commemoration and consolation which Chaucer in part inherited and in part created, and that remarkable engagement with French sources which made the poem what it is. By showing what he was working from, some precise idea of what he was working towards may be inferred (cf. pp. 100–12, 135–60 below). Having seen the way in which Chaucer renegotiated the construction of the feminine offered by Machaut's *jugement* poems, it will become harder to regard the English poet as enacting the encryptment of Blanche, of whiting out her name, in his text.

Talk of the 'annihilation of the identity of individual women' may call to mind the *Legend of Good Women*, for it could be suggested that the editorializing process which brought this poem into being is doing precisely that. No matter how the selected women are represented in Chaucer's sources, he chooses to emphasize (if not create) their sameness. For the most part they are kindly and sympathetic creatures, generous to a fault, certainly not promiscuous, and quite admirable in their pagan piety. Reductive these constructions certainly are, but that should not blind us to the point of the reduction; namely, that Chaucer is creating a series of female personae who are morally victorious even as their amatory hopes and plans are thwarted by male treachery. Here are no viragos, heroic women who succeed to the extent that they have become more like men (cf. pp. 423–34 below), but figures who have been given a distinct female ethic, a code of behaviour which is presented as being superior to the one followed by their male counterparts. The fact that this ethic, which ultimately presupposes an ideology of subservience to men in particular and to marriage in general, is hardly acceptable as an idealizing strategy in the 1990s should not be allowed to obscure the significance of what Chaucer, as a man of the 1380s, was trying to do within the cultural parameters which were his *données*. I believe that he was certainly being different, and perhaps even dissenting, in locating exemplary womanliness on a site which accommodates both earnest and game, and provokes the thought that literary play can have serious cultural implications. A poem like the *Legend* allows the thought that fictional females can get outside the given narratives which history fated many actual women to follow.

It must freely be admitted, however, that to speak of the literary effects under discussion in terms of dissidence may be at once simplistic and sensationalistic. Perhaps the quarrel functions within the culture—maybe as a sort of social safety-valve or even as a space which the dominant ethos cannot or does not wish to occupy—rather than against it.

Whichever of these visions one prefers, I would argue that in the *Legend* Chaucer presents a 'world upside down' in which gender games have been raised to the level of an alternative art, by which I mean an art which opens up fresh possibilities for the production of fiction and the business of living. 'Woman on pedestal' discourse the poem may be, in a sense; but it should be noted that pedestals come in different shapes and sizes, and have many uses and functions. The particular pedestal which Chaucer has chosen here is therefore of considerable importance, especially since it was not ready-made, but very much of the poet's own design, as I hope to show below.

To lift the poet from his period, eagle-like with our critical talons ('A thought may flee so hye', *HF* 973), is surely to render no service to the present-day imperative of comprehending the history of gender roles. The City of Ladies was not built in a day. Indeed, it is still very much under construction. Perhaps some of Chaucer's fictions of gender may be thought of as having helped to lay a few—just a few—of its foundations.

A useful introduction to our crucial term is provided by J. D. Burnley, '*Fine Amor*: Its Meaning and Context', *RES* NS 3 (1980), 129–49. For the process whereby the modern meaning of 'courtship' developed from the older sense of 'being at court' see Catherine Bates, *The Rhetoric of Courtship in Elizabethan Language and Literature* (Cambridge, 1992).
Gaston Paris, 'Lancelot du Lac: Le Conte de la Charrette', *Romania*, 12 (1883), 459–534.
C. S. Lewis, *The Allegory of Love* (Oxford, 1936). Lewis made a large claim for the cultural significance of courtly love: a 'real change in human sentiment', it erected a barrier between us and antiquity, in which love was seen as either 'merry sensuality' or a 'tragic madness', and transformed European ethics, imagination, and daily life. As compared with its invention, he declares, the Renaissance was 'a mere ripple on the surface of literature' (p. 4). For Lewis, the unattached knight who made his own way in the world through personal valour and courtesy and fell in love with other men's wives was a social reality in many countries, though (mysteriously) it was in Provence that this situation first gave rise to the composition of the poetry of courtly love (p. 12).
Violet Paget, 'Medieval Love', in *Euphorion, being Studies of the Antique and the Mediaeval in the Renaissance* (London, 1884), ii. 123–217.
See John F. Benton's articles 'The Court of Champagne as a Literary Centre', 'The Evidence of Andreas Capellanus Re-examined Again', and 'Clio and Venus: An Historical View of Medieval Love', all reprinted in his *Culture, Power and Personality in Medieval France*, ed. Thomas N. Bisson (London and Rio Grande, 1991), pp. 3–43, 81–8, 99–121. D. W. Robertson, *A Preface to Chaucer. Studies in Medieval Perspectives* (Princeton, NJ, 1962), pp. 393–448. For further discussion and references see below, pp. 295–307, 314–19. On Ovid as a champion of married love see pp. 360, 393.
E. S. Kooper, *Love, Marriage and Salvation in Chaucer's 'Book of the Duchess' and 'Parliament of Foules'* (Utrecht, 1985). See further John T. Noonan, 'Marital Affection in the Canonists', *Studia Gratiana*, 12 (1967), 481–509; J. J. Morgan, 'Chaucer and the Bona Matrimonii', *ChR* 4 (1970), 123–41; also Peter Biller, 'Marriage Patterns and Women's Lives: A Sketch of a Pastoral Geography', in P. J. P. Goldberg (ed.), *Woman*

is a Worthy Wight: Women in English Society c.1200–1500 (Stroud, Gloucestershire, 1992), pp. 60–107, esp. pp. 69–70.

Mathew, *Court of Richard II*. Aelred of Rievaulx, *Spiritual Friendship*, trans. Mary Eugenia Laker, Cistercian Fathers Series, 5 (Kalamazoo, Mich., 1974). On the interrelations of love and friendship see the relevant material in Robert R. Edwards and Stephen Spector (eds.), *The Olde Daunce: Love, Friendship, Sex and Marriage in the Medieval World* (Albany, NY, 1991).

Jill Mann, *Geoffrey Chaucer*, Harvester Feminist Readings (New York and London, 1991), pp. 165–85 (on 'The Feminized Hero'). Concerning my rule-of-thumb distinction between 'gender' and 'biological sex', it should be noted that Judith Butler's *Gender Trouble* (New York and London, 1991) argues that *both* these terms are unstable, 'biological sex' being just as problematic and constructed as 'gender'. The matter has been further complicated by Thomas Laqueur, *Making Sex: Body and Gender from the Greeks to Freud* (Cambridge, Mass., 1990), which argues that before the eighteenth century male and female were generally regarded as manifestations of a single, unified substance. I find Laqueur's 'one sex' model far too reductive as a template for reading the negotiations of gender in much medieval poetry. Besides, much of the material in Joan Cadden's utterly indispensable *Meanings of Sex Difference in the Middle Ages* (Cambridge, 1993) simply does not fit the Laqueur model, as she herself notes (p. 3). See further N. F. Partner, 'No Sex, No Gender', *Speculum*, 68 (1993), 419–43. (This entire issue of *Speculum*, edited by Partner, is devoted to 'Studying Medieval Women: Sex, Gender, Feminism'.)

D. W. Robertson, 'The Concept of Courtly Love as an Impediment to the Understanding of Medieval Texts', in F. X. Newman (ed.), *The Meaning of Courtly Love* (New York, 1972), pp. 1–18. The *Sermo Epinicius* has been edited by Oberman and Weisheipl (cf. p. 55 above).

Maud Ellmann, 'Blanche', in Jeremy Hawthorn (ed.), *Criticism and Critical Theory* (London, 1984), pp. 99–110. Gayle Rubin, 'The Traffic in Women: Notes on the "Political Economy" of Sex', in Rayna R. Reiter (ed.), *Toward an Anthropology of Women* (New York and London, 1975), pp. 157–210.

James I. Wimsatt, 'The Apotheosis of Blanche in *The Book of the Duchess*', *JEGP* 66 (1967), 26–44. Cf. the interpretation of Marcelle Thiébaux, *The Stag of Love. The Chase in Medieval Literature* (Ithaca, NY, and London, 1974), who argues that Chaucer 'attributes all the poem's celestial radiance to White'. 'The shaded hopelessness of the pagan tale [of Ceyx and Alcyone], in which Death triumphs over love', is set 'against the luminous descriptions of White whose love, immortalized in the poem, is as strong as death because of her light' (p. 124). See further Stephen Manning, 'Chaucer's Good Fair White: Woman and Symbol', *Comparative Literature*, 10 (1958), 97–105.

Elaine Tuttle Hansen, *Chaucer and the Fictions of Gender* (Berkeley and Los Angeles, 1992). It should be noted that the evidence amassed in Cadden's *Meanings of Sex Difference* affords some support for Hansen's reading of Chaucerian fiction as exploring medieval gender boundaries and the ways in which men may behave like women and women may behave like men. While the gender binary was rigidly affirmed and policed, Cadden demonstrates, the use of such labels as 'womanly men' and 'masculine women' raised the possibility that men and women could share or exchange certain types of activity. 'The words "woman" and "man" each encompassed a range of dispositions and behaviors, and a "masculine" man might share traits with a "masculine" woman' (Cadden, p. 225). Here and later in this book I challenge some of the details and specific moves of Hansen's approach, but certainly not its general validity.

The term 'homosocial', as used above, is not to be equated with 'homosexual': on the contrary, it may be applied to 'male bonding' of a kind which is characterized by fear and hatred of homosexuality. See Eve Kosofsky Sedgwick, *Between Men: English Literature and Male Homosocial Desire* (New York and Oxford, 1985). In *BD* a homosocial bond forms between the dreamer and the Man in Black, their mutual maleness being defined and affirmed through the perception of woman as contrast, absent, Other. On the development of masculine identity in the knightly class see especially David Aers, 'Masculine Identity in the Courtly Community: The Self Loving in *Troilus and Criseyde*', in his *Community, Gender and Individual Identity. English Writing 1360–1430* (London and New York, 1988), pp. 117–52.

Karl Vossler, *Medieval Culture. An Introduction to Dante and his Times*, trans. W. C. Lawton (London, 1929), i. 299–300; Robert Miller, 'The Wounded Heart: Courtly Love and the Medieval Antifeminist Tradition', *Women's Studies*, 2 (1974), 335–50; Charles Camproux, *Le Joy d'amour des troubadours* (Montpellier, 1965); Diane Bornstein, 'Courtly Love', in Joseph R. Strayer (ed.), *The Dictionary of the Middle Ages* (New York, 1983), iii. 668–74. See further the very helpful survey by Roger Boase, *The Origin and Meaning of Courtly Love* (Manchester, 1977). Boase comments: 'Women ruled the imaginations of men and motivated their conduct, but it is doubtful whether the position of women in society was greatly altered by Courtly Love' (p. 77). The claims made by Joan Kelly-Gadol for the 'courtly independence' of women within the feudal aristocracy, 'Did Women Have a Renaissance?', in Renate Bridenthal and Claudia Koonz (eds.), *Becoming Visible: Women in European History* (Boston, 1977), pp. 137–64, have been critiqued by Sheila Fisher and Janet E. Halley in the introduction to their anthology *Seeking the Woman in Late Medieval and Renaissance Writings: Essays in Feminist Contextual Criticism* (Knoxville, Tenn., 1989), p. 9. Compare the well-grounded scepticism expressed by E. Jane Burns and Roberta L. Krueger in their introduction to 'Courtly Ideology and Woman's Place in Medieval French Literature', special issue of *Romance Notes*, 25/3 (Spring 1985), 209–19. The view that courtly literature promoted the social welfare of the noblewomen to whom romances were dedicated or addressed has been trenchantly challenged by Krueger in her monograph *Women Readers and the Ideology of Gender in Old French Verse Romance* (Cambridge, 1993).

R. Howard Bloch, *Medieval Misogyny and the Invention of Western Romantic Love* (Chicago and London, 1991). On the theory of mutual marital consent and the woman's right to choose see the discussion and references on pp. 302, 307, below.

It was generally held that women should not be taught deep matters of theology, but be instructed only in those things which were essential for their salvation. Moreover, women were not permitted to teach theology, except in the most special and limited of contexts. See A. J. Minnis, 'The *Accessus* Extended: Henry of Ghent on the Transmission and Reception of Theology', in Mark D. Jordan and Kent Emery (eds.), *Ad Litteram: Authoritative Texts and their Medieval Readers* (Notre Dame, Ind., and London, 1992), pp. 275–326 (pp. 311–16 is on Henry's view of 'Female Frailty'); Alcuin Blamires (ed.), *Woman Defamed and Woman Defended: An Anthology of Medieval Texts* (Oxford, 1992), pp. 250–60 (on the trial of the Lollard Walter Brut, who dared to suggest that women can preach and administer the sacraments). On Christine de Pizan see below, pp. 427–30, 433–4.

For an excellent treatment of the idea that 'women in medieval literature and sometimes in real life find subtle or hidden ways to exercise . . . power, to manipulate people and situations, and to spin out fictions which suit them better than their reality, fictions by which they can, or hope to, control reality', see Joan Ferrante, 'Public Postures and Private Maneuvers: Roles Medieval Women Play', in Mary Erler and Maryanne Kowaleski (eds.), *Women and Power in the Middle Ages* (Athens, Ga., and London, 1988), pp. 213–29. To the speculation that some medieval women may have found aspects of 'pedestal discourse' susceptible to collusion, negotiation, appropriation, and exploitation may be added the suggestion (which I owe to Ruth Evans) that certain courtly fictions could have been pleasurable and narcissistically gratifying to women as well as men. See, for example, the way in which the 'Antigone's Song' episode in *Troilus*, ii. 813–903, thematizes the notion of a *community* of ladies finding the fictional representation of love a source of shared pleasure. This scene, and others like it, may be seen as asserting a Barthesian disruptive plurality. To protest that here we are dealing with an episode within a masculinist fiction, wherein women are merely represented in ways in which patriarchal culture wants them to be, would be to miss the point that sophisticated textual configurations regularly exceed the boundaries which they appear, indeed which they may palpably seek, to delimit (cf. pp. 443–54 below).

On the 1277 Paris condemnations see pp. 43, 54, above. See further A. J. Denomy, 'The *De Amore* of Andreas Capellanus and the Condemnation of 1277', *MS* 8 (1946), 107–49, though this article is over-eager to match up certain condemned propositions with Andreas's text.

Very aware of my subject position as a male writing about Chaucer's textual constructions of women, I share many of the feelings expressed by Stephen Heath in his article 'Male Feminism', in Alice Jardine and Paul Smith (eds.), *Men in Feminism* (London, 1987), pp. 1–32.

# The Book of the Duchess

Blanche of Lancaster died on 12 September 1368, perhaps of the plague. Two major monuments were constructed to preserve her memory. One was a poem by Geoffrey Chaucer, this being (as far as we know) his first substantial composition; he was probably in his mid-twenties at the time of Blanche's death. The other was the work of her husband, John of Gaunt, the third surviving son of King Edward III. In 1374 he commissioned from master mason Henry Yevele a splendid alabaster tomb, surmounted by sculptures of the duchess and himself. Perpetual masses were to be said for her soul at an adjoining altar, and a memorial service held on 12 September of each year. Gaunt's will contained the directive, 'My body to be buried . . . beside my most dear late wife Blanche, who is there interred'. And that was done. However, the tomb of Gaunt and Blanche, which was located in the north arcade of the choir of old St Paul's cathedral church in London, perished in the Great Fire. Chaucer's poem has survived. Is it a record, however idealized, of a genuine love-affair, or an elaborate piece of princepleasing which plays fast and loose with the facts, assuming that the poet knew them? Many critics have felt obliged to speculate on the nature of the royal relationship, since on it hangs—or at least they have made to hang—their views on the negotiations between artifice and life, conventional discourses and emotional integrity, which are made by the *Book of the Duchess*.

It has been argued that Gaunt's first marriage was dictated by political expediency every bit as much as his second, to Constance of Castile. Worse still, in some medieval accounts he appears as an inveterate womanizer: having fathered an illegitimate daughter before he met Blanche, during the time of his marriage to Constance he took Katherine Swynford as his mistress (they were to marry in 1396). Indeed, it has even been suggested (though hard evidence is lacking) that this affair began while he was married to Blanche. Katherine had been one of Blanche's ladies-in-waiting and the governess of her daughters. Chaucer could hardly have been unaware of such events, if it is true that his wife Philippa was the sister of Gaunt's long-time mistress.

One would give much to know what the poet had in mind as he wrote the *Book of the Duchess* and as he looked back on it in later years. But that knowledge will, of course, never be forthcoming, and in the absence of such intimate biographical detail we may isolate the appropriate critical issues by means of a modern meditation on a medieval tomb—

not Blanche's lost tomb, to be sure, but one belonging to the Howard family, once earls and countesses of Arundel, which may be seen in Winchester Cathedral. Philip Larkin's poem 'An Arundel Tomb' raises questions concerning the artistic imitation (or is it illusion?) of feeling and the needs of the audience which confronts such an image, questions which lead us into vital regions of the aesthetics of Chaucer's poem.

> Side by side, their faces blurred,
> The earl and countess lie in stone,
> their proper habits vaguely shown
> As jointed armour, stiffened pleat

What these people really felt for each other has also become 'blurred', as the poem will make abundantly clear. In what sense do they 'lie in stone'? The earl's left-hand gauntlet is empty, and

> One sees, with a sharp tender shock,
> His hand withdrawn, holding her hand.

But this serves to perplex as well as please. Is this a true or false image of historical reality? 'They would not think to lie so long', the repetition of 'lie' underlining the double meaning of the word: the sculptures lie together there as part of the tomb, and yet they may be perpetuating an untruth. (The fact that the hand-clasp is the result of later 'restoration' of the tomb serves to reinforce Larkin's point!) The next line, 'Such faithfulness in effigy', is similarly ambiguous. That particular effigy could be an accurate representation of genuine fidelity; yet, taken in its entirety, the phrase also suggests something grimly static and cold, the life-affirming quality of fidelity in love being impossible to preserve artificially.

The role of the artist, the sculptor responsible for this fabrication, is then considered. Maybe the holding of hands was simply a grace-note ('A sculptor's sweet commissioned grace') which he added on his own initiative (though of course he had been paid to display his skill), in the hope that its rarity would aid the memory of the beholders. If so, it would seem that time has reversed such priorities. Now tourists stare uncomprehendingly at the Latin names 'around the base', not being able to understand this dead language. What seems to be familiar, what they fancy they recognize, is that hand-clasp; here is something which transcends temporal and linguistic differences. 'Only an attitude remains'—the configuration of the sculptures, existing irrespective of, and maybe even despite, what the original attitudes of the medieval lord and lady may have been. It seems to affirm that human love is durable. Certainly, that is what (the poem's assumed) 'we' *want* to believe; what is seen on the tomb appears

to prove
Our almost-instinct almost true:
What will survive of us is love.

But the poem will not allow 'us' to luxuriate in such a sentiment, tempting though that may be. It persists in asking, *does* love survive, in general, and is this what has happened in the case of the Howards, whose identities are lost in the past?

Time is not passive; it has not merely permitted the effigy to travel unhindered in its 'supine stationary voyage' down to the present. Rather, it is a power which effects transformation.

Time has transfigured them into
Untruth. The stone fidelity
They hardly meant has come to be
Their final blazon

In this case it may have exercised a heightening, and hence a distorting, effect on something which owes more to art than to life, more to fiction than to truth. The medieval aristocrats may not have lived up to their image; 'hardly meant' evinces at once possible misunderstanding and firm affirmation—the hard stone declares its own meaning. The 'attitude' of love has thus been created by art; art has the power, as it were, to 'make' love. But are we dealing, then, with a lie? In terms of historical truth, maybe—though we shall never know. But the desire of human beings to believe in the survival of love in itself constitutes a major truth. Hence one can justifiably speak of an 'almost-instinct' as being 'almost true'. The agnostic modern, seeking to avoid sentimentality and dubious of the existence of a destiny which shapes our ends, is not prepared to go any farther than that. Yet this almost-truth is, in Larkin's terms, a fact of the first magnitude.

Due to the carefully wrought ambiguity of this poem, neither element of the balance is allowed to dominate. It cannot be said that this has always been the case in modern interpretation of Chaucer's 'lie' in verse, the *fabula* of the *Book of the Duchess*. Some have been convinced that time, with the help of Chaucer's artistic 'grace' (whether specifically 'commissioned' or not) has transfigured Gaunt and Blanche into untruth. The possibility that John of Gaunt had committed adultery with Katherine in Blanche's lifetime has occasionally been raised, with Gaunt's wish to be buried beside his first duchess being taken as indicative of his thankfulness for her acquiescent forbearance. Then there is the question, did Gaunt do enough on Blanche's death? One may contrast, for example, Richard II's order, on the death of his queen in 1394, that the royal manor at Sheen be destroyed; he had once enjoyed happiness with her there. (As Clerk of the Works, Chaucer had overseen alterations to that royal residence.) But, even by the standards of the age, this was an extravagant expression of grief; it can hardly be taken as a norm against which to measure Gaunt's behaviour and find it wanting.

Others have perceived an even more elaborate web of intrigue, which included Chaucer's own wife and the poet himself. For instance, it has been suggested that Gaunt may have had an affair with Philippa, the issue of which was Thomas Chaucer. Such a claim, however, rests on an extraordinarily partial interpretation of such evidence as does exist and a determination to make gaps in the historical record into significant silences. Moreover, it is quite unnecessary: such links as we know Chaucer to have had with Gaunt certainly did not require him to have been in the position of a 'contented cuckold' (as B. J. Whiting puts it) who merited some compensation, and 'in later years the fact that the duke truly loved Chaucer's sister-in-law may be reason enough why he granted financial favors' to her kin, to quote Donald Howard (p. 95).

But let us concentrate on the relationship between Gaunt and Blanche. It has often been declared or implied that love is the most important thing that has survived of them. Sydney Armitage-Smith, in his 1904 biography of John of Gaunt, saw Blanche's death as marking the end of the best years of Gaunt's life. 'Of the sincerity of the Duke's grief there need be no question'; his 'gratitude to the memory of his first wife never failed' (p. 77). Monkish attacks on Gaunt's subsequent affair with Katherine are trivialized as 'merely the venom of the cloister', and there is special pleading with reference to the 'standard of English society in the fourteenth century', which is supposed to have been 'not exacting' in matters of personal morality. Gaunt's conduct, Armitage-Smith believes, was 'if no better . . . certainly no worse' than that of others (pp. 138–9). Writing over eighty years later, Howard follows in Armitage-Smith's footsteps by seeing Gaunt's life with Blanche as marking the end of his golden age: 'Her death . . . wrought a change in his character. He was to be thereafter a man possessed by ambitions' (p. 123). Concerning the quality of Gaunt's first love, while noting that 'Medieval knights of royal lineage are often depicted as unfeeling military leaders whose relationships with women were exploitative and wanting in sentiment', Howard prefers to throw his own weight behind the belief that 'they could love their wives with towering and noble emotion', and unhesitatingly takes the commemorative masses and services which Gaunt ordered, along with his declared desire to be buried beside Blanche, as firm evidence that he

'loved her deeply' (p. 40; cf. p. 94). A similar dichotomy pervades Derek
Brewer's approach. Evincing a robust willingness to accept medieval
*realpolitik* and mores, he refuses to be surprised by Gaunt's prompt
remarriage: 'Private sentiment could not weigh against public policy; and
there was anyway a hardboiled acceptance of death in the fourteenth century.' However, these general facts of late medieval life certainly do not,
in Brewer's opinion, rule out the possibility that profound 'private sentiment' could have existed in this case: 'Lancaster's genuine love for
Blanche and his grief at her death are not to be questioned' (p. 112).
Chaucer's poem, he continues, is 'not so much an idealized account
of life as the ideal truth to which life was so fortunate to approximate'
(p. 116).

George Kane, *pace* Chaucer's poem, is determined to portray Gaunt
with warts and all, and to remind us that they were clearly visible before,
as well as after, his time with Blanche. 'There was nothing [in the *Book
of the Duchess*] about the daughter Gaunt fathered before he married
Blanche'; nor could one know from it that 'Gaunt's marriage to Blanche
had in fact been arranged by his father to consolidate the kingship' (pp.
27–8). Yet, later, Kane declares that although this was an arranged marriage, 'It turned into a love match' (p. 71). 'Lovely Blanche . . . never
lost her place in his heart', as is manifest by his wish to be buried beside
her (p. 70). However, Chaucer's latest biographer, Derek Pearsall, has
challenged such reasoning. 'It was usual to be buried next to one's first
wife', he claims, 'especially when she was the foundation of one's fortune.' And the phrase 'my most dear late wife', apparently so appropriate as applied to Blanche, is also applied to Constance of Castile (who
died in 1394). Anyway, declares Pearsall, here we are dealing with 'the
routine commonplaces of inky clerks' (p. 90).

How, then, can one possibly sum up Gaunt's behaviour in love? 'A
spectacular man to whom the rules might not seem to apply' is Kane's
verdict (p. 71). Thus, Gaunt's best side is presented to the beholder: here
is one who was not numbered in the roll of common men. And this is,
of course, precisely what the *Book of the Duchess* shows and says, inasmuch as its Man in Black is an idealized figure of Gaunt. In the final
analysis, we cannot claim familiarity with Gaunt. Similarly, there is considerable distance between the observer and the observed in the *Book of
the Duchess*, the poet persona and the Gaunt-surrogate being divided by
rank and experience. These matters will be discussed below. Suffice it to
say here that Chaucer's portraits of Gaunt and Blanche, though idealized
representations, are no effigies upon which the narrator can project his
meditations—which is what is happening in the Larkin poem. For in the
*Book of the Duchess* it is the black knight who is dominant, who imposes

his meditations on a beholder, the narrator, a subordinate who can listen and learn even if he cannot fully understand. He, the marvelling reporter, invites his audience to share in his admiration. And in Chaucer's poem, art, far from turning feelings into stone, serves to conserve them—but here too the pleat has stiffened, inasmuch as they are presented in forms which owe much to the ritualizing processes of literary decorums and conventions. Whether or not this is a 'lie' or an approximation to ideal truth (to echo Brewer's phrase) is impossible to tell. History allows either opinion, and gainsays neither. 'Only an attitude remains.' The following sections will attempt to describe it.

The date of Blanche's death was firmly established by J. J. N. Palmer, 'The Historical Context of the *Book of the Duchess*: A Revision', *ChR* 8 (1974), 253–61. Previously it was generally thought that she died on 12 September 1369. For Gaunt's arrangements regarding the anniversaries of her death see Sydney Armitage-Smith (ed.), *John of Gaunt's Register*, Camden Third Series, 20–1 (London, 1911), items 915, 918, 943, 1091, 1122, 1394, 1585, 1659. For his will see Sydney Armitage-Smith, *John of Gaunt* (London, 1905), pp. 420–36. A succinct account of Gaunt's reputation and of Katherine Swynford may be found in Chris Given-Wilson and Alice Curteis, *The Royal Bastards of Medieval England* (London and Boston, 1984), pp. 147–53. On Henry Yevele see John Harvey, *English Medieval Architects* (London, 1954), pp. 312–20.

Philip Larkin, 'An Arundel Tomb', in *The Whitsun Weddings* (London, 1964), pp. 45–6.

For the yarn about Thomas Chaucer being Gaunt's illegitimate son see Russell Kraus, *Chaucerian Problems: Especially the Petherton Friendship and the Question of Thomas Chaucer* (1932; repr. New York, 1973), pp. 50–6. Cf. F. W. Bateson, *Essays in Critical Dissent* (London, 1972), pp. 89–90.

Howard, *Chaucer and the Medieval World*. D. S. Brewer, *Chaucer and his World* (London, 1978). Kane, *Chaucer*. Pearsall, *Life of Chaucer*. For Whiting's remark see *Speculum*, 8 (1933), 535. For excellent recent scholarship on Gaunt and his affinity see Simon Walker, *The Lancastrian Affinity, 1361–1399* (Oxford, 1990), and Anthony Goodman, *John of Gaunt* (Oxford, 1992).

Good introductions to *BD* include David Aers, 'Chaucer's *Book of the Duchess*: An Art to Consume Art', *Durham University Journal*, 69 (1976–7), 201–5; Bertrand H. Bronson, '*The Book of the Duchess* Re-opened', *PMLA* 67 (1952), 863–81; repr. in Edward Wagenknecht (ed.), *Chaucer: Modern Essays in Criticism* (New York, 1959), pp. 271–94; Wolfgang Clemen, *Chaucer's Early Poetry*, trans. C. A. M. Sym (London, 1963), pp. 23–66; Robert R. Edwards, *The Dream of Chaucer. Representation and Reflection in the Early Narratives* (Durham, NC, and London, 1989), pp. 65–91; P. M. Kean, *Chaucer and the Making of English Poetry* (Oxford, 1972), i. 31–66; Kooper, *Love, Marriage and Salvation*, pp. 161–99; Dieter Mehl, *Geoffrey Chaucer: An Introduction to his Narrative Poetry* (Cambridge, 1986), pp. 22–36; Pearsall, *Life of Chaucer*, pp. 82–93; Spearing, *Medieval Dream-Poetry*, pp. 49–73; also his *Readings in Medieval Poetry* (Cambridge, 1987), pp. 94–106.

In addition to the edition of *BD* by L. D. Benson and C. Wilkinson, as included in the *Riverside Chaucer*, the edition by Helen Phillips is recommended, particularly for its notes.

*Text, Date, and Circumstances*

The *Book of the Duchess* survives in only three manuscripts, all of which are now in the Bodleian Library, Oxford (Fairfax 16, Bodley 638, Tanner 346), along with the text which William Thynne included in his 1532 edition of Chaucer's works. Thynne's text includes some lines which are not found in the manuscripts, the most important being the section formed by lines 31–96, containing the narrator's account of how he came to read the story of Ceyx and Alcyone and the beginning of the summary of its narrative. The loss may have been due to a leaf which was lost early in the transmission of the work. The scribes of Fairfax 16 and Bodley 638 know that something is missing, because they leave a space; in Tanner 346 a clumsy attempt has been made to patch the pieces together. Clearly, this passage or something like it is essential to the sense of the poem at this point, and there has been a large body of opinion in favour of the theory that Thynne represents a textual tradition which is superior to that reflected by the manuscripts. Norman Blake, however, has suggested that lines 31–96 could nevertheless be spurious. Helen Phillips has reasserted the authenticity of these lines, in a manner which I find convincing. Moreover, she suggests that the problem may have come about as a result of Chaucer's attempt to dovetail an earlier work, an independent version of the story of Ceyx and Alcyone, into the poem as we now have it.

That Chaucer was writing to commemorate Blanche of Lancaster there need not be any doubt. This is confirmed by his entitling the poem 'the Deeth of Blaunche the Duchesse' in the prologue to the *Legend of Good Women* (F 418, cf. G 406). Chaucer's method of encoding her name in the text itself seems to follow a technique used by Guillaume de Machaut in a major source of the *Book of the Duchess*, the *Remede de Fortune* (composed *c.*1340). The lady who governs the action therein is identified as Bonne, daughter of King Jean of Bohemia, through a pun on her name— 'beautiful and *Bonne*, everyone properly gives her this name':

> . . . ma dame, qui est clamee
> De tous sur toutes belle et bonne.
> Chascun par droit ce non li donne.                    (54–6)

As Wimsatt and Kibler point out, Chaucer seems to have recognized what Machaut had done, and to have substituted his own pun on 'Blanche', anglicized as 'White', who like Bonne 'hadde not hir name wrong' (948–51). This word-play is of course confirmed by the more elaborate one in lines 1318–19, wherein Chaucer links the names of 'White' of 'Long castel' (= Lancaster) and 'Johan' of 'Ryche hil' (= Richmond;

Gaunt was Earl of Richmond in Yorkshire until 1372, which helps to confirm the poem's *terminus ad quem*).

According to a note in the Fairfax manuscript, the poem was written at the specific request of John of Gaunt. There is no substantiating evidence for that statement, but we do know that Blanche died on 12 September 1368. This is thanks to a letter written by Louis de Mâle, Count of Flanders, to Queen Philippa, which tactfully deflects the queen's suggestion that Gaunt, her son, should marry Louis's daughter Margaret—clearly, he was then a widower. Having put together the pieces of information, Derek Brewer (p. 112) concluded that 'at the latest two months after the death of Blanche', the English were seeking to arrange a politically expedient marriage for her former husband, and hence Chaucer must have written the poem in a hurry, between Blanche's death on the 12 September 1368 and November of the same year, by which time the English proposal that Gaunt should marry Margaret of Flanders would have been made. Meeting with no success here, Gaunt and his advisers sought a wife elsewhere: in 1371 he married Constance, daughter of Pedro I of Castile.

However, many Chaucerians, including Brewer, refuse to believe that Gaunt's love for Blanche ever died. If we take this as a serious possibility, then there is no reason to suppose that the period within which Chaucer might have composed the *Book of the Duchess* was very brief. Indeed, Edward Condren has argued that it was possibly written for, and read, at one of the annual commemorations of the duchess's death as much as eight years later. There is no definitive way of disproving this, though the 'Ryche hil' (= Richmond) pun would have been redundant after 1372, as already noted. Besides, the occasional immaturities in the poem would suggest that it is an early work, composed before the much more technically accomplished *House of Fame*. And the lack of any Italian influence would seem to confirm the dating of 'before 1372'.

N. F. Blake, 'The Textual Tradition of *The Book of the Duchess*', *English Studies*, 62 (1981), 237–48.
Phillips (ed.), *BD*. Machaut, *'Behaigne' and 'Fortune'*, ed. Wimsatt and Kibler. Palmer, 'Historical Context'. Brewer, *Chaucer and his World*. Edward Condren, 'The Historical Context of the *Book of the Duchess*: A New Hypothesis', *ChR* 7 (1971), 195–212.
See further the relevant discussion and references in the two preceding chapters, which have allowed the treatment above to be brief.

## Verse-form, Rhetoric, and Style

Chaucer's use of the octosyllabic couplet also encourages the feeling that we are in the presence a young poet who is heavily influenced by French fashion. This was the verse-form used in the *Roman de la Rose*. Chaucer seems to have translated this extraordinarily influential poem into English, at least one fragment of which may have survived. It was also the measure of several of the direct sources of the *Book of the Duchess*, most notably Guillaume de Machaut's *Remede de Fortune* and *Dit de la Fonteinne Amoureuse* (*c.*1360), and the *Ovide moralisé*, which was written between 1316 and 1328 by an anonymous Franciscan.

Some lines have one syllable more and others one syllable less. This cannot be put down to inexperience, however, since this variation is found also in the later *House of Fame*. Moreover, sometimes a trochee functions as the first, second, or indeed the third foot in place of the iambus. And on occasion Chaucer allows an extra syllable before the caesura and a short foot after it. All this indicates Chaucer's preference for a looser verse-form—by contrast with Gower, who in his *Confessio Amantis* creates octosyllabic couplets of exceptional regularity with apparent ease. The current consensus is that Chaucer cannot be judged strictly by French metrical standards, given that he seems to have been influenced by the freer English tradition of four-beat lines. Certainly there is no justification for thoroughgoing editorial attempts to 'restore' smooth octosyllabics.

Further, there is, perhaps, a general tendency to regard the octosyllabic couplet as a highly reductive measure, cramping and homogenizing in its limited scope. This should be resisted. An effective antidote is offered by the work of a contemporary master of the form, Tony Harrison. To take but two examples, his controversial poem on the Gulf War, 'A Cold Coming', and his film poem 'The Gaze of the Gorgon' prove beyond any shadow of a doubt that octosyllabics can accommodate both savage satire and subtle sensitivities, and are eminently capable of ranging from hope to horror, from the sublime to the ridiculous, from the tender to the obscene, even within a few lines. All the more reason to give Chaucer the benefit of the doubt.

At two points in the *Book of the Duchess* a more complicated rhyme scheme is used. This is in the case of the 'enclosed lyrics', the Man in Black's initial 'compleynte' about his lost 'lady bryght' (475–86) and the very first 'song' which, according to his reminiscences, he wrote in expression of his feelings for her (1175–80). The latter rhymes *aabbaa*. The former has a more elaborate scheme, *aabbaccdccd*, which seems to be imperfect. All the manuscripts agree here, but normally one would expect a second couplet rhyming on *a*, though as a genre the complaint can take many forms. In William Thynne's 1532 edition of Chaucer the line 'Now have I tolde the, sothe to say' appears after the indubitably authentic line 1180, but Thynne may simply have made it up.

By including lyrics in this way and highlighting them as discrete units within the narrative (we are told when a recital is about to begin, and some comment is made to mark its completion), Chaucer was following in the footsteps of the Old French poets. The fiction of overhearing and recording a superior's lyric was almost certainly indebted to Machaut's *Fonteinne Amoureuse*, in which the patron's accomplished complaint is transcribed admiringly by the narrator. But the 'intercalated lyric' is a common feature of the *dit amoreux* genre. To take one of the most influential *dits* of them all as an example, in Machaut's *Remede de Fortune* the narrator composes a lay about his feelings for his lady (431–680) and a complaint about Fortune (905–1480). (At the end of the latter Machaut presents the I-persona as debating and struggling alone ('per moy debatus', 1481–2). That particular phrase calls to mind Chaucer's statement that the Man in Black's complaint is 'to hymselve' (464), and later, in *Troilus and Criseyde*, iv. 1084, Troilus will be described as 'disputyng with hymself' in the 'matere' of fate and fortune.) Subsequently Hope sings a *chant royal* (1985–2032) and a *baladele* (2857–92) to comfort and cheer the lover. Duly revitalized, he composes a *ballade* to his lady (3013–36), and prays to Love (3205–348). The climax comes when he actually performs a *chanson baladee* (3451–95) before her, after which she consents to be called his beloved; overjoyed, he sings a *rondelet* (4106–16) as he takes his leave. It could be said that here poetic production is being put in place of amatory experience, an effect which is even more obvious in Machaut's *Voir Dit* (*c*.1364), wherein the lover-narrator and the beloved, Toute-Belle, exchange poems and verse letters, and when their relationship blossoms, each writes a lyric by way of celebration. Jean Froissart's *Prison Amoureuse* (*c*.1360), which is fundamentally a sequence of lyrics and letters, is an obvious attempt to surpass the *Voir Dit*; similarly, Froissart's *Paradys d'Amours* (*c*.1362–9) includes examples of the *rondel*, *rondelet*, *lay*, *virelay*, and *ballade*, which the characters sing with pleasure and much self-congratulation. Nominally these lyric performances record and reflect the psychological history of the narrator and/or some authority figure, but above all else they are an ostentatious display of technical virtuosity, the narrative functioning as a show-case.

Chaucer is rather more interested in having the intercalated lyric fulfil a definite narrative function. Thus, it is the Man in Black's complaint that first tells us that his beloved is dead; thereby the scene is set for the lengthy conversation which follows. And the composition of his very first song in honour of the lady White is also presented as an event of real significance in the furtherance of the story. Knowledge of the bereaved lover's past emotions helps us to understand his present ones. The fact that there are only two lyrics, rather than a formidable arsenal, makes them all the more effective in these terms; they function symmetrically as a neatly contrasting pair. The point which I want to emphasize, however, is that these lyrics keep the action moving rather than hold it up; to some extent this is due, of course, to the fact that they are a lot shorter than most of the effusions in the French *dits*, but different literary priorities are the major determining factor. When John Lydgate came to produce his own version of Chaucer's poem, the *Complaynt of a Loveres Lyfe* (written during the period 1398–1412), he returned to the French manner of doing things which we have just described, the result being a poem which comprises a sequence of quite static set pieces. The actual complaint of 'a man / In black and white, colour pale and wan' (130–1) occupies some 356 lines within a poem of 681 lines, thus constituting over half its total length. Lydgate's eavesdropping narrator does not actually converse with the grieving knight, but carefully records what he said—to entertain the audience!

> A pene I toke and gan me fast[e] spede
> The woful pleynt[e] of this man to write,
> Worde by worde as he dyd endyte:
> Lyke as I herde and coud him tho reporte
> I haue here set, youre hertis to dysporte.          (598–602)

And he utters a twenty-five-line prayer to 'lady Venus' on the knight's behalf. The poem ends with two envoys, of eight lines each, the first to 'Princes' and 'womanhede' in general and the second to his 'luyves quene' in particular. Here direct human contact is avoided, Lydgate being more interested in the aureate encrustation of disembodied emotions than the creation of selfhoods or with their interaction. The contrasts with the *Book of the Duchess* are striking.

Chaucer's interest in the intercalated lyric was by no means confined to the *Book of the Duchess*. *Anelida and Arcite* contains an elaborate 'compleynt' (211–350), and a 'roundel' in praise of St Valentine's Day appears near the end of the *Parliament of Fowls* (680–92). In the F Prologue to the *Legend of Good Women* a 'balade' beginning 'Hyd, Absolon, thy gilte tresses clere' is recited ('seyn') by the I-persona (249–69), while in the G Prologue it is sung by the group of ladies which accompanies the God of Love (203–23); these performances have an ornamental function in the main. Moreover, in *Troilus and Criseyde* there is a *Canticus Troili* at i. 400–20 (on the contrary emotions characteristic of love) and another at v. 638–44 (on the torment caused by Criseyde's absence). In the second book Antigone sings 'cleere' a 'Troian song' (ii. 827–75), which encourages Criseyde to sympathetic to Troilus, while the final book includes two verse letters, one from Troilus to Criseyde (v. 1317–421), the other,

Criseyde's reply (1590–631). More unusually, in the third book Boethian philosophy is recast in the form of yet another *Canticus Troili* (1744–71), sung by the overjoyed prince in celebration of the consummation of his love. As Ardis Butterfield has argued so well, this may be regarded as a development of the French practice of lyric enclosure, less surprising given the manifest debt of some of the *dits amoreux*, particularly the *Remede de Fortune*, to the *Consolatio philosophiae*. Clearly, Old French verse-forms and intercalating techniques exercised an influence on Chaucer which lasted well into his so-called Italian period.

Moving on now to discuss the poem's style, with special reference to its rhetoric, it may be said that Chaucer took a calculated risk in introducing idiomatic dialogue, which is generally awkward to handle in verse. Lines 1042 ff. work very well, the tricky exchange at 1045–7 being handled with especial skill. Then again, a wonderfully comic effect is achieved at lines 184–6, when Juno's messenger wakes up Morpheus ('Who clepeth ther?' / 'Hyt am I'). But lines 1309–10 pose problems even for some of the poem's greatest admirers.

> 'She ys ded!' 'Nay!' 'Yis, be my trouthe!'
> 'Is that youre los? Be God, hyt ys routhe!'          (1309–10)

For a climax to a long apotheosis of love and the lady, is not this rather disappointing? Of course, it could be said that here at last the poem's displacing and ritualizing decorums have been left behind, as the plain fact of death is confronted in plain speech. But there is a hint of something else, something which feels uncomfortably like bathos. The chime of the rhyme diminishes the emotional force of the exchange, making it sound inappropriately pat and curt. A similar effect occurs at the end of the 'poem within the poem', the story of Ceyx and Alcyone, when the traumatized queen is dismissed rather brusquely:

> . . . 'Alas!' quod she for sorwe,
> And deyede within the thridde morwe.          (213–14)

Here, however, the effect can be justified as part and parcel of the 'game' which the narrator may be playing with the ancient text (cf. pp. 146–55 below). Alternatively, Chaucer could have been striving to construct a blunt statement of the facts of death, a theory which can claim support from the emphasis on earthly transience that is characteristic of the entire passage (195–214) which culminates with this couplet.

The prevailing impression given by the poem, however, is of an enthusiastic and highly ambitious writer who is in love with rhetoric. This may be illustrated with reference to Chaucer's long *descriptio* of 'faire White', which occupies lines 817–1041, with a brief continuation at lines 1052–87,

making a grand total of some 261 lines of verse. Chaucer took the account
of a beautiful lady (who, incidentally, proves unfaithful) as seen through
the eyes of her lover from Machaut's *Jugement dou Roy de Behaingne*
(composed before 1342), and embellished it further, developing its theme
with devices of *amplificatio* (amplification, enlargement) and enriching its
language with the ornaments of style. Both descriptions follow a set pattern, as recommended by the medieval arts of poetry and followed with
extraordinary consistency by generations of medieval poets writing in the
several European vernaculars as well as in Latin. Medieval gentlemen
certainly preferred blondes, and ladies with golden hair, thin brown eyebrows, slender waists, swelling bellies (suggesting child-bearing potential), and of lily and rose complexion are ubiquitous in literature and
painting.

The rhetoricians had listed the personal attributes which should be
included in a description, including name, nature, style of life, fortune,
quality, diligence, and the like. Chaucer is particularly interested in the
lady's name, whereas in the *Behaingne* Machaut was not:

> And goode faire White she het;
> That was my lady name ryght.
> She was bothe fair and bryght;
> She hadde not hir name wrong.                    (948–51)

By the interpretation of a person's name something good or bad about
them may be intimated, declares Matthew of Vendôme in his *Ars
versificatoria* (written before 1175). For example, Maximus lives up to his
great name in nobility and soul (Ovid, *Epistulae ex Ponto*, i. 2.2), whereas
Caesar 'takes his name from his achievement' (a reference to one of
Matthew's own examples of *descriptio*; trans. Parr, p. 44). Similarly, 'faire
White' is white by name and white and bright by nature. Moreover, she
is determined to live up to her good name: 'She loved so wel hir owne
name' (1018). The *artes poetriae* advocate an emphasis on a person's rank,
and that certainly is being placed here: the lady White knows who she is,
and the poem makes sure that we know it too. Her beauty functions to
confirm her high birth and impeccable breeding.

Chaucer takes Machaut's statement that the lady's hair 'was like
strands of gold, neither too blond nor too brown' (302–3; trans. Wimsatt
and Kibler, p. 74), and builds it up into a *circumlocutio* or roundabout
statement, which ends with an affirmation of his conclusion:

> For every heer on hir hed,
> Soth to seyne, hyt was not red,
> Ne nouther yelowe ne broun hyt nas;
> Me thoghte most lyk gold hyt was.                    (855–8)

In his *Documentum de modo et arte dictandi et versificandi* Geoffrey of Vinsauf—the 'Gaufred, deere maister soverayn' referred to in the *Nun's Priest's Tale* (VII. 3347)—says of this device, 'instead of speaking of a thing directly, we move about [it] in a circle' (trans. Parr, p. 47). And certainly that is what is happening here.

*Exclamatio*, exclamation which expresses vehemently some emotion, occurs at lines 895–7 and 919–20 (cf. 1075, etc.). Chaucer employs *repetitio*, repetition of a word or phrase at the beginning of several lines, at 827–9 ('Of . . .'), 869–70 ('Hyt . . .'), 906–7 and 911–12 ('And . . .'), 927–8 ('Ne . . .'), 988–9 ('And . . .'), 1025–6 ('To . . .'), 1038–40, ('My/Myn . . .'), etc. Then there is *interrogatio*, where a question is asked for rhetorical effect and not as a request for information (830, 1034, etc.). The comparison of White to the phoenix in order to emphasize her uniqueness (981–4) is of course an *exemplum* (cf. 1052–87, where a formidable arsenal of *exempla* may be found, White being likened to Penelope and Lucrece). The older poet was to exploit the funny side of the ponderous use of *exempla* in *Troilus and Criseyde*, i. 759–80. There Troilus, having been warned against excessive weeping like Niobe (who turned into stone when grieving), tells Pandarus that he has had enough:

> 'What knowe I of the queene Nyobe?
> Lat be thyne olde ensaumples, I the preye'.

But that is some time away in the future, and of course the context is very different. To be sure, the Man in Black is hardly impressed with the role model of Socrates as recommended by the dreamer (715–20), but he is too polite to protest much, even when his companion provides him with five further *exempla* for good measure (721–41). Later, he himself demonstrates a fatal attraction to the device (1056–87).

There are, however, aspects of Machaut's account in the *Behaingne* which Chaucer abbreviates rather than amplifies. The descriptions of the lady's 'forehead, eyebrows, nose, mouth, teeth, chin, haunches, thighs, legs, feet, flesh' and the statement of her age are all omitted, as Derek Brewer succinctly puts it (p. 37). This was probably due to decorum: Chaucer could not be too familiar in textualizing the wife of the powerful Gaunt, a woman who had been one of the most eminent heiresses throughout England. Indeed, some of the specimen descriptions provided in the *artes poetriae* include rather salacious passages, as when Matthew of Vendôme, having described a woman's ivory teeth, milky forehead, snowy neck, star-like eyes, rosy lips, narrow waist, and 'luscious little belly', moves on to consider her 'sweet home of Venus': 'The sweetness of savour that lies hid in the realm of Venus / The judging touch can fortell' (trans. Parr, p. 38). This voyeurism (fairly standard in Matthew) sees the female body very much in terms of its sexual attractions to the male. Machaut's lover was more circumspect: 'Of the rest, which I did not see, I can assure you . . . that it was in perfect accord with Nature, pleasing in shape and contour. This remaining part, which I wish to speak no more of here, must be held without comparison to be sweeter and more beautiful than any other' (379–87; p. 78). Chaucer took discretion even further—

> I knew in hir noon other lak
> That al hir lymmes nere pure sewynge     *perfectly proportioned*
> In as fer as I had knowynge.                                    (958–60)

—even though he is putting these words in the mouth of the man who, within the narrative, subsequently wins her. The Man in Black is, of course, speaking of White as she was when he first knew her, rather than from the point of view of a husband married to her for nine years (the length of time that Gaunt was married to Blanche).

Not that Chaucer is averse to elaborating on the traditional physical attributes: he moves away from Machaut in adding plumpness to the arms and red fingernails to the customarily white hands and in noting her straight flat back (956–7) and long body (952). Moreover, he describes her speech, as goodly, friendly, soft, and reasonable (852, 919 ff.); here he was following another poem of Machaut's, the *Remede de Fortune* (217–30). Matthew of Vendôme recommends the inclusion of this attribute, for someone's character can be established through reference to a 'cultivated manner of speaking', as when Ovid says that grace was not absent in the 'eloquent speech' of Ulysses (*Metamorphoses*, xiii. 127; trans. Parr, pp. 50–1). Of course, some aspects of Machaut's description simply did not apply to Blanche, as, for example, her age. The Machaut lady, the subject of so much male praise and the cause of so much sorrow on account of her infidelity, is fourteen and a half years old. Heroines in medieval literature can be, by today's standards, surprisingly young, probably a reflection of the medieval belief that women matured and died earlier than men. For instance, Emilia in Boccaccio's *Teseida* (the primary source of the *Knight's Tale*) is only 15 when she marries Palemone. By contrast, Chaucer makes no comment about how old his Emelye was, and professes ignorance of the age of Criseyde (*Troilus and Criseyde*, v. 826). He also avoids mentioning White's age. Blanche was 27 when she died, and thus past her prime (as envisioned in Chaucer's day), and so it may have been delicacy which prompted him to avoid that matter. Against this, it may be noted that Froissart described her as having died 'fair and young'— but then, he was vague about her age, remarking that she was 'about twenty-two years old', which is a considerable underestimate. Returning to Blanche as textualized by Chaucer, there is another possible reason for his silence. She was slightly (at the most one year) younger than Gaunt, and so the specification of her age might have made her greater maturity seem implausible, even allowing for the belief that women were thought to mature earlier. But of course, it would be quite naïve to talk as if White *is* Blanche or the Man in Black *is* Gaunt, for we are dealing with fictions which maintain some distance from their real-life equivalents, in a manner which owes much to the practice of the *dits amoreux*.

Moreover, certain aspects of White which Chaucer wished to describe simply had no precedent in the *Behaingne*. Her moral qualities are emphasized, qualities markedly absent in the case of the lady in Machaut's poem, who left her adoring knight for another man. Once again, Chaucer follows the precepts and the practice of the rhetoricians. Matthew of Vendôme includes in his series of model *descriptiones* an account of the virtuous woman, here identified as Marcia, wife of Cato. This paragon is said to reject 'feminine deceits', display understanding, and radiate trustworthiness. 'The honesty of her speech portends / The value of her virtue'; she 'lacks guile', the 'goodwill of her gaze' not being 'a craving for Venus' sport . . . Marcia is strong in mind' (trans. Parr, pp. 36–7). Similarly, White is friendly but not forward; no prude (she enjoys dancing and modest 'pleye') but certainly no flirt. Her glance is direct, quite lacking in coquettishness and sexual allure, as is her behaviour in general. Her intelligence is disposed to all goodness, and she is incapable of wronging anyone. In her dealings with men she is honest and straightforward, giving no encouragement where none is meant and not being the type to set a suitor elaborate tests of love, sending him off to foreign lands to win 'worshyp' before he can enter her presence again (1019–33). However, she is not to be won easily; the black knight has to 'serve' her for a year before she takes him into her 'governance', thereby making a man of this rather callow youth. Marcia, Matthew of Vendôme concludes, is a fit wife for the wise Cato. White, Chaucer's poem implies, was the perfect match for the Man in Black.

Geoffrey of Vinsauf, in his *Poetria nova* (composed between 1200 and 1213), recommends that *descriptio* be delightful as well as large, 'handsome as well as big'. In order that the mind should be 'fully refreshed', he continues, 'her conventional nature should not be too trite' (trans. Kopp, p. 53); 'more unusual usages' should therefore be sought (p. 55). In similar vein, Matthew of Vendôme declares that a writer is at fault when he employs 'a superfluous flourish of words and ornamented speech and grasps at clouds and vacuities' (p. 25). In the *Book of the Duchess* Chaucer's verse sometimes comes perilously close to doing just that. It must be said, of course, that medieval vernacular poetry is generally

designed for oral performance, or at least circumscribed by strategies
which had developed to enhance oral delivery. Here is literature composed above all else to be *heard*, when read aloud to a company or indeed
to oneself (whether the words were declaimed or mouthed), 'silent reading' being a rarity. Hence the rhetorical nature of so much medieval literature. We are dealing with 'performance texts' *par excellence*, works
which require room to create their effects, long periods to build up their
descriptions, since the writer cannot rely on his public reading and
rereading a passage until all its significance is grasped (this being the
usual means in which poetry is experienced in an age of print rather than
script).

After all due allowance is made for these factors, however, it may be
said that Chaucer has not as yet learned that big may not be beautiful and
that more can mean less. On the other hand, certain passages in the *Book
of the Duchess* have an exquisite charm which is scarcely rivalled by anything he was to write later: the lightsome dream-chamber (290–342), the
lush landscape through which the mysterious dog leads the dreamer
(387–442), White dancing 'so comlily' and laughing with her friends
(848–54), the black knight's description of how he and she lived as one
(1285–97), and so forth. And as a whole the poem has retained its power
to move.

On Chaucer's octosyllabics see especially Paull F. Baum, *Chaucer's Verse* (Durham, NC,
1961), pp. 27 33; Howard, *Chaucer and the Medieval World*, pp. 143 7; Edgar F.
Shannon, 'Chaucer's Use of the Octosyllabic Verse in the *Book of the Duchess* and the
*House of Fame*', *JEGP* 12 (1913), 277–94. Moreover, there are also pre-Chaucerian
English verse romances in octosyllabics, such as *King Horn*, *Havelock*, and *Floris and
Blauncheflor*. A good introduction to the subject of Chaucer's merging of European
and native verse traditions, which includes discussion of *BD*, is provided by Derek
S. Brewer, 'The Relationship of Chaucer to the English and European Traditions',
in his *Chaucer: The Poet as Storyteller* (London, 1984), pp. 8–36. All the Tony
Harrison poems here cited are published in his collection *The Gaze of the Gorgon*
(Newcastle, 1992), pp. 48–54, 57–75. Other exceptional poems written in octosyllabic
couplets include Milton's *L'Allegro* and *Il Penseroso*, and Marvell's *To his Coy
Mistress*.
Chaucer's prosody has been the subject of heated debate. See e.g. Alan T. Gaylord,
'Scanning the Prosodists: An Essay in Metacriticism', *ChR* 11 (1976), 22–82, and
Steven R. Guthrie, 'Prosody and the Study of Chaucer', *ChR* 23 (1988), 30–49.
On the *Romaunt* fragments see especially C. D. Eckhardt, 'The Art of Translation in *The
Romaunt of the Rose*', *SAC* 6 (1984), 41–63.
The 'intercalated lyric' is discussed thoroughly by Ardis Butterfield, 'Interpolated Lyric
in Medieval Narrative Poetry' (Ph.D. diss., University of Cambridge, 1988), to which
my own account is indebted. Some of her ideas have been published as follows: 'Lyric
and Elegy in the *Book of the Duchess*', *MÆ* 60 (1991), 33–60; 'Froissart, Machaut,
Chaucer and the Genres of Imagination', in André Crépin (ed.), *L'Imagination médiévale: Chaucer et ses contemporains: Actes du Colloque en Sorbonne*, Publications de
l'Association des Médiévistes Anglicistes de l'Enseignement Supérieur, 16 (Paris,

1991), pp. 53–69, and (involving discussion of Old French intercalated lyrics) 'Medieval Genres and Modern Genre-Theory', *Paragraph*, 13/2 (1990), 184–201.

The love-affair in the *Voir Dit*, as Butterfield says, is 'aesthetically conceived': the protagonists' exchanges are 'as full of commentary on the style of their lyric poetry as of protestations of their feelings for each other' ('Interpolated Lyric', p. 140). Similarly, at the end of Nicole de Margival's *Panthère d'Amours* (*c*.1300), a partial analogue of Chaucer's *House of Fame*, the narrator offers the lady a *rondeau* which professes his love for her, to which she responds positively with a second poem of this kind, whereupon the narrator joyfully confirms with a third *rondeau* the understanding they have reached. Even more remarkably, Froissart's *Meliador* manages to incorporate no less than seventy-nine *ballades*, *virelais*, and *rondeaux*.

For the Lydgate poem see John Lydgate, *Poems*, ed. John Norton Smith (Oxford, 1966), pp. 47–66, 160–76.

Machaut, *'Behaingne' and 'Fortune'*, ed. Wimsatt and Kibler; Derek S. Brewer, 'The Ideal of Feminine Beauty in Medieval Literature, especially the Harley Lyrics, Chaucer, and some Elizabethans', in his *Tradition and Innovation in Chaucer* (London and Basingstoke, 1982), pp. 30–45. He believes that 'the interest lies in watching Chaucer enliven the traditional description' (p. 37).

Matthew of Vendôme, *Ars versificatoria*, trans. Roger P. Parr (Milwaukee, 1981). Geoffrey of Vinsauf, *Documentum de modo et arte dictandi et versificandi*, trans. Roger P. Parr (Milwaukee, 1968); also his *Poetria nova*, trans. J. B. Kopp, in J. J. Murphy (ed.), *Three Medieval Rhetorical Arts* (Berkeley, Calif. 1971), pp. 29–108. The Latin texts are printed in Edmond Faral (ed.), *Les Arts poétiques du XIIe et du XIIIe siècle* (Paris, 1924). J. J. Murphy, 'A New Look at Chaucer and the Rhetoricians', *RES* 15 (1964), 1–20, emphasizes that Chaucer did not have to go to manuals like these in order to acquire such technical knowledge of rhetoric as he displays; he could well have obtained it from the basic textbooks which he had studied at grammar school. Having taken this point fully, here and later in this book I use the quotations from the *artes poetriae* simply to illustrate typical late medieval thinking about the stylistic devices in question. (Murphy's article was a response to J. M. Manly's study, 'Chaucer and the Rhetoricians', *PBA* 12 (1926), 95–113.)

In his *Documentum* Geoffrey remarks that 'It is common to describe beauty', so 'more difficult and less ordinary descriptions' should be used (p. 46), a principle which may help to account for the elaborate detail of some medieval *descriptiones* of beautiful women, wherein the superlatives coagulate. Medieval gender construction treated men very differently; often their bodies were off limits. 'The giving of approval to the form of the feminine sex ought to be amplified,' declares Matthew of Vendôme (*Ars versificatoria*, p. 41), 'but it ought to be restrained in [the case of] the masculine sex'; as Ovid says, 'a virile form loves to be honoured in moderate bounds' (*Heroides*, iv. 56). Of course, medieval poets were far from restrained in expressing their approval of the inner qualities of males, including their intellectual and emotional prowess. For females, bodily externals remained a dominant aspect of the stereotyping discourse. On gender stereotyping see further pp. 434–43 below. On 'the body' in medieval literature see especially Karma Lochrie, *Margery Kempe and Translations of the Flesh* (Philadelphia, 1990); Linda Lomperis and Sarah Stanbury (eds.), *Feminist Approaches to the Body in Medieval Literature* (Philadelphia, 1993); E. Jane Burns, *Bodytalk: When Women Speak in Old French Literature* (Philadelphia, 1993).

On orality see especially John Burrow, *Medieval Writers and their Work* (Oxford, 1982), pp. 47–55; Derek S. Brewer, 'Orality and Literacy in Chaucer', in Willi Erzgräber and Sabine Volk (eds.), *Mündlichkeit und Schriftlichkeit im englischen Mittelalter* (Tübingen, 1988), pp. 85–119. See further H. J. Chaytor, *From Script to Print* (London, 1945), pp. 5–21; Marshall McLuhan, *The Gutenberg Galaxy* (Toronto, 1962); Walter Ong, *Orality* and Literacy: The Technologizing of the Word (London, 1982); Brian Stock, The Implications of Literacy (Princeton, NJ, 1982).

## Sources

The extent to which the Book of the Duchess is indebted to Old French poetry, particularly Machaut's Jugement dou Roy de Behaingne and Remede de Fortune, is quite remarkable. From there Chaucer appropriated many structures, expressions and images, and it is perfectly fair to regard his composition as an English dit amoreux wherein the traditions of 'the school of Machaut' are being continued. Yet Chaucer imposed his own impress and agenda on those borrowings.

The 'narrative within a narrative', the story of Ceyx and Alcyone (62–214), has its ultimate source in the eleventh book of Ovid's Metamorphoses, but additional details may have come from the Ovide moralisé (a translation, with added allegorizations, of the entire Metamorphoses), and from the partly humorous handlings of the tale in Machaut's Dit de la Fonteinne Amoureuse and Froissart's Paradys d'Amours. Some have also postulated the influence of the De consolatione philosophiae of Boethius (which Chaucer was to translate in the late 1370s or early 1380s), but there are no close literal parallels to support this; the descriptions of fickle Fortune derive rather from his French sources, particularly the Remede de Fortune, 2379–734, and the Roman de la Rose, 4739–6870.

The following discussion will concentrate on Chaucer's retelling of the Ceyx and Alcyone story and his rewriting of the Behaingne, the latter being his single most important precedent. Our investigation of Chaucer's sources cannot, however, end with this section, because later we must return to the dits amoreux to clarify the positions which Chaucer was taking, the compositional options he chose, and those he rejected— a form of criticism which is possible only when a text is composed within a highly formal genre which has a precisely defined range of subjects.

### OVID UNMETAMORPHOSED

Ovid's Metamorphoses, xi. 410–750, recounts how King Ceyx sets sail to consult the Delphic oracle concerning his brother Daedalion, who had been transformed into a fierce hawk by Apollo when he threw himself from a high cliff. Ceyx leaves behind 'his most faithful wife Alcyone' (415–16; trans. Miller, ii. 151), who laments his departure, fearing the devastating power of the winds. Ceyx is just as devoted to her, being deeply moved when she asks him to take her with him, so that they may share the risks of the journey: 'the fire of love burned no less brightly in his heart' (445; p. 153). However, he does leave Alcyone behind, and her fears prove to have been well founded, for the ship bearing Ceyx is indeed destroyed and he is drowned, his last thoughts being of his wife. Alcyone, not knowing that he is dead, continues to pray to the deities, particularly Juno, for his safe return, until that goddess, no longer able to endure these entreaties for a 'man who is no more' (579; p. 161), orders her messenger Iris to go quickly to the 'drowsy house of Sleep, and bid him send to Alcyone a vision in dead Ceyx' form to tell her the truth about his fate' (585–8; p. 163). An eerie description of the Cave of Sleep follows. In its central space the God of Sleep lies, himself asleep, on 'a high couch of ebony, downy-soft, black-hued, spread with a dusky coverlet' (610–12). When Iris enters, the awesome house is lit up with the gleam of her bright garments. Then the god, 'scarce lifting his eyelids heavy with the weight of sleep, sinking back repeatedly and knocking his breast with his nodding chin, at last shook himself free of himself and, resting on an elbow, asked her (for he recognized her) why she came' (618–23; p. 165). Iris delivers her message and departs quickly, for she can feel drowsiness stealing upon her. Then the god rouses Morpheus, one of his thousand sons, 'a cunning imitator of the human form' (634); he 'takes the face and form of Ceyx, wan like the dead, and stands naked before the couch of the hapless wife' (653–5). Speaking as if he actually were Ceyx, Morpheus tells Alcyone that her prayers have been in vain: ' "I am dead. Cherish no longer your vain hope of me. . . . And this tale no uncertain messenger brings to you, nor do you hear it in the words of vague report; but I myself, wrecked as you see me, tell you of my fate". . . . These words spoke Morpheus, and that, too, in a voice she might well believe her husband's' (662–72; p. 167). Alcyone groans, sheds tears, 'and in sleep seeking his arms and to clasp his body, held only air in her embrace' (674–6). Wide awake, she laments his loss, and vows to die with him. Gazing seawards, she sees a corpse floating slowly towards her, which proves to be her husband's. The gods change first her, and then her husband, into seabirds, the halcyons who are said to brood over their nest on the surface of the waters for seven peaceful days during winter. In turning Daedalion into a hawk, Apollo had left his 'old-time courage and strength greater than his body' (343; p. 145); likewise, the metamorphosis of Ceyx and Alcyone has left their love intact: 'Thus though they suffered the same fate, still even thus their love remained, nor were their conjugal bonds loosened because of their feathered shape' (742–4; p. 173). To that extent, therefore, Ovid's story can be said to have a happy ending.

Chaucer made highly selective use of Ovid's narrative in turning the original's 340 lines of verse into his 153 (*BD* 62–214); some parts were cut drastically, whereas others were amplified, or changes and substitutions were made. Ovid had devoted 64 lines (410–73) to Ceyx's departure, concentrating on the lovers' mutual sorrow, with most space being given to Alcyone's griefs and fears. A vivid description of the storm followed (474–572), these 99 lines representing well over a quarter of the entire narrative. All this Chaucer rushed through in a mere 14 lines (*BD* 62–75). In the English poem Alcyone gives voice to her feelings only *after* her husband has departed, in a long passage of 55 lines (76–130), the emphasis therefore having shifted considerably, particularly since this passage represents almost one-third of Chaucer's entire retelling. Chaucer's Alcyone demands to know if her husband is alive or dead; in Ovid she innocently continues to pray for his safety, though we readers know that he is already dead. Chaucer was obviously very taken with Ovid's account of the Cave of Sleep, for he spent 57 lines on it (135–91), proportionately far more than Ovid's 58 (592–649). Morpheus is identified with the God of Sleep, whereas in Ovid he is merely one of the god's sons (a fact which is clearly registered by the other versions of the tale known to Chaucer). And Iris becomes an (unnamed) male messenger. But of course the most striking feature of Chaucer's narrative is its ending. Morpheus actually takes up Ceyx's dead body and bears it to Alcyone (in Ovid, only a representation is involved). The recovery of Ceyx's corpse is not afforded separate treatment, but prophesied by the dream-Ceyx; this allows Alcyone's own death to be treated with extraordinary (perhaps too drastic?) economy, in two lines (*BD* 213–14).

Most important of all, there is no metamorphosis and hence no relatively happy ending. Ceyx is dead, and that is the end of it; all his grieving widow can do is bury him and recognize that their worldly bliss is over. Chaucer's unmitigated materialism, particularly his emphasis on the dead body of Ceyx, is quite remarkable:

> [Morpheus] Took up the dreynte body sone      *drowned*
> And bar hyt forth to Alcione . . .
> Hys wif the quene, ther as she lay . . .
> And stood ryght at hyr beddes fet,
> And called hir ryght as she het      *she was called*
> By name, and sayd, 'My swete wyf,
> Awake! Let be your sorwful lyf,
> For in your sorwe there lyth no red;      *remedy*
> For certes, swete, I am but ded.
> Ye shul me never on lyve yse.      *see me alive*
> But, good swete herte, that ye
> Bury my body, for such a tyde
> Ye mowe hyt fynde the see beseyde;

And farewel, swete! my worldes blysse!
I praye God youre sorwe lysse.
To lytel while oure blysse lasteth!'                    (195–211)

There is no remedy ('red') in Alcyone's 'sorwe'; love is in no way salvific.
No pitying gods return Ceyx and Alcyone to life in different shapes,
thereby allowing their relationship to continue. In marked contrast, John
Gower, who includes the metamorphosis in his version of the story, treats
it as a divine reward for 'the trowthe of love, / Whiche in this worthi lady
stod' (*Confessio Amantis*, iv. 3090–1). Here Ovid's assurance that their
transformation has not affected their ability to love is elaborated as seen
from the queen's point of view:

. . . sche mihte hirself conforme
To do the plesance of a wif,
As sche dede in that other lif:
For thogh sche hadde hir pouer lore   *lost her [human] power*
Hir will stod as it was tofore,
And serveth him so as sche mai.                    (3110–15)

But such an ending would have been quite inappropriate to the circumstances in which Chaucer wrote his poem. As a 'wonder thing' (61) the
Ovidian fable has little relevance to the harsh realities of earthly transience. It may also be suggested that Chaucer preferred to make this, his
bluntest statement of the brutal fact of death, at an early stage of his poem
because he wished to distance such sentiments from the idealized inscription of Gaunt's feelings for Blanche which was to follow.

In the tenth book of the *Thebaid* (84–136) Statius had improvised on
Ovid's description of the Cave of Sleep (though he did not include the
Ceyx and Alcyone legend itself), and it has been suggested that a few of
his details may have influenced Chaucer. Far more important, however,
are Chaucer's debts to the vernacular tradition of the entire story. The
fact that he worked not from Latin sources alone is intimated by the narrator's description of his bedtime book as a 'romaunce' (48). At this time
the term usually referred either to the French language or to a literary
work of a particular kind written *in the vernacular*—that is, in French or
indeed in Middle English, certainly not in Latin. Lines 47–51 could
therefore be referring to the *Ovide moralisé*. Of course, 'romaunce' would
also be an appropriate description of Machaut's *Fonteinne Amoureuse*,
which contains a version of the Ceyx and Alcyone story that Chaucer certainly used in writing the *Book of the Duchess*, and James Wimsatt has
argued that the I-persona's 'book' was a Machaut compendium manuscript which included that *dit*. There is no indication, however, that
Chaucer had a compendium manuscript in mind, and so it seems prefer-

able to opt for a single text which fits every aspect of the description he provides: namely, the *Ovide moralisé*.

Particularly significant is Chaucer's identification of the 'book' as a book of fables, which not only fits the *Ovide moralisé* considered as a discrete work but also echoes the discussion of fables with which it begins. Chaucer's brief account of the historical origin of fables (as written down to be read and committed to posterity 'While men loved the lawe of kinde'; 52–6) reads like a paraphrase of the anonymous Franciscan's justification of his translation of 'les fables de l'ancien temps' into Romance ('en romans'): 'it pleases me to undertake to translate from Latin into Romance [i.e. French] the tales of ancient times—and I'll say what I understand by them—in accordance with the way in which Ovid hands them on' (i. 15–19). This idea of Ovid as participating in a process of transmission of myths which were not exclusively his chimes with Chaucer's view of ancient 'clerkes' and 'poetes' as being involved in a collective process of recording and versifying 'fables' (52–4); indeed, in his day the *Metamorphoses* was often described as a collection of diverse materials rather than as a work by a single author. The *Ovide moralisé* preface continues with the explanation that, from the very first beginning of the world until the arrival of Christ (i.e. the period in which men lived under the Natural Law, what Chaucer calls the 'lawe of kinde'), mention is made of fables which, although they all seem false, contain nothing but truth. If one gets to know the sense of such things, the truth they contain is obvious (*Ovide moralisé*, 37–46). Also of interest is Chaucer's declaration that his source is a repository of stories about illustrious men and women (57–8). The fact (at least, I think it is a fact) that he used the *Ovide moralisé* in his subsequent collection of stories 'of quenes lives, and of kinges', the *Legend of Good Women*, may indicate that he thought of the French poem in that way.

Turning now to the specifics of Chaucer's 'Seys and Alcyone', several striking verbal parallels (as noted by Wimsatt) indicate that some of its details came from the *Ovide moralisé*; here we are talking, of course, of material not found in the original Latin. But it is impossible to tell exactly how much Chaucer took from the *Ovide moralisé* and how much from the *Metamorphoses* itself, because almost all of Ovid's text is translated *verbatim* by the anonymous Franciscan, though with a few omissions which, since Chaucer includes them, serve to reassure us that he consulted the Latin as well as the French text.

What he certainly did *not* take from the *Ovide moralisé* was its allegorization of the Ceyx and Alcyone story. The French poet's ambition was to bring out the moral (and often specifically Christian) truth which he believed to be hidden in the pagan fables. Indeed, he opens the work with a citation of Romans 15: 4, 'all that is written is written for our doctrine', which he takes to mean that books provide their readers with ethical instruction, showing them what to do and what to avoid. Whoever God has graced with wisdom and knowledge should not be reluctant to share this, adds the friar; the thousands of verses which follow indicate that there was no serious risk of him hiding his intellectual treasure in the earth (8–14). In the case of the specific *fable* of Ceyx and Alcyone, this entails interpreting the ship in which Ceyx sails as the human body, the sea as mortal life, the wind that causes the storm as sin, and so forth. Most drastic of all, Alcyone is reduced to worldly vanity. Thus the story is read as a warning against putting one's trust in earthly things, for the pleasures of this life are fleeting, like birds. Here Chaucer had in his hands the seed of a poem which would counsel John of Gaunt to recognize that ephemeral things, however beautiful they may be, are ultimately worth little, and therefore should be relinquished the more easily.

But Chaucer chose not to cultivate a growth of that kind. What he did instead was to turn to the relatively humorous adaptations of the Ceyx and Alcyone story included in two Old French *dits*. At the beginning of Froissart's *Paradys d'Amours* the insomniac lover recounts how recently he got some sleep by praying 'to Morpheus, to Juno, and to Oleus'. 'I did a wise thing', he declares, 'for if I had not asked them and made sacrifice to Juno of a golden ring, I think I would still be lying awake without sleep' (13–22; trans. Windeatt, p. 42). The first part of this passage is the direct source of lines 242–7 of the *Book of the Duchess*. Froissart goes on to tell of how the sweet God of Sleep sent one of his sons, Enclimpostair, into the narrator's bedroom, whereupon he fell asleep. This figure was probably invented by the French poet, and must be the explanation of Chaucer's otherwise puzzling reference to 'Eclympasteyr, / That was the god of slepes heyr' (167–8).

In the *Fonteinne Amoureuse* Chaucer found both a more elaborate form of wit and a more complicated framing of the Ceyx and Alcyone story. Machaut's version (which has the *Ovide moralisé* as its source) pictures the queen trying to discover the truth of what has befallen her husband—a development of the narrative which, along with a marked lack of interest in the events which lead up to Ceyx's death, clearly influenced the English poet. Machaut's account of the Cave of Sleep is generally true to the spirit of Ovid's original, though he picked up on one glimmer of humour to have the God of Sleep open 'one of his eyes just a little' as he asks Iris the purpose of her visit (631–4; trans. Windeatt, p. 32). Chaucer improved on the joke by having the messenger blow his horn in the god's ear and shouting 'Awaketh!' loudly in order to rouse him to action (179–85). Chaucer also took from Machaut the offer to the God of

Sleep (or, he adds, to Juno—professing ignorance of which deity to
address) of a feather bed with rich accessories (240–69). Thus Chaucer—
with some help from the Froissart *dit* as well—got the idea of the 'game'
of a contemporary Christian appealing to a pagan god (cf. the somewhat
heavy-handed humour of *BD* 234–9).

But whereas Chaucer's I-persona simply wants to sleep, the speaker in
the *Fonteinne Amoureuse* has rather more in mind. His professed ambition
is to enlist Morpheus as an accomplice in the pursuit of his love-affair
(along with the more usual personifications—Love, Pity, Desire, and the
like—who inhabit the Old French allegory of love). If Morpheus would
assume his half-dead form and appear to the lady 'five or six times', then
she would know fully 'my heart, my sadness, my grief' (708–16; p. 32).
Indeed, Morpheus is treated rather like the male confidante figure who
appears in so much love-poetry of the period (see especially the figure
'Ami' in the *Roman de la Rose*), as when the lover imagines Morpheus
saying to him as he sleeps, 'never regret your sadness, for you have conquered the richest treasure that there is in the world' (952–4; p. 35).

The lover who would have Morpheus as his friend is not the Machaut
persona but a highly cultured construct which images Jean, Duc de Berry
(Jean is identified in an acrostic near the beginning of the poem). The
occasion of the *Fonteinne Amoureuse* was Jean's departure in 1360 for
England, where, in accordance with the Treaty of Brétigny, he was to live
as a hostage, thus leaving behind the woman he had recently married,
Jeanne d'Armagnac, who presumably is represented by the lady in the
poem. It begins with the Machaut persona, half-asleep in his bed, overhearing someone 'lamenting very bitterly' and certainly not pretending,
because he was 'complaining and groaning so deeply that I felt a shiver
of horror and fear at it' (70–6; pp. 26–7). The narrator carefully tran-
scribes this complaint, which includes the version of the Ceyx and
Alcyone story discussed above. It becomes clear that the speaker's anxiety is due to uncertainty concerning his lady's feelings towards him; this
has brought him close to death. At daybreak the narrator seeks out this
exquisite sufferer, to come face to face with a physically perfect individual (more handsome than anyone, whether man or woman, he had ever
met before), with 'a very gracious, pleasant, cheerful, simple and gentle
face'—albeit a little pale, 'since he had stayed awake and suffered all night
long' (1097–116; p. 36). The lord's alleged brush with death has, so to
speak, left him remarkably unscathed, at least to judge by appearances.
He proceeds to receive graciously, and just as graciously give away again,
several expensive gifts: a well-saddled horse, a very fine sparrow-hawk,
and a dog. The narrator is then honoured with his exclusive attention.
When the lord reads the complaint which he himself composed, his heart

is troubled, because this was very much a private matter: he 'kept it so secret' that he 'cannot think or understand how any man alive can know of it' (1528–34; p. 39). Clearly, a *sujet* of such mental gifts and psychological balance is eminently capable of seeing both the pain and the possibilities for humour in the story of Ceyx and Alcyone.

The narrator's act of service in transcribing his superior's secret yet artful thoughts seems to have provided the basis for warm (though status-conscious) companionship. Their intimacy is confirmed later in the *dit* when the lord and the poet, in an act of homosocial intimacy which verges on the homoerotic, actually fall asleep together, the lord's head and arms resting on the poet's lap, and share one and the same dream. This may be regarded as the culmination of the narrator's self-feminization in the *Fonteinne Amoureuse*; earlier (1261–73; p. 37) he had put himself very much in the inferior subject position by affirming his love for his superior, 'such as a poor man can love'—a protestation which elicits the response, 'Sweet friend, by my troth, you are very welcome' (the 'Sweet friend' idiom being reminiscent of a common form of heterosexual address in the *dits*). There is nothing like this in the *Book of the Duchess*, to be sure, but there we do meet another ideal male, a 'man for all seasons' who suffers profoundly in private, but is utterly urbane and charming in public.

Machaut's *Fonteinne Amoureuse*, then, helped Chaucer to see how an Ovidian narrative could be placed in the context not of moral allegory but of amatory protestation of the most fashionable kind, how a text could move from ancient fable to a contemporary dialogue in which maleness is affirmed and a degree of male bonding achieved (within firmly defined limits) through the construction of woman as Other. But there is a major difference. The Man in Black is not the teller of the tale of Ceyx and Alcyone: this task falls to the dreamer. Does *he* have the right to smile? And to juxtapose the 'game' of half-jesting narration with the pain of bereavement is perhaps a rather daring thing to do—arguably more of a risk than juxtaposing it with the less acute, and *deo volente* temporary, pain of departure. Pain there certainly is in the Duc de Berry's parting from his wife Jeanne, as fictionalized by Machaut, but where there is life there is hope, and that hope (it may be argued) is being encouraged by the element of game in the *Fonteinne Amoureuse*. There is, after all, every prospect of Jean's return from England across the channel. But Blanche of Lancaster has journeyed to that undiscovered country from whose bourne no traveller returns.

The worst that could be said here is that Chaucer was misled by the humour in the above-mentioned *dits*, or that he followed them without sufficient thought regarding the fact that his main narrative was of a very different kind from theirs. Alternatively, as Helen Phillips has argued, he composed 'in youthe' an earlier version of 'Ceys and Alcione' (referred to in the *Introduction to the Man of Law's Tale*, II(B¹) 57) which he had trouble accommodating to the larger structure of the *Book of the Duchess*.

On the other hand, it may be claimed that the occasional witticisms in this part of Chaucer's poem do serve its larger needs: for instance, as a device which helps to construct the dreamer and distinguish him from the Man in Black, and as a partial counterbalance to the highly charged emotion of melancholic sorrow which at several points in the poem threatens to dominate—after all, is it not 'agaynes kynde' to suffer too much for too long? 'Mesure' (moderation) 'is medicine', though you long for much, to borrow a phrase from William Langland (*Piers Plowman*, B i. 35). And White herself was a model of moderation.

> In alle thynges more mesure
> Had never, I trowe, creature.                    *believe*
>                                                   (881–81)

In any case, Chaucer's manners of mourning should not be judged by later, more narrowly puritanical, standards.

Ovid, *Metamorphoses*, ed. and trans. F. J. Miller (London and Cambridge, Mass., 1921). *Ovide moralisé*, ed. C. de Boer (Amsterdam, 1915–38). Good accounts of the Old French poem are included in Paul Demats, *Fabula*, Publications romanes et françaises, 122 (Geneva, 1973), pp. 61–113; Rita Copeland, *Rhetoric, Hermeneutics and Translation in the Middle Ages: Academic Traditions and Vernacular Texts* (Cambridge, 1991). Parallels with Pierre Bersuire's *Ovidius moralizatus* (completed by 1362) are pointed out in the notes to Phillips's edition. On this work see Minnis and Scott (eds.), *Medieval Literary Theory*, pp. 317–18, 323–4, 366–72; also M. Twycross, *The Medieval Anadyomene: A Study in Chaucer's Mythography*, Medium Ævum Monographs, NS 1 (Oxford, 1972).

James Wimsatt, 'The Sources of Chaucer's "Seys and Alcyone"', *MÆ* 36 (1967), 231–41; see further A. J. Minnis, 'A Note on Chaucer and the *Ovide moralisé*', *MÆ* 48 (1979), 254–7. Compare the possible influences of the *Ovide moralisé* on *LGW*, discussed on pp. 348–9 below. However, Helen Cooper is sceptical about Chaucer's use of the Old French poem; 'Chaucer and Ovid: A Question of Authority', in Charles Martindale (ed.), *Ovid Renewed* (Cambridge, 1988), pp. 71–81. On Machaut and the *Ovide moralisé* see C. de Boer, 'Guillaume de Machaut and l'*Ovide moralisé*', *Romania*, 43 (1914), 335–52. The idea that 'Most of the knowledge medieval authors had of what we call the classics was limited and secondhand' is emphasized by Götz Schmitz; while believing that Chaucer was 'steeped in Ovidian . . . lore', he criticizes John Flyer (cf. reference below) for taking for granted 'Chaucer's intimate acquaintance with all of Ovid's writings'. 'Gower, Chaucer and the Classics: Back to the Textual Evidence', in R. F. Yeager (ed.), *John Gower: Recent Readings* (Kalamazoo, Mich., 1989), pp. 95–111.

On the meaning of the phrase 'lawe of kinde' see especially Lynn V. Sadler, 'Chaucer's *Book of the Duchess* and the "Law of Kynde"', *AnM* 11 (1970), 51–64, and John Fyler, *Chaucer and Ovid* (New Haven, Conn., 1979), pp. 65–81.

Froissart, *Paradys d'Amours*, trans. Barry Windeatt in *Chaucer's Dream Poetry: Sources and Analogues* (Cambridge, 1982), pp. 41–57. For the French text see *Oeuvres*, vol. 1:

*Poésies*, ed. A. Scheler (Brussels, 1870), pp. 1–52. See further N. R. Cartier, 'Froissart, Chaucer and Enclimpostair', *Revue de littérature comparée*, 38 (1964), 18–34.

Machaut, *Le Dit de la Fonteinne Amoureuse*, trans. Windeatt, *Sources and Analogues*, pp. 26–40; French text in *Œuvres*, ed. E. Hoepffner, SATF (Paris, 1808–21), iii. 142–244. See further A. T. Kitchel, 'Chaucer and Machaut's *Dit de la Fonteinne Amoureuse*', in C. F. Fiske (ed.), *Vassar Medieval Studies* (New Haven, Conn., 1923), pp. 217–31.

Deschamps composed a 'Balade de Ceix et Alcyone', in *Œuvres*, vol. 1, ed. Marquis de Queux de Saint-Hilaire (Paris, 1878), pp. 118–19. According to Christine de Pizan, poets were so impressed by the loving marriage of Ceyx and Alcyone that they likened them to the loyal halcyon birds; thus she demythologizes their metamorphosis. See Christine de Pizan, *The Epistle of Othea, translated from the French by S. Scrope*, ed. C. F. Bühler, EETS OS 264 (London, 1970), pp. 96–7.

On the textualization of homosocial bonding compare the discussion and references above on pp. 63, 70–71.

Several modern readers of *BD* have been unnerved by its 'hints of the absurd', to apply one of Larkin's phrases. Lewis, *Allegory of Love*, complains of 'comic effects which are disastrous, and which were certainly not intended' (p. 170), while Charles Muscatine, *Chaucer and the French Tradition* (Berkeley, Calif., 1957), remarks that 'for some, he brings into the most serious part of the poem a tasteless vein of humour' (p. 107).


REWRITING MACHAUT: A *JUGEMENT* REVERSED

There has been in much Chaucer criticism a tendency to believe that the major French progenitors of the *Book of the Duchess*, the *dits amoreux*, were too trivial to cope with such a serious and demanding subject as death; this has led to a lopsided view of Chaucer's achievement in this, his first major, poem. For instance, Charles Muscatine's highly influential *Chaucer and the French Tradition* contains only a few cursory remarks on them, declaring that herein the courtly style of Guillaume de Lorris tends 'to lose that ultimate, delicate contact with human concerns that gives it meaning, to reduce itself to a collection of shiny but valueless trinkets, symbols without reference' (p. 40). In particular, Machaut's style is judged to be facilely fluent and 'too rich to be functional'; the 'poetry too often converts device to ornament, making of its materials something trivial and banal' (p. 99). Similarly, Derek Brewer speaks of the poets of the *Roman de la Rose* and their fourteenth-century successors as being 'not without their charm, but they are artistically in the doldrums'; 'they wrote mostly about love at what now seems excessive length' (p. 14). Chaucer's poem is then hailed for the new directions it is supposed to have taken or at least presaged. 'The death of the Duchess Blanche whom it mourns, is like the first menacing roll of thunder from the storm which must shatter the Garden of the Rose' (p. 28). But in fact such subjects had been confronted in many of the French poems which followed in the train of the *Rose*; death had already entered the *locus amœnus*.

An interesting case in point, and one close to Chaucer's early milieu, is offered by Jean de la Mote's dream-vision allegory *Le Regret Guillaume*, an elegy on the death of William of Hainault, directed to his daughter Philippa, wife of Edward III and Queen of England. This consists basically of a sequence of laments: thirty female personifications of the various chivalric qualities bemoan the passing of William, emphasizing what has been lost, an element of variation being provided by the different natures and hence the differing emphases of the weepers (though in practice the distinctions between them often vanish). Far more ambitious in their elaboration of the lyric impulse to produce challenging dialogic discourse, and assuredly more complex in their attitudes to death, are Machaut's *Jugement dou Roy de Behaingne* and *Jugement dou Roy de Navarre* and Froissart's *Le Joli Buisson de Jonece* (1373). However, these works are in no way elegiac; they do not celebrate the life and mourn the death of some specific noble person, which is the brief of *Le Regret Guillaume*. Chaucer's tacit task was to bring together elements of both types of poem.

One should not, therefore, look for Chaucerian originality in terms of his widening the scope of the *dits amoreux* by introducing the unpalatable and shocking subject of death, for this was already very much on the agenda of the Old French courtly poets. Rather, it is to be found in the manner in which Chaucer approached this subject, especially the roles which he has his *dramatis personae* (the Man in Black and the dreamer) play in creating a delicate pattern of telling contrasts whereby full experience of life and love is set against detached inexperience, and the pleasures of recollection are pitted against the pains of loss. An essential part of this argument rests on the premiss that the *dits* can be far more sophisticated and profound than their 'pretty but precious' stereotyping has allowed for. This point is ably demonstrated in recent criticism by William Calin, Kevin Brownlee, James Wimsatt, J.-P. Badel, and Ardis Butterfield, among others, but much recuperation remains to be done, particularly in view of the persistence of the belittling views which have been illustrated above.

Chaucer's subjectivities, and the inspiration for their deployment, seem to derive in no small measure from Machaut, in particular from his *Behaingne*; so we must consider this *dit* in more detail. It begins with the conventional May morning setting (which directly influenced *BD* 339–43). Machaut's narrator, who has concealed himself in order to hear the sweet sound of the birds, overhears a knight and a lady debating which of them has the worse fate: the knight, whose love is unrequited (his lady, after swearing that she would always love him loyally, having transferred her affections to another), or the lady, whose lover has died. From this Chaucer took details for his own spring landscape (339–43) and the elaborate civilities which his characters exchange on meeting (519–28, 532–8). The lady's dog, which barks at the narrator as he emerges from his hiding-place and then sinks his teeth into his clothes, may have given Chaucer the idea for the rather different dog in the *Book of the Duchess*, whose ownership is unclear and indeed slightly mysterious; however, this creature's friendliness and function as a guide to the central figure may owe more to the dog-like lion in another Machaut poem, *Le Dit dou Lyon* (which, incidentally, may have been the source of the lost 'book of the Leoun' which in the 'Retractions' Chaucer tells us he wrote). There is no doubt, however, that the woman's protestation of the extent to which she loved her 'sweet friend' and the man's description of his beloved and account of their courtship provided Chaucer with materials for the Man in Black's memories of his white lady. (For example, 475 ff., 487 ff., 599 ff., 749–52, 754–76, 805–13, 817 ff., 848–74, 904–13, 939–47, 952–60, 1035–41, 1183–98, 1203 ff., 1219–20, 1226–30, 1236–8, 1241–4, and 1258–97 pick and mix lines from the *Behaingne*.)

From that point onwards the two poems diverge sharply. Chaucer had no specific use for the climax of the argument between Machaut's protagonists or the King of Bohemia's adjudication between them. But the influence of the *Behaingne* does not stop there; nor is it simply a matter of specific verbal borrowings. Chaucer went to other French poems for purple passages (Machaut's *Remede de Fortune*, *Dit dou Lyon*, and *Dit de la Fonteinne Amoureuse* and Froissart's *Paradys d'Amours*): from the *Behaingne* he derived his poem's dramatic form and many of its methods of creating selfhoods.

A comparison of the remaining part of the *Behaingne* with the *Book of the Duchess* should make this clear. Having tried to shift the blame for his lady's infidelity on to Fortune and Love, Machaut's jilted lover proceeds to defend vigorously his claim that his suffering is the greater: '"Therefore I say, if you've listened well and heard me, that the sorrow in which I languish, whose rigour has disfigured me and made me pale, is a hundred thousand times greater than yours; for your troubles are like pure joy and perfect sweetness compared to the sorrows that martyr me"' (872–80; trans. Wimsatt and Kibler, pp. 102, 104). The lady responds by pointing out that at least he still has desire for his beloved, and there is no desire without hope; moreover, through memory he can enjoy happy thoughts of her. Finally, she concludes, 'it is possible for you to regain your lady, but Nature has made it impossible for me to regain my beloved' (926–8; p. 106). The knight compliments her on her 'wisdom, honor and moderation', but refuses to accept her arguments. There is no hope in his desire, just despair; his memories are unhappy ones. The possibility of his ever having his lover again is discounted, since the lady has proved her unreliable nature beyond all doubt. Something which never ceases to move but 'instead is constantly fickle and changing—now here, now there, now by the fire, now at table, then elsewhere—is something not to be trusted' (1069–77; pp. 112, 114). Like Lady Fortune (it is implied), the lady who once said she loved him changes and varies, 'gives and then takes back' (1082–3). Chaucer transferred some of these phrases to Lady Fortune herself, there being no question of the fidelity of 'faire White' (see 645–9). The knight brings his speech to an end by emphasizing, with a somewhat surprising directness, the freedom from former vows which death brings (Behaingne, 1108–23). By contrast, he cannot put his old flame behind him, because he sees her often in his memory, and indeed quite often in the flesh (1123–33). At this point the narrator intervenes to recommend that they bring their dispute before the King of Bohemia. His judgement, which is very much in line with the views of the personification Reason who counsels him, is that 'more pain is concentrated in this lover than in this lady' (1930–1; p. 156. Cf. Reason's speech, 1776–8; 148). Eventually the lady will forget her dead lover, and Youth will reassert herself; for the spurned lord, however, time can bring no such relief.

This was by no means Machaut's last word on the subject, for in his later *Jugement dou Roy de Navarre* (1349) he presents himself as being taken to task by a lady (later identified as Bonneürte, Happiness) who declares that the poet 'grievously erred' in giving a 'conclusive judgment' (1015–30; trans. Palmer, p. 47) in favour of the knight. Another king, the King of Navarre, is chosen as judge, and after hearing both sides of the argument he decides against the poet who, however, defends his earlier opinion well, and shows no real sign of having been convinced by the counter-arguments. In this work the debate is more impersonal than in the more richly dramatic *Behaingne*, where the *sujets* are presented as having first-hand knowledge of the losses which they lament. In the *Book of the Duchess*, it may now be argued, Chaucer espouses the expert opinion given in the later Machaut poem but chooses to express it through a dialogic framework and juxtaposition of subjectivities which were based on the earlier one.

The *Book of the Duchess* begins with the identification of the I-persona as an unrequited lover who has been longing for his lady for eight years. We are not told that in so many words, but the conventional symptoms are, in my view (though some would disagree), too obvious and specific to be mistaken. He is sleepless and suffering from melancholy, his mind being full of sorrowful imaginings and fantasies; despite the length of time he has suffered this 'sicknesse',

>       my boote is never the ner,                          *remedy*
>   For ther is phisicien but oon                           *doctor*
>   That may me hele; but that is don.                        *heal*
>
>                                                            (38–40)

The 'that is don' means simply 'that is enough of that', as is reinforced by the next lines:

>   Passe we over untill eft;
>   That wil not be mot nede be left;
>   Our first mater is good to kepe.                          (41–3)

—the 'first mater' being his insomnia, as opposed to the underlying cause thereof about which he has just digressed. (Line 42 means that 'what will not be, must be done without'.) There is neither evidence nor justification for the argument that the narrator, as well as the Man in Black, is a bereaved lover. For general parallels to all the major ideas and expressions in question may be found in Guillaume de Lorris's discourse of the pains attendant on loving a living but aloof lady. There the dreamer is warned by the God of Love himself that he can expect 'more than a thousand torments' at night. Unable to sleep, he will vainly fantasize about holding his lady in his arms, thus building mental 'castles in Spain' and taking 'joy in nothing as much as in going around deluding' himself 'with this delectable thought that contains only lies and fables'. But this affords little comfort, for the lover will soon begin to weep and despair of all help. His lady is the only person who could cure his 'sickness of love': 'God help me, I should like very much to see her at this instant. He who saw her now would be cured' (*Roman de la Rose*, 2423–90; trans. Dahlberg, pp. 64–5).

All this is clear enough; but there is a more direct source for the opening lines of the *Book of the Duchess*. As has long been recognized, Chaucer was influenced by the beginning of Froissart's *Paradys d'Amours*. The narrator's initial expression of wonder that he is still alive, the following statement of his sleepless torment, the specification of his sad and melancholic thoughts—all are to be found there. What is in Froissart's poem but not in Chaucer's is this identification of the root cause of his suffering: 'They [sad thoughts and melancholy] often come to torment me. They bind my heart tightly, and I cannot loosen them, for I do not want to forget the fair one, for love of whom I entered into this torment and suffer such sleeplessness' (7–12; trans. Windeatt, p. 41).

Why did Chaucer omit this? Not, I think, because he had any serious doubts concerning the stereotype on which he based his persona, but rather because he wished to place his emphases elsewhere, with a view to the overall plan of his poem. The wonder 'How that I lyve' will give way to the Man in Black's expressed wonder at what he has lost and the dreamer's (delayed but palpable) participation in that emotion; the emphasis on the narrator's insomnia sets the stage for his subsequent *somnium*, and the broad hints that the persona's mental images are those characteristic of a suffering lover, to a medieval dream-psychologist would have chimed perfectly with the content of his dream, which images the most extreme form of lover's suffering known to man (cf. pp. 40, 42–4 above). And, of course, in more general terms one can say that the opening of Chaucer's poem is far more enigmatic than that of Froissart's, where the terms of reference are immediately declared, thereby precluding the effect of journeying towards the poem's centre which is such a pleasing aspect of the trajectory of the *Book of the Duchess*. (One may compare the slow and subtle way in which the *Pearl* poet proceeds to his specific topic.) But, perhaps most important of all, by minimizing his persona's individual importance as a lover and concentrating on feelings which the Man in Black will both share and surpass, Chaucer has set in motion that strategy of deference which will dominate the entire text.

This deference is palpable in the persona's account of how he met the Man in Black. Here, once again, we have cause to note that Chaucer is ritualizing the plight of the Gaunt surrogate in amatory and class-reflexive discourses that are characteristic of 'the school of Machaut'. In the *Navarre* the narrator comes across as socially inferior to the richly attired and accompanied 'lady of great nobility' (545), who mocks, reproaches, and contradicts him (593–4), and it is no surprise that the final judgement goes her way. In the *Fonteinne Amoureuse* the surrogate for Jean, Duc de Berry, is established as a figure with a great retinue, whose moral virtue, princely prowess, and emotional sensitivity are as superlative as his physical beauty. The Machaut persona kneels in his presence—whereupon the lord generously reproves him for so doing, though of course it is utterly appropriate—and addresses him as the one he wishes to see more than anyone else in the world, 'because of the good that abounds in you'. 'I should never have dared to come to you like this if it did not please you,' the narrator gushes; 'I love you a great deal, such as a poor man can love, even if the love of a poor man is worth little or nothing' (1239–42, 1259–64; trans. Windeat, p. 37). The situation is somewhat different in the *Behaingne*, for there the lord and lady who are in dispute are on a par socially, but the poet persona is deferential to his chosen judge in a way which most modern readers can only regard as *de trop*. The King of Bohemia is stated to surpass Alexander in largess and Hector in prowess and Ovid in love-doctrine; moreover, he is 'the pillar of all gentility' and a great advocate of the Church and justice. In sum, 'there has never been, nor ever will be, another as perfect in every respect, both in words and deeds, as he' (1296–335; trans. Wimsatt and Kibler, pp. 124, 126). Froissart often adopts a similar stance in his poetic encounters, the main difference being that in such situations he sometimes evinces a greater sense of self-irony than Machaut does. A good example of this may be found in *Le Paradys d'Amours*, when the poet persona, fearful of being discovered in his amatory despair, conceals himself in some bushes, only to be flushed out by 'two of the most refined and courtly ladies', 'most regally attired' and of 'great beauty' (236–44; trans. Windeatt, pp. 43–4). To be sure, these are personifications—namely, Plaisance and Hope—who have come to take the melancholic lover to task for railing against their lord, the God of Love. But the differences of degree and the imperative of deferring to one's superiors were doubtless real enough. In all these examples we are being offered the transparent (especially in the Machaut examples) literary equivalences of that deference which the historical courtier-poets owed to their (potential or actual) patrons.

In the *Book of the Duchess* the Man in Black's social and natural eminence is quickly and firmly established. He is a man great enough to be approached with caution and courtesy, though the dreamer does show a degree of daring; hence there is a social tension in their dialogue which is unprecedented in the *Behaingne*. The dreamer comes from behind the lamenting lord to stand at his feet, and makes his presence felt, doffing his hat in the best social manner and greeting him with all due decorum:

> . . . at the last, to sayn ryght soth,
> He was war of me, how y stood
> Before hym and did of myn hood,   *took off*
> And had ygret hym as I best koude,   *greeted*
> Debonayrly, and nothyng lowde.   *courteously, vulgar*
> He seyde, 'I prey the, be not wroth.
> I herde the not, to seyn the soth,
> Ne I sawgh the not, syr, trewely.'
>  'A, goode sir, no fors,' quod y,
> 'I am ryght sory yif I have ought
> Destroubled yow out of your thought.   *disturbed*
> Foryive me, yif I have mystake.'
>  'Yis, th'amendes is lyght to make,'
> Quod he, 'for ther lyeth noon therto;   *nothing of the kind is needed*
> There ys nothyng myssayd nor do'.   (514–28)

These formal gestures, particularly the play with the hat, may remind us of the passage in *Hamlet* where Osric's foppish formalities arouse the contempt of the Prince of Denmark: 'Your bonnet to his right use; 'tis for the head' (III. ii). But that would be unfortunate. In the Chaucer poem the exchange of civilities marks the good breeding and *gentilesse* of the participants—which is precisely the point in the specific source of the lines quoted above, the beginning of the dialogue between the lord and lady in Machaut's *Behaingne*. Chaucer's version is more elaborate, however, and the overall effect is quite different.

First, here the relationship between the dreamer and the Man in Black comes across as being that of inferior and superior, this being much more in line with the encounters described in Machaut's *Navarre* and *Fonteinne Amoureuse* and Froissart's *Paradys d'Amours* (as summarized above) than the one in the *Behaingne*, where the protagonists are very much on a par in terms of degree, as we have said. In particular, the fact that it is the Man in Black who takes the lead in the exchange of apologies, rather than the dreamer—who is, after all, in the weaker position because he has been eavesdropping—is probably intended to be a mark of his superior breeding. *Noblesse oblige*; no true gentleman needs to stand on his dignity, for that is beyond question. By contrast, in the *Behaingne* the person in the reverie, the lady, is indeed in the wrong in terms of good manners, because she walks past the lord without returning his greeting; this moves him to take her by the edge of her gown and gently ask, 'Fair lady, do you hold my greeting in contempt?' (66–7; p. 62); whereupon she appropriately asks for his pardon. Apologies having been exchanged, the lord goes straight to the point by asking what is upsetting her. Despite her expressed wish to be left in peace, he persists, whereupon she declares 'you shall know what you seek to learn about my thoughts' (112–13; p. 64), and tells him the whole sad story, on the condition that he tell her all about his own sorrow. Such directness and reciprocity are utterly lacking in the way in which Chaucer's constructs initiate their conversation. The narrator seeks a 'tale' (536), a pretext, whereby he may gain by oblique means 'more knowynge of hys thought', and begins to talk to the Man in Black about the hart-hunting. This diffidence is in marked contrast with what happens in the *Behaingne*, where the poet persona makes himself known to the disputing couple with utter self-confidence, without the slightest doubt regarding the value of his presence and opinions. Not at all 'shy or abashed', he greets the company with a smile, declares that he has heard all their discussions, assures them that his eavesdropping was utterly well-intentioned, and presumes to nominate their judge (1220–3, 1267–348; pp. 120, 122–6).

Even more importantly, as they appear in the *Book of the Duchess*, the lines in which Machaut's knight promises to do all in his power to redress the other's grief take on a new import: part of a pact between equals has become what seems to be an offer of service from the inferior to the superior.

'. . . certes, sire, yif that yee
Wolde ought discure me youre woo,                          *reveal*
I wolde, as wys God helpe me soo,
Amende hyt, yif I kan or may.                              *relieve*
Ye mowe preve hyt be assay;                            *prove, trial*
For, by my thouthe, to make yow hool                       *healthy*
I wol do al my power hool'.*                                 *whole*
(548–54)

The grief-stricken stranger makes no request to hear about the narrator's suffering; indeed, the narrator does not mention it, let alone suggest that it is worse than the other's. The only 'condicioun' that the Man in Black sets upon telling the dreamer the cause of his sorrow is that the other should

'. . . hooly, with al thy wyt,                    *wholly, intelligence*
Doo thyn entent to herkene hit'.                     *purpose, listen to*
(751–2)

In Chaucer's poem the speakers and their respective sorrows are certainly not on a par, the flow of emotions being in one direction, from high to low. As Louise Fradenberg says in a different but related context, 'The servant ceases to be an individual and becomes a symbol in the service of his master's meanings' (pp. 89–90).

Secondly, in this first exchange the Man in Black's politeness is given more point by the fact that he is able to present such a face to the dreamer despite his heavy sorrows—the persona's civility being managed, one cannot but feel, with much less effort. Here is someone who is suffering in a way which is commensurate with his station, and the dreamer instantly acknowledges this. The lyric he overhears is, he assures us,

The most pitee, the moste rowthe,               *most piteous thing*
That ever I herde . . .                                    (465–6)

Yet this is essentially private suffering; the Man in Black's 'compleynte' is very much 'to hymselve' (464). So involved is he with his own thoughts that at first he is unaware of the presence of another. But when he becomes aware of this, he is instantly all geniality; so sudden is the transition, and so patently is the Man in Black's demeanour achieved without strain, that the dreamer admiringly declares that it is as if another person were standing before him:

Loo, how goodly spak thys knyght,
As hit had be another wyght;

* Chaucer's repetition of 'hool' should not be deemed a failure: rhyme which used a homophone with two different meanings was a device valued in French poetic theory, and is often found in Machaut.

He made hyt nouther towgh ne queynte.   *behaved in neither an awkward*
And I saw that, and gan me aqueynte                    *[nor affected way*
With hym, and fond hym so tretable,                              *affable*
Ryght wonder skylful and resonable,
As me thoghte, for al hys bale.

(529–35)

Like Shakespeare's Duncan (cf. *Macbeth*, IV, iii), he both feels his sorrow like a man and bears it like a man—and like the exceptional man he is. This represents the sum total of the poem's explicit praise of the Man in Black: by the standards of Machaut, it is extraordinarily restrained. Chaucer moves from such modest praise to tacit praise, allowing the Man in Black to commend himself out of his own mouth. His apotheosis of White has a reflexive aspect (not deliberate on his part, and therefore decorous), in that in praising her he is revealing his own true nature, proving that he is noble in behaviour as well as by birth.

And here is the key to the essential difference between the subjectivities inscribed in Chaucer's poem, a difference which disrupts the homosocial aspect of their dialogue (as discussed above, pp. 63, 70–1). The text intimates that it is the Man in Black's greater experience and depth of feeling which fundamentally set him apart from a lesser mortal like the dreamer, rather than simple social status—Chaucer is not prepared to 'pull rank' explicitly on the reader. Of course, the other side of the coin is that the black knight would have been incapable of the fine feelings which his lady's tuition released in him, had he not been from the very 'top drawer' of society in the first place. 'Gentle is as gentle does' is an excellent sentiment, and was recognized as such by Boethius, Dante, and the Wife of Bath, but the more fundamental medieval belief—as evinced in legions of romances and lyrics—was that someone who was not a gentleman would not be *gentil*, and degrees of rank were related to degrees of sensitivity, as with other chivalric virtues. Thus, the higher the rank, the greater the sensitivity. The quality of the Man in Black's grief reflects the quality of his pedigree; the precious nature of what he has lost affirms the superlative worth of the figure who once possessed it. We, along with the dreamer, are being allowed a privileged glimpse of how the other half lives, loves, and reacts to loss. In other words, the class-determined power and privilege of Gaunt's social position have been textualized in terms of a superiority of sentiment and emotional capacity.

Such difference and deference, quite obvious in the constructs' initial reactions to each other, are consolidated in the lines which follow. In the *Behaingne* Machaut gave the woes of the lord and the lady equal weight, each figure being allowed to present his/her case fully. In the *Book of the Duchess*, however, the argument is one-sided—and yet we are never given any cause for feeling that this is less than proper. The Man in Black's declaration to the dreamer, 'I have lost more than thou wenest' (744, 1138, 1306), is not challenged; indeed, everything that the latter says and does evinces its truth. In place of the aggressive knight who gets the better of the debate though he is defending what is inherently the weaker position (only within the charmed circle of courtly love would his casuistry hold sway) stands a self-abnegating figure who prefers to listen rather than speak. The dreamer does not think to raise the objection that his own woe could be regarded as the worse, on the grounds that the Man in Black once enjoyed his lady's love whereas his own position may be hopeless. That, to be sure, would hardly have been tactful, given the special circumstances in which the poem was written. John of Gaunt would hardly have taken the point; besides, such argument was appropriate only in a very different kind of poem, certainly not in the mode of secular elegy which Chaucer was striving to create (about which, more later).

Neither is there any place for the most devastating proposition found in the *Behaingne*, as introduced by the unrequited knight, reiterated by Reason, and accepted by the King of Bohemia, that when the beloved's body dies, so also must the human love which it attracted. For the dreamer's role is to ask questions rather than make affirmations like that, to learn from the other's experience rather than dispute its validity or advance his own case. The Man in Black makes a tremendous 'first impression' on him, as we have already noted, and its force is maintained throughout the text. A relationship of subordination underpins their dialogue, the objective being that the reader should leave Chaucer's poem feeling convinced that the Man in Black has at once achieved far more in life and love, and suffered far more, than the dreamer.

The question inherent in the poem (who is the worse off, the unrequited lover or the bereaved lover?) therefore elicits the answer that it is the Man in Black who has the heavier burden to bear. The woes of bereavement are 'a hundred thousand times greater' than those of unrequited love, the dreamer's pain being 'pure joy and perfect sweetness compared to the sorrow' which martyrs the Man in Black. Those words come from the *Behaingne* (877–80; p. 104); they belong to the dejected knight, being part of his argument that rejection is more painful than bereavement. But in respect of the *Book of the Duchess* one could imagine the Man in Black saying them to the dreamer. Chaucer's poem therefore constitutes a rewriting of Machaut—and, more specifically, a reversal of the *jugement* which had been offered in the *Behaingne*.

In sum, the English poem's basic narrative plan and images of selfhood (however much Chaucer may have embroidered upon them) were derived from Machaut and his French contemporaries, but the polarities and priorities of his specific sources have been rethought substantively. The result is something rich and strange, a text which goes far beyond the mere translation of French matter and manners into English.

Muscatine, *Chaucer and the French Tradition*. Brewer, *Chaucer*. Similarly, G. L. Kittredge, *Chaucer and his Poetry* (Cambridge, Mass., 1915), contrasts 'French fashions of allegory and symbolism and pretty visions' with 'the language of the heart' (p. 54), while Norton Smith, *Geoffrey Chaucer*, aggressively denies the significance of the parallels with Old French sources for comprehension of Chaucer's text (pp. 2, 11). More balanced and nuanced positions are taken by Barbara Nolan, 'The Art of Expropriation: Chaucer's Narrator in *The Book of the Duchess*', in Donald W. Rose (ed.), *New Perspectives in Chaucer Criticism* (Norman, Okla, 1981), pp. 203–22; and Kane, *Chaucer*. However, Kane's wish to emphasize the merits of Chaucer's first major literary venture leads him into disparagement of the French poems which were its inspiration (see esp. p. 31).

William Calin, *A Poet at the Fountain* (Lexington, Ky., 1974). Brownlee, *Poetic Identity*. Wimsatt, *French Love Poets*; also his *Chaucer and his French Contemporaries*. P.-Y. Badel, *Le 'Roman de la Rose' au XIVe siècle* (Geneva, 1980). Butterfield, 'Interpolated Lyric', 'Lyric and Elegy', 'Genres of Imagination', and 'Medieval Genres' (cf. pp. 89–90 above).

On the narrator in Machaut see the relevant discussions by Brownlee, Badel, and Calin; also Daniel Poirion, *Le Poète et le Prince* (Paris, 1965), pp. 204–5; Sarah Jane Williams, 'Machaut's Self-Awareness as Author and Producer', in M. P. Cosman and B. Chandler (eds.), *Machaut's World: Science and Art in the Fourteenth Century* (New York, 1978), pp. 189–97. Poirion and Badel also discuss the self-constructions of other French poets.

Machaut, *'Behaigne' and 'Fortune'*, ed. Wimsatt and Kibler. Machaut, *The Judgment of the King of Navarre*, ed. and trans. R. Barton Palmer (New York and London, 1988). *Roman de la Rose*, ed. Langlois, trans. Dahlberg. Froissart, *Paradys d'Amours*, in *Œuvres*, ed. Scheler, trans. in Windeatt, *Sources and Analogues*. Machaut, *Le Dit de la Fonteinne Amoureuse*, in *Œuvres*, ed. Hoepffner, trans. in Windeatt, *Sources and Analogues*.

On Guillaume de Lorris's self-construction see especially Hult, *Self Fulfilling Prophecies*.

Louise Fradenberg, 'The Manciple's Servant Tongue: Politics and Poetry in *The Canterbury Tales*', *ELH* 52 (1985), 85–118. With Chaucer's account of the Man in Black's composure, compare the chronicler Adam Murimuth's description of King Edward III as 'so great-hearted that he never blenched or changed the fashion of his countenance at any ill-hap or trouble soever that came upon him'; moreover, he was 'affable and gentle in courtesy of speech, composed and measured in gesture and manners'. Quoted by G. G. Coulton, *Chaucer and his England*, 8th edn. (London and New York, 1950), pp. 155–6.

Regarding the question raised by the *Behaingne*, of which of the two sorrowing figures is the worse off, compare the *demande d'amour* tradition, as discussed in the chapter on *PF*.

On Chaucer and Machaut see especially John Lawlor, 'The Pattern of Consolation in *The Book of the Duchess*', in R. J. Schoeck and J. Taylor (eds.), *Chaucer Criticism* (Notre Dame, Ind., 1961), ii. 232–60; originally printed in *Speculum*, 31 (1956), 626–48. Also C. B. Hieatt, '*Un autre fourme*: Guillaume de Machaut and the Dream Vision Form', *ChR* 14 (1979–80), 79–115; G. L. Kittredge, 'Guillaume de Machaut and *The Book of the Duchess*', *PMLA* 30 (1915), 1–24; M. M. Pelen, 'Machaut's Court of Love Narratives and Chaucer's *Book of the Duchess*', *ChR* 11 (1976–7), 128–55.

On other sources or possible sources see V. Langhans, 'Chaucer's Book of the Leoun', *Anglia*, 52 (1928), 113–22; C. L. Rosenthal, 'A Possible Source of Chaucer's *Book of the*

*Duchess—Li Regret de Guillaume* by Jehan de la Mote', *MLN* 48 (1933), 511–14; James Wimsatt, 'Machaut's *Lay de confort* and Chaucer's *Book of the Duchess*', in R. H. Robbins (ed.), *Chaucer at Albany* (New York, 1975), pp. 11–26; W. O. Sypherd, '*Le Songe Vert* and Chaucer's Dream-Poems', *MLN* 24 (1909), 46–7, cf. J. B. Severs, 'The Sources of *The Book of the Duchess*', *MS* 25 (1963), 355–62. However, the anonymous *Songe Vert* may be later than *BD*: see Wimsatt, *French Love Poets*, pp. 139–43, and Ethel Seaton, '*Le Songe Vert*: Its Occasion of Writing and its Author', *MÆ* 19 (1950), 1–16.

See further N. R. Cartier, '*Le Bleu Chevalier* de Froissart et le *Livre de la Duchesse* de Chaucer', *Romania*, 88 (1967), 232–52. By contrast, Wimsatt suggested that Chaucer's poem was the source of *Le Bleu Chevalier*; recently Susan Crane has argued convincingly that the dependency was the other way around, in an article which also critiques Cartier (see p. 18 above). Crane emphasizes that Froissart may have written his poem in Queen Philippa's household, 'in Chaucer's literary milieu', and just a few years before Chaucer wrote *BD* in memory of Philippa's daughter-in-law. The similarities between the two poems are certainly marked. Given that no account of *Le Bleu Chevalier* is provided in either Windeatt's anthology or Phillips's useful appendix (pp. 168–88, containing a précis of poems by Machaut and Froissart, along with the *Songe Vert*), the following summary may be helpful. The Froissart persona, walking alone in the woods to enjoy the song of the birds, overhears a knight (who is dressed entirely in blue) singing joyfully and sorrowfully in turn. He is involuntarily separated from his lady-love, yet unable to win glory, which might justify his absence from her. (Crane notes that here the text is describing what may have been the situation of the French hostages held in London in accordance with the Treaty of Brétigny of 1360.) Exclaiming against Fortune, his attempts at self-consolation fail, and he swoons, at which point the narrator intervenes in an attempt to help him. When the knight recovers, he welcomes the company and counsel of his companion, who, abashed, realizes that he is in the company of a person of high rank. Encouraged by the narrator, the blue knight reiterates at greater length the causes of his grief, to be assured that one must accept whatever Fortune decrees and that true love will last. Comforted, the knight asks the narrator to record this encounter in verse, in the hope that his lady will hear it and learn of his feelings.

Dress symbolism features in the *Songe Vert* also. Here a bereaved and black-clad lover walks in a garden, longing for death, whereupon the Queen of Love appears to him in a dream. Fortune is to blame, he is assured, and he receives the promise of a new lady; this hope for the future is symbolized by the green clothes in which Love's attendants proceed to clothe him.

## Structure and Strategy

The narrator/dreamer is the major and most obvious of the cohesive devices which define the poem's structure. It is he who reads and makes 'play' of the 'romaunce' of Ceyx and Alcyone, and then dreams his way into three main locations. First, there is a rich chamber, the interior of which is dominated by the iconography of love's pains and pleasures; this space, however, is in no way enclosed or cut off from the world outside, for it is filled with joyous bird-song, sunlight, and fresh air. Moving into the temperate springtime landscape, the dreamer joins the Emperor Octavian's hunt, which quickly proceeds to a forest in search of its game, the hart. But the animal escapes, and the hunters are obliged to regroup, at which point a 'whelp' leads the dreamer through a little used 'floury grene', to the third and main location—a remote part of the 'woode', where he encounters, in the midst of all this exquisite natural beauty, the utterly incongruous and contrasting Man in Black. After the grieving knight's disquisition returns to the point from which it began, the statement that his lady-love is dead, the narrative returns quickly and briefly to the 'hert-huntyng', declaring simply that it is over; 'this kyng' (presumably Octavian, though some have found here a reference to the Man in Black as a figure of Gaunt) then rides home to his castle, the topographical details of which Chaucer employs to affirm the union of Gaunt and Blanche of Lancaster (cf. pp. 79–80 above). The dreamer, for his part, wakes up to find himself in bed with his book, whereupon he vows to put his wonderful 'sweven in ryme' immediately (1332).

Certain aspects of the action of the *Book of the Duchess* may now be discussed in more detail, with regard to their significance for the structure and strategy of the poem as a whole. Since they are mediated by the dreamer's consciousness as constructed in the text, we must begin with a discussion of the nature of that consciousness itself, a topic which has been the subject of some controversy.

DREAMING CONSCIOUSNESS AND POETIC COHESION

First of all, it must freely be admitted that the principle which I invoked at the beginning of this section    that is, that the narrator/dreamer functions as a cohesive device in the poem—has come under pressure in some recent Chaucer criticism. For instance, David Lawton argues that the Chaucerian narrator is radically unstable, an 'open persona' or 'apocryphal voice' who engages in a range of relationships to his subject-matter and audience. There is no single identity (fictional or social) represented by the poetic 'I', but rather a modulation of tones is represented through him. And Morton Donner sees a play of subjectivity and objectivity centring on the narrator: 'Chaucer narrates subjectively through the medium of "I" but objectively by de-emphasizing the role of "I" in his narratives in favor of ideas, characters and actions presented for their own sake and speaking to universal values' (p. 190). I fully accept the notion that Chaucer, whether over a range of poems or even within a single poem, can create the appearance of a single, controlling consciousness, which in the details of the text constantly breaks down; this can be regarded as mere confusion or intriguing indeterminacy, depending on the reader. But such views as these, while they may fit well the *House of Fame* and to a lesser extent the *Parliament of Fowls*, are in my view of limited value in a reading of the *Book of the Duchess*. For there the I-persona has definite work to do, a sociopolitical agenda which is fixed to an extent that Chaucer would not replicate in the narratives of the other Shorter Poems.

Of course, the points made by Lawton and Donner are well taken. Chaucer criticism has suffered from a kind of character analysis which derives its values from the Victorian novel. (And the views of Lawton and Donner, in their turn, are influenced by contemporary literary theory of a kind which places a premium on faultlines rather than achieved architecture, on discord and discrepancy as opposed to concord and integration.) But the reading offered below may, I believe, be justified with reference to literary attitudes current in Chaucer's day. At least some late medieval readers were skilled in seeking out the values embodied in fictional personae; what was said was very much judged with regard to who said it. To cite a few examples among many, there is Chaucer's plea that the words of the Canterbury pilgrims not be mistaken as his own, and the situation engineered in the *Pardoner's Prologue and Tale*, wherein the morality of what a preacher has to say is seriously called in question by his blatant personal immorality. Moreover, in the early fifteenth century 'quarrel' over the ethics and import of the *Roman de la Rose*, Jean de Meun's defenders argued that certain objectionable statements found therein characterized the personae who made them and were not to be taken as representative of the views of the author himself, whose voice was essentially that of the figure Reason. Amant the I-persona was certainly not, it was asserted, the spokesman for Jean, but rather a fiction which typified the follies and excesses of young love (cf. pp. 2, 7 above). Here, then, are the specifications of the several *sujets*, and their semantic space within the poem is assigned accordingly; they function consistently in relation to each other to help form the poem's literary patterns (to adopt Lacanian language of the kind explained on p. 3 above). In the *Book of the Duchess* the I-persona is a figure who is removed from any image of a unified and originary authorial self (whilst being self-recommendingly illustrative of the author's courtier virtues), whose significance, like Amant's, is delimited by the position he has to adopt in relation to something outside himself. In the Chaucer persona's case the relationship is that of a subordinate sufferer whose function (at once textually implicit and, inasmuch as it is self-aware, complicit) is to do all in his 'power' to 'make . . . hool' the paragon whose 'woo' he receives and records. What 'he' is, is therefore very much determined by what 'he' has to do in the poem. And this may be identified as one of the major grounds of its structure and general strategy.

In anticipation of his later function, initially and fundamentally the I-persona is presented as an unrequited lover (cf. my earlier discussion, in the previous section). The fact that Chaucer's narrators deny personal involvement in love elsewhere in the minor poems (and beyond, as in *Troilus and Criseyde*, ii. 12–14, 19–21) should not pressure us into minimizing the initial impact which the conventional discourse of unrequited love is designed to have in the first forty-three lines of the *Book of the Duchess*: there are obvious dangers in making a reductively composite figure out of 'the Chaucerian narrator', then finding that very creature in each and every text. Besides, Chaucer does speak *in persona amantis* elsewhere: in the *Complaint unto Pity*, *A Complaint to his Lady*, *To Rosemounde*, and *Womanly Noblesse* (cf. the final chapter). The first three of these dwell on the pains of unrequited love, and the beginning of *A Complaint to his Lady*, with its description of the lover's insomnia, has obvious affinities with the beginning of the *Book of the Duchess*:

> The longe nightes, whan every creature
> Shulde have hir rest in somwhat as by kynde,
> Or elles ne may hir lif nat longe endure,
> How I so fer have broght myself behynde
> That, sauf the deeth, ther may nothyng me lisse,        *apart from, relieve*
> So desespaired I am from alle blisse.                   *deprived of all*
>
>                                                          (1–7)

In the third stanza of the complaint the source of this suffering is unambiguously declared to be 'This Love, that hath me set in such a place / That my desir [he] nevere wol fulfille' (15–16). In view of all this, the claim which I am making here regarding the narrator of the *Book of the Duchess* can hardly be called radical. So, then, the narrator is described in terms specific enough to enable us to identify him as an unrequited lover. This specificity need not, of course, undermine the more general effect which the poem's opening lines are supposed to have: of setting the scene for an exploration of different kinds of sorrow, with the main emphasis subsequently falling on grief of a kind which quite transcends the sufferings of unrequited love. Perhaps that is why Chaucer did not wish to be *too* precise at the outset. (Besides, he may well have been influenced by the more global and non-amatory *melancholia* attributed to the Machaut persona at the beginning of the *Navarre*, on which more later.)

This unrequited lover, as here identified, reads the tragic tale of Ceyx and Alcyone. As he mediates it, some of its sadness is certainly left intact—

> '. . . farewel, swete, my worldes blysse!
> I praye God youre sorwe lysse.                            *relieve*
> To lytel while oure blysse lasteth!'
>
>                                                          (209–11)

—and this prepares us for the serious notes to come. Neither is he devoid
of pity and sympathy:

> . . . trewly I, that made this book,
> Had such pitee and such rowthe
> To rede hir [i.e. Alcyone's] sorwe that, by my trowthe,
> I ferde the worse al the morwe
> Aftir to thenken on hir sorwe.                          (96–100)

But for the inexperienced dreamer, wrapped up in his own limited subjectivity, this is hardly an important failure, to adopt a term from W. H.
Auden's poem 'Musée des Beaux Arts'. As interpreted by Auden,
Brueghel's *Icarus* depicts the tiny white legs of that classical pioneer of
flight vanishing into a wide ocean, while the ploughman, who appears in
the foreground of the painting, goes about his own business, and the
ship—depicted sailing in the opposite direction from Icarus—casually
and detachedly notes that 'Something amazing' has just happened.

> . . . everything turns away
> Quite leisurely from the disaster; the ploughman may
> Have heard the splash, the forsaken cry,
> But for him it was not an important failure; the sun shone
> As it had to on the white legs disappearing into the green
> Water; and the expensive delicate ship that must have seen
> Something amazing, a boy falling out of the sky,
> Had somewhere to get to and sailed calmly on.

'About suffering they were never wrong, / The Old Masters,' concludes
Auden. Chaucer may be numbered among them. It is painfully obvious
why in the *Book of the Duchess* the narrator can, to some extent, treat
Ovid's tale in a detached, even rather jocular, fashion. Real tragedy has
not touched him, as yet. Thus mediation becomes transformation, as the
ancient text is made to reflect his own fluctuating—indeed, somewhat
immature—emotions. The feelings of young lovers were notoriously
unstable, as in the case of Troilus:

> 'Thus possed to and fro,                              *tossed*
> Al sterelees withinne a boot am I               *rudderless, boat*
> Amydde the see, bitwixen wyndes two,
> That in contrarie stonden evere mo.
> Allas, what is this wondre maladie?
> For hote of cold, for cold of hote, I dye'.        (*T&C* i. 415–20)

This is very far from the cruel sea in which such figures as Ovid's Ceyx
and Brueghel's Icarus actually end their lives. Clearly, the dreamer is ripe
for instruction, in a position analogous to that occupied by the Man in

Black before he met his edifying 'faire White'. Soon the black knight will demonstrate what suffering for love is really like in its purest, deepest form. Whatever the local interest of the 'playful' narration of the adventures of Ceyx and Alcyone may be, it serves the poem's larger interests by definitively establishing the dreamer as a foil against which the Man in Black will soon show to best advantage. (Moreover, the dreamer's easily treatable woe, functioning in contrast with the black knight's more advanced condition, serves the poem's ultimate strategy of consolation, a topic which must be reserved for later.)

Chaucer's Old French sources had shown him how to make mock of Morpheus, and their narrators were certainly capable of appearing in somewhat ridiculous poses, without compromising the serious aspects and/or the princepleasing objectives of the works in which they featured. From these paradigms and his own political experience Chaucer crafted an I-persona who maintains a remarkable degree of consistency throughout the poem, and who may therefore be regarded as a source of its unity, as should become clearer below, as we consider what happens when that figure settles down to become a 'social subject' largely determined by the obligations of service which he must perform in relation to his social superior.

Lawton, *Chaucer's Narrators*. Morton Donner, 'Chaucer and his Narrators: The Poet's Place in his Poems', *Western Humanities Review*, 27 (1973), 185–95. See further Edwards, *Dream of Chaucer*, pp. 68–73, and R. W. V. Elliott, 'Chaucer's Reading', in A. C. Cawley (ed.), *Chaucer's Mind and Art* (London, 1969), pp. 46–68.

My argument for the functionality of the first part of the poem within the work as a whole is in opposition to the views of, for example, John Furnivall, *Trial Forewords* (London, 1871), and John Fisher (ed.), *Complete Poetry and Prose*. Furnivall went so far as to suggest that it was written 'for another ending and then used for the piece of death-work ordered by John of Gaunt' (p. 36), while Fisher declares that despite 'attempts to show how appropriate it is as an introduction', it 'remains a distraction. The poem does not really get started until the dream begins at l. 291' (p. 543). Those who have found it an anticipation of, and preparation for, the poetry to come include Clemen, *Early Poetry*, pp. 27–37, and Spearing, *Medieval Dream-Poetry*, pp. 59–74.

HUNTING THE HERT(E)

The hart-hunting in the *Book of the Duchess*, occupying lines 344–86, and referred to again at lines 539–42 and 1311–13, has two major strategic functions. It emphasizes the Man in Black's alienation from the normal pleasures of the aristocratic life, hence highlighting the depths of his pain. And, through the obvious but unlaboured punning on *hert* ('deer', 'hart', 'red deer') and *herte* ('heart'), it establishes a subtext of the chase of love, which intimates that for the bereaved knight this particular 'game' is indeed 'doon', his amatory hunting days being over (cf. 539).

Sleep frees the dreamer, however temporarily, from his 'hevyness', replacing 'sorwful' with joyful 'ymagynacioun' as his consciousness is released into an activity in which he can take genuine pleasure—the hunt. The joys of this sport are regularly described in the hunting manuals which circulated in the later Middle Ages, and are also evoked in poems in which hunts play a significant part in the narrative, such as *Sir Gawain and the Green Knight*, the *Awntyrs off Arthure*, and—most relevantly for the *Book of the Duchess*—Machaut's *Jugement dou Roy de Navarre*. There hunting (in this case, hare-hunting) is described as an activity at once honourable and noble, pleasurable and improving:

> . . . it is an honour, diversion, and joy;
> It's an activity that the noble choose,
> Something of gracious enterprise,
> And quite advantageous to undertake
> For it improves one nicely;
> So the thing itself is pleasant enough to do,
> And honor comes with its completion.
>
> (510–16; trans. Palmer, p. 25)

Moreover, the pleasure of hunting is linked with the pleasure which the sensitive aristocrat may take in the countryside. Thus the Machaut persona tells us that he goes 'riding for pleasure' and 'to claim for my own the sweetness that came from the country' (492–5). He watches a group of hares running across the fields, and enjoys 'the songs of the birds which were lovely to hear, and the air of the temperate weather which soothed all my body' (526–9).

A similar connection is made in Chaucer's poem, though there the landscape description occurs in lines 397–442 *after* the hunt has ended (at least temporarily, the hart having thrown the hounds off the scent), and a dog leads the dreamer away from its scene to the Man in Black. This desolate figure is not soothed by Nature, and his sorrows are deeper than hunting can reach.

> 'Y do no fors therof', quod he;
> 'Myn thought ys theron never a del'.                    (542–3)

The inference may be drawn that the dreamer's sorrows, since they are assuaged the more easily, are therefore the less profound. Here is yet another device by means of which the Man in Black's superiority is established.

Chaucer makes careful use of hunting terms, clearly intending their technical senses, as, for example, when the quarry is said to have 'rused' (381, cf. 539–41), or doubled back on its scent to confuse its pursuers, or when the 'forlyn' (386) is blown, this being a call signalling that the hounds are nowhere near the game. 'Strake' (1312) is more difficult. Obviously, it denotes the signal for going home, but with what outcome? There were different types of *straking*: one type would indicate that the hart had been slain, while another would indicate that the king wished to hunt no longer, whether the chase had been successful or not. The manner in which the notes were sounded was what made the difference, but Chaucer is silent on this. To approach the problem in a different way: at line 380 and lines 540–1 we are told in no uncertain terms that the stag had eluded the hunters; but are we meant to suppose that time has stood still in the world of the hunt whilst the dreamer has been talking with the Man in Black, the *straking* simply being a restatement of the fact that 'this game is doon' (539)? Or is the implication rather that the hunt has continued during the central dialogue, but with no change in the participants' fortunes? On the other hand, it could be argued (following Marcelle Thiébaux' study) that the stag has indeed been slain: it may have escaped at one stage of the proceedings, but this does not mean that the hunt ultimately proved unsuccessful. The poet may have been too tactful to mention the animal's death, she suggests, but the implication is obvious enough. In my view it is simply not that obvious, and surely the loss of one object of desire, the stag, counterpoints well the loss of another, the lady. Alternatively, the irreducible ambiguity regarding the outcome of the chase (to read the lines differently) reinforces the bittersweet quality of a narrative which comprises both pain and pleasure, gain and loss. These possibilities are preferable to the invocation of Christ as hunter in search of the soul of man (on which, more later) or the idea of Death as a hunter with rather less noble motives.

The main puzzle, however, is the identity and the significance of the leader of the hunt, the mysterious 'emperour Octovyen' named at line 369 and almost certainly to be identified with the 'kyng' of line 1314. He has variously been identified as a hero of medieval romance, a king of the other world, or an 'Octavian' of British history (Eudalf in Welsh myth), who in the *Mabinogion* is described as sitting in an ivory chair carving chess-pieces. Then there could be at least an allusion to the Roman Emperor Augustus, who, it should be remembered, was a judge of poetry, in that he valued Virgil whilst sending Ovid into exile because (on one theory current in Chaucer's day) his love-poetry was subversive of public morals. Chaucer, then, could have been subtly offering to Gaunt a (flattering, to be sure) image of himself as patron—an image which, if accepted, would certainly have been of advantage to a courtier who had to make his way in the world.

Moreover, with the rather exotic Octovyen Chaucer creates what Thiébaux has well described as a sense of majesty, authority, remoteness—and, I would add, timelessness—which is of considerable importance in the establishment of an appropriate tone here at the beginning of the narrator's dream-vision proper. A bridge has been created between the tragicomic narration of, and response to, the tale of Ceyx and Alcyone and the sombre, but ultimately celebratory, encounter with the Man in Black.

The hunt in the *Book of the Duchess* does not, of course, function in a merely literal way, but also metaphorically, to veil the Man in Black's initial pursuit and subsequent loss of his lovely quarry. The love-hunt was a common topos in much medieval literature, and has classical roots. It appears in several forms. In Virgil's *Aeneid*, for instance, Dido is presented as a victim hunted by love. Venus appears to Aeneas in huntress's guise, and has her son Cupid make Dido his victim. Once smitten, she is described as wandering throughout Carthage like a hind struck by an arrow (iv. 68–73). The chase which Dido organizes actually serves the purpose of the huntress Venus, inasmuch as it provides the queen with the place and occasion for the consummation of her love for Aeneas; thus she is the hunted rather than the hunter. Then again, imagery of hunts of all kinds occurs in Ovid's *Ars amatoria*, women being seen as the prey or spoil (*praeda*, i. 126) of men. The hunter knows full well 'where to spread his nets for the stag', in what glen the boar may be found (i. 45–6; trans. Mozley, p. 15), and likewise lovers first of all must learn the habitats of their quarry. Women's gatherings are 'fit occasions for hunting' (i. 253–4; p. 31). 'All women can be caught,' continues the narrator; just 'spread your nets and you will catch them' (i. 269–70; p. 31). Press home the attack, he urges: once the bird's wings are limed, it cannot escape; the boar will not easily leave the entangling nets (i. 391–2). But women's hearts are various, and so therefore must be the methods of pursuing them. Here fish are caught with spears, there with hooks, elsewhere with drag-nets. 'A grown hind' requires special treatment, since she 'will regard the snare from further away' (i. 755–6, 763–6; p. 65).

Imagery such as this pervaded late medieval love-poetry, as written in Latin and the European vernaculars. To take but one example, from an actual source of the *Book of the Duchess*, Froissart's *Paradys d'Amours* includes a scene (916–56) in which the God of Love, his limerers, and his company enjoy 'l'amoureuse chace': 'The hunt of love pleases them so much that each one seeks after his delight where he thinks to have it' (945–7; trans. Windeatt, p. 50). And of course the God of Love was often equipped with bow and arrows with which he would shoot his victims, through the eye and into the heart, thereby turning them into his devotees (as in the *Roman de la Rose*, 1681–776). It was in the context of the early fifteenth-century *querelle* over the meaning of the *Roman* that

Christine de Pizan, who criticized Jean de Meun as a scurrilous 'Modern Ovidian' who had defamed women, attacked the literary practice of presenting women as animals to be hunted or enemies to be deceived; she makes an appeal for women to be treated as human beings (cf. pp. 429–30 below). These iconoclastic sentiments have, quite understandably, found favour with contemporary gender critics, who are challenging that fundamentally Freudian thinking which holds that aggression and eroticism are essentially connected; that hunt, pursuit, and capture are biologically programmed in male sexuality. The literary situation is complicated, however, by the fact that sometimes it is the woman rather than the man who is presented as the hunter—though the situation is generally viewed through the 'male gaze', and the female *sujets* are very much created in man's image of what they should be. Thus, Ovid warns women that their 'hare', or lover, will be hunted by other women. This statement appears in the third book of the *Ars amatoria* (iii. 662), wherein Ovid offers advice to women, having spent the first two books advising men. He jocularly remarks that he is being indiscreet, quite letting the side down; after all, 'The bird does not show the fowlers where it may be hunted; the hind does not teach the enemy hounds to run' (iii. 667–70; p. 165).

This imaging of gender is perpetuated in the French love-allegories which have the chase of love as their fundamental structural principle. In the thirteenth-century *Dis dou cerf amoreus*, the beloved is the stag, and Love is the hunter who shoots the animal and has his hounds drink its blood. However, the male lover becomes the quarry in Jean Acart de Hesdin's *L'Amoureuse Prise* (1332). When that particular stag is killed, its body is divided in three parts and eaten by the beloved's hounds— namely, Pleasure, Will, and Thought—while its heart and will are given to the ultimate cause of the hunt, the lady. These poems read as extreme, indeed macabre, elaborations of the commonplace notions of the power of Love and the sufferings incumbent upon lovers.

In lines 344–86 of the *Book of the Duchess* Chaucer avoids such excesses. An elaborate account of the death of the *hert*, of the type illustrated above, would have been in the worst possible taste in his elegy. Neither is there any risk of the Ovidian dehumanization of woman as spoil of male desire (of the type illustrated above), since the text works through allusion and implication rather than by direct statement of any connection between loving and hunting. The link is rather implied through word-play with the terms *hert* and *herte*.

Chaucer first refers to the *hert* at line 351, where the animal's death at the hands of the hunters is forecast—perceived, interestingly, as an act of forceful, almost brutal, aggression ('they wolde slee the hert with strengthe'). The finding of the 'hert' is noted at line 378, and when the dreamer first meets the Man in Black, he remarks, as a conversational gambit, that the 'hert be goon' (540). Finally, near the end of the poem, we have the muted announcement that the 'hert-huntyng' is over (1313).

The term *herte*, denoting the physical organ supposed to be the seat of the affections, appears more often. For example, the black knight tells how the love-songs that he composed in honour of his lady gladdened his 'herte' (1173); similarly, the first line of the first of these pieces, as he quotes it, declares that his 'herte' becomes 'lyght' when he thinks of 'that swete wyght' (1175–6). When he debates with himself regarding whether or not he should declare his love, it seems that his 'herte' will 'braste atweyne' (1193); with 'sorweful herte and woundes wide' he eventually attempts such a declaration (1210–11). A connection between *heart* and *hurt* is implied when the besotted lover proudly declares that his mistress 'herte' many with her beautiful look, but this affected her 'herte' very little (883–4). (Punning use of one word-form with two meanings was highly valued in French poetic theory.) But she has won him entirely: since she possesses his 'herte', he may not 'asterte' (i.e. escape; 1153–4). Subsequently their hearts become such a mutual pair ('Oure hertes wern so evene a payre . . .') that there was no difference of emotion between them (1289–91). In the full sense of the term, White is the Man in Black's sweetheart ('herte swete', 1231). Looking back at the earlier part of the poem, Alcyone figures as the 'goode swete herte' (206) of King Ceyx, and here heartache ('her herte began to erme', 80) is caused by the queen's realization that her husband has been away for an ominously long period of time.

These idioms therefore link the two major parts of the poem. And in between is the richly suggestive hunt of Octavian with all its implications of 'l'amoureuse chace'. Was the dog which led the dreamer to the Man in Black part of the hunting party, and if so, what relationship does that require between the bereaved man's 'herte' and Octavian's hunt? The text is silent. Particularly intriguing is the fact that when the bereaved aristocrat finally admits to the narrator (or, better, to the narrative) that his beloved is 'ded', the hunt breaks up—that dreadful word signals, perhaps even commands, its ending:

> And with that word ryght anoon
> They gan to strake forth; al was doon,
> For that tyme, the hert-huntyng.               (1312–13)

Faced with the news of White's death, the text could hardly allow the hunt to continue. The 'game' is well and truly 'doon' (to adopt terms from line 539), not just for the black knight but for Octavian's hunting-party: this returns to its home, that 'long castel with walles white' which is the house of Lancaster. The 'hert' is 'goon' (540); ultimately (in my view) the hunting has been unsuccessful. The Man in Black's 'herte swete' has also 'goon'. And this can be regarded as a victory of Fortune the champion chess-player—perhaps even of Death, conceived of as a hunter (to return to Thiébaux' suggestion).

If so, and I personally think that we cannot be so specific, this thought is left unspoken. Chaucer is content to tantalize. He concentrates on the fate of fair White, forgetting what happened to the *hert*. One death is enough—indeed, more than enough, as will be demonstrated by the next section of the poem, wherein the narrator encounters love and loss of a superlative kind, of which he himself can only dream.

On hunting imagery in medieval literature in general and in *BD* in particular, see Thiébaux, *Stag of Love*, esp. pp. 115–27, to which the above account is indebted. The crucial *hert/herte* pun is discussed on p. 116 n. 35. See further Anne Rooney, *Hunting in Middle English Literature* (Cambridge, 1993), who notes that the love-hunt did not feature strongly in late medieval English texts. 'The most pervasive use of the hunt in Middle English literature is as a figure of worldly bliss,' she argues; in *BD* 'the hunter-king conjures up the image of worldly pleasure—the worldly pleasure from which the Black Knight is excluded by his grief' (pp. 145, 154).

Machaut, *Navarre*, ed. and trans. Palmer.

For different views on the 'emperour Octovyen' see Mother Angela Carson, 'The Sovereignty of Octovyen in *Book of the Duchess*', AnM 8 (1967), 46–57; A. S. Cook, *Chaucerian Papers* (New Haven, Conn., 1919; repr. New York, 1973), pp. 31–2; Phillips (ed.), *BD*, pp. 35 6; Rooney, *Hunting*, pp. 143–5; Thiébaux, *Stag of Love*, pp. 124–5. For the allegorical reading of B. F. Huppé and D. W. Robertson see pp. 137–8 below. As Phillips notes, the Emperor Augustus regularly features in medieval literature as a 'type of worldly power and wealth'; he also had a reputation for wisdom, as when, on hearing the Sibyl's announcement of the birth of Christ, he refused to be deified by his people (according to the *Legenda Aurea*, on which text see the chapter on *LGW*).

Ovid, *The Art of Love and Other Poems*, ed. and trans. J. H. Mozley (Cambridge, Mass., and London, 1939). The I-persona declares that he is the prey of Cupid in the *Amores*, I. ii. 19. Women are said to make men their prey in *Amores*, I. ii. 1–2, *Ars amatoria*, iii. 560. The *Remedia amoris* prescribes actual hunting as a good way of helping one to forget about love (199–212).

Froissart, *Paradys d'Amours*, ed. Scheler; trans. Windeatt.

Marcelle Thiébaux, 'An Unpublished Allegory of the Hunt of Love: *Le dis dou cerf amoreus*', SP 62 (1965), 531–45; Jean Acart, *La Prise Amoureuse*, ed. E. Hoepffner, Gesellschaft für romanische Literatur, 22 (Dresden, 1910). See further Thiébaux, *Stag of Love*, pp. 145–60.

The suggestion that, while this particular hunt is finished, another one is imminent, is offered by Rooney, *Hunting*, who places special emphasis on 'al was doon / For that tyme, the hert-huntyng' (1312–13). After the Man in Black's emotions run their natural course, 'the bereaved may perhaps re-enter the joyful life represented by the hunt' (p. 174).

DEATH DEFERRED: THE CENTRAL DIALOGUE

Why, having overheard the Man in Black's lyric, which makes clear that his lady is dead, does the narrator proceed to ignore this fact, and have to be told again at the end of his interchange with the bereaved knight? Is he stupid and uncomprehending, or actually quite sensible, considerate, and tactful? Naïve or knowing?

The range of critical responses to these questions is quite extraordinary. Some have affirmed that the I-persona is perfectly aware that White is dead, but conceals this knowledge from the Man in Black, then proceed to offer various reasons for this reticence. For example, the narrator has been praised for his tact, and in similar vein his ostensibly obtuse comments have been seen as 'gently but firmly forcing the mourner to the full confession which will ease his sick heart', as P. M. Kean puts it (i. 61). In Dieter Mehl's reading the emphasis is placed on the dreamer's admiration, his 'incredulous queries' being regarded as 'not an expression of slow comprehension, but rather an indication that he is genuinely moved and only now begins to grasp the full extent of the knight's grief (p. 31). It is the dreamer's search for specific information, rather than the broadening of his emotional horizons, which was singled out in John Lawlor's highly influential essay of 1956 on the poem's pattern of consolation. The dreamer wants to know which of two possible reasons for the stranger's grief is correct, suggests Lawlor: has death intervened to make the fulfilment of his love an impossibility, or is it rather the case that death has interrupted 'love in its fulfilment'? But surely the text does not allow us to be specific in quite that way.

Others have been perplexed by the apparent contradiction between 'a childlike dullard stupefied with sorrow and sleeplessness' and that apparently different 'character who knows the facts, understands what he hears and sees, and puts his knowledge to use with tact and diplomacy, with the kindly purpose of enabling the stranger to ease his heart' (to borrow phrases from B. H. Bronson, p. 273). Solutions have been sought in the distinction between a knowing poet and a naïve I-persona, one of the consequences of this approach being the location of the tact and diplomacy in the author's mind rather than in his character's. One of the most sophisticated versions of this type of argument is advanced by A. C. Spearing, who believes that those who see the dreamer as tactful have confused his nature 'with the nature of the poem': it is rather *the poem* which is 'supremely tactful', this being effected by Chaucer's establishment of 'a contrast between his patron's transcendent grief and his own clumsy and uncomprehending attempts to grasp its nature' (pp. 69–70). We do not have 'to believe that he is so stupid as not to understand the knight's lay when he hears it', continues Spearing; but for him this is really beside the point, which is that the 'lay must be in the poem so that we, the audience, shall know all along what is the cause of the knight's sorrow', thereby being enabled to sympathize with him. For 'the convention of the dream-poem does not demand that we should be *conscious* [Spearing's italics] of the dreamer as the witness of every event in his dream' (p. 70): only when the narrator says something definitely dreamerish should we be aware of him as dreamer; for the rest, his voice is that of the poet who is reading the work to an audience which he must fully inform, while leaving (for such is the implication of this argument) the intermittent *sujet* of the dreamer in the dark.

Assuming for the moment that he is not in the dark (at least in the relevant passages), another possible reason for his reticence could be natural caution: the dreamer wants to learn more before committing himself to an opinion. In the closed, dangerous world of the court, one could pay dearly for a *faux pas*. It is to be expected that such worries should often be reflected in courtly literature. There was a general realization that appearances can be deceptive, as is well illustrated by an episode in Machaut's *Jugement dou Roy de Behaingne*. The hidden poet at first believes the two people in the encounter to be lovers, but further eavesdropping reveals that this is not the case. In the *Book of the Duchess*, then, the overheard lyric might be not a personal protestation of grief but a dramatic rendition of a lyric by a performer who has not necessarily experienced the emotions he is expressing. In the later Middle Ages (and beyond) love-poems were held in common by courtiers: lyrics produced by one individual could be performed by another, either *verbatim* or with significant alteration, and the uses to which such poems were put were also various, including the praise of some actual or potential patroness and the demonstration—to observers of both sexes—of one's intelligence and sensibility (always a shrewd move in the competition for preferment), as well as the pursuit of a genuine passion. If one encountered a man in mourning clothes singing a lament for a dead lady, one could not, therefore, immediately conclude that the performer was the bereaved lover himself. Donald Howard offers a vivid modern analogy:

If you came upon a cowboy in a field singing to himself a typical cowboy song about death, would you conclude that someone had really died? That is exactly the narrator's circumstance: he wants to know why the knight is sad, wants to help him, tells him it may ease his heart to tell his story, but doesn't see that the conventional song stated the facts. (p. 156)

In similar vein, on may recall the Prince of Denmark's musings on the way in which an actor can counterfeit feelings on request. Is it not extraordinary, he asks himself, that a player, who is only in 'a fiction, in a dream of passion' rather than in a state of personal grief, can weep so convincingly for Hecuba, while he, who has a major 'motive' and 'cue for passion', 'can say nothing' (*Hamlet*, II, ii)? 'Saying nothing' is, of course, the traditional lot of the attendant lord rather than of the prince (which is part of Hamlet's problem). How much more heavily, then (so the argument would run), should the necessity of discretion weigh on the shoulders of the dreamer. Like T. S. Eliot's Prufrock, he is wary of having an impetuous expression of sympathy being met with a curt 'That is not what I meant at all. That is not it, at all.'

There, in a nutshell, are the major problems of interpretation relating to the central dialogue of the *Book of the Duchess* and in particular to its deferral of death, the participants' refusal to speak its name to each other until line 1309. In order to make our own way through this forest of conflicting opinion, we shall once again go back to Chaucer's creative roots—to the Old French courtly poetry which lies behind his earliest literary efforts. The reading offered here takes the view that, *pace* Spearing, the poem's personae are fairly well fixed, not fluctuating to any marked degree. The narrative keeps no secrets from the dreamer. It is rather that the dreamer wishes to probe the inner secrets of the Man in Black's mind, this quest having as its objective the discovery not of the basic cause of the other's grief (for that is already known) but of its circumstances and significance, and hence ultimately of its essential value. The narrator/dreamer is not Prince Hamlet; nor is he meant to be in this text. Rather, he is an attendant lord, a role which is subordinate without being servile, the distance between master (who has a major 'motive' and 'cue for passion') and man being defined in terms of inequality of experience and emotional accomplishment rather than of rank *simpliciter*—though high degree is of course the *sine qua non* of the nature of the lover and of his love.

The part played by the overheard lyric in the narrative process may be elucidated by the contrast with Machaut's practice in the *Behaingne*. In the earlier poem there is no lament for the knight to overhear, and so he has no means of knowing what lies behind the lady's grief. So he asks her outright what is wrong, and, overcoming her initial reluctance to tell, draws out the information from her. In giving a direct answer to his direct question, she reserves the fact that her beloved is dead for the end of her speech, where it has maximum impact; only at this point does her interlocutor learn of the root cause. Chaucer's persona, on the other hand, tells us that he wants to have 'more knowynge' of the Man in Black's 'thought' (538), the 'more' surely implying that he already has *some* knowledge, gained by overhearing the lyric, but wants more. He does not have to wait until the end of the Man in Black's speeches to discover the fundamental problem, for this has been revealed to him, by indirect means, at the outset. The suggestion, as made by Howard, that the dreamer is worried lest he should mistake a mere performer for a person—maybe its author, maybe not—who is using a poem to convey a personal grief which may have nothing to do with death, is ultimately unsatisfying in view of what we have described above (pp. 108–9) as the essentially private nature of the Man in Black's protestation. That this is in no way audience-oriented is surely evinced by the fact that, as soon the bereaved lover realizes that he has an audience—the dreamer—he instantly stops behaving in that manner, his grief not being a matter for public display. Yet the basic impulse behind this suggestion—namely, that some sense of the caution which courtiers, including poets, necessarily had to exercise in their dealings with the great, should be brought to bear in criticism of the *Book of the Duchess*—is certainly a sound one. And it is fully accommodated in the view, which will be developed further below, that the Chaucer persona is deferentially sympathetic to the Man in Black, while Chaucer, within the plan of his poem as a whole, strives to subordinate the emotion and experience of that persona to those of his natural superior.

The dreamer, then, offers to do the Man in Black some service—by offering him such relief as a sympathetic hearing can afford. In the *Behaingne* the lord had offered to do all in his power to redress the lady's grief, but this stance was soon superseded as they engaged in what might be called their trial of emotional strength. Such competitiveness is utterly lacking in Chaucer's text, the initial offer of Machaut's lord being elaborated in words which have no parallel in the *Behaingne*:

'Paraunter hyt may ese youre herte,          *Perhaps*
That semeth ful sek under your syde'.          *sick*
(556–7)

(I fully endorse Helen Philipps's view that here is a 'very simple explanation' of the dreamer's motivation in asking 'ostensibly obscure questions'; p. 37). The dreamer certainly tries his best to help, never declaring that he knows full well the fact of the other's bereavement, but rather drawing him out with tact and assumed ignorance. Likewise, the Man in Black never realizes that his lyric has been overheard (again this contrasts with the *Behaingne*, herein the lord and lady soon learn that the persona has 'heard our whole discussion', as the former puts it; 1266), and so his responses are natural, appropriate, unindulgent. Thus, for example, the dreamer's remark that no one would 'make this woo' for a 'fers' (a queen in chess) has its desired effect, as the Man in Black stops being cryptic

and promises to reveal all (740–57). And here may be found the reason
for what was described above as the deferral of death—which is largely
due to the contrivance of the dreamer, and may be regarded as being to
his credit. Once the two figures admit to each other that 'She ys ded',
the dreamer's line of questioning cannot continue as before, and the Man
in Black's responses can never be the same again. At that point, they have
nothing left to say to each other. The dialogue stops short of the silenc-
ing admission as long as it can, in order that the poem's special kind of
consolation (on which see pp. 155–60 below) may be effected.

But let us return to the dreamer's attempt to 'ese' the 'herte' of the
Man in Black. Having started with that commendable intention, so to
speak, the dreamer soon genuinely finds himself out of his emotional
depth, and the text establishes the truth of the Man in Black's statement
that he has lost more than his interlocutor can understand—such is the
force of this repeated statement that it rings in the mind like a refrain.
'Thow wost ful lytel what thow menest' (743, 1305; cf. 1137); that is, the
dreamer does not appreciate the full import of his words in this particular situation. He is constructed as a figure who has made the classic mistake of trying to judge someone else's experience by his own, his own
being determined by the discourse characteristic of the unrequited lover.
This goes a long way towards explaining the choice of the questions and
statements which are used as 'tales', ploys to gain more knowledge of the
Man in Black's thought.

'How and in what way can these lovers endure the woes that you have
told me about?' cries Jean de Meun's lover to the God of Love (*Roman
de la Rose*, 2583–5; trans. Dahlberg, p. 66). In similar vein, Froissart's
*Paradys d'Amours* opens with the exclamation 'I can only be amazed that
I am still alive, when I am lying awake so much' (1–2)—lines which, as
we have already remarked, directly influenced the portrait of the I-persona at the beginning of Chaucer's poem. Such are the boundaries of the
dreamer's experience and expectation, as may be illustrated by two of his
interventions, which are significant events in the central dialogue inasmuch as they initiate changes in the direction and address of the Man in
Black's reminiscences.

First, on hearing how the Man in Black saw and fell in love with his
white lady, he remarks that his emotions were certainly well placed; he
could not have done better. This elicits the emphatic response that no
one else could have done as well. I truly believe that, declares the
dreamer, adding the slight qualification:

> 'I leve yow wel, that trewely
> Yow thoughte that she was the beste

> And to beholde the alderfayreste,          *most beautiful of all*
> Whoso had loked hir with your eyen.'
>
> (1048–51)

This relativity is comprehensible if one assumes that the dreamer must
think, from his own point of view, that *his* lady is 'the beste'. But the
Man in Black will have none of it; his beloved's beauty was not in the
eye of a single beholder.

> 'With myn [eyen]? Nay, all that hir seyen
> Seyde and sworen hyt was soo'.   (1052–3)

Then he charmingly admits that, even if his lady had not won such universal acclaim, *he* certainly would have loved her best: thus he tacitly
admits that the dreamer has a point. But only for a moment.

Secondly, having heard at length how and where the Man in Black saw
his beloved, the dreamer eagerly asks to be told what he said to her and
how she reacted to him at first, the crucial question 'what ye have lore'
being somewhat swamped by these enquiries. The dreamer proceeds to
speculate:

> 'What los ys that?' Quod I thoo;
> 'Nyl she not love yow? Ys hyt soo?
> Or have ye oght doon amys,
> That she hath left yow? Ys hyt this?
> For Goddes love, telle me al'.   (1139–43)

Of course, this is far off the mark, the objective being to enable the Man
in Black to 'telle . . . al'. And inevitably he undertakes to do so (1144).
Considered in terms of the poem's narrative movement, then, these lines
constitute yet another successful ploy. Considered in respect of the
dreamer's designated role, he is viewing the Man in Black's sorrow
through the filter of his own pain; it seems reasonable to infer from his
portrait at the beginning of the poem that he fears his lady will not love
him. The dreamer responds most fully to what his companion is saying
when the pleasures and pains which he is viewing from the outside seem
to be consonant with his own. It is by this means, rather than having him
openly describe his own situation, that Chaucer maintains his persona's
role as unrequited lover. Reports of his stupidity have been much exaggerated. The fact that he lacks the experience to fully understand does
not make him an idiot; one may compare the not dissimilar 'communication gap' between the Pearl-maiden and the dreamer in *Pearl*. Moreover,
in both these dream-poems such failure is utterly functional in that it
accentuates the magnitude of what is there to be understood.

This argument should not be interpreted as implying that the dreamer is a mere sounding-board for the Man in Black's protestations. For Chaucer developed that figure in a quite different, and uncompeting, direction—as enquirer into dreams, respondent to the classical (at least in origin) 'tale' of Ceyx and Alcyone, and so on. What he is not, however, is a self-recommending love-poet. Here is yet another significant divergence from Machaut, which may be regarded as another aspect of Chaucer's strategy of deference, his subordination of the dreamer to the dreamed.

Kean, *Making of English Poetry*. Mehl, *Narrative Poetry*. Lawlor, 'Pattern of Consolation'. Bronson, '*BD* Re-opened'. Spearing, *Medieval Dream-Poetry*.

Machaut, *'Behaigne' and 'Fortune'*, ed. Wimsatt and Kibler.

Howard, *Chaucer and the Medieval World*. On courtiers' use of love-poems see John Stevens, *Music and Poetry in the Early Tudor Court* (London, 1961; repr. Cambridge, 1979), pp. 154–202.

Phillips (ed.), *BD*. *Roman de la Rose*, ed. Langlois, trans. Dahlberg. Froissart, *Paradys d'Amours*, ed. Scheler, trans. Windeatt.

Lewis thought that in *BD* Chaucer attempts 'to do better than he is yet able' in trying to dramatize 'the impatient self-absorption of grief on the part of the lover [i.e. the Man in Black], and his demands on the dreamer's close attention', for this is done 'so clumsily that he sometimes makes the one seem a bore, and the other a fool' (*Allegory of Love*, p. 170). And Kittredge believed that the 'mental attitude of the Dreamer is that of childlike wonder. He understands nothing, not even the meaning of his dream' (*Chaucer and his Poetry*, p. 50). Yet 'Speech eases his [i.e. the Man in Black's] soul. . . . It is a relief to him that the Dreamer seems not to comprehend' (p. 51). J. S. P. Tatlock, *The Mind and Art of Chaucer* (New York, 1950), found the narrator indifferent to 'human reality'; his practice of ignoring the fact of the lady's death, which he has told us 'so bluntly at the beginning', is a 'really inexplicable blur' (p. 30). In marked contrast, Strohm speaks of 'Chaucer's subtle delineation of the Knight's and the dreamer's respective social positions. At every point in their interaction, we are reminded of a certain amicable equity, on the one hand, and of a considerable social gulf on the other; of a polite egalitarianism in that both are gentlepersons and a decided limitation of egalitarianism in that one is an aristocrat and the other is not' (*Social Chaucer*, p. 52).

## THE PATRON AS POET

One of the ways in which the poet-personae in the Old French *dits* (especially Machaut's) keep their end up when faced with authoritative kings and nobles who are the arbiters of the relevant amatory and moral issues is by emphasizing their profession as poets, which is presented as prestigious. The narrator of the *Navarre*, for instance, maintains his position with considerable self-confidence, even though he is judged to be in the wrong, and the penance subsequently imposed on him—the composition of a lay, a song, and a ballade—actually serves to confirm his privileged status and skill. We are a long way from a poem which was definitely influenced by the *Navarre*, the prologue to Chaucer's *Legend of Good*

*Women*, where the offending poet is presented as having merely translated without understanding what he was writing about. To return to Machaut, the situation in another source of the *Book of the Duchess*, the *Dit de la Fonteinne Amoureuse*, is complicated by the fact that there the patron is flatteringly cast in the role of accomplished poet. On reading through the overheard lover's complaint as he has written it down, 'to see if he repeated any rhymes', the Machaut persona is impressed to discover that he cannot find a single one; on the contrary, 'there were one hundred different rhymes' (1046–52; trans. Windeatt, p. 35). A little later, the lover (a fictionalization of the Duc de Berry, as already noted) asks the poet to make for him a lay or complaint about his sad situation, where-upon the poet presents the lover with his own poem word for word as he himself had composed it (1521–4; p. 39). Here, then, the lamenting lord has beaten the poet at his own game. And yet, one leaves the Machaut poem with the utter conviction that the game is essentially the poet's. It is he, after all, who has judged the patron's poetry to be excellent. Moreover, of course, he is the real author of the poetry with which he has credited the patron; in ostensibly praising the patron's artistry, he is actually praising his own.

In the *Book of the Duchess*, Chaucer gives his main Gaunt persona the literary credit in a manner which is far less fulsome but none the less effective for that. The Man in Black, on his own account, busied himself with making 'a gret del' of 'songes' about his lady (1155–9), this state-ment being followed first by a brief excursus on the historical origins of song (1160–70) and then by the text of the very first song he ever com-posed about his lady (1175–80). He often sang 'loude' (1158), he tells us, and significantly in his first song the emphasis falls on the fact that thoughts of 'that swete wyght' gladdened his heart, even though at that stage she had not yet accepted him 'for hir knyght'. This contrasts sharply with the 'dedly sorwful soun' of the Man in Black's private 'com-pleynte to hymselve' (464); that sombre

> lay, a maner song,
> Withoute noote, withoute song          (471–2)

which he declaims with a 'ful pitous pale' face (470). The dreamer sim-ply 'rehearses' (cf. line 474) his words—that is, reports without making any contribution or alteration to what has been overheard. This stance is maintained at the end of the *Book of the Duchess*, when the narrator declares,

> Thoughte I, 'Thys ys so queynt a sweven          *remarkable*
> That I wol, be processe of tyme,
> Fonde to put this sweven in ryme

>       As I kan best, and that anoon.'
>       This was my sweven; now hit ys doon.          *dream*
>                                                   (1330–4)

Here the emphasis is definitely on involuntary dreaming rather than vigorous composition of poetry—though it could be said that the reference
to 'processe of tyme' hints at the long labours required to make satisfactory 'ryme'. Quite clearly, however, it is with reference to the Man in
Black's *makynge* that we have the mention of poetic genre and technique,
the remark that his lay is without 'noote' or 'song' being especially interesting in that it may imply Chaucer's knowledge of one major aspect of
the poetics of 'the school of Machaut'. In Deschamps' *Art de dictier*,
accompanying melody is regarded as 'artificial music', while the actual
words of a poem are supposed to make 'natural music'. 'Natural music',
it is explained, may be heard in situations where the melody of artificial
music would not always be appropriate, as between lords and ladies who
have set themselves apart and are meeting privately; alternatively it may
issue from the mouth of a single person, or be read to someone who is
sick. In these and similar situations a performed song would be out of
place because of its loudness. It could be argued, therefore, that the 'natural music' of the Man in Black's 'compleynte to hymselve' is utterly
appropriate to the singular and private circumstances of its recital.
Indeed, the *Book of the Duchess* in its entirety could be described as a
composition of 'natural music' designed to be read before someone who
was 'sick' in a manner of speaking, the sorrowing John of Gaunt. But
more on that later.

Turning to the matter of the connection between emotion and expression, and hence to another branch of medieval literary theory, it may be
added that being in love was regarded as a necessary condition for successful composition of love-poetry, at least according to the thirteenth-
and fourteenth-century *vidas* ('lives') of the troubadour poets. To take
but two examples, Guiraudo lo Ros is supposed to have fallen 'in love
with the countess, daughter of his lord, and his love for her taught him
how to invent poetry', while Aimeric de Peguilhan 'sang very badly' until
'taught to invent poetry' by love (*Vidas*, trans. Egan, pp. 61, 62). Similar
attitudes are found in Old French love-poetry, as when the I-persona in
Machaut's *Remede de Fortune* says that he 'learned to compose chansons
and lais, ballades, rondeaux, virelais, and songs, according to my feelings,
about love and nothing else; because he who does not compose according to his feelings falsifies (*contrefait*) his work and his song'. His lady, he
adds, is 'the charming inspiration for my song' (401–8, 412; trans.
Wimsatt and Kibler, p. 188). And in the *Vita nuova* (xxv) Dante portrays
himself as being directed and compelled by Love to write about Beatrice

and subjects related to her. Indeed, at one point Dante claims that the first person to write as a vernacular poet was moved to do so because he wished to make his verses comprehensible to his beloved, who could not understand Latin. Verses written to his 'screen ladies'—that is, the women to whom (he would have us believe) he addressed certain poems in order to conceal the real object of desire—are included in the *Vita nuova* not for their own sake but because of their relation to Beatrice, the clear implication being that the quality of the poetry is directly related to the quality of the passion. The same could be said of the Man in Black's poetry; *fin' amors* makes for fine verse. Moreover, different experiences produce different genres: love leads him into song, while the beloved's death directs him into noteless complaint. Those love songs were written out of his own innermost feelings, expressive of transformative sentiment—

> . . . songes thus I made
> Of my felynge, myn herte to glade . . .                    (1171–2)

—while, conversely, his lay resulted from the pain of deep personal loss. The Man in Black's works might seem conventional—indeed, technically speaking, they *are* conventional—but the context makes it clear that they are to be taken as highly personal, even autobiographical, within the poem's fictional space.

By contrast with all this personal engagement and expression, the narrator's role is conceived of as essentially passive; he is the receiver and transmitter of the Man in Black's rhymes and rhetoric and, more generally, of the 'queynt sweven'. The Man in Black, then, is 'il miglior fabbro' ('the better craftsman', as Dante said of Arnaut Daniel, at *Purgatorio*, xxvi. 117), or at least the figure with whom the technical vocabulary of the craft is associated, and his emotions give him a literary insight which the I-persona (the figure one would have expected to champion the craft of verse) can record but cannot share.

A major consequence of this point of view is that criticism of the *Book of the Duchess* must be sensitive about the relative importance it allocates to the two protagonists. To take a case in point, part of Bronson's reading intimates a very narrator-centred view of the poem, the awake narrator's 'private grief' being taken as having 'been renounced by the Dreamer'

to reappear externalized and projected upon the figure of the grieving knight. The modern analyst, indeed, would instantly recognise the therapeutic function of this dream as an effort of the psyche to resolve an intolerable emotional situation by repudiating it through this disguise. The knight is the Dreamer's surrogate; and in this view it would be significant that the force which keeps the surrogate from his lady is the far more acceptable, because decisive and final, fact of death. (p. 281)

Thus, by helping the Man in Black, the dreamer is essentially helping himself. Similarly, Spearing suggests that while 'externally' the Man in Black is certainly John of Gaunt, considered 'internally'—in terms of his operation within the poem—'he is a projection of the narrator himself, though of course on a far grander and more aristocratic scale' (p. 59). In my view, however, any reading which would have the I-persona's subjectivity dominate that of the bereaved lover is working against the power structure of the poem. For it is the Man in Black who must ultimately be recognized as dominant; his claim on our attention is to be recognized as far surpassing the dreamer's, and anyone who thinks otherwise may well be judging the poem a failure, at least as far as its original purpose (in so far as we may presume to infer that) is concerned. Thus, the 'external' identification of the Man in Black with Gaunt dictates and delimits the sphere of 'internal' operation of this his main persona. The narrator may, technically speaking, have dreamed up the Man in Black, but he is no narrator surrogate, his origins being a lot more distinguished, in terms of social and emotional status—and indeed of literary creativity as well, as we have just seen. Chaucer has, so to speak, bestowed his finest garments upon his superior; what is left for his own persona looks far less attractive.

In the *Book of the Duchess*, then, an idealized figure of the prince is given the best lines and the better of the tacit argument. Indeed, somewhat paradoxically, the very fact that the Man in Black is not identified too closely with John of Gaunt makes the total effect even more complimentary, for this allows the Man in Black's natural (i.e. class-reflexive) superiority, and by implication Gaunt's, to be conveyed primarily in terms of superlative quality of life experience and noble sentiment. Here is princepleasing of a sophisticated kind, far more subtle than heaping flattery on named kings and ostentatiously giving them the final word (and/or the literary prize) in one's poems. The grief of Chaucer's narrator is subordinated to the greater grief of his interlocutor, and generally is deployed in such a way as to counterpoint the Man in Black's virtues. This may be seen as the fictive metamorphosis of the actual service which Chaucer the young courtier rendered, or at least wished to present himself as capable of rendering, to John of Gaunt.

Machaut, *Navarre*, ed. and trans. Palmer. *Idem, Fonteinne Amoureuse*, in *Œuvres*, ed. Hoepffner, trans. in Windeatt, *Sources and Analogues*. The statements of some critics regarding Machaut's self-denigration in the face of patrons and an audience of courtiers (e.g. Poirion, *Le Poète et le prince*, p. 198; Lawton, *Chaucer's Narrators*, p. 50; Spearing,

*Medieval Dream-Poetry*, pp. 44–5) should not disguise the fact of his aggrandizing self-fashioning as *poète*, on which see especially Brownlee, *Poetic Identity*, pp. 3–23.

On Deschamps' *Art de dictier* see Glending Olson, 'Deschamps' *Art de dictier* and Chaucer's Literary Environment', *Speculum*, 48 (1973), 714–23; also his 'Making and Poetry in the Age of Chaucer', *Comparative Literature*, 31 (1979), 272–90, and of course Wimsatt, *Chaucer and his French Contemporaries*, in which the distinction between 'natural' and 'artificial' music is of central importance.

*The Vidas of the Troubadours*, trans. Margarita Egan (New York and London, 1984). Dante, *Vita nuova*, in *Opere di Dante Alighieri*, ed. E. Moore and P. Toynbee (Oxford, 1924), pp. 205–33; trans. B. Reynolds (Harmondsworth, 1969). A useful commentary on aspects of this work of Dante's—including those 'screen ladies'—is provided by R. P. Harrison, 'Approaching the *Vita nuova*', in Rachel Jacoff (ed.), *The Cambridge Companion to Dante* (Cambridge, 1993), pp. 34–44. Machaut, *'Behaigne' and 'Fortune'*, ed. Wimsatt and Kibler.

Bronson, '*BD* Re-opened'. With my final remarks compare Strohm, *Social Chaucer*, who describes *BD* as to some extent 'an exploration of Chaucer's own existing and potential relations with Gaunt, in a form at once tactful and quietly self-promotional' (p. 52). The poem shows that Chaucer is 'a fit interlocutor—at once a gentleperson worthy of intimacy and friendly exchange, and a person of discretion who can be trusted not to forget aspects of social difference' (p. 54).

## *The Consolation of Experience*

We are now in a position to confront that central crux of criticism of the *Book of the Duchess*: in what ways—if at all—can the poem be regarded as a consolation? Starting with the most widely read of all the literary consolations which circulated in the Middle Ages, the *De consolatione philosophiae* of Boethius, we will proceed to view Chaucer's work within the perspective of models and modes of Christian consolation which he chose *not* to follow, either explicitly or implicitly. Finally, some conclusions will be offered regarding the value system of the *Book of the Duchess*, with reference to the intertextual position it occupies in relation to the Old French *dits*, these being the 'locating' texts against which Chaucer's poem must be measured.

### AVOIDING ALLEGORY

The *Consolatio philosophiae* teaches that the usual sources of human happiness—wealth, honour, power, glory, bodily pleasure—should ultimately be dismissed as inferior, limited goods which are under the control of Fortune, which is utterly fickle, her unreliability being the essence of her nature. Man's quest for stability and sufficiency can be satisfied only by God, who is the *summum bonum*. In particular, the longing for the pleasures of the body is full of anxiety, and their satisfaction is full of regret (III, pr. vii). Such delights have a bitter end, declares Lady Philosophy, as anyone will understand who is willing to recall his own lusts. The pleasure derived from wife and children is certainly not wholly good, for it was well said that children were invented to be tormentors. Besides, 'who would not despise and reject the service of so very base and frail a thing as the body?' (III, pr. viii, 12–13; trans. Tester, p. 261). The brightness of beauty is brief, continues Lady Philosophy, and passes swiftly, more quickly than the changing loveliness of spring flowers. Physical beauty is only skin deep. If, as Aristotle says, men had vision as powerful as that of Lynceus the Argonaut, 'so that their sight penetrated obstacles, would not the superficially very beautiful body of Alcibiades seem most vile when his inwards could be seen?' (22–6; p. 261). Medieval readers misunderstood this as referring to an animal, the lynx, and (quite understandably, given their sexual politics) often turned Alcibiades, the male lover of Socrates, into a woman—specifically, a beautiful prostitute about whom Aristotle delivered a homily on the deceptiveness of appearances. The message, then, was abundantly clear. Men could not place their trust in earthly beauty in general or in beautiful women in particular. Rather, they were advised to turn away from all earthly things, taking a warning from the behaviour of Orpheus, who looked back at his wife Eurydice (III, met. xii), thereby lapsing into involvement with *temporalia* and failing to escape from concupiscence, according to a host of medieval commentaries on the *Consolatio*.

In Machaut's *Jugement dou Roy de Behaingne* something of the same spirit of contempt for the body beautiful pervades part of the narrative, though of course this functions in a quite un-Boethian way, to privilege the love of the knight for his faithless beloved over the love of the bereaved lady for her dead partner. Machaut has this knight emphasize the freedom from former vows which death brings:

'it is common for both men and women that when the soul has left the body and the body is interred beneath the gravestone, it is soon forgotten, although it may be mourned. I've seen no man nor woman weep so long that he'd not found joy again before the year was out, no matter how true his love—and I make no exception for powerful or poor. Truly, I believe that this is reasonable. You'll hold to the pattern; you'll not break it, and you'll not be reproached for this by anyone, though you pray for his soul sincerely.' (1109–22; trans. Wimsatt and Kibler, pp. 114, 116)

The personification Reason, who acts as an adviser to the King of Bohemia (not only an expert in love-lore but also the possessor of a larger wisdom), is even more ruthless than is the knight in identifying the love of man and woman as essentially a thing of the flesh and concluding that therefore it cannot survive the grave. 'Love comes from carnal affection, and its desires and essence all incline to pleasure' (1709–11; p. 147).

Regarded in such terms, human love stands in opposition to the things of the spirit and the soul; its pleasures can lead an individual into vice or sin. The logic of this argument is that when the body dies, love dies also, whereas the soul is unscathed: 'as soon as the soul leaves the body, love withdraws and sets off. As God is my witness, this is what I see everywhere. Therefore the love of this lady of great worth is constantly diminishing from day to day, and in like measure is her sorrow diminishing' (1717–23; p. 147). Out of sight is out of mind: 'Since she will not see him again, it will happen that I [i.e. Reason] will make her forget him; for the heart will never love anything so much that it won't forget it after separation' (1677–81; p. 145). Time heals, and youth will soon reassert its natural vitality. Such is the consolation that may be extracted from Machaut.

Chaucer could have taken a similar line in the *Book of the Duchess*. John of Gaunt could have been reminded, with the best possible taste and tact, that while all due credit should be given to his wife, his love for her (inasmuch as it had a corporeal basis) has to be accepted as a thing of the past. He is free to love again. Besides, the things of the soul are more important. Blanche's soul is enjoying its heavenly reward, that being a motive for spiritual satisfaction rather than earthly sentiment, and he himself should not give way to excessive grief in mourning a creature whose existence on earth—like his own—is so transitory. Indeed, to borrow a phrase from the *Troilus* epilogue,

> . . . al nys but a faire,
> This world that passeth soone as floures fair.          (v. 1840–1)

Here, then, would have been Boethian counselling, a consolation of transcendence. But of course the *Book of the Duchess* says nothing of the kind. Yet the question remains: are the values we have just invoked *implicit* in the poem, functioning as a subtext which an audience has to be knowledgeable in a certain way in order to read correctly? Should the text be interpreted allegorically?

D. W. Robertson certainly thought so. In his 1965 study of the *Book of the Duchess* the dreamer is likened to the Boethius persona in the *Consolatio*, as in a condition of despair arising from the loss of Blanche perceived as a sensible object, this loss being attributed to the agency of Fortune. In Boethian terms, he declares, 'this kind of sorrow, although it occurs spontaneously in all of us, is actually a kind of foolishness' (p. 241). Chaucer carefully distanced the Man in Black from the historical John of Gaunt, the argument continues, making him into a beardless adolescent who gave himself up to love 'in ydelnesse' (798) before he met Blanche—a figure very much in need of the instruction which Boethius offers so well. When we first encounter the Man in Black, he is unaware of the essential selfishness of his passion (which Robertson sees as 'basically lustful'), and fails to realize that Blanche's virtues—which, according to this reading, are the real point of Chaucer's description of her—belong to the realm of the intelligible, and hence are not subject to Fortune. In the figure of the Man in Black, then, Chaucer is actually addressing 'the initial reaction of the mourners for Blanche generally', here 'somewhat exaggerated for poetic purposes' (p. 251). This audience has set in front of it an *exemplum* of how *not* to react, what *not* to think. Similarly, in the earlier (1963) study which Robertson undertook in association with B. F. Huppé, the 'one key' to the poem's interpretation is found in a theory of tacit Christian consolation. The dreamer is seen as taking to his horse in preparation for spiritual battle; he encounters the hunt of 'Octovyen', symbolizing Christ coming to save mankind ('Octo' means the number 8, which signifies Christ's resurrection, while 'vyen' means 'coming'). But the hart escapes, since the speaker's will is too overwhelmed by worldly cares to accept at once the formal consolation of the Church. His wilful grief is then epitomized in the black knight, who is in a culpable state of despair—a condition which is unworthy of Blanche's memory. The poem moves to achieve an extraordinary appreciation of the beauty of the lady, along with the understanding that her death is not a cause for grief; rather, comfort and joy may be taken in her memory. This memory, Huppé and Robertson continue, can be revered only by turning to the Physician who is Christ, the source of her virtues and the ultimate exemplar of the kind of love which she encouraged.

In my own view, if Chaucer had wanted to say that, he would have done so. The fact that he did *not* should be respected, and values which he judiciously left out of the *Book of the Duchess* should not be read into it. This argument may be advanced by the demonstration that Chaucer had many models and modes of writing available to him for the composition of Christian consolation; hence the fact that he resisted their pressures may be taken as a clear indication that he was attempting something different. The fable-plus-moralization treatment of the story of Ceyx and Alcyone which Chaucer found in the *Ovide moralisé* could easily have formed the basis of a poem which demonstrated that the pleasures of earthly love and life are as fleeting as birds (cf. pp. 95–6 above). But Chaucer was not tempted by that model, even though two of his contemporaries, Thomas Walsingham and Walter of Peterborough, apparently were, since they produced allegorized versions of the *Metamorphoses* (cf. pp. 26, 34, above). Neither did he follow the example of any of the allegorized 'game' texts which were available in his day, whether the game in question was hunting or playing at chess, as I now hope to show.

The best known of all the allegories based on the chess-game was the late thirteenth-century *Liber de ludo scaccorum* by the Dominican friar Jacques de Cessoles, an investigation of the hierarchical structure of society and the correct relationships between its constituent parts. Jacques describes three causes of the origin of chess. First, it was invented by the philosopher 'Exerses' as a means of correction: through this game the evil king of Babylon was shown the proper roles and offices of the ruler, nobles, and common people, whereupon he changed his life and manners and all his evil characteristics. Secondly, it keeps people from idleness. Those who are fortunate in the things of this world often become idle, whence spring many evils and great sins. Thirdly, every man naturally desires to know and to hear of novelties and new things (or 'tydynges', as William Caxton put it in the English translation which he printed in 1474). The *Liber de ludo scaccorum* was one of the two main inspirations for the anonymous Old French poem known as the *Echecs amoureux* ('The Chess of Love'; cf. pp. 44–5 above), the other being the *Roman de la Rose*. Its narrator is presented as experiencing in his youth a springtime vision of the goddess Nature, who tells him about the two paths between which he must choose, the way of reason and the way of sensuality. Subsequently he meets Mercury and the goddesses Venus, Juno, and Pallas. In a re-enactment of the Judgement of Paris he declares his preference for Venus, who rewards him by setting him on the road for the Garden of Delight, where he will find a mistress. On the way he is upbraided by Diana for his foolish choice, but her efforts are in vain. In the garden he meets Delight playing a game of chess with a beautiful lady. Each chess-piece represents a quality, disposition, or activity associated with love, there being one set for the man and a different set for the woman. Having been checkmated by the lady, the young man is instructed in the *ars amatoria* by the God of Love. After all this, the narrator finds himself alone; he looks for the lady, anxious to play another game of chess with her, but instead he meets the third goddess involved in the Judgement of Paris, Pallas, the goddess of Reason. She explains the conflict between the passionate life and the life of reason, and offers him the principles whereby he can pursue the good life, here following Giles of Rome's *De regimine principum*—which, incidentally, was a source of the *Liber de ludo scaccorum* as well. That is all we have of the *Echecs amoureux*, because the unique surviving manuscript breaks off at this point; but it is very clear that the poem had an unequivocally moral ending.

There is no evidence, however, that Chaucer was directly influenced by either of these works; neither does he show any interest in their methods of allegorization. The Man in Black's complaint about having been checkmated by Fortune (652–89) may have been prompted by a brief reference in Machaut's *Remede de Fortune*: 'Everywhere she [i.e. Fortune] wanders she gets such pleasure from her tricks that in victory she exclaims proudly "Checkmate"!' (1189–92; trans. Wimsatt and Kibler, pp. 232, 234). But the technical details relating to the playing of chess, along with the notion that 'Athalus' was its inventor (*pace* Jacques de Cessoles), seem to be largely derived from the *Roman de la Rose*, lines 6619–710, where the chess allegory has a very different application, to the battles between Charles of Anjou and his enemies which resulted in Charles's defeat. Jean de Meun cited John of Salisbury's *Policraticus* on the connection of chess with arithmetic (i. 5); Chaucer may have followed up that reference, because Pythagoras (667) is mentioned by John of Salisbury but not by Jean. At any rate, it would seem that Chaucer's use of the imagery of chess works within parameters which are far more literal-minded and limited in didactic terms than those found in either the *Liber de ludo scaccorum* or the *Echecs amoureux*.

A comparison of the *Book of the Duchess* with hunting allegories yields the same result. We need look no further than a work composed by Blanche's father, the *Livre des Seyntz Medicines* of Henry of Lancaster. This includes an allegorical fox-hunt, in which the female fox is read as 'Peresce'—that is, sloth or idleness, the mother of the vices. Henry compares the fox's den, with its entrances, to the human body and its orifices. Within is a corner, a man's heart, where the vixen cohabits with the male, 'Orgoil' or Pride, to bring forth their cubs, these being the five other deadly sins. Foxes hide in their dens during the day, but roam abroad by night, seeking their prey. Henry allegorizes this in terms of how the evil of the human heart is generally kept concealed, but at night the vices issue forth secretly to do harm. The fox-hunter is interpreted as the father confessor. After he has drawn forth a confession of the sins—that is, forced the foxes out of their holes and killed them—this figure has their pelts displayed on the wall of the lord's hall. This is to be seen, according to Henry, as the perpetual memory, which is painful and shaming, of the sins which is to be kept always before the eyes of the heart.

Clearly, here we are in a quite different realm from the one in which Chaucer's poem operates. However, particularly in view of the emphasis which Robertson and others have placed on the idleness in which the Man in Black first gave himself up to love, it is essential that we look at another, more literal feature, which occurs in so many of the late medieval treatises on hunting that Thiébaux can describe it as a commonplace—the belief that hunting is a cure for idleness. It is very much present in Henry of Lancaster's *Livre des Seyntz Medicines*, for instance, wherein Peresce is described as an evil enchantress who causes the loss of many a good thing. Henry imagines the slothful man, who should be rising to perform some service for God or to do some other good, protesting that it is too early to get up, that the weather is too bad to go hunting or hawking. He will murmur, 'Laissez moi dormir ou penser en mes amors!' Similarly, according to the *Master of Game* which Edward, second Duke of York, compiled between 1406 and 1413, hunting enables men to avoid the seven deadly sins, for if they linger in bed or indoors, they incline to 'ymagynacioun of fleshly lust & plaisere'. Should the Man in Black, then, be seen as wilfully refusing to take part in the hart-hunt, preferring to indulge his overcharged imagination? I think not, believing (as argued above) that this refusal quietly implies his withdrawal from the game of love, due to the absence of his lady. As for his original idleness, Chaucer has taken pains to contrast it with the emotional and moral maturity which the Man in Black has achieved thanks to the tutelage of fair White. In this regard he is heavily indebted to Machaut's *Remede de Fortune*. There, as the lover himself readily admits, once 'Youth governed me and kept me in idleness, my works were fleeting, my heart was changeable' (47–50; p. 170). But his mistress becomes the 'model and guide' in all he does (3585–6), and so, with the aid of Hope, he makes himself worthy of her, and she gladly accepts him into her service. Looking back, he can condemn his earlier self as being 'young and small, silly, childish and infantile, void of sense and quite naïve, of very weak understanding' and 'accustomed to idleness' (3573–7; pp. 366, 368). Chaucer's black knight boasts a similar *curriculum vitae*, and he too has left idleness behind.

What, then, of Chaucer's description of this figure as being only 24 years old (455) when he laments his loss, a fact which is often seized on by those modern allegorizers who wish to argue that the Man in Black is definitely not Gaunt but a figure of unrighteous and inappropriate grief? The age specification can be explained, with varying degrees of plausibility, in quite different terms. In his note on line 455 W. W. Skeat suggested a textual corruption: instead of reading .xxiiij it should read .xxviiij, Gaunt being 29 in 1369, a year which in earlier scholarship was often suggested for the death of Blanche. But the convincing argument that she died in 1368 (cf. p. 80 above), when Gaunt would have been 28, undermines that argument, unless of course one invokes the principle that medieval citations of dates are often rather approximate or accepts Phillips's suggestion that 29 could be taken as 'the age of Gaunt as a mourner, at the time the poem was written' (p. 153 n.). The problem could be solved with the suggestion that what Chaucer actually wrote was .xxviij, which was corrupted to .xxiiij (a v/i substitution being easier than the omission of the v which Skeat postulated). Alternatively, since 1374 may have been the first year in which Gaunt personally attended the annual commemoration of his first wife's death, it could be argued that a scribal error turned .xxxiiij (Gaunt's age in 1374) into .xxiiij. The second of these three theories is, for me, the most attractive. 'Of the age of eighte and twenty yer' seems, and sounds, feasible.

If such number games are left aside, other possible solutions present themselves. For example, that the emphasis on the Man in Black's youth may distance the poem from the present (say, 1374, when Gaunt had remarried), thus reactivating the feelings of loss and grief so intense at that time in the most tactful and decorous way possible. Or that Chaucer employed the age specification to contrast the character encountered by the dreamer with the even younger self who first set eyes on White, as a man in his 'firste youthe' (799). It is a means whereby her achievement in bringing her lover from callow youth to relative maturity may be emphasized. Now without her, the man dresses in black and adopts the trappings of old age; he brings the cold breath of winter into the Maytime garden, as Mary Dove argues. In this way the passage of time and the ageing process are intimated. It should be noted that he is described as being 'ryght yong' *both* when he first sees his lady *and* when the text brings him forward to tell his story to the dreamer (1090 and 453). But this need not undermine the suggestion we have just made, since the adjective may be used loosely, and certainly does not contradict the strong impression here given that the figure who is addressing the dreamer is older, wiser, and certainly sadder than the very young *sujet* who first fell in love with White.

This theory gains some support from one of the methods of computing and describing the ages of man which was current in Chaucer's day, the scheme of seven ages as promulgated, for instance, in Ptolemy's *Tetrabiblos*. Here youth is supposed to last from the ages of 14 to 22. This is when a man first feels the stirrings of love: 'At this time particularly a kind of frenzy enters the soul, incontinence, desire for any chance sexual gratification, burning passion, guile, and the blindness of the impetuous lover' (trans. in Burrow, *Ages of Man*, p. 198). The following period, however, of 'young manhood' or 'middle' age (which lasts until one is around 40), is a time in which the soul seeks 'the mastery and direction of its actions, desire for substance, glory, and position, and a change from playful, ingenuous error to seriousness, decorum, and ambition'. Applying this scheme to the *Book of the Duchess*, it may be argued that the 24-year-old Man in Black, enjoying his period of serious and decorous 'young manhood', is looking back on his 'youth', when he first felt love's stirrings; White's example and advice eased his passage to a state of relative maturity. There is no indication of how old he was when he first met her. However, we are told that a 'longe tyme' passed before the

Man in Black's initial declaration of love (1148), that 'another yere' elapsed between White's rejection and subsequent acceptance of him (1258), and that they lived happily together 'ful many a yere' (1296). Therefore, we can, as it were, subtract enough years from 24 to infer a 'firste youthe' well within Ptolemy's period which ends at 22.

Against this, however, it may be pointed out that there were other medieval schemes of the ages of man, which postulated three (following Aristotle), four, or six stages; according to all these the 24-year-old Man in Black would be located as still in his *adolescentia*. For instance, the medical writer known to the West as Johannitius (who specifies four ages) has 'adolescence' end in 'the twenty-fifth or thirtieth year' (trans. in Burrow, p. 23); while the encyclopaedist Isidore of Seville (who believes that there are six) says that it 'extends up to twenty-eight years' (trans. in Burrow, p. 201). It could be replied, however, that according to these schemes the real-life John of Gaunt, 28 at the time of Blanche's death, was still well within *adolescentia* if we apply Johannitius's model and just within it if we apply Isidore's. So Chaucer may simply have thought of Gaunt's age as falling within a broad 'band' (i.e. of 'adolescence'), which he chose to mark as 'foure and twenty yer'. To expect him to have known Gaunt's actual birth-date, and hence his actual age, is to apply modern standards; after all, as already noted, Froissart thought that Blanche was 'about 22 years' when she died, whereas she was probably 27 (cf. p. 87 above). And it may be added that medieval people set aside clerical expertise when it suited them, as when in his *Lay de Franchise* (1385) Deschamps flatteringly alludes to the 16-year-old Charles VI, 'a King, who indeed should be loved, for nowhere is there one more handsome or with gentler manner. Nature could well give him sixteen years of age, who—before he was thirteen—won such great renown when he overcame 26,000 men in battle' (149–56; trans. Windeatt, p. 154. This passage refers to the Battle of Rosebech, fought in November 1382). So the degree of influence which the above-mentioned schemes really had on men's thoughts and actions is very debatable. In sum, it is dangerous to identify Chaucer's term 'firste youthe' with *adolescentia* unless one specifically has the 'seven ages' scheme in mind. What is sufficiently clear is that the poet definitely wanted to make a distinction between the Man in Black's early youth, when he first fell in love with White, and his later youth, when he describes to the dreamer what he has won and lost.

In this distinction may be found the key to the positive value bestowed upon youth (or, at least, later youth!) in the *Book of the Duchess*, this being in marked contrast to the more negative way in which it is regarded generally in the *Behaingne*. There the personification Youth is described as very cheerful and full of happiness, incapable of holding to any pledge or promise unless it is in accord with her desires. A lover, she declares, would be a fool to listen to Reason—at which point the King of Bohemia laughs heartily, recognizing that she 'spoke only as she ought', which I presume means that she is speaking in accordance with her nature as he perceives it (1848–99; trans. Wimsatt and Kibler, pp. 152, 154). Reason is rather less polite to her, as when she declares that Youth is feeding the jilted knight 'with folly' in encouraging him to persist in loving the woman who wronged him (1755–7; p. 148). Most important of all, one of the reasons why Reason is so confident that the sorrowing lady will promptly forget her past love is that Youth, who by nature is cheerful and joyous, will soon assert herself and thus ensure such oblivion, for Youth 'soon forgets what she doesn't see' (1683–7; p. 144). Chaucer's Man in Black might have felt like that in his 'firste youthe'—but that was some time ago, and a gulf of experience separates the present figure from the callow character he once was. He is still quite young—after all, youth is the time for love, and the speaker is still deeply in that state—but not *that* young.

Perhaps even more remarkable is the difference between the *Book of the Duchess* and what is arguably the most sophisticated treatment of youth (and in particular of its relationship to love) in all the Old French *dits*, as found in Froissart's *Le Joli Buisson de Jonece* ('The Fair Arbour of Youth'). Here an older I-persona (some 35 years of age, well into his maturity on any medieval theory of the ages of man) dreams his way back to past youth and love. But the personification Youth is confronted and interrogated: why, the persona asks, can his one-time mistress now be so young and fresh, as she was in the past? By way of reply, Youth offers two *exempla*: one, featuring the lovers who were blinded by love to their own ageing; the other, concerning a dead mistress who stays young only in her lover's dreams. This is hardly reassuring: it would seem that love, together with the youthfulness which seems necessary for its existence, survives only in the eyes of beholders who are intent on ignoring reality. Thus the limitations of Youth's arguments and point of view are very obvious, and there is no real room left for doubting the conclusion towards which the whole poem moves: namely, that one cannot live in the past; Nature will take her course, and this fact must be accepted. The persona awakens to thoughts of approaching death and divine judgement; the poem ends with a prayer to the Virgin.

Youth—or at least 'later youth', as I have termed it—has a higher value than that in the *Book of the Duchess*, and the didacticism of the *Joli Buisson* is not shared by Chaucer's poem, either explicitly or (in my view) implicitly. This is not to deny that Chaucer's poem is didactic, however, but rather to claim that it is didactic in a different sort of way, which we may now investigate. It may indeed be read as offering a remedy—but in my view the cure in question is not of a spiritual condition (excessive love of the temporal) but rather of a psychological and physical one, a condition which is the concern of the doctor of medicine rather than the doctor of divinity. The ailment in question is *melancholia*. Methods of treating it are inscribed in the text, and the text itself seems to function in some measure as a cure for melancholy, in a manner which is resolutely secular rather than religious. Earthly causes are indicated for earthly ills, and ultimately the poem prescribes moderate and restorative recollection of pleasant experiences which, however wonderful they were, are yet of this world. It should never be forgotten that when, in the *Retracciouns*, Chaucer came to make his peace with his Maker, he included 'the book of the Duchesse' in his list of 'enditynges of worldly vanitees'. Had he not avoided allegory, it might have been a different story.

Boethius, *The Theological Tractates and 'The Consolation of Philosophy'*, ed. and trans. H. F. Stewart, E. K. Rand, and S. J. Tester (Cambridge, Mass., and London, 1973). At II, pr. iv, 18–24, Boethius's own wife is portrayed as living only for him, though she detests this present life: 'she is wasting away in tears in her grievous longing for you.' The best that can be said about her is that she is like her father, the noble Symmachus.

On the medieval Alcibiades see Minnis (ed.), *Chaucer's 'Boece'*, pp. 127–8, 192, 194, 195 n. Interestingly, in *BD* Chaucer seems to regard him (accurately, of course) as a man: see lines 1056–67, where beautiful Alcibiades is followed by two obviously male exemplars, strong Hercules and worthy Alexander. This passage is indebted to Machaut's *Remede de Fortune*, 107–27, but Alcibiades is not included in this particular list, Absalon being the representative of attractive manhood. For the commentary tradition on the Boethian version of the Orpheus myth see Minnis and Scott (eds.), *Medieval Literary Theory*, pp. 121, 320–1, 332–6; also the relevant discussion in J. B. Friedman, *Orpheus in the Middle Ages* (Cambridge, Mass., 1971).

Machaut, *'Behaigne' and 'Fortune'*, ed. and trans. Wimsatt and Kibler.

D. W. Robertson, 'The Historical Setting of the *Book of the Duchess*'; originally published in 1965, repr. in *idem, Essays in Medieval Culture* (Princeton, 1980), pp. 235–56, from which the above citations are taken. Robertson goes so far as to say that 'There is no probability whatsoever' that the Man in Black 'was meant to represent literally anyone in Chaucer's audience, least of all John of Gaunt' (p. 242). B. F. Huppé and D. W. Robertson, *Fruyt and Chaf: Studies in Chaucer's Allegories* (Princeton, NJ, 1963), pp. 33–99. See further Robertson's contribution on *BD* in Beryl Rowland (ed.), *Companion to Chaucer Studies* (Toronto, New York, and London, 1968), pp. 332–40, and of course the remarks on the poem in his highly influential study, *Preface to Chaucer*, esp. pp. 463–7. Part of his interpretation is contested by Rooney, *Hunting*, who argues that the 'hunt of Christ and His Church is not a motif which was developed in Middle English Literature outside a satirical context' (p. 144).

Caxton, *The Game and Playe of the Chesse* (1474), reprinted with an introduction by William E. A. Axon (1883, repr. St Leonards-on-Sea, Sussex, n.d.). Caxton begins his translation with a quotation from St Paul (Romans 15: 4): 'all that is written is written for our doctrine' (pp. 3–4). As already noted, this is also how the *Ovide moralisé* begins.

*Echecs amoureux* references are given on p. 54 above. The text and commentary are discussed by A. J. Minnis, 'Late-Medieval Vernacular Literature and Latin Exegetical

Traditions', in J. Assmann and B. Gladiglow (eds.), *Text und Kommentar. Archäologie der literarischen Kommunikation IV* (Munich, 1994), pp. 309–29.

It is important to note that in the medieval game of chess the status of the queen was rather lower than in the modern version, its possible movement being far more restricted (one square diagonally). Thus Caxton, in his translation of Jacques de Cessoles, says that 'when she is meuyd ones oute of her place she may not goo but fro oon poynt to an other and yet cornerly whether hit be foreward or backward takynge or to be taken' (p. 170). This restricted movement is explained in gender terms: 'hit is not fittynge ne couenable thynge for a woman to goo to bataylle for the fragilite and feblenes of her.' In view of this, how can the Man in Black say that, once his 'fers' was taken, he can 'no longer playe' and is checkmated (655–61)? The medieval strategy may have been to keep the queen in close attendance on the king; therefore, when the queen is taken, the king will soon be checkmated. Alternatively, the point could be that, even though the loss of a queen is not in itself serious, the special affection which the black knight has for this piece renders him incapable of playing properly after it has gone, and so he is soon checkmated. For discussion see S. W. Stevenson, 'Chaucer's Ferses Twelve', *ELH* 7 (1940), 215–22; F. D. Cooley, 'Two Notes on the Chess Terms in the *Book of the Duchess*', *MLN* 63 (1948), 30–5; W. H. French, 'Medieval Chess and the *Book of the Duchess*', *MLN* 64 (1949), 261–4; Beryl Rowland, 'The Chess Problem in Chaucer's *Book of the Duchess*', *Anglia*, 80 (1962), 384–9. See further H. J. R. Murray, *A History of Chess* (Oxford, 1913), esp. pp. 396–402, 421–8. Chaucer's reference to *twelve* 'ferses' (723) remains an intractable problem.

*Roman de la Rose*, ed. Langlois, trans. Dahlberg. John of Salisbury, *Policraticus*, ed. Webb, trans. Pike.

Henry of Lancaster, *Livre des Seyntz Medicines*, ed. E. J. Arnould (Oxford, 1940), pp. 22–3. Cf. Thiébaux, *Stag of Love*, pp. 79–80; for a more detailed account see her article, '*Sir Gawain*, the Fox Hunt and Henry of Lancaster', *NM* 71 (1970), 469–79. Edward, second Duke of York, *The Master of Game*, ed. W. A. and F. Baillie-Grohman (London, 1909); cf. Thiébaux, *Stag of Love*, p. 79, and also V. J. Scattergood, '*Sir Gawain and the Green Knight* and the Sins of the Flesh', *Traditio*, 37 (1981), 347–71 (esp. pp. 357–8).

Skeat (ed.), *Works*, i, note to line 455; cf. Kooper, *Love, Marriage and Salvation*, p. 163. Phillips (ed.), *BD*.

Mary Dove, *The Perfect Age of Man's Life* (Cambridge, 1986); for her elegant discussion of *BD* see pp. 141–7. 'Suffering from an excess of melancholy', she comments, the Man in Black 'is like a man in his old age; cold and on the verge of death, he is under the malign influence of Saturn; his stage of life corresponds to the depths of winter' (p. 143).

John Burrow, *The Ages of Man: A Study in Medieval Writing and Thought* (Oxford, 1986). Deschamps, *Lay de Franchise*, in *Œuvres*, ed. Marquis de Queux de Saint-Hilaire and G. Raynaud, ii. 203–14; trans. Windeatt. My comments on Blanche's age rest on the assumption that she was born in 1341.

Froissart, *Le Joli Buisson de Jonece*, ed. A. Fourrier (Geneva, 1975). It includes an elaborate exposition (in lines 1611–707) of the Ptolemaic seven ages. See Burrow, *Ages of Man*, pp. 40–3, 179–80, to which my own discussion of this poem is indebted.

AVOIDING MELANCHOLY: 'PLAYE' VERSUS PLAGUE

In the later Middle Ages various ideas circulated concerning the beneficial effects of the reading of literature, most of which fall into one or other of two large categories. As a break from more serious occupations, literature was supposed to relieve mental tension, ensuring that the spirit remained strong and supple (this constitutes the 'recreational' justification of literature). Moreover, as decorous entertainment, it was believed to promote physical and mental well-being (the 'hygienic' justification). Too little literature, it seems, can damage one's health.

The second of these theories of healthy reading, the 'hygienic' rationale, is of most interest to us here. According to the medical lore found in the *Secretum secretorum*, a popular treatise belonging to the 'instruction of princes' genre, proper and moderate joy and gladness ensure a man's good health and digestion. These emotions may be aroused by, for example, looking at beautiful people, hearing pleasant songs—and reading delightful books. In the full-scale medical manuals, reasonable and moderate cheerfulness is recommended as a remedy against melancholy, this being a condition which was then regarded as pathological and a possible cause of death. When at the beginning of the *Book of the Duchess* the suffering dreamer declares, 'drede I have for to dye' (24), this is no exaggeration, but a prognosis which would have seemed utterly plausible to any physician of Chaucer's day. The basic principle involved here is that all illnesses are cured by their contraries, an idea which is stated, and illustrated, with admirable clarity in one of the *exempla* included in Machaut's *Jugement dou Roy de Navarre*. The personification Temperance recounts how a young woman, on learning that her beloved has been killed in a tournament, suffers a mysterious illness. The doctors are baffled until one of them affirms the 'cure by contrary' axiom, explaining that maladies can arise from great sorrow or overwhelming joy. If sorrow is the cause, then

> One should make merry
> In her presence, do whatever would please her
> And whatever she asks for,
> And also minstrels should be summoned
> To entertain her and make her laugh.
>
> (1944–8; trans. Palmer, pp. 87, 89)

That is precisely what Dorigen's friends do, when in the *Franklin's Tale* the 'Desir' of the 'presence' of her husband Arveragus

> . . . hire so destreyneth
> That al this wyde world she sette at noght.        (V(F) 820–1)

Arveragus's absence is temporary rather than permanent, though of course Dorigen is grief-stricken lest it should indeed be permanent—in which case she would, so to speak, be partly re-enacting the role of Queen Alcyone in respect of her beloved King Ceyx. Anyway, her persistent friends 'conforten hire in al that ever they may', telling her that she is killing herself needlessly with her sorrow (823–5), and offering her 'every confort possible in this cas . . . Al for to make hire leve hire hevynesse' (826–8). One of their attempts at cheering her up, walking along the sea-shore 'Hire to disporte' (849), proves counter-productive, however, as her 'darke fantasye' (844) focuses on the 'grisly' black rocks which, she believes, will wreck her husband's returning ship. Realizing what is happening, her friends try other forms of therapeutic play: they take her to delightful places, involve her in dancing, and play at chess and backgammon—

> Hire freendes sawe that it was no disport
> To romen by the se, but disconfort,
> And shopen for to pleyen somwher elles.                    *arranged*
> They leden hire by ryveres and by welles,
> And eek in other places delitables;
> They dauncen and they pleyen at ches and tables    (895–900)

—those board-games being, of course, the ones which the dreamer of the *Book of the Duchess* passed over in favour of the 'better play' of reading (50–1). The notion that an entertaining book could improve one's health is confirmed by the *Tacuinum sanitatis*, an Arabic hygienic manual which was translated into Latin in the thirteenth century. Here it is stated that the teller of tales should know well the type of fictions in which the soul takes delight, and

be a good judge of discourses (not only histories of great princes but also delight-ful stories that provoke laughter), and be conscious of verses and rhymes, so that through these things a prince may gain an abundance of pleasures. For his diges-tion will improve because of them, and his *spiritus* and blood will be purified, and he will be freed from all sort of troubling thoughts. (trans. in Olson, pp. 82–3)

Two specific applications of such theory are of crucial importance for criticism of the *Book of the Duchess*, relating to the efficacy of play (including literary pleasure) as a remedy for sleeplessness and as a means of reducing one's chances of becoming ill—including falling prey to the plague, the disease which (according to most historians) had killed the Duchess Blanche.

At the beginning of Chaucer's poem the narrator is portrayed as a man desperately suffering from 'Defaute of slep and hevynesse' (25); in this unnatural state he has 'felynge in nothyng' (11), and is beset by all kinds of 'ydel' thoughts (4) and 'fantasies' (28). Clearly, he is suffering from 'melancolye' (23), apparently induced by unrequited love (cf. pp. 103–5 above). Whether by accident or design he manages to apply the 'cure by contrary' principle to himself, and looks for some 'play' (albeit to 'drive the night away' rather than as a specific antidote to insomnia; 44–51). He chooses to read a tale of long ago, something of a curiosity, and certainly remote from his own experience to date. His melancholy abates somewhat as this fiction awakens his sense of humour. He can see the funny side of, for example, the awakening of Morpheus, and soon he is jocularly praying to this god for the gift of sleep. 'Sodeynly', 'Such a lust' comes over him to sleep that he falls asleep immediately (272–5). The pleasant book has done its job remarkably well. (Later the narrator will learn, of course, to be rather more respectful of the sufferings of loss and bereavement which are the Ovidian tale's central concern.) In his dream he encounters another type of healthy game—the hart-hunt, which also invigorates him; he is 'ryght glad' when he hears the sounds of the hunt (354–6), and soon he is enjoying the thrill of the chase and the beauties of the countryside. The 'ydel' thoughts to which he confessed at the beginning of the poem (4) have been dispelled; as has already been noted, the hunting manuals regularly recommend hunting as a cure for idleness, and as a health-bestowing activity in general. It would seem that the dreamer is, quite sensibly, cultivating a spirit of reasonable and moderate cheerfulness.

This poetic movement from the portrait of a melancholic I-persona to a vivid hunting scene appears to have been directly influenced by Machaut's *Navarre*, which opens with a graphic account of the ravages of the plague, and so we must consider the implications of this connection in some detail. The central notion involved here is that there were two main predisposing causes of the plague against which one could take precautions; sad thoughts and bad air (a poisoned atmosphere was then believed to cause the disease) were to be avoided at all costs. John Lydgate's ballade on the pestilence sums it up well:

> Who will been holle & kepe hym from sekenesse
> And resiste the strok of pestilence.
> Lat hym be glad, & voide al hevynesse,
> Flee wikkyd heires, eschew the presence          *avoid*
> Off infect placys . . .
> Smelle swote thynges, & for his deffence          *sweet*
> Walk in cleene heir; eschewe mystis blake.

With these thoughts in mind, we may turn to the *Navarre*.

Machaut begins this poem with an extensive account of his persona's *merencolie*, seen in the wide perspective of a time of death and disorder. The setting is November; the cold north wind has destroyed summer's greenery and cut down many a flower with its sword (32–6). The world is ruled by Avarice, laments the narrator, and all is vanity. These general musings give way to 'a much greater melancholy' (142; p. 9) as his mind focuses on specific calamitous events. grim portents in the heavens, including a lunar eclipse (presumably a reference to the eclipse of 17 January 1348) and a comet; a great earthquake which destroyed many villages and cities in Germany and Carinthia (this actually occurred on 25 January 1348); a new outbreak of wars and 'savage killings'; the alleged poisoning of the water supply by the Jews (a reference to an outbreak of anti-Semitism which was triggered by the early manifestations of the plague in northern Europe). There follows a description of the ravages of the plague itself. Seeing mankind bent on self-destruction, Nature makes her displeasure known by creating terrible storms, which give rise to filthy vapours that poison the air, making it 'vile, black and heavy' (here Machaut is invoking the common medieval explanation of the origins of plague). 'Five hundred thousand died' (332; p. 17); family bonds break down, and friendships dissolve as everyone tries to save themselves. 'In order to exact justice and vengeance' (354), God unleashes Death, a monster so rapacious that he cannot be satisfied until he has consumed everything. Machaut does not spare us any of the gory details: great heaps of corpses (of young and old, male and female, high and lowly) are thrown together into mass graves; once infected, no one lasted more than three days; men who carried the dead to the church themselves did not return; so many died that it was impossible to make an accurate reckoning.

At a time at which even 'the bravest trembled' (435; p. 21), the narrator tells of how (having made a full confession of his sins) he shut himself away in his house, cutting himself off from what was happening in the city, thereby feeling less melancholy because he had no idea of how many of his friends were dying. This passage should probably not be read as heavily self-denigratory: after all, the Machaut persona is simply following the advice which was offered so regularly in the plague tracts and the literature which they influenced: 'Flee wikkyd heires, eschew the presence / Off infect placys.' As well as escaping from that poisonous air, he is also avoiding as much 'hevynesse' as he can: seeing his friends die would only make him intensely depressed, thereby increasing his own chances of infection. The plague treatise of the Florentine physician Tommaso del Garbo advises against occupying 'your mind with death, passion, or anything likely to sadden or grieve you, but give your thoughts over to delightful and pleasing things'. 'Associate with happy and carefree people and avoid all melancholy,' he continues; 'Spend your time in your house, but not with too many people,' and enjoy 'gardens with fragrant plants, vines, and willows, when they are flowering' (trans. in Olson, p. 175). At the beginning of Boccaccio's *Decameron*, which opens with an equally detailed and horrific account of the ravages of the plague of 1348 (in Florence in this case), the lady Pampinea justifies her proposal to move to the countryside in similar terms. 'How can it possibly be wrong', she asks, 'for us or anyone else to do all in our power to preserve our lives?' (trans. McWilliam, pp. 59–62). If they remain, all they can do is count the number of corpses or hear whether or not the friars (those who are left) are continuing to chant their offices or 'exhibit the quality and quantity of our sorrows, by means of the clothes we are wearing, to all those whom we meet'. Moreover, they would continue to hear accounts of who is dead or dying, 'and if there were anyone left to mourn, the whole place would be filled with sounds of wailing and weeping'. Pampinea admits to sorrowful thoughts even in her own house: there she seems to be 'haunted by the shades of the departed, whose faces no longer appear' as she remembers them 'but with strange and horribly twisted expressions' that frighten her out of her senses. In the countryside, by contrast, they will see 'fresh green hills and plains', lovely 'fields of corn', and 'trees of at least a thousand species'; moreover, 'the country air is much more refreshing.'

Statements like these might encourage us to read Chaucer's descriptions of natural beauty in, to revivify the cliché, a new light. His beautiful dream chamber is filled with the merry and sweet sounds of bird-song; through his windows bright and clear light shines, and the air is 'clere' (291–343). There is not a cloud in the sky, no hint of any infection in the atmosphere. Later, after the narrator has ventured out of doors to take part in the hart-hunt, we are treated to a description of a landscape blessed with beautiful trees and flowers of every kind and teeming with all types of wildlife (397–442). To an audience which had suffered the trauma of plague, and was obsessed with the advantages of 'clere', country air, those lines would have a resonance which is rather lost on us. 'Conventional' such statements may be (within the traditions of the Old French *dits*), but within the cultural poetics relevant to the *Book of the Duchess*, they take on new life and definite connotations.

But let us return to the *Navarre*. At last, the horrors of the pestilence have passed; it is all over. The Machaut persona hears horns, trumpets, and drums: the survivors are celebrating, and he himself marks the joyful occasion by going hunting.

> I went quickly through the fields
> Riding for pleasure,
> In order to entertain and solace myself (*jouer et soulacier*)
> And to claim for my own the sweetness
> That came from the country and from that enjoyment
> In which the heart willingly delights
> Which has no concern for the pain
> That is a part of trouble or strife
>
> (491 9; trans. Palmer, p. 23)

Soon, he has forgotten all 'those former melancholic thoughts' (543). Then, the *Navarre* changes tack, as the persona encounters a noble lady who is later identified as Bonneürté (Good Fortune, Happiness). Here Machaut is, to some extent, celebrating his own good fortune in being alive; the specific way in which the fiction develops, however, is through a challenge to a judgement offered in his *Jugement dou Roy de Behaingne*. The terms in which the subsequent debate is initiated and conducted are quite crucial for an understanding of what Machaut is about: for this, too, is presented as a kind of game. One type of honourable and edifying recreation, the hare-hunt, has been exchanged for another, the decorous argument about which person has the more ill fortune, the man whose lady has been unfaithful to him or the lady whose beloved has died. For the Machaut persona welcomes the idea of a debate and the judgement of some wise and discreet individual as affording joyful entertainment: 'it will be a pleasant task,' he declares, to hear all the arguments (1084–5; p. 49). And the lady laughingly agrees (1089–93). In a very real sense, Happiness (Bonneürté) instigates and organizes the entire discussion. Without in any way undervaluing the genuine profundity of many of the matters over which the discussion ranges or wishing to deny that on occasion its participants genuinely are upset or feel anger, it may be accepted that the recreational parameters within which it is conducted are firmly in place.

Similarly, in the *Decameron* the ten noble young men and ladies opt to tell tales in preference to playing chess or other board-games, an activity which develops into a sort of debate as narrators tell tales in a spirit of competition. 'Embrace cheerfulness in a reasonable way,' advises Tommaso del Garbo in his plague treatise, and here music and story-telling have their part to play: 'make use of songs and minstrelsy and other pleasurable tales without tiring yourselves out, and all the delightful things that bring anyone comfort' (trans. in Olson, p. 175). Boccaccio's characters seem to be doing precisely that. Reviewing the fortnight they have spent together, Panfilo remarks on how they 'departed from Florence to provide for our relaxation, preserve our health and our lives, and escape from the sadness, the suffering and the anguish continuously to be found in our city' (trans. McWilliam, pp. 824–5). 'These aims we have achieved', he continues, 'without any loss of decorum.' The tales may have been somewhat risqué, perhaps, and they have eaten well, played music, and sung many songs, but the 'proceedings have been marked by a constant sense of propriety'. Clearly, here the principle of 'reasonable cheerfulness' prevails.

In the *Decameron*, as in the *Navarre*, literary pleasure (whether in telling tales and/or recounting *exempla* or debating the merits of a poem)

is frequently 'enjoyment in which the heart willingly delights which has
no concern for the pain that is a part of trouble or strife'. Indeed, the
*avoidance* of such pain is at the very centre of these works which, having
begun with the horrors of contemporary trouble and strife, proceed to do
their very best to purge and dispel them through pleasing fiction. We are
dealing not with some sort of naïve escapism, however, but with a rational strategy for reducing the risk of illness, as approved by late medieval
medical science. And in the *Navarre* to some extent the Machaut persona
is being offered, so to speak, as a psychic role model for the reader. In its
entirety this poem offers a cure for melancholy which has much in common with the remedies which are shown within its text to prove
efficacious for its I-persona.

In the *Book of the Duchess* too, the narrator is shown as attempting to
cope with his melancholy through decorous 'pleye' (in reading and hunting), this being a matter of some importance since, as already noted, it
provides a rationale for those elements of humour in the poem which
some have found incongruous. But here the psychic role model is the
Man in Black rather than the narrator, an argument I offer in diametric
opposition to the view that the fictional character's behaviour is (at least
in part) unworthy of the memory of the real-life Blanche. My basic point
is that while the Man in Black is suffering from melancholy just like the
narrator, the ways in which he is portrayed as coping with it are shown
to be more admirable than are the narrator's tactics.

Initially the black knight is presented as avoiding the company of men
and isolating himself in a lonely part of the woods, impervious to the
beauties of nature and the pleasures of the hunt. He can produce a poem
(the 'compleynte to hymselve'), but this is expressive of 'pitee' and
'rowthe' rather than of any joyful theme (461–6). The dreamer comments
on how the 'spirites' of this noble figure 'wexen dede' (490) and his woes
lie 'colde upon hys herte' (490, 508); his condition is so desperate that he
is lucky to be alive.

> Hit was gret wonder that Nature
> Myght suffre any creature
> To have such sorwe and be not ded.    (467–9)

But it is far less desperate than that of the lady who, according to the
*exemplum* narrated by Machaut's Temperance, becomes gravely ill on
hearing that her lover has been killed in a tournament (*Navarre*,
1863–2012; trans. Palmer, pp. 84–91; cf. p. 147 above). All that the physician who correctly diagnoses her ailment can do is say that 'Her heart is
locked within the tower of Love, by the key of Sadness'; 'In this place
she suffers great distress, and thus she shall die soon; she'll never escape'

(1991–6; pp. 89, 91). And die she does. Moreover, unlike Dorigen and her obsession with those black rocks which may kill her husband, the Man in Black has not fallen the utter victim of depression. For he can greet the dreamer with a politeness, even a cheerfulness, which seems quite unforced. Clearly, there is much hope for him yet. While he takes no interest in the hunt, he does engage in conversation with the dreamer—and conversation, according to the medieval medical treatises, has a medical value. Talk about delightful things, for example, was supposed to encourage sleep which is health-inducing and free from bad dreams. Certainly the Man in Black recovers something of his vitality in the very telling of his story, a tale which celebrates life rather than morbidly indulging in thoughts about death. For its subject is something which is highly pleasant—fair White's beauty of body and mind and the conduct of their delightful love-affair.

To equate the Man in Black with John of Gaunt would be absurd, while to deny the connection would be perverse. The character's extraordinary self-control and reasonableness mark out flattering similarities between the two figures, the one fictional and the other historical. Thanks to his own remarkable mental powers, the Man in Black is in no real danger of dying. Thus Gaunt is being represented as a man of impressive mental stability, who is therefore not at 'high risk' of becoming seriously ill or indeed of catching the very disease which killed his wife. And here the *Book of the Duchess* may help, if only a little; as a pleasing fiction, it is 'better play' than any board-game or even hunting, an appropriate entertainment by which an aristocrat may drive the night away and have his sorrow assuaged. Inasmuch as the Man in Black is *not* Gaunt, this constructed selfhood offers Gaunt and his household a model for mourning, a model which is striking in its consummate nobility and secularity. Or, to read in a slightly different way, the extent to which the Man in Black elaborately suffers, and is at least initially said to be in some danger of death, may serve as a gentle warning of the dangers of dwelling on the past with the wrong kind of attitudes and feelings, while at the same time giving voice to the quite understandable grief of those who knew and loved Blanche. The manner in which the *Book of the Duchess* offers a positive way of dwelling on the past will be considered next.

*Secretum secretorum. Nine English Versions*, ed. M. A. Manzalaoui, EETS OS 276 (Oxford, 1977), pp. 4, 8–9. Machaut, *Navarre*, ed. and trans. Palmer. John Lydgate, *Minor Poems*, ed. H. N. MacCracken, EETS ES 107 and OS 192 (London, 1910, repr. 1961–2), ii. 702. Boccaccio, *Decameron*, trans. G. H. McWilliam (Harmondsworth, 1972).
The above discussion was inevitably influenced by Glending Olson's major study, *Literature as Recreation in the Middle Ages* (Ithaca, NY, and London, 1982), from which

the citations of the *Tacuinum sanitatis* and Tommaso del Garbo's treatise were taken. Tommaso was a friend of Petrarch's. His father, the physician Dino del Garbo, had written a learned commentary on the *Canzone d'Amore* of Guido Cavalcanti, a treatise which Boccaccio mentions approvingly in the commentary he wrote on his own *Teseida*, on which see below, pp. 283–4, 289–90.
See further the excellent discussion by Giuseppe Mazzotta, *The World at Play in Boccaccio's 'Decameron'* (Princeton, NJ, 1986), esp. pp. 16–46 on 'Plague and Play'. For *melancholia* in general see R. Klibansky, E. Panofski, and F. Saxl, *Saturn and Melancholy. Studies in the History of Natural Philosophy, Religion and Art* (London, 1964); see further the major English Renaissance treatise on the subject, Robert Burton's *Anatomy of Melancholy* (first published in 1621; enlarged editions followed), which has recently been edited by H. Jackson (New York, 1977). On melancholy and lovesickness see John M. Hill, 'The *Book of the Duchess*, Melancholy, and that Eight-Year Sickness', *ChR* 9 (1974), 35–50; John L. Lowes, 'The Loveres Maladye of Hereos', *MP* 11 (1913–14), 491–546. On lovesickness more generally see Cadden, *Sex Difference*, pp. 139–41; Danielle Jacquart and Claude Thomasset, *Sexuality and Medicine in the Middle Ages*, trans. M. Adamson (Cambridge and Oxford, 1988), pp. 84–5; and especially Mary W. Wack, *Lovesickness in the Middle Ages: The 'Viaticum' and its Commentaries* (Philadelphia, 1990).

## CONSOLATION AND THE KEY OF REMEMBRANCE

Instead of chronicling the horrors of the plague which cut down Blanche in her prime, the *Book of the Duchess* metamorphoses the duchess into the very quintessence of life and love. Far from being walled-up within the poem, as Ellmann and Hansen would argue (cf. pp. 61–3, 68 above), fair White is 'conserved' therein, not buried alive but given a literary after-life, through a process which was well known and well described in medieval literary theory.

At the beginning of Guido delle Colonne's *Historia destructionis Troiae* (completed in 1287), a text on which Chaucer drew in writing *Troilus and Criseyde* and the *Legend of Hypsipyle and Medea*, the common notion that writing could preserve the past is expressed with economy and elegance:

Writings of the ancients, faithful preservers of tradition, depict the past as if it were the present, and, by the attentive readings of books, endow valiant heroes with the courageous spirit they are imagined to have had, just as if they were alive—heroes whom the extensive age of the world long ago swallowed up by death. (trans. Meek, p. 1)

What is said here about heroes applies equally well to lovers, of course; hence the *Book of the Duchess* can be said to endow Blanche with the spirit she is imagined to have had, when alive; her relationship with John of Gaunt, as constructed in the text, is therefore rescued from oblivion. If 'olde bokes' did not exist, declares Chaucer in the prologue to his *Legend of Good Women*, 'Yloren were of remembrance the keye' (F and G Prol. 25–6). Chaucer's first major poem may therefore be said to offer to

Gaunt and his household a key which will unlock remembrance of their duchess.

The crucial concepts here are imagination and memory. It is by means of *imaginatio* that writers 'depict the past as if it were the present'. Images, phantasms, or mental 'pictures' were supposed to be formed by the imagination and transmitted to the memory, where they were stored; the imagination could summon them up again at will, putting them into various combinations and relationships. Literature was created when such imaginations were put in writing. The *Book of the Duchess* is particularly interesting in that it presents a character, the Man in Black, illustrating that process of imaginative recall of the past which (to apply the traditional rationale) is responsible for its very existence as a poem; here, then, is a literary imagination, or fiction, which contains within itself a (fictional) imagination.

Chaucer's presentation of the Man in Black's imaginings may be seen as yet another aspect of his rewriting of Machaut's *Jugement dou Roy de Behaingne*. Here the bereaved lady claims that, through memory, the rejected knight can enjoy happy thoughts of the woman who loved and left him. His bitter response is that memory brings thoughts of his lady, certainly—but particularly of her faithlessness. 'If Reminiscence (*Pensee*) is engendered in me by Memory (*Souvenir*), what is it like? It is disconsolate, sad, worthless, sorrowful, and dejected' (1048–51; trans. Wimsatt and Kibler, p. 112). And he 'can neither imagine (*ymaginer*) or conceive' that he might regain her (1065–6). Therefore to say that his original joys, which were great, should be remembered is no help, since the greater his former happiness, the worse is his present wretchedness. The *Book of the Duchess* affirms that present wretchedness does not destroy past joys. The Man in Black's memories are of a lady who was as true as she was beautiful; hence they can only be happy—as soon as he moves away from the sad, weary, mournful, and desperate thoughts which are prompted by her death. That movement is enacted by Chaucer's poem. The happy memories are allowed to dominate, in marked contrast to Froissart's extraordinarily sobering *Joli Buisson de Jonece*, which relates the continuation of human love to a blindness to, or ignorance of, reality. There, the mental processes of imagination and memory which allow the perception that love will survive are called in question by ruthless rationalization (cf. p. 144 above). In the *Book of the Duchess* they are left unchallenged. Chaucer seems to be saying that, no matter what the figure Reason in Machaut's *Behaingne* may say, human love does not die with the body, and is more than a matter of bodily affection and fleshly delight. Out of sight is *not* out of mind: the image of fair White will remain in the memory of the Man in Black, just as the image of Blanche will remain in the memory of John of Gaunt (or such is the poem's agenda).

> '. . . while I am alyve her,
> I nyl foryete hir never moo'.                    (1124–5)

But the memories of men, however noble and superior those men may be, are notoriously unreliable, according to medieval faculty psychology. 'Memory is fragile and cannot cope with the whirling storm of things,' declares the preface to a popular reference book, Thomas of Ireland's *Manipulus Florum* (1306); and Vincent of Beauvais, whose 'Estoryal Myrour' was certainly known to Chaucer (cf. *LGW*, G Prol. 307), refers to its slippery nature (*memorie labilitas*). And that was where the writers came in: their books could repair some of the deficiencies of the human mind by functioning as a sort of 'artificial memory' or conservatory of past things. The English Benedictine Ralph Higden summed it up well in the prologue to his 'universal history', the *Polychronicon* (which was finished *c*.1352). A 'schort lyfe, a slawe soule, and a slipper memory' hinder us from knowing many things, declares its fifteenth-century English translator, 'obliuion' being the enemy of memory. Thankfully, God in his mercy has 'provided vse of letters in to the remedy of the imperfeccion of man'. History (*historia*), here bearing the sense of the written record) is 'the testimony of tymes' and 'the memory of life' (*memoria vitae*), 'renewenge as thro immortalite' things which are likely to perish, being in a manner of speaking 'a conseruatiue perpetualle to thynges mortalle'. As a literary *memoria* which exceeds the mental capacity and longevity of any human being, the *Book of the Duchess* may therefore be seen as 'a conseruatiue perpetualle' to one mortal thing of great worth, the duchess Blanche. An act of superlative service, then, to nourish the fragile memories of those who knew and loved her.

The 'truth' of Chaucer's text is therefore fundamentally the same as that of Tennyson's *In Memoriam*:

> This truth came borne with bier and pall,
> I felt it, when I sorrow'd most,
> 'Tis better to have loved and lost,
> Than never to have loved at all                    (lxxxv)

On this argument, the fact that the lady is dead (whether she be fictional White or historical Blanche) does not retrospectively devalue her life and love. The fundamental strategy is to show the Man in Black, and by implication John of Gaunt, that his memory of the beautiful beloved will not die; no one can take that away from him. It *is* better to have loved and lost than not to have had the experience at all. One only has to look at the (apparently unrequited) dreamer to be assured of that, and to appreciate more fully the consolation of experience. *Pace* the Robertsonian reading, the Man in Black's 'passion hath not swerved / To works of weakness', for, thanks to Chaucer, he has found 'An image comforting the mind', and in his 'grief a strength reserved' (to quote *In Memoriam* further). And here we confront the limitations of the medical 'cure by contrary' principle as a reading strategy for the *Book of the Duchess*, despite its descriptive purchase and theoretical relevance. For its oppositions of grief and joy—cheer up someone who is sad, sadden someone who is excessively joyful—are simply too neatly dichotomaic to provide an adequate discourse for criticism of the poem in its entirety. Chaucer's objective was rather to negotiate an area between the joys of Blanche's life (as seen by her fictionalized grieving lover) and the sorrow of her death. And he seems to have succeeded remarkably well.

Whereas Tennyson, like so many elegists, felt obliged to include in his work an affirmation that the dead one 'lives in God, / That God, which ever lives and loves' (*In Memoriam*, cxxxi), Chaucer stayed within the bounds of a secular consolation which encapsulates the conviction that one 'cannot but remember such things were, that were most precious to me' (to draw on Macduff's wonderful words concerning his dead wife and children again; *Macbeth*, IV. iii). This is of the essence of the remembrance which the *Book of the Duchess* illustrates and offers. Its consummate simplicity puts the poem on a par with *Le Lay de Plour*. This 'Lay of Weeping' evidently represents Machaut's penance as assigned at the end of the *Jugement dou Roy de Navarre*, in which (speaking through constructs other than the I-persona) he affirms the view that the sadness of loss through death is, after all, worse than that of unrequited love. Written from the point of view of the bereaved lady in the *Behaingne*, the *Lay de Plour* takes on additional poignancy from the fact that it may well be a veiled commemoration of an actual person—not a man but a woman, Bonne of Luxembourg. Bonne, who died in 1349 or shortly thereafter, was the daughter of the King of Bohemia, who was praised in the earlier poem, and the mother-in-law of the King of Navarre, who is the judge in the later one. (Her name may be echoed in the title of the central personification in the *Navarre*, Bonneürté, which has often been regarded as, in part, an idealized portrait of Bonne.)

'Qui bien ainme a tart oublie', declares the *Lay*. Whoever loves well forgets slowly,

> And the heart that slowly forgets
> Is like the fire that burns
> But cannot easily be put out.
>
> (2–4; trans. Palmer, p. 191)

The better the love, it would seem, the slower the forgetting. For the poem proceeds to valorize the remembrance of past love, something which had been discouraged in the *Behaingne*, as we have seen. Day by day the I-persona's memory of her dear friend grows rather than fades; her weeping nourishes her recollection, just as water nourishes those roots which have survived even after the huge tree to which they remain attached has fallen. When a heart is bent on a noble love-affair,

> It can hardly forget its loved one,
> Rather, always, through memory
> Inclines toward him.
> For the water flowing down
> To the root that remains
> Makes it green again and flourish,
> Bearing fruit:
> Just the same, my heart, weeping
> Bitterly all the time
> Makes my memory grow
> Both day and night.               (26–36; pp. 193, 195)

'The beautiful memory [*bon recort*] that recalls him' to her makes the lady determined never to have another lover (95–9). Seeing him in her thoughts, she finds pleasure (132–3). 'With a heavy heart' she mourns and recalls his 'great worthiness' which she prized so much. In imagination she sees him

> Face to face, so I think,
> Sweet lover,
> And always
> I remember you.                    (180–4; p. 211)

The poem ends with the speaker beseeching God that, before her own life ends, their love may find life in a book: 'Qu'en livre soiens de vie' (210). This prayer has clearly been granted, for the *Lay de Plour* is itself that very 'livre'.

Similarly, in the *Book of the Duchess* the love of John of Gaunt and Blanche finds life, this poem being the *memoria vitae* of Blanche and a remedy against that *memoriae labilitas* which is one of the ills to which the flesh is heir. It is, then, not a book of death but a book of life—in a fundamentally secular sense, for the poem has an agenda which is very different from that of the supreme *Liber vitae*, which is the Bible. The consolation offered by the *Book of the Duchess* is not the consolation of philosophy or theology but the consolation of experience, and the memories of that experience which are evergreen—or forever young, if we may give Shakespeare (almost) the last word.

> ... do thy worst, old Time; despite thy wrong,
> My love shall in my verse ever live young.

(Sonnet 19, 13–14)

Perhaps, after all, 'What will survive of us is love.' And, in total opposition to Larkin's 'Arundel Tomb', the *Book of the Duchess* seeks to prove that this is not an 'almost-instinct' but a genuine instinct. And not 'almost true' but utterly true.

Guido delle Colonne, *Historia destructionis Troiae*, ed. N. E. Griffin (Cambridge, Mass., (1936); trans. M. E. Meek (Bloomington, Ind., and London, 1974).

Machaut, *'Behaingne' and 'Fortune'*, ed. and trans. Wimsatt and Kibler. Froissart, *Joli Buisson*, ed. Fourrier.

R. H. and M. A. Rouse, *Preachers, Florilegia and Sermons: Studies on the 'Manipulus florum' of Thomas of Ireland* (Toronto, 1979); this includes a text of the Preface. Vincent of Beauvais, *Speculum Maius*, Apologia totius operis, ed. A.-D. v. den Bricken, 'Geschichtsbetrachtung bei Vincenz von Beauvais', *Deutsches Archiv für Erforschung des Mittelalters*, 34 (1978), 465. Ralph Higden, *Polychronicon*, ed. C. Babington and J. R. Lumby (London, 1865–86), i. 4–7.

For further information on *imaginatio* and *memoria* as understood in the later Middle Ages see the references on pp. 53–4 above.

Machaut, *Le Lay de Plour* ('Lay of Weeping'), trans. Palmer, with Hoepffner's text, as an appendix to his edition and translation of the *Navarre*, pp. 190–210.

Obviously, my reading differs from that of Mehl, who thinks that 'it seems wrong to overemphasize the significance of the poem as an act of consolation. . . . it does not attempt—or only very hesitatingly—to reach out to those areas from which alone lasting consolation can be hoped for by the true Christian' (*Narrative Poetry*, p. 36). This seems to me to underestimate Chaucer's achievement in using the courtly *dit amoreux* as a vehicle for secular consolation. An elegant reading of that consolation is offered by Philippa Tristram, *Figures of Life and Death in Medieval Literature* (London, 1976). For her, the 'delicate emotions of loss and regret prove finally more durable than the bracing Boethian consolations that the dreamer offers. Imagination prevails over reason, both in persuading the dreamer that the dead still live, and, through that persuasion, finally rendering his advocacy of resignation irrelevant.' In a poem such as this, she continues, 'the dead, in terms of art, do not die' (pp. 119–20).

On Chaucer's lament for the dead in *BD* and other poems see Renate Haas, 'Chaucer's Use of the Lament for the Dead', in J. N. Wasserman and R. J. Blanch (eds.), *Chaucer in the Eighties* (Syracuse, NY, 1986), pp. 23–37. The conventionalized lament (in the Ceyx and Alcyone episode) is said to have, 'among other things, the function of placing the Black Knight in the great community of mourners', this being necessary in order that we can 'appreciate the uniqueness of his personal loss' (p. 25).

*BD* does not draw on the *ars moriendi* ('art of dying') tradition, on which see M. C. O'Connor, *The Art of Dying Well: The Development of the Ars Moriendi* (New York, 1942), and R. Rudolf, *Ars Moriendi* (Cologne, 1959). See further the anthology of essays edited by J. H. M. Taylor, *Dies Illa. Death in the Middle Ages*, Proceedings of the 1983 Manchester Colloquium (Liverpool, 1984). There is an abundance of stimulating material, with the emphasis on later periods, in Philippe Ariès, *The Hour of our Death*, trans. Helen Weaver (1981; repr. Harmondsworth, 1983). More specifically, Chaucer's treatment of death may be better appreciated through comparison with post-medieval literary practices. See the well-organized quotations in D. J. Enright (ed.), *The Oxford Book of Death* (Oxford, 1983), especially the section on 'Love and Death', pp. 243–67.

# The House of Fame

No! I am not Prince Hamlet, nor was meant to be
                (T. S. Eliot, *The Love Song of J. Alfred Prufrock*)

'I neyther am Ennok, ne Elye,
Ne Romulus, ne Ganymede,
That was ybore up, as men rede,
To hevene with daun Jupiter'

                                                        (*HF* 588–91)

Both poets seem to have had in mind Dante's lines:

'Io non Enëa, io non Paulo sono;
me degno a ciò né io né altri 'l crede'.

['I am not Aeneas, I am not Paul,
Of this neither I nor others think me worthy'.]
                                                        (*Inferno*, ii. 32–3)

In the *Inferno* such reticence is short-lived. Dante presents himself as
travelling farther than Virgil in paradise and in poetry. When Virgil can
serve as his guide no longer, the now glorified Beatrice takes over, she
in turn giving way to St Bernard of Clairvaux, the great authority on
Christian love. The implication that the Christian *Comedy* transcends
the pagan *Aeneid* is obvious. Dante's reference to St Paul recalls 2
Corinthians 12: 2–4, where Paul describes how he was elevated 'to the
third heaven', 'whether in the body, or out of the body, I know not:
God knoweth'. 'Caught up into paradise', he 'heard secret words which
it is not granted to man to utter'. In the fourth canto of the *Inferno*,
Dante, welcomed into the distinguished dead poets' society, which has,
along with *l'altissimo poeta* Virgil, Homer, Horace, Ovid, and Lucan as
its most prominent members, enjoys the poetic equivalent of that divine
rapture:

Così andammo infino a la lumera,
parlando cose che 'l tacere è bello,
sì com' era 'l parlar colà dov' era.

[Thus we went onward to the light,
talking of things it is well to pass in silence,
even as it was well to speak of them there.]

                                                        (iv 103–5)

In short, the Dantean *sujet* is 'not Aeneas' nor does he want to be; for in several ways he is his superior; and while he is 'not Paul', his literary exstasis may be recognized as an experience analogous to the saint's. Here is Prince Hamlet after all; a hero-poet determined to take the leading role.

In the *House of Fame*, however, when the Chaucerian *sujet* echoes 2 Corinthians, the emphasis is on his ignorance rather than any heightened understanding:

> Thoo gan y wexen in a were,                    *to grow perplexed*
> And seyde, 'Y wot wel y am here,
> But wher in body or in gost                          *spirit*
> I not, ywys, but God, thou wost',                *don't know*
> For more clere entendement                    *understanding*
> Nas me never yit ysent.
>
> (979–84)

Neither does 'Geffrey' (as the eagle familiarly calls him) go back on his declaration that he is unsuitable material for stellification. 'Artow com hider to han fame?,' asks the mysterious 'oon' who in Fame's hall claims the English poet as a 'Frend'. The (somewhat startling) response is that the story-teller is quite content to have his name perish after his death.

> 'Nay, for sothe, frend,' quod y;
> I cam noght hyder, graunt mercy,
> For no such cause, by my hed!
> Sufficeth me, as I were ded,
> That no wight have my name in honde'.          (1873–7)

And yet, a curious profession of independence follows. The narrator is his own man, who will drink life's experiences as deeply as his ability ('art') will allow. His own opinion of himself is good enough for him.

> 'I wot myself best how I stonde;
> For what I drye, or what I thynke,
> I wyl myselven al hyt drynke,
> Certeyn, for the more part,
> As fer forth as I kan myn art.'          (1878–82)

'Is there anythyng more precyous to the than thiself?,' Dame Philosophy had asked the despondent Boethius. He will answer in the negative, she predicts; in which case, if he has command over himself (by dint of 'tranquillite of thi soule', Chaucer's gloss explains), then he has something in his power that he will never lose, which Fortune can never take away (*Boece* II, pr. iv, 128–49; cf. the Latin text, l. 75). But the narrator's statement in the *House of Fame* does not sound as grand as that.

In his rewriting of the medieval poem, Alexander Pope catches something of Chaucer's tone in the lines,

> Nor Fame I slight, nor for her Favours call;
> She comes unlook'd for, if she comes at all.
>
> *(The Temple of Fame, 513–14)*

Yet Pope's narrator is altogether more analytical and balanced in his reaction to the 'one' who asks if he is 'a Candidate for Praise':

> Tis true, said I, not void of Hopes I came,
> For who so fond as youthful Bards of Fame?
> But few, alas! the casual Blessing boast,
> So hard to gain, so easy to be lost:
> How vain that second Life in other's Breath,
> Th'Estate which Wits inherit after Death! (501–6)

This deliberation ends with a plea for an 'honest' game, the persona asking only for his just deserts:

> Then teach me, Heaven! to scorn the guilty Bays;
> Drive from my Breast that wretched Lust of Praise;
> Unblemish'd let me live, or die unknown,
> Oh grant an honest Fame, or grant me none! (521–4)

The *House of Fame* is not as open and direct as that. Chaucer's narrator denies any claim to fame in a manner which is brusque and unreflective. He is just a visitor to Fame's domains, having come on a simple errand, to collect 'Somme newe tydynges' of love, this being the gift which his guide, Jupiter's eagle, has promised him for the service which he has rendered love's servants.

Once again, the contrast with Dante is instructive. In the passage which forms the epigraph to Eliot's *Prufrock*, *Inferno*, xxvii. 61–6, Guido de Montefeltrano speaks freely to Dante's self-construction only because he believes that no report of what he says will reach the earth. The privileged status of the narrator is thereby indicated: not himself dead, yet a traveller among the dead, he will report their private speech to living men. Chaucer's narrator is also an outsider, uninvolved with the passions and ambitions which move the denizens of his other world. His honouring of love is 'causeles' (667)—that is, not motivated by personal emotion. He is 'in the daunce' of those that Cupid does not advance (639–40). However, unlike Prufrock, the ever unrequited and frustrated lover, the Chaucer persona seems quite content with his distance from love and from the overwhelming question of fame which Pope's narrator was to personalize.

But, how 'fer forth' can his 'art poetical' go? 'The very book in which the poet proposes to eschew the poetic art', argues J. A. W. Bennett, 'is in part devoted to enumerating the great poets of old time, and essentially to the discovery of new poetic *matière*. In one sense the whole work is a vindication of poetry' (p. xi). This, he adds, is 'the one work' of Chaucer's 'that dwells on the nature and rewards of poetic achievement; the work in which he follows in the footsteps of poetry's two greatest princes (Virgil and Dante) and gives due honour and regard to lesser writers; the work in which he presents himself as a seeker after fresh poetic inspiration, new poetic "tidings"' (p. 3). Similarly, Piero Boitani believes that Chaucer's invocation of the Muses implies that he considers himself the heir of the ancients and is seeking to follow Dante's example in claiming admission to the élite company of poets who are united by mastery of their craft and the bond of superlative wisdom which they share (cf. *Inferno*, iv. 94–102).

It may freely be admitted that the range of literary reference in the poem is extraordinary: Ovid, Virgil, Boethius, Claudian, Alan of Lille, Martianus Capella, Dante . . . not to mention the writers listed in book iii as bearing on their shoulders the 'matters' of 'Jewerye', Thebes, and Troy. Further substantiation for the view that Chaucer took his poem very seriously indeed is afforded by its division into books. This, as John Burrow says, is a definite neo-classical or learned feature, a novelty in English poetry around 1380. (Chaucer was to use the device again in his *Troilus*.) Then again, in many respects the *House of Fame* is quite uncompromising intellectually; it does not suffer fools gladly. For instance, only someone with a reasonable grasp of the detail of the *Aeneid*—whether obtained from the original, the French romanticized version, or some summary—could appreciate the significance of a poem about Fame beginning with the story of Dido and Aeneas. Nowhere does Chaucer make clear the fact that Virgil's description of Fame forms an excursus within the Roman poet's account of the doomed love-affair (its point of departure being the rumours about the relationship which are said to circulate throughout Libya). On the contrary, Chaucer actually distances the description of Fame from the story of Dido and Aeneas (with the exceptions of lines 305–6 and 349–50, which are not particularly obtrusive), placing the former mainly in book iii and the latter in book i. The sense that Chaucer was deliberately making his poem difficult supports the impression that it evinces a labyrinthine aesthetic, the 'Domus Dedaly' (1920) being a model—or at least an emblem or logo—for the whole work.

There are, however, plenty of reasons to feel uneasy about the view that, in the final analysis and all joking aside, the poem affirms the value of poetry in a manner akin to Dante's efforts at valorizing 'the illustrious vernacular'. In *De Vulgari eloquentia* Dante had identified love, together with arms and moral fortitude, as a fit subject of the high or tragic style (cf. pp. 229–30 below). But there is nothing high or tragic about the love described in the *House of Fame*. It is difficult to have confidence in Venus as a presiding deity, particularly when her temple is made of brittle glass. Moreover, rather than ennobling its servants, love seems to bring out the worst in them. Aeneas stands condemned as a traitor to Dido (who in her turn is reductively criticized for loving a stranger too soon), and this episode initiates a long list of liars in love which points the depressing moral that vulnerable women should not trust their mendacious menfolk. Love, then, does not offer a firm basis on which to build a poetic; it is as unreliable as that foundation, ice, on which the House of Fame itself rests. Can such a basis be found in dream-vision theory? The 'long, eager and breathless sentence' (as G. L. Kittredge termed it, p. 75) in which Chaucer rushes through the types, times, causes, and effects of dreams strikingly contrasts with the confident and more controlled openings of the *Roman de la Rose* and other French dream-visions, where authorities are often quoted to prove that dreams are worthy of belief (though occasionally more negative theories about their origin and credibility are alluded to as well; cf. pp. 43–4, 49 above). The narrator is himself quite lacking in confidence as to the truth of the matter ('noght wot I'), and manages to imply that the experts on the subject are in disagreement and disarray. The effect of all this is to undermine the form, rather than elevate it. Morpheus, it would seem, is not a reliable Muse; the fact that he is invoked as one is unsettling. Turning to the several great poetic 'matters' described in book iii, security can hardly be found there. The poets who support the fame of Troy disagree among themselves, and one of them (yet another anonymous 'oon') accuses the great Homer of being a liar. Here fame in general, and literary fame in particular, come in for tough questioning.

Along with all this uncertainty, an air of good humour pervades the poem, produced by effects which range from obscure learned jokes through literary parody to the coarsest of jests. Nowhere is Chaucer's lack of 'high seriousness' (as Matthew Arnold termed it) more in evidence than in this ambivalent artifice. Take the theory of sound retailed in book ii, for instance. In itself this is highly respectable lore, as found in Boethius's *De musica* and Macrobius's commentary on the *Somnium Scipionis*, as well as in medieval textbooks on linguistics and semiotics; it was the staple fare of the medieval grammar school. Yet here Chaucer just might be making one of the most elaborate farting jokes of all time— surpassed only (perhaps) by the enquiry in the *Summoner's Tale* into the difficult matter of how a fart can be divided into twelve equal parts, which is conducted with all due scholastic rigour. And in the pedantic eagle who treats his captive audience to an in-flight lecture on this and other subjects, 'Chaucer's genius for comedy . . . reached a height of achievement which he never surpassed and rarely equalled', as Kemp Malone says (p. 55).

However, a certain kind of seriousness is necessary when the highest literary prestige, or *auctoritas* as it was termed in Chaucer's day, is being solicited. Dante most certainly had that quality. 'This magnificent poet', Giovanni Boccaccio declares in a wonderfully constructed sentence which is a masterpiece of tact, had 'an accurate sense of self-worth; nor (as his contemporaries report) did he think himself to be worth less than he actually was' (*Trattatello in laude di Dante*, 165; trans. Minnis and Scott, p. 501). Certainly, Dante sought to ensure that his poems would be treated with scholarly seriousness, put on a par with the classical *auctores*, and admitted into the canon. But Chaucer fails to express an interest in loading the canon, and has no obvious desire to set himself up as an English Dante, *pace* John Lydgate's view of him as a 'Dante in Inglissh' (or so I would interpret the equivocal remark in the *Fall of Princes*, Prol. 302–3). Chaucer's eagle soars not to heavenly regions of immutable truth and total certainty, but to gossip-filled dwellings of rumour and dubious reportage. Here, then, is the challenge of the *House of Fame*.

J. A. W. Bennett, *Chaucer's Book of Fame* (Oxford, 1986). Piero Boitani, *Chaucer and the Imaginary World of Fame* (Cambridge, 1984). John A. Burrow, *Ricardian Poetry* (London, 1971), discusses book-division as a learned feature on p. 51. Kemp Malone, *Chapters on Chaucer* (Baltimore, 1951). Minnis and Scott (eds.), *Medieval Literary Theory*. Kittredge, *Chaucer and his Poetry*.

The significance of Dante's appropriation of 2 Cor. 12: 2–4 is elucidated by Steven Botterill, ' "Quae non licet homini loqui": The Ineffability of Mystical Experience in *Paradiso I* and the *Epistle to Can Grande*', MLR 83 (1988), 332–41. He points out that both Paul (see 2 Cor. 12: 5) and Dante move beyond ineffability to expression, actually rejoicing in the fact that the visions and revelations of the Lord which they narrate are *arcana verba*. On the 'ineffability' or 'inexpressibility' topos see further E. R. Curtius, *European Literature and the Latin Middle Ages*, trans. W. R. Trask (London, 1953), pp. 159–62.

On Pope's rewriting of *HF* see especially John M. Fyler, 'Chaucer, Pope, and the *House of Fame*', in J. M. Dean and C. K. Zacker (eds.), *The Idea of Medieval Literature: New Essays on Chaucer and Medieval Culture in Honor of D. R. Howard* (Newark, Del., London, and Toronto, 1992), pp. 149–59. Here Fyler concludes that 'Pope's imitation of Chaucer, and his reworking of that imitation in the *Dunciad*, show that he has assimilated Chaucer's troubling thoughts about the centrality and central ambiguities of language' (p. 157).

There are four recent book-length studies of *HF*: the monographs of Bennett and Boitani cited above; B. G. Koonce's allegorical reading, *Chaucer and the Tradition of Fame* (Princeton, NJ, 1966), and Sheila Delany's elegant and influential *Chaucer's 'House of Fame': The Poetics of Skeptical Fideism* (Chicago and London, 1972). Good short introductions include P. Boitani, 'Chaucer's Labyrinth: Fourteenth-Century Literature and Language', *ChR* 17 (1982), 197–220; Clemen, *Chaucer's Early Poetry*, pp. 67–121;

R. R. Edwards, *Dream of Chaucer*, pp. 93–121; Fyler, *Chaucer and Ovid*, pp. 23–64; Mehl, *Narrative Poetry*, pp. 73–89; Jacqueline T. Miller, 'The Writing on the Wall: Authority and Authorship in Chaucer's *House of Fame*', ChR 17 (1982), 95–115; Spearing, *Medieval Dream-Poetry*, pp. 73–89.
In addition to John Fyler's edition of *HF* for the *Riverside Chaucer*, the individual edition by N. R. Havely is highly recommended, particularly for its notes.

## Text, Date, and Circumstances

The state of the text of the *House of Fame* is a matter of some debate. Chaucer may simply have left the poem unfinished, as with—if appearances are not deceptive—so many of his other works. Alternatively, he actually did write a conclusion (perhaps only a few more lines were necessary to bring the work to a satisfactory close), but this was lost, its final verses having been written on a new folio which became detached from the rest of the book. The mysterious 'man of gret auctorite' (2158) is about to be identified, the argument could run, this being evidence that Chaucer had the conclusion clearly in his mind, making it improbable that he would stop composing at that crucial point. However, the two best manuscripts, Oxford, Bodleian Library MSS Fairfax 16 and Bodley 638 (which are closely related), end in mid-folio, and so this theory has to be related to an earlier copy. In the only other surviving manuscript, Cambridge, Magdalene College MS Pepys 2006, the poem ends at line 1843, while the text which William Caxton printed ran out at line 2094. Norman Blake has stressed the point that, because Chaucer left some works incomplete, we should not assume that he habitually failed to finish them, ever keen to explore pastures new. When a poem is incomplete because it lacks an ending, it is eminently possible that this has been lost in its transmission: and that may well have happened to the *House of Fame*. On the other hand, Larry D. Benson and others who think that Chaucer *meant* to break off abruptly as soon as he mentioned the man of great authority, believe that we have the whole poem as the poet intended it—complete in its very incompleteness, as it were. The question of whether or not the poem we possess is complete in the sense of having a cohesive argument and structure will be addressed later, in the light of a review of the sources of its several elements.

The poem is usually dated between 1379 and 1380, during the period in which Chaucer was Controller of the Wool Custom, a post which he had held since 1374. Its dialogue with Dante can be taken as one of the literary results of Chaucer's Italian voyage of 1372–3. This date would account for the poem's transitional character: though still displaying a substantial debt to the French love-visions, it points to Chaucer's future horizons and things unattempted yet in English verse or rhyme. The octosyllabic couplet is still being used, which would have been a natural choice at that point in the poet's career, particularly since it appears in the *Book of the Duchess*. However, the greater mastery of this verse-form manifested by the *House of Fame* (on which, more below) can be taken as indicating some temporal distance between it and Chaucer's first substantial poem.

The precise specification of the date of the narrator's vision ('The tenthe day now of Decembre' (63; cf. line 111)) has occasioned much comment, though it should be noted that this device has precedents in Old French courtly poetry. For example, Machaut's *Jugement dou Roy de Navarre* is dated 9 November 1349, and Froissart's *Joli Buisson de Jonece* is dated 30 November 1373.

Some have tried to relate it to historical events. This approach has often involved an attempt at identification of the 'man of gret auctorite' as some noble personage. The tidings which 'Geffrey' seeks, Kittredge declares, 'cannot be a story out of a book'; most likely, they concern some contemporary affair, which would be of interest to the English court (p. 103). But which affair? It has been suggested that it was intended to celebrate the announcement in late 1380 of the betrothal of Anne of Bohemia to Richard II, or perhaps an announcement in the following year of Anne's imminent arrival in England—good tidings indeed, whatever the details. Alternatively, the poem could mark the expected betrothal of John of Gaunt's daughter Philippa to Charles VI of France, an event which in fact did not happen. Chaucer had a precedent for this in Froissart's *Le Temple d'Honneur*, a dream-poem which celebrates figuratively the wedding of two prominent (though unnamed) personages, perhaps Humphrey de Bohun and Joan of Arundel, who married in May 1363. Here there is a similar promise of new tidings (*aucune nouvelle*). Who, then, is the authoritative figure who is about to appear at the poem's end? Perhaps John of Gaunt, perhaps even the king himself?

There are major objections to such theories. A poem which castigates 'pious Aeneas' as a philanderer and offers a long reading list of stories of credulous women being deceived by mendacious men makes an unlikely prothalamium. Moreover, the fact that the expected tidings emanate from the House of Rumour, where truth and falsity are compounded, renders it unlikely that some definite—and prestigious—event is being anticipated; surely no noble couple would have welcomed their wedding plans being publicized in such a way. Then again, as Benson says, given that 'the entire poem has comically deflated the whole idea of "auctorite"', one 'can hardly imagine that either Richard II, who insisted on being treated with elaborately ceremonial respect, or John of Gaunt, would-be "King of Castile", would have been pleased to have been placed in so indecorous a setting' (p. 7). So, then, maybe the historical events about to be revealed were unpleasant rather than pleasant? After all, this is a December dream, far away from the Maytime setting which is *de rigueur* for visions of true love and beauty. Perhaps, as Bertrand H. Bronson suggested, the trust of some noblewoman had been betrayed, and Chaucer had completed the poem, satirically naming, or alluding to, the guilty party—then thought better of it, and suppressed the ending. Or could he have been leading up to a criticism of John of Gaunt for his womanizing? But why would Chaucer court professional suicide? Further, the most obvious woman in question, Katherine Swynford, was probably the poet's sister-in-law, so perhaps that particular affair was altogether too close to home.

Very few critics, however, have agreed with Robert B. Burlin's view that there is 'a faintly unpleasant tone' in the *House of Fame* (p. 47), taking the line, rather, that it was written in the spirit of comedy rather than satire. Hence R. J. Schoeck can seek to identify it as an Inns of Court Christmas revel, perhaps written for one of the ritualistic functions of the Inner Temple. This, he argues, provides a reason for 'the whole grand playfulness' of the poem, even for its 'suggestion of parody . . . of intellectual pomposity and pedantic portentousness' (p. 192). On this reading, the man of great authority is the Constable-Marshal. One can only wonder what this audience would have made of the poem's emphasis on tidings of love. This fact, and the essentially comic nature of the *House of Fame*, are accommodated in Benson's approach. The scene in the House of Rumour, he declares, is of the very stuff of 'slapstick comedy',

a raucous scene in which everyone is leaping up and down, stomping on one another's feet, and climbing on backs in riotous disorder. It is a setting in which a man who appears to be 'of gret auctorite' can only seem ridiculous, like a dignitary in a top hat and tails suddenly appearing in a similar scene in a Marx brothers comedy. (p. 7)

He proceeds to offer a particularly elaborate hypothesis concerning its circumstances, involving the public shaming of a 'lesser—but still authoritative—dignitary', one Nicolò, a messenger sent by Cardinal Pileo da Prato with the unwelcome tidings that the negotiations concerning the marriage of Richard II to Caterina Visconti had come to nothing. On 10 December 1379 Nicolò received a payment of ten pounds, which Benson takes as evidence that he was present at the English court on that day— when he might have received a very different kind of reward, delivered by Geoffrey Chaucer.

when Chaucer got to the final lines about the one who 'semed for to be / A man of gret auctorite', he paused, turned, and slightly bowed in the direction of

Cardinal Pileo's nuncio. Poor Nicolò, puzzled but pleased after sitting through over two thousand lines of verse in a language he probably could not understand, politely acknowledged the unexpected honor, and smiling, bowed in return. (p. 19)

Whereupon the poet closed his book and sat down to rapturous applause from an audience which was smarting from the snub it had just received. A wonderful theory, but utterly unprovable . . . and one which rests on two assumptions: that Chaucer performed his poem before the court, and that his listeners could have made more of those two thousand lines of difficult verse than the hapless Nicolò had done. Both are highly debatable.

We can, of course, liberate ourselves from all these speculations by taking the line that the poem is essentially about literary art and authority rather than true-life tidings of love, and that the 'man of gret auctorite' was not a historical personage at all, but rather a literary *auctor*, as Bennett has argued (p. xii). But that provides us with a new set of puzzles and problems, as we will see later.

Others have explored the astrological implications of dreaming in December, which have given rise to several hypotheses concerning the date, circumstances, and subject of the poem. For example, David Bevington points out that 10 December is just before the winter solstice (12 December according to the Julian calendar), and argues that the 'obtuse narrator' has chosen the day least 'suggestive of love and springtime' (p. 292)—but why, as John Fyler has asked (*Riverside Chaucer*, p. 979), should he pick the 10th rather than the 12th? John Leyerle notes that in December the sun approaches the constellation Aquila, the Eagle, and on 10 December is in Sagittarius, 'the house of dreams, tidings, and travels' and also 'the night domicile of Jupiter, the most benevolent of the planets' (p. 249). The configuration here suggested corresponds most closely to the actual conditions of the night of 10 December 1379. He adds that in 1379 or 1380 Chaucer would have been 35 years old, the same age as Dante when he had his vision *nel mezzo del cammin di nostra vita* (*Inferno*, i. 1). However, if it is supposed that Chaucer was born in 1340, then that particular parallel disappears.

Chaucer's reference to a full moon ('the faire white Mone', 2116) is what is significant for J. D. North (p. 351). 'When we search for a full moon on 10 December, between, say, 1375 and 1390, only for 1383 do we find exactly what we need.' Moreover, he continues, there is 'a hint of a conjunction of Jupiter with Venus' in book i (219): these planets were in conjunction on 20 April 1383. But, as North himself admits (p. 13 n. 11), this is 'a weak hypothesis'. It is even weaker than he supposes; for line 2116 is not referring specifically to a full moon at all, but rather is making a vague and general point about its beauty; what *is* being specified here is the unremarkable fact that the moon waxes and wanes (cf. 2115).

In conclusion, there seems to be no compelling reason to abandon the dating of 1379–80. Yet there seems to be no utterly compelling reason in favour of it either. It is somewhat unnerving to be faced with the remark of 'Geffrey' that he is 'olde' (995), which contrasts with the Man of Law's statement that the poet composed the *Book of the Duchess* in his youth; though such details should perhaps not be taken too literally. Personally I believe that the *House of Fame* just might have been composed after *Troilus and Criseyde*, these two works constituting an elaborate creative engagement with Italian literature, wherein Chaucer moved from Boccaccio to Dante, away from the *roman antique* genre to confront the *Comedy* and all it implied for vernacular poetics.

N. F. Blake, 'Geoffrey Chaucer: The Critics and the Canon', *Archiv*, 221 (1984), 65–70. Kittredge, *Chaucer and his Poetry*, Larry D. Benson, 'The "Love Tydynges" in Chaucer's *House of Fame*', in Wasserman and Blanch (eds.), *Chaucer in the Eighties* pp. 3–22. B. H. Bronson, 'Chaucer's *Hous of Fame*: Another Hypothesis', *University of California Publications in English*, 3 (1934), 171–92. Robert B. Burlin, *Chaucerian Fiction* (Princeton, NJ, 1977). Burlin feels that the poem 'takes on the quality of an *insomnium*, a nightmare governed by uncertainties and the deep fear that comes from dislocation in a sterile or unstable atmosphere' (p. 47). R. J. Schoeck, 'A Legal Reading of Chaucer's *House of Fame*', *UTQ* 23 (1954), 185–92. David Bevington, 'The Obtuse Narrator in Chaucer's *House of Fame*', *Speculum*, 36 (1961), 292. It should be noted that here we are dealing with the Julian calendar which, as Bevington says, was becoming increasingly inaccurate. John Leyerle, 'Chaucer's Windy Eagle', *UTQ* 40 (1971), 247–65. North, *Chaucer's Universe*.

Koonce, *Tradition of Fame*, p. 65, states that on 10 December the sun is in the sign of Sagittarius, the mansion of Jupiter (a highly benevolent plante), and the ninth of the twelve houses of the Zodiac, this being the house of faith and religion, which may be taken as exerting its power in (*inter alia*) prophetic dreams.

Blake, 'Critics and the Canon', argues that 'The manuscripts themselves suggest that there was a progressive loss of final folios . . . It is consequently not difficult to imagine that one or more final folios were lost before the earliest extant copy was made. It should be added that Chaucer in other works twice refers to this poem and never suggests it is unfinished' (pp. 66–7). Similar views are expressed by Bevington, 'Obtuse Narrator', pp. 289–90. Those who believe that Chaucer abandoned the poem include Dorothy Everett, *Essays on Middle English Literature*, ed. Patricia Kean (Oxford, 1955), p. 101; Kittredge, *Chaucer and his Poetry*, p. 103; John Lawlor, 'The Earlier Poems', in D. S. Brewer (ed.), *Chaucer and Chaucerians* (London, 1966), p. 48; Payne, *Key of Remembrance*, pp. 137, 139. Kittredge (p. 107) professed that he was glad the poem was unfinished, for this gave him 'a chance to guess at the story that should conclude it'! With Benson's hypothesis cf. Donald K. Fry, 'The Ending of the *House of Fame*', in Robbins (ed.), *Chaucer at Albany*, pp. 27–40, who envisages Chaucer reading aloud the final lines as we have them, then closing the book, and sitting 'down smiling, to a rising crescendo of shocked surprise, laughter, understanding, and finally applause' (p. 39), thereby emphasizing the ironic nature of the man of great authority: 'there is no authority, much less great authority, possible in secular human affairs' (p. 38). Several theories are usefully summarized in K. Stevenson, 'The Endings of Chaucer's *House of Fame*', *English Studies*, 59 (1978), 10–26.

Other textual matters are discussed in the editions by Fyler (*Riverside Chaucer*) and Havely. See further A. S. G. Edwards, 'The Text of Chaucer's *House of Fame*: Editing and Authority', *Poetica*, 29–30 (1989), 80–92, who states that here, in a way unique in Chaucer's poetry, 'the editor is . . . often adrift in a sea of indeterminacy, lacking satisfactory means to resolve questions of textual authority'.

If, as D. R. Howard notes, one supposes (with Condren; cf. p. 80 above) that *BD* was written for one of the anniversaries of Blanche's death, in the late 1370s, then *HF* could be Chaucer's first important poem—an intriguing possibility. 'Flying through Space: Chaucer and Milton', in J. A. Wittreich (ed.), *Milton and the Line of Vision* (Madison, Wis., 1975), p. 22 n. 16. On the other hand, John Fisher believes that *HF* is later than *PF*: *PF* dealt with the 'unsuccessful effort to secure' Richard II's 'betrothal to Marie, daughter of King Charles V of France, in 1377', while *HF* was written 'to celebrate his actual betrothal to Anne of Bohemia in 1380' (*Complete Poetry and Prose*, p. 564). Neither theory has found much support. Blake declares that 'there is no reason why it should not be dated immediately before the *Legend*, in which it is mentioned ('Critics and the Canon', p. 69).

## Verse-form, Rhetoric, and Style

Chaucer's handling of the octosyllabic couplet is much more assured than it was in the *Book of the Duchess*. A comparison with the earlier poem reveals a sharp decrease in the number of irregularities (assuming that the metrics of the *Roman de la Rose* can be taken as a gauge by which to measure English practice). There are fewer cases in which an extra syllable occurs before the caesura or a short foot after it, or the trochee is substituted for the iambus in the first two feet (though a trochaic third foot appears more often in the *House of Fame* than in the *Book of the Duchess*).

That slurring of syllables which occasionally created roughness in the *Book of the Duchess* is far less frequent. On the other hand, here Chaucer has used more, rather than fewer, seven-syllable lines (the bulk of them occurring in the third book). Indeed, he actually draws attention to this feature of his verse at one point:

> Nat that I wilne, for maistrye,          *desire, impressive achievement*
> Here art poetical be shewed,                              *displayed*
> But for the rym ys lyght and lewed,
> Yit make hyt sumwhat agreable,
> Though som vers fayle in a sillable                        (1094–8)

Leaving humorous self-denigration aside, it is obvious that Chaucer regarded 'failing in a syllable' not as a blemish but as a means of achieving pleasurable and attention-holding variation. This may be illustrated by lines 896–903, where several of the irregularities noted above may be seen in action:

And y adoun gan loken thoo,
And beheld feldes and playnes,
And now hilles, and now mountaynes,
Now valeyes, now forestes,
And now unnethes grete bestes,                    *with difficulty*
Now ryveres, now citees,
Now tounes, and now grete trees,
Now shippes seyllynge in the see.                 (896–903)

Here there are three seven-syllable lines (897, 899, 901), and a trochee forms the second foot in line 898 and the third foot in line 897. Skilful management of the pauses and the sentence stress ensure that this passage runs smoothly, its variation creating interest in what might otherwise be just one more in a long line of Middle English descriptions of lovely landscapes. The contrast with Gower, whose octosyllabic couplets in the *Confessio Amantis* are remarkably regular, is revealing. The characteristic vice of the verse-form—its tendency to produce a monotonous and droning effect—is far less common in Chaucer, particularly in the *House of Fame*. In fairness to the fundamental measure of this poem, however, it must be emphasized that Chaucer often uses regular octosyllabics to good effect. Wolfgang Clemen has praised their deployment in the Dido episode, for example, where they underline and reinforce what is being said.

Chaucer's handling of another aspect of his 'art poetical', the figures and tropes of rhetoric, has also matured. The *House of Fame* is brim full of *descriptio*: of the temple of Venus and the houses of Fame and Rumour, together with all their ornaments and inhabitants; of those extraordinarily original creations, the eagle and Fame herself; of the bird's eye view of earth and heaven, of imaged sound. Geoffrey of Vinsauf recommends that when using this method of *amplificatio*, the writer should avoid the trite and banal, and enable 'the eye and the ear' to 'rove amid variety' (*Poetria nova*, trans. Kopp, pp. 53–4). In the *House of Fame* Chaucer spectacularly achieves precisely that. Another amplifying device, apostrophe, appears to good effect in, for example, the invocation at the beginning of book iii, where the address to Apollo begins with the *exclamatio* 'O God of science and of lyght' (1091), and also in Dido's comprehensive lament, at lines 315–63. Here the distraught heroine apostrophizes, in turn, herself, Aeneas, men in general, her own birth, and, finally, wicked Fame, with an *exclamatio* marking each change of subject.

Turning to just one of the many uses of *figurae verborum*, here Chaucer indulges his fondness for *repetitio* (also known as *epanaphora* or *anaphora*), the longest example extending over 17 lines (1960–76), with 'Of' being the word which is repeated at the beginning of each line. This expansive passage conveys forcefully the wide range of 'tydynges' which fill the

House of Fame. Moreover, particularly in book ii, Chaucer has discovered the pleasures of exploiting rhetoric to achieve richly comic effects. For example, the eagle's amusingly egotistical statement that he has conveyed many facts to his pupil in speech which is simple and lacking in subtlety, prolixity, philosophical terminology, poetic figures, and rhetorical colours (853–63) is in fact a masterpiece of rhetorical expression. Here is an *interrogatio* (a strong affirmation in the form of a question) which uses *circuito* or *paraphrasis* inasmuch as the same point is being reiterated in various ways. Lines 856–9, each of which begins with 'Of', constitute a *repetitio*. The whole thing parodies the rhetoricians' insistence that a speech should be carefully suited to its audience: 'A ha', declares the eagle triumphantly, 'lo, so I can / Lewedly to a lewed man / Speke' (865–7).

The rhetorical device in the *House of Fame* which has attracted most interest, however, is apostrophe; specifically, the invocations of the Muses which occur at the beginnings of books ii and iii. Piero Boitani responds to these passages by hailing Chaucer as 'the first English poet to invoke the Muses' (p. 203); it is more accurate, however, to describe him as the first poet to invoke the Muses in Middle English, since this device, as a long-established feature of learned medieval Latin poetics, sometimes appears in Latin verses composed by Englishmen. At the very beginning of an anonymous and undated verse *vita* of St Hilda of Whitby, Clio, Muse of History, is invoked. The Muse of Tragedy, Melpomene, is invited to sing the 'tragica gesta' of the Tartars in John of Garland's eight-book poem on the crusades, *De triumphis ecclesiae* (*c.*1245–52). Thalia, Muse of Comedy, features in the six-book epic on the desert saint Malchus which Reginald of Canterbury produced in the late eleventh century and also in the *Hypognosticon* of Lawrence of Durham (*c.*1100–54), a verse epic on the redemption of man. A single unspecified Muse appears in an anonymous thirteenth-century goliardic satire, *De grisis monachis*; while at the end of Joseph of Exeter's *De bello Trojano* or *Iliad* (*c.*1188) Apollo figures in a sort of anti-invocation (on which, more below). Chaucer seems to have known Joseph's work. But the indubitable source of the invocations in the *House of Fame* was Dante's *Comedy*.

Having met Virgil, the Dante persona prepares himself for his poetic odyssey in the following terms:

> O Muse, o alto ingegno, or m'aiutate;
> o mente che scrivesti ciò ch'io vidi,
> qui si parrà la tua nobilitate.
>
> [O Muses, o high ingenuity, help me now!
> O memory that wrote down what I saw,
> here shall your worthiness appear!
>          (*Inferno*, ii. 7–9; trans. Singleton, with one alteration) ]

Similarly, in the Proem to the second book of the *House of Fame* Chaucer refers obliquely to those 'that on Parnasso duelle' (521), and proceeds to apostrophize 'Thought', that wrote everything that he dreamed, and enclosed it in the treasury ('tresorye') of the poet's brain; now men shall see if there is 'any vertu' therein to recount his entire dream properly (523–7). 'Now', he adds in an *exclamatio*, make known 'thyn engyn and myght'! 'Engyn' renders Dante's 'ingenio', in the sense of creative power, ingenuity, and skill; 'vertu' probably corresponds to 'nobilitate', 'Thought' may translate 'mente', which here means 'memory', as in Singleton's translation.

Composing poetry involves copying the original text as written in the book of memory, thereby manifesting what was already in the poet's mind so that it may be experienced by others and its worthiness appraised. Similarly, in a famous passage at the beginning of his *Vita nuova* Dante explains the production of this work by saying that in the book of his memory he found a rubric which said 'Incipit Vita nuova', under which were 'written the words which it is my intention to copy into this little book; and if not all, at least their substance' (trans. in Singleton, p. 26). However, Howard H. Schless has argued that Chaucer was thinking 'not in terms of *memory* but rather in terms of the considerative power of the mind' (p. 51). 'Thought has noted down all his [i.e. the Chaucer persona's] dream and shut it up in the treasury or storehouse of his brain; now he wants to see whether Thought has the ability to recount that dream.' This does not take full cognizance of the fact—which is well documented in Carruther's comprehensive study—that memory is, so to speak, a book that writes itself, both author and text, at once considerative and recordative. More specifically, the task of 'recounting' a dream which one has had can easily be regarded as a job for memory; after all, it was in the memory that the details of his dream were recorded, and this mental faculty is now being asked to produce them. Besides, the notion that the *memoria* is a storehouse or treasury for images of things past is a medieval commonplace. For instance, in an oft-quoted passage, Cicero (*De oratore*, i. 18) had described memory as a treasure-house (*thesaurus*) of everything the rhetorician needs, the repository of those *verba* and *res* required in thought and invention. John of Salisbury spoke of it as 'the mind's treasure-chest (*mentis arca*), a sure and reliable place of safe-deposit for perceptions' (*Metalogicon*, i. 11; trans. in Carruthers, p. 113). Still, Schless does have a point. Lines 523–5 can certainly be interpreted as meaning that the poet initially thought about his subject, then deposited it in the 'tresorye' of his memory, and now is externalizing that thought, transferring it from memory to narrative. This very process is well described in a sermon of St Augustine's. 'Before I come to you,' he tells his audience, 'I mentally compose [*cogitavi*] in advance what I will say to you. When I have composed what I will say to you, then the word is in my memory. Nor would I speak to you, unless I had previously composed in my mind' (*Sermo* 225, 3; trans. in Carruthers, p. 207). But there is not, in my view, the distance between those specific Italian and English passages which Schless postulates. For both bespeak a concern with poetic composition and the role of memory therein.

Even more important, both highlight the role and contribution of the poet himself—the Muses by no means get all the credit. However, this is done in different ways, which may now be explored. One of the most remarkable things about the *Inferno* passage is the speed with which it moves from the Muses to the self, from 'alto ingenio' to Dante's own 'mente', what *he* saw. Whereas Dante saw ('io vidi'), Chaucer dreamed ('I mette'). But this does not necessarily imply a greater passivity on the English poet's part. For earlier in the Proem an impressive list of no fewer than six virtuoso dreamers was provided (514–16), and the Chaucerian *sujet* roundly declared that his 'avisyon' or 'drem' was better than theirs (517). However, this heaping up of distinguished predecessors has an effect similar to that of the breathless multiplication of dream types and classifications at the very beginning of the *House of Fame*—namely, one of hyperbole which is so *de trop* that it produces bathos. Also quite un-Dantean is Chaucer's appeal to 'Cipris' (Venus) to be his helper at this time (518–19), which precedes the invocation of the Muses, and seems to make the point that this is (or will be) a poem about human love. Here, then, is a project far less ambitious than Dante's. (Similarly, in the *Parliament of Fowls*, 113–19, Venus will be addressed as a quasi-Muse, to borrow a term from N. R. Havely.) The statement that the Parnassus-dwellers live by 'Elicon, the clere welle' (521–2) blurs together Helicon, the Muses' mountain, and Hippocrene, the Muses' well; but no deliberate irony should be sought here, since this confusion is common in medieval literature, appearing in many French lyrics as well as in Walter Map's *De nugis curialium* (dist. 4, ch. 2) and Boccaccio's *Teseida* (ii. 63). Far more significant is the poet's request that he should be helped 'to endite and ryme' (520), which seems a relatively trivial thing to ask of so powerful an agency. Clearly, the Dante and Chaucer passages are following different trajectories. The Englishman's concerns seem to be those of the skilled craftsman, or *makere*, rather than the inspired, innovative *poeta*.

This difference is even more marked in the second invocation, at the beginning of the third book of the *House of Fame*. Here Chaucer is echoing *Paradiso*, i. 13–36, particularly the following lines which address

Apollo, god of music (especially the lyre) and prophecy, and 'the leader of the Muses', as Macrobius termed him:

> O buono Appollo, a l'ultimo lavaro
> fammi del tuo valor sì fatto vaso,
> come dimandi a dar l'amato alloro. . . .
> Entra nel petto mio, e spira tue . . .
> O divina virtù, se mi ti presti
> tanto che l'ombra del beato regno
> segnata nel mio capo io manifesti,
> vedra'mi al piè del tuo diletto legno
> venire, e coronarmi de le foglie
> che la materia e tu mi farai degno.

[O good Apollo, for this last labor make me such a vessel of your worth as you require for granting your beloved laurel. . . . Enter into my breast and breathe there . . . O divine Power, if you do so lend yourself to me that I may show forth the image of the blessed realm which is imprinted in my mind, you shall see me come to your beloved tree and crown me with those leaves of which the matter and you shall make me worthy. (Trans. Singleton, pp. 2–5) ]

Dante's words underlie Chaucer's praise of the 'myght' of 'Appollo'; he too wishes the 'devyne vertu' (1101) to 'entre' into his 'brest' (1109) so that he might 'shewe now' what is 'ymarked' in his 'hed' (1102–3). But Dante's 'beloved tree' is a bush of a quite different kind in lines 1105–8 of the *House of Fame*. If only you will help me, the poet promises Apollo, I will happily go up to the next laurel that I see, 'And kysse yt, for hyt is thy tree'! This is reminiscent of Chaucer's promise to the 'god' Morpheus in the *Book of the Duchess*: he will give him a bed feathered with pure doves' down, and the like (242–69), if he will only make him sleep. Both these Chaucer passages are amusing, and both raise the issue of whether such a tone is appropriate in the circumstances. Dante had in mind his metaphoric coronation as poet laureate by Apollo, the transference of the honorific wreath of laurel from the heads of ancient Roman dignitaries to his own distinguished crown, as a fit reward for the resuscitation of dead poetry which his vernacular masterpiece had effected. Far from engaging in such self-aggrandizement, Chaucer seems intent (not for the first or last time) on making his persona look ridiculous. As Havely points out in his note on these lines, Chaucer may have been influenced by Ovid's *Metamorphoses*, i. 452–567, the fable of how the nymph Daphne, on being pursued by the lovelorn Apollo, was metamorphosed (at her own request) into a laurel tree. The god continues to love her in this form, and even kisses her:

But even now in this new form Apollo loved her; and placing his hand upon the trunk, he felt the heart still fluttering beneath the bark. He embraced the branches as if human limbs, and pressed his lips upon the wood. But even the wood shrank from his kisses. And the god cried out to this: 'Since thou canst not be my bride, thou shalt at least be my tree. . . . With thee shall Roman generals wreathe their heads.' (i. 553–61; trans. Miller, i. 41)

Chaucer seems to have moved behind and beyond the Dante passage, to locate the source of the laureation rite in an amatory escapade which has its amusing elements. If it be granted that this allusion exists, it may be recognized as quite fitting in a poem which is allegedly under the auspices of Venus, goddess of love.

Though he begins with Apollo as 'God of science and lyght' (1091), Chaucer ends up with Apollo the lover. And inserted into the very middle of the invocation, bisecting the panegyric of the god's 'grete myght' and 'devyne vertu', is an extraordinary disclaimer. It is not, Chaucer declares, that he wants to show off; he is not planning to display 'art poetical' in a way which evinces or implies 'maistrye' (in the sense of admirable and grand achievement). Given that his rhyme is easy ('lyght') and 'lewed' (unlearned), the height of his ambition is that it should be agreeable. Some of his verses may be faulty; he may give the substance or meaning ('sentence') alone, without wrapping it up nicely in an elaborate style—at least, that is how I understand the statement 'I do no diligence / To shewe craft' (1099–1100). Here we are back in the world of the 'modesty topoi' so beloved of medieval poets and rhetoricians, that formulaic self-denigration which Dante's egotistical sublime had brushed aside. Little wonder, then, that David Wallace should remark: 'Heard against the sonorous background of Dante's magisterial *terzine*, Chaucer's English couplets [i.e. in lines 1091–8] amount to little more than a nervous squeak' (p. 23).

I myself would not go quite that far, preferring Havely's view that Chaucer's text is reflecting the 'double' nature of the Muses, those symbols of the dignity of poetry which, on the one hand, were lauded by Dante and later by Boccaccio (in both the *Filostrato* and *Teseida*), and on the other, were lambasted and banished by Boethius as 'theatrical tarts' or 'scenic strumpets' (depending on how one translates the untranslatable *scenicas meretriculas*; *De consolatione philosophiae*, I, pr. i, 29). To the 'poeticas Musas' Lady Philosophy had opposed her own Muses ('meisque Musis'). In the thirteenth-century revision of William of Conches' commentary on the *Consolatio*, one of the explanations provided for the *scenicas meretriculas* is that they are 'scenic in the sense of shady, because they are the shadow of knowledge rather than true knowledge', as H. A. Kelly puts it (p. 71). Boethius commentators generally gloss *meisque Musis* as the arts and sciences which offer true knowledge. This tension between the Muses interpreted *in malo* and *in bono* is apparent in many writers, including Joseph of Exeter. At the beginning of *De bello trojano* he declares that his mind, concerned with historical truth (and indeed with truth in general), has 'banished far from it the poet who plays with fictions' (trans. Roberts, p. 3), while at the end of the work he looks forward to a more serious enterprise, the composition of a Christian epic about the wars of Antioch. No pagan Muse will help him there; 'a more glorious Apollo will come down from heaven and fill the void of my trusting heart' (pp. 86–7). And when Gower, at the end of the *Confessio Amantis*, follows the advice of a Muse ('My muse', viii. 3140) who wants the poet to understand that he should 'take reste' from writing about love, perhaps he was thinking of the proper and personalized Muses of Philosophy (*meisque Musis*), as Havely suggests. In the light of such negotiations, Chaucer's convolutions seem far more comprehensible.

The doubleness deepens when Chaucer's description of Apollo as god of science and light (not found in the corresponding Dante passage) is investigated. In Greek mythology Apollo was the god of light, whence his epithet 'Phoebus', meaning 'the bright'. In Roman religion he became prominent as a god of oracles and prophecy, and it is that type of knowledge to which Chaucer's term 'science' must pre-eminently refer. But in Christian tradition Apollo was often criticized for his duplicitous and misleading answers. When discussing ambiguity (*amphibolia*) as a form of speech, Isidore of Seville offers as his first example the response of Apollo to Pyrrhus: 'I say that you, O man sprung from Aeacus, the Romans can defeat' (*Etymologiae*, I. xxxiv. 13–16). Here it is uncertain who will be the victor, the Romans or Pyrrhus. Similarly, in his *Livre de Divinacions* Nicole Oresme warns that 'the words of the diviners are sometimes of double meaning, amphibolic, two-faced, as we see in many histories; and they can be applied to more than one event or person . . . And the diviner who has a mind to prophesy in obscure terms as to a man's fortune can hardly fail to find something happening to which his forecast will apply.' He proceeds to quote Cicero's declaration, 'Apollo, thy responses are sometimes true, sometimes false, according to chance, in part doubtful and obscure, so much so that the expositor has need of another expositor' (*De divinatione*, ii. 56). That, Nicole explains, 'is what Tully says of the responses of Apollo, which were at that time more renowned than any, and they are all alike in this respect' (trans. Coopland, pp. 94–7). Little wonder, then, that Chaucer's Criseyde, with her father's devotion to Apollo in mind, should protest that

'. . . goddes speken in amphibologies,
And, for a sooth, they tellen twenty lyes'.

(*Troilus and Criseyde*, iv. 1406–7)

In similar vein, Guido delle Colonne recounts how Achilles and Patroclus visit the temple of Apollo at Delphos to ascertain the outcome of the war against the Trojans which is in the offing. Here is found a great image in honour of the god, made entirely of gold, that has been entered by an unclean spirit which, through its answers, ensures that men are 'kept in the perpetual blindness of error' (*Historia destructionis Troiae*, x. 105–17; trans. Meek, p. 91). Its response is that in ten years Troy will fall to the Greeks (260–6; p. 95). There is no need for Guido to labour the point that this oracle, although accurate, is deceptive: the Greeks did indeed win the war after ten years, but their loss both during and after the siege of Troy was a terrible price to pay. What else can one expect from an unclean spirit?

It may be recalled that 'Guydo . . . de Columpnis' (1469) appears in Chaucer's list of authorities who support the matter of Troy. The fact that writers with such different views of the Muses can be accommodated in the *House of Fame* is highly revealing. And Apollo's sinister side is explicitly intimated by Chaucer's brief mention of how Marcia (a female version of the satyr Marsyas) lost her skin—that is, was flayed as a punishment for having beaten Apollo in a piping competition (1229–32). In short, Chaucer's two invocations of the Muses are microcosms of the fissured texture of the *House of Fame* as a whole, wherein 'amphibologies' run riot.

Moving on to attempt an overall view of the poem's style, it may be said that the distinctions, as reiterated by generations of rhetoricians, between high, middle, and low styles count for little here, because Chaucer can move from one register to another within the space of a few lines, this being accomplished with a dexterity and grace which is breathtaking. If the poem has a 'motley texture', to use Muscatine's phrase (p. 108), that garb is infinitely more impressive than the best clothes of many another poet. In his magisterial study of style and meaning in Chaucer's poetry, Muscatine also speaks of the 'choice and widely prized accomplishments' of the *House of Fame*, which are limited by the poet's failure to fit them into a pattern. 'Structurally', he pronounces, 'it is most charitably seen as an experiment', wherein Chaucer's 'energy and imagination by far outrun his sense of form'. But for all we know, Chaucer did finish his poem, complete the pattern, fill out the form, whether in the 'tresorye' of his 'brayn' or in a full text which has been maimed in transmission. It is all too easy to find fault with the fragmentary. Taken as it stands, what we have got is quite extraordinary.

Of course, Chaucer vacillates between the sublime and the ridiculous. That is one of the great strengths of the poem, which has as its real muse Thalia, the Muse of Comedy, though Chaucer does not acknowledge her. And the *House of Fame* does indeed move from confidence to diffidence and back again, exploring the literary landscape which forms the border-land between poetry as inspiration and versifying as craftsmanship. But what other English—or indeed, French—poem composed around 1380 (if we may accept that dating) could have got this far? In its own right the work evinces considerable 'maistrye'—dull would he or she be of soul that took its modesty formulae literally—and *inter alia* it contains 'the germ of the whole central tradition of high poetical language in England', to bestow upon it the praise which C. S. Lewis (p. 201) gave to the (per-haps) later *Anelida and Arcite*. Yet simultaneously it nurtures that 'low style' which was to pass from the discourse of the lower-order birds in the *Parliament of Fowls* to the speech of churls like the Miller and the Reeve in the *Canterbury Tales*. Here, then, is God's plenty, Apollo's blended dream.

Shannon, 'Chaucer's Use of the Octosyllabic Verse'. Baum, *Chaucer's Verse*, pp. 27–33. Clemen, *Chaucer's Early Poetry*, esp. p. 121.

Geoffrey of Vinsauf, *Poetria nova*, trans. Kopp. See further the discussion on pp. 188, 190 below of the distinction between natural and artificial order, as found in certain *artes poetriae*. The eagle's use of rhetoric is discussed by F. E. Teager, 'Chaucer's Eagle and the Rhetorical Colors', *PMLA* 47 (1932), 410–18. On apostrophe in *HF* see especially A. C. Spearing, *Medieval to Renaissance in English Poetry* (Cambridge, 1985), pp. 24–7.

Boitani, *Imaginary World*. On the Muses in the Latin poems of Englishmen see Rigg, *Anglo-Latin Literature*, pp. 22–3, 25–8, 57, 173, 230. Also Joseph of Exeter, *The Iliad of Dares Phrygius*, trans. Gildas Roberts (Cape Town, 1970), pp. 3–4. The Latin text has been edited by L. Gompf in *Joseph Iscanus: Werke und Briefe*, Mittellatcinischen Studien und Texte, 4 (Leiden and Cologne, 1970).

Dante, *The Divine Comedy: Inferno*, ed. and trans. Charles S. Singleton (Princeton, NJ, 1977). C. S. Singleton, *An Essay on the 'Vita nuova'* (1949; repr. Baltimore, 1977).

Howard H. Schless, *Chaucer and Dante: A Revaluation* (Norman, Okla., 1984), pp. 50–2, 68–70. Carruthers, *Book of Memory*: 'The metaphor of memory as a written surface', she suggests, 'is so ancient and so persistent in all Western cultures that it must . . . be seen as a governing model or "cognitive archetype"' (p. 16). On the nature of mem-ory storage as understood in the Middle Ages see Carruthers, pp. 46–60. More specifically, she discusses the 'storehouse model' on pp. 14, 33–45, 145, 146, 192, 246, 247. On the term *thesaurus* ('storage-room', 'strong-box') as applied to memory see pp. 33–5, 38, 82, 160–1, 251, 261. For the memory as a treasure-house see pp. 73–4, 85, 113, 160–1, 204, 207, 246. Quintilian described memory as the treasury of eloquence ('thesaurus hic eloquentiae'; cited on p. 74).

Dante, *The Divine Comedy: Paradiso*, ed. and trans. Charles S. Singleton (Princeton, NJ, 1977). Ovid, *Metamorphoses*, ed. and trans. Miller. Francis Petrarch was actually crowned with laurel for his poetic achievements—though in Latin rather than the ver-nacular—at Rome on Easter Sunday 1341, having stood a public examination before King Robert of Naples. Chaucer refers to him as 'lauriat poet' at *CT* IV(E) 31.

Medieval topoi of affected modesty are discussed by Curtius, *European Literature*, pp. 79, 83–5.

David Wallace, 'Chaucer's Continental Inheritance', in Boitani and Mann (eds.), *Chaucer Companion*, pp. 22–4. I have drawn on notes in Havely's edition of *HF* and also his unpublished paper, 'The *House of Fame*: Italian Muses and English Poetry'. H. A. Kelly, *Ideas and Forms of Tragedy, from Aristotle to the Middle Ages* (Cambridge, 1993). For further discussion see P. Hardman, 'Chaucer's Muses and his Art Poetical', *RES* 37 (1986), 478–94, and P. B. Taylor with S. Bordier, 'Chaucer and the Latin Muses', *Traditio*, 47 (1992), 215–32.

On Chaucer's invocations in *HF* compare the valuable comments by J. A. W. Bennett, 'Chaucer, Dante and Boccaccio', in Boitani (ed.), *Italian Trecento*, pp. 89–113 (pp. 107–10); Burlin, *Chaucerian Fiction*, pp. 52–3, 56; John P. McCall, *Chaucer among the Gods: The Poetics of Classical Myth* (University Park, Pa. and London, 1979), pp. 56–8.

Macrobius refers to Apollo as the 'leader of the Muses' in *In Somnium Scipionis*, II. iii. 3; trans. Stahl, p. 194. Medieval attitudes to Apollo are usefully reviewed by M. Twycross, 'The Representation of the Major Classical Divinities in the Works of Chaucer, Gower, Lydgate and Henryson' (B. Litt. diss., University of Oxford, 1961), pp. 275–80. On the classical sources of traditions relating to the Delphic oracle see Joseph Fontenrose, *The Delphic Oracle: Its Responses and Operations, with a Catalogue of Responses* (Berkeley and Los Angeles, 1978). Ambiguous pagan prophecies are discussed by A. J. Minnis, *Chaucer and Pagan Antiquity* (Cambridge, 1982), pp. 33–7, 135–9, 181 n. 83. *Re* idolatry see the relevant discussion in Michael Camille, *The Gothic Idol: Ideology and Image-Making in Medieval Art* (Cambridge, 1989).

Isidore of Seville, *Etymologiae*, ed. W. M. Lindsay (Oxford, 1911). Coopland, *Oresme and the Astrologers*. Guido delle Colonne, *Historia destructionis Troiae*, ed. Griffin, trans. Meek. Similarly, Macrobius had stated that 'all portents and dreams conform to the rule that their announcements, threats or warnings of imminent adversity are always ambiguous'. He takes a relatively positive view of this, however, citing the *Iliad*'s story of how a dream sent from Zeus encouraged King Agamemnon to engage in a battle with the enemy in which he was heavily defeated. We cannot say, Macrobius declares, that 'the deity had sent him a deceitful vision'. For there was 'a hint concealed in the words of the dream which, if carefully heeded, could have enabled him at least to avoid calamity, and perhaps even to conquer'. Besides, the king did not follow all of the deity's commands, and thus absolved him 'from blame of falsehood'. *In Somnium Scipionis*, I. vii. 1–6, trans. Stahl, pp. 118–19. On the ambivalence of dreams see further pp. 47–49, above.

Chaucer's female Marsyas may result from a confusion found in a sub-branch of the manuscripts of the *Roman de la Rose*, on which see Alfred David, 'How Marcia Lost Her Skin: A Note on Chaucer's Mythology', in Larry D. Benson (ed.), *The Learned and the Lewed* (Cambridge, Mass., 1974), pp. 19–29. However, particularly in view of Chaucer's knowledge of *Paradiso*, i. 13–36, it is possible that he was influenced by Dante's appeal to Apollo to 'enter into my breast and breathe there as when you drew Marsyas from the sheath of his limbs' (19–21; trans. Singleton, p. 5), which he partly misread. But the two passages are utterly different in nature and effect; Apollo is anything but impressive in the *HF* passage. (See further Chaucer's anti-heroic vulgarization of Phoebus Apollo in the *Manciple's Tale*.) Once again the English poet has turned Dante's elevated symbolism into something which is quite literal and earth-bound through the provision of narrative details from the fable in question which are not present—and which would be utterly inappropriate—in the text of the *Comedy*.

Muscatine, *French Tradition*. Lewis, *Allegory of Love*. My final sentence appropriates a phrase from a poem by the young Louis MacNeice, which is quoted by a critic who uses it in the title of his monograph: William McKinnon, *Apollo's Blended Dream: The*

*Poetry of Louis MacNeice* (Oxford, 1971), p. 52. The reference is to poetry which does not reflect only the world of roses and rosemary, but accepts and expresses the blended dream that includes a wide range of experiences and events (particularly those that are far from what traditionally is conceived of as 'poetic'). This agenda for modern poetry, as recommended by MacNeice, has intriguing similarities to the one followed over 500 years previously by *HF*.

## Sources, Images, Sounds

All the things which men say, because they are made of air (which rises according to its very nature), travel upwards to the House of Fame, a reputation factory in which they are duly processed and their posterity determined. It is to this rarefied land of reified language that 'Geffrey' travels, the basic genre within which Chaucer's poem falls being that of the intellectual or mental flight. That is to say, the *House of Fame* belongs to the same category as Cicero's *Somnium Scipionis* (which in the Middle Ages circulated in association with Macrobius's commentary on it), Martianus Capella's *De nuptiis Mercurii et Philologiae*, and indeed Dante's *Comedia*. There are, moreover, several important passages in 2 Corinthians, the Book of Revelation, Boethius's *De consolatione philosophiae*, and Alan of Lille's *Anticlaudianus*. All these works are named or alluded to in this the most bookish of Chaucer's books; he was to experiment further with the genre at the beginning of the *Parliament of Fowls* and the end of *Troilus*. In particular, the arts subjects touched upon by the eagle (physics, metaphysics, astronomy/astrology, grammar, music, rhetoric, poetics) as he carries his corpulent cargo aloft, distantly echo 'Marcian's' (985) narrative of philologia ('love of language') ascending to heaven to be married to the god of eloquence, accompanied by her handmaidens the Seven Liberal Arts. But Chaucer's account of a flight to Fame is unique.

Three vernacular poems which are sometimes compared with the *House of Fame* centre on human love, and confine themselves to earthbound journeys through allegorical regions. In Nicole de Margival's *Dit de la Panthere d'Amours* (probably *c.*1300) the God of Love directs the dreamer to a house of Fortune, where he hopes to further his love-suit; Jean Froissart's *Temple d'Honneur* (*c.*1363) contains, as its title suggests, an elaborate description of a temple of Honour. Boccaccio's far more ambitious *Amorosa Visione* widens the scope of the love-vision, but a love-vision it remains (and sometimes a scurrilous one at that). This poem bears some interesting resemblances to Chaucer's, including the use of pictures to tell stories, in this case frescoes of the triumphs of Wisdom (which includes a depiction of the great poets, wherein Dante appears in the company of the ancients), Worldly Glory, Riches, and Love respectively. There is, however, no definite evidence of direct influence,

and in any case, it is Fortune rather than Fame who occupies a key position in Boccaccio's work. Indeed, in marked contrast to the well-established tradition of Fortune, Fame occupied only a minor position in the
repertoire of medieval poets, her iconography being scarcely developed.
Chaucer seems to be breaking new ground.

On the apotheosis tradition, which includes many accounts of heavenly journeys, see John
   M. Steadman, *Disembodied Laughter: 'Troilus' and the Apotheosis Tradition* (Berkeley
   and Los Angeles, 1972); also Howard, 'Flying through Space'. On the significance of
   this tradition for the beginning of *PF* see pp. 266–71 below.
Nicole de Margival, *Dit de la Panthère d'Amours*, ed. H. A. Todd, SATF (Paris, 1883);
   excerpts trans. Windeatt, in *Sources and Analogues*, pp. 127–32. Froissart, *Temple
   d'Honneur*, in *Dits et Débats*, ed. A. Fourrier (Geneva, 1979); excerpts trans. in
   Windeatt, pp. 133–5.
On *HF* and Boccaccio's *Amorosa Visione* see especially Boitani, *Imaginary World*, pp. 20,
   82, 93–5, 100, 113, 121, 129, 159, 168, 205, and David Wallace, 'Chaucer and
   Boccaccio's Early Writings', in Boitani (ed.), *Italian Trecento*, pp. 141–5; also Wallace's
   monograph *Chaucer and the Early Writings of Boccaccio* (Cambridge, 1985), pp. 5–22.
   Both admit that the case for direct influence is not strong. Petrarch's *Trionfi* has a similar status as a possible source: there are parallels, but nothing to clinch the matter. See
   J. A. W. Bennett, *Book of Fame*, pp. 109–10; Boitani, *Imaginary World*, pp. 20, 93, 104,
   112, 121–4, 205.
The influence of Dante's *Comedy* has been considered in the previous section; other possible parallels are collected in the editions by Fyler (*Riverside Chaucer*) and Havely. For
   a minimalist view of the matter see Schless, *Chaucer and Dante*, pp. 29–76. The suggestion that Dante's *Convivio* may have influenced certain passages in *HF* was made
   by John L. Lowes, 'Chaucer and Dante's *Convivio*', *MP* 13 (1915–16), 19–33, and
   amplified by J. P. Bethel, 'The Influence of Dante on Chaucer's Thought and
   Expression' (Ph.D. diss., Harvard University, 1927). Schless (pp. 60–4, 74–6) critiques
   the suggestions *re HF* 936–59 and 2060–75, and takes a more positive line in respect
   of the latter, 'although the passage in the *Convivio* cannot be definitively offered as a
   source' (p. 76).


THE FAME OF FAME: OVID, VIRGIL, BOETHIUS, AND THE
*ROMAN D'ENÉAS*

The primary sources for Chaucer's conception of the goddess were indubitably the accounts of Rumour (*fama*) in the *Aeneid*, iv. 173–90, and the
*Metamorphoses*, xii. 39–63, both of which relate to what the Middle Ages
regarded as 'the matter of Troy'.

   Ovid's version occurs in the narrative context of the Greek ships coming to attack Troy. The Trojans are prepared for this invasion, because
they have had advance warning of it from Rumour. She lives in the middle of the world, situated between earth and sky and sea, 'a place from
which everything the world over can be seen, however far away, and to
its listening ears comes every sound' (39–42; trans. Innes, p. 269). 'There
Rumour lives, in a home she has chosen for herself on a hilltop' (43).

This is why the narrator has to make such a difficult climb ('with alle payne') to the House of Fame on its 'hygh . . . roche' (1115–19). From this vantage-point she sees everything that 'is done in heaven, on the sea and land, and searches throughout the world for news' (62–3). This seems to have influenced Chaucer's account of the place

> Ther as Fame lyst to duelle,
> Ys set amyddys of these three,
> Heven, erthe, and eke the see,
> As most conservatyf the soun.                    *preserving*
>                                                                          (844–7)

An even clearer parallel appears earlier in the scholar-eagle's lecture to its captive audience:

> 'First shalt thou here where she duelleth,
> And do thynn oune bok hyt tellith:
> Hir paleys stant, as I shal seye,
> Ryght even in myddes of the weye
> Betwixen hevene and earthe and see,
> That what so ever in al these three
> Is spoken, either privy or apert,               *privately, publicly*
> The way therto ys so overt,
> And stant eke in so juste a place                        *exact*
> That every soun mot to hyt pace;                       *proceed*
> Or what so cometh from any tonge,
> Be hyt rouned, red, or songe,                        *whispered*
> Or spoken in suerte or in drede,           *confidently, fear*
> Certeyn, hyt moste thider nede'.          *must needs go there*
>                                                                          (711–24)

Chaucer's 'oune bok' must be the *Metamorphoses*.

His description of the House of Rumour (1925–85) is heavily indebted to Ovid's account. 'Night and day', Ovid explains, the house of Rumour 'stands open' (46; cf. *HF* 1951, 1953), for *Fama* has given it 'countless entrances, a thousand apertures' (44–5; cf. *HF* 1948–50), 'with no doors to close them' (45). Chaucer's edifice does have doors, but they are always open (*HF* 1951–5). The whole structure is of 'echoing brass', and is full of confused noises (45–6; cf. *HF* 1957, 1960); it 'repeats all words and doubles what it hears. There is no quiet within, no silence in any part' (47–8; cf. *HF* 1956), 'and yet there is no loud din, but only murmured whisperings' (49; Chaucer has both whisperings and loud tidings, 1958), whisperings 'like the sound of the sea's waves, heard at a distance, or the last rumbles of thunder when Jupiter has crashed dark clouds together (50; those images appear at *HF* 1034–42; cf. 608, 1025–31). Crowds fill the hall, 'shifting throngs come and go, and everywhere wander thousands of rumours, falsehoods mingled with the truth, and confused reports flit about' (53–8). (Here I have drawn on the translations of both Innes and Miller.) Similarly, Chaucer's eagle informs his reluctant passenger that Fame's house is

> full of tydynges,
> Bothe of feir speche and chidynges,
> And of fals and soth compouned.        *truth compounded*
>                                          (1027–9)

Some of these inhabitants, Ovid continues, 'pour their stories into idle ears, others carry off elsewhere the tales they have been told, the story grows, and each new teller [*novus auctor*] adds something to what he has heard. Here live Credulity, and hot-headed Error, groundless Joy and craven Fears, Sedition newly-born, and Whispers whose origin no one knows' (trans. Innes, p. 269). There is no precedent here, however, for a twirling house made of twigs in the shape of a beehive. Whirling houses do occur in romances; the building material presents a greater problem, and it has been suggested that Chaucer knew of the existence of such houses in Ireland or Wales. 'Chaucer would not need to wander in Wales or Ireland to find such dwellings,' protests Bennett; 'They were a part of any rural scene' (p. 169). He adds the suggestion that Chaucer may have had in mind the cage in which, according to the medieval Alexander legend, birds carried the king up through the aerial regions (cf. the reference to 'Alixandre Macedo' at line 915).

Whereas Ovid concentrated on Fame's dwelling, Virgil focused on her very nature. The Virgilian account is of more obvious relevance to the *House of Fame*, given its concern with 'the matter of love' in general and the specific subject of book i. For Virgil's description immediately follows his account of how Dido and Aeneas consummate their love in a cavern. After this, he declares, Dido ceases to care for her appearance 'or her good name' or for maintaining 'secrecy in her love' (170–1; trans. Knight, p. 102). Whereupon rumour (*fama*) spreads. She races through Libya's great cities (could that have influenced *HF* 488?), 'for of all pests she is the swiftest' (174). As Chaucer puts it,

> thorgh yow [Fame] is my name lorn,        *lost*
> And alle myn actes red and songe
> Over al thys lond, on every tonge.
> O wikke Fame!—for ther nys
> Nothing so swift, lo, as she is!         (346–50)

Rumour, Virgil continues, is 'fleet of foot, and swift are her wings; she is a vast fearful monster, with a watchful eye miraculously set under every feather which grows on her, and for every one of them a tongue in a mouth which is loud of speech, and an ear ever alert' (180–3). Clearly, this lies behind Chaucer's description of the creature with as many eyes as birds have feathers (1381–2) and as many ears and tongues as beasts have hairs (1389–90).

Yet Chaucer does not allow his Fame to degenerate into something totally grotesque. She remains a 'femynyne creature' (1365), and owes a lot to the much more common medieval iconography of Dame Fortune— a family resemblance which Chaucer acknowledges by presenting them as sisters (an original touch).

> Ryght as her suster, dame Fortune,
> Ys wont to serven in comune.                          (1547–8)

In other words, neither female is any respecter of persons or of personal merit, and Chaucer's account of Fame's capricious decrees reveals that they are also alike in being constant only in their very inconstancy (cf. *De consolatione philosophiae*, II, pr. i; also *Troilus* i. 843–4: "Woost thow nat wel that Fortune is comune'). Chaucer's description of her feet reaching the earth while her head touches heaven (1374–6) is an obvious parody of the appearance of Dame Philosophy at I, pr. i, 8–13, of the *Consolatio*, and clear echoes of this work occur elsewhere in the poem; most striking perhaps is the citation of the statement of 'Boece' that a thought may fly beyond the elements 'Wyth fetheres of Philosophye' (972–8; cf. *De consolatione philosophiae*, IV, met. i, 1–5).

But let us return to Virgil's account. Fame 'strikes dread throughout great cities, for she is as retentive of news which is false and wicked as she is ready to tell what is true'. And so she spreads 'various talk among the peoples of Libya, repeating alike facts and fictions [*facta atque infacta*]', telling how Dido and Aeneas 'were now spending all the long winter together in comfort and self-indulgence, caught in the snare of shameful passion, with never a thought of their royal duty. Such was the talk which this foul goddess everywhere inserted into the conversations of men' (187–95; p. 103). That last sentence may have influenced Dido's speculation concerning what 'seyth the peple prively' (360). What most struck Chaucer about these two accounts, however, seems to have been the notion that fame mixes fact and fiction: certainly this is fundamental to his conception of the *House of Fame*.

That fine twelfth-century French *roman antique*, the *Roman d'Eneas*, elaborated upon Ovid's remark about tales growing with every telling. Even though Fame knows little of something, she makes much of it, enlarging 'it more and more'. 'She enlarges with equal speed the false thing, as well as the true.' 'From a little bit of truth', the French poet continues, 'she tells such lies that it seems like a dream, and she exaggerates it so that there is not the least truth in it' (trans. Yunck, p. 87). Moreover, the monster Fame is developed into a creature who neither stops nor rests, having 'a thousand mouths with which she speaks, a thousand eyes, a thousand wings with which she flies, a thousand ears with which she listens for any wonder that she might spread about'.

However, this romance is not necessarily a source. The main argument in favour of this hypothesis seems to be that both Chaucer and the French poet begin at the beginning of the narrative rather than, as did Virgil, *in medias res* by putting the fall of Troy (as recounted by Aeneas to Dido) in the second book rather than in the first. But this could be simple coincidence; Chaucer did not have to take such a lesson from the French poet in how to re-order a narrative, particularly since the notion that there were two types of order, *ordo naturalis* and *ordo artificialis*, was a commonplace of medieval literary theory, and usually illustrated with reference to the *Aeneid*. In his twelfth-century commentary on Virgil 'Bernard Silvester' defines 'natural order' as occurring 'when the work is set out in accordance with the sequence of events', the narrative following the order in which the events really happened, while 'artificial order occurs when we begin the narrative artificially right in the middle, and subsequently return to the beginning' (trans. Minnis and Scott, p. 151). Chaucer would have had no trouble in determining the *ordo naturalis* of his story, such as was sufficient for his needs. He was also quite capable of independent recasting of the story as having love rather than 'arms and the man' as its high subject. In this regard the influence of Ovid's *Heroides* is paramount; with good reason is 'the Epistle of Ovyde' (379) mentioned alongside 'Virgile in Eneydos' (378). *Heroides* vii, wherein Dido cries out against her faithless lover, inspired Chaucer's version of her complaint, and her fate leads the narrator to think of other women who have been 'forsworn' by 'fals' men. They are all heroines from Ovid's work, and they appear in roughly the same order. Chaucer was to explore the similarities between them at greater length in the *Legend of Good Women*.

Finally, a few further words on 'Boece'. The eloquent critique of earthly glory in *De consolatione philosophiae*, II, pr. vii–met. vii, probably influenced Chaucer's own thinking on that subject. Of special significance is the statement by the airborne poet that the entire world seemed no more than a pinpoint or 'prikke' to him (907), which is probably indebted to *De consolatione philosophiae*, II, pr. vii, 11 and 21 (the Latin *punctus* is translated as 'prykke' in these passages in the *Boece*). The limited, inferior status of worldly ambition within the grand scheme of things may be gauged through recognition of just how small the earth is in relation to the heavens, Boethius declares. Moreover, only a quarter of the earth is habitable (some regions being wasteland, like the 'desert of Lybye' referred to in *HF* 488), which narrows even further the limits within which fame can spread. The diversity of languages and the difficulties of travel hinder the process of transmission. Besides, fame is relative: since there is a wide variety of customs in the world, what one race approves of may be condemned by another. The best that one can hope for is to have one's 'glory well-known among his own people', fame necessarily being 'restricted within the bounds of one nation'.

But, he continues, 'how many men famous in their own time are now completely forgotten, for want of written record?' (trans. Tester, p. 219). As Boethius asks in the following metrum, who now remembers the good Fabricius or Cato or Brutus? Names written in a few letters are all the fame that is left to them, and by reading these letters we cannot gain knowledge of the people themselves. 'The thynne fame yit lastynge of here idel [i.e. valueless] names is marked with a fewe lettres' (*Boece*, p. 420). One may compare Chaucer's vision of the fading letters on the rock of ice which forms the feeble foundation of the House of Fame:

| | |
|---|---:|
| wel unnethes koude I knowe | *hardly* |
| Any lettres for to rede | |
| Hir names by; for, out of drede, | *no question* |
| They were almost ofthowed so | *thawed* |
| That of the lettres oon or two | |
| Was molte away of every name, | *melted* |
| So unfamous was woxe hir fame. | (1140–6) |

While the 'Boethian resonances of reducing the world to a "prikke"' may well be, as Fyler suggests (p. 56), 'undercut by the Eagle's naturalism' (here he is referring to the creature's reduction of 'language and meaning to their lowest naturalistic common denominator'), their serious aspects are given considerable space in the third book of the *House of Fame*, in lines like the ones we have just quoted.

Moreover, problems which Boethius had adumbrated regarding the status of writings and writers are obviously on his mind there also. What is the value of such records as do survive from the past, when they and their *auctores* 'are lost in the obscurity of long ages?' (II, pr. vii, 47–9; trans. Tester, p. 219). Which may be taken as asking, what sort of fame can literature itself expect? Secondly, how powerful is the writer's role as recorder? Many a man 'that was ful noble in his tyme' has been 'put out of mynde and doon away' by 'the wrecchid and nedy foryetynge of writeris', declares the *Boece* (p. 419), giving the writer a more definite role than Boethius's Latin would seem to allow here. ('Scriptorum inops' probably has the more passive sense of the general deficiencies of written records, as per Tester's translation.) Chaucer's depiction of Lady Fame goes further than this, in suggesting that, as well as causing certain names to be forgotten (the emphasis from her standpoint being of course on *deliberate* ignoring rather than accidental omission), she can create or destroy reputations. And writers are her agents in this process. Indeed, they may be regarded—in every sense of the term—as *makeres* of fame.

Ovid, *Metamorphoses*, trans. Miller. Ovid, *Metamorphoses*, trans. Mary M. Innes (Harmondsworth, 1955). J. A. W. Bennett, *Book of Fame*. Virgil, *Aeneid*, trans. W. F. Jackson Knight (Harmondsworth, 1958). Boethius, *De consolatione philosophiae*, ed. and trans. Tester. Chaucer seems to have thoroughly assimilated the *Consolatio* by now, using expressions from it easily and naturally, often in ways far removed from their original contexts.

*Eneas: A Twelfth-Century French Romance*, trans. John A. Yunck (New York and London, 1974). For the Old French text see the edition by J.-J. Salverda de Grave (Paris, 1925–9). Useful discussions of this work include R. J. Cormier, *One Heart, One Mind: The Rebirth of Virgil's Hero in Medieval French Romance*, Romance Monographs (University, Miss., 1973); Louis Brewer Hall, 'Chaucer and the Dido-and-Aeneas Story', *MS* 25 (1963), 149–53; and especially Barbara Nolan, *Chaucer and the Tradition of the 'Roman Antique'* (Cambridge, 1991), pp. 71–4, 77–96. It should be noted that Ovidian complaint exercised a major influence on the laments of pagan women in this and other romances of antiquity, as Nolan demonstrates superlatively well.

Minnis and Scott (eds.), *Medieval Literary Theory*. Alternatively, see Bernard Silvester, *The Commentary on the First Six Books of the 'Aeneid' of Virgil commonly attributed to Bernardus Silvestris*, ed. J. W. Jones and E. F. Jones (Lincoln, Nebr., and London, 1977); trans. E. G. Schreiber and T. E. Maresca (Lincoln, Nebr., and London, 1979), pp. 3–4. The attribution to Bernard has been contested; see especially Christopher Baswell, 'The Medieval Allegorization of the *Aeneid*: MS Cambridge, Peterhouse 158', *Traditio*, 41 (1985), 181–237.

The distinction between natural and artificial order is also found in *artes poetriae*. See Geoffrey of Vinsauf, *Poetria nova*, trans. Kopp, pp. 39–40; also Geoffrey's *Documentum*, trans. Parr, pp. 39–40.

Fyler, *Chaucer and Ovid*. Contrast the resolutely serious use of Boethius made in the approach of Koonce, *Tradition of Fame*, pp. 159–61, 166–9, 186–8, etc. A more nuanced Boethian reading has been provided by C. P. R. Tisdale, 'The *House of Fame*: Virgilian Reason and Boethian Wisdom', *Comparative Literature*, 25 (1973), 247–61.

'FIGURES OF OLDE WERK': PICTURES TELLING STORIES

Many of Chaucer's images for the insubstantiality of fame (ice, glass, wind, etc.), which appear and combine throughout the poem, are traditional. One of the most pervasive was the image of wind. This has biblical precedent (Hosea 12: 1, Ecclesiasticus 34: 1–2), but is also characteristic of medieval scholarship on the classical poets. Hence 'Bernard Silvester' in his *Aeneid* commentary can gloss Boreas, the wind, as 'glory', citing in support Juvenal, 'Whom glory has borne to the stage in the windy car' (*Epistles*, ii. 1. 77), and a *sententia* which seems to derive ultimately from Euripides' *Andromeda* (319–20), 'Glory is nothing but a great wind in the ears' (trans. Schreiber and Maresca, p. 72). Similarly, Dante's Oderisi da Gubbio speaks of earthly fame as being 'but a breath of wind, which now comes hence and now comes thence, changing its name because it changes quarter' (*Purgatorio*, xi. 100–2; trans. Singleton, p. 115). This notion lies behind the 'grete soun' that 'rumbleth up and doun' in the *House of Fame* (1025–7) and also, of course, Chaucer's hilarious account of Aeolus, the god of wind, with his two clarions, one which sounds the praise of those of whom Fame approves, and the other which is universally called 'Slander' (1567 ff.).

The poem's remarkably rich use of imagery often demands a visual response, the beholder being invited to imagine with the mind's eye various murals, sculptures, and architectural structures which beggar description. In book i the temple of Venus is described as being filled with

| | | |
|---|---|---|
| ymages | | |
| Of gold, stondynge in sondry stages, | | *stands* |
| And moo ryche tabernacles, | | *decorated niches* |
| And with perre moo pynacles. | *precious stones, pinnacles* | |
| And moo curiouse portreytrues, | | |
| And queynte maner of figures | | *elaborate* |
| Of olde werk | | (121–7) |

This 'portreyture' includes a depiction of naked Venus, floating on the sea with her characteristic accoutrements of rose garland and doves. Chaucer then guides us through the narrative of Troy as 'writen' (and also depicted?) on a brass tablet. In book iii 'Geffrey' explores 'queynte' architectural structures which range from the sublime to the ridiculous: Fame's castle and great hall, with its many pillars supporting the several poetic subject-matters; the rotating wicker dwelling of Rumour which is, we are assured, more wonderful and elaborately wrought than the labyrinth, the design of the master-craftsman Daedalus.

Bennett had no doubt that the interior structure and design of the temple of Venus resemble 'less a classical temple than a Gothic church of the late decorated or early perpendicular period when stained glass was at its richest and stone grew plastic in the hands of the sculptors of the Percy tomb at Beverly or the carvers of the pillars at Strassburg'. He speculates that the phrase 'Ymad of glas', which describes the exterior appearance of the temple, would be an appropriate way of referring to 'the window-walls that the new perpendicular style made possible', and offers the example of the (now destroyed) chapel of St Stephen at Westminster. The Sainte-Chapelle in Paris has also been suggested as a possible model.

Moreover, with reference to the depiction of the Dido and Aeneas story, Bennett reminds us that the art of mural painting, either on stone or on wood panels, 'reached its peak in Chaucer's lifetime' (pp. 12–13).

But the poem's architectural antecedents are largely literary. For a start, there is, as Bennett freely accepts, classical precedent in the first book of the *Aeneid*, where Virgil describes how, upon his arrival in Carthage, Aeneas visits the temple of Juno and sees 'pictured there the Trojan War, with all the battles round Ilium in their correct order, for their fame had already spread over the world'. Indeed, he even 'recognized himself hotly engaged among the Greek chieftains' (i. 456–7; trans. Knight, p. 41). However, Virgil only gives the merest hint of a temple of Venus (*Aeneid*, i. 416–17), and besides, in the *House of Fame* the determining influence is surely medieval rather than classical. We are looking at the legacy of the mythographers who enlisted supposedly pagan images in the service of Christian truth by elaborately moralizing them. Chaucer's iconography of Venus seems to have its primary source in the second redaction of Pierre Bersuire's *Ovidius moralizatus* (completed by 1362); he also may have drawn on this account in his fuller description of the temple of Venus in the *Knight's Tale*, a version of which he had written sometime before 1386–8.

For Chaucer the large amount of glass in the temple of Venus is a symbol of the very insubstantiality of the structure—which is *entirely* made of glass—rather than a literal description deriving from Chaucer's recollection of 'the window-walls that the new perpendicular style made possible'. This is the sense brought out in John Lydgate's reworking—and simplification—of Chaucer's poem, the *Temple of Glass* (probably written before *c*.1412).

> me þou3te þat I was
> Rauysshid in spirit in a temple of glas—
> I nyste how, ful fer in wildirnes—　　　　　　*don't know*
> That foundid was, as bi liklynesse,
> Not opon stele, but on a craggy roche,
> Like ise ifrore.　　　　　　　　　　　　　　*frozen*
> 　　　　　　　　　　　　　　　　　　　　　(15–20)

Clearly, not a structure—or a goddess—to rely on. But how deep should the audience's suspicion of Chaucer's Venus actually be? Bersuire, following the fifth-century *Mythologiae* of Fulgentius, allegorizes Venus as the voluptuous life or a certain voluptuous person, said to be a woman because of woman's inconstancy. Her nakedness indicates indecency; her doves, the lecherous people whom she nourishes; her roses, vain curiosities. She is said to have been born in the sea because she always wishes to be in delights; Bersuire compares her with another 'daughter of the sea', the harlot described in Isaiah 23: 10 and 16. All this Chaucer omitted—just as in the *Book of the Duchess* he had found no place for the allegorical interpretation of the tale of Ceyx and Alcyone as provided in the *Ovide moralisé* (see pp. 95–6, 138 above). And this was done, I think, precisely for the same reason: namely, that as a poet he was not interested in writing within the tradition of 'moralised mythography'.

Is he, however, *implying* a moral of some kind, expecting his readers to supply what he has not, for whatever reason, made explicit? D. W. Robertson, defending his allegorical reading of the temple of Venus in the *Knight's Tale*, argues that 'since all the details are consistent with the traditional meanings attributed to Venus by medieval mythographers', it 'would be mere critical waywardness to consider the temple as a whole to be just so much decoration on the surface of a "story", or to regard it as a blind accumulation of detail without significance' (p. 373). An allegorical reading of the similar temple in the *House of Fame* is included in B. G. Koonce's Robertsonian *Chaucer and the Tradition of Fame* (1966). Boccaccio had made a (now much-quoted) distinction between two Venuses in his own gloss on the temple of Venus as described in the *Teseida* (a passage which Chaucer was to use directly in the *Parliament of Fowls*; see pp. 283–7 below). One Venus represents 'all worthy and legitimate desires' and is associated with marriage, but the other is she 'who causes all kinds of lust to be desired' (trans. Havely, p. 131), and it is her temple, Boccaccio continues, which is described in his poem. Having quoted this, Koonce proceeds to argue that as a symbol Chaucer's temple of Venus points to the contrast between carnal and spiritual love. Allegorically, he says, 'the "chirche" of Venus is an inversion of the Church of Christ'. This 'false temple symbolizes not only the mind's estrangement from God but also the end of such estrangement. Anagogically, therefore, it is an image of Hell, the dwelling of Satan' (p. 102). The I-persona 'must learn to distinguish between appearance and reality and thereby perceive the nature and end of the wrongful love typified by Venus and her glittering temple' (p. 103); that lesson is the purpose of book i. In a much milder version of this approach, Brewer suggests that the temple in question belongs to the lascivious Venus of 'painful betrayed love', which of course would form an appropriate context for the betrayal of Dido by Aeneas and the appended list of other women who have suffered a similar fate (p. 74).

Against such views it may be argued that a writer has as much right to leave out as to leave in, and it is perfectly possible for imagery which signifies something in a particular context to be made to signify something quite different within a different context. The Venus of the *Knight's*

*Tale* can be regarded as a single but ambiguous goddess: she brings division, but she also unites Palamon and Emily (who eventually enter into the pagan equivalent of holy matrimony). Similarly, the naked goddess in the *House of Fame* can bring pain and pleasure, and may be regarded as a mixture of good and bad qualities—perfectly appropriate for a poem which sees poetic fiction and fame itself as a compounding of truth and falsehood. After all, Virgil's narrative had revealed her dualistic nature. In the *Aeneid* she is at once a good mother to Aeneas and quite ruthless in her treatment of Dido. In the *House of Fame*, moreover, it is Aeneas rather than Venus who gets the blame for Dido's demise—and likewise with the other tales of disloyal menfolk. Thus, the ultimate culpability of Venus is simply not brought out, and the relationship between 'lore' and 'game' which the poem seems so anxious to maintain—with the emphasis falling on the latter—is left undisturbed.

Furthermore, there is a real sense in which it is profitable (*pace* Robertson and Koonce) to claim that what one sees in the *House of Fame* is what one should get. The mythographic tradition is only one of several in which medieval Christians sought to come to terms with their classical heritage. It would be quite reductive, not to say rather boring, to presume that there was only one road to Rome—and how better to illustrate that than to consult the major medieval guidebook to the continuing city, the *Mirabilia urbis Romae*? written around 1143 by one Benedict, a canon of St Peter's, this served as a guide for pilgrims long into the fifteenth century. While it scrupulously relates the various Christian martyrdoms and triumphs to their proper locations, the *Mirabilia* betrays no anxiety about contemplating the beauty of the city's classical marvels. And the conclusion of the book declares its purpose of preserving such wonders for posterity:

These and more temples and palaces of emperors, consuls, senators and prefects were inside this Roman city in the time of the heathen, as we have read in old chronicles, have seen with our own eyes, and have heard the ancient men tell of. In writing we have tried as well as we could to bring back to the human memory how great was their beauty in gold, silver, brass, ivory and precious stones. (trans. Nichols, p. 46)

It would be grossly unfair to call Benedict's account of the marvels of Rome 'a blind accumulation of detail without significance' (to reiterate Robertson's phrase). Yet his interests were quite different from those of the moralizing mythographers: he was concerned with topography rather than tropology. And this 'humanism' is every bit as important—indeed, I would say even more so—than the brand identified by Robertson as being essential for an understanding of Chaucer's painterly poetry.

Many of the details in the *Mirabilia* are analogous to those of the iconography of the House of Fame. For instance, Castel Sant' Angelo is said to be 'all covered with stones *and adorned with different stories*' (pp. 35–6), while the palace of Trajan and Hadrian is 'adorned throughout with marvelous works. The ceiling was of many different colours. Here is a pillar of marvelous height and beauty, *carved with the stories of these emperors* like the Pillar of Antoninus at his palace' (p. 39; italics mine). Since Benedict does not feel obliged to provide elaborate allegorization of the great 'temples and palaces' of the heathen, why should we expect Chaucer to do so? And when such interpretation does not form part of the actual text, why should it be said to be implicit or to be found on some more hidden, deeper level of meaning? Moreover, in the light of these descriptions, the view of Bennett that Chaucer's temple of Venus looked more like a medieval church than a classical temple stands out as being anachronistic: Chaucer was depicting his heathen architecture in accordance with the then current state of knowledge concerning the appearance and proportions of such 'queynt' constructions. And, like Benedict, he expected his reader to marvel at the wonders of Fame's domain rather than criticize them for being ideologically unsound. Indeed, the 'wonder tale' element of his journey through space to strange lands inhabited by personified sounds and governed by an all-powerful and utterly unpredictable queen does not always receive the attention it deserves.

But Benedict sought to record actual structures and images, whereas Chaucer did not; Chaucer's iconography is, to reiterate this crucial point, primarily 'literary', and here his art is in accord with the mythographic tradition of 'poetic pictures'. When Bersuire or those English 'classiciz- ing friars' of the early fourteenth century, John Ridevall and Robert Holcot, say that an image of some pagan deity or personification of some abstract quality 'is painted' by the ancients, often they are imagining con- structs which defy actual representation in painting. For instance, in Ridevall's *Fulgentius metaforalis*—which amplifies the moralizations pro- vided by Fulgentius in his *Mythologiae*—any notion of reference to real paintings or carvings is dispelled when he ascribes his *picturae* to the poets in idioms like 'poetic picture', 'according to the poetic image', and 'it is painted by the poets'. 'All this fancy is verbal, not visual,' suggests Beryl Smalley, inasmuch as the 'pictures' (which are justified with refer- ence to their alleged usefulness to preachers) have many abstract and sometimes conflicting traits which would defeat even the most skilled of illustrators (p. 118). In the 'table' of images of the heathen gods which introduces Bersuire's *Ovidius moralizatus* and in Holcot's popular *Moralitates* the technique is developed to produce more unified images, which were easier to draw or paint, but the 'poetic' aspect remains strong.

This iconography is proof positive of the perceived connection between what, in his *Li Bestiaire d'amour* (*c.*1250), Richard de Fournivall termed the 'two doors' of memory, the senses of sight and hearing (literary language being conceived of as primarily spoken and heard rather than 'read' in the modern sense of silent reading). These are the two routes to remembrance; they are alternatives, yet comparable in that they have the same end and share some of the same means:

Painting (*painture*) serves for the eye, speech (*parole*) for the ear. And the manner in which one may make one's way to the house of memory, guardian of the treasure won by man's senses through the excellence of the imagination, makes what is past seem as if it were present. And to this same end, one can come either by painting or by speech. For when one sees a story painted, whether a story of Troy or of some other thing, one sees the deeds of the brave men who were there in past times as if they were present. And so it is with speech. For when one hears a tale read, one perceives the wondrous deeds as if one were to see them taking place. And since what is past is made present by those two means, that is by painting and by speech, therefore it is clear that by these two things one can come to remembrance. (trans. in Kolve, p. 25)

V. A. Kolve, whose translation this is, finds in book i of the *House of Fame* important evidence concerning the way in which Chaucer held the verbal, the visual, and the memorial to be linked (pp. 41–2). The long section devoted to the story of the *Aeneid* is, he declares, remarkable for the ambiguity with which it registers the kind of experience which is involved. First comes reading. The narrator reads, as engraved upon a tablet of brass, the initial lines of the *Aeneid*—lines which, unremarkably in medieval terms, relate to sound, the oral performance of poetry. 'I wol now synge', the inscription says, of 'armes and also the man' (143–4). Yet the account of the story which follows 'is narrated in terms of seeing rather than reading':

> First *sawgh* I the destruction
> Of Troye thurgh the Grek Synon                    (151–2)

At lines 209–11 the narrator 'specifies a new medium altogether' in describing a fearful tempest as being 'peynted on the wal',

and then resumes the 'graven' designation until that point at which he identifies his own act of poetic composition with those temple decorations, by using a verb that belongs to neither poets or 'gravers' by first right: 'What shulde I speke more queynte, / Or peyne me my wordes peynte / To speke of love?' (*HF* 245). Rhetoric, too, has its colours. (pp. 41–2)

After Dido's lament, the verb 'graven' dominates 'the narration of the story until the very end, when what the narrator has been seeing is defined unequivocally as pictorial rather than verbal' (see lines 471–3). In sum, Chaucer's version of Virgil 'begins with words on brass and ends with pictures, perhaps on brass, perhaps on glass, perhaps painted on the wall; between those two points we have at best a shifting sense of what mode of artistic experience is being reported. Reading, seeing, hearing, remembering, and even writing (see ll. 381–2) are rendered as interchangeable'.

Such shifting, remarks Kolve with good reason, is quite 'disorienting'. However, here we may be dealing with difficulties which the text presents to modern rather than medieval readers. For *parole*, spoken speech, or 'voice' (*vox*, on which more later) was supposed to be signified or imaged by the combinations of letter-forms or graphemes. *Painture* could also signify those same sounds, as well as physically replicating mental pictures or *imagines* first seen before the mind's eye; similarly, verbal compositions were sometimes said to be 'written' in the mind before being committed to paper, as already noted (cf. pp. 175–6 above). Both *parole* and *painture* supposedly stimulated the imagination to produce images which were stored in the memory, as Richard de Fournivall indicates. An account more detailed than his may be attempted here. Written language enabled another speech-act, the performance or reading (whether aloud or 'to oneself') of the text, which in turn would lead to the storage of literary 'words and pictures' in the memory of the reader, and, if the reading were public, in the auditors' memories. Similarly, physical images (and/or verbal descriptions of such images, with or without illustrations attached) could provoke the construction of mental images and their memory storage, a process sometimes described explicitly in treatises on contemplation which sought to encourage the production and remembrance of devout imaginations. It would seem, then, that sounds, letters, and pictures interpenetrated in late medieval discourses which mingled the scientifically literal and the pedagogically metaphoric; and, of course, the moralizers of the properties of things elaborated further the ways in which one could be thought of as hearing, seeing, reading, and writing.

Chaucer roams happily in this rich semantic field, perhaps his most striking perception being expressed in an extraordinary depiction of the 'red or blak' colours worn by the sounds which travel from earth to the House of Fame. The ostensible point is, of course, that the various sounds take on the very likenesses of their earthly speakers, whether male or female. But Chaucer also visualizes how, as inscribed in the manuscript book, the *voces* are clothed in either black ink or red (he probably had rubrics in mind):

Whan any speche ycomen ys
Up to the paleys, anon-ryght
Hyt wexeth lyk the same wight
Which that the word in erthe spak,
Be hyt clothed red or blak;
And hath so verray hys lyknesse
That spak the word, that thou wilt gesse
That it the same body be,
Man or woman, he or she                              (1074–82)

Here are words incarnate, in a sense which defies neat classification, but is certainly secular—or secularized. It would seem that sounds can be taken as the souls of language, while written words are the bodies. Personified rumours are found in Ovid's account of Fame's house (*Metamorphoses*, xii. 53–8), but the detail about the preservation of sexual difference is unique to Chaucer. I suspect that he was influenced by the theological commonplace that on the occasion of the Last Judgement souls will return to the same bodies (duly purged of those aspects which make them naturally corruptible) which they inhabited while alive on earth. In this *resurrectio carnis* men will rise as men and women as women, to be glorified or punished in those outer forms which they now occupy. (The argument that women should resurrect in male bodies, since the male body was deemed the more perfect, was generally rejected.) This suggestion regarding the inspiration of lines 1081–2 finds some support in Chaucer's clear echo of a passage from the main biblical pronouncement concerning the Last Things, the Book of Revelation: the four beasts which will honour God's judgement-seat are referred to at lines 1383–5 (cf. Rev. 4: 6). And of course the account of Fame's judgement in book iii of the poem may be seen as a parody of the Last Judgement, with Aeolus serving as a secular substitute for the trumpeter-angels, and Fame's throne being somewhat reminiscent of God's.

But let us return to Kolve's account. It would be 'inadequate and finally off the point' to describe Chaucer's reiteration of the *Aeneid* narrative simply as an instance of *ut pictura poesis*, he concludes. And so it would: for *ut pictura poesis*, 'a speaking picture', (to cite Sir Philip Sidney's definition), is a Renaissance notion. The quite different, if superficially similar, medieval notion of ancient 'poetic painting', as held by the mythographers and 'classicizing friars', is far more to the point, the influence of this tradition on the *House of Fame* (and the *Knight's Tale*) being unmistakable. The interplays of words and image, of reading and seeing, which Kolve perceives in the Chaucer passage are quite commonplace in the hermeneutics of Bersuire, Ridevall, and Holcot, among others. There the two routes to remembrance as described by Richard de

Fournivall have merged to form a single path. Yet Kolve is dismissive of the 'more remote corridors' of 'the mythographic treatises', and actually ignores Bersuire, despite the fact that he may well have been a direct source. Moreover, his implication that the *Ovidius moralizatus* was recherché is rather unfair, given the treatise's popularity in the later Middle Ages, and indeed (in a printed redaction) in the Renaissance.

Kolve believes that his own approach comes somewhat nearer to the 'popular centre' of Chaucer's 'art and audience' (p. 73). In practice this means that the sensory synthesis in the *House of Fame* may be taken as paradigmatic of how narrative poems are made, received, and subsequently remembered. Kolve envisages large, controlling images forming in the minds of medieval readers as the narrative proceeds, thanks to the skill of the poet. These images, so his argument runs, determine the way in which the audience responds to the several parts of the narrative and how the whole work is stored in the memory. In the *Knight's Tale*, imagery of the prison/garden and of the amphitheatre is said to dominate; in the *Miller's Tale*, of nature, youth, and Noah's flood, and so forth. I, for one, am reluctant to follow Kolve that far, given that there are no medieval discussions which treat the matter with the degree, and type, of sophistication which he brings to it—and one would expect something of the kind in the scholastic age of thoroughgoing textual commentary, were the method of imagistic composition and reception as pervasive as he claims. Certainly, as far as the *House of Fame* is concerned, the mythographers' methods seem to afford the most obvious procedural parallels with Chaucer's pictures which tell stories.

Bernard Silvester, *Commentary on the 'Aeneid'*, trans. Schreiber and Maresca. Dante, *Purgatorio*, ed. and trans. Singleton.

J. A. W. Bennett, *Book of Fame*. See also M. F. Braswell, 'Architectural Portraiture in Chaucer's *House of Fame*', *JMRS* 11 (1981), 101–12, and Laura Kendrick, 'Chaucer's House of Fame and the French Palais de Justice', *SAC* 6 (1984), 121–33.

On Bersuire see Minnis and Scott (ed.), *Medieval Literary Theory*, pp. 317–18, 323–4, 366–72; also Minnis, *Chaucer and Pagan Antiquity*, pp. 20–1, 109–14 *passim*, 116–18. On the medieval iconography of Venus, including Bersuire's contribution, see especially Twycross, *Medieval Anadyomene*.

My discussion of Bersuire's Venus picture is based on my own reading of the Latin text, as edited and published by J. Engels and the Instituut voor Laat Latijn of Utrecht, *Petrus Berchorius, Reductorium morale, liber xv: Ovidius moralizatus, cap. i, De formis figurisque deorum*, Wekmateriaal, 3 (Utrecht, 1966), p. 22.

*Temple of Glass*, in Lydgate, *Poems*, ed. Norton Smith.

Robertson, *Preface to Chaucer*. Koonce, *Tradition of Fame*. Boccaccio, *Teseida*, trans. N. R. Havely, *Chaucer's Boccaccio* (Cambridge, 1980). Brewer, *Chaucer*.

*The Marvels of Rome (Mirabilia urbis Romae)*, trans. F. M. Nichols, 2nd edn. by Eileen Gardiner (New York, 1986). This translation is unreliable as a guide to the original *Mirabilia*, since Nichols includes much additional material from later revisions of the text. The passages quoted above are, however, to be found in the original *Mirabilia*, as edited by Roberto Valentini and Giuseppe Zuchetti, *Codice topographico della Città di Roma*, Fonti per la Storia d'Italiano per il medio evo (Rome, 1940–53), iii. 17–65 (see pp. 65, 46, 53).

Beryl Smalley, *English Friars and Antiquity in the Early Fourteenth Century* (Oxford, 1960). On the 'poetic pictures' of these friars see further Frances A. Yates, *The Art of Memory* (London, 1966; repr. Harmondsworth, 1969), pp. 105–9; Carruthers, *Book of Memory*, pp. 230–1.

V. A. Kolve, *Chaucer and the Imagery of Narrative* (London, 1984). See further the important discussion by Carruthers, *Book of Memory*, pp. 221–5, which covers both the Richard de Fournivall passage and *HF* 1074–82. Also J. T. Miller, *Poetic License*, pp. 55–9. Richard's original French text has been edited by C. Segre, *Li Bestiaires d'Amours di Maistre Richard de Fornival* (Milan, 1957), and there is an English translation by J. Beer, *Master Richard's Bestiary of Love and Response* (Berkeley and Los Angeles, 1986).

The visual element in *HF* is also emphasized by Marilynn Desmond, *Reading Dido: Gender, Textuality and the Medieval 'Aeneid'* (Minneapolis, 1994), who emphasizes that Carruthers's evidence derives from Latin textual communities that are entirely masculine. Her argument is that for the dreamer of *HF*, as for his counterpart in the *Roman de la Rose*, 'the masculine identity of the viewer is essentially authorized and clarified by the iconic representation of women'; Geffrey's 'construction as a masculine subject depends on the specular gestures of reading the images of Dido, Venus and Fame' (pp. 132, 134). Thus, Venus is a 'reified figure of female sexuality' (p. 140) which pleasures the male gaze, while Dido is 'primarily represented as the object of the male gaze and thereby the *object* of desire despite the dreamer's insistent awareness of *Aeneid* 4 and *Heroides* 7 as a set of texts which situate Dido—and several other classical women—as the *subject* of desire' (p. 150; my emphases). Moreover, Chaucer emphasizes that Fame is a 'femynyne creature' (1365): 'Geffrey's uncertain and unfocused search for fame is particularly undermined by this sight', Desmond argues; 'this female image . . . challenges his authority as a viewer and makes a fixed interpretation impossible' (p. 136).

The doctrine of the resurrection of the body (cf. Job 19: 26: 'And I shall be clothed again with my skin; and in my flesh I shall see my God') was held as an article of faith. It is alluded to by Dante, *Paradiso*, xiv. 43–5. St Augustine and St Thomas Aquinas, among many others, affirmed that sexual difference will be preserved in risen bodies. See Augustine, *De civitate Dei*, xxii. 17; Aquinas, *Summa contra Gentiles*, iv. 88 ('De sexu et aetate resurgentium'), in *Opera omnia* (Parma, 1852–72), v. 378–9. 'While all defects will be removed' from those risen bodies, Augustine explains, 'their essential nature will be preserved. Now a woman's sex is not a defect: it is natural. And in the resurrection it will be free from the necessity of intercourse and childbirth. However, the female organs will not subserve their former use; they will be part of a new beauty, which will not excite the lust of the beholder—there will be no lust in that life—but will arouse the praises of God for His wisdom and compassion, in that He not only created out of nothing but freed from corruption that which He had created' (trans. in Blamires (ed.), *Woman Defamed*, pp. 82–3). On the age (believed to be the 'perfect age' as intimated by the age at which Christ died), qualities, and stature of the risen body see Augustine, *De civitate Dei*, xx. 20–1, xxii. 13–21; Aquinas, *Summa contra Gentiles*, iv. 82–95 (pp. 372–83); also the major theological textbook of the later Middle Ages, Peter Lombard's *Sentences*, iv, dist. 44, 1–8, in *Magistri Petri Lombardi Sententiae in IV libris distinctae*, 3rd edn. (Grottaferrata, 1971–81), ii. 516–22. See further Dove, *Perfect Age*, pp. 57–9.

Possible echoes of the Book of Revelation in *HF* are discussed by Koonce, *Tradition of Fame*, though some of his alleged parallels seem far-fetched, as is his assumption that

Chaucer's intent was serious. I myself believe that Chaucer is occasionally engaging in biblical parody, of the kind which he was to do so brilliantly in the *Summoner's Tale* (cf. pp. 223–4 below).

On medieval theory of memory and imagination see further the discussion and references on pp. 39–45, 48–9, 53–5, 156–60 above.

### THE DESCENT OF CHAUCER'S EAGLE

Chaucer's funny fowl has a complicated line of descent. Having its ultimate origin in the brief accounts of Jupiter's elevation of Ganymede in the *Aeneid* and *Metamorphoses*, it bears clear marks of descent from Dante's eagle in the *Purgatorio*, and embodies several notions about the nature of the creature as commonly found in bestiaries. The eagle, says Bartholomew the Englishman in his encyclopaedic account of the properties of things (as translated by John Trevisa in 1398), is 'riȝt strong, bolde, and hardy, passyng þe strengþe and boldenes of oþur briddes' (pp. 602–3). This is just as well, given the weight of the portly poet, about which it complains (573–4; cf. 660). 'Geffrey's' refusal to look at the bright stars, lest this would 'shenden' all his 'syghte' (1015–17), probably alludes to the eagle's ability to do just that. Indeed, this bird was supposed to be capable of looking directly at the sun, which emphasizes the power and keenness of its eyesight (hence it is a good astronomer, by contrast with the narrator, who is happy to read about, rather than look directly at, the stars). The eagle's skill as a hunter was therefore prodigious—little wonder that the bird of Jove feels obliged to reassure its passenger that no harm will come to him. Alternatively, as Fyler suggests (p. 48), he may be worried because of the eagle's reputation for carrying its young aloft and dropping them if they refuse to face the sun's brilliance, another property noted by Bartholomew.

Most relevant to Chaucer's conception of this creature, however, is the eagle's status as a contemplative symbol, a fact which links it directly to the Boethian 'fetheres of Philosophye' referred to at lines 972–8, which symbolize how 'hye' a 'thought may flee', as Chaucer himself explains. In that much used guide to decoding the sacred symbolism of the Bible, the fifteenth chapter of the *Celestial Hierarchy*, 'Saint Denis' (Pseudo-Dionysius the Areopagite) explained that

The figure of the eagle signifies the royal dignity and the ascent aloft of the divine, and the swift flight of contemplation, and the power of penetrating acutely, soberly, nimbly, and with wisdom to the draught of the divine sweetness which truly strengthens and nourishes. It also signifies the ability to exercise one's powers of contemplation without any let or hindrance, . . . an ability which acts through the most salutary and clear-sighted elevation of one's own contemplative powers towards the most abundant and clear ray of the eternal wisdom. This ray God the Father gives forth in the fullness of spiritual light and heat, just as the sun is a full expression and source of all physical light and heat. Just so, the eagle sees its prey minutely from afar off, and flies to it swiftly and directly with wings drawn together, and gazes on the rays of the sun with sight which remains unimpaired. (trans. Minnis and Scott, pp. 189–90)

Moreover, the eagle was the symbol of St John, the evangelist who wrote not only a gospel (which begins with an affirmation of the pre-eminence of the divine word, or logos) but also, according to medieval belief, the Book of Revelation, the supreme example of heaven-sent vision in the scriptural canon. (As already suggested, its imagery of the Last Judgement seems to be reflected comically in the third book of Chaucer's poem.) Such traditions lie behind Dante's silent but imposing eagle.

Virgil had alluded to Ganymede 'being carried aloft in hooked talons by the bird which is armourer to Jupiter' (*Aeneid*, v. 252–7); and at *Metamorphoses*, x. 155–61 Ovid refers to how the king of the gods, 'fired with love for Ganymede', changed into a bird (this being a shape which enabled him to carry his thunderbolts), snatched him away, and made him his cup-bearer (cf. Chaucer's 'botiller', 592). This story is also cited in *Purgatorio*, ix. 19–33, the most direct source of *House of Fame*, 534–9. There Dante dreams of an eagle, with feathers of gold, poised in the sky, ready to swoop. 'Having wheeled a while, it descended terrible as a thunderbolt and snatched me upwards as far as the fire.' Dante then awakes from his dream, which has imaged his ascent to the sphere of fire (supposed to exist between the sphere of air and the sphere of the moon). But 'Geffrey' remains in his, remarking (in very un-Dantean language) that the eagle bore him up as lightly as if he were a lark. What with the suddenness of the flight and his fear, the poet swoons, whereupon the eagle cries 'Awak!' Chaucer had already used this joke in the *Book of the Duchess*, 178–83, where Juno's messenger has difficulty in awakening the God of Sleep, Morpheus. It was worth repeating. And it serves as a measure of the distance between the *Divine Comedy* and Chaucer's human comedy of the *House of Fame*.

Dante, waking from his dream of the eagle, had likened himself to Achilles, who had 'turned his awakened eyes about him', not knowing 'where he was, when his mother carried him off, sleeping in her arms from Chiron to Skyros' (*Purgatorio*, ix. 34–8; cf. Statius, *Achilleid*, i. 104–241, 247–50). In reality, he has been borne aloft by St Lucy, symbol of illuminating grace. But the Chaucer persona, being neither Prince Hamlet nor Dante Alighieri, thinks instead of how the sound and tone of the eagle's voice remind him of 'oon' he could name (perhaps his wife, stereotypically shouting to get him up in the morning? or perhaps a servant, performing that same duty? Certainly not St Lucy).

This domestic note is followed by the eagle's grumble about the poet being rather heavy to carry, and then the assurance that his master Jupiter has no intention whatever of turning 'Geffrey' into a star, but is simply willing to reward him for his thankless task of honouring love—by giving him even more material to honour love with. Is that a *reward*? Surely bathos can go no deeper.

Bartholomew the Englishman, *On the Properties of Things*, trans. John Trevisa, ed. M. C. Seymour *et al.* (Oxford, 1975). Fyler, *Chaucer and Ovid*. Minnis and Scott (eds.), *Medieval Literary Theory.*

John M. Steadman has plausibly argued that Bersuire's *Ovidius moralizatus* may be the source of both the epithet 'goddes boteler' (*pincerna deorum*, 'cup-bearer of the gods') and the reference to 'stellifye' (*in celo stellificatus*). See ' "Goddes Boteler" and "Stellifye" (*The Hous of Fame*, 581, 592)', *Archiv für das Studium der neuren Sprachen*, 197 (1960), 16–18.

On Chaucer's eagle see especially Leyerle, 'Chaucer's Windy Eagle', who describes the humour exceptionally well; also J. A. W. Bennett, *Book of Fame*, pp. 49–51, 61–4, 71; Reginald Berry, 'Chaucer's Eagle and the Element Air', *UTQ* 43 (1974), 285–6; Fyler, *Chaucer and Ovid*, pp. 45–8; John M. Steadman, 'Chaucer's Eagle: A Contemplative Symbol', *PMLA* 75 (1960), 153–9.

The apocalyptic elements in the poem are brought out well by Lisa J. Kiser, *Truth and Textuality in Chaucer's Poetry* (Hanover, NH, and London, 1991), pp. 25–41.

BROKEN AIR AND SPOKEN FICTION: THE GRAMMAR OF SOUNDS

The eagle has promised his charge 'lore' (579) as well as 'disport and game' (664), and his version of standard medieval doctrine concerning the nature and transmission of sound offers both in abundance. Chaucer's 'Soun ys noght but eyr ybroken' (765) is paralleled by Macrobius's statement that 'Sound is produced only by the percussion of air'. Also, Chaucer's reference to the air being twisted and rent by a 'sharpe' blow on a pipe, and broken when men strike harp-strings, whether the blow be stout or light, is reminiscent of Macrobius's remarks on how 'the blow regulates the pitch of sound: a stout blow swiftly dealt produces a high note, a weak one lightly dealt produces a low note'; later he refers to the different notes which may be struck on a lyre (II. iv. 2, trans. Stahl, p. 197). Similar ideas are found in the *De musica* of Boethius.

Such theory is in fact common to medieval textbooks of music and grammar, but the latter are the most relevant to our poem, particularly in view of the fact that one major aspect of medieval grammar was the study of the ancient poets (*enarratio poetarum*). The *Speculum naturale* (iv. 14–18) of Vincent of Beauvais is sometimes cited as a possible source, and the verbal parallels are certainly close, but the ideas found in these chapters are commonplaces of conventional grammar teaching, as Martin Irvine has demonstrated so well.

In his *Institutiones grammaticae* Priscian cites the definition of 'spoken utterance [*vox*] as very thin struck air or its property perceptible to hearing, that is, what property strikes the ears' (trans. in Irvine, p. 855). The first part of this definition relates to the substance of *vox*, he continues. Some grammar teachers agonized over the notion that the substance of sound was air. If this were true, could not human speech, considered simply as mere sound ('so breketh it [the ayr] when men speketh', 780), simply be reduced to a form of air—an apparent absurdity? What Priscian actually meant, they suggested, was that a percussion of air is the *cause* of a spoken utterance and not actually its substance. Chaucer's eagle does not worry about such niceties:

> every speche that ys spoken,
> Lowd or pryvee, foul or fair,
> In his substaunce ys but air                              (766–8)

If Chaucer knew of the debate on the substance of air (and I strongly suspect that he did), it was very much in his interest here to suppress that knowledge. Certainly he seems to relish the element of *reductio ad absurdum*. Indeed, some would argue, he carries it further—reducing sound, the speech of men, and literature (as visible and recorded speech) to a lot of broken air.

Chaucer's explanation of how sound-waves (as we would call them) travel, by analogy with the motion of a series of actual waves caused by a stone being dropped into water eventually reaching the river-bank (787–822), is also found in standard grammatical teaching. By this ripple effect or 'multiplicacioun' of air, whereby

> Everych ayr another sterteth
> More and more, and speche up bereth,
> Or voys, or noyse, or word, or soun                       (817–19)

all sounds, including human speech, rise upwards until they reach the House of Fame. Indeed, speech is utterly necessary for the very existence of fame. Medieval grammarians believed (correctly, as it turns out) that the word *fama* 'is derived from *fando*, meaning "speaking"', to cite Isidore of Seville's well-known etymology. 'It is, however', he warns, 'the name of both good and bad things' (*Etymologiae*, V. xxvii. 26; trans. in Irvine, p. 862). Chaucer himself accentuates this connection by having his eagle remark that 'every soun, / Be hyt eyther foul or fair' (832–4) has its natural place in air, which recalls the statements of Virgil and Ovid concerning fact and fiction coming together in rumour, these of course being the sources of the second part of Isidore's definition, and the notion of the 'multiplicacioun' of air is consonant with the sequential and amplifying operations of fame.

The connection between speech, fame, and literature which Chaucer assumes to exist, may be further clarified by another grammatical definition, this one being of *litterae*. 'Letters', explains Isidore, 'are the indices of things, the signs of words, in which there is such great force that they speak to us without spoken sound [*vox*] things said by those absent. The practice of letters was invented for the memory of things. Things would vanish into oblivion unless they were bound by letters' (*Etymologiae*, I. iii. 12; trans. in Irvine, p. 870). Books, therefore, have their own voiceless speech, a speech which allows the absent or dead to speak, thereby conserving what time would otherwise destroy (cf. above, pp. 155–60). Without letters, declares John of Salisbury in the Preface to his *Policraticus*, 'things worth knowing' would not have been experienced; 'arts would have perished, laws would have disappeared, faith and all religious duties whatsoever should have shattered, and even the correct use of eloquence would have declined, save that divine compassion granted to mortals the use of letters as a remedy for human infirmity'. 'The examples of our ancestors', he continues, 'never would have encouraged and been heeded by everyone, unless, through devotion, care and diligence, writers triumphed over idleness and transmitted these things to posterity.'

Who would know of Alexander or Caesar, or would respect the Stoics or the Peripatetics, unless they had been distinguished by the memorial of writers? . . . Triumphal arches advance the glory of illustrious men whenever inscriptions explain for what cause and for whom they have been erected. It is only because of the inscription on a triumphal arch that the onlooker recognises that Constantine (who was of British stock) is proclaimed liberator of his country and founder of peace. No one would ever be illuminated by perpetual glory unless he himself or someone else had written. The reputation of the fool and the emperor is the same after a moderate period of time except where the memory of either is prolonged by the beneficence of writers. How many powerful kings have there been of whom there is nowhere a word or thought? Therefore, there is no better counsel to those who seek glory than to be worthy of the greatest thanks of men of letters and scribes. There is nothing to be gained from the excellence of their conduct, which would be enveloped in a perpetual darkness unless illuminated by the light of letters. (trans. Nederman, pp. 3–4)

All this is vividly illustrated in the *House of Fame*. The letters inscribed on the side of the ice-mountain which are unprotected by the shade of Fame's castle are fading away (1136–46). By contrast, the inscriptions on the side which Fame shades are as fresh as if men had written them that very day or hour (1151–8).

But how can we believe what we read? For fiction, too, is a kind of speech—speech concerning things which are made up, which therefore have their only existence in speech. 'The fables [*fabulae*] of the poets', explains Isidore, 'are named from *fando*'—that is, speaking—'because they are not true things [*res factae*] but only spoken fictions [*loquendo fictae*]' (*Etymologiae*, I. xl. 1). This sets them in stark opposition to the transmission of accurate reporting which was expected of history. Thus Isidore defines *historia* as 'the narration of an action performed, by which the things done in the past are known'. It is derived 'from the Greek *historein* which in Latin is *videre* ["to see"] or *cognoscere* ["to know"]. For among the ancients no-one wrote history except one who had been present and had seen the events which had to be written about' (*Etymologiae*, I. iv. 1). However, many authorities seemed to have intermingled truth and fiction, a problem addressed directly in the preface to the *Historia destructionis Troiae* of that Troy-supporter Guido delle Colonne (cf. line 1469). 'It is fitting', Guido declares, 'that the fall of Troy should not be blotted out by a long duration of time. To keep it alive in the minds of succeeding generations, by means of continuous records, the pen of many writers described it in a trustworthy account.' But 'certain persons' have dealt with the story,

dealing with it lightly as poets do, in fanciful inventions by means of certain fictions, so that what they wrote seemed to their audiences to have recorded not the true things, but the fictitious ones instead. Among them Homer, of greatest authority among the Greeks in his day, turned the pure and simple truth of his story into deceiving paths, inventing many things which did not happen and altering those which did happen. (Prol., trans. Meek, p. 1)

Thus, Homer could be accused of having mixed poetical fictions in with historical truths.

> Oon seyde that Omer made lyes,
> Feynynge in hys poetries,
> And was to Grekes favorable;
> Therfor held he hyt but fable.               (*HF* 1477–80)

However, 'Homer was not the only author of falsehoods [*uitiorum auctor*]', continues Guido. For Ovid wove truth and fiction together in his many books: 'He added many inventions to what had been invented and did not omit the truth mixed in with them.' Even Virgil, 'that highest of poets' (p. 265), had erred in this respect in his *Aeneid* (cf. p. 231 below). Guido proceeds to attest to the reliability of the eyewitness testimony of Dictys and Dares, who were, he declares, actually present at the Trojan war, and hence 'the most trustworthy reporters of those things which they saw' (cf. Isidore's definition of *historia*).

    It should now be abundantly clear why a poem about fame might take its point of departure from a retelling of the *Aeneid*, include an explanation of the theory of sound and human speech, and confront the nature of poetic fable as spoken fiction. The poets seem to be the agents of fame in the fullest possible sense (cf. p. 190 above). In poetry, as in fame, fact and fiction, truth and lies, are brought together. As Robert J. Allen puts it, 'Poets set forth what "meyn seyn", not knowing whether it is true or false. They are, in fact, the dispensers of Lady Fame's capricious decisions on the fate of tidings' (p. 405). Are the poets, then, monsters, just like Virgil's winged creature with its proliferation of eyes, tongues, and ears? The problem does not end there. The achievements of the great, as John of Salisbury remarked, 'would be enveloped in a perpetual darkness unless illuminated by the light of letters'. It would seem that writers have the fame of those they write about, or choose to ignore, in their hands. The *House of Fame*, it should be emphasized, depicts the poets as bearing the fame of the great subject-matters, along with the names of their protagonists. Without the poets, the key of remembrance (to borrow that term again from the *Legend of Good Women*) would be lost. All these things considered, what possible value can be claimed for their activities? That question is at the very centre of Chaucer's meditation on 'art poetical'.

Macrobius, *In somnium Scipionis*, ed. Willis, trans. Stahl. Vincent of Beauvais, *Speculum quadruplex*, vol. 1: *Speculum naturale* (Douai, 1624; repr. Graz, Austria, 1964), cols. 241–4.

Martin Irvine, 'Medieval Grammatical Theory and Chaucer's *House of Fame*', *Speculum*, 60 (1985), 850–76. This section is inevitably indebted to Irvine's crucially important article, though my interests sometimes diverge from his.

Isidore of Seville, *Etymologiae*, ed. Lindsay. Cf. Minnis, *Chaucer and Pagan Antiquity*, pp. 22–4.

John of Salisbury, *Policraticus. On the Frivolities of Courtiers and the Footprints of Philosophers*, trans. Cary J. Nederman (Cambridge, 1990).

Guido delle Colonne, *Historia destructionis Troiae*, ed. Griffin, trans. Meek. For other challenges to Homer's reliability see pp. 230–1 below. It should be noted that Guido's claim that Homer 'turned the pure and simple truth of his story into deceiving paths' suggests the image of a labyrinth or maze, on which see our next section.

Robert J. Allen, 'A Recurring Motif in Chaucer's *House of Fame*', *JEGP* 55 (1956), 393–405.

## Structure and Strategy

| | |
|---|---|
| Tho saugh y stonde in a valeye, | |
| Under the castel, faste by, | *close by* |
| An hous, that Domus Dedaly, | |
| That Laboryntus cleped ys, | |
| Nas mad so wonderlych, ywis, | *Was not, indeed* |
| Ne half so queyntelych ywrought. | *elaborately* |
| | (1918–23) |

Thus Chaucer emphasizes the complexity of the House of Rumour, by saying that it excels that of the Labyrinth in its wonderful construction. Here he is alluding to the myth which tells how, on the orders of King Minos of Crete, the Minotaur (the result of his wife's copulation with a handsome bull) had been imprisoned in the labyrinth specially built for this purpose by Daedalus, the master-artificer of antiquity. The bewildering complexity of its paths ensured that the Minotaur would remain trapped inside, and that the Athenian youths who were sent into it to be eaten by the monster would not escape their fate. Eventually, Theseus was chosen as a sacrifice, but Ariadne, the king's daughter, fell in love with him, and resolved to save his life. She gave him some thread, which he tied to the entrance of the labyrinth and unwound as he moved towards its centre; having killed the creature, he made his escape from the maze by rewinding the thread. However, the story ended sadly for Ariadne, who was subsequently abandoned by the ungrateful Theseus (cf. *HF* 405–26 and of course the *Legend of Ariadne*).

Virgil described the labyrinth as 'a bewildering work of craft with a thousand ways', with a 'baffling plan, which none might master and none retrace', the trail of any guiding clues being foiled (*Aeneid*, v. 588–91); whereas Ovid described it as a 'maze, confusing the usual marks of direction, and leading the eye of the beholder astray by devious paths winding in different directions' (*Metamorphoses*, viii. 162–4; trans. Innes, p. 183). As such, it is an apposite image to find in the *House of Fame*, and may be taken as emblematic of the poem itself. The following discussion will examine the threads with which various critics have sought to enter and escape from its textual maze. Many have got lost in the ambivalence of its thousand ways. The pleasure of the text, however, has replaced the fear of the monster.

FAME AND FORM

Is it, or would the finished poem have been, about love? On the face of it, this theory has much to commend it, given the French analogues (cf. p. 183 above) and certain features of the poem itself. The *House of Fame* begins with an account of the temple of Venus (who can be said to be the work's presiding deity) and depicts 'Geffrey' as the servant of her son, Cupid. Book i then focuses on the love-affair of another son of Venus, namely Aeneas. In book ii the eagle says that Jupiter has sent him to reward the poet's service to love, and to provide him with the 'tydynges / Of Loves folk' which he lacks. Once into book iii, however, the problems of lovers are, in general, subsumed under broader categories; but they resurface in Chaucer's account of the sixth company of lovers who appear before Fame. These people have, they admit, been idle all their lives, but they want to be known as great and fortunate lovers of women, even though in fact they received neither brooch nor ring nor anything else from women. Fame readily agrees. But when the seventh company, who are of the same character, ask for the same boon, the inconsistent goddess attacks them as being 'ydel wrechches' who do not deserve to 'Be famous good'. The woman that grinds at a hand-mill (the innuendo is obvious) would be far too good for them, she declares with utter contempt. The narrator then declares to the anonymous figure who greets him that, although he came here for 'newe tydynges' of 'love or such thynges glade' (1886–9), he has been disappointed so far. Finally, in a corner of the House of Rumour he hears men telling of 'love-tydynges'. There is a considerable commotion among them—some major piece of news seems to be afoot. Then a 'man of gret auctorite' appears: can he be the bearer of such news? We will never know; there the poem, as we have it, stops.

But has Chaucer, in any case, strayed too far from the subject of love? W. O. Sypherd thought not; his reading makes a brave attempt to uphold the dominance of the love-theme and affirm the poem's unity on that basis. What Chaucer was 'most interested in is the idea of the worship of Love' (p. 169), he declares, this being the poem's 'determining factor'; despite the work's length, 'his original idea is by no means forgotten (p. 171). Against this it may be argued that the poem lacks the spring garden setting characteristic of so many love-poems. This December dream may remind us of Froissart's *Le Joli Buisson de Jonece*, wherein the year's midnight (30 November 1373) is identified as the time of its dream, a poem which, as we have seen (cf. p. 144 above), takes rather a sceptical view of human love, viewing it from the perspective of mature wisdom. And the autumn dream in *Pearl* comprises a vision of a dead child who is spiritually mature, a beautiful bride of Christ; here human love of however natural and commendable a kind, in this case the love of father for child, is transcended. Did Chaucer, one can only wonder, intend to leave love behind in the *House of Fame*, rather than make new love-tidings his *matière*? Alternatively, one may speculate that a *negative* rather than a positive view of love was the controlling theme (which the work's conclusion would have clarified); in this vein John Leyerle, who emphasizes Chaucer's ability to create unity from diverse sources, suggests that the 'poem is a subtle and forceful attack on private love, for it shows that the necessary condition of secrecy is contradicted by natural order and so such love will, in consequence, inevitably be liable to be exposed' (p. 260). Since all sound ends up in the House of Fame, there can be no hiding-place for the tidings of lovers.

Recognizing that the identification of love as the poem's main theme (whether it be presented in positive or negative terms) hardly resolves its contradictions and anomalies, Alfred David offers as his thread the idea that the *House of Fame* has literary satire on love-poetry as one of its major purposes. Taken as 'a serious dream-vision poem', he argues, 'this is certainly an unwieldly and sadly disproportionate piece of work. But parody is a form in which the laws of literary craftsmanship are suspended' (p. 333). The poem is, then, 'planned chaos', its 'lack of unified sense' being in fact 'calculated nonsense', meant to reduce the earnestness of courtly love to absurdity. Only in this special sense, according to David's reading, can love be said to be the dominant theme.

Others have sought the thematic thread in the nature of fame itself, as understood in Chaucer's day, the principle being that the poem is in large measure reflecting the ambivalence and complexity of this its central concept, and therefore understanding of that concept will lead us out of its literary labyrinth.

In Virgil, as in Ovid, Rumour (*fama*) is duplicitous and deceitful, composed as it is of truths and falsehoods mixed together. Glory (*gloria*), on the other hand, functions as a positive term to express the notion of deserved renown and superlative reputation, of the kind that is won by pious Aeneas, founder of the New Troy at Rome. In the fourth book of the *Aeneid*, Aeneas is presented as a man who must leave behind the pleasures of life with Dido to endure toil for personal glory, to fulfil the high destiny which Jupiter has assigned to him. If he will not stir himself to any exertion for his own good name, Mercury declares, he should think of his son Ascanius and all that can be expected of him as a future ruler of Rome (265–76; cf. Jupiter's instructions to Mercury at 232–4).

The Church Fathers eroded this distinction between *fama* and *gloria*, as when Augustine identifies a major limitation of pagan virtue as the 'thirst of praise'. To be sure, their desire for earthly glory and love of country did indeed set the Romans 'upon admirable action', and Christians should be shamed from boasting of their deeds for the eternal country by the many *exempla* of Romans who performed superhuman feats of virtue for their temporal city and for earthly glory (*De civitate Dei*, v. 18). But there is no doubting the priorities: the farther we are from the impurity of the desire for human honour, the nearer we are to God, the glory of the righteous being wholly in God. In contrast, the heathen,

living in an earthly city, wherein the end of all their endeavours was by themselves propounded to themselves, the fame and domination of this world and not the eternity of heaven; not in the everlasting life, but in their own ends, and the mouths of their posterity: what should they love, but glory, whereby they desired

to survive after death in the memories and mouths of such as commended them.
(v. 14; trans. Healey, i. 163)

Similarly, Boethius identifies 'the desire for glory and the reputation of
having deserved well of the state' as 'the only thing that could attract
minds which are naturally outstanding, but not yet brought to the per-
fecting of their virtues to their finished condition' (*De consolatione
philosophiae*, II, pr. vii, 4–7; trans. Tester, p. 217). The mind thus completed will recognize that fame is one of those inferior goods which must
be transcended on the journey towards the *summum bonum*.

But, for the 'classicizers' and/or 'proto-humanists' of the later Middle
Ages, that virtue which resulted from the desire for glory was not necessarily a bad thing. Both these discourses are well represented in
Boccaccio's *Amorosa Visione*, wherein the narrator is guided to a noble castle which has two gates: one leads to high and glorious things, to that
immortal virtue which lives on in the collective memory; whereas the
other leads to worldly glory and success (including success in love). A
splendid triumph of Worldly Glory is presented; she sits resplendent with
gems and gold on her chariot, which is decorated with laurel leaves. In
Boccaccio's earlier *Teseida*, however, worldly glory is presented in a less
ambivalent way, this being possible because the story is set in pagan antiquity. In particular, Theseus is constructed as a historically correct (by the
standards of Boccaccio's day) heathen warlord. In his speech in memory
of Arcite, Theseus maintains that the valorous man need not be concerned
about his death, because 'Fame will render him the honour that is due'.
Arcite's death is such that 'it bore the delectable fruit of fame after its
blossoming time. And if we paid good heed to that we would set aside our
miserable grief' concerning Arcite's fate 'and address ourselves to the kind
of noble actions that would gain us a glorious reputation' (*Teseida*, xii. 9
and 12; trans. Havely, p. 148). Following this lead, Chaucer presents his
'Duc Theseus' as praising the late lamented Arcite, 'of chivalrie flour', for
having won great fame for himself. For such a warrior to die 'Whan he is
siker [sure] of his goode name' is right and fitting; it is 'best'

> as for a worthy fame
> To dyen whan that he is best of name.
>
> (*Knight's Tale*, CT I(A) 3055–6)

This is surely intended as commendation rather than criticism: although
the limits of heathen knowledge and virtue are definitely implicit in the
*Knight's Tale*, the achievements of such as Arcite may justly be celebrated.

Neither was such commendation limited to ancient flowers of chivalry.
Jean Froissart, in the last redaction of the first book of his *Chronicles*,

declares that valorous men fight in order to conquer glory and win fame in this world; then clerks write and record their deeds in perpetual memory. Sir John Clanvowe, 'Lollard Knight' and friend of Chaucer, took the opposite line. In *The Two Ways* he attacks those who pride themselves on being 'greete werreyours and fiȝteres', and complains that the world respects those who insist on being avenged for every wrong. 'And of swyche folke men maken bookes and soonges and reeden and syngen of hem for to hoolde by mynde of here deedes be lengere heere vpon eerth, ffor þat is a þing þat worldely men desiren greetly þat here naame myghte laste loonge after hem heere vpon eerth' (493–6). But in the eyes of God, who is sovereign and true judge, this is shameful. Would it not be better, then, for the good Christian to actually neglect his fame, to be utterly unconcerned about his reputation? That question is considered in Robert Holcot's commentary on the Book of Wisdom, his conclusion being that fame *can* be a good thing if sought in the right manner and to the right extent. But he attacks those who are wholly preoccupied with fame, with the aid of arguments from *De consolatione philosophiae*, II, pr. vii (as summarized above, pp. 188–90). He who hopes to live in the memories of men, reiterates Holcot, suffers two deaths—one of his body, the other of his name.

Fame, then, 'is the spur that the clear spirit doth raise' to superlative feats of virtue and valour; but it is also, as Augustine and Boethius emphasized, the 'last infirmity of noble mind' (cf. Milton, *Lycidas*, 70–1). Because of this inherent paradox, it is little wonder that the imagery of fame is so rich and indeed so richly ambivalent, as is brought out in Boitani's magisterial study *Chaucer and the Imaginary World of Fame*. This abundance of ideas is certainly reflected in the poem; but are they synthesized? Do they work together, or pull apart?

The crux of the matter is surely Chaucer's creation of *two* houses for *fama* or rumour. Are both really necessary? Would a single domain not have been enough? Is Chaucer guilty of repetition and redundancy of material? G. L. Kittredge did not doubt that the poem is 'admirably constructed. Everything is to the point and in good proportion' (p. 93), the subject being a 'humorous study of mankind from the point of view of a Ruling Passion'—namely, the obsession with reputation. In his view Chaucer has successfully harmonized what he takes to be 'the two senses of the Latin *fama*':

Fame, of course, is *reputation* or *renown*. The whirling wicker house, to which come all the words that are spoken on earth, is the factory or laboratory where rumours are compounded. These fly up to the castle close by, where Fame holds court. Thither all the world resorts . . . to take whatever reputation the freakish goddess may assign them. (p. 106)

Boitani takes what is basically a similar view to this, but emphasizes that here we are dealing with 'the raw material of tales—events, sayings, facts, forecasts, hearsay'. Initially 'they mirror the world of nature, of animals and men', but they are 'governed by Chance' (i.e. 'Aventure, that is the moder of tydynges', 1982–3), and so the whirling wicker house distorts them from their original state, amplifying them to the point of exploding (2065–80), and then each is joined to its contrary so that it 'leaves the House inextricably true *and* false' (2087–109), even though when it entered, it could be identified as either true *or* false. These compounds then fly to the House of Fame, where they are 'somehow ordered by Fame' (in however arbitrary a way) and 'spread all over the world by her ministers'. Thus 'The Castle-Palace of Fame works like a clearing station' (p. 211).

This reads as a reversal of the priorities of Bennett's analysis. For him, Fame's house is 'a transmitter as well as a receiving centre; more strictly, the palace proper is a royal broadcasting station, the adjacent, but subordinate, house of twigs a kind of office for miscellaneous business' (p. 122). Though Bennett certainly canvasses the idea that the differing abodes of Fame and Rumour indicate the duplicity of one and the same phenomenon, he proceeds to contrast the 'grandiose temple of Fame with its self-contained life and action' with 'the inferior house of Rumour composed of commonplace materials and thronged with commonplace people' (pp. 106–7). It is just not in the same *class*: 'The more marvellous Fame's castle is, the more striking will be the contrast with the suburban, not to say plebeian, abode of Rumour, her Cinderella sister' (p. 115). But surely this quite misrepresents the nature of the relationship between the two constructions. Although Fame's castle may look a lot more grand than Rumour's dangerous roundabout, this is the merest façade. In fact, Fame's establishment is utterly dependent upon Rumour's; it is not 'self-contained' in any way. Therefore, it is the whirling wicker which has the most right to be regarded as the dominant dwelling. As Sheila Delany says, 'Fame's court could not exist without the House of Rumour, for there originate the events which fame either commemorates or condemns to oblivion' (p. 110). The movement from Rumour to Fame is the process in which experience becomes tradition—and contamination, it would seem, is an unavoidable part of that process.

This theory of a sort of 'fame factory' wherein the chief executive chooses the labels for the products which her subordinate has compounded seems eminently plausible. But the question remains, should the unity of the *House of Fame* be sought not in the idea (however complex) of fame itself but in a more comprehensive and elevated moral vision of the mutable? That certainly is the view of Paul Ruggiers, who has suggested that a serious philosophical meaning underlies and unifies Chaucer's 'high comedy', as he terms it. All three of the poem's books are regarded as variations on the theme of earthly mutability, and it is suggested that the man of great authority may have been Boethius, arriving to deliver a homily on the falseness of worldly glory. The most extreme version of this view is undoubtedly that offered by Koonce, who propounds a Dantean movement in the poem from Hell through Purgatory to Paradise, the eagle functioning as 'a symbol of the intellect illumined by grace, directing the mind to the path of salvation', and the man of great authority being identified as Christ himself (pp. 266–73). In complete opposition to this aggrandizing of the imminent *auctor* is Donald Fry's claim that the man of great authority, standing in the middle of the mad activities of the 'insanely' spinning house of Rumour, does not—indeed, cannot—have any real authority, since this is just not possible in the realm of human affairs. And so, to emphasize this fact, Chaucer abruptly cuts him off—a brilliant *coup de théâtre* and an 'ending' which, in its deliberate fragmentation and irresolution, at once squares with and sums up the poem's central concerns.

Faced with these quite extraordinarily varied attempts to find the poem's *sine qua non*, one might find rather refreshing the view of J. S. P. Tatlock, who doubted whether the *House of Fame* 'was begun with any clear-cut purpose or meaning, except irresponsibly for fun' (p. 64). A 'striking but unfair case' can be made for *any* theory concerning the poem's subject, he asserts, 'by picking out seemingly favourable evidence and disregarding all else' (p. 57). Similarly, Robert Jordan emphasizes that many subjects—poetry, 'dreams, love, fame, auditory physics, cosmology, mythology, epistemology'—are jostling for position in Chaucer's text (p. 34). Those who have concentrated on the apparent lack of 'clear-cut purpose or meaning' in the poem have, however, tended to reject the idea that it was written purely and simply 'for fun', as may be exemplified by Sheila Delany's reading.

Delany believes that the *House of Fame* does indeed have a theme and a significant form, but in her view this cannot be defined in terms of a single topic. It is more appropriate to speak of a 'repeated structural pattern' as being the meaning of the poem, this being governed by the principles of medieval 'skeptical fideism', which holds that the 'truths' of history, philosophy, and poetry are not absolute, and may even conflict with Christian doctrine. (One fourteenth-century English theologian often credited with such views, incidentally, is Robert Holcot, whom we have already cited above.) According to Delany, Chaucer perceives that 'tradition, or fame' offers no certain truth; he is therefore 'reluctant to commit himself to a traditional role or to any single traditional point of view' (p. 67). Thus, initially he displays a scepticism about dreams, undercutting traditional authorities on the subject. Then, in book i he highlights the differences in the accounts of Dido provided by Virgil and Ovid, granting 'the validity of conflicting truths' and recognizing that there is no rational way of choosing between them (p. 57). 'Geffrey' asks to be delivered from 'fantome and illusion' (493); the term 'fantome' could mean, in the Macrobian sense, a kind of nightmare devoid of valid instruction. Yet, *phantasmata* or *imagines* ('images') were the basic units of thought; as Aristotle and his followers declared, man cannot think without images.

This ambivalence hardly inspires confidence in the normal processes of human thinking. In particular, poetic discourse was supposed to be 'imaginative' (according to the main medieval version of Aristotle's *Poetics*), and the *poetae* were often attacked as purveyors of fantasies (in the derogatory sense of the term) and lying fictions—a subject to which we will return. The eagle's disquisition reveals science as being limited also, while the narrator's experiences in the House of Fame itself demonstrate the unreliability of history. In this way Delany emphasizes the contradictions which inhere within the specific subject-matters, and between the accounts of the different authors, here named. However, she believes that a way out of the labyrinth is offered, that its confusions may be transcended by appeal to 'the highest authority', the leap of faith to 'God or Christ' (pp. 37, 41). But can we really accept the notion that with one such bound the narrator will be free? Clear traces of transcendence in the poem are markedly lacking. Does he, then, remain in the labrinyth? And, if so, is this imprisonment, empowerment, or what? These crucial issues must now be addressed.

Virgil, *Aeneid*, trans. Knight, p. 137, and also Virgil, *Aeneid*, ed. and trans. H. R. Fairclough, rev. edn. (Cambridge, Mass., 1934), i. 485.

W. O. Sypherd, *Studies in Chaucer's 'Hous of Fame'*, Chaucer Society, 2nd ser., 39 (London, 1908). Leyerle, 'Chaucer's Windy Eagle'. Alfred David, 'Literary Satire in the *House of Fame*', *PMLA* 75 (1960), 333–9.

The Virgilian distinction between *fama* and *gloria* is discussed by J. A. W. Bennett, *Book of Fame*, p. 39; see further Boitani, *Imaginary World*, pp. 21–4. An excellent review of medieval usages of the terms is provided by Boitani, pp. 40–8, 52–71, 72–150. The *MED*, s.v. fame, defines it as reputation (whether good or bad); (wide-spread) reputation or renown; any report, rumour, or widely circulated opinion; also a tiding or rumour. As an example of the last of these senses the *Man of Law's Tale*, II(B) 995–6 is cited: 'The fame anon thurgh Rome toun is born, / How Alla kyng shal comen in pilgrymage.'

Augustine, *De civitate Dei*, trans. Healey. Boethius, *De consolatione philosophiae*, ed. and trans. Tester. On Boccaccio's *Amorosa Visione* see Boitani, *Imaginary World*, pp. 93–6, and Wallace, *Early Writings*, pp. 5–22.

Havely, *Chaucer's Boccaccio*. On fame and glory in the *Knight's Tale* see Minnis, *Chaucer and Pagan Antiquity*, pp. 92–3. On Chaucer's exploitation of pagan settings see further

B. Nolan, 'Chaucer and the 'Roman Antique', and Spearing, Medieval to Renaissance, pp. 21, 40–58, especially his challenging statement on p. 57. See further the splendid article by Morton W. Bloomfield, 'Chaucer's Sense of History', repr. in his Essays and Explorations (Cambridge, Mass., 1970), pp. 12–26, which highlights Chaucer's respect for cultural diversity.

Jean Froissart, Chroniques, ed. G. T. Diller (Geneva, 1972), p. 37.

Clanvowe, The Two Ways, in Works, ed. Scattergood, p. 69.

Robert Holcot, Sapientiae Regis Salomonis praelectiones (Basel, 1586), lectio 18 (on Wisdom 2: 4), pp. 68–9. Cf. Minnis, Chaucer and Pagan Antiquity, pp. 129–30; Boitani, Imaginary World, pp. 143–7.

Kittredge, Chaucer and his Poetry. Boitani, Imaginary World. J. A. W. Bennett, Book of Fame. Delany, Chaucer's 'House of Fame'. Paul Ruggiers, 'The Unity of Chaucer's House of Fame', SP 50 (1953), 16–29. Koonce, Tradition of Fame. Fry, 'Ending of House of Fame'. Tatlock, Mind and Art of Chaucer. Robert Jordan, Chaucer's Poetics and the Modern Reader (Berkeley and Los Angeles, 1987). The most important version of Aristotle's Poetics to circulate in the later Middle Ages was Hermann the German's translation of the Muslim scholar Averroës' 'Middle Commentary' on that work, on which see Minnis and Scott (eds.), Medieval Literary Theory, pp. 277–313. On Averroës' view of imagination see pp. 280–4. There is a modern English translation from the Arabic by C. E. Butterworth, Averroes' Middle Commentary on Aristotle's 'Poetics' (Princeton, NJ, 1986).

## EXPLORING THE LABYRINTH: SOME MODERN NEGOTIATIONS

On Delany's approach, and others like it, the lack of single and clear-cut purpose or meaning becomes, in a sense, the actual structuring principle of the poem. And the perfect symbol to express this paradox is one which Chaucer himself has offered us: namely, 'Domus Dedaly', the labyrinth.

Its efficacy is not limited to this early poem. The 'interlaced thematic structure' of the Canterbury Tales, Donald Howard has suggested, 'is like a maze or labyrinth in which it is easy to get lost, but the dominant form of the work—may I say the idea of the work—never permits us to come to a dead end' (p. 326). Howard proceeds to describe the central image of the House of Fame, which the poem leads up to and presents near its end, as 'an idea of a world of stories or "tidings" like a labyrinth in design' (p. 331). Here Howard has in mind a labyrinth which is different in design from the one best known today; he believes that the 'unicursal' type, with a single winding path leading inevitably to the centre and then back out again, is the one commonly known in Chaucer's day. '"Multicursal" labyrinths or mazes', he continues, 'in which one comes to forks in the path and must make blind choices, were as far as I know a later development' (p. 329).

However, Penelope Doob's admirably thorough study, The Idea of the Labyrinth (1990), has demonstrated that both types of labyrinth identified by Howard were known in the Middle Ages. The 'unicursal' type was the model for most medieval mazes in the visual arts; however, the written tradition presupposed the 'multicursal' type, with its different paths and many dead ends, designed to confuse and frustrate. If in visual art the labyrinth is largely a thing of pleasure, 'an image of perfect human and divine creation', in verbal art the house of Daedalus is often an image of moral error, of how unstable and sinful men stray from the right path. These ethical implications are very relevant, she argues, for our reading of the *Aeneid*, *De consolatione philosophiae*, and the *Divine Comedy*, which she regards as forming a self-consciously continuous expression of the idea of the labyrinth in Western literature. By contrast, the *House of Fame* is held to be a parodic poem which, breaking away from the highly respectful treatment afforded metaphorical labyrinths by those distinguished predecessors, highlights 'the issues raised by labyrinths of *words*, of texts, of complex and sometimes misleading artistry' (p. 312). That is to say, 'labyrinthine errors in the *House of Fame* are not moral but epistemological; they may ultimately have profound spiritual consequences, but Chaucer does not let us see them.' The primary focus is turned away from the moral tradition stressed by the poem's models, the implication being that the interpretations of critics like Ruggiers and Koonce are inappropriate. The text is said to move from one confusion to another, ending with a

significantly nameless man, who merely *seems* a likely guide, never says a word; and had he spoken, what authority could he have had in such a place, in such a poem? . . . transcendence and true authority alike are unthinkable. Order collapses into disorder, simplicity into multiplicity, dazzling artistry into dazed confusion, one statement into its opposite: the only world we know is a labyrinth without a center and perhaps without an end.

'The multicursal labyrinths' described in the poem *are* endless when one cannot escape them, argues Doob; there is no way out for 'Geffrey', 'trapped in his dream of recurrent mazes' (p. 331).

When critics call the work 'planned chaos' (David), note its 'bewildering uncertainty of direction' (Spearing), puzzle over its 'air of deliberate obscurity' (Koonce), or complain that it is 'all process' (Burlin), they are actually, in Doob's view, sensing its labyrinthine qualities. But is it appropriate to adopt any particular symbol, however flexible and multifaceted it may be, to convey—and thereby rationalize—the poem's apparent lack of a single and clear-cut purpose or meaning? Why not take the daring step of declaring that the poem is simply chaotic? What price the obsession with thematic unity which has been evident so often in our discussion thus far? Should we stop grasping at threads?

These questions are made the more acute by the associations which the labyrinth symbol has in postmodernist thought. For Jorge Luis Borges, the library images the world, the world as labyrinth, the order of which is blocked to the human mind. 'For one reasonable line or one straight-forward note there are leagues of insensate cacophony, or verbal farragoes and incoherencies' (p. 80). The labyrinth is ordered according to laws which are incomprehensible to human intelligence and which are there-fore undecipherable, though librarians offer conjectures about the lan-guage in which the books of this cosmic library are written, and interpret them incessantly. Readers of the *House of Fame*, and more particularly of its critics, may well respond to these sentiments with considerable sym-pathy, and it is arguable that contemporary literary theory holds out many possibilities for the interpretation of this poem—a path which we may now explore. At the outset, however, the caveat should be entered that, as far as Chaucer was concerned, the universe was conceived of in terms of order rather than disorder (as the eagle's heavenly journey indi-cates), however it might look from the human point of view (Boethius said it all, of course, in his *Consolatio philosophiae*). But the world of fame, with the reputations of men as its primordial matter, might well be seen as chaotic, and a poem could reflect such chaos or simply slide into chaos itself.

That having been said, we may consider the idea that the problem lies not so much with the poem as with the thematic approach itself. The issues may be clarified by reference to Terry Eagleton's trenchant criti-cism of 'reception' or 'reader response' theory, which has Wolfgang Iser as one of its most eloquent exponents. The Iser approach envisages read-ing as interactive, creative—not just a passive imbibing of authorial mean-ing. Eagleton describes this as springing from a liberal humanism which is not as liberal as it looks, inasmuch as it assumes a reader equipped with the 'right' capacities and responses. A 'literary' work turns out to be a work which can profitably be illuminated by this kind of enquiry, which fits in with its ideological agenda—hence a 'hermeneutical circle' is cre-ated. To his credit, Iser believes that there is no single correct interpre-tation. But 'one rigorous instruction' remains: 'the reader must construct the text so as to render it internally *consistent*'; textual indeterminacies must be 'normalized'—a revealingly authoritarian term. The ultimate goal of this approach, then, is completion and cohesion—the creation of a reliable structure with stable meaning, all the gaps having been filled in and the inconsistencies reconciled. '[T]he "openness" of the work is something which is to be gradually eliminated, as the reader comes to construct a working hypothesis which can account for and render mutu-ally coherent the greatest number of the work's elements' (p. 81).

Much *House of Fame* criticism has sought to construct such hypothe-ses, and the identification of love, politics, fame, *ars poetica*, literary authority, or whatever as the poem's central theme or themes could easily be identified as yet another enterprise of this type. But more than any other work of Chaucer, the irreducibly 'polysemantic' *House of Fame* stubbornly resists such enforced closure. The same could even be said of the attempt to locate the thematic centre of the poem in the very absence of fixity—as with the specifications of pluralism, diversity, literary scepticism, or the 'labyrinthine aesthetic' as the controlling principle. However large and accommodating such categories may be, on Eagleton's argument they could be seen as products of the Iser mould: once again, the interpretative key which opens most of the poem's literary locks is being sought, or, to revert to an earlier metaphor, the gaps are 'normalized' by being regarded as an essential part of the very structure.

Suspicion concerning the thematic approach pervades Robert Jordan's attempt to negotiate the *House of Fame* for the modern reader. Those who mine the 'rich veins' of the work 'for traces of a single theme' are reproved. 'We must recognize how little thematic continuity tells us about this poem,' he declares. 'However firm or fragile we may deem the thematic thread to be, the poem is more disjunct and disparate than continuous and integrated' (p. 33). Yet he cannot resist stating that the poem 'probably possesses more thematic continuity than either the *Book of the Duchess* or the *Parliament of Fowls*'—an obvious case of trying to eat one's cake and have it.

The *House of Fame* has suffered at the hands of realist critics 'in search of referentiality' Jordan argues (p. 24); thanks to 'our relatively recent recognition of realism as a convention rather than the standard of literary value, we are better able to recognize the differing aesthetic values and epistemological implications of a rhetorical poetics' (p. 25). This poetics has as its aim 'not truth but persuasive discourse' (p. 32); meaning is secondary to rhetorical brilliance, and the rhetorical brilliance is ostentatious, self-aware, and self-regarding. Furthermore, the aesthetic values of the *House of Fame* are said to be 'expressed through segmentation and multiplicity'. For all these reasons the poem bears analysis in the same terms as those deemed appropriate to the post-realist contemporary novel. Chaucer is not so much writing about the world as writing about writing about the world, sharing the postmodernist's dissociation from the realist assumption that truth is unambiguously accessible through language.

But, in the final analysis, Jordan's standards are very much those of the traditional canon. Chaucer is supposed to have 'delighted in the resources of his vernacular language and its capacity to emulate the classics in elegance and range of expressiveness' (p. 42). Similarly, 'The *House of Fame* is a brilliant mosaic, a literary entertainment, sanctioned by its classical—

and in Book ii its "scientific"—erudition and rendered ceaselessly engaging by the narrative skills of its presentation' (p. 46). It could be responded that the radicalism of the *House of Fame* consists in its very subversion of such classical standards. If 'deconstruction' may be defined as destroying conventional assumptions by demonstrating their inherent inconsistencies and contradictions, then it can be argued that Chaucer's poem is doing just that to received ideas concerning, *inter alia*, dreams and visions, noble love, fame, and literary *auctoritas*. For his poem erodes the distinctions between mere noise, human speech, and literature (as visible and recorded speech), and threatens to reduce them to a lot of broken air. Meaning is cut off from sound, the link between signifier and signified disrupted. On this approach the *House of Fame* intriguingly opens itself up to post-structuralist interpretation. For, by contrast with reader-response theory which seeks to smooth out the text's disjunctions and fill in its gaps, post-structuralism accepts the text's disruptions of stable meaning and sees art as transgressive. As Eagleton puts it, 'There is absolutely no need to suppose that works of literature either do or should constitute harmonious wholes, and many suggestive frictions and collisions of meaning must be blandly "processed" by literary criticism to induce them to do so' (p. 81).

In the case of the *House of Fame* the danger of bland processing may perhaps be averted if the critic adopts Jacques Derrida's notion of the play of *différance* (i.e. the conflict of textual elements which refuse to yield cohesive, unitary meaning). Throughout the poem we are constantly encountering what Derrida calls *aporias* (impasses, dead ends), where our quest for meaning becomes blocked, leaving us with a tissue of inconsistencies, discontinuities, fissures, and lacunae; the possibility of coherent communication is thus denied. Jesse Gellrich has responded admirably to the challenge of such ideas. In his view the text inscribes the broad 'subject of how language signifies, where it originates, how it is authorized, and how it is received' (p. 174); here is 'a work of provocative experiments in structure, authority, and the determinacy of meaning', authority having been dislocated 'from the voice of the past to the play of signifying in the text' (p. 199). Alternatively, following a suggestion by Vincent Gillespie, we could appropriate Roland Barthes's notion of the 'orgasmic text', which 'dislocates the reader's historical, cultural and psychological assumptions, the consistency of his tastes, values and memories and brings to a crisis his relation with language' (p. 255).

Does, then, the search of the *House of Fame* 'end in the absence of structure, the abandonment of a centreless void'? This is denied by Gellrich, whose Derridian reading addresses more directly than any other Chaucer's textual engagement with

the lie
The maze, the wild-wood waste of falsehoods, roads
That run and run and never reach an end,
Embowered in error

(from Edwin Muir, 'The Labyrinth')

For the labyrinth itself is disclosed as a durable structure, something 'founded to endure' (*HF* 1981). Its centre is a secret place, and its roads are eccentric, yet its very existence ensures that the wild wood of falsehoods (and truths compounded) does not become a wasteland. Here, then, is a theoretically adequate reading model for the *House of Fame*. The multiplicity and artifice of authoritative sources, and then the unreliability of authority figures, having been revealed, the labyrinthine text stands as its own authority. (These remarks constitute a meditation on Gellrich, pp. 196–9.)

But such approaches have their limitations. The extent to which one may speak validly of 'indeterminacy' of meaning in the case of medieval texts (even the *House of Fame*) is highly debatable; it could be said that here we are dealing rather with a known range of discourses, each of which is culturally marked and to a considerable extent fixed. At issue, then, is an *array* of competing determinations rather than indeterminacy *per se*. And as far as the 'textual erotics' of Barthes are concerned, it should be noted that the thrill is experienced by the reader without any reference to what the author may feel. There is something masochistic about this, as Eagleton says:

since there is no way to arrest it [the text] into determinate sense, the reader simply luxuriates in the tantalizing glide of signs, in the provocative glimpses of meanings which surface only to submerge again. Caught up in this exuberant dance of language, delighting in the textures of words themselves, the reader knows less the purposive pleasures of building a coherent system, binding textual elements masterfully together to shore up a unitary self, than the masochistic thrills of feeling that self shattered and dispersed through the tangled webs of the work itself. (pp. 82–3)

Such *jouissance* is highly personal and private. The work as sexual/textual object is rendered ineffective as a commentary on larger concerns (whether aesthetic, sexual, social, or political) as the reader has his/her wicked way with it.

More generally, it may be said that deconstruction in effect declares: the king is dead, long live the king. Having killed off the author, it proceeds to authorize the critic. The Derridian theory of *différance*, for instance, is essentially a reading strategy rather than an authorial one. By suggesting, as I have done above, that in the *House of Fame* Chaucer is engaged in the deconstruction of received ideas, I am in fact relocating the author as master-reader. But his chair is already occupied by the contemporary reader. It could be replied that it is Chaucer's deconstruction which makes his poem worth reading, that his particular *jouissance* is more fun than that of his contemporary readers—without of course supposing that 'we' can ever share that experience adequately.

What is at stake here may be further clarified by exploring the limitations of the distinction which Denis Donoghue makes between 'epireading' and 'graphireading'. The former hears the voice of the author 'as absent person' in the text, and believes that the author is communicating with the reader through the medium of the text—an attitude which (after Derrida) is described as 'logocentrism', the belief that texts say one thing only, which is what their authors intended them to say. By contrast, 'graphireading' is the reading strategy which follows naturally from the 'death of the author'; namely, that a written text, freed from the author's alleged control, yields up an inexhaustible semantic profusion. But in the *House of Fame* semantic profusion may be said (following Donoghue's terms of reference for the moment) to exist within what the author himself says, as he reviews a wide range of topics; and to imply that this is in some way monolithic would be inaccurate and indeed insulting. When an author like Chaucer is such an accomplished graphireader, perhaps the critic should, with all due humility, bow out and leave the stage to him. After all, to suggest this is simply to claim for the glorious gamester of the *House of Fame* what the followers of Derrida, Barthes, and the rest are tacitly claiming for their masters by their very discipleship.

Far more useful, in my view, is the approach promulgated by Mikhail Bakhtin, whose work combines many of the characteristics of the graphireader with those of the epireader. Much of what Bakhtin says about 'heteroglossia' ('different languages') in the comic novel can, with minimal effort, be applied to Chaucer's comic poem. (Indeed, Bakhtin regards medieval parody as having paved the way for the great Renaissance novels of Rabelais and Cervantes.) For the story-line of the *House of Fame* paradoxically re-processes many of the levels of literary language current in the later Middle Ages: the forms of scholastic debate, the eloquence of the court, the pedantic speech of scholars, the high epic style, visionary and biblical discourse, and finally 'the way one or another concrete and socially determined personality, the subject of the story, happens to speak' (*The Dialogic Imagination*, p. 301). 'Parodic-travestying literature'—a category within which, to some extent, the *House of Fame* falls—'introduces the permanent corrective of laughter, of a critique on the one-sided seriousness of the lofty direct word, the corrective of reality that is always richer, more fundamental and most importantly *too con-*

*tradictory and heteroglot* to be fitted into a high and straightforward genre' (p. 55). By contrast with the 'univocal' (single-voiced) Bible and epic, which share a presumption of authority and lay claim to an absolute language, the novel—as its antecedents—celebrates the riotous plurality of its meanings. Fully aware of the impossibility of total meaning, such a text offers a dialogue of many different voices, including those which are humorous, ironic, and self-ironic. Within this textual carnival there can be no place for the single, reasoned, and authoritative voice which silences all the others and establishes a fixed, reliable version of the narrative events; for the text is by nature anarchic rather than authoritarian. All this rings true for the festive *House of Fame*, a work which is too contradictory and heteroglot to fit into a straightforward genre.

Equally valuable is Bakhtin's discussion of medieval humour of a kind which survives, and has one of its richest exponents, in Rabelais. The unashamedly scurrilous and vulgar 'language of billingsgate' which is so often part of such literature is, he argues, antithetical to Renaissance 'aesthetics of the beautiful', which saw the human body in a very different light. In medieval 'grotesque realism' the unlovely bodily element is profoundly positive; its characteristic exaggeration is assertive and festive, brimming over with 'abundance', and above all else communal, a 'banquet for all the world', in which man is not regarded as an isolated biological individual or a single economic unit. The laughter thus provoked materializes and degrades, 'degradation' here meaning 'coming down to earth', involving a concern with 'the lower stratum of the body, the life of the belly and the reproductive organs; it therefore relates to acts of defecation and copulation, conception, pregnancy and birth' (*Rabelais and his World*, p. 21). And, of course, to acts of farting, as in Rabelais' episode of the 'Isle of the Winds', where 'people pass wind and gas in great abundance', even dying 'from swollen stomachs' so that 'their souls depart by the back passage' (*Quart Livre*, ch. 42 and 44). Here, Bakhtin says, 'The theme of "wind" and the entire complex of lofty motifs associated with it in literature and poetry—the wafting of zephyrs, the wind in sea storms, breathing and sighing, the soul as a breath, the spirit and so on are here, via the intermediary expression "to pass wind"', are pulled down into various types of 'degrading' narrative series relating to eating, defecation, and the quotidian (*Dialogic Imagination*, pp. 188–9).

A similar 'bringing down to earth' could well be part of the meaning of the *House of Fame*. I share John Leyerle's suspicion that the eagle's disquisition on the percussion of air may be, among other things, an elaborate farting joke, an idea which, if taken to its ultimate conclusion in conjunction with what has been said in our previous section, would have Chaucer threatening to reduce all human discourse (from love-tidings to the revered *sententiae* of the *auctores*) to a spectacular case of cosmic flatulence. But an important caveat must be entered here. The phrase 'break wind' that seems to be implied in Leyerle's reading is apparently not attested to until the mid-sixteenth century, as N. R. Havely points out (note on lines 761–822). 'The flatulence', he suggests, 'may well be a *ffantoume*.' But I think that there is more substance in it than that. The practice of using the terms *ventus* ('wind') and *flatus* ('the blowing of a wind') to refer to intestinal wind goes back to the first century AD at least, as the *Oxford Latin Dictionary* attests. And Leyerle points to a passage in Vincent of Beauvais' *Speculum naturale* (iv. 15), wherein sound is said to be produced 'through the constriction of air, as in the blowing of wind through a pipe' ('per flationem intra fistulam'), which could easily have been misread jocularly in a scatological sense, particularly since *fistula* could designate the back passage, as in John of Arderne's medical treatises of *Fistula in ano*. Certainly lines 1636–55, the account of how Aeolus blows a blast out of 'his foule trumpes ende', causing a stink like 'the pit of helle', supports this hypothesis, and there may be a pun on 'tu(w)el' (1649), which primarily means 'chimney-hole' here but probably connotes 'anus'. (In the *Summoner's Tale* (III(D) 2148) 'tuwel' designates the anus of the churl who farts into the hand of the unscrupulous friar who is seeking to extort money from him.) Moreover, this entire passage about Aeolus's trumpeting is reminiscent of the episode in Dante's *Inferno*, xxi. 139, where a devil makes 'a trumpet of his arse' to lead his troop of demons. 'Never to so strange a pipe', Dante continues, 'have I seen horsemen or footmen set forth!' (*Inferno*, xxii. 10–11).

Also common to the *House of Fame* and the *Summoner's Tale* is the image of the circle, as a means of describing the movement of sound (and smell also, in the case of the later text). Chaucer's explanation of how 'every cercle' or wheel causes the 'other' (*HF* 809–22) parallels the solution proposed in the *Summoner's Tale* to the mock-serious 'scholastic' problem of how a fart may be divided into twelve equal parts. The answer is: position the twelve friars in question in a circle around the rim of a cartwheel, one opposite each spoke, then have the churl who has offended the friar's dignity sit in its centre and 'lete a fart';

> And ye shul seen, up peril of my lyf,
> By preeve which that is demonstratif,
> That equally the soun of it wol wende,          *travel*
> And eke the stynk, unto the spokes ende          (III(D) 2271–4)

This tale, among other things, encompasses a brilliant parody of the ultimate 'heteroglossic' experience: namely, Pentecost, the historical occasion on which a quite extraordinary gift of speech, the ability to speak in

different tongues, was bestowed on Christ's disciples. 'Suddenly there
came a sound from heaven, as of a mighty wind coming' (Acts 2: 2–4).

Perhaps Chaucer had such 'degrading' vulgarities in mind for the climax of his poem on 'windy glory'; in which case it might have ended
something like this:

> But he semed for to be
> A man of grete auctorite.
> 'Geffrey' quod he, 'If thou wilt lere
> What thyng ys Fame, thanne listu here.
> For in thyn ere, if thou knelest doune
> A pistel thereof wol I roune'.
> And doun upon my knowes faste
> I fil; and in myn ere atte laste
> This man of grete auctorite
> (For so he semed unto me)
> Ful prively gan lete a fart.
> Ther nys no capul, in a cart                                    *nag*
> Koude lete a farte of swich a soun
> Ne swich a stynke; to my resoun
> Nat Joves, with his dent of thonder
> Nevere ne clefte the air asonder
> With half the ese and mageste
> As dide this grete auctoritee.
> And with the rumblynge of the soun
> And his reverberacioun,
> Doun goon the pilers of this halle,
> Toures, walles, roof and alle,
> And I awook, and that anoon.
> This was my sweven; now hit ys doon.\*

But should the 'man of gret auctorite' not be identified? Perhaps not—after
all, there are no less than three unidentified figures in the poem as we have
it, the 'oon' who asks 'Geffrey' if he is in quest of fame (1869), the 'oon'
who accuses Homer of being a liar (1477), and the 'oon' who usually calls
upon the narrator to 'Awak!' (562). The ending which William Caxton
wrote for the poem is of no help here, since his text stopped at line 2094,
and so he did not have to face that particular problem.

> And wyth the noyse of them wo
> I sodeynly awoke anon tho
> And remembryd what I had seen
> And how hye and ferre I had been
> In my ghoost and had grete wonder

---

\* Many thanks to the Rev. Dr. W. G. East, *auctour newe* of this *olde clerkis speche*.

Of that the god of thonder
Had lete me knowen and began to wryte
Lyke as ye have herde me endyte
Wherfor to studye and rede alway
I purpose to doo day by day
Thus in dremyng and in game
Endeth thys lytil book of Fame.

Whether the *House of Fame*'s final effect was due to accident or design (accident, I would say), it is appropriate that a work which so blatantly rejects the idea of 'univocal' discourse should in the final analysis fail to bring in an author to sort out the riotous plurality of its meanings. When the author's away, the signifiers will play—and what a 'game' it is, a truly festive occasion on which the normal hierarchies relating to (pagan) gods and men, signifying speech and mere noise, bird-calls and 'mannes vois', mighty *auctores* and mere minstrels, even the deserving and the unworthy, are suspended. Here there is no place for 'the reasoned, authoritative, single voice'. The 'man of grete auctorite' should not be admitted; he would only spoil the party. But, *pace* certain strands of postmodernist thinking, it is very definitely Chaucer's party. A carnival held in the midst of the maze.

Donald R. Howard, *The Idea of the 'Canterbury Tales'* (Berkeley, Calif., 1976), pp. 326–32. Penelope Reed Doob, *The Idea of the Labyrinth from Classical Antiquity through the Middle Ages* (Ithaca, NY, 1990). Cf. Boitani, 'Chaucer's Labyrinth', and *Imaginary World*, p. 210. Jorge Luis Borges, 'The Library of Babel', in his *Labyrinths*, ed. D. A. Yates and J. E. Irby (Harmondsworth; repr. 1981), pp. 78–86.

Terry Eagleton, *Literary Theory: An Introduction* (Oxford, 1983). Jordan, *Chaucer's Poetics*. Jesse M. Gellrich, *The Idea of the Book in the Middle Ages* (Ithaca, NY, and London, 1985). Vincent Gillespie, review of Boitani, *Imaginary World*, in *Notes and Queries*, 232 (1987), 255. Cf. Roland Barthes, *The Pleasure of the Text* (London, 1976). Denis Donoghue, *Ferocious Alphabets* (London and Boston, 1981), pp. 146–8, 199–201. On the Barthesian theory of 'the death of the author', to which I have here alluded, see below, pp. 249–50.

Mikhail Bakhtin, *The Dialogic Imagination: Four Essays*, ed. Michael Holquist, trans. C. Emerson and M. Holquist (Austin, Tex., 1981). My sentence about 'the forms of scholastic debate, the eloquence of the court', etc. is an adaptation of a passage from Bakhtin's discussion of 'heteroglossia' in Dicken's *Little Dorrit: Dialogic Imagination*, p. 301. The following account is indebted to Peter Barry's cogent remarks on Bakhtin, in Peter Barry (ed.), *Issues in Contemporary Critical Theory* (London, 1987), p. 17.

Mikhail Bakhtin, *Rabelais and his World*, trans. Hélène Iswolsky (Bloomington, Ind., 1984).

Leyerle, 'Chaucer's Windy Eagle'; cf. Doob, *Idea of the Labyrinth*, who envisages a tradition of classroom snickers on the subject (p. 321 n. 23). See further Fyler, *Chaucer and Ovid*, who suggests that from the eagle's 'point of view the *Aeneid* and *flatus* are essentially the same thing' (p. 54), since his proof seems to put the most elevated literary language on a par with the most vulgar of noises.

*Oxford Latin Dictionary*, ed. P. G. W. Glare (Oxford, 1982); *flatus* 3.c, *ventus* 4.b (pp. 711,

2031). An example of both usages in one and the same sentence is afforded by a passage in Suetonius's *Life of Claudius* (32.1) in which 'some' are reported as saying 'that he planned an edict to legitimize the breaking of wind at table, whether silently or noisily' (*quo ueniam daret flatum crepitumque uentris in conuiuio emittendi*).

On the farting joke in the *Summoner's Tale* see especially Alan Leviathan, 'The Parody of Pentecost in Chaucer's *Summoner's Tale*', *UTQ* 40 (1970/1), 236–46; also Paul E. Beichner, 'Non Alleluia Ructare', *MS* 18 (1956), 135–44; Bernard Levy, 'Biblical Parody in the *Summoner's Tale*', *Tennessee Studies in Literature*, 11 (1966), 45–60; Penn R. Szittya, 'The Friar as False Apostle: Antifraternal Exegesis and the *Summoner's Tale*', *SP* 71 (1974), 19–46.

## Chaucer's Crisis of Authority

Having explored some of the possibilities for contemporary criticism of the *House of Fame*, we may move to consider how aspects of medieval literary theory—the theory contemporaneous with the poem itself—can help us towards comprehension of it. Authority and *auctor*-ship constitute one of the main preoccupations of that body of hermeneutics, and this has often been taken as the major concern of Chaucer's poem. His position may be explored through a contrast with the rather different views of Dante, who, through the appropriation of some of the discourses of medieval literary theory and criticism, sought to establish himself as a 'vernacular author', one worthy to keep company with the great poets of antiquity.

### AUTHORS AND AUTHORITY

During the first decade of the fourteenth century, Dante worked on, and left unfinished, *De Vulgari eloquentia* and *Il Convivio*. Whatever differences of strategy and argument (and there are many) may exist between these two treatises, together they present a powerful manifesto for vernacular art. In *De Vulgari eloquentia* Dante claimed that the illustrious Italian vernacular could possess an eloquence impressive enough to rival that which had been achieved in Latin, the fact that all this is said in Latin serving to emphasize the point further. Writing in Italian in the *Convivio*, he claimed—more obliquely, but indubitably—that vernacular poetry can aspire to that *auctoritas* which traditionally had been enjoyed by Latin poetry.

This treatise is, quite clearly, based on the medieval genre of the commentary on an *auctor*. A preliminary excursus on exegetical techniques and on the appropriateness of vernacular texts receiving vernacular commentary is followed by exposition of three of his own *canzoni* which reveals their profoundly scientific subject-matter; exegetical techniques which for generations had been employed in commentary on ancient

Latin *auctores* are applied to the work of a living writer (and indeed by that writer himself). This is a highly political act. Never .before had poetry in any modern European language been taken with that kind of seriousness, and made to bear the burden of so much doctrine. The implication is that vernacular literature may merit this kind of treatment, can be strong enough to shoulder that burden. The *Convivio*, therefore, may be understood as Dante's *De vulgari auctoritate*.

Dante raises the issue of literary authority in the context of a discussion of imperial and philosophical authority. Having considered the roots of imperial authority, he proceeds to affirm the divine origin of the Roman Empire, one manifestation of which is the coincidence in time between the birth of David, the founder of the line whence Mary came, and the birth of the holy city with the arrival of Aeneas from Troy. God chose for such office 'the hallowed people in whom the high Trojan blood was infused', their empire having 'no limit of things nor of time', as Virgil says in the *Aeneid* (cf. i. 278–9), speaking in the person of God (*Convivio*, iv. 4–5, trans. Wicksteed, pp. 244, 246). Dante then moves on to consider philosophical authority, and begins by defining his terms *autoritade* and *autore* (cf. Lat. *auctoritas* and *autor/auctor*). Drawing on standard medieval etymologies, he explains that *autore* may be derived from two sources. The first is a defunct Latin verb *auieo*, meaning 'to tie', which refers 'only to poets', who tie their words together with the help of the Muse. The second, quite crucial, source is a Greek word, *autentim*, which denotes one who is 'worthy of trust and obedience'. And thus, in this sense *autore* is used for any person who deserves to be obeyed and trusted—whence the term *autoritade*, which denotes that 'to which trust and obedience are due'. Similarly, in the Latin dictionary of Giovanni de' Balbi of Genoa (completed in 1286), the same etymology is discussed, and the comment made that 'philosophers and discoverers of the arts such as Plato, Aristotle, Priscian and whoever is of excellent character ought to be called authors'. The *auctor*, then, must be utterly trustworthy and of excellent character, or else (the implication is obvious) the authority of his works will be undermined. In the case of the three named authors, the works in question are the philosophical and grammatical treatises of Plato, Aristotle, and Priscian, the surviving witnesses on which those writers' claims to authority were based.

But what, then, of the poets? Dante was not content to think of them as *auctores* only in the sense of men who had tied their words together; for him the great poets were men of great authority in the philosophical-moral sense of that term also. In the *Inferno* Virgil is hailed as 'my master and my author' who honours 'science and art' (i. 85, iv. 73; trans. Singleton, pp. 9, 39), and four distinguished members of his 'school' are

identified: namely, 'Homer, sovereign poet', 'Horace, satirist', Ovid, and
Lucan (iv. 88–90; p. 41). Such figures, like Virgil himself, occupy the
first, outermost circle of hell, not on account of any sins on their part but
because they lacked baptism or (in the case of those who lived before
Christ) 'did not worship God aright' (iv. 33–42; p. 37). Their merit is
obvious; their 'honoured fame' which resounds through human existence
is said to win 'grace in Heaven' (iv. 76–8; p. 39). They seem to occupy a
Castle of Fame, where the Dante persona encounters people with 'looks
of great authority' (iv. 112–13; could that passage have inspired
Chaucer?). There dwell also the souls of virtuous heathen warriors
(including Aeneas) and exemplary women, and of the great pagan
philosophers, with Aristotle as their master. Quite clearly, then, the poets
and the philosophers are happy in each others' company: indeed, the
poets are referred to as 'sages' (savi; iv. 110) who possess wisdom in large
measure. Certainly the poets of great authority appear as being in essential agreement, and they are unanimous in welcoming Dante into their
select club: 'they made me one of their company, so that I was sixth amid
so much wisdom' (iv. 101–2; p. 41).

These attitudes indicate that Dante was heir to an 'ethical poetic', to
use Judson Allen's felicitous term, a poetic which had been firmly established during the twelfth-century renaissance, and was perpetuated in the
way in which poetry was taught as part of the study of grammar (cf. pp.
203–7 above). The subject-matter treated by syllabus authors such as
Aesop, Horace, Virgil, Boethius, and even the dubious Ovid was usually
identified as falling within the sphere of moral philosophy or ethics, and
so those writers became regarded as authorities on human behaviour. The
poet got into the house of fame on the philosopher's ticket. Thus their
ideological credentials were established, their inclusion in a Christian curriculum justified, and their prestige and authority secured and affirmed.
The concomitant was that the poets had to be of trustworthy and excellent character, men worthy of respect and belief. Hence, for example, the
learning and prophetic powers of vatic Virgil were emphasized. Dante
saw all this very clearly; and when he produced his own 'autoexegesis',
he took care to provide himself with the right credentials. The reader of
his canzoni may have formed the impression that he had pursued a great
passion of love, Dante admits. But in fact virtue was his motivation, as,
he promises, the subsequent expositions will make clear. Any potential
threat to the authority of the text or the good character of its author is
refined out of existence by the techniques of allegorical exegesis.

The position which Dante takes with regard to human love in the
Convivio is, therefore, quite comprehensible in view of his objective of
elevating vernacular art, but rather different from the position found in

*De Vulgari eloquentia*, wherein love, together with arms and moral fortitude, are identified as the fit subjects of the high or tragic style. However,
since Dante's triumvirate of topics fits the *Aeneid* so perfectly, one may
infer that the 'love' in question was, in the main, the hopeless passion of
Dido for Aeneas—which is shown to be destructive. No *auctor*, and certainly no would-be *auctor*, could approve of such unbridled emotion (and
certainly Virgil himself did not, as medieval *Aeneid* commentaries emphasize). In the event, Dante himself did not write such a work, but in his
*Teseida* Boccaccio took up the idea, singing of arms and two men who
loved one woman. (He also followed Dante's precedent in writing a
learned, aggrandizing commentary on it as well; cf. pp. 283–5, 289
below). It was in the *Comedy* that Dante paid his profound but limited
homage to Virgil—as pre-Christian prophet and virtuous heathen, one of
those who were on the verge of full enlightenment. A man of great
authority, certainly, and a trustworthy guide for a substantial part of
Dante's progress to the paradise of his own making and to literary fame.

But where Dante saw firm footprints which could confidently be followed, Geoffrey Chaucer saw faint and confusing tracks. This comes
across very strongly in the two poems in which he professed to follow the
'lanterne' of 'Virgil Mantoan', to whose name he wished all due 'Glorye
and honour', the *House of Fame* and the *Legend of Dido* in the *Legend of
Good Women*. Who knew if all that Virgil, or Homer, or indeed any of
the major poets, wrote was true? That was the question which Chaucer
implied. The Middle Scots poet Robert Henryson was in turn to ask it
explicitly of Chaucer, coupling the *Troilus* with another putative source
(which almost certainly did not exist) of his own poem, the *Testament of
Cresseid*, in the following terms:

> Quha wait gif all that Chauceir wrait was trew?
> Nor I wait nocht gif this narratioun
> Be authoreist, or fenȝeit of the new
> Be sum poeit                                        (64–7)

Here poetic 'feigning' is placed in opposition to authorized narration,
a tension which pervades the *House of Fame*. Dante's 'sovereign'
philosopher-poet has become a purveyor of fiction ('fable'), indeed of lies.

> Oon seyde that Omer made lyes,
> Feynynge in hys poetries,
> And was to Grekes favorable;
> Therfor held he hyt but fable.                    (*HF* 1477–80)

In fact, not just 'oon' but several writers had accused Homer in these
terms, including two on Chaucer's list of the supporters of the fame of
Troy, 'Dares' and 'Guydo' (1467, 1469), as well as Benoît de Sainte-

Maure, whose Old French *Roman de Troie* was actually the primary source of Guido's *Historia destructionis Troiae*—although of course Guido did not admit that, any more than Chaucer admitted that the primary source of his *Troilus* was a work 'fenȝeit of the new / Be sum poeit', Boccaccio's vernacular *Filostrato*, rather than the authorized Latin narrations which he cited so ostentatiously at the beginning of his poem, 'Omer', 'Dares', and 'Dite' (*Troilus and Criseyde*, i. 146). And 'Virgil Mantoan' had been accused in similar terms. 'Even Virgil', declared Guido, 'although for the most part he related in the light of truth the deeds of the Trojans when he touched upon them, was nevertheless in some things unwilling to depart from the fictions of Homer' (trans. Meek, p. 2). At the very end of his *Historia* Guido speaks of the 'failure' of the great authors Virgil, Ovid, and Homer, 'who were very deficient in describing the truth about the fall of Troy, although they composed their works in an exceedingly glorious style, whether they treated them according to the stories of the ancients or according to fables, and especially that highest of poets, Virgil, whom nothing obscures' (p. 265).

What begins with criticism thus ends with commendation of the highest of poets. By contrast, Chaucer's *Legend of Dido* begins with commendation but proceeds to engage in quite extraordinary textual convolution and subversion (cf. pp. 306–7 below). And in the *House of Fame* the highest poet is knocked off his pedestal as his narrative is reduced to a tale of a faithless man and a woman who failed to recognize that all that glitters is not gold. Feathered philosophy, it would seem, has flown, having given up on the poets.

Dante, *Il Convivio*, ed. Bruna Cordati (Turin, 1968); trans P Wicksteed, *The Convivio of Dante Alighieri* (London, 1931). Dante's etymologies draw on Hugutio of Pisa's dictionary, the *Magnae derivationes*, s.v. *augeo*. For discussion see Albert Pogue Rossi's fine essay, 'The Unfinished Author: Dante's Rhetoric of Authority in *Convivio* and *De Vulgari Eloquentia*', in Rachel Jacoff (ed.), *The Cambridge Companion to Dante* (Cambridge, 1993), pp. 45–66. On Dante as self-commentator see A. J. Minnis, '*Amor* and *Auctoritas* in the Self-Commentary of Dante and Francesco da Barberino', *Poetica*, 32 (1990), 25–42.

Giovanni de' Balbi, *Catholicon* (Venice, 1495), s.v. *auctor*, fols. 73ᵛ–74ʳ. See further A. J. Minnis, *Medieval Theory of Authorship: Scholastic Literary Attitudes in the Later Middle Ages*, 2nd edn. (Aldershot, 1988), pp. 10–11.

Dante, *Inferno*, ed. and trans. Singleton. Judson B. Allen, *The Ethical Poetic of the Later Middle Ages* (Toronto, 1982). See further Minnis and Scott (eds.), *Medieval Literary Theory*, pp. 13–14.

Dante, *De Vulgari eloquentia*, ii. 4. 5, in E. Moore and P. Toynbee (eds.), *Le Opere di Dante Alighieri*, 4th edn. (London, 1963), p. 393.

Robert Henryson, *Testament of Cresseid*, in *Poems*, ed. Denton Fox (Oxford, 1981). Fox believes that this poem was in circulation by 1492.

Guido delle Colonne, *Historia destructionis Troiae*, ed. Griffin; trans. Meek.

On the significance of Dante for Chaucer's own poetics see especially Piero Boitani, 'What

Dante Meant to Chaucer', in Boitani (ed.), *Italian Trecento*, pp. 115–39, and the critique of Boitani's position by Steve Ellis, 'Chaucer, Dante, and Damnation', *ChR* 22 (1988), 282–94.

What Dido meant to Dante is a very intriguing question, particularly in view of the great interest in this figure among late medieval vernacular poets; the small space he allows her is atypical, and probably a reflex of his concern with the imperialistic and patrilineal (both political and poetic) qualities of the *Aeneid*. Specifically, Dido is found in the second circle of hell, among 'carnal sinners, who subject reason to desire' (*Inferno*, v. 38–9); here they are tormented by a 'hellish hurricane [*bufera infernal*], never resting', which 'sweeps along the spirits with its rapine' (v. 31–2; cf. v. 33, 42, 51; trans. Singleton, pp. 49, 51). This raging wind (which recalls *Aeneid* vi. 739–41) is a far cry from Chaucer's billingsgate blasts. Dante's Virgil speaks of Dido briefly and obliquely as 'she who slew herself for love and broke faith to the ashes of Sichaeus' (v. 61–2; cf. *Aeneid*, iv. 550–2), not owning her as his creation. She seems somewhat ill-placed between cruel Semiramis and 'wanton Cleopatra'. In his commentary on this passage, Pietro Alighieri (writing *c.*1340) supplies qualifying details of a kind which his father had so notably omitted. Dido's depiction here is 'according to Virgil's fiction', Pietro explains; however, according to Jerome's *Adversus Jovinianum* she 'remained chaste in her widowhood and killed herself because Iarbas . . . wanted to make her his wife by force' (trans. Minnis and Scott (eds), *Medieval Literary Theory*, p. 487). A challenging discussion of *Inferno* v in relation to *Aeneid* vi is offered by Rachel Jacoff, 'Transgression and Transcendence: Figures of Female Desire in Dante's *Commedia*', in Marina S. Brownlee, Kevin Brownlee, and Stephen G. Nichols (eds.), *The New Medievalism* (Baltimore, 1991), pp. 183–200.

This entire section on 'Chaucer's Crisis of Authority' draws upon and amplifies material in my article '*De Vulgari Auctoritate*: Chaucer, Gower, and the Men of Great Authority', in R. F. Yeager (ed.), *Chaucer and Gower: Difference, Mutuality, Exchange* (Victoria, B.C., 1991), pp. 36–74.

## AFFECTIVE DIDO AND THE ART OF LYING

One major area in which Virgil had intruded poetical fiction into historical truth was his invention of the love-affair between Dido and Aeneas. In that part of his *Genealogia deorum gentilium* (written *c.*1350–74) which constitutes a trenchant *ars poetica*, Boccaccio had admitted that 'the greatest Latin poet' had told 'the more or less untrue story of Dido', but proceeded to argue that poets are not in fact liars, for it is not their purpose to deceive anyone with their fictions. Virgil was well aware of the fact of Dido's impeccable chastity; but poets are not historians, and there were good reasons for what he did, including his intention of concealing 'within the poetic veil . . . with what passions human frailty is infested, and the strength with which a steadfast man subdues them'. So, Boccaccio continues, 'he represents in Dido the attracting power of the passion of love', and in Aeneas 'one who is readily disposed in that way and at length overcome'. But, Boccaccio continues, 'after showing the enticements of lust, he points the way of return to virtue by bringing in Mercury', who is interpreted as 'either remorse or the reproof of some outspoken friend', to rebuke Aeneas, 'and call him back from such indulgence to deeds of glory' (trans. Minnis and Scott, pp. 435–6). Here Boccaccio is following in the footsteps of those great allegorizing commentators on the *Aeneid*, Fulgentius and 'Bernard Silvester'.

Chaucer seems not to have known this particular excursus, but he was probably aware of the virtuous Dido presented by St Jerome in his *Adversus Jovinianum* (i. 43), a work cited in the G Prologue to the *Legend of Good Women* (281) and drawn on as a source in the *Wife of Bath's Prologue* and the *Franklin's Tale*. She is the saint's first example of women who were reluctant to survive their husbands' deaths for fear they might be forced into a second marriage—'This may teach us that second marriage was repudiated among the heathen.' 'Carthage', continues Jerome, 'was built by a woman of chastity, and its end was a tribute to the excellence of the virtue.' No mention is made, however, of Virgil's violation of chronology. That figures largely in Augustine's reference to the *Aeneid* in his *Confessions* (i. 13), wherein the story of Dido and Aeneas is criticized as a mere figment of the poet's imagination. But there is no evidence that Chaucer knew this passage. However, the fact that William Langland could use 'Dido' as a generic term for an old yarn, a mere minstrel's tale—

'It is but a dido', quod this doctour, 'a disours tale!'

(B XIII. 172)

—would seem to indicate that some people treated it with scant respect, perhaps at least in part because of its fictitious nature. And the English Benedictine Ralph Higden, compiler of the *Polychronicon*, certainly believed that what Virgil had said about Dido and Aeneas was untrue. 'Yf it is sooþ . . . þat Dido bulde Cartage þre score ȝere and twelve to fore þe byldynge of þe citee of Rome', as John Trevisa put it in his Middle English translation of Higden (1387), 'þanne it is sooþ þat Eneas sygȝ neuere Dido þe quene of Carthage,' for Aeneas lived earlier than she did, and died over three hundred years before the construction of Carthage. It is, therefore, reasonable to suggest that Chaucer was aware of the fictionality of the story, or at least that its historical truth was questionable.

This would have had many implications for him, not least the questioning of the emotional force of this moving tale—or indeed of any story which was demonstrably false. At the centre of Augustine's critique of Virgil's account of Dido is the charge that this fiction arouses human emotion in a way which leads the mind away from its true destiny.

What can be more pitiful than an unhappy wretch unaware of his own sorry state, bewailing the fate of Dido, who died for love of Aeneas, yet shedding no tears for himself as he dies for want of loving you? . . . I did not weep over this, but instead I wept for Dido, who surrendered her life to the sword, while I forsook you and surrendered myself to the lowest of our created things. (*Confessions*, trans. Pine-Coffin, pp. 33–4)

He proceeds to emphasize the fictionality of the story, thereby underlining its relative worthlessness. This may be compared with Petrarch's report of two reactions to Boccaccio's story of Griselda (*Seniles*, xvii. 4). A mutual friend of theirs, a learned man from Padua, was so sensitive that he was actually unable to read Boccaccio's tale to the end, being overcome by tears half-way through. Petrarch remarks that this friend was 'a man of the kindest disposition', and quotes Juvenal: 'Nature, by giving us tears, shows that she gives the gentlest hearts to mankind, and this is the noblest quality we have' (*Satires*, xv. 131–3). Some time later, Petrarch continues, another mutual friend, on hearing what had happened to the first one, read the story for himself. But he was unmoved, on the grounds that the story was utterly improbable and therefore a fiction, for which he could not possibly weep: ' "I too would have wept, for both the pitiable subject matter and the well-chosen words were enough to move to tears, and I am not hard-hearted. But I was convinced, and still am, that the whole thing is a fiction" ' (trans. Robinson, pp. 195–6).

In many of his works—most obviously in the complaints and the highly affective *Legend of Good Women*—Chaucer inscribed the belief that 'pitee renneth soone in gentil herte' (*Knight's Tale*, I(A) 1761). And book i of the *House of Fame* itself is suffused with pity (the second book being, in marked contrast, quite jolly). There the narrator is moved by the account of how the sad apparition of Creusa ordered Aeneas to flee from the Greeks and sail to Italy where he would fulfil his destiny : 'hyt was pitee for to here' (189). A little later, we hear of how the 'wepynge' Venus (213–14) pleads with Jupiter for the deliverance of Aeneas's navy. In his account of Dido, the pitiful aspects are emphasized. She wrings her hands (299) and demands to know if all men are faithless; then she tries to awaken pity in her lover:

> 'Allas!' quod she, 'my swete herte,
> Have pitee on my sorwes smerte,
> And slee mee not! Goo noght awey!
> O woful Dido, wel-away!'
> Quod she to hirselve thoo.
> 'O Eneas, what wol ye doo?
> O that your love, ne your bond
> That ye have sworn with your ryght hond,
> Ne my crewel deth,' quod she.
> 'May holde yow stille here with me!
> O haveth of my deth pitee!' (315–25)

But all this 'compleynt' and 'moone' is of no avail. Aeneas sets sail, whereupon Dido proceeds to a second complaint, this time to her sister Anne, whom she blames for having encouraged her affair. This being 'seyd and doo', she kills herself. Her tale, Chaucer continues, is not untypical; 'the harm, the routhe' which such 'untrouthe' brings about is inscribed in many other books. A list of tales of man's inhumanity to woman follows, several of which Chaucer revisited in the *Legend of Good Women*. 'Loo, was not this a woo and routhe?' According to some, it would seem, the answer to that had to be in the negative, given the fact that the story had no basis in historical truth. All the world knows the story of Dido's passion to be fiction, declares Macrobius in his *Saturnalia* (V. xvii. 5–6), yet the beauty of Virgil's narrative has so far prevailed that painters and sculptors and those who represent human figures in tapestry take it for their theme in preference to any other. 'Although all are aware of the chastity of the Phoenician queen and know that she laid hands on herself to save her good name, still they turn a blind eye to the fiction, suppress in their minds the evidence of the truth, and choose rather to regard as true the tale which the charm of a poet's imagination has implanted in the hearts of mankind' (trans. Davies, p. 359). Most medieval responses were less forgiving, as Boccaccio knew full well; hence his attempt to allegorize the problem away.

Alongside accounts of the un-Virgilian Dido who 'preferred to burn rather than marry' (to cite Jerome's ghastly inversion of 1 Corinthians 7: 9) circulated stories of an alternative Aeneas. In his *Historia destructionis Troiae* Guido delle Colonne associates Aeneas from the first with the plot to deliver Troy to the Greeks, and has Hecuba single him out for condemnation as *proditor* ('traitor'); hence the *Gest Hystoriale of the Destruction of Troy* describes him as 'The traytor with tene, vntristy Eneas' (11,973). He had been as unfair in love as in war. In *Heroides* vii Ovid had allowed the betrayed Dido to castigate impious Aeneas as a deceiver of women. 'You are false in everything!', she exclaims, adding that she was not the first woman deceived by his tongue—a reference to Creusa, his first wife, 'left behind by her unfeeling lord' in Troy, as Dido would have it (trans. Goold, p. 89). It was but a short step to Aeneas the traitor in love.

In neither of Chaucer's versions of the story of Dido and Aeneas did he resort to the allegorical rationalization of fiction as used by Boccaccio on Virgil in the *Genealogia* and by Dante on his own *canzoni* in the *Convivio*. The attitude implied by the *House of Fame* is rather that summed up so well in that much-read grammar school textbook, the *Distichs* of (Pseudo-) Cato:

Multo legas facito, tum lectis neglege multa;
Nam miranda canunt, sed non credenda poetae.

[Read much and much of it forget: 'Tis well
T'admire but not believe what poets tell.]

The major medieval dictionaries reiterated an etymology which explained *fabula* as denoting 'spoken fictions' or verbal artefacts in contrast to factual things which truly existed. 'The fables [*fabulae*] of the poets are named from *fando*, because they are not true things [*res factae*] but only spoken fictions [*loquendo fictae*],' to cite Isidore of Seville's succinct definition once again (cf. p. 206 above). In similar vein, the *House of Fame* implies that poetry is an art of lying. Moreover, Chaucer's actual 'feynynges' are themselves full of lies. He provides portraits of lying lovers—the impious Aeneas of the *House of Fame* and the feigning fornicators who deceive the virtuous heroines of the *Legend of Good Women*, those women who love not wisely but too well. The poets are liars, the lovers who poets write about are liars—and fame itself may be a pack of lies, or at best a mixture of truth and fiction, as Chaucer intimates in book iii of the *House of Fame*. Rarely has the alleged mendacity of poetry—in its form, content, and posterity—been revealed so ruthlessly. There seems to be no basis here on which to build a claim for vernacular *auctoritas*. For how can one think *de vulgari auctoritate* when the *auctoritas* of the revered Latin poets seems so shaky?

And that is not all. John Guillory, comparing literary authors with other 'workers in the medium of power', indicates as a major difference the fact that 'they have only chosen a strangely durable medium, the text, which has come to signify the very assurance of an afterlife' (p. vii). In the *House of Fame*, by contrast, Chaucer seems to be conveying a sense of the lack of durability of literary fame—and indeed of all fame (as book iii intimates), since fame rests on evidence which is invariably literary, the testimony of 'olde bookes'. Neither is there any belief in the durability of empire and civic fame, no vision of the *translatio imperii* to a 'New Troy', whether it be Rome or London, to correspond to Dante's faith in the divine origin and preservation of his continuing city. In view of such powerlessness, the *House of Fame* can be said to record Chaucer's crisis of authority.

Can he get out of it? A man of great authority is promised, but the poem as we have it breaks off at that point, just before he comes to the rescue. Who was this author with no name? Virgil, Boethius, and Boccaccio have been suggested; Ovid and Dante also have their claim. But in terms of the theoretical impasse which the poem has got itself into, it is appropriate to suggest Lollius—the author who never was.

Here it is not simply that the author is dead; he never existed in the first place.

Such is the wide gulf which, for Chaucer, the differences between Virgil and Ovid opened up. The Middle Ages had developed sophisticated techniques for reconciling authorities which seemed to be discordant, a classic statement of which is found in the famous prologue to Peter Abelard's *Sic et Non*. But Chaucer was more interested in the fact that, between those who bear up the heavy weight of the fame of Troy, there was 'a litil envye' (1476)—what an understatement!—and in his list of poets the 'Latyn poete Virgile' who has supported for so long 'The fame of Pius Eneas' is followed by 'Venus clerk Ovide' (*HF* 1481–9). Similarly, in the *Legend of Dido*, after his famous statement about wishing to follow Virgil's lantern, Chaucer identifies the subject of the *Aeneid* not as arms and the man but rather as 'How Eneas to Dido was forsworn' (927)—in other words, the theme of *Heroides* vii. Here we may recall the Man of Law's claim that in his 'Seintes Legende of Cupide' Chaucer had surpassed Ovid's 'Episteles' (= the *Heroides*):

> he hath toold of loveris up and doun
> Mo than Ovide made of mencioun
> In his Episteles, that been ful olde.          (*CT* II(B) 53–5)

Certainly, in book i of the *House of Fame*, as in the narratives of the *Legend*, Chaucer sided with Ovid, and that inevitably meant the subversion of the authority of Virgil. That is hardly surprising, since Ovid had set himself up as a writer who was diametrically opposed to Virgil; his retelling of the *Aeneid* in *Heroides* vii constitutes a refusal to ally himself with his elder contemporary's celebration of military glory and the distinguished lineage of the Emperor Augustus, ruler of the New Troy. But Chaucer went far beyond Ovid in this regard, thereby earning himself the respectful but firm reproof of the Scots poet Gavin Douglas (who completed his translation of the *Aeneid* in 1513), a very revealing account, to which we may now turn.

Boccaccio, *Genealogia*, xiv. 13, in Minnis and Scott (eds.), *Medieval Literary Theory*, pp. 434–6. Boccaccio amplifies Jerome's positive depiction of Dido in his *De mulieribus claris*: see below, pp. 404–5. In his Latin works Boccaccio consistently rejects the Virgilian Dido, though his vernacular writings accommodate her in various ways. Cf. the chapter 'Boccaccio's Two Didos' in Craig Kallendorf, *In Praise of Aeneas. Virgil and Epideictic Rhetoric in the Early Italian Renaissance* (Hanover, NH, and London, 1977), pp. 58–76.

The Latin text of the Jerome passage may be found in *PL* 23, col. 286; cf. the partial translation in Blamires (ed.), *Woman Defamed*, pp. 68–9. Augustine, *Confessions*, trans. R. S. Pine-Coffin (Harmondsworth, 1961), pp. 33–4, 25; for the original see CCSL, 27, pp. 11–12. Since Langland's usage is the only instance noted by the *MED* for this sense of the term 'dido', the *Piers Plowman* quotation should be used with caution. Higden,

*Polychronicon*, ed. Babington and Lumby, i. 166–7, ii. 432–5. Higden knew the relevant passages in Augustine's *Confessions* and Pompeius Trogus (in Justin's epitome) and also Papias, who in his dictionary entry on *Elissa* refers to the 'historical' Dido. The various presentations of this figure have been studied extensively by Mary Louise Lord, 'Dido as an Example of Chastity: The Influence of Example Literature', *Harvard Library Bulletin*, 17 (1969), 22–44, 216–32. James H. Robinson (ed. and trans.), *Petrarch. The First Modern Man of Letters* (1898; repr. New York, 1970). With this passage may be compared Boccaccio's remark in the *Amorosa visione* that no one 'would have been so cruel as not to have wept in compassion' in response to the Virgilian story of Dido (trans. Kallendorf, *Praise of Aeneas*, p. 59). However, 'Boccaccio did not sing the praises of Virgil's Dido after his meetings with Petrarca' (p. 63).

Macrobius, *The Saturnalia*, trans. P. V. Davies (New York and London, 1969).

On Chaucer's Dido narrative, see the useful discussion by J. A. W. Bennett, *Book of Fame*, pp. 24–45, which concentrates on its functions within the poem as a whole. Hall, 'Dido-and-Aeneas Story', praises Chaucer for having fitted in the story well as an *exemplum* of Lady Fame's general truth. For his negotiation of the space between Virgil and Ovid, see the relevant discussion in Desmond, *Reading Dido*, particularly her chapter '*Sely* Dido and the Chaucerian Gaze' (pp. 128–62); also Karla Taylor, *Chaucer Reads 'The Divine Comedy'* (Stanford, Calif., 1989), pp. 28–9; Mann, *Chaucer*, pp. 8–16; J. T. Miller, 'Writing on the Wall', pp. 105–6, and her *Poetic License*, pp. 52–62. Chaucer 'does not attempt to reconcile his sources', claims Taylor, 'but instead stitches them together with such obvious seams that they are shown to be irreconcilable' (p. 29). The fact that the attitudes of Virgil and Ovid 'toward truth itself are entirely disparate', says Miller, suggests the question, 'are there "absolute standards" that exist as authoritative or is the only authority available something more local, relative, and individual?' (*Poetic License*, p. 54). Mann, taking the poem's 'central concern' as being 'the question of literary authority', argues that what is at stake 'in these competing narrative versions is not only Dido herself, but the nature of poetic truth' (*Chaucer*, pp. 14, 15). Working from very different premisses, Gellrich, *Idea of the Book*, similarly suggests that 'Chaucer's text does not resolve the conflict of sources in order to establish the privilege of one over the other' (pp. 171–2, 190, 197–8).

An admirably lucid account of classical and medieval versions of the Dido story is provided by Götz Schmitz, *The Fall of Women in Early English Narrative Verse* (Cambridge, 1990), pp. 17–43. The most comprehensive treatment is Desmond's *Reading Dido*, which explores the various ways in which, by displacing the epic hero Aeneas, the medieval tradition of reading Dido often disrupts the patrilineal focus of the *Aeneid* as an imperial foundation narrative.

Chaucer's Dido may profitably be compared with her construction in a work which is, if not a source, at least a challenging analogue, of the Dido narratives in *HF* and *LGW*; namely, the *Roman d'Eneas*. See especially B. Nolan, *Chaucer and the 'Roman Antique'*, pp. 89–92, who demonstrates that, with the aid of categories derived from the medieval commentary tradition on Ovid, the French poet sets the foolish love of Dido and Aeneas in opposition to the legitimate love of Lavine and Aeneas. See further the articles by Nadia Margolis, '*Flamma*, *Furor*, and *Fol'Amors*: Fire and Feminine Madness from the *Aeneid* to the *Roman d'Eneas*', *Romanic Review*, 78 (1987), 131–47, and Simon Gaunt, 'From Epic to Romance: Gender and Sexuality in the *Roman d'Enéas*', *Romanic Review*, 83 (1992), 1–27. On Gower's Dido and the anonymous *Letter of Dydo to Eneas* which was printed with *HF* in Richard Pynson's edition (1526?), see Schmitz, *Fall of Women*, pp. 30–2, 39–43. A single but split Dido narrative is deployed to good effect by Christine de Pizan in her *Livre de la Cité des dames* of 1405. At I. 46. 1–3, 'Reason' speaks in praise of the prudence and attentiveness of Queen Dido; the narrative pauses at the point at which she has consolidated her position at Carthage and is ruling it well, as a *virago*—i.e. a woman with 'the strength and force of a man'. At II. 55. 1 the narrative resumes, as Dido appears at the head of a series of *exempla* of women who were constant in love in the face of male treachery. *The Book of the City of Ladies*, trans. Earl Jeffrey Richards (London, 1983), pp. 91–5, 188–9. The original French text has been edited by Maureen Cheney Curnow, *La Livre de la Cité des Dames of Christine de Pisan: A Critical Edition* (diss., Vanderbilt University, 1975). Christine's Dido is discussed in ch. 6 of Desmond's *Reading Dido*.

Guido delle Colonne's Hecuba accuses Aeneas of being a traitor in *Historia destructionis Troiae*, book 30; trans. Meek, p. 225. Cf. the *Gest Hystoriale*, ed. G. A. Panton and D. Donaldson, EETS OS 39, 56, repr. as one volume (New York, 1969), p. 390. Aeneas's treachery is described at length in book 29 of Guido's *Historia* (trans. Meek, pp. 209–19). Earlier, Guido had referred to the *Aeneid* concerning Aeneas's subsequent career, his 'continued fortunes and successes', and had praised his imperial line: 'From his race proceeded in great felicity that great and glorious Ceasar Augustus' (p. 107). But he makes no attempt to reconcile the different traditions concerning Aeneas, or indeed to confront them. One may contrast Otto of Freising, who cites Virgil as the authority for the view of Aeneas as a brave man, but notes that 'according to others' he is 'a betrayer of his country and a necromancer, inasmuch as he even sacrificed his own wife to his gods': Otto, Bishop of Freising, *The Two Cities*, trans. Charles C. Mierow (New York, 1928), pp. 142 3. According to yet another tradition, Aeneas was suspected of homosexuality, as is noted by Ralph J. Hexter, *Ovid and Medieval Schooling. Studies in Medieval School Commentaries on Ovid's 'Ars amatoria', 'Epistulae ex Ponto', and 'Epistulae Heroidum'*, Münchener Beiträge zur Mediävistik und Renaissance-Forschung, 38 (Munich, 1986), pp. 198–9. This may be a reflex of the ancient tradition, as found in the earliest *vitae* of Virgil, that the poet himself preferred boys. See R. Ellis (ed.), *Appendix Vergiliana* (Oxford, 1957), p. 11, for the relevant comment in the fourth-century *Vita* by Donatus.

*Heroides*, vii. 81–4, trans. Grant Showerman, 2nd edn. by G. P. Goold, *Ovid: 'Heroides' and 'Amores'* (Cambridge, Mass., 1986), p. 89. *Disticha Catonis*, ed. Marcus Boas (Amsterdam, 1952); trans. W. J. Chase, *The Distichs of Cato: A Famous Medieval Textbook*, University of Wisconsin, Studies in the Social Sciences and History, 8 (Madison, Wis., 1922), pp. 32–3.

John Guillory, *Poetic Authority: Spenser, Milton and Literary History* (New York, 1983). Chaucer's crisis of literary authority should of course be seen within the perspective of the many crises of authority (political, social, and ecclesiastical) which arose in the England of his day. These are well reviewed by Charles Muscatine, *Poetry and Crisis in the Age of Chaucer* (Notre Dame, Ind., and London, 1972); on social conflicts see further the comments by David Aers in the introduction to his *Community, Gender and Individual Identity. English Writing 1360–1430* (London and New York, 1988), pp. 1–19.

For Abelard's *Sic et Non* prologue see Minnis and Scott (eds.), *Medieval Literary Theory*, pp. 87–100.

Concerning the identification of the man of great authority, Donald Baker nominates Virgil in 'Recent Interpretations of the *House of Fame*: A New Suggestion', *Studies in English* (University of Mississippi), 1 (1960), 97–104. Boethius is offered by Ruggiers, 'Unity'; while Boccaccio is tentatively suggested by R. C. Goffin, 'Quiting by Tidings in the *Hous of Fame*', *MÆ* 12 (1943), 40–4. Koonce, *Tradition of Fame*, pp. 265–7, proposes Jesus Christ. The reading of David Lyle Jeffrey, 'Sacred and Secular Scripture: Authority and Interpretation in *The House of Fame*', in *idem* (ed.), *Chaucer and Scriptural Tradition* (Ottawa, 1984), pp. 207–28, follows in Koonce's footsteps. Drawing on the Book of Ezekiel as interpreted in medieval exegesis, Jeffrey regards the poem's end as 'opening the way to an authoritative conclusion not yet grasped by individual readings', with the man of great authority being 'the mysterious One before whom all things are to be uncovered, and from whom nothing is hid . . . the ultimate Judge, or interpreter'. This is the culmination of his argument that Chaucer is undermining the authority of the author and raising the question of ultimate trust, which can be only in God. By contrast with all this, Benson's 'The "Love Tydynges"' claims that the man of great authority was a historical personage (cf. pp. 169–70 above). My own proposal of the candidature of Lollius vacillates between earnest and game. I do not mean to suggest that Chaucer had intended *literally* to produce Lollius at this point (though, given Chaucer's humour, one certainly cannot rule out that possibility). My point is the more modest one that, given the way *HF* has been going, a non-existent *auctor*, or at least an *auctor* with no known book (it being impossible to determine how Chaucer regarded him), would be a highly appropriate person to introduce here. On the mysterious Lollius, referred to at *HF* 1468 and cited ostentatiously as an authority in *T&C*, see Windeatt, *OGC: T&C*, pp. 37–50. In *T&C* part of Chaucer's purpose was surely to exploit the high-sounding name of some allegedly ancient Latin authority rather than that of a 'modern' writer who had written in the Italian vernacular, even though Boccaccio's *Filostrato* is of course the primary source of the English poem.

### REASSERTING AUTHORITY: DOUGLAS ON CHAUCER'S VIRGIL

It may be presumptuous, Douglas admits, to take his master Chaucer to task—but Chaucer was even more bold when he claimed that he was following Virgil's lantern in narrating the story of how Aeneas perjured himself to Dido.

> My mastir Chauser gretly Virgill offendit.
> All thoch I be to bald hym to repreif,
> He was fer baldar, certis, by hys leif,      *bolder, leave*
> Seyand he followit Virgillis lantern toforn,      *ahead*
> Quhou Eneas to Dydo was forsworn.
> Was he forsworn? Than Eneas was fals—
> That he admittis and callys hym traytour als.
> Thus, wenyng allane Ene to have reprevit,      *alone Aeneas*
> He hass gretly the prynce of poetis grevit,
> For, as said is, Virgill dyd diligens
> But spot of cryme, reproch or ony offens
> Eneas for to loif and magnyfy,
> And gif he grantis hym maynsworn fowlely,      *perjured*
> Than all hys cuyr and crafty engyne gais quyte,    *care, ingenuity*
> Hys twelf yheris laubouris war nocht worth a myte.
>
>                                   (Prol. 410–24)

Clearly, this echoes the beginning of the *Legend of Dido* (924–7), and so it would seem that Douglas was reacting to the Dido of the *Legend of Good Women* rather than the one presented in the *House of Fame*. But both accounts are, in Douglas's terms, objectionable, and so they may usefully be considered together here. If, the Scots poet protests,

Chaucer's charge that Aeneas was a 'traytour' and perjurer were true,
then Virgil's construct would be utterly ruined and his twelve years'
labour on the poem rendered worthless (423–4). This charge is as powerful in the earlier poem as it is in the later. The credulous queen,
Chaucer declares in the *House of Fame*, believed

> hyt had al be so
> As he hir swor; and herby demed
> That he was good, for he such semed.
> Allas! what harm doth apparence,
> Whan hit is fals in existence!                    (*HF* 262–6)

Similarly, Aeneas is called a 'traytour' in both the *House of Fame*—

> For he to hir a traytour was
> Wherfore she slow hirself, allas!                 (*HF* 267–8)

—and in the *Legend*:

> as a traytour forth he gan to sayle
> Toward the large contre of Ytayle.
> Thus he hath laft Dido in wo and pyne,
> And wedded ther a lady hyghte Lavyne.    (*LGW* 1328–31)

Chaucer, it would seem, had 'gretly offendit' the 'prynce of poetis' on
two occasions.

Douglas saw with utter clarity that, whatever Chaucer's motives may
have been, his manipulation of material from the *Aeneid* struck at the very
heart of the poem's claim to greatness. For, in the terms of the 'ethical
poetic' which was as familiar to Chaucer as it was to Douglas, the basis
of a poem's excellence was its ethical usefulness. A poem which had an
unscrupulous oath-breaker as its hero was hardly likely to pass the test
of moral correctness, and the writer responsible for such a creation would
not be worthy of trust and obedience, that essential requirement for an
*auctor*. Far from following Virgil's lantern, Chaucer was in grave danger
of blowing it out.

The Scottish poet's fears, then, were very real ones (according to the
hermeneutic values of his age), and his wish to answer Chaucer's innu-
endoes is perfectly understandable. His fourfold defence of Virgil constitutes one of the finest pieces of literary analysis to survive from the later
Middle Ages. Specifically, it is an attempt to rehabilitate Virgil, to recuperate the *auctoritas* which the *Aeneid* had lost at Chaucer's hands.

First, Douglas protests, Aeneas was simply obeying the gods' command. *That* is where the responsibility lay; his departure from Carthage
was not of his own volition.

> gif that thar command maid hym maynsworn,          *perjured*
> That war repreif to thar diuinyte
> And na reproch onto the said Enee.                    (428–30)

Chaucer himself was aware of this argument, as he makes clear in the *House of Fame*:

> But to excusen Eneas
> Fullyche of al his grete trespas,
> The book seyth Mercurie, sauns fayle,          *without fail*
> Bad hym goo into Italye,
> And leve Auffrikes regioun,
> And Dido and hir faire toun.                    (*HF* 427–32)

The tone of these lines suggests that the excuse is not a very convincing one. The *Legend* goes even further by utterly destroying the basis on which such an excuse could be made, 'the said Enee' being directly and personally reproached. Here the divine decree is carefully confined within a dream which Aeneas claims to have had—a dream which he reveals only after being confronted by the (rightly) suspicious yet deeply loving queen (1290–1300). We have only his word for it, therefore, and that is just not good enough. His excuse is feeble at best, and at worst quite incredible.

Second, Douglas points out that Aeneas never concealed the fact that his destiny lay in Italy (431–6). In the *House of Fame* the ghost of Aeneas's first wife, Creusa, tells him just that (187–8), but Dido is not privy to such information, and in the *Legend* there is not a word of any of this; indeed, there—as in the earlier poem—the emphasis is placed on the vast amount which Aeneas conceals from his lover. Stealing away in the night while she is asleep, this 'traytour' sets sail for another country where he sets the seal on his infidelity by marrying another woman (*Legend of Dido*, *LGW* 1288–9, 1326–31).

Third, Douglas continues, Aeneas never promised to stay, and so he was not forsworn (437–40). But in both Chaucer's poems he apparently did make and break an oath. 'He betrayed hir,' declares the *House of Fame* in no uncertain terms (294). Indeed, here Chaucer's version of the *Aeneid* begins with a pointed reference to the treachery of Sinon:

> First sawgh I the destruction
> Of Troye thurgh the Grek Synon,
> [That] with his false forswerynge,
> And his chere and his lesynge,
> Made the hors broght into Troye          (*HF* 151–5)

The clear implication is that the poem continues in this vein by recording how Aeneas deceived Dido with his 'false forswerynge'; here, it would seem, is an appalling chronicle of deceit and downright lying. Moreover, in the *Legend* it is clearly implied—in a passage which, since it is located before Aeneas's report of his dream, suggests that the real reason for his departure is that he simply tired of a woman who had given him everything:

> This Eneas, that hath so depe yswore,
> Is wery of his craft withinne a throwe;                    *short time*
> The hote ernest is al overblowe.                           *blown over*
> And pryvyly he doth his shipes dyghte,
> And shapeth hym to stele awey by nyghte.        *prepared himself*
> (*LGW* 1285–9)

Which brings us to Douglas's fourth point: namely, that Aeneas, far from being unkind, was regretful and sorrowful on departing, but had no choice in the matter (441–4). There is no suggestion of this defence in either of Chaucer's poems. What does weaken the force of the character assassination in the earlier poem, however, is the clear suggestion that the lovers shared the blame for what happened—*pace* Bennett (p. 38), who believes that 'All of Chaucer's sympathies, even while he shows her folly, are with Dido':

> Loo, how a woman doth amys
> To love hym that unknowen ys! . . .
> For this shal every woman fynde,
> That som man, of his pure kynde,
> Wol shewen outward the fayreste,
> Tyl he have caught that what him leste . . .
> Al this seye I be Eneas
> And Dido, and hir nyce lest,
> That loved al to sone a gest . . .                    *guest*
> (*HF* 269 ff.)

There are thirty-seven lines (256–92) on this theme, with Dido's 'foolish desire' being made very obvious. In the *Legend of Good Women* this is reduced to a mere three lines, and here it is 'certain people'—not women in particular—who are said to be attracted foolishly by what is new:

> And, for he [i.e. Aeneas] was a straunger, somwhat she
> Likede hym the bet, as, God do bote,                *may God help us*
> To *som folk* ofte newe thyng is sote.               *sweet-smelling*
> (*LGW* 1075–7; italics mine)

And, as already noted, the earlier poem does refer to Aeneas's high destiny, though Dido is (reprehensibly) kept in ignorance of it. In the *Legend*, however, Chaucer presents us with the image of a self-motivated (and self-centred) man who sheds 'false teres' (1301), and, as already noted, subsequently sneaks away like a thief in the night (1288–9,

1326–7), apparently with no qualms about what he is doing. It was this impression which Douglas was so anxious to correct.

In sum, Douglas took very seriously what his predecessor had done to the reputation of Aeneas, along with the implications of this for the judgement of Virgil's entire poem according to principles characteristic of the academic literary theory of the later Middle Ages. However, he softened his critique of Chaucer with the florid declaration that his 'mastir' may be excused on the grounds that this was predictable behaviour from one who was a friend to all women:

> Bot sikkyrly of resson me behufis                           *behoves*
> Excuss Chauser fra all maner repruffis
> In lovyng of thir ladeis lylly quhite
> He set on Virgill and Eneas this wyte,                       *reproach*
> For he was evir (God wait) all womanis frend.        (445–9)

That famous, or infamous, remark has been interpreted in many ways. From our point of view, its prime significance consists in the fact that it highlights the intimate nature of the relationship between the two poems which Douglas's previous comments concern so directly, the *House of Fame* and the *Legend*. In the former work Chaucer approaches the unpalatable fact that we cannot always believe what we read through what is, in effect, a quite eccentric (if heavily Ovidian) retelling of the *Aeneid* in which the titular hero is anything but heroic and the over-passionate woman who first serves, then threatens to obstruct, his high destiny is allowed a large measure of credibility. This response to Dido causes a sort of chain reaction concerning other wronged women of the past (383–426); of the seven then named, four (Phyllis, Hypsipyle, Medea, and Ariadne) also figure in the *Legend*. Later in the *House of Fame*, it is in the area of the 'matter of Troy'—the band of the literary spectrum wherein the *Aeneid* is located—that the nub of the problem is confronted. Here is where the suggestion is made that Homer might have told lies, and may have been biased ('favorable') towards the Greek side (1477–80; cf. p. 230 above). Fame, as the subsequent section of the poem makes painfully clear, need not give people what they deserve. In the *Legend*, Chaucer pushed these speculations and suspicions to a sort of logical conclusion as far as the regular victims of history were concerned. He determined to do for women what Homer had done for the Greeks and Virgil (to Dante's applause) had done for the greater glory of Rome. He would consistently be 'favorable' to the female sex, adopting a deliberate and all-determining bias on behalf of women. The poets, even the very greatest of them, had engaged in 'feigning' (or, to speak bluntly, had told lies). So be it: Chaucer would 'lie' with the best of them. He would offer his own intermingling of poetic fiction with historical truth. This may be identified as a fundamental procedure of the *Legend of Good Women* (on which, more later). And this trajectory makes it clear that Virgil meant to Chaucer something substantially different than what he had meant to Dante.

Douglas's critique of Chaucer is quoted from A. M. Kinghorn (ed.), *The Middle Scots Poets* (London, 1970), pp. 162–3. The entire text has been edited by David F. C. Coldwell, *Virgil's 'Aeneid' translated into Scottish Verse by Gavin Douglas*, STS (Edinburgh, 1960).

The chaste 'historical' Dido is firmly excluded by Douglas from his own translation. In addition to Chaucer's he also criticizes William Caxton's version of the *Aeneid* (1490), for several reasons, including its 'perverse' treatment (as Douglas terms it) of the Dido story; this narrative is said to be amplified out of all proportion (Prol. i. 163–72). For this text, a close translation of the anonymous French *Livre des Eneydes*, see the edition by W. T. Culley and F. J. Furnivall, *Caxton's 'Eneydos'*, EETS ES 57 (London, 1890; repr. 1962). Herein the chaste Dido from Boccaccio's *De mulieribus claris* is immediately followed by the Virgilian version, which is briefly introduced as an alternative account.

On the 'all women's friend' claim and its implications for interpretation of *HF* see especially Hansen, *Fictions of Gender*, pp. 87–107, and Desmond, *Reading Dido*, ch. 4 and 5. Despite the protestation that she is 'no longer interested in defending' the Douglas view that Chaucer liked women (p. 10), Hansen reads the Chaucer persona 'Geffrey' as (initially at least) being like women in many ways, though presented as superior to the weak Dido. The 'instability or fluidity' of the narrator's gender is said to be intimated by his 'self-characterization as a womanly type in the Proem to Book 1', his 'sympathy and identification with Dido', and his 'relation to the manly (and preposterous) golden eagle' (p. 98). Near the end of the poem as we have it, however, Geffrey's affirmation of his autonomy as individual and artist ('As fer forth as I kan myn art', 1882) serves to proclaim that 'he is finally *not* a woman, and not like women/any woman/every woman'—certainly different from those 'wrechched wymmen' who, as Dido's essentializing statement has it, 'konne noon art' (335).

In her treatment of *HF* Desmond presents Chaucer as a spectator of women rather than as their friend. However, despite his representation of Dido as the object of the male gaze and therefore of desire, 'the memory of Dido's story offers Geffrey a momentary subject-position that calls into question the totalizing discourse' which is presented by the *Aeneid*, that 'mythic/historical' project which involves the construction and celebration of 'the fame of Pius Eneas' (p. 150). Here, then, are possibilities for critique rather than rigid closure. While Chaucer's rhetorical strategy in questioning the culturally normative premisses of the *Aeneid* plot through an exploration of Dido's point of view certainly does not make him 'women's friend', at least it does 'exhibit a set of possibilities for reading Dido in late medieval vernacular cultures', which Desmond regards as having culminated in Christine de Pizan's version of the Dido story.

UNAUTHORIZED CHAUCER?

Here, it would seem, is a poet with a highly developed sense of the relative, someone who instinctively shies away from those absolutes necessary for the creation of *auctoritas*, including the absolute agreement between *auctoritates* at (least at) the level of *sententia* or essential meaning. The four evangelists who narrated the greatest story ever told, the life of Christ, provided the ideal paradigm—

> ye woot that every Evaungelist
> That telleth us the peyne of Jhesu Crist
> Ne seith nat alle thyng as his felawe dooth;
> But nathelees hir sentence is al sooth,
> And alle acorden as in hire sentence,
> Al be ther in hir tellyng difference.                    (*CT* VII. 943–8)

—but Chaucer found in many of his source-texts not mere verbal discrepancies but crucial differences of sense and sensibility. This recognition lies at the centre of many of his most distinctive literary creations. But it inhibits any impulse towards self-authorization, since no common perception of value is affirmed as existing between the *auctores* which could enclose within its brackets a new poetic discourse.

Of course, in a passage near the end of *Troilus and Criseyde* Chaucer directs this 'litel book' as follows:

> no makyng thow n'envie,
> But subgit be to alle poesye;                              *subject*
> And kis the steppes where as thow seest pace
> Virgile, Ovide, Omer, Lucan, and Stace.          (v. 1789–92)

This seems to be quite modest, particularly if it is compared with the far more confident way in which, in *Inferno* iv, Dante made himself a member of that distinguished school of song to which Virgil had introduced him. There *l'altissimo poeta*, along with its four other most prominent members (Homer, Horace, Ovid, and Lucan), do honour to the Dante persona, who enjoys the poetic equivalent of Pauline rapture (cf. pp. 161–2 above). Chaucer's statement, however, is none the less striking and significant for that. He is firmly allying his modern, vernacular tragedy with the works of the great tragedians of the past, moving quite near (if with great deference) to those men of great authority. Here, in marked contrast with the *House of Fame*, there is no 'envie' between the authors— and Chaucer knocks on the door of their club.

The Man of Law's statement that Chaucer had sought to surpass Ovid in the ancient genre of amatory epistles by writing the *Legend of Good Women* should be given due weight, and other Canterbury characters display appropriate deference to those illustrious moderns, Dante 'the wise poete of Florence' (*Wife of Bath's Tale*, III(D) 1125–6) and Petrarch 'the lauriat poete' (*Clerk's Prologue*, IV(E) 31). To return to the *House of Fame*, it must never be forgotten that this is the first poem in English to invoke the Muses, and, according to Boitani, this implies that Chaucer considers himself the heir of the ancients and presents his candidacy for the place of 'sixth amid so much wisdom' (*Inferno*, iv. 101–2) which Dante had been accorded by the great poets of antiquity in his Castle of Limbo. And Chaucer's declaration that 'I wyl myselven al hyt drynke' (1880) has, naturally enough, been regarded as an affirmation of his status as artist.

Then again, the Chaucer persona interrupts his account of the 'grete peyne' of Dido (312) to declare that all this was revealed to him in *his* dream: 'Non other auctour alegge I' (314). The primary sense of *auctour* here probably follows the juridic connotation of the Latin term *auctor* as 'the person responsible' for something, but it is perfectly possible that Chaucer had literary authorship in mind. Assuming this, John Norton Smith points out that the poet is indeed his own *auctor* here, since of the sixty lines which constitute Dido's lament only a half-dozen or so have any parallel in Virgil. However, his refusal to allege any author other than himself is more likely to be self-ironical than self-asserting. In the *Parliament of Fowls* the foolish cuckoo is certainly not to be approved of when she attempts to solve the problem being debated in the assembly of birds 'of myn owene autorite' (507). Similarly, in the *Merchant's Tale* January stupidly chooses a wife 'of his owene auctoritee' (IV(E) 1597), while Melibee warns her husband not to take vengeance 'as of youre propre auctoritee' (VII. 1385). And self irony could also be the main motive behind that line about drinking 'al' himself. But, in general terms, can Chaucer be said to be emulating the Italians in their apologies for poetry? Petrarch's Laureate Oration, described by Fyler as 'the noblest fourteenth-century statement of the poet's high vocation' (p. 62), links the immortality of the names of those whom the poet celebrates with the immortality of the poet's own name; such immortality is, Petrarch argues, among the poet's major rewards. Chaucer did not get anywhere near saying that. Yet, as already noted, it is surely significant that it is *the poets* who support the various major subject-matters of literature in the House of Fame. As Bennett says, Chaucer makes this point 'so silently, almost imperceptibly, as if without knowing it, certainly without ostentation'. Yet he definitely does make it: 'If Chaucer anywhere departs from earlier medieval assumptions about the status of poets it is here' (pp. 143–4). And the subtlety of this departure, if such it is, marks its difference from the ostentatious claims of the Italians. Indeed, in general, the obvious contrasts between the views on literary authority implicit in the writings of Dante and Chaucer are far more striking than any alleged similarities.

In this regard Chaucer is best remembered for his (or at least his Wife of Bath's) claim for the authority of experience, albeit that her experience is often supported, whether in earnest or in game, by quotations from *auctores*. In sharp opposition to Dante, Chaucer seems to have found it difficult to make or imply a claim for the high status of his own art in the vernacular. He certainly knew Dante's extraordinary venture into self-commentary, the *Convivio*, by the early to mid-1390s, for he drew on a passage from it in the *Wife of Bath's Tale*, III(D) 1133 ff. Yet he did not follow Dante's lead in that respect, or indeed emulate his friend John Gower, who seems to have written the Latin commentary on the Middle English *Confessio Amantis* himself. There is no trace of an attempt at formal self-commentary by Chaucer. We can only guess at the reasons why he refused to engage in that particular process of authorization of himself and his vernacular art, of why he took a different path. The tale told by the *House of Fame*—which may or may not have much to do with the poet's own attitudes—seems to be as follows. If the men of great authority can disagree so irresolvably, how can—why should?—one associate with them? Indeed, no 'company' of mutually supportive *savants* seems to exist, and therefore no new member can be admitted. If the veracity of the literary *auctores* is so dubious, how can one possibly follow their lanterns; if the authority of the greatest Latin poet can be called in question, how can vernacular poetry be empowered?

Then there is the issue of the woman of no authority, the virtuous and wise Queen of Carthage who was occluded in the *Aeneid* and reduced to an allegory of 'the attracting power of the passion of love' (to reiterate Boccaccio's phrase) in the academic commentary tradition on Virgil. The relocation of the *disours tale* of Dido's love and suicide at the centre of the narrative may be taken as a sort of vernacular response to—perhaps to some extent a reaction against—the imperial Latin poem of great authority. Dante's enveloping of Virgil is an exception which helps to prove the rule; most other 'vernacular poets show less direct investment in the textual authority' of the *Aeneid*, as Marilynn Desmond says. 'One might read the medieval vernacular Dido', she continues, 'as a counter-tradition to the Latin commentary and allegory traditions, traditions colonized by the textual authority of elite, Latin literary culture.' These, of course, are the very traditions which Gavin Douglas was striving to maintain; hence his wish to police the textual perversions of Chaucer and Caxton. Chaucer's putative friendship with women may therefore be read as an aspect of his friendship with vernacular literature, within a poetic that was ostensibly transgressive of scholastic textual authorization in a manner quite foreign to Dante.

At any rate, Chaucer remained more interested in the poet as *fictor* (at once *makere* and liar) rather than as *auctor*. He refused to seek a self-authorizing 'final signified', to attempt to impose a single 'theological' meaning on his texts—to adopt terms from Roland Barthes. Indeed, what Barthes has to say about the author before pronouncing him dead in modern times is worth citing here at some length. Contrasting the 'traditional' Author with the present-day 'Scriptor', he declares:

We know now that a text consists not of a line of words, releasing a single 'theological' meaning (the 'message' of the Author-God), but of a multi-dimensional space in which are married and contested several writings, none of which is original: the text is a fabric of quotations, resulting from a thousand sources of culture. . . . Once the Author is distanced, the claim to 'decipher' a text becomes entirely futile. To assign an Author to a text is to impose a brake on it, to furnish it with a final signified, to close writing. This conception is quite suited to criticism, which then undertakes the important task of discovering the Author . . . beneath the work: once the Author is found, the text is 'explained,' the critic has won; hence it is hardly surprising that historically the Author's empire has been the Critic's as well.

'Literature', he continues, 'by refusing to assign to the text . . . an ultimate meaning, liberates an activity we may call countertheological, properly revolutionary, for to refuse to halt meaning is finally to refuse God and his hypostases, reason, science, the law' (pp. 52–3).

Barthes' conception of the erstwhile author is not, of course, to be equated with the standard medieval one, but these terms of reference are nevertheless useful. For it can be said that Dante's self-authorizing commentary (in the *Convivio*) and textualization (in the *Comedy*) move in the direction of 'closing' writing and halting its meaning (polysemous it may be, but the array of possibilities is firmly restricted). These strategies project the Author as the Critic of his own works, thereby gesturing towards a kind of impersonality (or pedagogic self-fashioning) which is very different from the cult of authorial personality that Barthes sought to bury. In the above-mentioned works of Dante the Author's empire is also the Critic's; indeed, in the *Comedy* Dante solicited the blessing of God himself for his Author–God operations. By contrast, several of Chaucer's works—the 'countertheological' *House of Fame* most of all—evince a sense of 'multi-dimensional space in which are married and contested several writings'. No brake is imposed on the text, and so an author is not assigned to it, the conditions for authority not having been created. The Chaucer of those works, then, is more of a 'Scriptor' than an 'Author', to apply Barthes' distinction.

Later, Chaucer was to have one version of *auctor*-ship, the paternity of English poetry, thrust upon him—mainly on stylistic and linguistic grounds, though Thomas Usk did praise him as the noble philosophical poet in English (the significance of which will be explored in our next chapter). But in the *House of Fame* at least, there is no sense of any 'auctour newe' triumphally emerging, certainly not Geoffrey Chaucer himself. There he was more interested in the craft of not being Prince Hamlet.

Norton Smith, *Chaucer*, pp. 38–9. Fyler, *Chaucer and Ovid*. J. A. W. Bennett, *Book of Fame*. Boitani makes a larger claim for *HF* as a manifesto for art poetical. In 'What Dante Meant', for instance, he states that while Dante may have been more 'ambitious', none the less Chaucer did kiss Apollo's tree, as being 'honour enough for him'—an unironical reading of lines 1106–8 (p. 124). Similarly, in *Imaginary World* Chaucer's address to Virgil in *LGW* 924–5 is described as an 'exulting "Gloria"' (p. 75), and elsewhere he is credited with views on poetry similar to Dante's (pp. 156–8, 193). Some critics take note of the possible ironies in the Chaucer passages in question, yet maintain that *HF* still 'asserts the dignity of poetry', as Brewer puts it (*Chaucer: The Poet as Storyteller* (London, 1984), p. 30, and cf. p. 29); see also Burlin, *Chaucerian Fiction*, p. 57. Others are more cautious, as when, for example, Wallace says that 'perhaps Chaucer recognises that serious claims to Fame cannot yet be upheld by his native vernacular' (*Early Writings*, p. 21), or Spearing speculates that possibly 'Chaucer's inability at this stage to come fully to terms with a Renaissance sense of the poet's calling was one reason why he did not finish' *HF* (*Medieval to Renaissance*, p. 29). Karla Taylor goes so far as to speak of 'Chaucer's skepticism about Dante's endeavour', and supposes that he 'implicitly counters the view of history that animates the *Commedia*' (*Chaucer Reads*, p. 39).

Fyler, S. Ellis, and J. T. Miller seek a middle way. Chaucer 'is no *vates*', declares Fyler in his earth-bound reading, which emphasizes the 'faulty' nature of Geffrey's vision and finds in his heavenly flight 'a sustained inversion of Dante's vatic pretensions'; however, he goes on to say that in the third book Chaucer actually indicates 'the nobility, however fragile, of the poet's calling' (*Chaucer and Ovid*, pp. 43, 62). Ellis, 'Chaucer, Dante, and Damnation', does not see Chaucer's attitude to Dante's metaphysics as consistently sceptical: 'there is obviously an urge to transcendence that manifests itself at key points in Chaucer's work' (p. 289). Miller charts superlatively well Geffrey's negotiation of various subject-positions, which culminates in lines 1873–82, 'the final and firmest expression of faith in self as artist . . . that the narrator delivers'. However, this confidence is 'not total', and subsequently is revealed as 'not fully satisfactory' (*Poetic License*, p. 67). A rather more positive view is taken by Gellrich. Arguing against the notion that the prevailing tone is of 'doubtfulness and skepticism', he declares that 'Chaucer has made his choice very clearly in favor of his own text'; shifting away from the tradition of writing as a '"copy" of the Text of the past', he is looking forward to the Renaissance (*Idea of the Book*, p. 174). In Gellrich's view, the text's emphasis on fictivity and artificiality does not preclude such an affirmation.

Desmond, *Reading Dido*. Roland Barthes, 'The Death of the Author', in *The Rustle of Language*, trans. Richard Howard (Oxford, 1986), pp. 49–55. Cf. the use of the Barthes passage here quoted in John A. Burrow, 'The Sinking Island and the Dying Author: R. W. Chambers Fifty Years On', *Essays in Criticism*, 40 (1990), 1–23. See further the notion of medieval '*écriture* without an author' as developed by Eugene Vance, 'The Modernity of the Middle Ages in the Future', *Romanic Review*, 64 (1973), 140–51.

The idiom 'auctour newe' as used in my penultimate sentence, is borrowed from the end of the *Manciple's Tale* (*CT* IX(H) 359–60), where the teller recounts how his mother told him to 'be noon auctor newe / Of tidynges'. This is reminiscent of Ovid's account of the House of Rumour, in which stories grow in each telling, 'each new teller (*auctor*) adding something to what he has heard' (*Metamorphoses*, trans. Innes, p. 269; cf.

p. 186 above). Here the *novus auctor* is not an authority (in the sense used in our previous discussion) but rather a gossip-monger, someone who repeats and adds to rumours. Would the figure who has the *appearance* of a man of great authority ('he *semed* for to be') have turned out to be a mere gossip? (I am grateful to N. R. Havely for valuable discussion of this point.)

# The Parliament of Fowls

As kingfishers catch fire, dragonflies draw flame . . .
Each mortal thing does one thing and the same;
deals out that being indoors each one dwells;
Selves—goes itself; *myself* it speaks and spells,
Crying *What I do is me; for that I came.*

Here Gerard Manley Hopkins celebrates what he called 'inscape'—the distinctive pattern and design which is the unique property of each and every creature, yet which links it to God, inasmuch as 'the fire that breaks from thee' is 'a billion / Times told lovelier, more dangerous' (as he puts it in 'The Windhover: To Christ our Lord'). Hopkins's formulation of his interest in individuality and personality owed much to the theory of 'thisness' (or *haeccitas*) as held by the medieval schoolman John Duns Scotus, the notion that there is an individuating difference, or final perfection, which makes every created thing 'this' and not 'that'.

This theory was very much Scotus's own, but his peers were equally convinced of the amazing diversity and variety of creation. The twelfth-century theologian Richard of St Victor, described by Dante as being more than human in his contemplation (*Paradiso*, x. 131–2), expressed his amazement at 'how many, how great, how diverse, how beautiful and joyful are these corporeal things that we imbibe by means of corporeal sense. Marvelling we venerate and venerating we marvel at the power, wisdom and generosity of that supernatural creator' (*Benjamin Minor*, i. 6). And St Bonaventure declared that 'Whoever is not enlightened by such brilliance of things created must be blind; whoever is now awakened by their mighty voice must be deaf; whoever fails to praise God for all His works must be dumb' (*Itinerarium mentis in Deum*, i).

The movement from earthly admiration to divine praise was not, however, always easy, particularly when the human mind had to accept that those great, diverse, beautiful, and joyful corporeal things were as mere veils and shadows which had to be left behind, even condemned, in the face of the incomparably greater—but probably quite alien—joys of heaven. This paradox came to preoccupy Hopkins; he wrestled with the obligation of accepting that all the variety of life would unravel on to just two spools, as creatures were classified as either sheep or goats, placed in one or another of the two categories which are all that will then apply: black / white, right / wrong.

Our tale, or oracle! Let life, waned,
    ah let life wind
Off her once skeined stained veined variety upon, all on
    two spools; part, pen, pack
Now her all in two flocks, two folds—black, white;
    right, wrong

                    (*Spelt from Sibyl's Leaves*)

What is particularly disconcerting about the *Parliament of Fowls* is that here we move from condemnation to celebration, from the black / white, right / wrong view of the imposing oracle of Chaucer's tale, Scipio Africanus, to the 'skeined stained veined variety' of the *locus amœnus* and the assembly of birds which speak and spell their individuality, in line with their several species. For the *Parliament* begins as *Troilus and Criseyde* ends, with a humbling vision of the earth as a mere speck as compared with the immensity of the universe, and of man as an insignificant creature whose memory will soon perish. Men should recognize the supreme importance of their immortal souls, declares Africanus, and work for the common good ('commune profyt'; 47, 75) in order to attain 'hevene blisse' (72); law-breakers and lecherous people, on the other hand, will suffer an afterlife fraught with pain. This is followed, however, by a joyful account of God's plenty which is surpassed only by the General Prologue to the *Canterbury Tales*. As in the *House of Fame*, the univocal pronouncements of men of great authority do not rule the roost; the bird parliament counters with a cacophony of conflicting voices.

Which, then, is more important, Ciceronian ethics or amatory escapades, earnest or game, profit or play—or is such binary thinking itself inadequate? Like the *Book of the Duchess*, the *Parliament of Fowls* is a dream-vision poem: but where did this dream come from? Initially the narrator speculates that it was caused by his reading of Cicero as expounded by Macrobius (106–12); yet, in the very next verse, he acknowledges to Venus ('Cytherea') that *she* 'madest me this sweven for to mete' (115), and asks for her aid in writing the poem. Is *amor*, then, rather than authoritative philosophy, the poem's subject? That would seem to be appropriate since its events are said to occur on St Valentine's Day.

But could Chaucer be offering a philosophical critique of love? Some believe that 'common profit' is the essential theme, earthly love being revealed as short-lived and superficial. According to R. M. Lumiansky, herein true felicity, as defined in the first part of the poem, is set against false felicity, as illustrated later by the events in the garden of love. Could there even be a theological critique? While the poem is certainly not a sermon, declares David Fowler, it does have a text, 'Increase and multiply, and replenish the earth' (Genesis 1: 28; cf. v: 22, particularly 'and let the birds be multiplied upon the earth'). Nature, he says, favours no union of the sexes that does not have reproduction as its goal. However, there is precious little multiplying happening in the poem itself, though that can be assumed to be the next task of the birds who have chosen their mates—all except the eagles, of course. Are they, then, out of step with Nature and in breach of the divine injunction? In Alan of Lille's *De planctu naturae*—a work ostentatiously cited in the *Parliament*—unnatural sexual practices are attacked; is the eagles' refusal to pair off and procreate therefore to be seen as some sort of perversion? Or is it simply the sort of thing which aristocrats get up to, a courtship ritual which is, quite predictably, more elaborate than anyone else's, and a marker of their high caste and good breeding? But others see satire here, the target being the affected aristocrats and/or their 'designer emotions'; though on another view it is the churlish lower classes who are being criticized for their lumpen pragmatism and narrow self-interest.

Then there is the issue of the female eagle's refusal to exercise her 'choys al fre' (649) of mate. Some critics have found here an image of the narrator's own amused or troubled indecisiveness. 'The poet avoids committing himself or taking any definite line,' argues Wolfgang Clemen, but rather indulges in his natural liking 'for holding aloof, for playing hide-and-seek with his reader' (pp. 123–4). John Fyler takes the matter more seriously: 'the formel mirrors the narrator's state of mind: half in paralysis before the alternatives of a choice, half tentative about even choosing whether or not to choose' (p. 85). But could the formel's indecision be in some sense culpable? David Lawton explores the idea that she could be 'in the wrong' inasmuch as 'she seeks an escape from love, an escape from experience, which cannot be granted outside the context of chaste sainthood', but proceeds to dismiss this as being 'too heavy an interpretation'. What we are being offered, he concludes, is actually 'a play or game', 'an inconclusive trifle, a polished inconsequentiality' (pp. 42–3): this trivialization of the notion of 'game' will be contested in my own discussion. Does the text tacitly predict which suitor the highly valued creature will choose? Dame Nature's recommendation that it should be the royal tercel has been echoed by many of the poem's recent readers, though D. S. Brewer has claimed that this is unimportant, the interest lying instead 'in the humour and interest of various attitudes to or ideas about love' (p. 7), while Lawton postulates a recurring cycle of deferral: 'next year's debate will be just as abortive as the one we have now overheard' (p. 42).

The *Parliament*'s appeal consists largely in the fact that such questions are not given a clear answer. Its very resistance to closure is its great virtue, though of course several resolutions are possible, and if a performance of the text was followed by courtly debate—a plausible theory, given its designation as a Valentine's Day poem—then at least some of its first readers or hearers may have discussed those very possibilities. However, the text itself avoids a last judgement in which the world is reduced to right and wrong, black and white, but rather preserves the bright colours of creatures and allows them to 'go themselves', while ensuring throughout that it is the manners and methods of men which are at the centre of attention.

Richard of St Victor, *Benjamin Minor*, in *PL* 196, 1–64. A complete translation is included in *Richard of St Victor: 'The Twelve Patriarchs', 'The Mystical Ark', Book Three of 'The Trinity'*, trans. Grover A. Zinn (New York and London, 1979). (*The Twelve Patriarchs* is an alternative title of *Benjamin Major*.) St Bonaventure, *Itinerarium mentis*, in *Opera omnia* (Quaracchi, 1882–1902), v. 293–313. Dante, *Paradiso*, ed. and trans. Singleton.

On the 'apotheosis tradition' of accounts of humans who have been released from their earthly life (and who are therefore in a position to make contemptuous observations about it) see Steadman, *Disembodied Laughter*, and the relevant discussion and references in my *HF* chapter.

R. M. Lumiansky, 'Chaucer's *Parlement of Foules*: A Philosophical Interpretation', *RES* 29 (1948), 82–9. David C. Fowler, *The Bible in Middle English Literature* (Seattle and London, 1984).

Clemen, *Chaucer's Early Poetry*; Fyler, *Chaucer and Ovid*; Lawton, *Chaucer's Narrators*; D. S. Brewer, 'The Genre of *The Parliament of Fowls*', in idem, *Poet as Storyteller*, pp. 1–7.

David Aers, *Chaucer*, New Readings Series (Brighton, 1986), p. 16, finds in the reactions of the lower-order birds a challenge to upper-class power and privilege. A far more light-hearted view is taken by Gardiner Stillwell, 'Unity and Comedy in the *Parliament of Foules*', *JEGP* 49 (1950), 470–95, who reads the poem rather simplistically as an amusing commentary on social tensions. At the other end of the spectrum is the allegorizing interpretation of Huppé and Robertson, *Fruyt and Chaf*, pp. 107–48, in which the differences between the *Parliament* and its morally bracing sources (Cicero–Macrobius and Alan of Lille) are drastically eroded. For the idea that love provides the means whereby Chaucer pursues his overriding concern with art poetical see Lawton, *Chaucer's Narrators*, p. 44, and especially Kiser, *Truth and Textuality*, p. 44. There is remarkable critical consensus on the poem's lack of explicit answers, though wide variation in how the significance of this is perceived.

On 'closure' in Chaucerian and other medieval poems see Rosemarie P. McGerr, 'Medieval Conceptions of Literary Closure: Theory and Practice', *Exemplaria*, 1 (1989), 149–79; also Larry Sklute, *Virtue of Necessity: Inconclusiveness and Narrative Form in Chaucer's Poetry* (Columbus, Oh., 1984). David Aers, 'The *Parliament of Fowls*: Authority, the Knower and the Known', *ChR* 16 (1981), 1–17, argues that the narrator's search in *PF* is 'open-ended, finely resistant to authoritative and dogmatic closures of all kinds' (p. 14). Stimulating material may be found in Robert Adams, *Strains of Discord: Studies in Literary Openness* (Ithaca, NY, 1958), and Frank Kermode, *The Sense of an Ending: Studies in the Theory of Fiction* (Oxford, 1966), though unfortunately they regard resistance to closure as a relatively recent development, which has emerged in modern fiction.

Good general discussions of the poem include Aers, 'Knower and the Known'; J. A. W. Bennett, *The 'Parlement of Foules': An Interpretation* (Oxford, 1957); Piero Boitani,

*English Medieval Narrative in the Thirteenth and Fourteenth Centuries*, trans. J. K. Hall (Cambridge, 1982), pp. 168–92; Edwards, *Dream of Chaucer*, pp. 123–46; Charles O. McDonald, 'An Interpretation of Chaucer's *Parliament of Foules*', *Speculum*, 30 (1955), 444–57, repr. in *Chaucer Criticism*, ed. R. J. Schoeck and J. Taylor (Notre Dame, Ind., 1961), ii. 275–93; Mehl, *Narrative Poetry*, pp. 37–53; Payne, *Key of Remembrance*, pp. 139–45; Spearing, *Medieval Dream-Poetry*, pp. 89–101.

In addition to the edition of *PF* by Vincent J. DiMarco and Larry D. Benson in the *Riverside Chaucer*, D. S. Brewer's well-annotated edition (which includes a useful discussion of its prosody) is recommended.

## Text, Date, and Circumstances

The *Parliament of Fowls* has more surviving witnesses than any of the other Shorter Poems. It is extant in Caxton's early print and in fourteen manuscripts, the best of which is Cambridge University Library MS Gg. 4. 27, an anthology of Chaucer's poems which also contains the unique text of the G Prologue to the *Legend of Good Women*. Some manuscripts have written above the text of the roundel 'Now welcome, somer' which appears near the end of the *Parliament* (680–92) the words 'Qui bien aime a tard oublie' ('Whoever loves well forgets slowly'). This may suggest that indeed its 'note . . . imaked was in Fraunce' (677); that is, that the roundel was composed to fit the tune belonging to the French song that is being identified with these words. But it is unclear which French song is meant. The phrase is in fact a proverb which, because it was common parlance, was inevitably used by several poets. Machaut's *Lay de Plour* (on which see pp. 158–9 above) begins in this way; it is also part of the refrain of a ballade by Deschamps, and occurs elsewhere.

Whether we have here a clue to Chaucer's intention for the roundel's performance, or to the setting chosen for it by someone else, is impossible to determine. However, it may be suggested that, on one or more of the first public readings of the *Parliament*, when the roundel was reached instruments would strike up and its words would be sung rather than merely recited. After this the reader would return to intone the final stanza, a brief reintroduction of the bookish narrator who, typically, is going off to read even more books, hoping to find some thing, some day, which will help him fare the better (perhaps the vagueness is meant to express bumbling). The listeners, remembering how long he spent with the *Somnium Scipionis* (maybe the wrong book?), would have been highly amused. Thus the joy of the song and its music would move into general laughter and applause.

The *Parliament* is referred to in the F Prologue to the *Legend of Good Women*, which the *Riverside Chaucer* editors have dated between 1386 and 1388. Like the *House of Fame*, it bears the influence of Chaucer's reading in Italian literature, which means that it could hardly have been written before the poet's first Italian visit, from which he returned in 1373. All things considered, it was probably written in the period between 1373 and 1385.

Many attempts have been made to narrow this gap. If the strange astronomical reference at lines 117–18, where Venus is said to be seen 'north-north-west', actually describes the planet's extreme northern position, then this could refer to April and May of 1374, 1377, or 1382. However, as J. M. Manly has suggested, the expression may simply mean something like 'in an unpropitious position'. At any rate, Chaucer may have begun the poem in May 1382, to have it ready for St Valentine's Day 1383 (according to the argument of D. S. Brewer). This would place it after the marriage of Richard II and Anne of Bohemia; but other critics, convinced that the poem is connected in some way with either the occasion of this marriage or the events leading up to it, would date it earlier. Recently Larry D. Benson has revived the theory that the poem reflects the negotiations for the marriage, Anne being represented by the formel eagle and her three suitors (Richard, Charles of France, and Fredrich of Meissen) by the three tercels, though he freely admits that he is offering speculation rather than actual proof. He suggests a dating of 1380, either before, or to mark the departure of, the embassy that set out in June of that year with authority to conclude a marriage settlement with Anne's brother Wenzel, the Holy Roman Emperor.

The argument that the poem was written as part of the celebrations of the royal marriage, or for the first Valentine's Day to follow it, has generally been refuted on the assumption that a poem which revealed Anne as being unable to make up her mind would have seemed somewhat insulting after the event. Against this, it may be noted that the formel seems to have a preference for the royal tercel: she blushes when he declares his love (442–8), a reaction which is not replicated when the other birds make their pleas. Reason and Nature would certainly approve of that preference (cf. 631–7). And the formel seems to wish to prolong the process of choosing (or of declaring her choice) rather than just being unable to make up her mind; she utterly accepts that she will marry, but not 'as yit' (652–3). After all, in medieval poetry a decorously long process of courtship often serves as an indicator of the quality of the love concerned, and in those terms a year's love-service is not too much to ask.

At the very least, it would seem obvious that, whatever the year or specific motivation may have been, Chaucer's poem was written for a St Valentine's Day. This puts it in the same category as his *Complaint of Mars* and the Valentine poems of Oton de Graunson, one of which, the

*Songe Saint Valentin*, includes an account of the birds choosing their mates on that day. Chaucer and Graunson were exact contemporaries, so it is not clear who influenced whom, or even if such influence existed at all. But where did the idea of St Valentine's Day as a special occasion for lovers come from in the first place? Some have spoken of ancient folk customs which go back far beyond Chaucer. Brewer, on the other hand, suggests that Valentine's Day observances probably began as courtly entertainments and perhaps were primarily English (see his edition, p. 6). Others have gone so far as to argue that it was Chaucer himself who effectively invented the lovers' festival, the fullest account being that of H. A. Kelly. Chaucer first introduced the love-cult of St Valentine, he suggests; but for him it was a springtime festival—to suppose that he was talking about 14 February is anachronistic, for this association came later. February is not mentioned in Chaucer's Valentine poems and in fact Chaucer had in mind the Maytime feast-day of the Genoese St Valentine; the mating of birds and humans at that time fitted in well with the traditional amatory associations of May. But this Genoese saint's feast was confused with the universally calendared St Valentine's Day of 14 February, that tradition being so strong that it was able to override the common-sense reaction that creatures could not possibly be thinking so enthusiastically of love at such an inclement time of year.

This solution eliminates the manifest awkwardness of Chaucer's birds seeming to welcome summer in the middle of February (680–92). Alternatively, this could be explained by the fact that there were conflicting traditions which placed the beginning of spring on various days in either February or March. J. A. W. Bennett takes yet another tack. What the birds are singing is their theme song, he suggests, this being merely a February *rehearsal* for the celebrations that rightly belong to April and May. It is on the first of May that in the *Legend of Good Women*, F Prologue 170, the same birds sing a song of welcome to 'somer, oure governour and lord', apparently *referring back* to St Valentine's Day, making the point that they certainly have not repented of the choices of mate which they made on that earlier occasion:

> 'Blessed be Seynt Valentyn,
> For on his day I chees yow to be myn,
> Withouten repentyng, myn herte swete!'
> (F Prol. 145–7; cf. G Prol. 131–3)

By the same token, the passage in the *Parliament* can be a reference forward to future festivities, when they 'don to May som observaunce' (to borrow an idiom from *Troilus*, ii. 112). Yet another persuasive interpretation is offered by Jack Oruch, who believes that, though he does not actually mention the February date, Chaucer deliberately chose it—thereby welcoming spring in the face of potential, even probable, bad weather—on account of the creative opportunities that it afforded him. Climatic variability, the paradox of spring in February, created space for treatment of, for example, the variability of human love, or at least its bittersweet nature (now hot, now cold), along with the tensions that arise when imagined or temporary joy is faced with a grim reality or sobering moral self-awareness. In the case of the *Parliament* the idea is particularly appropriate, inasmuch as it affirms the regenerative powers of nature after the hard, sterile season of winter, the rising of the sap and the arousal or renewal of love, leading to new mating which will result in new birth.

Kelly will have none of this: Chaucer had in mind a Maytime event, and it was his readers who moved the date too far back by confusing, as was very easy to do, the two St Valentines. But what, then, of the apparent reference back to St Valentine's Day as a past event in the *Legend* passage quoted above? Kelly suggests that 'when the little birds sing their blessings on St Valentine on this day' (i.e. 1 May, the date assigned to the action), 'we can easily believe that they are looking forward to celebrating' the day on which they choose their mates, this being imminent (p. 125). For the Genoese St Valentine seems to have died on 3 May, with his feast-day in Chaucer's time having been established on 2 May. But surely the birds are looking back rather than forward, as Bennett suggested? This would not locate Valentine's Day, as understood by Chaucer, on 14 February, but would certainly put it sometime before the period of 2–3 May.

And is it not significant that Chaucer's friend Sir John Clanvowe should, in a poem which was certainly influenced by the *Parliament* and perhaps also by the *Legend*, refer back to the birds' choice of mates 'In Marche, vponn Seynt Velentynes day' (*Book of Cupid*, 80), the poem itself being located on the morning after 'the thirde nyght of May' (55)? At the very least, one can say that this indicates considerable confusion about the date of the saint's festival; the 3 May date is tantalizing. Clanvowe's reference to March, suggests Kelly, is the result of his misunderstanding of the dating system commonly used in medieval calendars. But such a misreading is more plausible on the part of a modern scholar than on Clanvowe's. Moreover, as a friend and literary follower of Chaucer's, Clanvowe might well be expected to have known what Chaucer's view was—or that Chaucer lacked a clear view in this case. Is Clanvowe's confusion his own, then, or is it due to Chaucer?

Probably we will never know, and some of us are reluctant to accept the notion that Chaucer single-handedly invented the widespread and prevalent tradition of St Valentine's Day as a lovers' festival, on which the birds pair off (the mislocation by his readers of that day in February not being his fault, so to speak; here Kelly is appealing to the 'muddle' theory of history). This seems to be rather too much to claim for Chaucer, particularly since it implies a rapid and wide influence for his writings on that subject, on French poetry as much as on English. However, anyone trying to relate the *Parliament* to specific historical events or astronomical configurations would be well advised to investigate the case for Maytime connections as well as, or instead of, ones with some February or other. Kelly himself ventures into this type of enquiry, arguing in favour of the hypothesis that Chaucer was celebrating the betrothal of Richard II and Anne of Bohemia. Their marriage treaty was concluded in 1381 on 2 May, the actual feast-day of St Valentine as observed in Genoa and elsewhere, and 3 May seems to have been a significant date for the king (and for Chaucer, as is evidenced by other poems). It could be inferred that Chaucer wrote the poem for the first anniversary of this royal event, St Valentine's Day 1382. But this, of course, is pure speculation.

On CUL MS Gg. 4. 27 see especially the introductory material (by M. B. Parkes and R. Beadle) to the facsimile edition (for full reference see p. 6 above). The possibility of female involvement in the production of another MS containing *PF*, the 'Findern Anthology', has been much discussed; see Elizabeth Hanson-Smith, 'A Woman's View of Courtly Love: The Findern Anthology, CUL Ff.1.6', *Journal of Women's Studies in Literature*, 1 (1979), 179–94, and Sarah McNamer, 'Female Authors, Provincial Setting. The Re-Versing of Courtly Love in the Findern Manuscript', *Viator*, 22 (1991), 279–310. A more sceptical view, which I myself would endorse, is taken by Julia Boffey, 'Women Authors and Women's Literacy', in Meale (ed.), *Women and Literature*, pp. 158–82, esp. pp. 169–71. On this MS (which contains *inter alia* a text of Clanvowe's *Book of Cupid*) see further the facsimile edition (ref. on p. 6 above).

On the effect of the roundel near the end of the poem see especially James Dean, 'Artistic Conclusiveness in Chaucer's *Parliament of Fowls*', ChR 21 (1986), 16–25. He argues that although in terms of the narrative we experience the *PF* as unresolved, the 'roundel beguiles us into accepting, for a brief moment, that a resolution has occurred' (p. 23). Less optimistic views are taken by, for example, Aers, 'Knower and the Known', p. 14, and Hansen, *Fictions of Gender*, pp. 131–2.

A reading of the poem's concluding stanza which is very different from the one given here is offered by Lawton, *Chaucer's Narrators*, pp. 44–5. For him it is 'nothing short of alarming that academic critics can find something pathetic in the resolve with which the narrator concludes the poem' (695–700). This is quite 'affirmative', in his view; the narrator 'carries on in a civilised way with exactly what he was doing before he dreamt', being 'entirely satisfied and in harmony with his books and his dream' (pp. 44–5, 74–5). But the 'I hope' of line 697 can hardly be taken as part of a confident affirmation that he *will* 'mete som thyng for to fare / The bet' (699–700). It seems to me that the narrator is lost in the labyrinth of the library. Besides, if he carries on doing what he did before he dreamt, he will be constantly meeting 'thyng which that I nolde' and failing to meet 'that thyng that I wolde' (cf. 90–1).

J. M. Manly, 'What is *The Parlement of Foules*?', *Studien zur englischen Philologie*, 50

(1913), 279–90. Brewer, edition of *PF*. Larry D. Benson, 'The Occasion of *The Parliament of Fowls*', in L. D. Benson and Siegfried Wenzel (eds.), *The Wisdom of Poetry* (Kalamazoo, Mich. 1982), pp. 123–44.

The *Songe Saint Valentin* of Oton de Graunson (*c*.1340–97) has been translated by Windeatt, *Sources and Analogues*, pp. 120–4. The original text is included in A. Piaget, *Oton de Grandson, sa vie et ses poésies* (Lausanne, 1941). Grandson's life and possible links with Chaucer are discussed by Braddy, *Chaucer and Graunson*. The problem of who influenced whom is discussed by Wimsatt in his *French Love Poets*, pp. 143–50. At the end of Chaucer's *Complaint of Venus* (82) Graunson is called the 'flour of hem that make in Fraunce' (cf. pp. 466–8 below).

H. A. Kelly, Chaucer and the Cult of Saint Valentine (Leiden, 1986). J. A. W. Bennett, 'Some Second Thoughts on *The Parlement of Foules*', in E. Vasta and A. P. Thundy (eds.), *Chaucerian Problems and Perspectives. Essays Presented to Paul E. Beichner* (Notre Dame, Ind., and London, 1979), pp. 132–46. Jack B. Oruch, 'St Valentine, Chaucer, and Spring in February', *Speculum*, 56 (1981), 534–65. Clanvowe's *Book of Cupid* is quoted from Scattergood's edition of his works. North, *Chaucer's Universe*, pp. 326–66, concludes his highly ingenious analysis of the astronomical allusions in the poem with the suggestion that the time of the editing was meant to be either 1 or 3 May 1385, referring back to 14 February of that same year as the date of the bird parliament.

Others have tried to locate the poem historically with reference to practices and events in the English parliament of Chaucer's day. See for example Paul A. Olson, 'The *Parliament of Foules*: Aristotle's *Politics* and the Foundations of Human Society', *SAC* 2 (1980), 53–69. Given the dearth of convincing specific parallels, however, he reverts to the more general (and more critically useful, in my view) argument that the *Parliament* is 'a very great civic poem, concerned not only with British institutions but also with the foundations of human community in its recognition of the weakness of our physical nature, which makes the interdependency of corporate groups necessary' (p. 69).

## Verse-form, Rhetoric, and Style

Gone are the octosyllabic couplets of the *Book of the Duchess* and the *House of Fame* which, whatever their distinguished antecedents and inherent virtues, sometimes seem to interfere with certain effects which Chaucer is stretching their boundaries to create, especially in the case of the earlier poem. Pathos, for example, may be moderated or even converted into unintentional (or at least not utterly intentional) parody. Then again, the inevitability of their rhymes and occasional narrowness of their scope for expression render difficult the creation of genuine *gravitas*, of the sublime, in English poetry.

In the *Parliament* we see, for the first time in English, a much more sophisticated rhyme scheme: namely, rhyme royal, the form which Chaucer was to use to perfection in *Troilus and Criseyde*. Its *ababbcc* rhymes enable a great variety of effects. There is, to be sure, simple sequential narrative which is reminiscent of the couplet form (e.g. the account of how the 'day gan faylen' and the narrator went to bed to dream of Africanus, at lines 85–112, and the descriptive lists at lines

176–82 and 337–64, with a new item to every one or two lines). But far more is now possible.

A definite argument may be built up in the alternating rhymes of the first four lines, with a clinching pronouncement or some sort of resolution coming in the final couplet (e.g. 400–6, 435–41, 442–8, 456–62, 596–602; 85–91 is a particularly good example). Sometimes the sense units simply follow and reinforce the division into quatrain and couplet (162–8, 603–9). Alternatively, sense units can be played off against the rhyme scheme in interesting ways. For example, in lines 411–13 and 474–6 the last three lines (the last line of the quatrain along with the couplet) constitute a single discrete sentence. The last line of the quatrain can function as an elegant point of transition, enabling the stanza to move with ease and grace to its conclusion, as for example in lines 652–8, 666–72, 673–9, and 693–9. Elsewhere the first three lines of the stanza form the first sense unit, with the remaining four lines forming the second (64–70, 456–62). And sometimes the last line of the stanza is cut off from the rest (435–41, 463–9, 610–16, 652–8), enabling a series of devices including firm declaration (616), the addition of yet another item in a list (182, 343, 350, etc.), an ironic twist (140), the conclusion of a speech (441), and introduction of the following verse (658).

The very first stanza is particularly interesting, and has been much discussed. The first three lines heap up various defining characteristics which the fourth line reveals to be those of love; the second group of three lines moves to declaration of the personal feelings of the persona, who, it now becomes clear, has uttered those generalities, the emphasis here falling on the 'I'. Thus the verse is cut neatly in half, with love being placed at its very centre.

Moreover, Chaucer also uses the device of the intercalated lyric, absent from the *House of Fame* as we have it but employed in the *Book of the Duchess* and the *Legend of Good Women*. Unfortunately the text of the roundel (680–92), perhaps the first appearance of this form in English poetry (Chaucer also uses it in his *Merciles Beaute*), has suffered much in transmission. W. W. Skeat's reconstruction, on the analogy with a form used by Machaut and other French poets, is eminently plausible, and has been followed in the editions of Brewer and DiMarco/Benson. This produces a thirteen-line lyric with only two rhymes being used, the scheme being as follows: *ABB' abAB abb ABB'* (the upper-case letters indicating the lines used for the refrains).

A large body of critical opinion holds that the *Parliament* is the most accomplished of the Shorter Poems, 'the most perfect of Chaucer's Love Visions', as Dorothy Everett put it (p. 102). It is not only finished, but highly polished. The over-long and (to many modern ears) somewhat vacuous long rhetorical periods of the *Book of the Duchess* have been left behind; Chaucer displays a new mastery of his art poetical. '*Sententiae* [wise, pithy sayings] may lend splendour to the work,' declares Geoffrey of Vinsauf in his *Poetria nova* (trans. Kopp, p. 38), identifying this as one of the best possible ways of beginning a poem. Such statements bear themselves like elders because of their grave manner, to follow an anonymous thirteenth-century commentator on Geoffrey; the use of this device, we are assured, actually doubles the poet's art (trans. Woods, pp. 33, 35). It is surely significant, therefore, that Chaucer should begin the *Parliament* with the *sententia* 'Ars longa, vita brevis', which he renders brilliantly but naturally as 'The lyf so short, the craft so long to lerne'.

Turning to the amplifying device of *descriptio* (with which the early poetry of Chaucer is so concerned), Vinsauf, after having exemplified a full picture of feminine beauty, remarks that 'the description of physical appearance is . . . a thing trite and outworn', and recommends more unusual practice (p. 55). Similarly, in his *Documentum de modo et arte dictandi et versificandi* Vinsauf moves away from 'common' description of beauty to offer 'more difficult and less ordinary descriptions in order that the variety of examples may remove aversion, and the new difficulty, like food for the ears, may entice the listener' (trans. Parr, p. 46). Chaucer's elaborate descriptions of the features of his Garden of Venus offer enticing difficulty. For example, his list of trees (176–82) brings to English a venerable tradition which extends from Virgil and Ovid to Joseph of Exeter, Guillaume de Lorris, and Boccaccio (the *Roman de la Rose* and the *Teseida* have influenced the *Parliament* passage), and after Chaucer, to Spenser and Keats. Even more ambitious is Chaucer's extensive *enumeratio* or *accumulatio* of the various species of birds (330–64). (Note also the lists of the personifications who inhabit the love-garden, 214–29, and of famous lovers, 286–92.) We have moved very far away from the altogether more 'common' kind of *descriptio* of beauty, such as the account of White's physical appearance, as found in the *Book of the Duchess*.

Exemplification could be somewhat ponderous in that earlier poem; however, in the *Parliament* Chaucer succeeds in including no less than seven *exempla* (specific illustrations of the general truth that dreams reflect the dreamers' interests and emotions) in a single stanza, lines 99–105, with an extraordinary lightness of touch. Lines 36–84 represent a lucid *abbreviatio* ('abbreviation') of Cicero's *Somnium Scipionis*, in which 'the greete' part of the 'sentence' is conveyed (cf. 35). Apostrophe occurs at lines 113–19, when Venus is invoked as quasi-Muse. Moreover, the *figurae verborum* are out in force. There is much *exclamatio* (14, 171, 492,

494, 540, 547, 563, 598, 617, etc.), which serves mainly to mark the clamour of the bird debate, where, it must be added, *nominatio* or onomatopoeia is used with extraordinary skill, as the sounds of words mimic the characteristic noises made by the different birds. *Interrogationes* or rhetorical questions appear at lines 365 and 953–4; lines 17 ff. may be read as a version of *subjectio* or self-answering. *Repetitio*, repetition of a word or phrase at the beginning of a line, may be found at lines 66–70, 101–5, and 176–82; see especially the instance at lines 342–64, which extends over no less than twenty-three lines. Rather than launching into a formal *descriptio* of Nature, Chaucer refers his audience to the full account found in Alan of Lille's *De planctu naturae* (316–18), in a manœuvre which has the same effect as the formal *occupatio*, wherein a matter is passed over with only the briefest of mentions. Actually, *occupatio* itself is notably absent from the *Parliament* (but see the undeveloped case in line 229, and the possible hint of another at line 279), by contrast with, say, the *Knight's Tale* or the *Legend of Good Women* (cf. pp. 336–8 below); this may contribute to the impression of self-containment and amplitude which the poem achieves.

Even more remarkably, Chaucer provided much 'food for the ears' by actually going beyond the precepts of the rhetoricians, who firmly distinguished between *stilus grandiloquus*, the elevated and ornate style appropriate to lofty themes; *stilus mediocris*, the middle style which is to be used in treating persons or things of intermediate status; and *stilus humilis*, the low style associated with lowly persons or things. It is not simply that the *Parliament* contains all three styles in rich abundance, ranging from the elevated philosophy of Macrobius and the idealistic effusions of the aristocratic birds through the *stilus mediocris* characteristic of his account of the *locus amœnus* to the lowly vulgarisms of the goose and the duck. It is also that he is able to change register with (usually effortless) ease, moving from high to low, grand to plain, within a pair of verses and even within one and the same verse. Thus he created a lively interaction of different idioms which was to be bettered only in those passages in the *Canterbury Tales* wherein gentles and churls speak their own—and sometimes each other's—distinctive languages. Here is writing of extraordinary confidence and accomplishment. Around 1380 there was simply nothing like it in English poetry. The *Parliament* is setting new standards, making the point that English, like Italian, can achieve an 'illustrious vernacular'.

On Chaucer's use of rhyme royal in *T&C* see Windeatt, *OGC: T&C*, pp. 354–9. See further the relevant material in Michio Masui, *The Structure of Chaucer's Rime Words* (Tokyo, 1964).
Dorothy Everett, 'Chaucer's Love Visions, with Particular Reference to the *Parliament of*

Foules', in *idem*, *Essays on Middle English Literature*, ed. Patricia Kean (Oxford, 1955), pp. 97–114.

Geoffrey of Vinsauf, *Poetria nova*, ed. Faral; trans. Kopp in Murphy (ed.), *Medieval Rhetorical Arts*; also Vinsauf's *Documentum*, ed. Faral, trans. Parr; M. C. Woods (ed. and trans.), *An Early Commentary on the 'Poetria nova' of Geoffrey of Vinsauf* (New York and London, 1985).

On the rhetoric of the poem's first stanza see Brewer's edition, pp. 48–9, also F. W. Bateson, Editorial Appendix, *Essays and Criticism*, 11 (1961), 256–63, and M. Manzalaoui, 'Ars Longa, Vita Brevis', *Essays in Criticism*, 12 (1962), 221–4. More generally see Brewer's entire discussion, pp. 47–51; Dorothy Everett, 'Some Reflections on Chaucer's "Art Poetical"', in *idem*, *Essays*, pp. 149–74.

Stephen A. Barney, 'Chaucer's Lists', in Benson and Wenzel (eds.), *Wisdom of Poetry*, pp. 189–223.

Charles Muscatine discusses *PF*'s different styles in *French Tradition*, pp. 115–23.

## Sources

The *Parliament of Fowls* is a highly original work, and so it is impossible to speak of 'sources' in the normal sense of the term, though borrowings there certainly are, and debts to several genres, particularly to the literary dream-vision. Rather the work represents an intricate case of Chaucerian intertextuality, engaging as it does in an elusive but effective dialogue with the *Somnium Scipionis* as interpreted by Macrobius, Alan of Lille's *De planctu naturae* and to a lesser extent its transfiguration in Jean de Meun's part of the *Roman de la Rose*, Old French sources of the type which had fixed Chaucer's narrower horizons in the *Book of the Duchess*, and that new and challenging addition to his library, Boccaccio's *Teseida*. Several of these works—*De planctu naturae*, the French love-visions, and the *Teseida*—contain opulent accounts of beautiful gardens and idealized landscapes, and the *Somnium Scipionis* and *De planctu naturae* share a fundamentally Neoplatonic vision of the structure and moral significance of the universe.

As in the *Book of the Duchess*, wherein Alcyone's dream prepares the way for the narrator's dream about the Man in Black, an ancient dream from an old book, this time Scipio the Younger's nocturnal encounter with his grandfather, prepares the way for the narrator's dream of the parliament of birds. In the earlier poem the Chaucerian I-persona had appealed to a figure in his source, Morpheus, the god of sleep (as Chaucer regards him). Here he actually dreams about a figure in his source, Scipio Africanus—and not just that, for Africanus effects the transition to the main subject of the persona's own dream (namely, the Garden of Venus and its bird parliament), even though such an action is utterly 'out of character' with a construct as serious and sententious as the grandfather of Scipio the Younger. The *Book of the Duchess* had invoked a second example of dream-vision literature in addition to its deployment of the Ovidian tale of Ceyx and Alcyone: namely, the *Roman de la Rose*. This time it is Alan of Lille's vision of Dame Nature, the *De planctu naturae*, which is named, in addition to Cicero's *Somnium Scipionis*. Our following review of sources will begin with these two distinguished precedents for the narrator's own dream.

### CICERO AND COMMON PROFIT

At the beginning of the *Roman de la Rose*, Macrobius is named as one who 'who did not take dreams as trifles, for he wrote of the vision which came to King Scipio' (7–10, trans. Dahlberg, p. 31). It was perhaps this passage which led Chaucer to, quite erroneously, describe Scipio as a king in the *Book of the Duchess*, 284–7 and the *House of Fame*, 916. And it may also have encouraged him to read Macrobius for himself, to see what this authority had to say about dreams and love. With respect to the latter he would have been disappointed, for the only type of earthly love which interested Macrobius was the love of the state and the common good. Well might Chaucer have said, 'For bothe I hadde thyng that I nolde, / And ek I ne hadde that thyng that I wolde' (90–1).

The work in question here is the Neoplatonizing commentary of Macrobius on Cicero's *Somnium Scipionis*. This was the only part of Cicero's *Republic* which was known in the Middle Ages, having been preserved through its association with Macrobius's commentary. Therefore, while Chaucer does not actually say that he read the commentary (though he does allude to it at line 111) and confines himself to a summary of aspects of Cicero's text, he could hardly have avoided it. This summary adds a Christian colouring, as for example when hell is referred to in line 32, and divine grace is involved at line 84, anachronisms as far as Cicero and Macrobius, both pagans, were concerned. And Chaucer's *abbreviatio* is highly selective, as the following comparison will indicate.

Cicero presents the Roman general Scipio the Younger recounting the story of how, during his time in Africa as military tribune in the Fourth Legion, he was received joyfully by an old family friend, King Masinissa of Numidia, and they talked together until late evening (cf. *PF* 36–42). When Scipio sleeps, he dreams of his grandfather Scipio Africanus, who predicts a future for him which is in many respects glowing: he will overthrow Carthage, thus proving himself worthy of his ancestral name, and subsequently go as legate to Egypt, Syria, Asia, and Greece; then he will bring a great war to a close and destroy Numantia. But there is bad news as well, for members of his own family will conspire against him. And here Africanus becomes evasive: 'you will need to set the commonwealth in order, *if* you escape the wicked hands of your relatives' (trans. Stahl, p. 71). In his commentary Macrobius raises the question of why Africanus should express uncertainty here, since as a divine soul, long since returned to the heavens and in possession of certain knowledge of the future, he would not have any doubt about Scipio's fate. His answer is that all portents and dreams conform to the rule that their announcements, threats, and dire warnings are always ambiguous (cf. pp. 47–8, 179–80, 182, above).

Africanus exhorts his grandson to protect the commonwealth by reminding him of the considerable rewards which such service will bring. The supreme God who rules the entire universe is very much in favour of the political system of the commonwealth, this being defined as an association of men bound together by principles of justice. And therefore all those who have 'saved, aided, or enlarged' it have a special place reserved for them 'in the heavens where they may enjoy a blessed existence forever' (p. 71). Chaucer expresses this with reference to men who love 'commune profyt' (47).

Scipio, terrified by the fear of treachery amongst his kinsmen, then asks after his father Paulus, to be assured by Africanus that he is dead and well, having been freed from the chains of his body as from a prison. 'Indeed', declares Africanus, 'that life of yours, as it is called, is really death' (a sentiment which Chaucer succinctly translates with the phrase 'oure present worldes lyves space / Nis but a maner deth', 53–4). Paulus then appears, to emphasize to Scipio the importance of cherishing that justice and duty which are owing to parents and family, but most of all to country. Such a life, he asserts, is the path to heaven, and to the company of those who, having already lived it, now dwell in that circle of stars which is called the Milky Way. In Chaucer it is Africanus who shows Scipio 'the Galaxye'; perhaps he felt that two authority figures would have been confusing in so curtailed a summary of his source.

At this point Africanus resumes his role as Scipio's teacher, now concentrating on cosmological and metaphysical matters: the structure of the universe and motions of the planets, the harmony of the spheres (cf. *PF* 59–63). Scipio, however, keeps looking at the earth, prompting Africanus to explain the insignificance of earthly glory (cf. *PF* 57–8). All the stars will eventually return to the place from which they started off, the original configuration of the heavens thus being restored. Within this period of return, or 'year', many generations of men are contained—viewed on such a time-scale, the glory of men, who usually measure a year solely by the return of a single star, the sun, is seen to be of little value indeed. Chaucer conveys well this idea in somewhat different language at lines 67–70, though in the interests of clarity Macrobius's notion of the larger year is simplified by its transmutation into 'certeyn yeres space', the measure of earth-years being used.

The remainder of Scipio's dream is concerned with the nature of the soul. Here the principle is affirmed that Scipio should believe that it is not he who is mortal, but only his body; indeed, he should know that he is a god—that is, that his soul is a god which moves his body, just as God moves the universe. (Here Chaucer plays safe with the reductive but orthodox phrase 'Know thyself first immortal', 73). A soul thus stimulated will speed to its proper destination and region. On the other hand, 'the souls of those who have surrendered themselves to bodily pleasures . . . and who in response to sensual passions have flouted the laws of gods and of men', have 'long ages of torment' to endure before they may return to this region. Cicero is invoking Neoplatonic theory of the existence of souls prior to their incarnation; on the death of its burdensome body, each soul strives to return to that original blissful existence. Chaucer steers clear of these ideas, which amounted to heresy in his day, simply reiterating the basic sentiments in terms of that personal forgiveness of sins which is characteristic of the Christian God (78–84).

Whereas Cicero moves from politics to metaphysics, the latter science dominates Chaucer's account. It has been suggested that it was the political aspect of the *Somnium Scipionis* that encouraged Chaucer to engage it in a courtly poem like the *Parliament*, the idea being that while Cicero's work is certainly not a treatise of advice to princes, any more than is the *Consolatio philosophiae* of Boethius, such a work may be seen as serving the same tastes which made the 'regiment of princes' genre so popular among aristocratic readers. (And it may be added that the *Somnium Scipionis* and the *Consolatio* are very similar in their attitudes to worldly glory and the little spot of earth.) If that is what happened, it must be said that Chaucer has, so to speak, covered his tracks very well, by refusing to augment those socio-political aspects of his source which would have made it a better fit within the *Parliament* as a whole, and indeed by emphasizing those elements which set it apart from what follows.

Why should one be so concerned to serve the commonwealth, since it is an earthly institution, and as such should be treated with contempt, the city of God being infinitely more important than the city of men (to invoke St Augustine's distinction)? Perhaps that is why Chaucer played down the importance of service to the state, as found in Cicero's account. In the *Somnium Scipionis* there is a firm connection between what Chaucer calls 'commune profyt' on the one hand and heavenly reward on the other, the former being the path to the latter: the man who serves his country steadfastly finds a passage to the sky (cf. Stahl, p. 76). But Chaucer generalizes the moral principles of his source to apply to mankind in general. Whatever man, he says, 'lered other lewed', who loves common profit and is endowed with the virtues should journey to that place where there is endless bliss—there is nothing here about that privileged position in heaven which, according to Cicero, is specially reserved for those who preserve, assist, or enlarge the commonwealth. The idea that both uneducated ('lewed') and learned men can participate in this process is particularly interesting. Here Chaucer may have been influenced by the commonplace of medieval Christianity that the poor and uneducated have as much chance of attaining heavenly bliss as those who are rich (whether in monetary terms or in their abundance of learning) and famous—indeed, they may well go to their reward with greater ease, an idea which is advanced with great vigour in, for example, *Piers Plowman*. Plowmen and herdsmen and poor common labourers, the unimportant and the ignorant, are said to be able to penetrate with their prayer the palace of heaven, and on their death to pass through purgatory without punishment (B X. 456–62). This forms a marked contrast with the intellectual élitism of Cicero's text, wherein Africanus tells his grandson to ignore the chatter of the 'common herd' (trans. Stahl, p. 76). In fact, the *Parliament* is full of the chatter of the common herd, the varieties of birds representing the varieties of human beings, and it is amusing to note that the only creature who appeals directly to the principle of common profit is the cuckoo (505 8), whose motives are utterly un Ciceronian. In this respect at least, Chaucer may be said to have muted the *Somnium Scipionis* in the interests of the poem as a whole.

But there remains Cicero's grim affirmation of the inevitability of the judgement of the soul after the death of the body, when reward (73–7) or punishment (78–84) will be meted out to all as the fixed categories of black / white, right / wrong are applied, which is a sombre start to a colourful love-vision, to say the least. True, the hope of eventual redemption for sinners through a sort of purgatorial experience is held out, but that can hardly be regarded as a *major* softening of the source, for the idea is very much present in Cicero. Chaucer has merely updated it with reference to divine grace and forgiveness. Moreover, Chaucer's specification of 'likerous folk' puts lechers on a par with law-breakers (in Cicero it is the pleasure-seekers who *are* the violators of the laws of gods and men), thereby affording their sin a specific category and status which highlights both its importance and its nature. This is certainly an unusual prelude to a *locus amœnus*.

On this view, Chaucer was more interested in the differences between the *Somnium Scipionis* and the rest of his poem than in the similarities. Indeed, R. K. Root was so struck with the apparent contrast that he dismissed the summary of Cicero as 'an unfortunate piece of introductory machinery' (p. 66). Setting aside the issue of the poem's unity (or lack thereof) for the moment, it may be suggested that it is this very contrast which makes possible Chaucer's brilliant *coup de théâtre* of having Africanus seize the narrator and lead him to the garden of love, finally shoving him through its gates (154) and holding his hand to comfort him (169–70). Africanus, it seems, does not enter the garden along with the I-persona, which is hardly surprising, because, as already noted, the *Somnium Scipionis* has nothing to say on the matters which it contains. Africanus is simply here to express his thanks to the dreamer for having read his old book, in return for which he will take him to a place where the aspiring poet—now clearly identified as an aspiring love-poet—will find plenty to write about. The diffident dreamer cannot 'do' (i.e become one of love's servants, since he has lost his taste for it), but he can at least 'se', observe, and learn (162–8). If the previous summary of Scipio's dream had been less serious, then this scene would have been less amusing.

It is not that Chaucer has proceeded to parody the *Somnium Scipionis*; rather, that he is creating a comic effect through the extreme incongruity of a terribly sober and strait-laced individual doing something which is quite unexpected and rather silly (for him). This prepares the way for the laughter which is so essential to the rest of the poem: 'The laughter aros of gentil foules alle' (575). It is as if the Monk were to break off from his (apparently interminable) catalogue of depressing tragedies to adopt the 'myrie' tones of the Nun's Priest; this effect, located in the difference between the several tellers and tales in the *Canterbury Tales*, has been created within one and the same narrative here in the *Parliament*. Moreover, Chaucer is continuing that not altogether respectful treatment of men of great authority which is such a major feature of the *House of Fame*.

Macrobius, *In Somnium Scipionis*, ed. Willis, trans. Stahl. A translation of the *Somnium Scipionis* alone is included in Windeatt, *Sources and Analogues*, pp. 73–80. On Macrobius and medieval dream-vision theory see the discussion and references above, pp. 37–9, 44–5, 47–8. However, a more sceptical view regarding the importance of Macrobius than the one I myself have offered is urged by Alison M. Peden, 'Macrobius and Medieval Dream Literature', *MÆ* 54 (1985), 59–73. In her view 'Cicero's *Somnium Scipionis* . . . is arguably of greater importance to Jean de Meun and Chaucer than is Macrobius's *Commentary*' (p. 70).

On Chaucer's adaptation of Cicero/Macrobius see especially J. A. W. Bennett, *Parlement of Foules*, pp. 24–61; R. R. Edwards, *Dream of Chaucer*, pp. 130–4; L. D. Benson, 'Occasion', pp. 125–32. By contrast with the argument pursued above, Benson emphasizes what he sees as Chaucer's interest in the political aspect of the poem, as do, for example, B. K. Cowgill, 'The *Parlement of Foules* and the Body Politic', *JEGP* 74 (1975), 315–35; P. A. Olson, 'Foundations of Human Society'; and Russell A. Peck, 'Love, Politics and Plot in the *Parlement of Foules*', *ChR* 24 (1990), 290–305. Aers, 'Knower and the Known', argues that Chaucer's version of Cicero challenges the lack of 'moral or psychological self-awareness' in the dogmatic claims of the 'Roman patriots and militarists' whose interests are expressed by Scipio's dream; however, it is highly unlikely that anyone in Chaucer's audience (and perhaps not even Chaucer himself) would have had the knowledge of Roman history necessary to take such a subtle point. Hansen, *Fictions of Gender*, emphasizes that 'In legend, Carthage is the city ruled by Dido' (p. 114), but Chaucer does not make that connection in *PF*, despite his considerable interest in the Dido story, as evidenced by both *HF* and the *Legend of Dido* in *LGW*. Therefore there is no textual warrant for Hansen's assertion that here 'Male hegemony and patriarchal authority leading to a triumph for the privileged few . . . are explicitly based on the alleged conquest and destruction of the feminine place, the city ruled by a female who is both ruler and lover' (p. 115)

R. K. Root, *The Poetry of Chaucer*, 2nd edn. (Boston, 1922).

## COMPLAINTS OF NATURE

Alan of Lille was born at Lille in Flanders *c.*1116, and died sometime between 14 April 1202 and 5 April 1203. He came to Paris around 1136 to study, and may also have attended classes at Chartres; certainly his thought has many similarities with that of the major philosophers associated with that centre, including Bernard of Chartres, Bernard Silvester, and William of Conches. Later Alan taught at Paris and probably at Montpelier. Eventually he joined the Cistercian Order, entering Citeaux. His many works include the *Anticlaudianus* (on the construction of the perfect man), and the *De planctu naturae*, this being 'the Pleynt of Kynde' referred to in line 316 of the *Parliament of Fowls*. This work, a masterpiece of medieval classicism, presents a tacitly Christianized version of many of the Neoplatonic ideas to which Cicero had alluded and which Macrobius had explicated at length. Alan's fundamental source was the same as Macrobius's—the *Timaeus* of Plato.

Like the *Somnium Scipionis*, the *De planctu naturae* is written in the form of a vision. Its I-persona apparently experiences a waking vision of Dame Nature (just as Boethius had encountered Dame Philosophy in the work which was the model for Alan's prosimetrum, the *De consolatione philosophiae*), but, faced with this extraordinary spectacle, he faints: 'completely buried in the delirium of a trance, with the powers of my senses impeded, I was neither alive nor dead and being neither, was afflicted with a state between the two' (VI, pr. iii; trans. Sheridan, p. 116). Nature cures him of his illness of stupor and brings him back to himself, but the ending of the work would seem to indicate that he has experienced the rest of the vision in a dream-like state: 'I awoke from my dream and ecstasy and the previous vision of the mystic apparition left me' (XVIII, pr. ix; p. 221).

Chaucer, however, treats these two sources very differently. He merely states that his Nature appeared in his dream, just as she is described by

'Aleyn, in the Pleynt of Kynde', and leaves it at that; there is no extensive summary of *De planctu naturae* as there was of the *Somnium Scipionis*.
And the stance, perhaps even the status, of Chaucer's Dame Nature is
rather different from that of Alan of Lille's: the earlier figure is utterly
imposing and awe-inspiring, whereas for some readers Chaucer's creation
comes across as a well-meaning referee who has to struggle rather hard
to maintain order among her unruly charges. Personally I find this exaggerated, for when Nature calls for 'pes' in line 617, the entire assembly
shuts up and listens, in contrast to the ineffectual calls for peace made by
some of the birds (cf. 547, 563), and Nature's subsequent decision brooks
no dissent. But the scarcely controlled, and sometimes quite irrepressible,
reactions of the impatient birds in the *Parliament* certainly stand in
marked contrast to the fearful respect with which Alan's I-persona listens
to Dame Nature, letting her do almost all the talking. Moreover, at one
point Chaucer's Nature describes her role (in contradistinction to
Reason's) in a way which is sometimes taken as an admission of incompleteness or even of weakness (631 ff.). Whatever the significance of this
passage (I myself would dispute the view here cited), the fact remains that
Chaucer has allowed a response which is scarcely possible in the case of
Alan's text, wherein Dame Nature does not suffer from a sense of her
own limitations. A review of *De planctu naturae* will allow these points to
emerge more clearly, along with the crucial importance of this work for
an understanding of Chaucer's sexual poetics in the *Parliament*.

Alan celebrates 'the holy faith of marriage', and attacks all abnormal sexual practices which interfere with the 'unwearied continuation' of the
human race, particularly homosexuality. *De planctu naturae* is written in an
elaborate, allusive, and sometimes downright obscure style (Alan's Latin is
far from easy), with dazzling rhetoric, sporadic allegory, and heavy dependence on classical myth. A good example of this effect is afforded by the
phantasmagoric description of Dame Nature's costume (in II, pr. i; pp.
73–105). In her diadem are visible all the beauties of the zodiac and the
heavenly bodies; on her robe of state, which perpetually changes in colour,
is an animated picture of a parliament of birds; the many intricate folds of
her mantle show the colour of water, and on it a series of figures 'exquisitely imprinted like a painting' tells of the nature of aquatic animals, as
divided into their numerous species, while on her multi-coloured tunic 'a
kind of magic picture made land animals come alive'.

Practically all creatures obey her decrees as a general rule, Nature
declares (in VIII, pr. iv; pp. 130–48). 'The firmament in its daily revolu-
tion makes all things go round with it'; 'the stars, too, that shine to give
the firmament its glory by clothing it with their adornment as they complete the short stays in their journey, traverse in their rotation the many

roads alloted to this journey and serve as soldiers' in Nature's 'royal army'; the planets also, in keeping with her decree, 'hold the onward rush of the firmament in check as, pressing in the opposite direction, they wander back towards their place of rising'. Turning to creatures, Nature commends, among many other things, the orderly behaviour of birds: 'stamped' with their 'various natural qualities', by Nature's 'direction and guidance' they 'sail over the waves of air', as it were rowing with their wings, 'and look with heartfelt longing to my instructions'. Fishes and land animals all play their several parts, as do the various herbs and plants. The Earth never ceases in tireless generation to bring the various species of things to birth. But man—on whom she has lavished so many rich gifts—refuses to obey her 'universal law', daring 'to stir up the tumult of legal strife against the dignity of his queen, and, moreover, to fan the flame of civil war's rage against his mother', Dame Nature. Man 'hammers on an anvil which issues no seeds'; 'He imprints on no matter the stamp of a parent-stem: rather his ploughshare scores a barren strand' (I, met. i; p. 69). Meanwhile, 'kisses lie fallow on maidens' lips while no one wishes to harvest a crop from them' (pp. 70–1).

The imperative of procreation is explained in a passage in VIII, pr. iv, which also makes clear the relationship between Nature and Venus. It was the will of 'the artisan of the universe' that 'by a mutually related circle of birth and death, transitory things should be given stability by insta bility, endlessness by endings, eternity by temporariness and that the series of things should ever be knit by successive renewals of birth. He decreed that by the lawful path of derivation by propagation, like things, sealed with the stamp of manifest resemblance, should be produced from like.' Accordingly, he appointed Nature as 'his substitute, his vice regent, the mistress of his mint, to put the stamp on the different classes of things so that she 'should mould the images of things, each on its own anvil, not allow the product to deviate from the form proper to its anvil' (i.e. by engaging in homosexual acts). So she positioned Venus 'on the outskirts of the universe' to be the deputy in charge of her work, so that Venus, acting under the will and command of Nature, 'might exert herself in the reproduction of the varied animal-life of earth and, fitting her artisan's hammer to its anvil according to rule, might tirelessly maintain an unbro ken linkage in the chain of the human race lest it be severed by the hands of the Fates and suffer damage by being broken apart' (pp. 145–7). But man alone interferes with this arrangement: by trying to 'denature the natural things of nature', he is arming 'a lawless and discordant Venus' to fight against Dame Nature (p. 131). Alan itemizes men's sexual devi ations through a series of oblique, and somewhat obscure, metaphors drawn from grammar and logic. His targets include homosexuals in general and as specifically classed as either active or passive, bisexuals, and men who enjoy sexual pleasure without achieving penetration, together with those who sell sex for gain.

Nature, we learn later, has a priest called Genius. As 'god of generation' in pagan antiquity, he was believed to be in change of, and have power over, the birth of all things (cf. Augustine, *De civitate Dei*, vii. 13). Isidore of Seville adds that he brings about the birth of children, thus the beds prepared for the newly-wed husband were called 'genius' couches' (*Etymologiae*, VIII. xi. 88–9). Like Nature, then, he stands for the belief that sexual relations must follow the normal process of nature and that the species should survive and multiply. It is therefore quite appropriate that Nature should describe Genius as 'her other self' (XVI, pr. viii; p. 206), and, as Nature's priest, read the document which excommunicates mankind. Men who refuse Genius 'his tithes and rites, deserve to be excommunicated from the temple of Genius', declares Nature, and that is what happens at the end of the work. 'Let everyone who blocks the lawful path of Venus, or commits any of the mortal sins, be separated from the kiss of heavenly love as his ingratitude deserves and merits,' Genius intones; 'let him be demoted from Nature's favour, let him be set apart from the harmonious council of the things of Nature' (XVIII, pr. ix; p. 220).

Given this link between Genius and Venus, it is hardly surprising that he should become the priest of Venus in Jean de Meun's part of the *Roman de la Rose*. A largely 'demythologized' figure now, Nature describes her own creation, the planetary motions and powers, destiny and free will (following Boethius), the influence of the heavens, the properties of mirrors and glasses, dreams and frenzies, and true gentility, concluding with a reiteration of Alan's commendation of all creation—man excepted—for its ordered obedience and observance of the rule of procreation. Nature then sends Genius to encourage the God of Love; he exhorts all to fecundity, threatening to curse and excommunicate all who hold in contempt Nature's processes by which life is sustained (19,505 ff.). If everyone were to follow the example of those who refuse to beat their hammers on anvils, to plough and deeply delve the fertile, fallow ground, then within sixty years there would be no children born again evermore, and the earth would be deserted or peopled only with dumb beasts. Or, he adds, if all women held to their virginity, the same result would follow. Those who misuse their plows and lose their seed are attacked, along with those who chose to follow the example of Orpheus (who came to prefer the love of men). May those who thus despise their fair mistress Nature be condemned to hell—and lose their male parts before they die, since they refused to put them to their proper use! 'Plow, barons, plow—

your lineage repair!' commands Genius (19,701–2), and at the very end of the poem Jean's dreamer does his bit for the furtherance of the human race by sexually penetrating his virgin rose. There may even be a hint—though the passage (21,727–30) is so brief and ambiguous that it can hardly be built upon—that she has been impregnated. Even more explicit in this regard is John Gower's *Confessio Amantis*, where (under the influence of the *Rose*) Genius again appears as the priest of Venus, but he warns against the sin of incest in book viii, and book vii includes a crucial passage which affirms that the male is made for the female, the best form of association being monogamous married love. For when a man's wife may readily be found, why should he go elsewhere and seek to borrow another man's plow (vii. 4218–25)? As far as women are concerned, Gower's Genius marvels that maidens should waste any time in hastening to that feast 'Whereof the love is al honeste'—and honest love involves the begetting of children, 'whiche the world forbere / Ne mai, bot if it scholde faile' (iv. 1480–97). This declaration follows an *exemplum* of slothfulness in love, wherein we learn how Rosiphelee, a king's daughter, who desires 'nother Mariage / Ne yit the love of paramours' despite being of 'lusti age', is brought into the 'betre reule' of normative sexual participation (cf. iv. 1268–9, 1264).

Much of this is rather far from Chaucer's poem, and the contrasts are revealing. In the *Parliament* Genius does not appear at all; instead we have Priapus, whose interests are markedly different (253–6). And there is very little plowing of the fallow ground in evidence. The dreamer hears the birds singing on every bough, and sees *some* of them occupying themselves in the production of new members of their species: 'Some besyede hem here bryddes forth to brynge' (192). The rest, it would seem, have other things to do. Of course, it must be admitted that the purpose of the parliament is to enable the birds to choose their mates, which must precede the engendering of their species—though one may still wonder why Chaucer is so silent about that stage of the process. Perhaps we should detect here the influence of 'fyn lovynge', wherein love is everything and the partners' desires are carefully insulated from their natural consequences. Or, if the poem had anything at all to do with the marriage of Richard II and Anne of Bohemia, it would perhaps have been rather indelicate to hint at progeny so soon. At any rate, it is clear that all the birds who represent the various classes of men and women in medieval society are resolutely heterosexual. The only instance of sexual deviation—if that is not too strong a word—that could possibly be found in the poem is the refusal of the eagles to play the mating game and pair off like all the other birds, a point to which we will return.

Moreover, it is rather ironic that in Chaucer's poem the birds, who appear as exemplary servants of Nature's will in the *De planctu naturae*, are such an unruly company. This, to be sure, may be put down to the fact that they constitute 'a feathered version of fallen man', as Fowler nicely puts it (p. 165). Birds and beasts regularly represent the actions and attitudes of men in medieval beast-fable literature, a genre which may now briefly be investigated, along with the sources and analogues of Chaucer's actual avian lore.

Alan of Lille, *De planctu naturae*, trans. James J. Sheridan, Pontifical Institute of Medieval Studies: Medieval Sources in Translation, 26 (Toronto, 1980). There is another complete translation, by Douglas M. Moffat, *The Complaint of Nature by Alain de Lille* (New Haven, Conn., 1908; repr. Hamden, Conn., 1972), but this is less accurate. Windeatt includes a translation of Alan's description of Nature in his *Sources and Analogues*, pp. 79–80. The best edition of the Latin text is that of N. M. Häring in *Studi Medievali*, 3rd ser., 19/2 (1978), 797–879. On medieval doctrines of Nature see Bernard Silvester, *Cosmographia*, trans. Winthrop Wetherbee (New York and London, 1973), esp. pp. 6–12; also George D. Economou, *The Goddess Natura in Medieval Literature* (Cambridge, Mass., 1972); Winthrop Wetherbee, *Platonism and Poetry in the Twelfth Century: The Literary Influence of the School of Chartres* (Princeton, NJ, 1972), esp. pp. 158–219; Hugh White, *Nature and Salvation in 'Piers Plowman'* (Cambridge, 1988). See further the relevant material and references in Peter Dronke (ed.), *A History of Twelfth-Century Western Philosophy* (Cambridge, 1988); N. Kretzmann, A. Kenny, and J. Pinborg (eds.), *The Cambridge History of Later Medieval Philosophy* (Cambridge, 1982).

On Alan's sexual metaphors see Alexandre Leupin, 'Alan of Lille's Grammar of Sex', *Daigraphe*, 9 (1975), 119–30; Jan Ziolkowski, *Alan of Lille's Grammar of Sex: The Meaning of Grammar to a Twelfth-Century Intellectual*, Speculum Anniversary Monographs, 10 (Cambridge, Mass., 1985). His treatment of sexual transgression is cogently discussed by Cadden, *Sex Difference*, pp. 221–5. For the larger picture see Jacquart and Thomasset, *Sexuality and Medicine*, pp. 88–9, 124, 155–6, and 159–61, and of course John Boswell, *Christianity, Social Tolerance, and Homosexuality: Gay People in Western Europe from the Beginning of the Christian Era to the Fourteenth Century* (Chicago, 1980).

The 'demythologizing' process from Alan of Lille to Chaucer is discussed by Maureen Quilligan, 'Allegory, Allegoresis, and the Deallegorization of Language: The *Roman de la Rose*, *De Planctu Naturae*, and the *Parlement of Foules*', in M. W. Bloomfield (ed.), *Allegory, Myth and Symbol* (Cambridge, Mass., 1981), pp. 164–86. She remarks that 'Unallegorical Chaucer' (i.e. a poet who does not write allegories as such) is 'most vulnerable' to the 'invasive interpretive force' of allegoresis (i.e. allegorizing interpretation by readers), citing as an example the study of the *Parliament* by Robertson and B. Huppé (on which, see our discussion below).

*Roman de la Rose*, ed. Langlois, trans. Dahlberg. In this section I have also drawn on the lively translation by Harry W. Robbins (New York, 1962).

On Gower's ideas regarding married love see J. A. W. Bennett, 'Gower's "Honeste Love"', in John Lawlor (ed.), *Patterns of Love and Courtesy* (London, 1966), pp. 107–21; revised reprint in J. A. W. Bennett, *The Humane Medievalist and Other Essays*, ed. P. Boitani (Rome, 1982), pp. 49–66; also A. J. Minnis, '"Moral Gower" and Medieval Literary Theory', in *idem* (ed.), *Gower's 'Confessio Amantis': Responses and Reassessments* (Cambridge, 1983), pp. 50–78, esp. pp. 62–6.

Fowler, *Bible in Middle English Literature*.

### BEAST-LORE AND BEASTLY BEHAVIOUR

According to the medieval grammar master Conrad of Hirsau (*c.*1070–*c.*1150?), fable was invented 'so that by introducing the fictitious conversation of dumb animals or insensible objects, certain similarities in human morals and behaviour might be criticized'. Hence the intention of Aesop in writing his beast-fables was 'to delight and also to recall irrational human nature to its true self by a comparison with brute beasts', his material being derived from actual observations of human nature, which is subject to considerable change and variation. When it transgresses its proper bounds through malice, wiliness, folly, and madness, it may quite properly be compared with wild beasts and domestic animals, even with stones and pieces of wood (trans. Minnis and Scott, pp. 47–8). Conrad's position, then, is that when a man lives irrationally, he lives like a beast, and may with good cause be likened to one and described through the actions and ways of animals. This is very much the standard view, and is well expressed in the Middle Scots translation of Aesop's fables by a later teacher, Robert Henryson (a work which is in part indebted to Chaucer's beast-fable the *Nun's Priest's Tale*, which clearly was a source of Henryson's version of the fable of the cock and the fox). Aesop, explains Henryson, showed through *exempla* and similitudes how many men in their activities emulate the condition of animals, thereby in effect metamorphosing themselves into 'brutal bestis' (Prologue, 43–56).

This does not, however, necessitate a pessimistic view of nature in general. Henryson's praise of its beauties, as evocative of the wit and wisdom of God, is very much in the spirit of Alan of Lille's *De planctu naturae*, and indeed of Gerard Manley Hopkins in his more optimistic moments.

> The firmament payntit with sternis cleir
> From eist to west rolland in cirkill round,
> And euerilk planet in his proper spheir,
> In mouing makand harmonie and sound;
> The fyre, the air, the watter, and the ground—
> Till vnderstand it is aneuch, I wis,          *enough*
> That God in all his werkis wittie is.          *reasonable*
>
> Luke weill the fische that swimmis in the se;
> Luke weill in eirth all kynd off bestyall;          *animals*
> The foulis fair, sa forcelie thay fle,
> Scheddand the air with pennis grit and small          *cleaving, wings*
> (1657–67)

And it also catches something of the tone of the *Parliament of Fowls*, while marking major differences from that poem. Aesop's fables, declares Henryson, reprove you for your misliving, 'O man, be figure of ane vther thing' (Prologue, 6–7). This reproof is made utterly explicit in the moralities which, as is usual in medieval beast-fable collections, follow the narratives as night follows day. But there is, of course, no such declaration of *moralitas* at the end of Chaucer's poem—which could, as it were, be described as having inverted the normal beast-fable structure, with the animal *narracio* being placed actually *after* the didactic *moralitas*. But if Chaucer's poem were to be read 'in reverse', the caveat would have to be entered that the moral does not fit the fable in the manner characteristic of the beast-fable genre. 'Taketh the moralite, good men', Chaucer declares at the end of the *Nun's Priest's Tale* (VII. 3440). No long 'moralite' is provided there, though there are definite hints as to the (quite conventional) forms which such a treatment would take (see 3434–7, on the evils of indiscretion and flattery). But not even hints are offered at the end of the *Parliament*. Men may take a 'moralite' if they want to. But only if they want to. And what exactly is it anyway? Chaucer is silent on the matter; his text resolutely resists that sort of reductiveness.

Moving now to consider the various species of birds which Chaucer depicts, and their hierarchical relationship, it may be noted (following J. A. W. Bennett, 'Second Thoughts') that the poem utilizes an 'organic' classification of birds that goes back to Aristotle, who describes the various kinds according to their characteristic foods (cf. *Historia animalium*, 592–3$^b$), a division that the thirteenth-century encyclopaedist Vincent of Beauvais reduces to five categories (*Speculum naturale*, xvi. 14). This is essentially the system that Chaucer has in mind (cf. 323–9 and 500 ff.) The eagle and hawks (flesh-eaters) belong to class one, the turtle-dove (representing seed-fowl) to class two, the cuckoos (worm-fowl) to class four, and the goose (water-fowl) to class five. Chaucer may be alluding to this ordering specifically when, at 323–9, he puts the hunters first in the sequence and the water-fowl last, though here the worm-fowl come after the birds of prey, and there is some doubt regarding the social, if not the spatial, location of the seed-fowl:

> the foules of ravyne
> Weere hyest set, and thann the foules smale
> That eten, as hem Nature would enclyne,
> As worm or thyng of which I telle no tale;
> And water-foul sat lowest in the dale;
> But foul that lyveth by sed sat on the grene,
> And that so fele that wonder was to sene.               *many*
>                                                              (323–9)

However, at this point Chaucer may be constrained by the exigencies of rhyme, and it could be argued that in his view of the basic characters and

mental abilities of the birds he is actually following the Aristotelian peck-
ing order. The eagles are, naturally, the brightest and best; the fact that
the turtle-doves hold a high ideal of fidelity in love (576–88; cf. the modest but sensible comment at 509–17) could be taken as evidence that seed-
fowl come next. Moving down the scale of being, the cuckoo is selfish
but certainly not stupid, being in possession of a self-seeking cunning, as
is revealed by the 'class one' merlin or small falcon (603–16, cf. 505–8).
The goose is quite stupid (see 501–4 and 561–74, especially the knightly
hawk's castigation of her as a 'fol'; also the tercel's similar put-down, at
596–602). And another type of water-fowl, the duck, is clearly a bird of
the same feather (589–93).

If parallels to Chaucer's statements concerning the birds' natural properties are sought, Alan of Lille's bird parliament (or 'crowded convention
of the animals of the air', as he puts it) richly repays study (II, pr. i; trans.
Sheridan, pp. 86–94). There we find brief descriptions of the eagle as having the power of renewing its youth; the hawk as a violent tyrant; the kite
as hunter; the falcon as enemy of the heron; the ostrich as desert hermit;
the swan singing to herald its own death; the peacock as receiver of an
extraordinary number of nature's gifts; the phoenix as miracle of nature;
the stork(?) as 'bird of concord'; the cock as 'common man's astronomer';
the owl as 'prophet of grief', singing 'in advance psalms of lamentation for
the dead'; the crow as silly chatterer yet with knowledge of what is to
come; the jackdaw as thief; the dove as bird of Venus; the raven with
'repulsive and shameful jealousy'; the vulnerable partridge, shrinking from
attack on all sides; the turtle-dove who, bereft of her mate, rejects 'the
joys of a second mating with another'; the parrot as capable of human
speech; the quail as being deceived by the imitation of a friendly voice;
the woodpecker as architect of its home, using its beak as an axe; the
meadow pipit as mothering the eggs of the cuckoo, only to be repaid with
death; the nightingale making 'excuses for her dishonoured chastity as she
plays a sweet harmony' (cf. the myth of raped Philomela, metamorphosed
into a nightingale); the lark as nature's harpist. Brief mention is also made
of the sparrow, the crane, the duck, and the goose.

Alan's sequence almost certainly helped Chaucer to his own version of
the parliament of birds; that may have been more important to him than
the brief specifications of the birds' properties, though one should notice
the parallels with Chaucer's accounts of the goshawk (334–6), swan (342),
owl (343), turtle-dove (355), peacock (356), cuckoo (357), and crow (363).
Particularly close is the parallel between Alan's description of how the
crane, as she appears on Nature's robe of state, rises 'to the height of the
over-sized giant' (while the sparrow, by contrast, 'was reduced to the
minimal height of the dwarf') and Chaucer's designation of this same bird

as 'the geaunt' (344). And, looking beyond the *Parliament*, Alan's designation of the cock as 'common man's astronomer' is echoed in *Troilus and Criseyde* (iii. 1415); and in Chaucer's later beast-fable *The Nun's Priest's Tale* we find Chauntecleer taking careful note of the exact position of the sun in Taurus and its height in the sky (VII. 3193–9).

However, Chaucer could have obtained most of the very same details from many a medieval bestiary or encyclopaedia; indeed, in *the Nun's Priest's Tale* he cites one of the most popular of them, the *Phisiologus*, as his authority for the observation that cocks sing 'wel and myrily' (VII, 3271–2). Thus, in the *De proprietatibus rerum* of Bartholomew the Englishman he could have read that the eagle has 'principalite among foules', being the 'most liberal and fre of herte'; it dwells in high places, and possesses powerful eyesight (cf. *PF* 330–1, and see p. 201 above). And that the owl is a night-bird with an unpleasant voice which bodes evil and death (cf. *PF* 343); the dove is a sweet-natured creature without a gall and forgetful of wrongs (cf. *PF* 341); the goshawk is cruel to other birds, stealing their food and driving them out of their nests (*PF* 335–6); the sparrow-hawk is 'bold and hardy', preying on the smallest birds (cf. Chaucer's 'hardy sperhauk' who is the enemy of the quail, *PF* 338–9); the stork is loyal to his mate, but if she breaks 'spousehode' he will beat her with his bill and even kill her (which explains Chaucer's somewhat enigmatic reference to 'The stork, the wrekere of avouterye', *PF* 361); the crow warns of what will befall in the future, and can foretell rain with its crying (*PF* 363); the swan protects other birds against men, and when dying, instead of groaning, it sings (*PF* 342); the swallow is a 'ful hoot bridde and lecherous', and its flesh taken as an aphrodisiac excites 'seruyse to Venus' (cf. *PF* 351). Chaucer classifies bees as 'foules smale' who make honey (*PF* 353–4); similarly, Bartholomew, following a common practice of medieval writers on natural science, includes a chapter on bees among his chapters on birds.

Of particular importance is the bad press which the cuckoo receives in such accounts. It is generally perceived as unnatural because of its habit of laying its eggs in other birds' nests. The 'fol kokkow', 'ever unkynde' (*PF* 505, 358), is the bird who will, on its own authority, take on the charge of attempting to resolve the situation at a crucial stage of the proceedings in the bird parliament. Given the creature's nature, one cannot have much confidence in its suggested solution.

Minnis and Scott (eds.), *Medieval Literary Theory*. Henryson, *Poems*, ed. Fox. J. A. W. Bennett, 'Some Second Thoughts on the *PF*', Bartholomaeus, *De proprietatibus rerum*, trans. Trevisa, book xii; ed. Seymour *et al.*, pp. 596–645.

An excellent discussion of Henryson's beast-fables, which includes much of relevance for the reading of Chaucer's, may be found in Douglas Gray, *Robert Henryson* (Leiden,

1979), pp. 31–161. On animal imagery see further the general studies by Beryl Rowland, *Blind Beasts* (Kent, Oh., 1971), and *idem* (ed.), *Animals with Human Faces* (Knoxville, Tenn., 1973).

## FROM FRANCE TO ITALY? FRENCH LOVE-VISIONS AND THE *TESEIDA*

In the *Parliament of Fowls*, it may be suggested, the French influence still dominates, even though Chaucer has introduced versions of Latin Neoplatonism (as already noted), along with material from a major Italian poem which, at roughly the same time as he composed the *Parliament*, he was translating into English, namely Boccaccio's *Teseida*; this work was subsequently to become the *Knight's Tale*. The basic idea of the garden of love which is the setting for the major part of the poem took on its definitive form, as far as Chaucer and many of his contemporaries were concerned, in the *Roman de la Rose*; but even as we enter it, Chaucer reminds us, so to speak, that he has been to Italy—the verses 'of ful gret difference' written over its gates (123–47) probably echo, in their repeated 'Thorgh me men gon' idiom, the inscription over the portal of hell in Dante's *Inferno*, canto iii, 1–9. There is no positive side to Dante's inscription, of course; the 'difference' in Chaucer derives from standard, paradoxical accounts of love as simultaneously a source of pleasure and pain, of joy and grief.

In several French love-visions debating birds are a prominent feature of the garden of love. There are various parallels with the *Parliament*, but nothing to suggest specific sources. In the anonymous *Fablel dou Dieu d'Amors* (mid-thirteenth century) the garden of the King of Love is firmly forbidden to those of low birth, we are told at the outset; and soon we hear the sparrow-hawk complaining to the nightingale that love is not what it used to be, because low-born people are abusing it. Nobody should become involved with love, he protests, except clerks who know how to speak well about love and 'to sport with their loves, and knights who go to joust for them' (stanza 29, ed. Lecompte; trans. Windeatt, p. 86). This proposition is challenged; the nightingale listens to the differing views, then simply says that they should leave this dispute and get on with the business of loving. (The narrator's own beloved then appears on the scene, only to be carried off by a dragon, and the poem changes course accordingly.) Similarly, the *Parliament* relates the capacity for love to social position. The eagles' elaborate predilections are abundantly obvious, whereas the churlish goose cannot understand what all the fuss is about (501–4) and is simply blind, the 'gentil tercelet' tells her, in matters of love, just as owls cannot see in daylight: 'What love is, thow canst nouther seen ne gesse' (594–602).

Bird debates also appear in tellings of the tale of Florence and Blancheflor. For example, in a thirteenth-century French version these two young women enter a garden to amuse themselves, but end up debating, with more heat than light, the topic of who make the more courteous lovers, knights or clerks (Florence loves a knight, and Blancheflor a clerk). They seek judgement at the court of the God of Love, who in turn seeks the counsel of the birds. The sparrow-hawk pronounces in favour of knights; the nightingale, of clerks. The falcon contradicts the nightingale, and is in turn contradicted by the lark. And so it goes on, until the nightingale and the parrot engage in trial by combat. The nightingale emerges as the victor, which means that the clerks' case has won. Whereupon Florence promptly dies. Such histrionics are, thankfully, absent from the *Parliament*. No one dies for love or because a judgement fails to go in his or her favour. Everyone gets what they want, with the apparent (but predictable enough) exception of the eagles, and in their case any possible unpleasantness is postponed—for a year, which for the reader means forever.

The *Messe des Oisiaus* of Jean de Condé (who lived from *c.*1275–80 until 1345) is a far more sophisticated work than any of the love-visions considered so far. Here an assembly of birds is the main subject, rather than a mere part, of the poem, providing its occasion and grounding its structure. The birds gather—this time in a forest rather than in a garden—to sing mass in the presence of Venus, with the holy sacrament taking the form of a red rose. The nightingale is the officiating priest, and the parrot preaches on the virtues whereby lovers may attain perfection. The cuckoo (traditionally associated with adultery) tries to disrupt the proceedings by accusing many of the lovers who are there of being cuckolds, and the birds complain about him to Venus. The goddess proceeds to describe the bird's bad character according to the usual medieval traditions of beast-lore, concluding that its words must simply be ignored. A banquet of allegorical amatory delights is then served, after which the poem changes tack, as canonesses complain to Venus that 'the grey nuns' (presumably meaning Cistercians) are stealing away their lovers. Venus's judgement is that she will accept anyone's service: indeed, for her to reject the nuns would be against Nature, because Nature urges all the world's creatures to love. Finally—rather incredibly—comes an attempt at moralization, at making this elegant parody of ecclesiastical practices and practitioners (which bears comparison with the rather more robust Latin *Drunkards' Mass*) bear an edifying meaning. The singing birds represent those clerics who help in the service of God in church, while the cuckoo represents those who sin against Holy Church in so many ways that they are condemned. The rose, Jean admits, is really nothing like the

bread consecrated on the altar; he has, however, expounded the doctrine
of transubstantiation by means of this image. The ladies' dispute and
Venus's judgement are interpreted in terms of sacred rather than profane
love, though at the end of the poem Jean returns to the literal level to
attack the squabbling canonesses and nuns for having been deceived by
Venus, thereby damaging their souls and risking eternal damnation.
Rational love is possible within marriage; those in holy orders, however,
must banish worldly love from their hearts, in favour of the love of God
which has no end.

The volte-face of the *Messe des Oisiaus* may serve to remind us, yet
again, of what the *Parliament of Fowls* is *not*—a poem with a clearly
defined moral message. Jean de Condé declares that he will 'gloss' the
greater part of his poem before leaving; Chaucer, for his part, offers 'text'
with little if any explicit 'gloss', as will become even more apparent
through a consideration of his adaptation of the temple and image of
Venus from Boccaccio's *Teseida*, book vii, stanzas 50–66, this being the
single longest piece of close translation from that work that Chaucer ever
made.

Boccaccio provided an extensive marginal explanation of this part of
his text in the formal commentary which he wrote to accompany his
'modern classic'. There are two Venuses, the gloss tells us. One may be
understood in terms of every worthy and lawful desire, as is the wish to
have a wife in order to have children. This Venus is not the one which
appears in the text, Boccaccio continues; rather, we find there the second
Venus, commonly called the goddess of love, through whom all lust is
desired. The moral significance of the temple of Venus is then spelled
out. The ungirded and barefoot women who dance before it (some beautiful in themselves and others because of their clothing), and the spar-
rows and doves which fly thereabouts (cf. *PF* 232–6), 'are highly
stimulating when they are seen by the lustful; and some arouse by their
dress and gestures, such as ladies dancing ungirt and unshod'. The text's
coy allusion to Priapus, 'clad just as he was when any who wished could
see him' (trans. Havely, p. 130; cf. *PF* 253–9), is made utterly clear. As
he approached the goddess Vesta with lustful intent, an ass brayed, waking everyone, and the naked Priapus was seen by all (cf. the fuller version of the story as told by Ovid, *Fasti*, i. 415–40, which notes that
Priapus had his 'obscene member' prepared for action). He is portrayed
naked like this in the temple, continues the gloss, to indicate what the
cause of love in women is, just as 'the affection of men' is shown in the
account of the shape of Venus. The basic point here seems to be that men
and women are sexually stimulated by the sight of each other's bodies.

The gloss continues in this vein, demonstrating abundantly that this

Venus is not the chaste and lawful kind. When it explicates the passage which corresponds to lines 360–78 of the *Parliament*, this being the *descriptio* of the goddess of love herself, the place in which Venus lies is said to be dark because, 'those who are doing evil hate the light', while her reclining means 'the languor characteristic of pleasure-lovers and the life of ease'. By her beauty, 'which we know to be a frail and transient thing, he represents that false beauty of pleasure-lovers who through true reason we can very easily recognize and prove to be baseless'. The place is perfumed, because sex is such a smelly business; 'if the sense of smell were not soothed by perfumes the stomach and the mind would easily be put off' (trans. Havely, pp. 132–3). And so forth.

The manuscript of the *Teseida* which Chaucer used probably did not contain Boccaccio's commentary. The questions then arise: are the moral principles which the gloss emphasizes part of the obvious meaning of Boccaccio's text; and, assuming for the moment that they are, in translating the Italian did Chaucer mean to convey them as determining his own meaning? There are many, highly persuasive, critical accounts of the *Parliament* which confidently assert that Chaucer's Venus definitely stands for excessive sensuality. In his highly influential discussion Jack Bennett argues that, having used Cicero to formulate the initial doctrine that love of the common weal is the only earthly good, Chaucer then puts forward an opposing viewpoint by showing love as sexual desire. Then the figure of Dame Nature is skilfully deployed as a synthesizing device. She governs natural human desire as part of the divine creation in accordance with the principles of harmony and measure; love and mating are thereby related to the poem's initial concern with common profit. This view rests on the belief that Chaucer is keeping the sensual Venus he derived from Boccaccio under firm control, carefully subordinating her to Dame Nature, and ensuring that the latter lady appears as the more powerful figure.

Similarly, Derek Brewer believes that, while Venus is 'naturally' a part of 'the park where Nature is supreme', she 'represents corruption all the same, and lies apart'. 'The Venus passage', he continues, 'is clearly a moral allegory, signifying selfish, lustful, illicit, disastrous love' (his edition, p. 31). And George Economou, in his study of the goddess Natura in medieval literature, distinguishes between the Venus inside the temple, who embodies enticement and lasciviousness, and the Venus-Cytherea who is credited with having caused the narrator's dream in lines 113–16; in Chaucer, he argues, *she* is always identified as the goddess of legitimate love (and thus, one may add, may be compared with Boccaccio's first Venus, the embodiment of every chaste and lawful desire). On the other hand, Elizabeth Salter can speak of 'moral neutrality' in Boccaccio's text, and argue that there is 'very little evidence that Chaucer felt the necessity to remould the Italian in any very important way'. There is nothing in the English poem, in her view, which hints at the unsuitability of Venus and her company for inclusion in such an ideal landscape. Indeed, Chaucer even seems anxious to remove what might be hastily interpreted as moral censure in Boccaccio's poem, as when he ignores the statement that Venus 'held Wantonness by the hand'. In his rendering of Boccaccio's depiction of Venus, she continues, 'no breath of criticism disturbs the still scene' (pp. 134–6).

Moreover, it should be emphasized at this point that medieval commentary (of the formal, scholastic type which Boccaccio was practising) invariably moralizes the text which it is describing—that is of the very essence of its technique, something which it does unfailingly and inevitably. This becomes very evident if we look at, for example, the sporadic Latin commentary which appears in many manuscripts of Gower's *Confessio Amantis*, which is a lot more stridently moral than is Gower's English text. Therefore, to assume that because Boccaccio wrote both the *Teseida* and its commentary the latter must be a full and exact guide to the meaning of the former, would be hermeneutically naïve. Boccaccio's gloss—an instance of a specific critical discourse—does not determine the meaning of Boccaccio's text. And if this point be accepted, then the dangers of taking Boccaccio's account of the two Venuses as some sort of interpretative control for Chaucer's text—or assuming that here Chaucer was thinking like Boccaccio *qua* commentator rather than *qua* poet—will be quite evident.

That having been said, we may look at the most important specifics of Boccaccio's text which Chaucer altered.

1. Boccaccio's Priapus, as already noted, is clothed (actually, unclothed!) in such a fashion that anyone who wanted to see him—meaning, see him naked—at night could do so. Chaucer heightens the bawdy comedy inherent in his source, the line 'hys sceptre in honde' hinting at the lustful god's state of sexual arousal as he approaches the sleeping nymph (255–6). As Emerson Brown says, here Priapus is transformed into an example of that perennial stock character in bawdy jokes, the would-be ravisher caught with his trousers down. Boccaccio refers vaguely to garlands of many different flowers throughout the great temple. Chaucer makes his Priapus appear even more ridiculous by having men heap such garlands on his head (257–9).

More serious-minded readings are possible, however. Priapus could be taken as an unappealing symbol of lust; alternatively, a gender-critical reading might find in this apparent endorsement of what he stands for a reprehensible attitude towards rape, male worship of sexual aggression. But if aggression is indeed being embodied here, surely it is failed aggression, virility made to look ridiculous, male desire mocked. Priapus can therefore be read as a focus (perhaps even a sort of patron saint) for male fears of sexual failure.

2. Boccaccio places Venus in the most secret (and hence the most important) part of her temple, in a dark place. Chaucer reiterates that the place was dark, but somewhat demeans it by calling it a 'prive corner' (260), thereby diminishing its importance and, it could be said, robbing Venus of the central position which she occupies in the *Teseida* passage. Moreover, the long build-up in Boccaccio's description of the allegorical landscape, which culminates in the vision of the goddess herself, has quite disappeared. In Boccaccio the personifications and other figures who are described before Venus very much precede and herald her; in Chaucer one simply gets the impression of a rather crowded area. Indeed, he even makes Venus share a line with her porter Wealth ('Fond I Venus and hire porter Richesse', 261); in Boccaccio the goddess and her servant maintain a decorous distance, him doing his job by guarding her chamber door and she taking her divine pleasure on its other side.

3. Boccaccio simply says that Venus is 'taking her delight'; Chaucer specifies what her 'disport' consists of—she is resting to avoid the warmth of the sun (265–6). The idea that a goddess as powerful as Venus—and so used to hot passions—should have to do this is rather striking, perhaps even amusing (whether intentionally or not). Indeed, here Chaucer has been accused of clumsiness (by R. A. Pratt). The line 'Til that the hote sonne gan to weste' (266) seems to contradict the remark, made some eight stanzas previously, that in the garden there was 'nevere . . . grevaunce of hot ne cold' (205) and, even more markedly, the categorical statement that it enjoyed perpetual daylight, 'nevere wolde it nyghte, / But ay cler day to any mannes syghte' (209–10). Pratt also feels that Chaucer has some difficulty in filling out his stanzas, and it must be admitted that there are occasional awkwardnesses, such as at lines 263–4. Moreover, the filler 'unnethe it myghte be lesse' (264) is repeated from line 201, where it works much better.

4. Boccaccio's Venus has golden hair; Chaucer transfers the adjective to inanimate objects, her bed (265) and the thread which binds up her hair (267).

5. Some have suggested that Chaucer is trying, in prudish or mock-prudish fashion, to cover up at least the lower part of Venus, who is described by Boccaccio as being quite naked. However, lines 270–3 can be taken as a voyeuristic joke, the point of which is that the beautiful goddess is leaving little to the imagination. Indeed, it could be said that Chaucer's *locus amœnus* is something of a voyeur's paradise. Its beauties are certainly seen through the male gaze; indeed, Beauty herself (unsur-

prisingly female) is 'withouten any atyr' (225). (And, as already noted, the only naked male figure around, Priapus, is ridiculous and/or a figure of masculine fears rather than an object supposedly of interest to the female gaze—which does not get a look in, so to speak, in that garden.)

Chaucer's somewhat obscure reference to the 'cloth' from the French textile centre of 'Valence' is simply an attempt to localize the 'fine garment' worn by Boccaccio's Venus.

6. The way in which Chaucer rounds off his account of Venus and her surroundings, by remarking 'But thus I let her lye . . .' (279), has struck some readers as brusque and disrespectful, and therefore (if one wishes to pursue this argument) in keeping with an alleged strategy whereby Venus is denigrated in favour of Nature. It is, of course, possible that Chaucer meant something quite neutral (albeit cheerful and/or patronizing), like 'And thus I will leave her in peace'. Alternatively, if it be accepted that there is a hint of an *occupatio* here (as suggested earlier), this being a rhetorical figure which can mark the curtailment of a description that could be a lot longer, then the sense would be something like 'And that is all I want to say about her', with the implication that there is much more which could be said about this powerful goddess if one had world enough and time.

In sum, this comparison does not yield overwhelming evidence for the case that Chaucer is firmly demoting Venus to eliminate any competition with Nature. (Of course, Nature's dominance can be argued on other grounds, especially the fact that it is she, not Venus, who officiates and judges at the bird parliament, and therefore is afforded top priority in the text. That argument I do find convincing.) True, Chaucer takes Boccaccio's Venus down a peg or two, but one could say that he has done the very same thing with Alan's Dame Nature. Chaucer's Nature declares that she is not Reason (though her behaviour is utterly rational); neither does she accommodate either the admirable Venus-Cytherea or the dubious goddess of love in any explicit or obvious way (though sexual activity, whether within or outside marriage, is essential to her purposes). The nature of the relationship between Venus and Nature is, then, left partially open. And the portrait of Venus remains essentially ambiguous, full of dualisms.

The crucial distinctions between these figures should not, however, be eroded away, which is what Hansen's reading of the passage seems to be moving towards doing (p. 115). The garden of love, she declares, is ruled 'by two powerful female divinities', a statement which betrays a tendency to prefer accidents to substance, by which I mean an assumption that the outer form of the personification is the determining force in that fiction's activities and significance, rather than the idea or concept which has been reified. Surely this is to read the text against its grain, every bit as much as if the common gender of Langland's Holy Church and Lady Meed, or Spenser's Una and Duessa (in the first book of the *Faerie Queene*), were regarded as being more important than the utterly opposed qualities which they embody. True, Hansen goes on to say that the garden is 'not a matriarchy'. That statement, however, is concerned not to reassert the difference between the personifications/deifications of Nature and desire, but rather to indicate the limits which the text imposes on female presences and principles: the poem offers 'no essentially female voice or positively feminine counterprinciple that neatly contrasts with, complements, or corrects Scipio's vision' (p. 115).

Clear demarcation between the various abstractions is precisely what the mechanics of medieval personification allegory require. Hence Youth in the *Jugement dou Roy de Behaingne* speaks exactly as he is expected to, and it may be said that the same is true of Machaut's 'Reason' as she functions therein (cf. pp. 136–7 above); similarly, in the *Parliament* Nature is fully aware that she is not Reason (as already noted), and therefore is not obliged to take the line which that figure inevitably would— that is, come out firmly in favour of the royal tercelet's suit (632–3). Besides, can we actually speak of 'common gender' here? Is that not just a new version of the old fallacy of reading 'characters' as if they were 'real people' with complex subjectivities?

Chaucer also imported from the *Teseida* many of the personifications ('Wille', 'Plesaunce', 'Aray', 'Lust', etc.; see 214–32) who inhabit the *locus amœnus*. C. S. Lewis attacked them as having 'nothing to do'; 'each has his little bit of description and his recognised emblems. They are pure decoration—things to be carved on a mantelpiece, or pulled along the streets in a pageant'. These personifications are 'pretty enough', he continues, 'but they have given the word "allegory" a meaning from which it will, perhaps, never recover' (p. 175). Against this it can be argued that the personifications used here *do* have work to do inasmuch as they help to build up that fundamental ambivalence which is endemic to the entire landscape, not just to its most dubious feature, the goddess of love. Here is playful and jolly 'Youthe' but also 'Foolhardynesse', bribery as well as beauty (218–28).

The same can be said of Chaucer's list of trees (176–82). He brings together material from the long list of Guillaume de Lorris (*Roman de la Rose*, 521–776) and details from the account of the trees which are felled for Arcita's funeral pyre in book xi of the *Teseida*, taking over Boccaccio's device of characterizing trees by mentioning their qualities or uses. The extremes are sharply defined: the elm is used for coffins, while whistles and pipes are made from the boxwood tree; cypress relates to the lamentation of death, while the olive intimates peace, and the vine has an obvious association with drunkenness. The life of man is a negotiation of joy and sorrow, success and failure, and in the process of human love this universal condition manifests itself in a particularly acute form.

In sum, Chaucer's entire *descriptio* of his paradisal garden may be read as an elaboration of the paradox which is announced at its very entrance: through me men go, declare the inscriptions over the gates, into a region which is at once life-enhancing and deadening, fruitful and barren, to be greatly desired and to be utterly avoided. Here is heaven for some, hell for others. And that is the standard fare of the French love-visions, of every major account of the bittersweet nature of *fin' amors*. Perhaps in that sense Chaucer has not travelled beyond France after all.

On the parallels with Dante see J. A. W. Bennett, *Parlement of Foules*, pp. 56–7; Boitani, 'What Dante Meant', pp. 129–30; H. R. Patch, *On Rereading Chaucer* (Cambridge, Mass., 1939), pp. 46–7; Schless, *Chaucer and Dante*, pp. 89–100. I share Schless's opinion that 'Dante's contribution is not sufficiently extensive to have any fundamental effect on the poem as a whole' (p. 89). *Re* the parallel in *PF* 123–40, Everett suggests that 'what haunted Chaucer's mind was the repeated "Per me si va . . ." of Dante's lines', and that 'it is this, perhaps more than anything else, that constitutes his "debt" to the Italian poet' in this text ('Chaucer's "Good Ear"', in *Essays*, pp. 139–48, this quotation being on p. 43).

*Feblel dou Dieu d'Amors*, trans. Windeatt in *Sources and Analogues*, pp. 85–90. The French text is included in C. Oulmont, *Les Débats du Clerc et du Chevalier* (Paris, 1911), and has also been edited by I. C. Lecompte, *MP* 8 (1910–11), 63–86. *Florence et Blancheflor*, trans. Windeatt in *Sources and Analogues*, pp. 92–5; French text ed. Oulmont, *Débats*. Jean de Condé, *Messe des Oisiaus*, trans. Windeatt, *Sources and Analogues*, pp. 104–19; French text ed. J. Ribard (Geneva, 1970).

For translations of the relevant part of the *Teseida* and part of Boccaccio's gloss on the two Venuses see Havely, *Chaucer's Boccaccio*, esp. pp. 128–33. The complete gloss is translated by Bernadette Marie McCoy, in Boccaccio, *Teseida* (New York, 1974), pp. 199–208, but this work contains many inaccuracies. There are several good editions of the original Italian text; I have used the one produced by A. Limentani, in vol. 5 of *Tutte le Opere*, gen. ed. V. Branca (Milan, 1964). On the *Teseida* as a medieval epic which, due in part to the influence of medieval literary theory, renegotiates classical epic's position on love, see B. Nolan, *Chaucer and the 'Roman Antique'*, pp. 155–97, and David Anderson, *Before the 'Knight's Tale': Imitation of Classical Epic in Boccaccio's 'Teseida'* (Philadelphia, 1988). On Chaucer's debt to the *Teseida* see Piero Boitani, *Chaucer and Boccaccio*, Medium Ævum Monographs, NS 8 (Oxford, 1977), and his article 'Style, Iconography and Narrative: The Lesson of the *Teseida*', in Boitani (ed.), *Italian Trecento*, pp. 185–99. On this work as a source for the *Knight's Tale* see further the discussion and references in Cooper, *OGC: CT*, pp. 65–8.

R. A. Pratt, 'Chaucer's Use of the *Teseida*', *PMLA* 62 (1947), 598–621. Also his 'Conjectures Regarding Chaucer's Manuscript of the *Teseida*', *SP* 42 (1945), 745–63, which argues that Chaucer did not know Boccaccio's *chiose*, as does William E. Coleman, 'Chaucer, the *Teseida*, and the Visconti Library at Pavia: A New Hypothesis', *MÆ* 51 (1982), 92–101, and 'Chaucer's Manuscript and Boccaccio's Commentaries on *Il Teseida*', *Chaucer Newsletter*, 9/2 (Fall 1987), 1–6. Boitani, *Chaucer and Boccaccio*, pp. 113–16, expresses the opinion that Chaucer *did* know the glosses.

In addition to Brewer's comments in his *PF* edition, see further his article 'Chaucer's Venuses', in Juliette Dor (ed.), *A Wyf Ther Was: Proceedings of the Conference in Honour of Paule Mertens-Fonck* (Liège, 1992), pp. 30–40. Economou, *Goddess Natura*; see further his essay 'The Two Venuses and Courtly Love', in Joan M. Ferrante and George D. Economou (eds.), *In Pursuit of Perfection: Courtly Love in Medieval Literature* (Port Washington, Wis., 1975), pp. 17–50. Elizabeth Salter, 'Chaucer and Medieval English Tradition', in *idem, Fourteenth-Century English Poetry: Contexts and Readings* (Oxford, 1983), pp. 117–40. Accounts of *PF*'s Venus which view her as having been made subservient to Nature include J. A. W. Bennett, *Parlement of Foules*, pp. 107–32; McDonald, 'Interpretation'; and Brewer, 'Chaucer's Venuses'. For contrary views, in addition to Salter see Mehl, *Narrative Poetry*, pp. 44–5, who says that, without 'any moral undertone', the 'dangerously tempting aspects of love are "placed" merely by the contrast to the charms of the ideal landscape'. On medieval discourses relating to the control of desire see especially Pierre J. Payer, *The Bridling of Desire: Views of Sex in the Later Middle Ages* (Toronto and London, 1993).

On the value-laden strategies of interpretation operative in medieval commentary see Minnis and Scott (eds.), *Medieval Literary Theory*, pp. 374–82; also Minnis, '*De Vulgari Auctoritate*' (here with special reference to the Latin commentary on Gower's *Confessio Amantis*). The 'interpretative distance' which exists between text and gloss is emphasized by Minnis, '*Amor* and *Auctoritas*'. This is not taken into account in Robert Hollander's important article 'The Validity of Boccaccio's Self-Exegesis in his *Teseida*', *Medievalia et Humanistica*, 8 (1977), 163–83. On the one hand, Hollander wonders if Boccaccio was altogether serious in providing all of the *chiose*, while on the other, he believes that the gloss on the two Venuses indicates the definitive way in which the temple of Venus as depicted in the text should be read.

Emerson Brown, 'Priapus and the *Parlement of Foulys*', *SP* 72 (1975), 258–74. This study brings out the humour very well. Quoting Kate Millett's remark that 'Medieval opinion was firm in its conviction that love was sinful if sexual, and sex sinful if loving', Brown argues that the episode may also imply a serious point: that the bliss and joy which the birds express upon taking their mates would not last very long if Priapic forces were left behind in the temple. This point has to be made obliquely, he says, given the standard medieval difficulty in accommodating sexual pleasure and the insistence that the objective of marriage was procreation. There is much in this, I believe, but the male orientation of the sexuality presented by the text should be recognized. On voyeurism in this and other medieval poems, see A. C. Spearing, *The Medieval Poet as Voyeur: Secrecy, Watching and Listening in Medieval Love-Narratives* (Cambridge, 1993). And of course, Millett's notion of medieval views of sexual sin and pleasure is very reductive, as is made abundantly clear by the relevant material in Cadden, *Sex Difference*; Jacquart and Thomasset, *Sexuality and Medicine*; and Payer, *Bridling of Desire*.

On the mythographic traditions which lie behind the portrait of Venus see the references on pp. 199, 200, above, to which may be added Earl G. Schreiber, 'Venus in Medieval Mythographic Tradition', *JEGP* 74 (1975), 519–35; Windeatt, *OGC: T&C*, pp. 224–5. For broader ideological and aesthetic contexts see Camille, *Gothic Idol*, pp. 81–7, 220–2, 240–2, etc.

Hansen, *Fictions of Gender*. Lewis, *Allegory of Love*.


## Debate Form and Implied Audience

Ambivalence, dualism, and inconclusiveness are not limited to the *Parliament of Fowls* and some of its sources and analogues, but seem to be a frequent feature of medieval debate poetry in general and beast-debate poetry in particular. This may be illustrated by reference to two other Middle English bird poems which, unlike the decisive Florence and Blancheflor narratives, do not come down on one side or the other. First we may take the Early Middle English *Owl and the Nightingale*, perhaps a product of the twelfth century. Given the considerable amount of legal vocabulary which it deploys, this could well be a lawyer's rhetorical exercise, and may be the work of the Master Nicholas of Guildford whom the birds are setting off to consult as the poem ends. It is more interested in process and form than in conclusion and content, and thus is a perfect show-case for the legal talents and verbal virtuosity of a good lawyer. Master Nicholas may be recommending himself through the quality of the speeches of each pleader, as well as the fulsome praise lavished on him by the warring birds, this being one of the few things on which they agree. Their confidence in Nicholas as a judge who can resolve their apparently irresolvable conflict is remarkable—if he can do that, he must possess the wisdom of Solomon!

The options are more sharply defined, though the resolution is equally elusive, in a bird-debate poem which was indebted to the *Parliament*, namely Clanvowe's *Book of Cupid*. Its narrator, a *senex amans* like the I-persona of Gower's *Confessio Amantis*, attends a meeting of birds who are celebrating the month of May. The 'lewede cukkowe' (90) attempts to disrupt the proceedings by warning against love (here the poem is strongly reminiscent of Jean de Condé's *Messe des Oisiaus*); the nightingale attempts to defend it. When, unable to cope with the cuckoo's diatribe any longer, the hypersensitive nightingale bursts into tears, the narrator intervenes, throwing a stone at her opponent and driving him away. The nightingale then declares her intention of bringing charges against the cuckoo for the wrong he has allegedly done her, whereupon it is agreed that all the birds will hold a parliament at which the matter will be resolved. They agree on the time and place: the morning of St Valentine's Day next, on the lawn in front of the Queen's chamber at Woodstock (presumably a reference to Anne of Bohemia; there was a royal residence at Woodstock. Cf. pp. 32–3, 259, above). The ending is, then, tantalizingly inconclusive. The narrator's promise to the nightingale that he will never cease loving, despite the pain that it brings him, can be taken as an affirmation of the power of love; on the other hand that promise, coming as it does from a character who at the outset had identified himself as 'olde and vnlusty', may ring rather hollow in our ears. And which of the birds will be vindicated at the future parliament of fowls?

In both the *Owl and Nightingale* and the *Book of Cupid*, it is clear what attitude should be taken by the sensible reader, that *sapiens* or wise man so beloved of medieval allegories of the tribulations which the human soul experiences due to the perpetual conflicts between reason and desire. But this is just one possible response; the poetry does not—at least, not obviously—align itself unequivocally with the views of the moral respondent. It is alive to other possibilities, to natural beauty and human emotion.

This ability to define formally, and see the different sides of, a question was cultivated by the medieval educational system, and manifested itself in various academic procedures and pedagogic genres, a good example of which is the formal academic question (*quaestio*) or disputation (*disputatio*), a research method which attained a high level of sophistication in the late medieval schools of law and theology. The master began by stating a proposition with which he may or may not have agreed. Various arguments in favour of the proposition, and various arguments against it (*sed contra*), were then marshalled. This oppositional language is echoed by the dreamer in Langland's *Piers Plowman* when he wishes to take issue with a point of view which two friars have just offered him:

> '*Contra!*' quod I as a clerc, and comsed to disputen
>
> (B VIII. 20)

The contrary opinions were followed by the climax of the procedure: the master would come down firmly on one side or the other, affirming his own opinion (this being called the *solutio*, *determinatio*, or *responsio*). The two poets we have been discussing, like Chaucer in the *Parliament*, refuse to proceed to the solution, of course; they are content to describe the pros and cons, practise the *sic et non* method, and leave the question open. Within the fiction, it is up to some authority figure to make a *determinatio* in a future which never comes; within the social milieu of the text the audience is left to reach its own conclusions in the present.

This brings us to the perplexing matter of the audience—or at least the implied audience—of the *Parliament of Fowls* and how Chaucer expected its members to respond to his poem, to participate in its questionings. As Paul Strohm has emphasized recently, medieval poetry should be seen as a form of utterance which exists within a communicative situation. The requirements of an audience or audiences, as perceived by a writer, directly influenced literary creation. The audience's role entailed not passive consumption, but active participation; it was fully involved in both receiving and determining textual meaning and in influencing the forms which texts took. It may be added that another aspect of literature's participation in the historical process is the phenomenon whereby literary conventions are incarnated, the modes of sensibility inscribed in texts being enacted by their readers. Thus, to adapt a phrase of Oscar Wilde's, 'life imitates art'. Meaning entered the *Parliament* in ways which cannot simply be referred to the all-controlling intention of that god-like author which so much criticism has required.

This approach is a version of New Historicism, an interpretative method which rejects on the one hand the New-Critical belief in the autonomy of literature, the notion that texts can be read in isolation from the socio-political determinants of the culture in which they participate, and on the other the deconstructionist concern with the textual surface of poetry and insistence on its status as a discourse in a world of discourse. The structure of late medieval social relations is regarded as providing a valid interpretative context for events in Chaucer's life and themes in poetry. According to Strohm, the dominant hierarchical social mode insisted on a divinely sanctioned order of 'vertically' arranged estates (pp. ix–xi). Working against this was an alternative social paradigm which elaborated a view of social relations as 'horizontally arranged, communal, secular, and bound in finite time'; they were 'based less on domination and subordination and more on ties of common interest and experience', this being part and parcel of a movement which is often summarized as the transition from feudalism to capitalism. Chaucer and his associates—the company of gentlepersons and London intellectuals which probably formed his 'core' audience—were very directly exposed to these tensions, for 'they found themselves in a highly ambiguous social location'. Their position was at once precarious and promising, promising in that these new careerists had excellent opportunities to enter the upper ranks of the social hierarchy, not on the traditional bases of military service and land tenure but through the skilled and specialized services they were able to provide. Such an audience would presumably have been highly amused at Chaucer's avian replications of social divisions. If, with Strohm, we can regard Chaucer's poetry as embracing 'a lively contention between vertical and horizontal forms of social depiction', that contention may be seen as alive and well in the *Parliament*. And the readers here envisaged would have been acutely aware of the career advantages of participation in the social fiction of the 'game of love'. The necessity of princepleasing required them to strike fashionable attitudes, and by writing, speaking—and debating—about love, their skills and graces would have been displayed to excellent advantage.

The sorts of games which such people played, for entertainment and profit, are indicated by Gower's list of his lady's pastimes; he is always prepared to get involved in them to please her:

> And whanne it falleth othergate,          *otherwise*
> So that hire like noght to daunce,
> Bot on the Dees to caste chaunce          *dice*

Or axe of love som demande,
Or elles that hir list comaunde
To rede and here of Troilus　　　(*Confessio Amantis*, iv. 2790–5)

Here dancing, playing at dice, discussing problems of love (the so-called *demandes d'amour*), and reading or listening to poems are classed together as recreational activities of a fashionable kind (cf. the association of playing chess or backgammon and reading as means of driving the night away at the beginning of the *Book of the Duchess*, 47–51). Many poets offered amatory 'test cases' both in their lyrics and within their narratives, presumably in order to provide material for debate, perhaps also to encourage discussion of those very poems. Sometimes whole lists of topics for consideration are provided, as in Deschamps' *Pluseurs demandes entre les dames avecques les responses sur ce*, wherein ladies ask and answer a series of questions one after the other. Sometimes a whole poem is based on a *demande d'amour*, an excellent example being afforded by Machaut's *Jugement dou Roy de Behaingne*, which describes a debate on the question of which is the worse off, the person whose beloved is dead or the person whose beloved has been unfaithful (cf. pp. 101–3 above)?

The creative possibilities were manifold, as may be further illustrated by Chaucer's practice. As has often been noted, there are traces of the *demande d'amour* tradition in the respective claims of the three tercel eagles, the underlying question being, which one has the greatest claim on the formel? The question is a tough one (the standard of difficulty being high in the *demandes*), and we are left with no answer. Indeed, as Derek Brewer has suggested (*PF* edition, p. 11), the lower-class birds compound the problem by asking, what will happen to the suitors who are unsuccessful? Are they to remain faithful to the tercel, even though their love will never be requited (pp. 11–12)? Allowing for the occasional outbursts of churlish impatience or incomprehension by the goose and the duck, the questions raised in the *Parliament* are all very much on a par, and observe the same social decorum; indeed, the humble turtle-dove proves that amatory idealism is not confined to the upper classes. This is a far cry from Deschamps' *Pluseurs demandes*, wherein some of the *demandes* are quite indecent.

A clearer example of a Chaucerian *demande d'amour* is afforded by the passage in the *Knight's Tale* in which Chaucer poses the question of who is the worse off: Palamon, who is incarcerated in prison but able to see his beloved Emily walk nearby every day, or Arcite, who is free but exiled and hence unable to see the same woman, with whom he also is in love (I(A) 1347 ff.)? Similarly, at the end of the *Franklin's Tale*, the question is asked: which character is the most 'fre' or generous (V(F) 1621–3)? Here, once again, no answer is given; the question is probably designed to lead to a discussion by the assembled company, who are enjoying the poem together—in the way in which Criseyde and her friends are depicted as listening to a romance about Thebes. Pandarus, we are told,

> fond two other ladys set and she,
> Withinne a paved parlour, and they thre
> Herden a mayden reden hem the geste
> Of the siege of Thebes, while hem leste.          (*T&C* ii. 81–4)

The closest extant analogue to the *Franklin's Tale*, the 'Tale of Menedon' in Boccaccio's *Filocolo*, is included in a series of stories which are debated by a group of young aristocrats and resolved by the lady Fiammetta. Literary accounts like these must surely have had *some* relationship to social events. Here we may be regarding some of the features of the privileged 'textual communities' in which Chaucer's texts were first performed and received.

The issue of the nature and very existence of 'courts of love' has perplexed many scholars, particularly the question of what went on at the twelfth-century court of Champagne. Our informant, Andreas Capellanus (cf. pp. 56–7, 67 above), is now regarded as an unreliable witness. His *De amore* describes various difficult love-cases being referred to the judgement of Queen Eleanor of Aquitaine and her daughter Marie, Countess of Champagne; it is Marie who, faced with the question of whether true love can exist between husband and wife, answers in the negative. The lack of firm historical evidence for such courts of love has been emphasized, and Andreas's claim to have been a chaplain at the royal court has been vigorously challenged. These problems cannot detain us here. Suffice it to say that while it would certainly be naïve to suppose that Andreas was merely recording actual events, the supposition that he invented the whole social matrix presented in the *De amore*, with all its elaborate rituals and amatory attitudes, is on the face of it highly improbable. The contents of his book can, at the very least, be taken as testimony to points of views and methods of debate which, it would seem from other sources, were fashionable in some aristocratic circles.

We are on more secure ground with the elaborate *cour amoureuse* which was founded by the French king Charles VI, ostensibly to honour women. This had its first meeting on St Valentine's Day 1400. A 'Prince of Love' who was a professional poet presided; with him were 'musicians and gallants who could compose and sing all kinds of songs, balades, roundels, virelays, and other love-poems, and could play sweetly on instruments'. After mass, they enjoyed 'joyous recreation and conversation about love', with a competition for the best love-poem being judged by the ladies.

But what of the English scene? Given the fashionable status of most things French, it seems reasonable to assume that such diversions were also part of English courtly culture. The hardest evidence we have, however, is notoriously hard to interpret. This consists of the allusions in the two versions of the prologue to the *Legend of Good Women* to debates between those who follow the flower and the leaf respectively, those apparently being the emblems of two aristocratic companies or 'orders' who would engage in pastimes of the kind we have just been describing (F 71–2, G 70–3). Apparently this cult was known across the channel also, since Deschamps wrote several poems about it, one of which declares the poet's own preference for the flower and goes on to praise John of Gaunt's daughter, Philippa of Lancaster, as another flower-follower.

Another reference occurs near the end of Gower's *Confessio Amantis*, in the account of the company of young lovers who form part of Cupid's company. This is led by Youth—and it is tempting to find here some sort of echo of the youthful court of Richard II, though of course the limitations which are frequently associated with Youth as a personified quality must be remembered (cf. pp. 143–4 above). Its members wear garlands, but they are not of the same colour, for some consist of flowers, and others of leaves—and indeed, others are formed of large pearls. The new fashion of Bohemia was there, Gower continues: an allusion to the fashions introduced by Anne of Bohemia and her retinue, which may refer not only to clothes but also to manners. Their sole concern was desire and emotion ('lust' in Middle English); all their songs were about love:

> I sih wher lusty Youthe tho,
> As he which was a Capitein,
> Tofore alle othre upon the plein
> Stod with his route wel begon,  *company well prepared*
> Here hevedes kempt, and therupon  *heads combed*
> Garlandes noght of o colour,
> Some of the lef, some of the flour,
> And some of grete Perles were;  *pearls*
> The newe guise of Beawme there,  *Bohemia*
> With sondri thinges wel devised,
> I sih, wherof thei ben queintised.  *adorned*
> It was al lust that thei with ferde,  *were concerned with*
> Ther was no song that I ne herde,
> Which unto love was touchende  (viii. 2462–75)

They were entertained with piping and song, which resounded loudly; they danced, laughed, and enjoyed themselves, putting care aside. The main subjects of their discussion were arms and *amor*:

The moste matiere of her speche
Was al of knyhthod and of Armes,
And what it is to ligge on armes                    *lie*
With love, whan it is achieved.        (viii. 2496–9)

The account then moves far into the depths of literary fiction as Gower informs us that Tristram and Isolde were of that company, and Lancelot with Guinevere, Jason with Creusa, Hercules with Eole, and Troilus with Criseyde—but even though he joined in the play he was heavy of cheer because Diomede claimed to be his 'parconner' (i.e. his partner, in the sense that he wished to share Troilus's lady with him—which is, of course, what came to pass in the tale). How, then, should we interpret this passage? As evidence of actual aristocratic practices in Gower's day, or as an amplification of ideas which he had picked up from the prologue to Chaucer's *Legend*? (The nature of the relationship between the *Legend* and the *Confessio Amantis* is a controversial issue, it being unclear as to which poet influenced which, or whether Chaucer influenced Gower at some points and Gower influenced Chaucer at others, the two poems having been written in a spirit of co-operation and friendly exchange.)

In the Middle English poem *The Floure and the Leafe* (dating from the third quarter of the fifteenth century) the two orders have become allegorical categories; this work throws no light on aristocratic fashions. However, in two poems written by Charles d'Orléans around 1435, during his long imprisonment in England, the two orders reappear again. But, as Derek Pearsall shrewdly says (*FL* edition, p. 25), we cannot tell whether Charles is referring to English custom or recalling the practice of the cult in France before his capture. In both poems the imagery is personalized; one declares that the only flower the poet was interested in, his lady, is dead, while the other has him explaining that it was merely in play that he chose the leaf, for his real allegiance is to the flower. Here is no courtly context, no debating society.

This point may lead us to the thought that only a few people would be needed to have an informal and impromptu 'court of love', and so the scholarly concern to prove or disprove the actual existence of grand formal occasions in which such matters were debated is probably misplaced. Where three or four were gathered together, there could be a small-scale *cour amoureuse*, a 'textual community' sufficient to enable the performance and reception (perhaps also the production) of an appropriate poem. After all, the 'mayden' who reads the 'geste / Of the siege of Thebes' to Criseyde and her friends (as quoted above) has an audience of three, the total company comprising four women. And when Gower's beloved wanted 'To rede and here of Troilus' or to 'axe of love som demande', she would not have needed many helpers.

Even on the most sceptical of approaches, there seems no reason to doubt that some oral performances of poems were followed by discussions of the issues they raised, and that love and chivalry were regularly on the agenda. Chaucer provided poems for such occasions. In the *Parliament*, as in the later *Legend of Good Women*, his literary fiction serves the social fiction of the game of love. It may be said with equal force that that social fiction was a major determinant of his poetry. The *Parliament* was shaped by the very processes and preferences which were involved in its consumption.

But precisely what tastes are inscribed in the poem? In the absence of information about what went on at the debates of the companies of the flower and the leaf, illumination may be sought from a later text, which is nevertheless the product of a cultural formation which had many similarities with Chaucer's. This is Baldessare Castiglione's *Book of the Courtier*. Set in the Palace of Urbino during March 1507, when Castiglione was in the service of Duke Guidobaldo, though not published until 1528, it takes the form of a series of debates between men and women (the male presence being dominant) on successive evenings, which are presided over by the duchess, Elisabetta Gonzaga. In the rooms of the duchess, Castiglione explains, 'along with pleasant recreations and enjoyments of various kinds, including constant music and dancing, sometimes intriguing questions were asked, and sometimes ingenious games (*giochi*) played' (trans. Bull, p. 44).

Over and over again we are told that the debaters are laughing as they react to each other's pronouncements or begin their own. Indeed, a theoretical account of laughter is even offered, when Bernardo Bibbiena explains that it is 'naturally attracted to pleasure and desirous of rest and recreation'. Grave philosophers, holy men of religion, and even 'prisoners waiting in hourly expectation of death, all seek solace in light recreation'. Therefore, Bernardo continues, 'everything which provokes laughter exalts a man's spirit and gives him pleasure, and for a while enables him to forget the trials and tribulations of which life is full' (p. 155). Every attempt is made to avoid trial and tribulation throughout the text, as laughter defuses possible tension and takes the sting out of extreme views which could otherwise be offensive, thereby ensuring that the discussion never goes so far as to be displeasing and is not taken too seriously, or with the wrong kind of seriousness.

The implications of this anthropology of game (here a textual construct, certainly, but surely indicative of a wider 'cultural poetics') become very clear when the subject of the nature and dignity of woman is being debated. The Magnifico Giuliano refuses to go into the matter of 'how inferior are all other human creatures to the Virgin Mary' on the grounds that 'this would be to confuse divine things with these foolish discussions of ours' (p. 223). Apparently, religious profundities should be kept out of such recreational activities. The same is true of philosophical subtleties (p. 218). When Signor Gaspare cites the common medical notion that a woman is an imperfect male, the Magnifico Giuliano rises to the intellectual challenge, though pauses to reflect that 'this is not perhaps the right time to go into subtleties'. But go into them he does, and soon the women have had enough. Signora Emilia Pia demands that the discussion be conducted in a way that everyone can understand (p. 221). Authorities should be left, it seems, to preaching and to school of clergy (cf. Prologue to the *Friar's Tale*, VII(D) 1276–7).

One may recall the similar attitude taken in the epilogue to a work of which Castiglione is very aware, though he often denigrates it in order to display his own work to best advantage, namely Boccaccio's *Decameron* (the anxiety of influence is sometimes acute). Boccaccio declares that his 'stories were told neither in a church, of whose affairs one must speak with a chaste mind and a pure tongue . . . nor in the schools of philosophers, in which, no less than anywhere else, a sense of decorum is required, nor in any place where either churchmen or philosophers were present. They were told in gardens, in a place designed for pleasure, among people who, though young in years, were nonetheless fully mature and not to be led astray by stories' (Epilogue; trans. McWilliam, p. 830). Boccaccio's ostensible purpose here is to defend his use of material and language which some may find morally offensive; but clearly his larger ambition is to define the special criteria with reference to which fiction should be judged (certainly not according to the tenets of theology or philosophy), by elevating the pleasure principle, the therapeutic benefits of stories which temporarily liberate an audience from the pressures of real life. Such writing can, to be sure, play and sometimes even beat the theologians and philosophers at their own game. The arguments in both the *Decameron* and the *Courtier* are often of the greatest sophistication, as the debaters—for the *Decameron*, too, owes a lot to the debate form—display their skills in rhetoric and dialectic with studied effortlessness and controlled nonchalance.

Much of this could be said, with equal validity, of the *Parliament*. The same balance exists there, with serious matter being introduced, but laughter winning out in the end. The sombre initial vision is passed over in favour of the values of the *cour amoureuse*; Africanus takes a holiday, and ushers in 'joyous recreation and conversation about love'. Bernardo Bibbiena's defence of laughter follows in the footsteps of medieval discussions of the therapeutic value of recreation (including recreational reading of literature), which have been well described by

Glending Olson (cf. pp. 146–54 above). All work and no play makes Jack a dull moral being. The bow which is always bent will be unable to shoot powerful bolts when the testing time comes. And, as (Pseudo-) Cato says,

> Interpone tuis interdum gaudia curis,
> Ut possis animo quemvis sufferre laborem.
>
> [With pleasure lighten now and then thy care,
> That so life's burdens thou mayst better bear.]

In Benet Burgh's translation (printed by Caxton around 1477) this passage is amplified thus:

> Who that lakketh rest may no while endure.
> Therfore among take ese and disport.
> Delyte the neuer in gret besinesse and cure,         *care*
> But that whilom thou maist also resort         *sometimes*
> To playes, recreacions and al other comfort.
> Than schalt thou better laboure atte longe,
> Whan thou hast mirth thy besinesse amonge.

These arguments were associated with the genre of beast-fable; both the warning about the 'bow that ay is bent' and the advice about mixing 'merines' with 'sad materis' appear at the beginning of Henryson's translation of Aesop (22–7). In similar vein, it could be argued that the *Parliament* was meant to enable its hearers and/or readers to forget for a while the trials and tribulations of which their life was full. The emotions conjoured up may have been similar to those which Gower attributes to the company of Youth:

> Ther was ynowh of joie and feste,         *an abundance*
> For evere among thei laghe and pleie,
> And putten care out of the weie,
> That he with hem ne sat ne stod.         (viii. 2490–3)

'The laughter aros of gentil foules alle' (575). That could be taken as referring to superior aristocratic laughter at the stupidity of the lower orders (the sparrow-hawk has just accused the goose of being a fool), but I suspect it is meant to convey feelings of general merriment. The water-fowls are certainly not cowed, and give as good as they get; they do not defer to the birds of prey, but only to Dame Nature.

Laughter would certainly have 'aros' from the 'gentil' audience of Chaucer's poem (no human equivalents of the water-fowl being present, of course). They would have been made aware of the practical problems caused by the elaborate courtship rituals which they had elaborated, the sheer length of time it took to get anywhere near satisfaction of their desires. Chaucer's fictions heighten and idealize actual frustrations; for example, the long wait which is all the tercel offers in the end reflects those marriage negotiations which in the highest echelons of society could drag on for a long time. The text, then, does not offer naïve escapism, inasmuch as the members of the audience are enabled to laugh at themselves and declare loudly that the lower-class birds organize things rather better. But the vulgarity of the churls might then be held up to ridicule, for no eagle would want to be a water-fowl! The aristocrats are thus flattered at having their sense of their own superiority affirmed, while recognizing that their social position necessitates many elaborate, and sometimes tiresome, responsibilities, including emotional ones. Such affections and behavioural patterns would confidently be accepted as a result of their ancestry, a condition of their status, and a mark of their class. Thus the trajectory of the *Parliament* would momentarily problematize, but ultimately confirm, the processes and results of their self-fashioning.

On this reading, the possibilities for real subversion scarcely exist. It could be responded, of course, that such a hermeneutic move is all too common in certain recent versions of historicist critique. Here we may recall the charge that New Historicism tends to produce conclusions wherein the potentially subversive ends up being crushed or disempoweringly accommodated by the dominant institution. The defeat of the subordinate is 'almost inevitable', to reiterate Cohen's protest; 'unless one is an aristocrat, there is nothing to be done' (cf. p. 5). And the *Parliament* can certainly be read somewhat differently, as David Aers's fine work on the poem demonstrates. Quoting the Marxist historian Rodney Hilton's postulation of a loss of plebeian respect for the traditional élites in the age of Chaucer, Aers finds in the reactions of the lower-order birds to their betters an 'explosion' which 'challenges the upper-class monopoly of Parliament, power and speech'. The aristocratic birds, for their part, seek to 'monopolise the assembly (ll. 414–90) and make the needs of other groups in the community quite invisible, literally unspeakable'. These comments are balanced, however, by Aers's remark that Chaucer, as a privileged individual himself, does not suppose that the lower social groups are evincing more admirable values. It is rather a case of competing claims, each social grouping finding means to declare and justify its own self-interest (*Chaucer*, p. 16).

While I have much sympathy with Aers's view that the *Parliament* is subversive of all attempts to substitute impersonal knowledge and an absolute viewpoint (as argued in his article 'Authority, the Knower and the Known'), it seems to me that the sociopolitical, as opposed to the intellectual, assumptions which underpin the poem are incapable of much negotiation. Class distinctions and the supposedly typical characteristics of members of each class have been made the object of mirth, but that does not make them any less fixed; the poem can easily be deconstructed as a celebration of sociopolitical stasis. 'Unless one is an aristocrat, there is nothing to be done.' Indeed—though there is the occasional shock to the system, like the Peasants' Revolt of 1381 or those aspects of Lollardy which held out possibilities of radical social change. Aristocrats also have the privilege of doing nothing, of remaining aloof from the crowd, of practising long procrastination. They can afford to wait. For in general they have the power to ensure that things are done in the end. Chaucer, the rich wine-merchant's son, occupies a good vantage-point from which to regard the social spectrum in all its colours. But he who pays the poet ultimately calls the tune.

Should, then, subversion be sought in the poem's sexual politics? Several of the *Parliament*'s recent readers have suspected that there might be something at least unusual in Chaucer's presentation of the female eagle's refusal to choose a mate from the three on offer. J. A. W. Bennett suggested that he was here 'championing, or at least admitting the possibility', of a woman's right to choose her marriage partner, 'even when the maiden is of such rank that her betrothal is the whole common-wealth's concern' (p. 177). However, the notion was a legal commonplace, well known to medieval lawyers both canon and secular; we have good grounds for suspecting that often mere lip-service was paid to it, given the force of social, financial, familial, and dynastic pressures, though there are some documented cases wherein the woman's preferences were apparently taken into account.

A larger claim has been made by Elaine Tuttle Hansen. While (quite properly) emphasizing the extent to which the formel functions as an object which 'affirms masculine identity, in both senses: individual sub-jectivity and empowerment articulated (she is mine, not yours, and I am more manly than other men because I possess her), and common man-hood proved (I am a man, like all others, because I desire her)' (p. 126), Hansen also argues that this creature's behaviour may pose an actual *threat* to such gender construction. For her indecision raises the subver-sive spectre of the female who is 'indifferent to masculine desire', who wishes to love no man at all (p. 127). I cannot see any support for this in the text. The formel clearly asks for a 'respit for to avise me' (648), a respite or period of reflection wherein, the assumption is, she may con-sider the merits of the rival suitors. And 'after that' she will exercise her choice by selecting one of them (649); on that occasion she 'wol speke and seye' what is the result of her deliberations. I will not *yet* follow Venus or Cupid, she declares;

'I wol not serve Venus ne Cipide,
Forsothe as yit, by no manere weye'.                    (652–3)

The implication being that she *will* serve them in the near future (*pace* Lawton, who supposes that next year's debate will be as inconclusive for the eagles as this one was).

In short, the formel accepts the inevitable; all she can do is postpone it for a year, the only period in which that 'by no manere weye' appertains. But there is neither any suggestion that she is putting off an evil hour nor that what those deities represent is inherently distasteful to her. Here is no slothful Rosiphelee, who has to be intimidated into the 'comun cours' of normative behaviour by 'Venus the goddesse' and 'Cupide . . . with his miht' (*Confessio Amantis*, iv. 1260–5). A year hence, and the formel's broken bow will join the extensive collection of such trophies which hang 'in dispit of Dyane the chaste' (281) on a wall in the temple of Venus. But there was never any suggestion that the formel wished to be a lifelong follower of the chaste goddess. She is therefore rather different from Emily in the *Knight's Tale*, who declares that she wants 'to ben a mayden' all her life and 'noght to ben a wyf and be with childe' (*CT* I(A) 2305, 2310). Yet Emily does not rule out those possibilities altogether; if, she continues, her destiny is ordained so that she must 'have oon of hem two', Palamon or Arcite, let her have the one who loves her most (2323–5). A quite un-Amazonian thing to say, but utterly in keeping with that text's gendered values. Within the boundaries of the female subjectivities inscribed in these passages, feminine free choice does not extend to choosing not to marry. As in Shakespearean festive comedy, there is no ultimate threat (if threat there be at all) to heterosexual fulfilment or to the principle that the earth must be peopled.

Hansen also tentatively explores another, far more radical possibility of transgression when she steers her perception of the 'indifferent' formel into very deep waters with the suggestion that this construct 'might be satisfied . . . by her present preeminent position, *presumably a chaste one* [emphasis mine], as Nature's most beautiful creation. She sits, after all, on Nature's hand, and is caressed by the goddess':

Nature hireself hadde blysse
To loke on hire, and ofte hire bek to kysse                    (377–8)

'Why', Hansen continues, 'should the formel desire, instead of this divine adoration by one of her own sex, any of the three egotistical scrappy eagles?' (pp. 127–8). What exactly is being implied here, particularly with that 'presumably a chaste one' manœuvre? Apparently the relationship between Nature and the formel is being eroticized—a dubious procedure, in my view. The poet who kept homosexual male practices as critiqued by Alan of Lille well clear of his own text would hardly be interested in introducing or implying homosexual female desire in its stead. Besides, surely the discourse invoked by the brief reference to Nature's kisses is meant as a maternal one—Nature treats her creation just as a loving and proud mother would shower kisses on her child—rather than one which involves sexual desire. (Other instances of that discourse may be found, for example, in the Pseudo-Bonaventuran *Meditationes vitae Christi*, wherein the Virgin Mary—the very paradigm of perfect motherhood—repeatedly kisses the Christ-child.) Then again, the fact that it is a beak ('bek') which Nature is kissing is amusing rather than erotic (cf. Chauntecleer's praise of the beautiful 'scarlet reed' around his beloved Pertelote's eyes, *CT* VII. 3161), and marks a palpable physical difference between the two figures rather than the mutuality which Hansen seeks to disclose. And thus I let the argument lie. I can find few, if any, prospects of subversion here, but rather compulsory heterosexuality, which is assumed to be the norm to such an extent that affirmation thereof is simply not considered.

In the *Parliament of Fowls*, then, there is little space for 'dissident reading'. But often literature is 'overdetermined' (to use Althusser's term) and can textualize far more than the sum of its determinations, and this is certainly true, I believe, of the *Parliament*. Besides, it seems not unreasonable to envisage some readers/auditors—from privileged communities, to be sure—wrestling with the dilemmas posed by its initial belittling of earthly life and human fame. If anyone insisted on taking it all too seriously, however, a reply was at hand. This is the affirmation of the frivolous alternative, as rendered explicit in Chaucer's barnyard tale of Chauntecleer and Pertelote. In the face of those grave subjects of predestination and fate which are accommodated in that beast-fable but never allowed to dominate, the undermining declaration is made: 'My tale is of a cok . . .' (VII. 3252). In similar vein it could be said that the *Parliament* is about, and maybe strictly for, the birds.

In another sense, it was mainly for the eagles of this world. As far as they are concerned, laughter is always there as a possible reaction, serving to balance (or maybe circumvent) the poem's most serious moments, ultimately rendering its didacticism optional and ensuring that edification never threatens entertainment for long.

*The Owl and the Nightingale*, ed. E. G. Stanley (Manchester and New York, 1960). Clanvowe, *Book of Cupid*, in Scattergood (ed.), *Works*, pp. 33–53. On the inconclusiveness of much debate poetry see Thomas L. Reed, 'Chaucer's *Parliament of Foules*: The Debate tradition and the Aesthetics of Irresolution', *Revue de l'Université d'Ottawa*, 50 (1980), 215–22. The *quaestio* form is discussed by Minnis and Scott (eds.), *Medieval Literary Theory*, p. 212, and is illustrated in the selection of texts which follows.

Paul Strohm, *Social Chaucer*. For a good introduction to New Historicism see the introduction by H. Aram Veeser to his anthology, *The New Historicism* (New York and
London, 1988), pp. ix–xvi. Cf. Hayden White's essay therein, 'New Historicism: A
Comment', pp. 293–302. At best, due to the conviction that 'every expressive act is
embedded in a network of material practices', this approach can bring together aspects
of (for example) literature, ethnography, anthropology, art history, politics, and eco-
nomics in a highly illuminating way, breaking out of the narrow confines within which
more traditional practitioners of these disciplines have tended to operate. At worst, its
portmanteau quality can become extreme eclecticism, with heterogeneous ideas being
yoked together with violence in a combination which, as such, has little if any historical value, though each and every one of the parts of the collage may be historically
authentic.

On literature within the social context of courtly game see John Stevens, 'The Game of
Love', in his *Music and Poetry*, pp. 154–202. Anthropological discussions of the implications of social game playing are many and various; of particular interest to literary
critics are Eric Berne, *Games People Play: The Psychology of Human Relationships*
(London, 1968); Roger Caillois, *Man, Play, and Games*, trans. M. Barash (New York,
1961); Jacques Ehrmann (ed.), *Games, Play, Literature* (Boston, 1968); J. Huizinga,
*Homo Ludens: A Study of the Play-Element in Culture* (Boston, 1950).

On the *demande d'amour* tradition see especially Manly, 'What is the *Parlement of Foules?*'.
Deschamps' *Pluseurs demandes* has been edited by Marquis de Queux de Saint-Hilaire,
*Œuvres complètes*, viii. 112–25. For Boccaccio's 'Tale of Menedon' see Robert P. Miller
(ed.), *Chaucer: Sources and Backgrounds* (New York, 1977), pp. 121–35.

I have taken the term 'textual community' from Brian Stock's *Implications of Literacy*, pp.
90–1, but use it with considerable adaptation and modification, since he is dealing with
religious dissenters and is describing textual uses and absences which are sometimes
different from those which I am hypothesizing for communities which included aristocrats, nobility, 'new men', etc. However, since in both situations we are dealing with
comparable interactions of textuality and orality, it is appropriate to retain the term.

By a 'textual community' I mean a socially privileged group within which a text is
received, internalized, and interpreted. Just one reader/performer can effect a considerable dissemination of the text (depending of course on the number of listeners), so
widespread reading ability need not be an essential postulate for wide consumption.
The total audience (performer plus auditors) will then internalize the text, discussing
and interpreting it either immediately after the performance or on subsequent occasions where the text itself may or may not be present. Thanks to (*inter alia*) previous
performances of texts like the one in question, the minds of at least some members of
the existing audience are trained in certain expectations, possessed of various values
and principles (relating to love, chivalry, normative noble behaviour, and the like),
which constitute the parameters of the reception. With such shared assumptions, the
group members are free to discuss, debate, and disagree on matters raised by the text
and related issues. Interaction by word of mouth can create an interpretative environment within which the text is received in certain predictable ways, and reiterate and
indeed reshape the text itself, as internalized by its recipients—which may well lead to
the composition of a further, new text, which in its turn will be subject to the processes
here described.

For the *De amore* see the edition and translation by P. G. Walsh, *Andreas Capellanus on
Love* (London, 1982). This supersedes the translation of J. J. Parry, *The Art of Courtly
Love by Andreas Capellanus* (New York, 1941, repr. 1959). A review of scholarly opin-
ion on Andreas Capellanus is included in Toril Moi, 'Desire in Language: Andreas
Capellanus and the Controversy of Courtly Love', in David Aers (ed.), *Medieval
Literature: Criticism, Ideology and History* (Brighton, 1986), pp. 11–33, and also in Don

A. Monson's excellent article 'Andreas Capellanus and the Problem of Irony', *Speculum*, 63 (1988), 539–72.

John Benton and D. W. Robertson have offered highly sceptical views of Andreas's courtly connections and the subversive potential of *De amore* (see the references on p. 69 above); here they were reacting against the large claims made for Andreas by Gaston Paris and C. S. Lewis. A middle course is steered by Walsh, who suggests that Andreas may have had *some* sort of association with Marie, Countess of Champagne, and his treatise 'may well have been stimulated by the interest at the court of Champagne in theories of secular love' (Introduction, pp. 2–3, 4). The fact that the work is written in Latin (and an academic Latin at that) rather than in the vernacular indicates, he argues, that Andreas had written 'for the predominantly clerical audience which could cope with his elegant Latin, and which would relish the spicy and daring speculations apparently redolent of discussion at the court of Champagne' (pp. 4–5). The reception history of *De amore* seems to indicate that such people did indeed form its main readership: see Bruno Roy, 'A la recherche des lecteurs médiévaux de *De amore* d'André le Chapelain', *Revue de l'Université d'Ottawa*, 55 (1985), 45–73. This also demonstrates that the work was far more popular in Italy (and to a lesser extent in Germany) than in England or in the country of its origin, France. This was probably due to the condemnation of some of its doctrines in 1277 by Stephen Tempier, Bishop of Paris (cf. pp. 67, 72, above).

See further the major study by Alfred Karnein, *'De amore' in volkssprachlicher Literatur: Untersuchungen zur Andreas-Capellanus-Rezeption in Mittelalter und Renaissance* (Heidelberg, 1985); some of his main ideas may also be found in *idem*, *'Amor est passio*—A Definition of Courtly Love?', in G. S. Burges (ed.), *Court and Poet: Selected Proceedings of the Third Congress of the International Courtly Literature Society* (Liverpool, 1981), pp. 215–21. In Karnein's view *De amore* takes a quite negative view of the type of love which was being celebrated in vernacular literature; indeed, he argues, it originated in the chancellery of Philip II Augustus, King of France, during the 1180s, being intended for the entertainment of a highly learned and Latinate coterie which would have viewed the goings-on at the Court of Champagne with amusement and lofty scorn. A compelling critique of this position is offered by Monson, 'Problem of Irony', pp. 547–8, 550–4.

On Charles VI's *cour amoureuse*, see A. Piaget, 'La Cour Amoureuse, Dite de Charles VI', *Romania*, 20 (1891), 417–54, and 'Un Manuscrit de la Cour Amoureuse de Charles VI', 31 (1902), 597–603; cf. Brewer's edition, pp. 4, 132. Richard Firth Green, '*Familia Regis*', emphasizes the male-dominated nature of this and similar enterprises. '*The Floure and the Leafe*' and '*The Assembly of Ladies*', ed. Derek Pearsall (Manchester, 1962).

I have quoted the translation of the *Courtier* by George Bull (Harmondsworth, 1967), and used the edition of the original by Carlo Cordié in *Opere di Baldassare Castiglione, Giovanni della Casa, Benvenuto Cellini* (Milan and Naples, 1960), pp. 5–361. On the importance of laughter in the *Courtier* see R. W. Hanning and David Rosand (eds.), *Castiglione. The Ideal and the Real in Renaissance Culture* (New Haven, Conn., and London, 1983), pp. 9, 11, 14–15, 22, 92. 'It is extraordinary', declares Thomas M. Greene, 'how many speeches are introduced with the participle *ridendo*' (ibid., p. 9). See further Wayne A. Rebhorn, *Courtly Performances: Masking and Festivity in Castiglione's Book of the Courtier* (Detroit, 1978), pp. 137–44. On Castiglione's notions of 'game' (*gioco*) see Rebhorn, *passim*, and Greene's entire article '*Il Cortegiano* and the Choice of a Game', in Hanning and Rosand (eds), *Ideal and the Real*, pp. 1–15.

Boccaccio, *Decameron*, trans. McWilliam.

G. Olson, *Literature as Recreation*. Pseudo-Cato, *Distichs*, ed. and trans. Chase. *Paruus Cato, Magnus Cato*, trans. Benet Burgh, ed. Fumio Kuriyagawa, Seijo English Monographs, 13 (Tokyo, 1974), p. 35. Henryson, *Poems*, ed. Fox.

Aers, *Chaucer*, and 'Knower and the Known'.

J. A. W. Bennett, *'Parliament of Foules'*. On the woman's 'right to choose' *versus* familial and other pressures see especially Beatrice Gottlieb, *The Family in the Western World from the Black Death to the Industrial Age* (New York and Oxford, 1993), pp. 52–6; see further Elaine Clark, 'The Decision to Marry in Thirteenth- and Early Fourteenth-Century Norfolk', *MS* 49 (1987), 496–516; John T. Noonan, 'Power to Choose', *Viator*, 4 (1973), 419–34; Sue Sheridan Walker, 'Free Consent and Marriage of Feudal Wards in Medieval England', *Journal of Medieval History*, (1982), 123–34. Cf. pp. 65–6 above.

Hansen, *Fictions of Gender*. While Alan of Lille's Dame Nature does not treat of sexual contact between women, in *De planctu naturae* it is evident that such relationships would thwart her procreative plans every bit as much as sexual liaisons between men. There seems to have been a general lack of concern about lesbianism in Chaucer's day (women's mad sexual passions for men being perceived as presenting much more of a problem for social control), but, as Cadden notes, 'women making love to women *were* sometimes seen as behaving "like men" and *were* prosecuted by lay authorities in the late Middle Ages' (*Sex Difference*, p. 224). See further Louis Crompton, 'The Myth of Lesbian Impunity: Capital Laws from 1270–1791', *Journal of Homosexuality*, 6 (1980/1), 11–25.

## Structure and Strategy

### THE GENUS AND SPECIES OF LOVE

The central interpretative crux of the *Parliament* should by now be clear. Are we to allow the poem to occupy a site apart from the church and the schools of philosophers (although their doctrines may make guest appearances), a secular pleasure-garden—whether actual or metaphorical—in which responsible people may be entertained by writing which is fundamentally secular? Boccaccio explicitly made that claim for his *Decameron*; is it implicit in Chaucer's poem? The answer to that question will determine how one reads the *Parliament*.

Take the poem's two most enigmatic lines, for example: 'For bothe I hadde thyng which that I nolde, / And ek I ne hadde that thyng that I wolde' (90–1). What does he have which he does not want, and what does he want which he does not have? The exact source for these lines is well known. It is *De consolatione philosophiae*, III, pr. iii, 19–21, the point at which Lady Philosophy asks the Boethius persona, 'Was it not either because something was missing that you wanted, or because something you did not want was present?' (trans. Tester, p. 241). In his *Boece* Chaucer translates the sentence as, 'And was nat that . . . for that the lakkede somwhat that thow noldest nat han lakkid, or elles thou haddest that thow noldest nat han had?' The answer is in the affirmative, and so Dame Philosophy proceeds to dismiss all those inferior goods (wealth, high office, earthly power, fame, and bodily pleasure) which men are drawn towards but which are fundamentally flawed and hence not really wanted. Men who possess them recognize that something is missing, for they lack the true end of happiness, the *summum bonum* which is the high God. Now, should this be taken as an interestingly intricate line which Chaucer, as a craftsman always on the look-out for a purple passage or a good turn of phrase, lifted from Boethius to use here for his own, very different, ends? On this view, what is important is how the stone has been sculpted rather than the quarry whence it came. And the line can be taken as meaning that Cicero gave the narrator much which he, as a love-poet in search of new matter, does not want, and that very matter is what he wants but does not have. This reading seems to be supported by the behaviour of Chaucer's Africanus, whose conveyance of Chaucer to the *locus amœnus* may be seen as the amusingly grateful *auctor*'s attempt to provide the poet persona with what he sought but did not find in the *Somnium Scipionis*. The narrator's experience of the bird parliament does give him plenty to write about, the result being a poem of the kind he had wanted to compose in the first place.

On another view, the original Boethian context of the enigmatic remark is in some way operative in the text of the *Parliament* itself, and the allusion provides a vital clue to Chaucer's attitude to his material and/or the way in which he expects his audience (or the heavily learned section of it at least!) to respond. This reading takes the narrator as a somewhat bewildered seeker after truth (not unlike the Boethius persona himself, as presented in book iii of the *Consolatio*), who does not fully realize the profound significance of his reading of the *Somnium*. What Chaucer is implying—so the argument would run—is that in Boethius, as in Cicero, may be found a reliable account of where true happiness lies.

The most uncompromising version of this approach is probably the analysis of B. F. Huppé and D. W. Robertson, who believe that in the *Parliament* the futility of earthly love is set against the true love of the seeker after wisdom. The garden is seen as a fallen Eden in which the deceptive nature of the pleasures of earthly love is intimated, the worshippers of Venus being revealed as unsatisfied and sterile. Even Dame Nature comes in for criticism, for her lack of reason: she does not understand either the blind idolatry of the eagles (who are not obeying the divine command to increase and multiply) or the blind haste of the waterfowl. Nature cannot remedy what is unnatural; that remains for God and for man when guided by God-given reason and grace. The Valentine song with which the poem ends is pretty, they concede, but above and beyond that may be found the high comedy which comes in seeing the folly of man who chooses blindly to cherish the summer of his earthly joy. The poem's laughter aims to restore to man a sense of proportion, which consists in the recognition that human passion is trivial. Huppé and Robertson profess to respect the poem's humour, but the laughter they imagine sounds very much like the humourless kind which is heard at the end of *Troilus and Criseyde*, where Troilus looks down on the 'little spot of erthe' (enjoying a view very similar to the one taken in the *Somnium Scipionis*) and, recognizing that all is vanity, laughs at those who are lamenting his death (v. 1814–25). This would make the poem ludic in a way very different from that explored in our previous section. The rules of the divine comedy, rather than those of the game of love, are now operating. The philosophers and theologians have invaded the pleasure-garden.

A poem which begins with *contemptus mundi* and ends with praise of a lovers' festival naturally lends itself to such extremes of interpretation. The question must therefore be asked: what, in a text of that age, should we expect of literary structure and poetic unity anyway; precisely what criteria should be invoked? At the outset it may be recognized that the device of a sombre backdrop against which the main action is thrown into sharp relief is a device common to much late medieval vernacular literature. Good examples are afforded by Machaut's *Jugement dou Roy de Navarre* and Boccaccio's *Decameron*, both of which begin with graphic accounts of the plague (in Rheims and Florence respectively) before proceeding to the pleasurable matters which are the texts' main concern (cf. pp. 149–51 above). Gower's *Confessio Amantis* in some measure follows the same basic pattern, starting as it does with a long prologue about the condition of England and the decline of moral standards within the three estates; though in this case it is probably more accurate to regard the initial excursus as the beginning of a 'frame' which is completed at the very end of the work, where the sociopolitical concerns are reiterated and a 'beau retret' is made from human love, the main subject of the greater part of the poem. In the *Parliament* Chaucer makes the move from philosophy to play with considerable panache; indeed, far from ignoring or trying to paper over the crack, he makes fun out of fissure by having the austere Africanus behave in a way which is highly amusing because it is so utterly unexpected from the authority figure who has been depicted so imposingly at the beginning of the poem.

But the structural problem remains, of course. Solutions to it have been sought in the notion of *discordia concors*, that harmony which arises from opposing forces, accommodating them and achieving a synthesis on a higher level. A good account of the contraries present both in the universe and within man is found in Alan of Lille's *De planctu naturae*. Nature, as she herself explains, formed man as a microcosm so that he would mirror the universe itself. 'For just as concord in discord, unity in plurality, harmony in disharmony, agreement in disagreement of the four elements unite the parts of the structure of the royal palace of the universe, so too, similarity in dissimilarity, equality in inequality, like in unlike, identity in diversity of four combinations' (i.e. the four humours) 'bind together the house of the human body.' Moreover, she continues, just as the planets fight against the regular motion of the heavens by going in a different direction (a reference to the retrograde motion of the planets), 'so in man there is found to be continual hostility between sensuousness and reason'. 'The movement of reason, springing from a heavenly origin', seeks to return to its source: 'in its process of thought' it 'turns back again to the heavens'. The 'movements of sensuality', however, move in a different direction: 'planet-like' they go 'in opposition to the fixed sky of reason', and 'with twisted course slip down to the destruction of earthly things' (i.e. the corrupting forces of sensuality pull down man's reasoning powers, thereby hindering his ascent to heaven). These forces corrupt man, change him into a beast; the movement of reason, on the other hand, has the power to transform him into a god (VI, pr. iii; trans. Sheridan, pp. 118–19).

'Concord in discord, unity in plurality, harmony in disharmony, agreement in disagreement': those terms would, on the face of it, seem to apply very well to such a diverse and apparently discordant poem as the *Parliament*. Indeed, this could serve as a means of describing the poem's own aesthetic, and critics have not been slow to exploit its possibilities. John McCall, for instance, believes that the poem presents a broad picture of the mysterious but genuine harmony of this sublunar world against the background of Africanus's authoritative report on the heavenly music of the spheres. Taking a positive view of Chaucer's Nature, he sees her as ordering the scene of strife so that a harmonious balance is achieved. The effort to find an ultimate 'answer' or point of reconciliation for the entire *Parliament*, however, is misdirected, because that answer or point is in heaven, and not in the gardens of earthly love. David Chamberlain adopts the same basic approach, but is highly critical of the eagles, arguing that they actually represent disharmony, due to their failure to achieve a worthy accord or music between their rational and irrational appetites. Planet-like, they are going in opposition to the fixed sky of reason. And David Fowler also makes good use of the theory of *discordia concors*, though he is inclined to be dismissive of the *De planctu naturae* and Neoplatonic tradition as the determining source for it. From Alan of Lille Chaucer takes little more than the figure of Nature, he argues; the Platonists have no really large role, philosophically, to play here. The *Parliament* is in his opinion actually a 'Creation' poem, with its organizing principles derived from commentaries on the first chapter

of Genesis, a body of medieval theology generally known as the hexameral tradition. It is there that one may find what Chaucer chose as his
underlying theme, the love of God which holds the universe together—
that is, the laws of concord and love which, according to St Ambrose's
*Hexameron* (of which Fowler makes much use), form a union of discordant elements. The sombre warning of Africanus, he continues, is in harmony with this theme, directing our search away from the tyrannical love
of the senses towards the love that governs heaven. All things considered,
then, Chaucer's vision is of a harmony that transcends the discord of
human conflict embodied in the parliament of birds, a concord that is the
same throughout the universe, whether in the music of the spheres or in
the sublunar song of the birds.

Such a totalizing approach certainly affirms the poem's unity—but for
many of its readers (myself included) its contraries are rather more
intractable than that. Differences and disjunctions can easily be multiplied. For instance, while Chaucer certainly did 'Christianize' Cicero's
vision (as I have suggested above), it could be said that this does not go
very deep, and the resulting effect is one of juxtaposition rather than
assimilation. Hence, a sharp contrast may be postulated between the
crabbed, limited, pagan vision offered by Cicero (which, one could argue,
seems incapable of accommodating many areas of human existence and
experience) and the joyful liveliness of a world which combines the exuberant twelfth-century version of Neoplatonism, as channelled by Alan of
Lille, with the secular, fashionable ethos of a lovers' festival. Even more
important, while the idea of *discordia concors* has enabled much appealing
criticism of the poem, a lot of it depends on the importation of material
(from Boethius, Alan, Ambrose, or whoever) which is simply not in the
text; thus Chaucer's work is being completed, if not rewritten, the supposed gaps being filled in and the whole made to look a lot neater than
when he left it.

Suspicion of this procedure is reasonable, surely, and one may be for-
given for scepticism when faced with the statement that an ultimate
'answer' or point of reconciliation cannot be found within the *Parliament*
itself because that answer or point is in heaven. Or with Fowler's declaration that the hexameral tradition which governs the poem's structure
functions at a level so deep that it scarcely ever shows itself on the textual surface. Or indeed with Bennett's suggestion that the very shadow-
iness of Bishop Valentine permits the introduction of his name as a
pointer to the heavenly bliss that the bird-song, however distantly, anti-
cipates. Implications, hints, echoes, distant anticipations, answers
deferred or referred upwards and out of sight, influences buried so deep
that they rarely surface—such language permeates discussion of the

*Parliament*, and much of it can sound uncomfortably like special pleading. What is remarkable, however, is the wide unanimity of the intuition
that one must go outside the poem to find some missing element or *deus
ex machina* to bring back to it. To add to the illustrations already offered,
it was that feeling which encouraged L. D. Benson to argue that the
*Parliament* is comprehensible only with reference to the betrothal of
Richard II and Anne of Bohemia.

My own response is to urge that the poem be seen as a performance
text, a work meant to open rather than close debate. The advantage of
this approach is that it respects the poem's incompleteness, and indeed
identifies this as an essential part of its strategy. Thereby the *Parliament*
is made more comprehensible *as it stands*, nothing being offered by way
of supplementation or supposed completion. Or, to develop the same
idea in a different way, it holds out the possibility of several possible
determinations, in the positions taken by various hearers. These
'answers' are elusive, but are many rather than one, and to be found in
medieval textual communities rather than in heaven; as such, they are
rather more available and imaginable. The poem itself, to be sure,
remains incomplete, and thus capable of provoking such 'completions'
indefinitely.

It is possible, however, that some of the poem's recent readers have
been rather unrealistic about the form, type, and degree of completeness
which the poem *could* possess, given the strains within the cultural formation of Chaucer's time. Hugh White, in his study of nature and salvation in *Piers Plowman*, argues that, while Chaucer and Gower seem to
be very sympathetic to the idea of the natural as a force for good, in the
end neither of them is able to sustain this view. In White's opinion, 'there
does not seem to be much credibility left to the high moral claims made
for natural sexual love in *Troilus and Criseyde* at the end of the poem,
while the reconciliation between sexuality and morality Gower is continually attempting in the *Confessio Amantis* is finally made to appear impossible' (p. 133). The same principle would, of course, apply to the
*Parliament*, where once again there seems to be a failure to reconcile sexuality and morality. It could be replied that within late medieval culture,
love and reason, *amor* and authoritative doctrine, were inevitably at odds;
and precisely because this tension was perpetual, there were no easy
answers, no 'fast fix' in literature as in life. Of course, scholastic writers
often dismissed desire in their elevations of *caritas*, but it was, after all,
the single most important subject of vernacular poetry. Indeed, in his
*Vita nuova* (xxv) Dante declared that it had its origin in human love: the
first to write as a vernacular poet was moved to do so because he wished
to make his poetry comprehensible to a woman who found it difficult to

understand Latin. Such poetry had, by Chaucer's time, developed its own discourses and rationales, and it was rarely the mere mouthpiece for clerical condemnations of lust (*pace* certain pan-allegorizing critics), even when it drew on aspects of the philosophical and historical lore which scholasticism had made available. The only poet who came anywhere near to resolving the dilemma was Dante, in his portrait of Beatrice in the *Comedy*. But there Beatrice is physically dead, thus enabling sexual desire to be transmuted, through quite exceptional sleight of hand, into the love of immortal soul for soul. Living ladies were a lot more problematic, and poems which concentrated on the pleasures and pains of earth-bound love had to confront the immovable object: love and reason were difficult, perhaps even impossible, to reconcile.

It is hardly surprising that such poems should display fissures. The *Troilus* epilogue does indeed encourage young folk to give up insecure worldly emotions in favour of the utterly reliable love of Christ, who will never let them down (v. 1835–48). But surely that does not retrospectively condemn out of hand what has been the poem's main subject, or eradicate the impression given by, for example, the end of the third book, where the love of Criseyde seems to have helped Troilus, in his post-coital philosophizings, to attain a vision of that love which is the very bond of the entire universe, ordering the elements and the seasons, reconciling the differences between nations, and bringing together good friends and virtuous couples (1744–71). Similarly, while at the end of the *Confessio Amantis* the aged persona does indeed beat a retreat from love, it seems abundantly clear that, due mainly to his debilitating old age, he is leaving behind an emotion which has brought him much pleasure as well as pain, something which (despite all the dangers) helps to make human life worth living. After all, human love shows to excellent advantage in the imposing figure of Apollonius of Tyre, who has dominated the final book of the *Confessio* prior to the 'beau retret' episode. Apollonius is the good lover, the good man, and the good ruler all rolled into one, these qualities being seen as mutually reinforcing and quite compatible. At the end of the poem a Latin gloss (probably written by Gower himself) can declare that 'the pleasure of all love apart from charity is nothing. For whoever abides in charity, abides in God' (ed. Macaulay, ii. 475). But the corresponding English text is making a far more complicated and ambiguous statement.

Similarly, Boccaccio's depiction of Venus and her temple in book vii of the *Teseida*, as already noted in our discussion of the *Parliament*'s sources, follows a discourse quite different from the one which constitutes his allegorizing gloss on the two Venuses. The formal literary commentary was a major site on which medieval thought built the moral hermeneutics which it derived from philosophy and theology. Glosses, then, had their hidden agenda, their own values to assert, and these did not have to be the same as those of the text which they were interpreting. Indeed, quite often they could be markedly divergent, as is evident in many medieval commentaries on works which had been handed down from pagan antiquity. Boccaccio's auto-exegesis, which is self-consciously following that same agenda, cannot therefore be taken as unlocking the definitive meaning of the *Teseida* or (by inference) offering the vital clue to the meaning of the *Parliament*. Poets wrote sometimes like philosophers; narrators talked sometimes like commentators. But that is not the same as saying that poets were governed by philosophy or that narrators were dictated to by commentary. One consequence of this situation is that there is no overriding need to provide a facsimile of a medieval commentary on the *Parliament*, in the manner of Huppé and Robertson. Even if this were the best reproduction possible, it could, at best, be regarded as the kind of thing which only a very well-educated member of Chaucer's audience (and almost certainly a churchman) could have thought. This meaning, then, would not have been determinate, and would hardly have prevailed within a largely secular audience of the highly privileged, which, whatever its moral disposition, certainly wanted to be entertained. At the very least, poets like Chaucer and Gower should not be blamed for failing to bridge major value gaps which were endemic to the cultural formation within which they wrote, and incapable of change until the culture itself changed.

The incompleteness of the *Parliament*, it would appear, is to some extent reinforced, rather than remedied, by appeal to its intellectual milieu; allegory, that great channel for the conveyance of philosophy and theology into poetry, is incapable of providing meaning which neatly fills the spaces in the text as we have it. As a hermeneutic method, it simply cannot normalize textual indeterminacies, 'render coherent the greatest number of the work's elements' (to reiterate phrases of Terry Eagleton's; cf. p. 218 above). Having recognized, then, that the work's incompleteness is irreducible, it may be possible to throw some light on its actual strategy.

Help is at hand in the possibilities for comparison afforded by an appropriation of scholastic method by one of the most controversial of all medieval writers on human love, Andreas Capellanus. The structure of the first part of book i of *De amore* is of interest here, because it initially uses the form of the *quaestio* (cf. p. 292 above) in asking about love's nature, participants, effect, and so forth, and then adopts the dialogue form in order to illustrate the different forms of love which are possible. This hierarchical sequence firmly relates the type and level of love to the class and social position of the constructed 'persons' who are in love or at least taking about it.

1. What love is.
2. Between what persons love can exist.
3. Where love gets its name.
4. What the effect of love is.
5. What persons are suited for love.
6. In what manner love may be acquired and in how many ways.

   1st dialogue: A bourgeois man addresses a bourgeois woman.
   2nd dialogue: A bourgeois man addresses a noble lady.
   3rd dialogue: A bourgeois man addresses a woman of the higher nobility.
   4th dialogue: A noble addresses a common woman.
   5th dialogue: A nobleman addresses a noblewoman.
   6th dialogue: A man of higher nobility addresses a common girl.
   7th dialogue: A man of higher nobility addresses a noble lady.
   8th dialogue: A man of higher nobility addresses a lady of higher nobility.

Similarly, in the *Parliament* the implicit *quaestio* of 'What is love?' (cf. *PF* 602), precipitated by the juxtaposition of a Ciceronian vision which fails to accommodate it and the narrator's own vision of a garden which is dominated by it, is followed by dialogues which vividly illustrate the different types of love, once again firmly linked to social position and status.

I am not, of course, suggesting that Chaucer knew the *De amore*, which actually seems to have had a poor reception in England (cf. p. 57 above). The point is rather that similar conceptualization is operative in both texts, though of course it is more obvious in Andreas's. This scholastic mode of thinking is, in my view, more important for the structure and strategy of the *Parliament* than that associated with the *demande d'amour* tradition, which is more concerned with specific test cases than with abstract definition and comprehensive review. Chaucer's poem therefore raises two distinct but related questions: what is love? and what are the kinds of love? It seeks to initiate, and offer much material for, a debate on the nature and species of love. This, I suggest, may be identified as the fundamental strategy of the *Parliament*.

On this view, the bird parliament does not hold out the possibility of any creature changing its mind, capitulating in the face of another's argument, or adopting a point of view different from the one with which he or she began. Rather, it is a device to set out an array of views about love which are irresolvably different in so far as the creatures themselves are different. This method of reading seems also to be required by another Middle English beast debate which refuses to come down formally on one side or another, *The Owl and the Nightingale*. That poem works well at the level of self-publicity (cf. p. 291 above), though on reflection one can but wonder if even the egregious Master Nicholas of Guildford could provide a definitive judgement in favour of one of the parties. (Maybe therein lies a joke, of course.) For the distinguishing features of the owl and the nightingale are developed from the traditional attributes of these birds as described in beast-fable and the moralized natural science found in medieval surveys of the properties of things. How, then, can there be a winner when each bird is acting true to its own nature? If the owl stopped doing the things that the nightingale is complaining about, it would cease to be an owl; the same is true of the nightingale in relation to the owl's criticisms.

This same point applies with equal validity to the *Parliament of Fowls*. Birds will be birds. If, for example, the eagles ceased their elaborate love-rituals, they would cease to be eagles; likewise, the water-fowl cannot change their attitudes any more than they can change their plumage. As clearly distinguished by their manifest differences of colour and markings, feeding habits, and behavioural patterns, the species of birds who present the species of love emphasize in the clearest possible way the differences between human beings, and reinforce the belief that socio-political distinctions are firmly fixed. It is not simply that the aristocratic eagle would not wish to be a low-born water-fowl: he simply *could* not be such, according to the hierarchical values which were so ingrained in the culture that they seemed to be simple common sense. The advantages which accrued from privilege and nurture were mistaken for part of nature itself.

This genetic determinism is often encountered in medieval romances and their later derivatives, as when the knight's son who is brought up by a widowed farmer's wife in a wild, desolate forest nevertheless plays at casting javelins (cf. Chrétien de Troyes' *Perceval*); a farmer's son brought up in a castle would want to sow and harrow oats. By the same token, 'fyn lovynge' is the prerogative of the privileged classes. 'Farmers', declares Andreas Capellanus firmly, 'can scarcely ever be found serving in Love's court. They are impelled to acts of love in the natural way like a horse or a mule, just as nature's pressure directs them. So for a farmer regular toil and the continuing uninterrupted consolations of ploughshare and hoe are enough.' If, in exceptional cases, such men are indeed 'roused in a way transcending their nature', he continues, 'it is not appropriate to instruct them in love's teaching' (trans. Walsh, p. 223). By concentrating on behaviour which is naturally alien to them, they will neglect their proper work, and the harvest will be ruined. What then of peasant women? In Andreas's book they do not know anything about civilized love either, and so fine courtship would be a waste of time: so, if you absolutely must have one of them, simply find a suitable spot and take her by force.

Within the privileged classes themselves, supposedly natural distinctions are real and to be respected, as is made abundantly clear by Andreas's hierarchical sequence of dialogues, as summarized above. Similarly, the *exempla* collection which Geoffroy de la Tour-Landry compiled in 1371 for the edification of his three daughters—a particularly interesting contribution to the literature of social control—includes a chapter in which men are advised to love 'after their estate and degree'. Then again, when Chaucer's Nature tells the three eagles to spend the next year serving their lady as best they can—

> ech of yow peyne him in his degre
> For to do wel                                            (662–3)

—the assumption is that the potential for well-doing is intimately related to the 'degre'. The greater the nobility, the better the action. And, by implication, the finer the loving. Chaucer complicates the matter slightly by suggesting that the formel just might not choose the royal tercel. (The clear implication being that if the girl has any sense, of course she will. Unfortunately, love's blindness, irrational desire, and/or general female waywardness can sometimes hinder the making of the best match.) But there is no chance whatever of the formel announcing a year hence that she wishes to partner, say, a duck or a goose.

In the *Parliament* such attitudes are presented in the best possible light. The various species are revealed not as sides in competition with each other, but rather as constituents of one and the same social spectrum. This ranges from the eagles' aristocratic airs and graces to the lower-class birds' plain speaking and directness, affirming that it takes all kinds to make a world, and that there is a place for everything. The bad news, it could be retorted, is that everything has to stay in its place, in order to make the total (and totalizing) structure operate. But let us go along with the text's mythologizing of power relations and social control for the moment. *Vive la différence* becomes the order of the (Valentine's) day. This is a festive occasion on which the concerns and cares of normal life have been set aside.

Inconclusiveness and resistance to closure are therefore part and parcel of a textual strategy which illustrates and affirms plurality. The differences between the species are vividly and noisily presented. Moreover, the birds are not narrowly circumscribed by their species, any more than in the *Canterbury Tales* the Miller (for example) could be regarded as just another miller or the Knight could be taken as the stereotypical knight. The principle of individuation is functioning in the

*Parliament*. The eagles, the cuckoo, the goose, and the other birds certainly display the natural properties which are associated with them in traditional beast-lore (and amplified by Chaucer), but they are allowed some subjective features which exceed those parameters. Each manifests his or her *haeccitas* (to revert to Hopkins's terminology); what they do is them, for that they came.

But what of the view from the eighth sphere, and those judgemental categories of black / white, sheep / goats which have been invoked at the very beginning of the poem? All that too has been set aside for the moment, for this lovers' special day; the main function of the summary of the *Somnium Scipionis* might be the encouragement of the audience to consider the genus of love and its place in the universe. And what of the ending of the *Parliament*, which seems to be unhappy from the eagles' point of view? 'Jack hath not Jill', to borrow a phrase from Shakespeare's *Love's Labour's Lost*. Chaucer, however, conveys the sense that love's labours have not been lost, but are simply continuing. In Shakespeare the grand project of founding a Platonic academy flounders as the central characters fall in (human) love. In Chaucer the Platonic philosophers (and theologians) do not have the last word either. The *Parliament*, I am convinced, presents a negotiation of discourses of a kind which they have little control over. The resultant hybrid belongs neither in the schools of philosophers nor in a church, but in a gathering of nobles, intellectuals, and 'new men', who could then engage in a pleasurable and self-displaying discussion of the genus and species of love. Chaucer offers not gloss but text; he has written not as a philosopher but as a poet.

And poets, as the reader of the *House of Fame* will know very well, are mouthpieces of Apollonine amphibologies, purveyors of the contingent and even the mendacious. Dame Philosophy may have driven out the Muses, but in the *Parliament* they have been welcomed back. Ironically, in this case the embodiment of philosophy, a man of great authority if ever there was one, leads the poet not away from them but to the garden in which they are jostling for position.

Boethius, *De consolatione philosophiae*, ed. and trans. Tester.

Huppé and Robertson, *Fruyt and Chaf*. On the laughter heard at the end of *Troilus* see especially Steadman, *Disembodied Laughter*.

Alan of Lille, *De planctu naturae*, ed. Häring, trans. Sheridan.

John P. McCall, 'The Harmony of Chaucer's *Parliament*', ChR 5 (1970), 22–31; David Chamberlain, 'The Music of the Spheres and *The Parlement of Foules*', ChR 5 (1970), 32–56; Fowler, *Bible in Middle English Literature*. Other relevant discussions include Aers, 'Knower and the Known'; Stillwell, 'Unity and Comedy'; Dean, 'Artistic Conclusiveness'; Reed, 'Debate Tradition'; and Larry M. Sklute, 'The Inconclusive Form of the *Parliament of Fowls*', ChR 16 (1981), 119–28, who speaks well of the work's 'complete-incompleteness' and 'conclusive-inconclusion'. The elements of disharmony and irresolution are emphasized by Aers, 'Knower and the Known', and also by H. Marshall Leicester, who argues that 'instead of seeing a single, unfolding vision, we hear many voices': 'The Harmony of Chaucer's *Parlement*: A Dissonant Voice', *ChR* 9 (1974), 15–34. Michael R. Kelley attempts to make critical virtue of textual necessity in arguing that antithesis is the key to the poem's structure: 'Antithesis as the Principle of Design in the *Parlement of Foules*', *ChR* 14 (1979), 61–73.

J. A. W. Bennett, 'Second Thoughts'. Benson, 'Occasion'.

White, *Nature and Salvation*. For further discussion of some of the issues he raises see Minnis, '*De Vulgari Auctoritate*'. Dante, *Vita nuova*, in E. Moore and P. Toynbee (eds.), *Opere di Dante Alighieri* (Oxford, 1924), p. 223. The difficulties of reconciling love and reason in the post-lapsarian world are well brought out by Payer, *Bridling of Desire*. On the methods of medieval literary commentary see the references on p. 290 above; for Andreas, pp. 305–6.

Andreas Capellanus, *De amore*, ed. and trans. Walsh. *The Book of the Knight of La Tour-Landry, translated from the Original French into English in the Reign of Henry VI*, rev. edn. by Thomas Wright, EETS OS 33 (London, 1906), pp. 178–9. With my account of noble nature and nurture compare Aers, 'Masculine Identity', in which the importance of the 'cultural formation of knightly love and the social construction of specific forms of sexuality' is emphasized (p. 121). What Aers says of the Man in Black in *BD* characterizes well the assumptions held by the eagles in *PF*: 'So internalized is the education which makes a courtly male of him that he can assert it must be a product of nature, . . . confirming a characteristic move in the self-representations of the dominant class, attributing features that are the product of a training based on massive privileges of economic and social power to "natural" qualities beyond the potential of "common" people. . . . love is a "craft" (l. 791), a discipline which was one of the markers of full membership in that upper-class community, one to which he [Chaucer] gained access but was not to the manner born' (p. 122)

R. R. Edwards, *Dream of Chaucer*, argues well that 'Chaucer's artistic and conceptual achievement consists in defining a unified poetic substance without refining away the singularities and discordant individualism of the particulars' (p. 141).

### 'The Noble Philosophical Poet in English'

Also, who was hier in philosophie
To Aristotle, in our tonge, but thow?                              (2087–8)

asked Thomas Hoccleve in the lament for Chaucer in his *Regiment of Princes* (of 1412). Similarly, Deschamps begins the ballade (1386?) which he addressed to Chaucer with 'O Socratès plains de philosophie', and Thomas Usk (writing shortly before 1387) had described him as 'the noble philosophical poete in Englissh'. The philosophical purchase of the *Parliament of Fowls* is undeniable—and yet, Chaucer does not offer any solutions. Given the debate form (and, I believe, the occasion) of his poem, that is hardly surprising. He does not resolve the endemic tensions between sapience and sex (in any case a virtual impossibility, given the prevailing cultural formation), or attempt an ideological reconciliation of the right / wrong, black / white Macrobian vision with the visual and aural riches of the bird parliament.

At the beginning of Macrobius's commentary Chaucer could have read the statement that philosophy does not reject all stories, nor does it accept all. Fables, explains Macrobius, are of two kinds, those which please (by gratifying the ear and generally entertaining) and those which encourage the reader to good works. The whole category of fables that promise only to please is to be avoided in a philosophical treatise and relegated to children's nurseries (trans. Stahl, p. 84). Macrobius singled out the beast-fables of Aesop as one type which drew the reader's attention to virtue, but in his refusal to provide explicit *moralizatio* Chaucer did not follow the conventions of that genre. Neither (*pace* the poem's allegorizing readers) did he attempt to compose a fiction of the other type which Macrobius judged to be philosophically acceptable, the *narratio fabulosa*, wherein a kernel of solid truth is to be found within the shell of fiction. This marks the *Parliament* off from, say, Jean de Condé's *Messe des Oisiaus*, which culminates with a (rather strained) attempt to allegorize its imagery, as we have already noted. I myself can find no evidence for the view that Chaucer expected his audience, or the clerkly part of it, to impose such a meaning on his text—if he had wanted this, surely he would have done it himself. But that is not to imply that the *Parliament* should be relegated to children's nurseries, for there are more things in heaven and in earth than are dreamed of in Macrobius's philosophy. They include the project of offering earnest and game, *sentence* and *solas*, to various audiences—in the first instance, almost certainly to an audience of aristocrats and other high-ranking people, on some special occasion which included a debate on questions of love.

Moreover, it could be suggested that in his poem's avoidance of philosophical resolution Chaucer is exercising one of the poet's distinctive prerogatives, as recognized in medieval and later criticism. Arnulf of Orléans, on being confronted with an astrological crux in Lucan's *Pharsalia*, comments that 'in the manner of the philosopher' Lucan is putting forward various opinions here, 'but in the manner of the poet he neither resolves nor affirms any of them' (trans. Minnis and Scott, p. 115). The poet, then, merely propounds; it is the task of the philosopher to resolve or affirm. As Sir Philip Sidney was to declare much later, 'the poet . . . nothing affirms, and therefore never lieth.' That is a good answer to Macrobius's charge that, when considered from a philosophical point of view, much poetry is a pack of lies.

Chaucer, then, is content to put forward various opinions, and leave it up to the audience to engage in philosophical discussion (very much following his lead), to resolve or affirm the issues as they wish. In the *Parliament* he at once makes a case for poetry's independence from philosophy and reminds us that the composition of poetry is above all else a social act, the artefact itself being shaped by the audience which it is designed to serve.

All the references to Chaucer as philosophical poet are conveniently given in Brewer (ed.), *Critical Heritage*, i. 63, 40, 43, and also in J. A. Burrow (ed.), *Geoffrey Chaucer: A Critical Anthology* (Harmondsworth, 1969), pp. 26, 29, 41.

Macrobius, *In Somnium Scipionis*, ed. Harris, trans. Stahl. Minnis and Scott (eds.), *Medieval Literary Theory*. Sir Philip Sidney, *An Apology for Poetry*, ed. Geoffrey Shepherd (London, 1965), p. 124 (cf. p. 123).

# The Legend of Good Women

In his song 'Go and catch a falling star', John Donne declares that of all the outlandish things he can think of (impregnating a mandrake root, learning to hear mermaids singing, etc.), quite the most unlikely is the existence of a woman who is at once fair and faithful.

> If thou be'st borne to strange sights,
> Things invisible to see,
> Ride ten thousand days and nights,
> Till age snow white hairs on thee,
> Thou, when thou return'st, wilt tell me
> All strange wonders that befell thee,
> And swear
> Nowhere
> Lives a woman true, and fair.

And if such a paragon actually existed, the poem continues, she could not maintain that rare state for long:

> If thou findst one, let me know,
> Such a pilgrimage were sweet;
> Yet do not, I would not go,
> Though at next door we might meet;
> Though she were true, when you met her,
> And last, till you write your letter,
> Yet she
> Will be
> False, ere I come, to two, or three.

Thus, traditional anti-feminism has its wicked way. This particular version of the discourse was alive and well in Chaucer's England. In the *Wife of Bath's Tale*, the loathly damsel gives her lusty young husband the choice of having her fair and faithless or foul and faithful—the implication being that no woman can be both fair and faithful. Here, however, the impossible occurs, and the knight is rewarded for his (belatedly) good behaviour with everything that his heart and body could desire, exclusive possession of a young and beautiful lady. (The woman pays the price of his moral reformation, transforming from powerful sage into submissive wife who obeys her husband in everything.) But what happens in a fairy-tale has little consequence for real life. There, one can assume—indeed, is encouraged to assume by the way in which the Wife is presented—that

the monstrous regiment of women, led by viragos like Dame Alice herself, act true to the types in which men have cast them.

The contrast with the material that Chaucer offers in the *Legend of
Good Women* seems striking. The poet, the God of Love declares, owns
no less than sixty books which are full of stories (both Roman and Greek)
about good women (G Prol. 273). Moreover, there are plenty of good
women that he doesn't know about—twenty thousand more, no less, are
here sitting in the present company!

> For here ben twenty thousand moo sittynge
> Than thou knowest, good wommen alle,
> And trewe of love, for oght that may byfalle.
>
>                    (F Prol. 559–61; no parallel in G Prol.)

On this evidence it would seem that, far from being the impossibly rare
species as mockingly envisaged by Donne, the true female lover exists in
large numbers. Or is this to read the poem in a naïvely literalistic way,
to take its 'naked text' (G Prol. 86) too seriously? After all, Solomon had
said that he could not find one good woman in a thousand: 'One man
among a thousand I have found: a woman among them all I have not
found' (Ecclesiastes 7: 29). Could Chaucer have been alluding to that passage of Scripture? Perhaps, but even if it was in his mind, that would not
necessarily have implied agreement with its *auctor*. Albertano of Brescia
(*c*.1193–?1260), for instance, had quibbled with him on this matter.
Although Solomon could not discover one, many others have found good
women. Then again, perhaps Solomon was thinking in terms of the highest possible order of excellence, which cannot be found simply because it
does not exist, since no one except God alone is perfect in everything.
The figure speaking at this point in Albertano's *Liber consolationis et con-
silii* is Dame Prudence. Chaucer translated her praises of women into
Middle English in his *Tale of Melibee*: 'I shal shewe yow by manye
ensamples that many a womman hath ben ful good, and yet been, and hir
conseils ful hoolysome and profitable.'

Here, then, is what purports to be a seriously meant medieval defence
of the female sex. Much of the earlier modern criticism of the *Legend* took
the line that if Chaucer's portrayal of good women was meant seriously,
then the poem is 'very medieval' but repetitive and boring (and Chaucer
himself got bored with it, leaving it unfinished). If it is a 'travesty on
female virtue', however, it instantly becomes more interesting, as is witnessed by the first, exuberant though extreme, advocacy of this theory by
H. C. Goddard. With this approach, one has to cope with the suggestion
that Chaucer was being subtly but certainly misogynistic, a problem (certainly for modern post-feminist audiences) which can neatly be side-

stepped with the idea that the poet was satirizing the misogyny of his persona, he himself being ideologically sound. (Similar attempts have been made to distance Chaucer from the anti-Semitism of his Prioress.) Hence Carolyn Dinshaw, who has given us what might be termed 'a *Legend* for the 1990s', argues that the narrator 'domesticates the alien woman', 'produces a dull text and wearies of it', thus serving Chaucer's larger purpose of demonstrating that to constrain the feminine is 'eventually to silence men, too', *all* human experience thereby being reduced (pp. 86–7). But should we place all the blame on the shoulders of 'the Chaucerian narrator', who has long been burdened with the rejects of modern taste? Elaine Tuttle Hansen is surely right to feel suspicious about 'the attempt to recuperate a feminist Chaucer who does not threaten the humanist Chaucer', which is based on assumptions such as the belief that 'Chaucer is sympathetic to woman's problems'. Indeed, she goes so far as to describe this enterprise as being fundamentally 'misguided' (p. 12).

The project of this chapter is to prove that the *Legend* is at once very medieval and very interesting, particularly inasmuch as it serves as a locus for interweaving and sometimes contesting discourses relating to the 'woman question' in its late medieval formulation. (The extent to which the text manipulates these discourses, rather than being driven by them, is very debatable.) My central argument is that the *Legend* works through inversion, as it turns the world upside-down to present a regiment of good women and bad men. Here is essentially a celebratory work which, with remarkable *bonhomie*—the emphasis being on the *homme*—focuses the minds of its audience (or, more accurately, several of its potential audiences) on traditional gender roles and the ways in which women may attain heroic status. Such male/self-referential wit is all the more remarkable in view of the pain and the pathos which the reader/auditor of the stories is openly invited to feel, and it certainly does not devalue those emotions. For an essential part of that celebration is ritual commemoration: the *Legend* turns the key of remembrance to provide access to records that have been laundered or lost in the house of fame, that being its implicit agenda. However, Chaucer was not concerned, as was Christine de Pizan, to put the record straight (in her terms), but rather to put it differently and provocatively. And he certainly succeeded.

In the *Tale of Melibee* Chaucer was working from a French abridgement, by Renaud de Louhans, of Albertano's treatise. Extracts from the Latin original are included in Blamires (ed.), *Woman Defamed*, pp. 237–42.

H. C. Goddard, 'Chaucer's *Legend of Good Women*', *JEGP* 7 (1908), 87–129; 8 (1909), 47–112. Carolyn Dinshaw, *Chaucer's Sexual Poetics* (Madison, Wis., 1989). Hansen, *Fictions of Gender*. We have come a long way from the time when Paull F. Baum could say of some of Chaucer's heroines, 'in the language of the vulgar they ask for it'. 'Chaucer's "Glorious Legende"', *MLN* 60 (1945), 381.

Estimates of the literary quality of Chaucer's legends have differed widely, ranging from Burlin's charge that here he made 'a colossal blunder' to R. W. Frank's admiring claim that the stories create 'a sense of the variety and violence of love, its capacity to evolve in powerful and unexpected forms'. See Burlin, *Chaucerian Fiction*, p. 34, and R. W. Frank, 'The *Legend of Good Women*: Some Implications', in R. H. Robbins (ed.), *Chaucer at Albany* (New York, 1975), p. 74. Most critics, however, have found something good to say about the Prologue(s) at least; thus Priscilla Martin can remark that 'The Prologue is as lovely, subtle and suggestive as anything Chaucer wrote but the stories are wooden and vexing'. *Chaucer's Women: Nuns, Wives and Amazons* (London, 1990), pp. 196–7. However, some have patronized it for what they perceive as its Frenchified charm.

Discussions which bring out the major issues of the poem include Ruth M. Ames, 'The Feminist Connections of Chaucer's *Legend of Good Women*', in Wasserman and Blanch (eds.), *Chaucer in the Eighties*, pp. 57–74; Janet M. Cowen, 'Chaucer's *Legend of Good Women*: Structure and Tone', *SP* 82 (1985), 416–36; Fyler, *Chaucer and Ovid*, pp. 96–123; Steven F. Kruger, 'Passion and Order in Chaucer's *Legend of Good Women*', *ChR* 23 (1989), 219–35; Carol M. Meale, 'Legends of Good Women in the European Middle Ages', *Archiv*, 144 (1992), 55–70; Mehl, *Narrative Poetry*, pp. 98–119; And A. J. Minnis, 'Repainting the Lion: Chaucer's Profeminist Narratives', in Roy P. Eriksen (ed.), *Contexts of Pre-Novel Narrative* (Berlin, 1994), pp. 1–23. Four book-length studies have been published: R. W. Frank, *Chaucer and 'The Legend of Good Women'* (Cambridge, Mass., 1972); Lisa J. Kiser, *Telling Classical Tales: Chaucer and the 'Legend of Good Women'* (Ithaca, NY, and London, 1983); Donald W. Rowe, *Through Nature to Eternity: Chaucer's 'Legend of Good Women'* (Lincoln, Nebr., and London, 1988); and Sheila Delany, *The Naked Text: Chaucer's 'Legend of Good Women'* (Berkeley and Los Angeles, 1994).

The recommended edition is by A. S. G. Edwards and M. C. E. Shaner, in the *Riverside Chaucer*.

## Text, Date, and Circumstances

The *Legend of Good Women* survives in twelve manuscripts and Thynne's early printed edition. On the face of it, that is a quite impressive number of witnesses, particularly as compared with the three manuscripts and one early print of the *Book of the Duchess* and the three manuscripts and two early prints of the *House of Fame*. Moreover, it does not seem to lag far behind the best attested of all Chaucer's Shorter Poems, the *Parliament of Fowls*, which survives in fourteen manuscripts and Caxton's edition. Unfortunately, none of the manuscripts is complete. Two are mere fragments, another a series of fragments. A further manuscript preserves only the *Legend of Thisbe*, yet another only the *Legend of Dido*. All the other copies have lacunae of various kinds.

The parlous state of the text as we have it lends additional force to the major question: do we have everything which Chaucer wrote of this poem, or was the final portion lost early in transmission? I say 'early' because John Lydgate, who refers to the *Legend* in the *Fall of Princes* which he began around 1431, seems to know it only in its imperfect state.

Would Chaucer really have broken off writing this poem in mid-sentence (which is, I believe, how line 2723 must be read)? Once, it was widely held by Chaucer's critics that the poet had got bored with the work, perhaps a commission for which he had no personal relish, particularly when he became fully engaged with another (far more challenging) collection of tales, the *Canterbury Tales*. On that hypothesis, it is just possible to imagine him throwing down his pen in disgust, unable to write a single word more. But that rather sensationalistic theory does not square with the other facts that we may glean about the *Legend* from Chaucer's other works.

The most pertinent of these references is the Man of Law's description of the poem in the introduction to his Canterbury tale (II(B$^1$) 53–89). There it is described as a 'large volume' (60), with the possible implication that it is complete (see especially lines 58–9). The names of sixteen heroines are listed. Eight of these appear in the *Legend* as we have it (if we may include the account of Alceste in the Prologue), whilst seven do not. Moreover, three figures who have legends devoted to them— Cleopatra, Phyllis, and Philomela—are not included in the Man of Law's account. The exclusion of Cleopatra might be explained on the grounds that the Man of Law is comparing Chaucer with Ovid, who of course did not tell the story of Cleopatra, though it could be countered that he might have thought of citing her legend as a specific instance of Chaucer's having written 'Mo than Ovide made of mencioun' in the *Heroides* (54–5). The Man of Law does say that Chaucer deliberately excluded the 'wikke ensample' of Canace's incestuous love (77–80); however, it should be noted that she is included as one of the twenty-one women who briefly figure in the ballade 'Hyd, Absolon' which is enclosed within the *Legend*'s Prologue (cf. p. 339 below).

Can the Man of Law's account be regarded as an over-optimistic recommmendation of a 'large volume' on which Chaucer was working but with which he never got very far? The evidence of the 'Retracciouns' which follow the *Parson's Tale* would seem to rule that out, for there the *Legend* is referred to as 'the book of the XXV. Ladies'. Three manuscripts have 'XIX' rather than 'XXV' at this point, and two editors, W. W. Skeat and F. N. Robinson (in his first edition of Chaucer's works), have followed that reading, on the grounds that it fits in with the nineteen ladies who appear in both versions of the Prologue (F 283, G 186), but this hardly makes the emendation necessary.

I myself incline to the belief that Chaucer completed the work, or at least wrote a lot more of it than we have now, comprising the twenty-five legends that are clearly attested to by the 'Retracciouns' (after all, this excursus names works which have been lost completely) and lent general support by the introduction to the *Man of Law's Tale*. Then there is the intriguing reference to the *Legend* in the hunting treatise *The Master of Game* which Edward, second Duke of York, produced between 1406 and 1413. A citation of Chaucer's *sentence* about writing being 'the keye of alle good remembraunce' (cf. F and G Prol. 25–6) is introduced with the remark, 'as Chaucer saith in this prologe of the XXV good wymmen'. Could Edward have seen a copy of Chaucer's poem which contained all twenty-five legends?

At any rate, the 'boredom' theory (whether applied to Chaucer himself or transferred to his long-suffering narrator) should be allowed to pass gently away from Chaucer criticism. It is highly unlikely that a poet would engage in the extensive revision of the Prologue to a work in which he had lost interest (here I assume that the G Prologue is a revision of the F version). Moreover, it is quite obvious that the *Legend* had a lasting fascination for its author, for to the two references which we have already cited may be added the eager anticipations of the poem in book i of the *House of Fame* (cf. pp. 244–5 above) and at the end of *Troilus and Criseyde* (v. 1772–85). (Moreover, lines 726–34 of the *Book of the Duchess* make abundantly clear his early interest in the stories of Medea, Phyllis, and Dido, though his comments there are less than respectful.) Chaucer mentions no other work of his so often, allows it so much significance, or describes it in such detail. Lydgate, faced with the imperfect text of the *Legend*, used it as the hook on which to hang the misogynistic joke that Chaucer could not find enough women who excelled in goodness and fairness to write about (*Fall of Princes*, i. 330–6). The truth of the matter may be that Chaucer did indeed find them, but they were lost again because of those ravages of fortune and injustices of fame which he recognized with such clarity and described so well in the *House of Fame*.

Now we may come to consider the date and circumstances of the *Legend*. In the F Prologue Chaucer takes the side of the flower (82), and singles out for praise one particular species, the daisy, which is elaborately identified with the part-historical, part-emblematic Queen Alceste of Thessaly, the poem's quintessential 'good woman'. Both these images—of light-loving flower and exemplary wife—seem to be, at least in part, figures of King Richard's queen. When the poet has completed the work, Alceste says, he should present it to 'the quene, / On my byhalf, at Eltham or at Sheene' (F Prol. 496–7; not in the G Prol.). Lydgate goes so far as to say that Chaucer actually wrote the work 'at request off the queen' (*Fall of Princes*, i. 330). Is this simply his own speculation concerning the lines we have just quoted, or did he have information which enabled him to identify Alceste's command with the queen's will? What is clear is that the G Prologue, presumably written after Anne's death on 7 June 1394, omits the reference to 'the queen' and the two royal residences (it is worth remembering that the grief-stricken king ordered the destruction of Sheen). Moreover, the I-persona's declared bias in favour of the flower has been replaced by the protestation that he is not taking sides, and indeed does not know who serves the leaf and who serves the flower, a typically Chaucerian profession of ignorance (71–7). It seems reasonable to infer that, at the time the F Prologue was written, Queen Anne championed the cause of the flower, or at least was interested in the entertainments which were generated by the servants of the flower and the leaf. When she died, and the relevant lines in the *Legend* ceased to be topical, Chaucer reverted to the (quite characteristic) stance of non-partisan teller of tales from the remote past, 'Of olde story, er swich strif was begonne' (G Prol. 80).

This argument, of course, depends on several assumptions, including the priority of the F Prologue (which has sometimes been challenged, most recently by Sheila Delany, who believes that the G version was composed first, with F being the revision) and Chaucer's authorship of both versions of the Prologue, which M. C. Seymour would deny. If it is granted that Queen Anne is being referred to in F Prologue 496–7, then the poem must post-date her arrival in England in early 1382. Alceste's allusion to *Troilus and Criseyde* would seem to indicate that the Prologue could not have been written much earlier than 1385, though, as M. C. Shaner and A. S. G. Edwards note, it is perfectly possible that some of the legends themselves were composed before that date. These editors would place the F Prologue between 1386 and 1388.

It should be emphasized that there is no reason whatever to assume that the poem was addressed to Queen Anne as principal recipient—simply that this is a poem of a kind which would have found favour with her, and therefore a presentation copy could be projected. But would the Bohemian lady have understood a poem of this length and complexity in English? Gervase Mathew's words may serve as a reply: 'It is probably a mistake to conceive of Anne as a German or a Bohemian. Queen Anne was cosmopolitan and it is characteristic of the period that the international culture that formed her background had strong North French inflections' (p. 16). She was fluent in French, the international language of court poetry and song, and the prologue to Chaucer's *Legend* reads very much like a French *marguerite* or daisy poem which just happens to have been written in English, so to speak. Even if the queen had been unable to understand all the words, she certainly would have sympathized with many of the sentiments. Then again, if the poem was first performed to an aristocratic audience (which perhaps included the respective followers of the flower and the leaf), the queen would have had plenty of helpers to hand to explain and interpret it. St Valentine's Day is praised by the singing birds (F Prol. 145–7; G Prol. 131–3), but there is no indication that this was the occasion for Chaucer's poem.

The cult of the flower and the leaf was of French origin, which was probably part of its appeal for ladies of the English aristocracy. It is from a poem by Deschamps that we learn that John of Gaunt's daughter Philippa was a supporter of the flower. In a related ballade, Deschamps gives a list of distinguished Frenchmen who belong to the order of the leaf. Such elegant entertainments, as practised on both sides of the English Channel, afford yet another example of how the international (i.e. French-dominated and oriented) court culture found fertile soil in England (cf. pp. 14–19 above), and the *Floure and the Leafe* manifests how that culture continued to thrive in the fifteenth century. It would, therefore, be quite fallacious to think of the *Legend* as a backward-looking poem which fails to capitalize on the accomplishments of *Troilus and Criseyde*. True, Chaucer has returned to the dream-vision form, and (most obviously in the Prologue) to the concerns of the *dits amoreux*. But there was much life left in those traditions, as the *Legend* itself amply demonstrates.

The manuscripts are briefly described by Shaner and Edwards in the *Riverside Chaucer*, pp. 1178–9; a fuller account is provided by George Kane and Janet Cowen in the introduction to their *LGW* edition (East Lansing, Mich., 1994). For the facsimile of MS Gg.4.27 see the reference on p. 6 above. Malcolm Parkes would date it *c.*1420, which would make it the earliest surviving copy of the *LGW* (Introduction, pp. 44–56).

John Lydgate, *The Fall of Princes*, ed. H. Bergen, EETS ES 121 (London, 1924).

Even R. W. Frank, who did so much to refute the 'boredom' theory, finds it impossible to 'deny that once [Chaucer] hit upon the scheme of the *Canterbury Tales* he devoted much more time and energy to it than he did to the *Legend*' (*Chaucer and 'The Legend of Good Women*', p. 210). But Blake, 'Critics and the Canon', emphasizes the point that the *Canterbury Tales* 'may conceivably have got started before the *Legend*'. He also argues against the 'boredom' theory, and asserts that 'Since Chaucer twice gives information about his poem which indicates that it was a large work and contained the stories of twenty-five ladies, we have no business to assume that he twice made a mistake or was indicating only what he intended to include in the poem' (pp. 79, 73). Similarly, M. C. Seymour, 'Chaucer's *Legend of Good Women*: Two Fallacies', *RES* NS 37 (1986), 528–34, believes that 'the final quires of the completed work have been accidentally lost' (p. 530). However, his argument that the G Prologue is the work of an anonymous reviser (pp. 531–4) is more notable for the confidence of its assertion than for the substance of its argument.

At the other end of the scholarly spectrum is Rowe, *Nature to Eternity*, who argues that, at the time he wrote the introduction to the *Man of Law's Tale*, either Chaucer 'had realized that he was not going to complete the originally intended sequence of legends and took advantage of this fact for some humour—partly at the Man of Law's expense, partly at his own—or he never intended to include all the women mentioned' (p. 110). Rowe proceeds to explore the possibility that the poem as we have it is 'a deliberate fragment', a 'finished work that appears incomplete' (p. 112), thereby partly echoing and partly altering Goddard's view that Chaucer left the poem unfinished to highlight the absurdity of the project and the lack of women who merited praise.

Edward, *Master of Game*, pp. 3–4. There are, of course, other possible explanations of this passage. Edward might have had an incomplete copy of *LGW* which nevertheless bore an inscription which announced that it was about 'XXV good wymmen'; or he could have remembered this title from the 'Retracciouns', and connected it to his citation of a work which he himself knew only in its incomplete form.

The Shaner and Edwards references are to the *Riverside Chaucer*, pp. 1059, 1060. Delany argues that the G Prologue precedes the F version, in the first chapter of her monograph *Naked Text*.

Mathew, *Court of Richard II*. On the companies of the flower and the leaf see the discussion and references above, pp. 296–8, 305. On the difficulties inherent in using references to St Valentine's Day to help date Chaucer's poems see pp. 257–61 above.

## Verse-form, Rhetoric, and Style

The *Legend* is written in couplets, now of not eight but ten syllables, the line being close to the French or Italian decasyllabic and the predecessor of the iambic pentameter. This was not the first time that Chaucer had used this verse-form, for it features in the work which we now know as the *Knight's Tale*, an earlier version of which seems to have pre-dated the *Legend*, since it is referred to in the Prologues as 'the love of Palamon and Arcite' (F Prol. 420, G Prol. 408). Moreover, as R. W. Frank points out, the last four lines of a rhyme royal stanza (the form used in the *Parliament of Fowls* and *Troilus*) are, as a matter of fact, a pair of decasyllabic couplets (*bbcc*) which are isolated in terms of rhyme from the preceding lines (the *abab* segment), and so Chaucer had, so to speak, plenty of practice at this kind of composition before he adopted it for the *Legend*.

It was to be the main type of versification in the *Canterbury Tales*, and after Chaucer its successor, the 'heroic couplet', was to enjoy a long and distinguished career in English literature. 'He found and used nearly all the liberties and the methods of obtaining variety which later poets have employed in the five-stress iambic line,' declared Paull F. Baum (p. 11), and a good number of those liberties and methods are found in the *Legend*. If Chaucer's style is sometimes cramped here, this is not the fault of his verse as such, but is due to the exigencies of the abbreviated yet highly emotive *exempla* which constitute the actual legends of good women.

The seven-line rhyme royal stanza is used for the enclosed lyric 'Hyd, Absolon' (F Prol. 249–69, G Prol. 203–23). This follows the usual requirements of the ballade form, having three stanzas, a linking refrain, and common rhymes—that is, the *a* rhyming words in the first verse rhyme with those in the second and third, and so forth. In other words, Chaucer had to produce six different words for the *a* rhyme, nine for the *b*, and four for the *c* (since the *c* rhyming words in the refrain are of course common to all three stanzas). However, this restriction does not produce an awkward or stilted effect (one may contrast some of the rather less felicitous rhymes in the ballade *To Rosemounde*), but rather one of quiet elegance. In the F Prologue the refrain addresses 'My lady'; the 'song' is said ('seyn', not sung) in praise of the daisy queen in the God of Love's company, who is identified as Alceste over two hundred lines later (432). In the G Prologue the 'Noble quene' is named at a much earlier stage, in line 179; some twenty-four lines later the ballade is sung like a carole or dance-song by a company of nineteen ladies, the refrain now announcing that 'Alceste is here'.

An obvious point of departure for a consideration of the *Legend*'s rhetoric and style is afforded by the statement, as found only in the G Prologue (86), that Chaucer's intention is to declare 'The naked text in English' of many stories as told by 'autours'. The relevant *MED* citations (s.v. *naked* adj., 5) make it clear that, as used here, the adjective 'naked' has the sense of plain, literal, and unadorned expression which requires no explanation or comment, there being nothing concealed, complicated, or obscure about it. In the Middle English lexicon it can function as a synonym of, or at least semantically overlap with, the adjective *plain(e)*. 'Plain' language is expression which is clear, direct, and to the point (perhaps even blunt), lacking in complexity or embellishment, innocent of the figures of rhetoric. (Approximately fifty years after Chaucer's death, Lydgate was using the phrase 'plain English'.) Chaucer's brief statement therefore invokes several discourses: of manifest literal meaning *versus* hidden or allegorical sense which requires commentary, of the process of translation from Latin to English, and of literary language which is (allegedly) lacking in ornamentation. Something must be said about each of them.

In the C fragment of the *Romaunt of the Rose* (probably not the work of Chaucer) the 'nakid text' is opposed to the 'glose' or interpretation of what is said in the text:

> And if men wolde ther-geyn appose          *consult*
> The nakid text, and lete the glose,          *leave*
> It myghte soon assoiled be                *disproved*
> (6555-7)

In medieval scholarship on certain classical poets and on the Bible, many a 'glose' was of an allegorical nature, and so this distinction may briefly be explored with reference to both those kinds of writing. In the twelfth-century renaissance certain philosophical truths were sometimes supposed to have been transmitted under a garment (*integumentum*) or veil (*involucrum*) of poetic fiction. An excellent example is afforded by William of Conches' interpretation of the birth of Venus. 'Consider Jupiter cutting off his father's testicles and throwing them in the sea so that Venus is born,' he requests. 'The testicles signify the fruits of the earth, through which, in the course of time, the seed from the bowels of the earth is diffused more and more . . . The fruits are cast into the sea, that is, into the hollow maw of the human belly, and thus Venus—that is, sensual delight—is born' (trans. Dronke, p. 26). This is the sort of interpretation which Jean de Meun had in mind when, in the context of Reason's discussion of the same fable, he has her remark that the Lover would understand its inner truth if he reviewed *les integumenz aus poetes*: 'There you will see a large part of the secrets of philosophy. . . . in the playful fables of the poets lie very profitable delights beneath which they cover their thoughts when they clothe the truth in fables' (7168–78; trans. Dahlberg, p. 136). Here Reason, it should be added, also defends her reference to Jupiter's 'balls' (*coilles*) 'according to the letter, without gloss' (7184–5), in plain French as it were! The coverings of fable are being rejected in favour of unashamed nakedness—nakedness both of the subject of the discourse and of the discourse itself—though Jean (typically) wants to drop the veil and keep it as well.

However, in the twelfth-century commentary tradition it was fully acknowledged that certain poets believed there was 'more enterprise / In walking naked' (to borrow a phrase from wicked Willie Yeats).* The Roman satirists Horace, Juvenal, and Persius had torn aside falsehoods and disguises to reveal facts about society which were unobscured by poetic invention or ornamentation. Hence, a representative twelfth-century commentator on Juvenal can declare that 'satire is naked . . . because it censures the vices of the romans nakedly, and openly, and clearly, and without circumlocution and periphrasis, and without an *integumentum*' (trans. Minnis and Scott, p. 116). And Conrad of Hirsau, in comparing satyrs with satiric poets, explains that while the former are not embarrassed to expose themselves publicly without care for clothing (*nichil tractantes de tegumentis*), the latter are not restrained from their objective of making 'the depraved suffer under the naked outspokenness of their words' (trans. Minnis and Scott, p. 61). That is to say, it is unnecessary to interpret Roman satire allegorically, because it conveys its moral message 'at the first, literal level of meaning', as Paul Miller puts it (p. 27).

Returning to Chaucer, it may be said that he is requesting an immediately literal understanding of his declarations of 'stories' as told by

---

* Here I cite Yeats' poem 'A Coat'. For the wickedness, see e.g. 'the Wild Old Wicked Man'.

'autours' (G Prol. 86); they do not need to be uncovered either by him, within his own discourse, or by the reader in some elaborate gloss. Chaucer's actual handling of sources bears this out. The *Ovide moralisé*, certainly a minor source of the *Legend* (cf. pp. 348–9 below), contains much integumental analysis, but Chaucer seems to have been quite uninterested in, say, its account of the joint burial of Pyramus and Thisbe as 'a figure of the dual nature of Jesus, whose suffering demonstrates the necessity for patience and for the love of God shown by martyrs' (to follow Sheila Delany's summary, p. 287), or Jason's winning of the Golden Fleece as a representation of Christ's incarnation, which enabled the salvation of mankind (*Ovide moralisé*, 799–820), while Creusa is the false beauties of the world which lead men and women astray, ensuring that they will perish in fire at the Last Judgement (1644–72).

This view may be supported further by evidence from the relevant tradition of Bible commentary. The *Summoner's Tale* affords a good point of departure. There a money-grabbing friar inflicts on his intended victim a sermon which does not completely follow 'the text of hooly writ', which (according to him) the uneducated find difficult to understand; rather, he will teach him 'all the glose' (*Summoner's Tale*, III(D) 1790–2). A specific instance of this privileging of interpretation occurs when 'frere John' explains that, while he cannot cite an actual biblical 'text' to prove that Christ was especially thinking of friars when he commended the poor in spirit, he can 'fynde it in a manner glose' (III(D) 1919–23). Little wonder, then, that this unscrupulous individual can exclaim,

> Glosynge is a glorious thyng, certeyn,
> For lettre sleeth, so as we clerkes seyn
> (*Summoner's Tale*, III(D) 1793–4)

This, of course, alludes to 2 Corinthians 3: 6, where St Paul declares that 'the letter kills, but the spirit gives life'. The Apostle was making a specific contrast between the spiritual and internal qualities of the New Law and the external 'tablets of stone' of the Old, but his words were often taken as a justification for allegorical exegesis of Scripture. However, some late medieval schoolmen came to believe that an excess of allegorical interpretations was killing 'the letter' of Scripture by smothering it. Near the beginning of his widely influential *Postilla litteralis* on the whole Bible, Nicholas of Lyre, OFM (*c*.1270–1340) complained that 'the literal sense of the text has been much obscured' by certain exegetes in the past. 'Although they have said much that is good, yet they have so multiplied the number of mystical senses that the literal sense is in some part cut off and suffocated among so many mystical senses' (trans. Minnis and Scott, p. 269). This is not to say, of course, that scriptural allegorization ceased: on the contrary, it flourished in preaching (Lyre himself compiled a *Postilla moralis* for 'readers of Bibles and preachers of the Word of God'), and indeed in monastic Bible study. But the status of the 'spiritual sense' had certainly been called in question, and thus a climate of opinion was created wherein, for example, certain kinds of glossing could be regarded suspiciously (as in the *Summoner's Tale*), and a theologian could commend his exegesis by saying that it paid close attention to the specific *textus* or *lettera* of Scripture, and to its 'literal sense' (*sensus litteralis*).

Some of Wyclif's followers took these ideas to what they regarded as a logical conclusion, in creating an 'open' English translation of the Latin Bible which could be widely understood. It was not, it should be emphasized, that the Lollards were against glossing as such; indeed, they produced a Bible commentary known as the 'Glossed Gospels', to cite but one testimony of their interest in earlier Bible commentary. And there is nothing specifically Lollard about the discourse of translation which we find reflected in the *Legend*; rather, we are dealing with commonplaces. Hence in the preface to *The Myroure of oure Ladye* (the Brigittine Breviary of Syon, translated between 1415 and 1450) the 'nakyd letter' is used as a point of contrast with the exposition which glosses provide; yet such exposition is seen as functioning in full co-operation with the text's literal statement, the shared and single objective being total clarity. 'In many places where the nakyd letter is, thoughe yt be set in englyshe, ys not easy for some symple soulles to vnderstonde; I expounde yt and declare yt more openly, other before the letter, or after or wlse fourthewyth togyther' (ed. Blunt, p. 3). Thus, a translator could commend his work by saying that it was literal, plain, and open, yet not so subservient to the letter of the Latin that it was barely comprehensible. This, then, is the way in which we should take Chaucer's assurance to little Lewis, that in the *Treatise on the Astrolabe* he will find 'full light reules [i.e. uncomplicated principles of language construction] and naked wordes in Englissh', since he has 'but small' Latin. And how we should read the God of Love's accusation of Chaucer for having translated 'in pleyn text, withouten nede of glose' the 'Romaunce of the Rose', which is a heresy against his law (F Prol. 328–30; cf. G Prol. 254: 'in pleyn text, it nedeth nat to glose'). Here the sense is that the text is open and plain to such an extent that it does not need the assistance of any gloss at all. And that, I believe, is the main point of Chaucer's statement of intent, 'The naked text in English to declare'.

The possibility that Chaucer was also implying that his text lacked rhetorical embellishment must, however, be considered as well. At the end of the *Confessio Amantis* Gower claims to have 'no Rethorique . . . /

Upon the forme of eloquence', but rather words which are 'rude' and 'pleyne' (viii. 3064–8*; cf. viii. 3115–22). Chaucer's Franklin excuses his 'rude speche' in similar terms:

> I lerned nevere rethorik, certeyn;
> Thyng that I speke, it moot be bare and pleyn
>
> (V(F) 719–20)

But both speakers are adopting a conventional 'modesty formula'; neither of them seriously wanted to produce a text which was stripped naked of all rhetorical colours and flowers. The same may be said about the *Legend*, which contains passage after passage wherein language is wearing its finest clothes. A few examples must suffice to substantiate this point.

Like the *Parliament of Fowls* the *Legend* begins with a *sententia* or profound, general statement (F Prol. 1–3, G Prol. 1–3). 'Let a well-chosen *sententia* incline in no respect to the particular, but rather raise its head higher, to something universal,' advises Geoffrey of Vinsauf in the *Poetria nova* (trans. Kopp, p. 37), and Chaucer's statement about there being joy in heaven and pain in hell certainly does that, being far removed from the particulars which he will treat later in the poem. It may be added that this *sententia* moves into *ratiocinatio*, which involves the posing of questions and the provision of answers by the narrator. Other *sententiae* occur at F Prol. 376–8, G Prol. 356–8; F Prol. 381–3, G Prol. 365–7; 735, 1187, 1389–93, etc.

Given the studied emotionalism of the writing, it is hardly surprising that there are many types of apostrophe (*apostrophatio*), wherein the speaker addresses himself or another person or thing: F Prol. 10–11, G Prol. 10–11; F Prol. 249–69, G Prol. 203–23; F Prol. 505–7, G Prol. 493–5; 658, 681–95, 756–66, 838–9, 905–7, 924–9, 1303–8, 1316–24, 1355–65, 1368–83, 1672–7, 1819–24, 1952–8, 2187–8, 2210–17, 2228–37, 2496–513, 2518–29, 2533–54, etc. And there are some splendid rhetorical questions, or *interrogationes*, for example at 742, 1027–32, 1086, 1098, 1254–9, 1797–803, 1819–24. *Repetitio* abounds, being one of the most highly used *figurae verborum*: F Prol. 22–4, G Prol. 22–4 ('Of . . .'); F Prol. 55–7 ('And . . .'); F Prol. 322–4, G Prol. 249–51 ('And . . .'); 717–18 ('That . . .'), 743–44 ('Ye . . .'), 813–16 ('And . . .'), 874–8 ('How . . .'), 1066–71 ('And . . .'), 1115–22 ('Ne . . .').

However, it must be admitted that the rhetoric of the prologues differs in certain respects from that of the narratives. For a start, the prologues are full of rich *descriptiones*, including the depictions of beautiful landscapes, the daisy queen Alceste, and the God of Love. In the legends themselves, however, this device appears very infrequently. The description of sunrise on that fateful day on which Pyramus and Thisbe decide to 'stele awey' (772–6) is too short to have much of an impact. Chaucer's account of the marriage of Hypermnestra and Lyno does manage to be significant despite the fact that it is only eight lines long (2610–17). Of a quite different order are the vivid account of the sea battle at Actium in the *Legend of Cleopatra* (where Chaucer's use of alliteration is particularly interesting; 635–53) and the two substantial *descriptiones* in the *Legend of Dido*, at 1114–27 (the queen's hospitality) and 1198–215 (Dido and Aeneas setting off to hunt). Within the curtailed and curtailing narrative which Chaucer is producing they are quite exceptional. *Descriptio* is of course one of the major constituents of *amplificatio*, the expansion and elaboration of material, whereas in the legends Chaucer is concerned with the opposite procedure—that is, with shortening or abbreviation (whether actual or alleged).

In abbreviation, explains Geoffrey of Vinsauf in his *Documentum de modo et arte dictandi et versificandi*, 'all those things which lead to prolixity are to be avoided' (*Documentum*, trans. Parr, p. 52). 'Let there be compressed into a modest circumference a little summary of the material,' recommends the *Poetria nova* (p. 58), and a thirteenth-century commentary on this work explains that here Geoffrey is teaching that in *abbreviatio* 'only the gist needs to be stated so that nothing is left out yet nothing superfluous is there in the brevity of the utterance' (trans. Woods, p. 65). Here, then, are the principles which, quite clearly, Chaucer was striving to follow. They guided him in the creation of 'relatively simple stories' which, as R. W. Frank has put it so well, must have 'events, sequence, memorability, meaning—but above all, events, action. . . . They are not very complex, but complexity is not essential to a tale, indeed not always desirable' ('Some Implications', p. 74). Here, then, is 'nakedness' of a kind. A distinctly relative kind.

One of the methods whereby Chaucer achieves his abbreviation involves considerable use of the figure of *occupatio* (otherwise called *occultatio* or *praelepsis*), which announces that certain details are being left out and/or that certain topics are being passed over hastily, with only the briefest mention. A frequent version of *occupatio* occurs when something is omitted on the grounds that there is a more important matter to consider. Geoffrey's commentator gives two examples of this, one of which is: 'I pass over the thefts, the betrayals, the crimes; I turn to the woman who has been uncovered' (p. 111). Similarly, Chaucer refuses to go into all the details of Cleopatra's wedding, on the grounds that he has to concentrate on what 'bereth more effect and charge' (616–20). 'Men', he adds, 'may overlade a ship or barge' (621), and he has no intention of so doing. Similarly, in the *Legend of Dido* the narrator says that he could follow Virgil word for word, but it would take too long

(1002–3; cf. 994–7, where he is concerned about 'los of tyme'). But *occupatio*, as Geoffrey's commentator makes clear, may be used 'when we say that we are silent about or pass over or do not know something that we are in fact emphasizing' (p. 111), and there are several good examples of this technique in the *Legend*. The narrator's refusal to recount all the details of Cleopatra's wedding (already cited) indicates that the queen's marriage to Antony was a proper and public event. Then again, in his account of Hypsipyle he ostentatiously wishes to God that he had the time to recount the entire 'proces' of Jason's wooing of the princess, and directs the reader to the 'orignyal, that telleth al the cas' (1552–8). Thus the impression is created that that particular courtship was long and complicated, which is precisely what Chaucer wants to emphasize, given his interest in depicting men who are capable of perpetrating the most elaborate forms of deceit and women who are (honourably and properly) slow to be won. Frank suggests that this should be regarded as a 'false *occupatio*' given that there is no actual 'orignyal' to follow here, since Chaucer is 'improvising from the sketchy outline of a story in the lyrical *Heroides*' (p. 202). But perhaps that slightly misses the point. *Occupatio* is not, or at least need not be, a marker of genuine omission of material by the author/translator. Rather, it is a rhetorical device which may have its own agenda, so to speak—and it definitely has in the two cases which I have just cited

The *figura verborum* of *occupatio*, as used by Chaucer in the *Legend*, certainly has its risks. As Frank has demonstrated so convincingly, most of the material which certain critics have cited in proof of their contention that Chaucer got bored with the poem actually appear in *occupationes* (see especially the narrator's statement that he is too weary to give a full account of the wedding of Tereus and Procne; 2255–8). The failure to recognize a rhetorical device for what it is thus contributed to what Frank (rightly I believe) would deem a highly dubious view of Chaucer's attitude to the *Legend*. Heavy use is made of *occupatio* in, for example, the *Knight's Tale* (for instance see I(A) 875–88, 994–1000, 1201, 1380, 1459–61, 1463–4, etc.), but no one has thought of arguing that Chaucer got bored with that poem.

Then there is the fact that *occupatio* may be used to create a comic effect, as was fully recognized by the theorists (see, for example, Geoffrey's *Documentum*; p. 93). Now, at certain points in the *Legend* that seems to be Chaucer's intention, as when he remarks:

> This honurable Phillis doth hym [i.e. Demophon] chere;
> Hire liketh wel his port and his manere.
> But, for I am agroted herebyforn                      *surfeited*
> To wryte of hem that ben in love forsworn,

And ek to haste me in my legende,
(Which to performe God me grace sende)
Therfore I passe shortly in this wyse.                    (2452–8)

The suggestion that the poet is wryly poking fun at his narrator here, in face of the enormity of the task which has been undertaken, is quite consonant with the apparent meaning of other passages of self-presentation in the poem, where *occupatio* is not being used. Elsewhere, however, the tone is harder to gauge, and it is all too possible to read *occupationes* which might have a serious purpose and/or standard rhetorical functions as amusingly curt dismissals of material which is embarrassing (because it does not support the profession of female virtue) or parodic.

When the rhetorical manuals discussed the *exemplum*, they were thinking primarily of a short-term and local comparison, and of course instances of such devices occur throughout Chaucer's poetry. However, in the fourteenth century exemplification was also practised as a large-scale narrative mode, which worked through careful restriction of meaning and judicious highlighting of only those aspects of a story which were most relevant to the general truth which the writer wished to illustrate. In other words, to make a story—which in its original form may include a wide range of themes and implications—into an *exemplum* is, as it were, to put the blinkers on that story, by directing it to a specific end in a way which entails the elimination of those features of the narrative which, to continue the metaphor, look to the left and the right of the straight and narrow path down which it is to be directed. This is not to claim that late medieval exemplary narratives are invariably simple in resonance and skeletal in significance. In fact, many of them contain elaborate and pleasurable detail, which contributes in no small measure to their success. A tale of this type, however, is 'seyd' for a specific 'conclusioun' (to adapt the very last line of the incomplete *Legend*), and that 'conclusioun' establishes the channel along which the story's energies should flow.

Exemplary narrative had, for generations, been used by preachers, and in their literary theory may be found much information about the relevant stylistic considerations. The necessity of careful control is emphasized in Humbert of Romans' remark to the effect that, when a long narrative is being adapted to point a particular moral, 'the useless or less useful things must be cut out, and only what is relevant to the subject must be narrated' (Welter, p. 73). The very real power exercised by the manipulator of narratives was fully recognized, as is revealed by the rhetorician Matthew of Vendôme's statement that 'examples must be referred back to the intention of the exemplifier [*mens exemplificantis*]' (*Arts poétiques*, ed. Faral, p. 150). To know the story-teller's purpose is to know the semantic limits within which his story operates. When poets like Jean de Meun, Deschamps, Froissart, Machaut, Chaucer, and Gower appropriated the methodology of exemplification to serve their own ends, their writing inherited the semantic restriction which is of the very essence of that methodology. One simply cannot say, therefore, that Chaucer's depiction of Medea (to take the toughest test case) must *inevitably* be ironic, for she was frequently placed in a good light in the *exempla* of Chaucer's predecessors, contemporaries, and successors. For instance, in Deschamps' *Lay de Franchise*, a poem which seems to have influenced the prologue to the *Legend*, the emphasis is on the considerable assistance which Medea rendered Jason because of her great love for him. Moreover, as J. L. Lowes pointed out long ago (in his attack on Goddard's 'travesty' theory), Medea, along with some of the other heroines who figure in the *Legend*, frequently appears in catalogues of ladies who define the standards of comparison necessary for praising one's own lady. Good examples are provided by Deschamps' *Lay de department* and the ballades which begin 'Judith en fais, Lucresse en voulenté' and 'Hester, Judith, Penelopé, Helaine' (cf. the discussion of the Medea story in the 'Sources' section below).

With these may be compared Chaucer's own ballade 'Hyd, Absolon, thy gilte tresses clere', in the two versions as they appear in the prologues to the *Legend*. The first stanza includes reference to Absolon, as a type of beauty, and Jonathan, as a type of friendship. If the reader applies information which is beyond the bounds of the exemplary specification— for example, the very basic fact that these people were men—the effect of the passage is undermined. In the same stanza, Isolde is advised to hide her beauty, because it cannot compete with that of the lady being praised by the poet. The remark that Isolde had an adulterous relationship (with Tristram) would be beside the point, and quite detrimental to the poem's objective of decorous compliment.

In sum, in exemplification subjectivities are conventionalized into representatives of particular attributes or qualities. Modern readers who value narrative abundance and ambivalence may, quite understandably, incline towards the reintroduction of what the exemplifiers have so carefully removed. But this is to go against the grain of the illustrative strategy and to misunderstand its *modus operandi*. The obvious inference is that Chaucer's legends of Cupid's saints should be accepted as taking on their meaning within the parameters which the exemplifier has defined, and read as stories of women who were true in love. After all, eight of those alleged saints are named in 'Hyd, Absolon, thy gilte tresses clere': are the actual legends not functioning in exactly the same way as this ballade functions, the only difference being one of scale?

This view has much to commend it, but a major caveat must be entered. There was no obligation to accept what a writer had made of a story. The best-known exemplary types and situations were very much 'in the public domain', and an author could take someone else's *exemplum* and rework it in such a way that its import was quite altered. Moreover, one could protest against an imposition of significance which seemed unsuitable, or even unfair, to the narrative in question. In his *Jugement dou Roy de Navarre*, for instance, Machaut had his persona accuse one of the other figures of using *exempla* which do not fit the meaning she is trying to draw from them. The treason of either Theseus or Jason has nothing to do with the issue under debate, he exclaims, adding, 'I wouldn't give two apples / For proving your point / By the introduction of *exempla* such as these' (2823–32; trans. Palmer, p. 127). On many occasions in his *œuvre* Chaucer reveals himself as being very aware of the limits and restrictions of exemplification; indeed, he can exploit those very limits to achieve sophisticated literary effects. Sometimes he emphasizes the contrast which, on the one hand, can exist between the tale and its alleged significance and, on the other, between the morality of the *exemplificans* and the *moralitas* of the *exemplum*. For instance, the Canterbury tale which the Physician tells of virtuous Virginia (like Lucrece, a clear candidate for secular sainthood) raises far more issues than are covered by its imposed and artificial 'conclusioun'. As Anne Middleton has demonstrated, we are encouraged to examine the moral problem surrounding the action of Virginia's father (in killing her rather than allowing her to be dishonoured) not by the force of external evidence—which, in accordance with our argument above, could be ruled out as being contrary to the spirit of exemplification—but 'because the tale itself offers incompatible ethical and generic systems for understanding it, and forces us to vacillate thoughtfully among them' (p. 23).

The *Legend* can be read in a similar way. Through the interactions of the poem's prologue and narratives we are offered value and generic systems which are in a state of tension; yet to say that they are incompatible would be reductive, since principles are in play which enable occasional and/or partial reconciliation. It is, moreover, essential to refer the amatory *exempla* back to the *mens exemplificantis*. The exemplifier who has made the legends (and who is still actively involved with them as both performer and respondent) is constructed as a figure with distinctive, and distancing, characteristics, which in large measure are familiar from the personae of the *Parliament of Fowls* and the *House of Fame*. Yet—in marked contrast with the narrators of those other poems—this persona does not bear the responsibility for what he makes, for here he is writing to order, carrying out a commission. To be more exact, he is attempting to serve two masters (or rather, a master and a mistress), the God of Love, whose directives are complicated by the same irony which raises questions about his own status, and Alceste, queen of good women, whose credentials as patroness and favoured topic of pro-feminist poetry seem to be impeccable. The differences between this less-than-mutual pair function as faultlines within the poem's entire structure and strategy. And because the directors of Cupid's exemplifier are not wholly in accord, it is to be expected that the poem he supposedly writes for them will contain elements which are not wholly in accord.

That argument will be pursued later (pp. 396–8 below); here other aspects of the larger stylistic procedures of the *Legend* must be considered. First, it should be noted that in medieval rhetorical and dialectical practice one and the same source could be cited both in support of, and against, a given proposition, and this was true of the treatment of materials relating to women. Indeed, this kind of manipulation of *auctoritates* (passages extracted from the *auctores*) was the corner-stone of medieval academic methodology. Alcuin Blamires, whose splendid anthology of medieval writings for and against women, *Woman Defamed and Woman Defended* (1992), contains many cases of such casuistry, suggests that 'the intelligentsia' sometimes regarded 'the rhetorical formulae of misogyny as a game', in so far as it provided a 'suitable arena in which to show off their literary paces' (p. 12). He goes on to cite the example of the extravagantly anti-feminist *Lamentations* of Matheolus, in the French translation (c.1371–2) of Jehan le Fèvre. This seems to have been the text which Christine de Pizan famously objected to at the beginning of her *Cité des Dames*, one of her criticisms being that it treated its subject frivolously ('en manière de trufferie'; cf. Blamires, p. 177). That is to say, she suspected Jehan le Fèvre of having produced a piece of writing which was more interested in showing off rhetorical skills than in seeking out the truth about women. And in his *Livre de Leesce* Jehan continued to play the game; this work systematically refutes Matheolus's anti-feminist arguments with the same force and vigour which he had employed in presenting them. Similarly, in the *Liber decem capitulorum* of Marbod of Rennes (c.1035–1123) a chapter on the destructive woman (*meretrix*) is followed by one on the good woman (*matrona*; trans. Blamires, pp. 100–3, 228–32). In two of its manuscripts the thirteenth-century *Blasme des Fames* ('The Vices of Women') is followed by the *Bien des Fames* ('The Virtues of Women'). Chaucer's discourse in praise of women in the *Legend* certainly presupposes its contrary. But the question raised by the texts we have just cited is: does it actually call it forth, the implication being that it is the contrary of Chaucer's presentation which is to be believed rather than the actual presentation itself? Or should the pro and the con be put on a par, and dismissed as equally extreme?

The crux of whether Chaucer has described women here *en manière de trufferie* can be confronted only after the sources and form of the *Legend* have been discussed. Suffice it to note here that *some* (that specification is important) of the extremely condemnatory things which he said in the poem—by which I mean of course his forceful attacks on men and male behaviour in love—can find a justification in medieval theory of satiric style. In the *querelle de la Rose* Jean de Montreuil advises an unknown opponent that Jean de Meun was 'an exacting satirist' (trans. Baird and Kane, p. 44). It was generally accepted that satire speaks in a way which is blunt and direct, indeed 'naked' (as was explained above). When reading works written in the genre, one should therefore expect, and accept, such a style. On the same argument, Chaucer's 'naked' text professes to tell the simple truth about menfolk, but this is utterly typical of satirical writing—outspoken statement is not necessarily fair comment, and therefore the meaning of the poem is not to be sought therein. So, the text's ambivalence cannot be resolved by such means.

Given that medieval satire, in conscious imitation of its Roman antecedents, set out to call a spade a bloody shovel rather than an agricultural implement, it claimed the right to use language which was indecorous (or rather, which would have been indecorous in a more elevated genre) and even indecent. The issue of whether there is obscene punning in the *Legend* has been raised by Sheila Delany (though not with reference to what was acceptable in satiric writing). For example, she argues that in the *Legend of Thisbe* Chaucer is improving on Ovid's image of the 'narrow crack' in the wall which separates the two lovers (*Metamorphoses*, iv. 65–6), as read obscenely by Alan of Lille, by having the word 'clyfte' appear no less than three times in eight lines (740–7) in a context which suggests the cleft in the buttocks. To this cleft the lovers apply their lips, and moreover they kiss the wall's 'ston' (768)—'two suggestions of unorthodox sexual contact' (p. 193). The statement made by Thisbe, on the brink of suicide, that her 'woful hand' is 'strong ynogh in swich a werk to me' (890–1) is read as an allusion to female masturbation, and the next couplet (where she says that love will make her wound large enough) is taken as alluding to the vulva. Because of these and other passages Delany concludes that there is 'plenty of snigger and leer' (p. 191) in the *Legend*.

The interpretative issues here are particularly vexed ones. It is made very clear by the courtesy books that people of noble birth (both men and women) were not supposed to take pleasure in scurrilities. The *Gawain* poet upholds 'clene cortays carp [conversation] closed from fylthe' as an ideal (*Sir Gawain and the Green Knight*, 1013), and Christine de Pizan's attack on obscenity in the *Roman de la Rose*, on the grounds that it debased women, is well known. Moreover, certain rhetorical manuals warn against the use of obscenity (see especially *Rhetoria ad Herennium*, iv. 34. 45). On the other hand, it should be noted that the enjoyment of *fabliaux*, which are often indecent, cut across gender barriers (and indeed class barriers). Yet even here explicit obscenities are uncommon, and in French courtly romance they are very rare indeed. However, some of the surviving *demaundes d'amour* are quite *risqué*, and the same can occasionally be said of other aristocratic pastimes, such as fortune-telling games. And troubadour poems can include blatant obscenities; as Simon Gaunt remarks, Marcabru's work has a 'surprisingly large number' of them (p. 59). Since he constructs himself as a moralist, no doubt he could have claimed the 'satire justification'. But Marcabru's interest in such devices verges on the obsessive, and it seems reasonable to assume that many poets would simply not have risked offending some of their auditors or readers with an obscene metaphor or euphemism.

   Would Chaucer have taken the risk of including a substantial amount of obscenity, of however hidden a kind, in a poem intended for a privileged audience which included at least some women (cf. my point, as made on p. 25 above, that a few female auditors in a courtly audience could have a significance quite out of proportion to their numbers), and might even have included the Queen of England? I very much doubt it. Had the poet engaged in blatant obscene punning, he would tacitly have included himself among the ranks of churlish men (cf. the careful location of churlish speech and 'harlotrie' in the *Miller's Prologue*, I(A) 3167 86) who are the villains of the legends, and, even more damagingly, have undermined the presentation of his 'gentil' and generous heroines. Then it could have been said of him, as Christine de Pizan said of Jean de Meun, 'you commit great wrong against the noble virtue of modesty, which by its nature bridles indecency and dishonourable conduct in words and deeds' (trans. Baird and Kane, pp. 48–9). Moreover, it would be difficult to reconcile Chaucer's valorization of marital and familial values (on which, more below) with 'plenty of snigger and leer'.

   I would not be so bold as to suggest that the *Legend* is utterly free from sexual innuendo; simply that the scale and extent of the implication which Delany postulates is unlikely. Besides, her disclosures of obscenity are, I believe, often far-fetched and evocative of modern rather than fourteenth-century sexuality. The ironic obscenities found, for example, by Simon Gaunt in troubadour poetry and by Jacquart and Thomasset in the *De amore* of Andreas Capellanus and its French translation by

Drouart la Vache are a lot more convincing. And Don Monson's critique of some of Betsy Bowden's suggestions regarding Andreas's use of obscenity may serve to remind us of the overriding importance of having unimpeachable linguistic grounds on which to base bawdy 'discoveries'. But of course, one's opinion on the question of obscenity in the *Legend* ultimately depends on the view taken on the overall strategy of the poem and the generic expectations which it sets up. In my view, the poem can be read as a *commendatio mulierum*, granted its instabilities of meaning and contestations of the normative (and with full recognition of the fact that other readings are quite possible, given the paradoxical and ambivalent nature of the discourses which the text deploys). At any rate, the 'satire justification' for the use of risqué language could apply only partially to the *Legend*; it reads very differently from the innuendo-laden *Wife of Bath's Prologue*, where Chaucer has, quite obviously, appropriated satiric discourse.

Finally, a word on Chaucer's cultivation of the pathetic style in his *Legend*. Though Chaucerian pathos makes its presence felt in many of the other Shorter Poems, as has been noted elsewhere in the present book, the *Legend* may be regarded as the poet's most consistent and sustained experiment in this *modus loquendi*. In attempting to locate its roots, it is important to acknowledge the importance of that sentimentalization of religious feeling, or 'affective piety' as it is often called, which was in full flow in Chaucer's day. Readers of texts like the Pseudo-Bonaventuran *Meditationes vitae Christi* were invited to empathize with the emotions of the main figures involved, to share (for example) the pains and pleasures of Mary as mother of the Christ-child, and particularly her suffering as she watched her son die on the cross. The plastic arts often invited similar involvement, making participation possible for literate and illiterate alike. One has only to think of the famous example of that most gifted of all weepers, Margery Kempe (*c*.1373–*c*.1440), who at the sight of a *pietà* 'was compelleyd to cryyn ful lowde & wepyn ful sor', as if she would have died (i. 60).

The secular *planctus* ('complaint') was a well-established genre by Chaucer's time; but as far as the *Legend* is concerned, the most important of the relevant stylistic models was indubitably Ovid's *Heroides*, that collection of emotive epistles which, the Man of Law tells us, the poet was seeking to surpass in this work. Chaucer was, of course, responding directly to the classical text, but it should be noted that Ovidian 'interior monologues' underlie many of the impersonations of female emotion in the French 'romances of antiquity' (the *Roman de Thèbes, Roman d'Eneas,* and Benoît de Sainte-Maure's *Roman de Troie*), as Barbara Nolan has pointed out. Therefore Chaucer would, so to speak, have been a beneficiary of Ovid's work indirectly as well as directly. But was the *Heroides* a beneficial influence on his style? Opinions have differed widely; Frank's generally positive view contrasts sharply with H. A. Kelly's belief that the poem's 'ceaselessly plaintive tone', which he finds 'oppressive', is in part due to Chaucer's 'excessive dependence on the *Heroides*'. 'The lamentations of Ovid's unfortunate heroines tended to be repetitive', Kelly continues, because 'they dealt for the most part with the disastrous aftermath of love, and not with love in the making'. Although Chaucer is free to tell his tales from their very beginnings, 'the incubus of catastrophe rarely allows the action to leave the ground' (p. 119).

Reactions to the *Heroides* itself have been just as divergent. For example, Florence Verducci has recently attacked that 'willful credulity' which has hindered understanding of the *Heroides*, as exemplified by Willa Cather's remark that they 'are the most glowing love stories ever told'. Verducci's own reading is an ironic one, which refutes the notion that Ovid was seeking to achieve 'melodramatic sentiment or sublime pathos' (p. 20). This is the antithesis of W. S. Anderson's view that in the *Heroides* 'a new note of genuine dramatic pathos' is heard (p. 67). In short, we cannot establish this Ovidian text as a secure site on which to base speculation about the implications of Chaucer's emotive style in the *Legend*, for that space is itself contested (a matter to which we will return in discussing the *Heroides* in the section on 'Sources'). The problems of historicizing both texts—the Roman collection and the medieval courtly construction—in terms of that very elusive cultural category, reader expectation, are formidable. Two generalizations may, however, be risked.

The first is that the intent to create genuine pathos may often be inferrable from the literary context and one's sense of the overall structure and strategy of the work in question. My discussion of the structure and strategy of the *Legend* (cf. pp. 378–99) supports the theory that Chaucer was indeed concerned with the creation of moments of great emotional intensity, wherein women who can be regarded as passive, innocent, and helpless (at least for the duration of the narrative) protest, in a manner at once private and public, about the suffering which unworthy, inferior men have inflicted upon them.

Secondly, tastes and fashions in sensibility often differ markedly, as between cultures and historical periods, and some cognizance should be taken of this. It is salutary to recall that Alfred Lord Tennyson was much affected by the pathos of the *Legend*. Having taken this poem by 'Dan Chaucer, the first warbler' and 'morning star of song' as his bedtime book, his 'heart, / Brimful of those wild tales',

Charged both mine eyes with tears. In every land
I saw, wherever light illumineth,
Beauty and anguish walking hand in hand
The downward slope to death.
Those far-renowned brides of ancient song
Peopled the hollow dark, like burning stars,
And I heard sounds of insult, shame, and wrong.

To dismiss that reaction as 'willful credulity' would be at best meaningless, at worst a judgement of considerable arrogance.

Charles Muscatine's summing up of the situation regarding pathos can hardly be bettered. 'To an extraordinary degree', he says, it is 'relative to individual taste and sensibility. One man's tenderness is another man's mawkishness. One generation is taught to weep, another to hold back the tears' (p. 128). In an age in which many readers are inclined to regard, say, the death of Little Nell as crass sentimentalism, a reaction which Dickens certainly did not expect from the public that he knew so well, it is quite possible that what Chaucer meant as pathos could be read as bathos. That would be to miss much, and to lose more.

Baum, *Chaucer's Verse*; Frank, *Legend of Good Women*.

Peter Dronke, *Fabula: Explorations into the Uses of Myth in Medieval Platonism* (Leiden, 1974); Minnis and Scott (eds.), *Medieval Literary Theory*; *Roman de la Rose*, ed. Langlois, trans. Dahlberg.

Paul Miller, 'The Mediaeval Literary Theory of Satire and its Relevance to the Works of Gower, Langland and Chaucer' (Ph.D. thesis, The Queen's University of Belfast, 1982); see further his article 'John Gower, Satiric Poet', in Minnis (ed.), *Gower's 'Confessio Amantis'*, pp. 79–105.

*Ovide moralisé*, ed. de Boer. Sheila Delany, 'The Naked Text, Chaucer's "Thisbe", the *Ovide moralisé*, and the Problem of *Translatio Studii* in the *Legend of Good Women*', *Mediaevalia*, 13 (1987), 275–94. On Nicholas of Lyre's literalistic exegesis see Minnis and Scott (eds.), *Medieval Literary Theory*, pp. 204, 266–76; also Minnis, *Medieval Theory of Authorship*, pp. 86, 108–9, etc. *The Myroure of oure Ladye*, ed. J. H. Blunt, EETS ES 19 (London, 1873), p. 3. Delany's claim that the phrase 'naked text' came to Chaucer *via* the Wycliffites is highly dubious: this is found in her forthcoming paper 'Chaucer's *Legend of Good Women*: The Relevance of Wyclif'. A more detailed and complicated picture is offered in the third chapter of her monograph *The Naked Text*.

Geoffrey of Vinsauf, *Poetria nova*, ed. Faral, trans. Kopp; *idem*, *Documentum*, ed. Faral, trans. Parr; Woods (ed. and trans.), *Early Commentary on the 'Poetria Nova'*.

Frank, 'Some Implications'. On abbreviation and *occupatio* in the *Legend* see especially Burrow, *Ricardian Poetry*, pp. 73–4, and Frank, *Legend of Good Women*, pp. 199–206. J. Norton Smith, *Chaucer*, pp. 73–6, discusses *sermocinatio* and *demonstratio* in the poem.

J. T. Welter, *L'Exemplum dans la littérature religieuse et didactique du moyen âge* (Paris, 1927). The Humbert of Romans text here cited is the *De habundancia exemplorum*. The best brief account of exemplification is by Burrow, *Medieval Writers and their Work*, pp. 107–18. Crucial issues relating to Chaucerian exemplification often arise in the context of discussions of Dorigen's *exempla*-laden complaint. See especially James Sledd, 'Dorigen's Complaint', *MP* 45 (1947), 36–45, and Gerald Morgan, 'A Defence of Dorigen's Complaint', *MÆ* 46 (1977), 77–97.

John L. Lowes, 'Is Chaucer's *Legend of Good Women* a Travesty?', *JEGP* 8 (1909), 513–69. For the Deschamps poems here cited see *ibid.*, pp. 560–1; also *Œuvres*, ed. Marquis de Queux de Saint-Hilaire and Raynaud, ii. 335–43, iii. 303–4, and x. xlix–l (this last poem invokes male paragons also—namely, Absalom, Solomon, and Alexander).

Anne Middleton, 'The *Physician's Tale* and Love's Martyrs: "Ensamples mo than ten" as a method in the *Canterbury Tales*', *ChR* 8 (1973), 9–32. By contrast, Kiser, *Telling Classical Tales*, sees Chaucer's exemplification in the *Legend* as a joking submission to the 'demanding stupidity' of his audience: 'When they can find classical literature palatable only through the medium of the moralized exemplum, he must let them have it that way' (p. 94). Here, it could be suggested, a reluctance to accept the medieval stylistics of exemplification has resulted in a low estimation of the capacities of the poem's audience (and of the fictional exemplifier who serves its alleged stupidity), the poet himself having been exonerated. The critic, it would seem, can trust no man but him.

Blamires (ed.), *Woman Defamed*. Blamires comments: 'quotations from (say) the Book of Proverbs about "wicked" or "strange" women were lifted quite without acknowledgement that an adjacent passage might be a commendation of the "good" woman, and the converse was also true' (p. 7). For the *Blasme des Fames* and *Bien des Fames* see *Three Medieval Views of Women*, trans. and ed. G. K. Fiero, W. Pfeffer, and M. Allain (New Haven, Conn., and London, 1989). Christine de Pizan, *Cité des Dames*, ed. Curnow, trans. Richards. *La Querelle de la Rose*, ed. Hicks, trans. Baird and Kane.

Sheila Delany, 'The Logic of Obscenity in Chaucer's *Legend of Good Women*', *Florilegium*, 7 (1985), 189–205; these ideas are reiterated in chapter 3 of her *Naked Text*. Simon Gaunt, *Troubadours and Irony* (Cambridge, 1989), pp. 20–2, 51–60. The work of William IX of Aquitaine contains many a *joc grosser* ('lewd game'). Jacquart and Thomasset, *Sexuality and Medicine*, pp. 96–110. Monson, 'Problem of Irony', critiquing Betsy Bowden, 'The Art of Courtly Copulation', *Medievalia et Humanistica*, 9 (1979), 67–85.

On Chaucerian pathos see especially Frank, '*Legend of Good Women*', pp. 95–6 and *passim*; also his article 'The *Canterbury Tales* III: Pathos', in Boitani and Mann (eds.), *Chaucer Companion*, pp. 143–58. *The Book of Margery Kempe*, ed. S. B. Meech, EETS OS 212 (London, 1940), p. 148. Chapters 79–81 of the first book form a quite extraordinary record of Margery's affective imaginings as she meditates on the Passion narrative from the betrayal of Christ to the Resurrection (pp. 187–97). One of the most extreme literary manifestations of 'affective piety' known to me is the Middle English 'tretys to lerne to wepe' (i.e. on the 'art of weeping'), which has been edited by R. Garrett as 'De arte lacrimandi', *Anglia Zeitschrift*, 32 (1909), 269–94. Rosemary Woolf, in her *The English Religious Lyric in the Middle Ages* (Oxford, 1968), regards its 'tone of enclosed, unrestrained emotion' as 'distasteful' (p. 259). Such a work, however, is quite useful in helping us to tune our sensibilities to respond to the (rather more restrained) emotionalism of poems like *LGW*.

B. Nolan, *Chaucer and Roman Antique*. H. A. Kelly, *Love and Marriage in the Age of Chaucer* (Ithaca, NY, and London, 1975). Florence Verducci, *Ovid's Toyshop of the Heart. 'Epistulae Heroidum'* (Princeton, NJ 1985). W. S. Anderson, 'The "Heroides"', in J. W. Binns (ed.), *Ovid* (London and Boston, 1973), pp. 49–83.

For the tradition of female lament after Chaucer see especially John Kerrigan (ed.), *Motives of Woe: Shakespeare and 'Female Complaint'. A Critical Anthology* (Oxford, 1991). Kerrigan comments: 'complaint fosters impersonation of the femine in ways which raise interesting questions about gender, but which also, frustratingly, make it difficult to judge the authorship and tone', particularly in the case of anonymous texts (p. 2).

Muscatine, *Poetry and Crisis*.

*Sources*

The Prologue to the *Legend*, in both its versions, represents a revisitation of major French poetic traditions. Chaucer's depiction of the daisy queen (whom he identifies with Alceste) has clearly been influenced by the *marguerite* or daisy poetry of the kind produced by Deschamps, Machaut, and Froissart, and the idea of the poet's repentance for his heresy against love owes much to Machaut's *Jugement dou Roy de Navarre*.

Turning to the narratives, the best candidate for the major source of the first of them, the *Legend of Cleopatra*, seems to be the *Speculum historiale* of the Dominican encyclopaedist Vincent of Beauvais (*c*.1190–1264). In the others, the influence of Ovid dominates. The *Heroides* was the primary source for the legends of Phyllis and Hypermnestra, and was drawn on for the endings of the stories of Dido, Ariadne, and Hypsipyle. Chaucer used the *Metamorphoses* in composing his tales of Thisbe, Ariadne, Hypsipyle, and Philomela, and perhaps also of Medea, though that has been questioned, and it is indubitable that here his main source was Guido delle Colonne's *Historia destructionis Troiae* (which may also have been used for the Hypsipyle narrative). Some believe that in addition he consulted the *Ovide moralisé*, most obviously in the *Legend of Philomela*, where there are parallels with Chrétien de Troyes' *Philomela* as incorporated into the later French poem, and perhaps in his accounts of Thisbe and Ariadne. The *Legend of Lucrece* is largely based on Ovid's *Fasti* (despite Chaucer's reference to Livy as well as Ovid). According to S. B. Meech, Chaucer made use of Filippo Ceffi's Italian translation of the *Heroides*, but as M. C. Edwards (now Shaner) has pointed out, many of the details are to be found in medieval glosses on the *Heroides*, and Chaucer may simply have been using what he found in the margins of his Ovid manuscript. Virgil's *Aeneid* (and maybe the *Roman d'Eneas* also) lies behind the *Legend of Dido*.

The invocation of the Neoplatonic deity with which the *Legend of Philomela* begins could have come from one of several sources, including *De consolatione philosophiae*, III, met. ix, 11–14, the *Roman de la Rose*, 15,995–6004, the *Ovide moralisé*, i. 71–97, or a medieval preface (*accessus*) to the *Metamorphoses* of the type which has been printed by Karl Young. Whatever its specific origin, the question of how the form-giver who 'wrought / This fayre world' could have allowed such a cruel creature as Teseus to exist (2228–43) is surely on a par with the other passages in Chaucer's *œuvre* wherein the doubts and anxieties of the Boethian I-persona are echoed, being of the same stuff as Palamon's suspicion that the cruel pagan gods may regard men as being of no more importance than sheep which cower in their fold (*Knight's Tale*, I(A) 1303–33),

Troilus's emotional speculation that his imminent parting from Criseyde must be the result of a divine predestination which allows no freedom to the human will (*Troilus and Criseyde*, iv. 957–1082), and (the closest parallel of all) Dorigen's bewilderment that a god who is perfect, wise, and stable could be responsible for those black rocks ('rather a foul confusion / Of werk than any fair creacion') which threaten her husband's ship (*Franklin's Tale*, V(F) 865–94). That is to say, it ranks with several of the most profound misgivings about the meaning—or lack of meaning—of life which Chaucer ever expressed. The range of the *Legend*'s concerns and tone colours is wider than has sometimes been acknowledged.

S. B. Meech, 'Chaucer and the *Ovide moralisé*', *PMLA* 33 (1918), 302–25; *idem*, 'Chaucer and an Italian Translation of the *Heroides*', *PMLA* 45 (1930), 110–28; *idem*, 'Chaucer and the *Ovide moralisé*: A Further Study', *PMLA* 46 (1931), 182–204. See further Sheila Delany's article, 'The Naked Text' (cf. chapter 3 of her monograph *Naked Text*), which notes parallels between the *Ovide moralisé* and the *Legend of Thisbe*. A more sceptical view of Chaucer's use of the French poem is taken by Cooper, 'Chaucer and Ovid', pp. 74–5, 264 n. 7, who emphasizes that Chaucer did not have to know the *Ovide moralisé* in order to know the *Philomela* attributed to Chrétien, and besides, some of the details in question might have come from Latin glosses in Chaucer's manuscript of the *Metamorphoses*. Commentaries on the *Metamorphoses* have been studied in relation to the *Canterbury Tales* by Judson B. Allen and T. A. Moritz, *A Distinction of Stories: The Medieval Unity of Chaucer's Fair Chain of Narratives for Canterbury* (Columbus, Oh., 1981).
The major study by Mary Shaner (née Edwards) of the *Legend* in relation to *Heroides* glosses, 'A Study of Six Characters in Chaucer's "Legend of Good Women" with reference to Medieval Scholia on Ovid's "Heroides"' (B.Litt. thesis, University of Oxford, 1970), has unfortunately never been published, but some materials from her research have been included in notes to the edition of the poem which she and A. S. G. Edwards prepared for the *Riverside Chaucer*.
Karl Young, 'Chaucer's Appeal to the Platonic Deity', *Speculum*, 19 (1944), 1–13.

FRENCH TRADITIONS REVISITED: *MARGUERITE* POETRY, THE
*ROMAN DE LA ROSE*, AND MACHAUT'S *NAVARRE*

Chaucer's depiction of love among the daisies in the *Legend*'s prologue follows the lead of poems like Machaut's *Dit de la Marguerite* and *Dit de la Fleur de Lis et de la Marguerite*. The first of these begins with an account of the appearance and properties of the daisy itself, moves on to praise its excellence in worth, sweetness, and colour, and proceeds to develop the implicit link between flower and lady, as when the poet remarks that 'every time I gather her with my hand and can look at her at my will and lift her to my mouth, to my eye, and kiss, touch, smell, and feel, and gently enjoy her beauty and sweetness, then I wish for nothing more' (37–44; trans. Windeatt, p. 145). The poetic skill involved here largely consists in the maintenance and prolongation of that link; the idea of the flower must never be occluded, even when the speaker declares his confidence that 'she will be a true lover to me until death, and will remain so if I die' (167–8; p. 146), which stretches the analogy somewhat. Similarly, in Froissart's *Dit de la Marguerite* the narrator protests that 'in each petal . . . the flower carries a piercing dart, through which I am so wounded by looking at her that there is no limb in my body where it has not spread. But I beg the power of the God of Love to cure me' (187–92; trans. Windeatt, p. 151).

We are far removed here from the pursuit of that rather more erotically significant flower, the rose, particularly as conducted by Jean de Meun. These are much gentler affairs, not interested in learned allegory or satire, but having as their obvious purpose compliment of the beautiful lady and display of the sensibilities of her eloquent lover. Chaucer derived the general idea of worshipping a flower-lady, along with various details such as the image of the daisy opening 'ayein the sonne' (F Prol. 48–9, G Prol. 48–9), from poems such as these.

The parallels between the *Legend*'s Prologue and Deschamps' *Lay de Franchise* are particularly substantial. The French poem opens with the narrator going out to honour the month of May, which 'prospers gentle hearts to delight in love with their ladies, who this day will listen to their complaints' (21–3; trans. Windeatt, p. 152). His own amorous sorrows are concentrated on the daisy, whose properties are emblematic of many of the virtues which were then believed to delimit the feminine. Walking further, he hides himself in a bush to observe the behaviour of ladies and young men, who sing new songs and gather 'flowers and leaves with which they were making garlands and chaplets. And all were clothed in green. The day itself was an earthly paradise, for many made wooden pipes and flageolets which they played continually, and others recited poems of love and spoke of honour and faithful love, with which every true heart must be taken' (121–30; p. 154). There is even the suggestion of a court of love: when some ladies raise the issue that a single unguarded look from a woman can cause suspicion and bragging, they are answered by the flower, who declares that there cannot be prowess without love, as the 'great example' of Troy proves, along with several lesser ones. A noble king who, slightly earlier in the poem, had been presented as an extraordinarily handsome and gentle 16-year-old (this alludes to Charles VI), approves of this judgement. A great feast follows, at which point the narrator jumps out from his bush and takes to the road once again. Then he encounters 'Marion and Robin' drinking from a stream and eating a little bread. Robin condemns feasting, which leads to bodily illness, and points to the fears and dangers which the high-ranking and high-living suffer. Duly chastened, the narrator meditates that 'courtly life is too uncertain a state', and prays that God may reward 'that flower, and the sweet May, which have warned me through Marion and Robin' (307–10; p. 155).

Chaucer was certainly influenced by this account of a May celebration which included the performance of poetry, discussion and debate about love, and the wearing of emblematic flowers and leaves. The consonance of the beautiful flower-lady and the powerful king, who agree so fully on matters of love and aristocratic behaviour, may have prompted his own presentation of the alliance between Alceste and the God of Love. His daisy queen's somewhat jaundiced view of aspects of court life may owe something to Robin's pastoral critique. However, for the ideas of a collection of stories of virtuous women and a poet's repentance for his supposed offence against Love we have to seek elsewhere.

At one point in Jean de Meun's portion of the *Roman de la Rose* (13,173–264) a series of *exempla* is offered of women who were betrayed by false men: namely, Dido, Phyllis, Oenone, and Medea. However, this passage functions within a framework which, it could well be argued, subverts its significance. For the speaker at this point is Jean's disreputable Old Woman, and her purpose is to prove that since all men betray and deceive women, women should deceive them in return. Any woman, she goes on to declare, who fixes her heart on a single man is a fool (13,269–72). Alceste would certainly not have approved of that. And Jean's *apologia* at lines 15,135–302, far from expressing repentance for having written ill about women, is rather a justification for such practice, on the grounds that this is what his sources say about them. Besides, he is writing for the purpose of instruction: while 'no one should despise a woman unless he has the worst heart among all the wicked ones', nevertheless 'we have set these things down in writing so that we can gain knowledge, and that you may do so by yourselves. It is good to know everything' (15,203–14; trans. Dahlberg, p. 259).

Far closer to the mark is Machaut's *Jugement dou Roy de Navarre*, wherein the ideas of poetic repentance and female panegyric are directly related. 'You have sinned against women' (811), the Machaut persona is told by the Lady, who will later be identified as Bonneürté; his 'false opinion' is 'so seriously biased against women' that a 'severe penance is called for' (918–20; trans. Palmer, pp. 37, 43). These criticisms are aimed at Machaut's *Jugement dou Roy de Behaingne*, and may seem rather surprising at first, given that none of the familiar anti-feminist diatribes appear in that poem. Perhaps it is inappropriate to seek such exactitude; Machaut, one might say, was creating an occasion for a new poem, not engaged in objective explanation of an earlier one, and hence he was obliged to reconstruct the old poem within the new. On the other hand, as William Calin has pointed out, it is quite possible to find reasons for offence in the *Behaingne*: 'Of his four main characters, two are men and two are women. One man lives and dies a perfect lover; the other, no less a paragon, will suffer possibly for the rest of his days because his love is so pure. Of the two ladies, we are told a different story. One is disloyal, vicious, and a liar, has abandoned the Knight for no good reason, and will be forever dishonoured; the other, despite good intentions, will forget her Lover' (p. 43). While 'Machaut says nothing to indicate that his characters' actions are conditioned by their sex', his male figures 'adhere more closely to *fin' amor*' than do his female ones, the implication being that the men love 'better' than the women (pp. 43, 44).

It is little wonder, then, that Bonneürté's companions should offer the poet persona various *exempla* which indicate that the opposite is true. After telling the story of Dido (2095–132), Peace declares that the male misery, pain, and torment which the poet had presented as the worst are nothing in comparison to what Dido 'was intent on paying out because she grieved for her lover' (2137–41; trans. Palmer, p. 97). A little later, Frankness offers the linked *exempla* of Theseus's abandonment of Ariadne and how Jason left Medea for Creusa (2707–822) to support her argument that women have proved to be truer lovers throughout the ages, and have been more loyal than men in every way (2699–703). Frankness concludes with the declaration that

> No man ever is as loyal
> As women are,
> Nor are men ever so powerfully inflamed
> With the spark of love
> As any noble lady can be.                    (2810–14; p. 127)

Women love better and more loyally than men; indeed, women have the greater capacity for love, and hence they have the greater suffering—the obvious implication being that the bereaved lady in the *Behaingne* experienced the greater sorrow.

But Machaut's I-persona disagrees, and soon his earlier professions of esteem for women are shattered as he declares that nothing is 'stable in a woman's heart' (3020; p. 135). Since she 'alters for the slightest reason', being prone to cry or laugh over trifles, 'great joy and immense suffering cannot remain with her for very long, because her nature convinces her to laugh quickly and lament nothing' (3027–30). Once a woman recognizes that she cannot have her lover back, no matter what she might do, she will forget him—for her nature is such that she 'forgets quite readily any creature out of her sight' (3039–41; p. 137). 'In contrast', he continues, 'a man's heart is firm, secure, wise, experienced, and mature, virtuous and strong enough to endure' (3047–9). This is the common opinion; everyone believes it, he declares, and that is why he put it in his poem.

> So I say in conclusion
> That, considering the nature
> Of men and women, no woman
> Can suffer so much torment,
> However much she screams and carries on,
> As any man can bear within his heart,
> For it is simply not in her nature.                    (3059–65)

Thus Machaut dramatizes the matter of his debate, the opposing viewpoints being presented with reason and sometimes with vehemence on both sides. And the beautiful *Lay de Plour* ('Lay of Weeping') which Machaut (at least initially, for he seems to have changed his mind later) presents as being a poem he wrote by way of repentance, following the King of Navarre's judgement against him, speaks in the voice of a sorrowful woman who is lamenting her dead beloved, this being of course the situation of the main female figure in the *Behaingne* (cf. pp. 101–3 above). The system of checks and balances which Machaut has created is, therefore, quite remarkable.

Chaucer learnt much from this, though what he did with it was singular. His *Legend* encapsulates the principle, as affirmed by Machaut's Frankness, that women love more and suffer more than men. No one in the English poem presents the counter-argument. By contrast with the Machaut persona, who protests his own rightness until the final judgement goes against him, the Chaucer persona argues less—indeed, he has less time to argue, for he receives his penance at a much earlier stage in the proceedings and accepts it meekly. The penance allotted to the Machaut persona (the composition of a lay, a chanson, and a ballade) is considerably lighter than what the Chaucer persona gets, the English text being far more concerned with what happens after the judgement than was the French one. Despite such differences, which are largely of scale and deployment rather than of fundamental principle, the influence of the French poem is pervasive. Indeed, the *Navarre* may be regarded as one of the major inspirations of the entire *Legend*, rivalled only by Ovid's *Heroides*, a point which will be substantiated more fully later.

Windeatt, *Sources and Analogues*, pp. 145–55. For the French text of Machaut's *Dit de la Marguerite* see the appendix to Jean Froissart, *Dits et débats*, ed. A. Fourrier (Geneva, 1979), pp. 277–84. For Froissart's *Dit de la Marguerite* see *ibid.*, pp. 147–53. Deschamps' *Lay de Franchise* is included in the *Œuvres*, ed. Marquis de Queux de Saint-Hilaire and Raynaud, ii. 203–14.
On the Machaut poems see especially J. I. Wimsatt, *The Marguerite Poetry of Guillaume de Machaut* (Chapel Hill, NC, 1970).

*Roman de la Rose*, ed. Langlois, trans. Dahlberg. Machaut, *Judgment of the King of Navarre*, ed. and trans. Palmer. See further John L. Lowes, 'The Prologue to the *Legend of Good Women* as Related to the French *Marguerite* Poems, and the *Filostrato*', *PMLA* 19 (1904), 593–683; R. M. Estrich, 'Chaucer's Prologue to the *Legend of Good Women* and Machaut's *Le Jugement dou Roy de Navarre*', *SP* 36 (1939), 20–39.
Calin, *Poet at the Fountain*.
Parallels with other French poems are pointed out in Shaner and Edwards' notes to their edition of *LGW*, in the *Riverside Chaucer*.

## 'STORYAL SOTH'? VINCENT OF BEAUVAIS

The *Legend of Cleopatra* has been claimed, by R. W. Frank, to be the 'first serious treatment of Cleopatra in English' (p. 37); similarly Dieter Mehl describes it as 'the first treatment of Cleopatra's story in English' (p. 107). However, the lively Old English account of the serpent of Old Nile in the Alfredian translation of Orosius's *Historia adversum paganos* (vi. 19) should be given due credit. Far more problematic is Cleopatra's reputation in the Middle Ages. According to Frank, her story was 'virtually unknown' (p. 39). The opposite view was taken by Beverly Taylor, who was criticized by V. A. Kolve for her anachronistic imposition on Chaucer's poem of 'a modern scholar's knowledge of the Cleopatra tradition—an enormous compilation of texts few of which could have been known to Chaucer or to his original audience' (234 n. 4). So, then, was Cleopatra a shadowy figure that Chaucer could manipulate with impunity, or a 'notoriously bad woman' (as Priscilla Martin supposes, p. 204) who would instantly have been perceived as out of place in a 'pak' of good women? What is quite clear is that Cleopatra was far less famous than, say, Dido or Medea. And if Chaucer could include them in his legendary, Cleopatra would have presented him with no real problem.

No source has been found which accounts for all the details in the *Legend of Cleopatra*, but the quest for such exactitude may well be unnecessary. I suspect that we are dealing with the result of elaborate *amplificatio* of a passage in Vincent of Beauvais' *Speculum historiale* (vi. 5), which may be quoted here in full:

Next, since the wanton Antony was seized by love for Cleopatra Queen of Egypt, having repudiated Augustus's sister, he joined that same Cleopatra in marriage to himself, and declared war on Augustus. But Augustus, at the first signs of these new disturbances, sailed from Brundisium to Epirus with three hundred ships; Antony indeed occupied the Attic shore. But when it came to battle, and the fleet of Augustus began to threaten the ship of Antony, Queen Cleopatra with her golden ship, and her purple sail, first began to flee, and Antony straightaway followed her. [Cleopatra] began to follow upon Augustus, and seeing this Antony killed himself by his own hand. The Queen indeed, falling at the feet of Augustus, tempted his sight, but, being rejected by him, abandoned hope. And when she realised that she would be kept for a triumph, when she was guarded in a less strict manner she placed herself next to her Antony in the Mausoleum that was filled with fragrances. Then she was lulled to death by serpents that she applied to herself. Then Augustus took possession of Alexandria.

Brief though this account may be, its distaste for the queen is evident. Antony's pursuit of her ornate ship away from the crucial battle clearly indicates the dangers attendant on his association with her. He commits suicide as the direct consequence of her attempt to change sides.

In Chaucer, however, Cleopatra was not the first in the 'flyghte': we are told that 'Antony is schent' and 'al his folk' are in retreat with him (652–3) before mention is made of the queen's action. Besides, it is little wonder that she should have fled, the narrator protectively declares, for the 'strokes . . . wente as thikke as hayl' (655). Antony dies not because his beloved is untrue, but out of 'dispeyr' at his defeat (Cleopatra's flight, as we have already noted, being only one aspect of that). In Vincent, the process leading to her suicide begins when her attempt to seduce Augustus is unsuccessful. Chaucer confines himself to the tactfully vague remark that she 'coude of Cesar have no grace' (663), the emphasis falling on the great 'routhe' which 'woful Cleopatre' made for her dead husband. There is nothing in the English poem about her wish to avoid being included in the emperor's triumph; apparently Chaucer did not want to include anything which would have marred the effect of an 'unreprovable' wife keeping her 'covenant' with Antony even to the extent of dying with him. Her suicide in the snake-pit—a detail apparently of Chaucer's invention, though conceivably he might have thought that that was what was meant by Vincent's statement that the queen applied serpents to herself—is a death as spectacular as that found in the most exotic of the *vitae Sanctorum*. It is also indicative of her total commitment to that central validating principle of the whole poem, namely 'wyfhood' (cf. pp. 412–22 below).

Within the *Legend of Cleopatra* itself, this principle validates the queen's actions and explains Chaucer's alterations of his source, *pace* Frank, who finds the story 'a failure . . . because it lacks imaginative unity' (p. 37). Nowadays Cleopatra is widely regarded as the most spectacular *femme fatale* of all time, thanks of course to Shakespeare, though Hollywood epics have had their impact too. But if we can manage to accept that Chaucer has presented her as an obsessively loyal wife (well, why not? Jean Rhys managed to rewrite *Jane Eyre*), then the rationale of the *Legend of Cleopatra* will become perfectly obvious.

The trajectory of Chaucer's version of the Cleopatra story is markedly different from that of the most vitriolic medieval depiction of the lass unparalleled, as found in Giovanni Boccaccio's *De mulieribus claris* (composed in various stages between 1361 and 1375). Since the argument that this work was a direct source of the *Legend of Cleopatra* is, to my mind, unconvincing—all the essential details may be found in the *Speculum historiale*, a work which, it should be remembered, is included in the God of Love's inventory of Chaucer's books (G Prol. 307)—it will be treated here as an analogue rather than a source.

In the *De mulieribus claris* Cleopatra is, as Peter Godman says, 'an incarnation of evil' (p. 285). 'Although she was the descendant of Ptolemy', Boccaccio writes, 'she nevertheless came to rule through crime. She gained glory for almost nothing else than her beauty, while on the other hand she became known throughout the world for her greed, cruelty and lustfulness' (trans. Guarino, p. 192). Indeed, she becomes 'almost the prostitute of oriental kings' (p. 193); and to prove this point, Boccaccio apparently invents the yarn of how she once urged the cruel King Herod to sleep with her, intending to rob him of Judea, which he had acquired not long ago from Antony. Herod 'not only refused through respect for Antony, but to free him from the shame of such a lewd woman he planned to kill her with his sword, but his friends dissuaded him' (p. 194). It was Cleopatra who caused Antony to repudiate Octavia: the queen was his mistress long before he married her (thereby Boccaccio devalues their marriage). Sumptuous banquets are the order of the day, an expression and symptom of debauchery and extravagance. By contrast, the one and only 'feste' in the *Legend of Cleopatra* is the lovers' wedding feast (616), yet another testament to the centrality of marriage in Chaucer's story.

In Boccaccio, Antony kills himself not on account of the queen's infidelity—in this version of the story it is inconceivable that he would set so high a value on her—but when he is unable to obtain peace terms from his enemy. (After his death, however, true to form, she tries 'with her old wiles to make young Octavian desire her', but in vain; p. 196.) This 'lustful man' must be kept noble enough for the audience to feel that he is being wronged by his rapacious consort, and Boccaccio conveys very strongly Antony's distrust of her. In Chaucer, he must be kept noble enough to sustain the excellence of Cleopatra's married love; for the rest, the narrator is content to cast him as the first of the many untrustworthy males who stalk the pages of Cupid's legendary. Recounting the death of Cleopatra, Boccaccio fires a parting shot. According to an alternative account, Antony forces her to drink the poison with which she had proved that his food-tasting precautions were no match for her cunning. Boccaccio admits that 'the other version', wherein Cleopatra 'follows her Antony' into death, is 'better attested', but the alternative account has done its work, in suggesting that the queen's one (partly) commendable action may never have happened (pp. 196–7). Chaucer's version, of course, demonstrates that 'Was nevere unto hire love a trewer quene' (695); indeed, she is portrayed as a veritable queen of love.

'This is storyal soth, it is no fable' (702), the I-persona assures us; but in fact the polarities of the 'Estoryal Myrour' have been reversed, though it should be noted that Vincent's remark that 'she placed herself next to her Antony in the Mausoleum' could have suggested another way of telling the tale. Adept medieval exemplifiers often made much out of far less than that. At any rate, Chaucer has created his own gynocentric and gamocentric narrative. Boccaccio's version follows the most natural direction for the story to take; he has consolidated and elaborated the biases of the standard narrative, as illustrated by Vincent (and also found in the Alfredian Orosius). But Chaucer has preferred to go his own way—or, rather, his narrator is following the path which Cupid and Alceste, acting in sometimes uneasy alliance, have indicated by their somewhat different gestures.

Frank, *Legend of Good Women*; Mehl, *Narrative Poetry*; Beverly Taylor, 'The Medieval Cleopatra', *JMRS* 7 (1977), 249–69. V. A. Kolve, 'From Cleopatra to Alceste: An Iconographic Study of *The Legend of Good Women*', in John P. Hermann and John P. Burke (eds.), *Signs and Symbols in Chaucer's Poetry* (University, Ala., 1981), pp. 130–78. Kolve's view is echoed by Lucy Hughes-Hallett, *Cleopatra: Histories, Dreams and Distortions* (London, 1990), pp. 113–14. See further W. K. Wimsatt, 'Vincent of Beauvais and Chaucer's Cleopatra and Croesus', *Speculum*, 12 (1937), 375–81, and Pauline Aiken, Chaucer's *Legend of Cleopatra* and the *Speculum Historiale*', *Speculum*, 13 (1938), 232–6, both of whom print Vincent's brief Latin text.
Martin, *Chaucer's Women*. Peter Godman, 'Chaucer and Boccaccio's Latin Works', in Boitani (ed.), *Italian Trecento*, pp. 269–95. Godman argues that Chaucer was following Boccaccio's story of Cleopatra.
Giovanni Boccaccio, *Concerning Famous Women*, trans. Guido A. Guarino (London, 1964). The Latin original has been edited by V. Zaccaria in Boccaccio, *Tutte le Opere*, vol. x. A partial (anonymous) Middle English translation was made around 1440; this has been edited by G. Schleich, *Die mittelenglische Umdichtung von Boccaccios 'De claris mulieribus'*, Palaestra 144 (Leipzig, 1924). For discussion see H. G. Wright, *Boccaccio in England from Chaucer to Tennyson* (London, 1957), pp. 28–36, and Janet M. Cowen, 'Women as Exempla in Fifteenth-Century Verse of the Chaucerian Tradition', in Julia Boffey and Janet Cowen (eds.), *Chaucer and Fifteenth-Century Poetry* (London, 1991), pp. 51–65.

### OVID AND INSTABILITY OF MEANING

With the knowledge of hindsight, Chaucer's homage to Ovid in the *Legend* may appear almost inevitable. In the *Book of the Duchess*, the *Parliament of Fowls*, and *Troilus and Criseyde*, in many of the short poems discussed in our final chapter, and perhaps also in the *House of Fame* (though its incomplete state makes this impossible to judge), Chaucer is presenting himself as *the* English poet of human love. What could be more natural, then, than an encounter with Ovid, the classical 'master of love'? After all, many a previous medieval writer on love had engaged in Ovidian self-fashioning, drawing on the contents of Ovid's poems and striving to imitate his style, tone, and realization of authorial presence: Andreas Capellanus, Juan Ruiz, and Jean de Meun are obvious cases in point. But Chaucer was not content merely to follow in their footsteps. According to the Man of Law's account of the *Legend*, his attitude to Ovid was competitive, perhaps even confrontational: Chaucer had said *more* about 'loveris up and doun' than Ovid 'made of mencioun / In his Episteles'—that is, the *Heroides*—'that been ful olde' (and therefore out of date?). But Chaucer, the Man of Law continues, avoided stories of incest, tales of a type which Ovid had certainly told (cf. especially *Heroides* xi, the letter of Canace to Macareus). This may be taken as another implicit claim that the English poet had improved upon his predecessor's work. Much of this may be said in jest, to be sure, but the humour cannot mask the serious aspect of these statements, which mark the negotiations in which an English poet engaged with his classical source and model.

   To imitate but yet to transform—that is the basic form which those negotiations took, to judge from the *Legend*. Chaucer seems to have been much affected by Ovid's tone colours, in particular the bravado with which he had presented himself as the *praeceptor amoris*: 'If anyone among this people knows not the art of loving, let him read my poem, and having read be skilled in love. . . . I am Love's teacher' (*Ars amatoria*, i. 1–2, 17; trans. Mozley, pp. 12–13). This passage almost certainly lies behind Chaucer's protestation, 'trusteth, as in love, no man but me' (2561). Opinionated intrusions of self feature prominently in the *Ars amatoria*, *Amores*, and *Remedium amoris*. These may be serious (cf. Chaucer's expression of his feelings regarding the 'foule story' of Tereus and Philomela, 2238–43) or suspiciously half-serious or downright cheeky, an affront to timid respectability and establishment mores. The tone of Ovid's more extreme effusions is well captured in Peter Green's translation of the following passages from the *Amores*:

> Arms, warfare, violence—I was winding up to produce a
> Regular epic, with verse-form to match—
> Hexameters, naturally. But Cupid (they say) with a snicker
> Lopped off one foot from each alternate line.*
> 'Nasty young brat', I told him, 'who made *you* Inspector of Metres?'
>
> (i. 1–5; p. 86)

---

* i.e. he is writing elegaics.

Warning to puritans: *This volume is not for you.*
I want my works to be read by the far-from-frigid virgin
On fire for her sweetheart, by the boy
In love for the very first time . . .
    . . . epic's a dead loss for me. I'll get nowhere with swift-footed Achilles . . .
    . . . Farewell, heroic figures of legend.        (ii. 5–7, 29, 35–6; pp. 111–12)

This cultivation of the mock-heroic is of course part and parcel of Ovid's ostentatious refusal to ally himself with Virgil's celebration of military glory and with Augustan values (cf. p. 237 above). Whatever its rationale in Ovid, it seems to have encouraged his English counterpart to indulge in rather frenetic hyperbole (the best example surely being the claim that Dido would make a suitable mate for God himself: see p. 386 below) or flat assertion which is so blunt that it is almost, or actually, bathetic. There are many examples of the latter effect, one of the most obvious being the curious relish with which he depicts Jason as a devourer of women: 'There othere falsen oon, thow falsest two!' (1377); 'Have at thee, Jason! Now thyn horn is blowe!' (1383). This effect is not, of course, limited to the narrator's personal protestations, but may be found often in his manner of narration. In the *Legend of Ariadne* the abruptness of certain stages of the narrative creates a somewhat jaunty effect, which is hardly conducive to pathos. Several critics have commented, for example, on the incredible haste with which Ariadne attempts to arrange a marriage not just for herself (with Theseus) but for her sister as well (with Theseus's son, Demophon; 2080–102), and the amusing speed with which the hero consents to swear anything the heroine asks in order that he may avoid being torn apart by the monster:

'Ye swere it here, upon al that may be sworn'.
    'Ye, lady myn', quod he, or ellis torn
Mote I be with the Mynotaur to-morwe!'        (2102–4)

As used here that 'sworn' / 'torn' rhyme seems to be subversive of romance, heroism, or of any impression of emotional sincerity, which may be why Chaucer introduced it.

Effects such as these may be regarded as results of the introduction of aspects of style from poems like the *Ars amatoria* and *Amores* into the world of the *Heroides*. But there is, of course, more to it than that. On the face of it, most of the letters in the *Heroides* side with the underdogs, the victims of militarism, those women who have been left behind whilst their menfolk pursue heroic destinies in which the feminine has little part. Yet anyone who seeks semantic security in the *Heroides* is likely to be disappointed, a point which we have already canvassed briefly. This collection, declares Florence Verducci, is 'guaranteed to challenge the reader who expects, or hopes, to find an assemblage of heart-rending apostrophes, tender litanies of anguish indited in the throes of despair by abandoned maidens or wives' (p. 21). According to her ironic reading of the text, 'Ovid's treatment of his heroines invites a disparagement and skepticism.' She goes so far as to claim that, in violation of the norms, Ovid has those arch-villainesses of antiquity, Phaedra and Medea, finally exert 'the richest claims upon our compassionate regard', while the figures who traditionally were best regarded 'least requite our sentimental and sympathetic expectations'. Many of these comments will strike a sympathetic chord with readers of the *Legend*, who have often suspected 'disparagement and skepticism' in Chaucer's poem also. My own point is simply that the primary model for the *Legend* has just as many interpretative problems—and interpretative problems of essentially the same kind—as has the *Legend* itself.

I cannot share the confidence of Verducci's pronouncements, however; the history of the reception of the *Heroides* induces uneasiness about guaranteeing anything to a generalized 'reader'. For a start, medieval commentaries on the *Heroides* regularly insisted that these poems affirmed the value of married love, as exemplified by the story of Penelope, and reprehended foolish passion of the type to which Phyllis succumbed, along with the unchaste love of a figure like Canace. The text therefore had a moral intention (cf. p. 393 below); even more interestingly, perhaps, readers were encouraged to 'read into' the love-letters details of the speakers' life-stories to which Ovid had merely alluded or deliberately omitted. What Ovid had brought together and homogenized, his commentators worked to put asunder—and here, it must be admitted, could be found a justification for an interpretative model for Chaucer's poem which similarly relied on imported information and prioritized the contrasts rather than the comparisons between the various subjectivities. But that approach has its limitations and *longeurs* also. Suffice it to say here that the notion that Ovid was a champion of married love is not an exclusively medieval opinion. It has been held, for example, by Brooks Otis, who remarked that 'conjugal love—the love of husband and wife' actually 'constitutes the ethical apex of Ovid's amatory scale' (pp. 266, 277), and more recently was treated with all due seriousness by H. A. Kelly in his monograph *Love and Marriage in the Age of Chaucer* (1975).

On the other hand, it should be realized that the 'Ovid' with whom we are dealing is not the figure constructed by twentieth-century scholarship, but the 'Medieval Ovid', the *auctor* of the much respected *Metamorphoses* and of those ethical textbooks of the grammar school curriculum. Any problems raised by the youthfully improper *Ars amatoria* were defused by reference to the allegedly apologetic *Remedium amoris*, which was read as a product of the poet's repentance. But of course the *Ars* and the *Remedium* could not be circumscribed in those ways; there is no reason to doubt that certain medieval readers noticed that the former said many negative things about love and women, while the latter could be as erotic as the poem which it was supposed to be recanting. Then there was the tradition of the allegorized Ovid, on which we have often touched already, wherein classical myths were made to bear the weight of a wide range of ethical, and sometimes specifically Christian, meanings. In sum, an *œuvre* which is marked by inherent instability of meaning was interpreted and augmented in ways which often accentuated that instability. The incidental became the essential, and vice versa. Hair-line cracks were widened into gulfs. Stabilizing structures were imposed, with only local or partial success.

It is little wonder, then, that all the major medieval writers who attempted to set themselves up as 'Medieval Ovids' (I am still thinking especially of Andreas Capellanus, Juan Ruiz, and Jean de Meun) produced works which are remarkable, if not notorious, for their irreducible ambiguities of tone and meaning, slipperiness of authorial viewpoint, and apparent inconsistencies of stance and purpose. Thus, Ovidian instability of meaning was made even more problematic, and was augmented with new materials which sat comfortably, or uncomfortably as the case may be, with the old ones. And such is the tradition of 'Medieval Ovidian' poetics in which the *Legend* may be placed—a tradition marked by its incorrigible refusal to fulfil expectation, be true to type, conform to rule, be reducible to neat critical aphorism. Which is, of course, a wonderful creative space for a writer to inhabit.

A full analysis of how Chaucer created his own versions of Ovid's tales is beyond the scope of this chapter, though the obvious point may be made that he took considerable liberties with the narratives of Medea, Hypsipyle, Philomela, and Ariadne as included in the *Metamorphoses* and reiterated in the *Ovide moralisé*. Seen from this perspective, Medea and Philomela are particularly unlikely candidates for pagan sainthood. The former, in addition to being a sorceress, robbed her father, and killed her brother, her two children by Jason, and Jason's new wife (*Metamorphoses*, vii. 1–396). The latter, who had been raped and mutilated by Tereus (the husband of her sister Procne), had, with Procne's aid, killed and cooked Itys (the son of Procne and Tereus), and served his flesh to his father (vi. 424–605). Ariadne, treacherously abandoned by Theseus, is considerably less culpable; however, out of love for him she had betrayed her father and her half-brother, the Minotaur, whom Theseus killed (vii. 456–8, viii. 6–176). Hypsipyle's behaviour was far better: in the seventh book of the

*Metamorphoses* she is depicted as sparing her father's life, thus refusing to take part in a female plot to murder the menfolk in her country. However, the fact that all the other women had no such qualms is a major feature of that narrative, this hardly being supportive of the stark contrast which Chaucer is positing between virtuous women and vicious men. On the other hand, in his *Heroides* Ovid had offered an alternative Medea, presented Ariadne and Hypsipyle (along with Thisbe, Phyllis, and Hypermnestra) in a flattering light, and constructed a Dido figure which is very different from Virgil's.

Strong 'double traditions' relating to Medea and Dido were in vogue during the later Middle Ages. The various versions of the Dido story have been discussed sufficiently in my chapter on the *House of Fame*. As far as Medea is concerned, while the negative depiction of her certainly continued (in, for example, *Le Roman de Troie en prose*, the *Ovide moralisé* (especially lines 705–8, 1487–95), Guido delle Colonne's *Historia destructionis Troiae*, and Boccaccio's *De mulieribus claris*), elsewhere she was treated more sympathetically, as in Benoît de Sainte-Maure's *Roman de Troie*, where she feels noble love (*fin' amor*, 1266) for Jason, and has 'le desire a mariage' (1278) as her honourable objective from the outset, and in Christine de Pizan's *Livre de la Cité des Dames* (cf. pp. 377–8 below). Indeed, the eighth ballade in Gower's *Traitié pour essampler les amantz marietz* is devoted to Jason and Medea. Happy in her husband's love she bore him two children, only to be abandoned, but 'God will avenge the broken marriage', as the refrain puts it. Since Chaucer's story of Medea is largely dependent on Guido's *Historia*, however, discussion of it must be postponed until the next section. Here we will concentrate on another Ovidian narrative with which Chaucer's modern readers have had great difficulty, the story of Lucrece, which has as its primary source the *Fasti*, ii. 685–852.

In Ovid the episode begins in a military camp. At a banquet held by Tarquinius Collatinus (son of the king, Sextus Tarquinius), men begin boasting about their wives. In their cups, the argument grows heated, and they decide to visit the city to find out what their womenfolk are doing. At the palace, the royal women are dissolutely 'keeping their vigils over the wine' (740; trans. Frazer, p. 111), but at the home of Collatinus his wife Lucretia is found busily spinning, along with her handmaids, and constantly lamenting the war; she weeps as she worries that her husband may be rash in battle. In Chaucer, there is no drunken banquet, no competitive boasting. 'Tarquinius the yonge', the villain of the piece, is singled out and immediately identified as an unsympathetic figure. Being 'lyght of tonge', he 'gan for to jape' about the state of partial idleness in which they are forced to live because of the siege, saying that no man here is doing anything more than his wife does (1694–1701). This is in effect an affirmation of male superiority, the clear implication being that his wife does very little and that such behaviour is unmanly (though perhaps stereotypically feminine). Having denigrated women, he then invites his companions to praise them. The only response we are given is Colatyn's warm commendation of Lucrece; his house alone is then visited, by himself and Tarquinius. Thus, the action concentrates, with admirable economy, on the central figures, whose roles have been established at the outset.

Colatyn and Tarquinius observe her for some time before the former makes his presence known. The initial, striking image is of a distraught woman sitting, dishevelled, beside her marriage-bed—the very bed that soon will be defiled by the false Tarquinius. (Ovid presents her as dishevelled *after* the rape, not before.) That image having been impressed on our memories, mention is made of what 'oure bok', presumably the *Fasti*, has to say about the 'softe wolle' which

> she wroughte
> To kepen hire from slouthe and idelnesse;
> And bad her servaunts don hire besyness,
> And axeth hem, 'What tydyngs heren ye?'          (1721–4)

Clearly, Lucrece is not 'idel'; hence Tarquinius's remark does not express a general truth about women. Yet this domestic business and bustle (probably intended by Ovid to reveal her command of the skills of household management, which she practises assiduously even in her husband's absence) have been carefully subordinated, in order that nothing should distract the reader from her singleness of mind and emotion. What is most important to her is her husband's safety (1725–31), which is why she is anxious to hear 'tydyngs' about the siege. The allusion which Ovid's Lucretia made to Colatyn's possible rashness in battle is omitted—it might have qualified her devotion to him. And Chaucer has added a reference to her 'wifly chastite', which is embellished by her 'honeste' tears (1736–7).

In Ovid's version of the story, Tarquinius then makes what is, to all appearances, a social call on Lucretia. 'He was welcomed kindly, for he came of kindred blood' (788; p. 115). But at 'the hour of slumber' he comes to her bed. In Chaucer, however, we do not see the heroine in the role of hostess. This is part and parcel of the effect of stealth and secrecy which the English poet wishes to create. His Tarquinius comes not as a guest but as a thief in the night ('And in the nyght ful thefly gan he stalke', 1781), gaining entrance through a 'privy' corner of the house (1780), an action which grimly travesties his first access to her, when he and Colatyn came 'prively into the hous' and saw her beside that great focal point of the narrative, her bed (1716). The rapist is further dehumanized when Lucrece, feeling her bed pressed, asks 'What beste is that?' (1788), an image which the narrator carries through by likening him to a wolf who has found a lamb alone (1798; all of this is an elaboration of *Fasti*, ii. 799–800).

Even more striking is the way in which Chaucer has altered Ovid's account of the rape itself. In the source Tarquinius plies her with 'prayers, bribes and threats', and finally threatens to kill both her and a slave, so that 'rumour will have it' that she was 'caught with him'. This is what causes her to yield, 'overcome by fear of infamy' (805–10; p. 115). In the *Legend of Lucrece* there is just the simple threat, yield or I will kill you, which causes the heroine to faint. This reaction, the narrative is at pains to assure us, is perfectly comprehensible in terms of the values then common among Roman wives, who were acutely conscious of their good name and were fearful of shame (cf. our discussion of Chaucer's presentation of virtuous heathen, on pp. 399–411 below). It cannot, therefore, be construed as a personal fault of Lucrece's, and is indicative of strength of character rather than typically feminine weakness. And so, Chaucer's Tarquinius takes advantage of the heroine whilst she is in a condition wherein she is not conscious of anything: 'She feleth no thyng' (1818). There is, therefore, no way in which she can be accused of collusion or complicity in her rape.

This is where Chaucer locates his main exoneration of Lucrece; it is all the more effective for being unlaboured. A little earlier, in lines 1789–811, he had imitated Ovid's exculpation of the heroine, that long list of reasons why she could not withstand her attacker (*Fasti*, ii. 795–809), to which he added the passage in which Tarquinius specifically threatens to kill her if she cries out, and puts his sword's point 'al sharp upon her herte' (1790–5). In Chaucer the scene functions to create pathos rather than to make a defence, though of course the apologetic element is definitely there. We should certainly not look for irony in these lines: I cannot accept the suggestion of Goddard that Chaucer 'has assigned four or five contradictory reasons for her failure to warn the house' (p. 78) or endorse Jonathan Sutton's opinion that the questions are 'blustery and intrusive' (p. 127). In my view, what Chaucer has written may fairly be compared with Shakespeare's quite serious imitation of the same Ovid passage in his *Rape of Lucrece*, 667–79.

In his description of Lucrece's suicide Ovid remarks that she took care to preserve her modesty even as she fell: 'Even then in dying she took care to sink down decently: that was her thought even as she fell' (*Fasti*, ii. 833–4; p. 117). This is considerably amplified by Chaucer:

And as she fel adoun, she kaste hir lok,
And of hir clothes yet she hede tok.
For in hir fallynge yet she had a care,
Lest that hir fet or suche thyng lay bare;
So wel she loved clennesse and ek trouthe.
Of hir had al the toun of Rome routhe                              *pity*
                                                          (1856–61)

R. W. Frank thinks that here 'the detail borders on the sentimental or
the grotesque and perhaps slips over that border' (p. 108). 'Chaucer's
audience', Brian Stone claims, 'would experience civilized amusement
at the sainted lady's concern' (p. 168). Dieter Mehl finds Lucrece's
action very prim, betraying a concern for mere appearance rather than
with 'more hidden values' (p. 115). And Florence M. Percival suspects
that 'Chaucer was here mocking the *verray trewe Lucresse* ever so
slightly'. Chaucer, like Ovid before him in her view, felt that Lucrece
was rather 'too good to be true' (p. 254). And yet the detail is used also
in John Gower's *Confessio Amantis*, vii. 5072–4, quite convincingly and
with no hint of irony (Gower may of course be imitating Chaucer here,
but that does not affect this point). Moreover, decorous arrangement of
garments while dying can be regarded as a saint's life motif. For example, the action was attributed to the 'hooly blisful martir' St Thomas à
Becket, who was believed to have arranged 'his gown decorously over
his feet, that his body might lie decently in his Father's house until it
was taken up for burial' (Duggan, p. 213). Therefore, it is hardly
surprising to find it (one might conclude) in a legendary of Cupid's
saints.

To get to the root of the matter, here we are up against a 'taste barrier': what can be read as exemplary (if somewhat superhuman) conduct
within one cultural formation can well look like deliberate irony in
another. In 1712, for example, if one may judge by the standards of
Addison and Steele's *Spectator*, 'Comeliness of Person and Decency of
Behaviour' were supposed to 'add infinite Weight' to one's words.

[T]he care of doing nothing unbecoming has accompanied the greatest Minds to
their last Moments: They avoided even an indecent Posture in the very article
of Death. Thus *Caesar* gather'd his Robe about him, that he might not fall in a
Manner unbecoming of himself; and the greatest Concern that appeared in the
Behaviour of *Lucretia*, when she stabb'd her self, was, that her Body should lie
in an Attitude worthy the Mind which had inhabited it.

The *Fasti*, ii. 833–4, is then quoted; the first reference was to the *De vita
Caesarum* of Suetonius. This may serve to reinforce our earlier comments
that what is pathos to one generation of readers may look like bathos to

another, and that the Ovidian tradition is beset with instability of meaning.

Chaucer, to be sure, sought to introduce some principles of order and control, as when he presents Lucrece as a martyr for marriage, an emphasis which is quite unprecedented in the *Fasti*. We have already noted the same emphasis in the *Legend of Cleopatra*, and it figures throughout the other narratives. If Ovid may be regarded as a champion of married love, so even more obviously may that English Ovid, Geoffrey Chaucer, in the *Legend* at least.

Ovid, *'The Art of Love' and Other Poems*, ed. and trans. J. H. Mozley, 2nd edn. (London and Cambridge, Mass., 1939); *Ovid: The Erotic Poems*, trans. Peter Green (Harmondsworth, 1982). W. Connely, 'Imprints of the *Heroides* of Ovid on Chaucer, *The Legend of Good Women'*, *Classical Weekly*, 18/2 (1924), 9–13. On Ovid's rewriting of Virgil's Dido see especially Schmitz, *Fall of Women*, pp. 24–8. In *Heroides* vii he finds a 'knowing Ovidian innuendo' which is 'directed as much against the heroine as against the hero'. But the fact that 'Ovid leaves his readers room for play does not', Schmitz believes, 'completely puncture the moving effects of the letter. The elegaic, being like the comic or mock-epic based on a lower ethical and stylistic plane, is capable of undermining the higher values that sustain the epic even without devaluing its agents' (p. 28). See further the lively discussion by Howard Jacobson, *Ovid's 'Heroides'* (Princeton, NJ, 1985).

Verducci, *Ovid's Toyshop of the Heart*. Brooks Otis, 'Ovid and the Augustans', *Transactions and Proceedings of the American Philological Association*, 69 (1938), 229; Kelly, *Love and Marriage*, pp. 97–100. On medieval commentary on Ovid and opinions regarding the life of a poet who presented a considerable challenge to the commentators by the apparent combination of transgressive eroticism and impressive learning in his *œuvre*, see Minnis and Scott (eds.), *Medieval Literary Theory*, pp. 20–30, 321–3, 360–72; F. Ghisalberti, 'Medieval Lives of Ovid', *Journal of the Warburg and Courtauld Institutes*, 9 (1946), 10–59; Frank T. Coulson, 'Hitherto Unedited Medieval and Renaissance Lives of Ovid (I)', *MS* 49 (1987), 152–207; Ralph J. Hexter, *Ovid and Medieval Schooling. Studies in Medieval School Commentaries on Ovid's 'Ars amatoria', 'Epistulae ex Ponto', and 'Epistulae Heroidum'*, Münchener Beiträge zur Mediävistik und Renaissance-Forschung, 38 (Munich, 1986).

Benoît de Sainte-Maure, *Roman de Troie*, ed. Léopold Constans (Paris, 1904–12). John Gower, *Traitié pour essampler les amantz marietz*, eighth ballade, in *Complete Works*, ed. G. C. Macaulay (Oxford, 1899–1902), i. 384.

Ovid, *Fasti*, ed. and trans. J. G. Frazer, Loeb Classical Library (London and Cambridge, Mass., 1931). Goddard, 'Chaucer's Legend'. Jonathan Sutton, 'A Reading of Chaucer's *Legend of Good Women*' (diss., University of Indiana, 1979).

Frank, *Legend of Good Women*; Brian Stone, *Chaucer: A Critical Study* (Harmondsworth, 1978); Mehl, *Narrative Poetry*; Florence M. Percival, 'Contextual Studies in Chaucer's *Legend of Good Women*' (Ph.D. diss., University of Sydney, 1988). Ian Donaldson has written a general history of literary realizations of Lucrece, *The Rapes of Lucretia: A Myth and its Transformations* (Oxford, 1982). The versions of the story by Gower and Shakespeare are compared by Richard Hillman, 'Gower's Lucrece: A New Old Source for *The Rape of Lucrece*', *ChR* 24 (1990), 263–70.

Alfred Duggan, *Thomas Beckett of Canterbury* (London, 1952).

*The Spectator*, ed. Donald F. Bond (Oxford, 1965), iii. 41 (no. 292, 4 Feb. 1712).

MISOGYNY RAMPANT: GUIDO DELLE COLONNE

'In Tessalie, as Guido tellith us . . .' (1396), begins Chaucer's account of
Hypsipyle, and her story generally follows the Jason narrative in the
*Historia destructionis Troiae* as far as line 1461, when it is announced that
the hero's meeting with the 'fayre yonge Ysiphele', daughter of King
Troas, is not to be found in Guido, but 'Yit seyth Ovyde in his Episteles
so' (1464–5)—that is, in *Heroides* vi. This Ovidian text is certainly alluded
to at line 1564 ('A letter sente she to hym') and probably also at line 1558,
where 'Th'origynal' is cited (in late medieval academic parlance the *orig-
inalia* were the 'authentic' texts of the *auctores*, in their entirety rather
than in extracts). When Chaucer comes to tell the tale of Jason's second
victim, King Aeëtes' daughter Medea, he returns to Guido, who seems
to be the main (if not the only) source of the remainder of the narrative,
apart from the very condensed version of *Heroides* xii, the 'lettre' of
Medea to Jason, as well composed in verse by 'Ovyde', with which the
story ends. Given that the *Historia destructionis Troiae* is notable for its
rampant anti-feminism, Guido presented quite a challenge to Cupid's
hagiographer. In order to appreciate fully how that was met, it will be
necessary to examine the way in which he brought the stories of
Hypsipyle and Medea together within a single legend, merging Ovidian
material with material from the *Historia*.

Ovid had linked *Heroides* vi and xii by having Hypsipyle make several
bitterly jealous references to the whore (*paelex*) who had robbed her of
her husband, and finally curse the 'barbarian poisoner' (19) in a fulsome
and foreboding manner (151–64; trans. Showerman, pp. 79–83). Medea
did not win him by her beauty or merits, Jason is assured, but by qualities which are as unwomanly as they are unnatural: this is the enchantress
who strives to 'draw down from its course the unwilling moon' and to
eclipse the sun; she can control the seas and streams, and move woods
and rocks from their places. Moreover, Medea stalks among sepulchres
and gathers bones from freshly cremated corpses, practises witchcraft,
and performs other deeds which it were better not to know. 'Ill sought
by herbs [i.e. the herbs she gathers for her magic] is love that should be
won by virtue and by beauty.' Can you really embrace a woman like this?
Jason is asked. 'Can you be left in the same chamber with her and not
feel fear, and enjoy the slumber of the silent night?' (85–96).

The way in which Medea became Jason's bride was shameless, whereas
the bond that united him with Hypsipyle was chaste (133–4). Consult
your parents, she entreats him; they certainly cannot approve of the
match. Doubtless they would have approved of Ovid's Hypsipyle, however, who is presented as a paragon of the traditional female virtues, being

a dutiful and loving daughter, wife, and mother. She saved her father from death, whereas Medea betrayed hers (135). So loyal a wife is she that, even now, if unfriendly gales were to drive Jason and Medea into her harbour, she would offer safety and protection to the man who deserved only death. But to her hated rival, Hypsipyle would become 'a Medea to Medea' and kill her with her own hands (141–51). Hypsipyle also evokes the attractions of parenting, and even goes so far as to say that she had considered sending her twins to Jason 'as their mother's ambassadors', but was frightened of what Medea might do to them, her hands being 'fitted for any crime' (119–28). Someone who could dismember her own brother (this having been done to delay her father's pursuit of Jason and herself) can hardly be trusted as a stepmother (125–30)! There is a grim irony here, of course: subsequently Medea will add to the long list of her crimes against nature by murdering the two children she has by Jason, a deed darkly hinted at in Hypsipyle's curse (159–60). The contrast between the two women, then, is complete and even symmetrical, each of Hypsipyle's virtues being opposed to one of Medea's vices. Indeed, it could be said that for the most part Ovid's Hypsipyle defines her character by reference to, and contrast with, that of Medea. And her case is certainly a strong one: Jason must have been mad when he 'slighted the wedding bed with Hypsipyle!'

Chaucer could not make use of the link between Hypsipyle and Medea which Ovid had forged. Guided by his I-persona's professed *entente*, he must reduce the moral differences between the two figures and concentrate on what they share, the fate of having been loved and left by Jason. Hypsipyle cannot be allowed to assassinate the character of the wronged woman who will follow her in the long line of love's martyrs. Thus, Medea is never mentioned by name, not even in the last lines of Hypsipyle's legend, which briefly echoes the passionate course which forms the climax of *Heroides* vi. Chaucer has Hypsipyle pray to God that, before long, the woman who has snatched away his heart from her will find him untrue to her also,

> And that she moste bothe hir chyldren spylle,          *kill*
> And alle tho that suffrede hym his wille.     *bowed to his desires*
> (1574–5)

Even allowing for the distorting effects of *abbreviatio*, this stands as being rather different from the text of Ovid, whose Hypsipyle wants her rival to suffer in each and every respect the woes in which she now groans (151–4), and for the unnatural tendencies which she has amply demonstrated already to manifest themselves afresh in the future: 'and as I am now left alone, wife and mother of two babes, so may she one day, bereft

of as many babes, lose husband too! . . . A bitter sister to her brother, a
bitter daughter to her wretched sire, may she be as bitter to her children,
and as bitter to her husband!' (155–60; p. 81).

The reported speech used by Chaucer lacks the passionate immediacy
and intensity of Ovid's verses; indeed, it reads almost as a factual
prophecy rather than as a *cri de coeur*. Whereas Ovid's Hypsipyle hopes
that her rival will be abandoned even as she has been, Chaucer's reporter
speaks as if this were a foregone conclusion. Moreover, quite unparalleled
in Ovid is the suggestion that those who let Jason have his 'wille' will die.
Since that term can carry a sexual implication, as in the *Miller's Tale*,
where the *wille/spille* rhyme again occurs—

> 'Ywis, but if ich have my wille,
> For deerne love of thee, lemman, I spille'.          (I(A) 3277–8)

—it may refer to (or at least include reference to) the death of Jason's
third conquest, Creon's daughter Glauce (briefly referred to later, in line
1661). So, anyone who is the object of Jason's sexual attentions will die.
Alternatively, if we take line 1575, 'alle tho that suffrede hym his wille',
to mean 'everyone who bowed to his desires' in the broadest sense of the
term rather than highlighting the specifically sexual one, then Jason
becomes even more dangerous: give this man what he wants, and you will
wind up dead. The fact that it is Medea who will do the killing is carefully occluded, the responsibility having been transferred to Jason as
*homme fatal*.

The rivalry between Jason's first two conquests having been eliminated, along with the contrast between Hypsipyle the good wife and
Medea the unwomanly witch, Chaucer portrays them as fellow sufferers
with a faithless lover in common. Hypsipyle's bitter jealousy is replaced
by goodness and lack of guile, the resultant effect being one of simple
pathos. For instance, Hypsipyle's statement that her children

> ben lyk of alle thyng, ywis,
> To Jason, save they coude nat begile          (1569–70)

—is simply pathetic, whereas in Ovid (*Heroides*, vi. 123–4) it also serves
to introduce Hypsipyle's fear that Medea might prove to be a cruel stepmother to those same children. It is out of goodness that Chaucer's
Hypsipyle offers help to the Argonauts, this being perfectly typical
behaviour on the part of a noble queen who wishes to assist everyone:

> Of hire goodnesse adoun she sendeth blyve          *energetically*
> To witen of that any straunge wight
> With tempest thider were yblowe a-nyght,
> To don him socour, as was hire usaunce          *help, practice*

> To fortheren every wight, and don plesaunce
> Of verrey bounte and of curteysye.                    (1473–8)

This princessly 'goodnesse' is underlined by the messenger's speech (1485–9), and acknowledged in Jason's response:

> 'My lady', quod he, 'thanke I hertely
> Of hire goodnesse'                                    (1492–3)

Hypsipyle's bounty and hospitality are manifested by her subsequent entertainment of the 'straunge folk', particularly Jason and Hercules.

Since they are all gentlefolk 'of gret degre' together, naturally Hypsipyle comes to confide in Hercules, expecting him to be 'sad, wys, and trewe, of wordes avyse [discreet]' (1521). His praise of Jason and professed concern for his friend's sloth in love (a topic on which Gower has much to say; see *Confessio Amantis*, iv. 1083–501) are accepted at face value by Hypsipyle, though the element of exaggeration in the statement that Jason

> hadde lever hymself to morder, and dye,        *rather*
> Than that men shulde a lovere hym espye.    *perceive to be*
>                                                        (1536–7)

should make us pause, particularly in the light of the narrator's introductory condemnation of Jason as a counterfeiter of emotion, wherein his 'wordes, farced with pleasaunce', along with his 'feyned trouthe' and 'contrefeted peyne and wo', are specifically attacked.

> O, often swore thow that thow woldest dye
> For love, whan thow ne feltest maladye
> Save foul delyt, which that thow callest love!
>                                                        (1378–80)

To swear to die if love is not requited, is of course rather different from threatening to die rather than love: but such protestations are equally hyperbolic and, the definite implication is, equally insincere. Events prove the truth of this. Hypsipyle's good nature is being exploited, for Jason and Hercules have conspired to entrap her with tactics which the I-persona of the *Ars amatoria* might have admired. In Chaucer's text such behaviour is presented as despicable:

> Of these two here was a shrewed lees,      *wicked deception*
> To come to hous upon an innocent!    *to become intimate with*
>                                                        (1545–6)

Whereas Hypsipyle is a credit to her class, her good breeding manifesting itself in, and being confirmed by, actions which are in the highest traditions of aristocratic behaviour, the antics of these two self-seeking males who have ganged up on her brand them as traitors to that same class, particularly to its ideals of chivalry and manly conduct.

After all this, we come to the story of Medea—and are instantly suspicious when the narrator praises Jason (1603–8), having been doubly alerted by the condemnation with which the entire *Legenda Ysiphile et Medee* opens and the male plot against Hypsipyle which is at the very centre of her story. Medea is seen as falling into the same trap as Hypsipyle; history—as rewritten by Chaucer—is repeating itself. The consistent depiction of Jason as chief traitor in love (cf. 1659) makes for considerable cohesion between the two short narratives. To pick up Chaucer's own introductory metaphor, the two women must in turn play the part of tender capons to Jason's sly, devouring fox (see 1369–70, 1383–93; echoed at the beginning of the Medea narrative, 1581). (Capons, or castrated roosters, were valued for their succulence in cuisine, and that might have been all that Chaucer had in mind, but the note of gender confusion chimes with several others in the *Legend*.) Hypsipyle's tenderness takes the form of goodness and innocence, as already noted; Medea's, of 'trouthe' and 'kyndenesse' (1664). These are constituents of a single pattern of figuration.

At this point we may also consider how Chaucer has used the story of the pursuit of the Golden Fleece, derived largely from Guido (as far as one can tell), as a framing device for the *Legenda Ysiphile et Medee*. Near the end of Medea's story Jason's actual winning of this prize is briefly announced (1651). This links up with lines 1396–1460, the initiation of the quest by King Pelleus. The entire escapade reads as a saga of male deception: the plot of Pelleus, who thinks he is sending Jason to his death (1414–19), paves the way for the plot of Jason and Hercules against Hypsipyle and Jason's subsequent intrigue at Medea's expense. The insincere words of Pelleus to Jason (1442–50) constitute the first of a series of deceiving speeches which the reader is warned (before and/or after they are delivered) not to trust, the others being Hercules' alluring words to Hypsipyle (1538–42) and Jason's false promise to Medea (1620–8). And Pelleus's false appearance, his 'Gret chere of love and of affeccioun' (1421), will of course also be replicated. The narrative symmetry is further enhanced by the fact that both stories end with a partial synopsis of the letter which the wronged lady sends to her false lover.

This completes our examination of how Chaucer, obliged to dispense with Ovid's links between the stories of Hypsipyle and Medea, skilfully manufactured his own. We are now in a position to investigate his editorializing of what 'Guido tellith us' about Medea. Guido introduces her as someone who 'although she had already reached marriageable age and was indeed ripe for marriage, had nevertheless from her childhood given herself up eagerly to the study of the liberal arts' (trans. Meek, pp. 13–14), the obvious implication being that this is most unusual for a woman. In those days there was nobody, whether man or woman, more learned than she, Guido admits, but then proceeds to devalue her learning by speaking of her skills as a necromancer and enchantress. The pagans of antiquity, he declares with heavy condescension, were willing to believe that she could very often force the sun and moon to go into eclipse against the order of nature—but this, he continues, is a fiction wrought by Ovid, which is unfitting for the belief of Catholics faithful to Christ.

Having undermined Medea's scholarly achievements, and labelled her a benighted pagan, Guido proceeds to attack her as a woman. Her father was foolish to place her next to Jason at dinner, given the nature of the whole female race:

Oh, unfortunate and infatuated generosity, what do you owe to politeness in the hazard of your reputation and the loss of your honor for courtesy? Is it wise to trust to feminine constancy or the female sex, which has never been able, through all the ages, to remain constant? Her mind always remains in motion and is especially changeable in girlhood, before the woman, being of marriageable age, is joined to her husband. (trans. Meek, p. 15)

In his translation of this passage in the *Troy Book*, John Lydgate rams the moral home:

| | |
|---|---|
| For who was euer ȝit so mad or wood, | *yet, crazy* |
| þat ouȝt of resoun conne ariȝt his good, | *that anything, rightly* |
| To ȝeue feith or hastily credence | |
| To any womman, with-oute experience, | |
| In whom is nouther trust ne sikernesse. | *security* |
| þei þen so double & ful of brotilnesse, | *instability* |
| þat it is harde in hem to assure; | *be confident* |
| For vn-to hem it longeth of nature, | |
| From her birth to hauen alliaunce | |
| With doubilnes and with variance. | (i. 1845–54) |

King Aeëtes paid heavily for his unthinking generosity, Guido continues; through it he lost his only heir and much of his treasure, which Medea stole when she fled with Jason.

Medea, on being placed in such close proximity to Jason, immediately falls in love with him: 'she suddenly burned with desire for him, and conceived in her heart a blind passion for him' (p. 16). Alone in her room after the feast, she is tormented by great anguish on account of the strength of her emotions, and thinks of 'how she could put an end to the flames of passion by satisfying her desire' (p. 17). Torn between love and

shame, she gives in to boldness. A week later she immodestly makes the
first move by speaking to Jason.

In the corresponding passage in Chaucer, there is no mention of
Medea's magical arts, her limiting paganism, or her typically feminine
weakness. Neither is her father described as a fool for not knowing what
women are like. Instead, Chaucer concentrates on the king's perfectly
commendable wish to honour a noble guest, which leads him to make
his daughter 'don to Jason companye / At mete' (1609–12). Medea herself is summarily described as being wise and fair, with the emphasis on
the fair:

> Medea, which that was so wis and fayr
> That fayrer say there nevere man with ye          *saw*
>                                                   (1599–1600)

Of Medea's emotional excesses in her own room, Chaucer makes no mention. Whereas in Guido the over-ardent female is very much the prime
mover of the affair, in Chaucer the emphasis is placed on Jason's winning
ways and his skill in 'al the art and craft' of love. Little wonder, then,
that Medea should fall in love with him. Thus, the responsibility for the
affair rests firmly with Jason. And Fortune too is blamed, for inflicting a
'foul myschaunce' on Medea (1609). In these ways, Chaucer rather deftly
absolves his heroine of blame.

Medea takes the initiative, in Chaucer as in Guido, but the significance
of her action is totally different. Guido was concerned to construct a
figure gripped by a sexual obsession which she could barely control.
Hence, when she wishes that Jason might be joined to her in marriage,
Guido harshly describes this as a transparent attempt to put her lusts in
the best possible light (one wonders if he was influenced by Virgil's condemnation of Dido for calling her illicit affair with Aeneas a proper marriage: cf. *Aeneid*, iv. 227–8, and pp. 386–7 below). Generalizing, as is his
wont, from the individual female case, Guido comments that 'it is always
the custom of women, that when they yearn for some man with immod-
est desire, they veil their excuses under some sort of modesty' (p. 17).
Lydgate reworks this passage by having Medea herself say that her wish
for marriage is 'honest',

> 'For my menyng is with-owten synne,
> Grounded and set vp-on al clennes,
> With-oute fraude or any doubilnes—
> So clene and pure is myn entencioun!'          (i. 2068–71)

—and then declares roundly that this is rubbish:

Loo, ay þe maner and condicioun
Of þis wommen, þat so wel can feyne,             *these*
And schewen on, þou3 þei þinke tweyne;    *think duplicitously*
And couertly, þat no þing be seyn,              *thing*
With humble chere and with face pleyn,
Enclose her lustis by swyche sotilte,
Vnder þe bowndis of al honeste
Of hir entent                              (i. 2072–9)

(He seems to be pulling away from Guido's crucial point: it is self-deception, rather than the deception of others, which is mainly at issue in the *Historia* passage.) In these accounts the import of Benoît's narrative is quite altered, for he had presented Medea's wish for marriage as the natural and honourable objective of the relatively controlled *fin' amors* which she is experiencing (cf. p. 362 above). But Chaucer is working to reinstate Benoît's emphasis, so to speak. He devotes some eleven lines (quite a lot, given the attenuated nature of the narrative) to an account of how Medea and Jason plan to get married. Jason makes solemn vows to become her husband for the rest of his life; only after that do they go 'to bedde'. (On the possible legal status of this union, cf. pp. 416–18 below.)

Guido's Medea, having protested too much about her reputation, offers Jason her expertise in exchange for marriage. By contrast, Chaucer's Medea gets down to the business of his quest right away, declaring that no one can succeed in the venture without her help, and that it is her will that he should survive (1611–19). Her manner here is curiously devoid of self-interest. Jason responds with the (somewhat bargaining) suggestion that since he is her man, she should be his helper. Medea tells him what he needs to know, and it is only then that the text begins to speak of their marriage. This lady, it would seem, is altogether more decorous, and certainly less driven by passion, than her prototype.

It should also be emphasized that, in Chaucer's account of their marriage agreement, pride of place goes to Medea's insistence that Jason should swear, upon the gods, that he will never be false to her. This comes from Guido, but within Chaucer's *abbreviatio* it has relatively more weight, the effect being that Medea is presented as having secured a solemn vow of lifelong fidelity before sleeping with Jason; by no means has she cheapened herself. Jason's eventual betrayal is, of course, thereby rendered all the more reprehensible. Guido had made this very point, but it is remarkable just how much criticism of Medea he manages to obtrude in what is ostensibly a condemnation of Jason. Since Chaucer reworked parts of this passage substantially it must be quoted at some length:

But oh, the deceiving falsity of the man! Say, Jason, what more could Medea ever have done for you, who, when she had set aside all honorable consideration

of decency, gave up her body and soul together to you, because of a quite mistaken confidence in your promise alone, not considering the signs of her rank
nor heeding the greatness of her royal dignity? For love of you she deprived herself of her hereditary sceptre and shamelessly left her old father, after having
robbed him of a mass of his treasure, and leaving her ancestral home, because of
you chose exile . . . Did she not preserve you unharmed from the annihilation
of death, and draw you away from the stain of perpetual scorn? . . . What lack
of shame made you dare to mock the bond of your oath so that you, defiled by
the disgrace of ingratitude, might deceive a credulous young girl? [Cf. *Heroides*,
xii. 89–90.] When you had taken her away from her ancestral hearth and had put
aside fear of the gods, whom you choose to scorn by foreswearing, you were not
afraid to betray the confidence of the woman from whom it is certain you
received such great benefits. (trans. Meek, pp. 22–3)

First and foremost, Chaucer emphasizes the benefits that Jason received
from Medea. It was she who saved his mission, his life, and his honour;
without her he would not have won fame as a great conqueror (1646–50).
The statement that this was done 'thourgh the sleyghte of hire
enchauntement' (1650) is the only occasion on which Medea's involvement with magic is mentioned in the whole of the *Legenda Ysiphile et
Medee*; here it serves to indicate the greatness of Medea's efforts on
Jason's behalf rather than being an object of censure. Then Chaucer
states:

> Now hath Jason the fles, and hom is went          *Fleece*
> With Medea, and tresor ful gret won;
> But unwist of hire fader is she gon          *unknown to*
> To Tessaly                                                        (1651–4)

There is no suggestion here that she has betrayed her father (as claimed
by Guido in the above passage, and cf. *Heroides*, xii. 109–10) and robbed
him 'of a mass of his treasure'. A little later the statement that Medea
'lafte hire fader and hire herytage' (1666) indicates just how much she
gave up for her worthless lover: it is she who has suffered the loss, not
her father.

Guido adds insult to injury by wondering why a woman so accomplished in astrology did not foretell her own fate, but of this there is not
a whisper in Chaucer. Guido does not chronicle what happened to the
lovers after their elopement, on the grounds that this has no bearing on
the present treatise. Chaucer's narrator, true to his professed *entente*, limits himself to the statement that Jason afterwards 'brought hire to
myschef' (1655). Here, once again, the blame is being laid on the shoulders of Jason, whom Chaucer proceeds to condemn for a reason which
would have been regarded as frivolous by Guido—namely, that he was
always a traitor in love. John Gower's handling of the Medea story, it

may be added, is very different at this point, because, although he presents her sympathetically throughout the narrative, at its end Gower does not shrink from mentioning the atrocities which she perpetrates—namely, the murder of Creusa and Jason's two sons—after which comes the extraordinary statement that Medea, thanks to her love-sufferings, is elevated into the heavenly court of Pallas, thereby escaping the wrath of the horrified Jason (cf. *Confessio Amantis*, v. 4190–222).

The way in which a single phrase from Guido may take on quite different resonances within the context to which Chaucer has assigned it, may be illustrated by Medea's eulogy of Jason as being dearer to her than herself. In the *Historia destructionis Troiae* the first words which Medea says to her lover after 'a whole night in the delights of voluptuous pleasure' which whets her appetite for more of the same (her lust having been revealed as insatiable) are: 'Dear friend, dearer to me than myself' (p. 24). In Chaucer the expression appears as the opinion of the narrator within a passage which depicts Medea as victim:

> This is the mede of lovynge and guerdoun       *reward*
> That Medea receyved of Jasoun
> Ryght for hire trouthe and for hire kyndenesse,
> That lovede hym better than hireself, I guesse
>
> (1662–5)

But of far greater significance is Chaucer's reversal of the import of a substantial passage of Guido, this being the most spectacular liberty which he took with his source. Near the beginning of his account of Medea, Guido attempts to establish a scientific basis for his belief in woman's inconstancy, by appropriating the common scholastic view of the relationship between matter and form. 'The heart of woman', he declares,

always seeks a husband, just as matter always seeks form. Oh, would that matter, passing once into form, could be said to be content with the form that it has received. But just as it is known that matter proceeds from form to form, so the dissolute desire of women proceeds from man to man, so that it may be believed without limit, since it is of an unfathomable depth. (p. 15)

In Chaucer, however, the faithless Jason is the matter which must always seek form:

> To Colcos comen is this duc Jasoun,
> That is of love devourer and dragoun.
> As mater apetiteth forme alwey,       *desires*
> And from forme into forme it passen may,
> Or as a welle that were botomles,
> Ryght so can false Jason have no pes.
>
> (1580–5)

This flies in the face of a whole tradition of scientific imagery: just as the seal was male while the wax it stamped was female, so form (pattern, order, structure) and matter (mere inchoate material, requiring form to become anything) were seen as expressive of the male and female principles respectively.

Although that may seem somewhat extreme (and raises the issue of whether Chaucer meant it to be regarded this way or not), his negotiations of the *Historia* were, for the most part, carried out with considerable subtlety. In marked contrast is what Lydgate made of Guido's account of Medea. At one point the Monk of Bury, having rendered his source-text's rampant misogyny with some vigour, feels obliged to protest against it:

> þus liketh Guydo of wommen for tendite.                *compose*
> Allas, whi wolde he so cursedly write
> Ageynes hem, or with hem debate!
> I am riȝt sory in englische to translate
> Reprefe of hem, or any euel to seye;
> Leuer me wer for her loue deye.                *I would rather*
> (*Troy Book*, i. 2097–102)

Going to the other extreme, Lydgate declares that women are perfect:

> þei ben so god and parfyte euerechon,
> To rekne all, I trowe þer be nat on,                *reckon, believe*
> But þat þei ben in wille and herte trewe.                (i. 2105–7)

If they take new lovers, he continues in the same sycophantic vein, this is because they have learned this promiscuous practice from men. Besides, he adds with ponderous jocularity, a woman cannot live alone—a remark which highlights the insincerity of the defence in which he is now engaged. Lydgate cannot leave well (or ill) enough alone, but must return to say that he himself should not be regarded as having transgressed in merely following what was written in his 'original'. Were Guido alive today and he were to shrive him, a bitter penance would be given! As we have already noted, extravagant praise, like extravagant blame, of women could serve as a rhetorical show-piece; Lydgate's swing from one to the other is therefore hardly surprising (cf. pp. 341–2). Moreover, there is the possibility that Lydgate could have learned from Chaucer's manner of protesting against the harsh literary treatment of women, in *Troilus and Criseyde*, v. 1772–85. If so, he has imbibed nothing of his master's tact and judgement. Whereas Lydgate loudly defamed and then loudly defended, Chaucer quietly drew the poison from the 'original' (cf. *Legend*, 2241).

Others worked by similar stealth, of course, most notably Christine de

Pizan, who in her *Cité des Dames* presented Medea as a figure who 'In learning . . . surpassed and exceeded all women' (trans. Richards, p. 69). This material came from *De mulieribus claris*, Christine having omitted what followed in Boccaccio's narrative, an attack on Medea for having allowed her eyes too much freedom when she gazed longingly and shamelessly at Jason (Boccaccio may have been inspired by Guido's remark that 'she could not control the glances of her eyes'; trans. Meek, p. 16). Given the trajectory of his narrative, Chaucer has no place for either Medea's extraordinary learning, which would (though possibly commendable in itself) have set her apart from his other 'good women' who are epitomes of aristocratic rather than clerkly virtues, or (to place those same accomplishments in the worst possible light) those sinister magical powers which are the very quintessence of heathen error and superstition. His agenda is a different one. The value which was bestowed upon marriage in *Heroides* vi actually permeates the entire *Legenda Ysiphile et Medee*; that Ovidian paragon of wifely and familial virtue, Hypsipyle, is followed by a figure who, having left behind her books and her barbarous revenge-lust, now cares as much about noble 'wyfhod' as she did.

Ovid's *Heroides*, ed. and trans. Showerman. Guido delle Colonne, *Historia destructionis Troiae*, trans. Meek; Latin text ed. Nathaniel E. Griffin (Cambridge, Mass., 1936).

John Lydgate, *Troy Book*, ed. Henry Bergen, pt. 1, EETS ES 97 (London, 1906). Benoît de Sainte-Maure, *Roman de Troie*, ed. Constans. Christine de Pizan, *Cité des Dames*, ed. Curnow, trans. Richards. On Christine's use of *De mulieribus claris* see especially Patricia A. Phillippy, 'Establishing Authority: Boccaccio's *De Claris Mulieribus* and Christine de Pizan's *Le Livre de la Cité des Dames*', *Romanic Review*, 77 (1986), 167–93.

For discussion of Chaucer's Medea narrative see especially Frank, *Legend of Good Women*, pp. 79–92; Fyler, *Chaucer and Ovid*, pp. 103–4; Meale, 'Legends of Good Women', pp. 59–66; R. K. Root, 'Chaucer's *Legend of Medea*', *PMLA* 24 (1909), 124–53; Rowe, *Nature to Eternity*, pp. 59–62.

A wide-ranging review of the medieval fortunes of the story has been carried out by Joel Nicholas Feimer, 'The Figure of Medea in Medieval Literature: A Thematic Metamorphosis' (Ph.D. diss., City University of New York, 1983).

## Structure and Strategy

It is difficult to speak with conviction of the *Legend*'s structure because the poem, as we have it, is incomplete, and therefore comment about Chaucer's overall plan can only be speculative. But various speculations have indeed been offered, some being far more persuasive than others. I myself have much sympathy with W. W. Skeat's suggestion (as strongly supported by V. A. Kolve) that Chaucer intended the poem to end with the legend of Alceste, she being the superlative example of virtuous womanhood, and a means of bringing the poem back to where it began, the dream-encounter with Alceste in the company of the God of Love. But the only formal instruction given to the I-persona was that

> At Cleopatre I wol that thou begynne,
> And so forth                    (F Prol. 566–7; cf. G Prol 542–3)

—in order to 'wynne' the God of Love's benevolence. Given that we will never know what Chaucer had in mind as he wrote that 'And so forth', the following section will concentrate on ideas put forward in the Prologue(s) which seem to offer clues as to the general directions which the subsequent narratives are supposed to be taking, and as such may be taken as intimating the poem's overall strategy.

### DRAWING INTO MEMORY: WOMEN AND THE WRITTEN RECORD

Is the God of Love's claim that good women may be numbered in their thousands made in a context which disposes the reader to call it in question? Let us explore this possibility. The poem begins with the narrator saying that he has heard men say that there is joy in heaven and pain in hell, and he is perfectly prepared to believe this, even though there is no one alive 'in this contree' who has actually been in either place. Apparently one can know of them only by hearsay—that is, from what one has heard or read. Such matters are unprovable by experience, then, but God forbid that men should refuse to believe anything unless they have seen it with their very own eyes. For here written authority comes in. Books, as the key of remembrance, strive to remedy the deficiencies of our first-hand knowledge: they preserve for the present age authentic histories ('olde aprovcd storyes') of many things, including holiness, love, and hate, records which command respect and demand belief.

> And if that olde bokes weren aweye,
> Yloren were of remembrance the keye.                    *lost*
> Wel oughte us thanne on olde bokes leve,                    *believe*
> There as there is non other assay by preve.                    *test*
>                                        (G Prol. 25–8)

Or, to cite other versions of this traditional doctrine, history provides 'accounts of actual occurrences removed in time from the recollection [or 'memory', the Latin being *memoria*] of our age'; the term *historia* derives 'from the Greek *historein* which in Latin is *videre* (to see) or *cognoscere* (to know). For among the ancients no-one wrote history except one who had been present and had seen the events which had to be written about' (cf. p. 206 above). In other words, old books record things seen in the past, and 'maken us memorie' (*CT* VII. 1974) in the sense of bringing them into the contemporary consciousness. This is the process which, in the *Legend of Lucrece* (1685), is described as 'drawing into memory'.

Chaucer's formulation implies that it is only the exceptional and/or remote subjects for which books are the sole source of knowledge. Now, the heroines who are his subject are both exceptional (in their virtue) and remote (because they lived long, long ago in heathen times), even though they cannot, of course, compete with the mysteries of heaven and hell in terms of difficulty and importance. It could be inferred, therefore, that such creatures are a thing of the past and nowadays are found, for the most part, only in books. Certainly, all Chaucer's heroines are from 'old story', from a period long before the present-day strife between the parties of the flower and the leaf (G Prol. 80). Here one may recall the claim made in Walter Map's *Epistola Valerii ad Rufinum*, a work apparently alluded to in line 280 of the G Prologue, that nowadays one cannot find a Lucretia, a Penelope, or a Sabine woman—the entire sex is to be feared. 'Lucretia, Penelope, and the Sabine women carried the banners of chastity and (with few followers) brought back their prizes. My friend, there are no Lucretias, Penelopes or Sabine women now: beware of them all' (trans. Blamires, p. 106). Similarly, at the end of the Clerk's tale of patient Grisilda, having been presented with the image of woman as long-suffering yet devoted wife, enduring all the trials of fidelity her husband puts her through, we are faced with the firm declaration that both Grisilda and her patience are dead and buried:

> Grisilde is deed, and eek her pacience,
> And bothe atones buryed in ytalle;       *together*
> For which I crie in open audience
> No wedded man so hardy be t'assaile      *foolhardy, test*
> His wyves pacience in trust to fynde
> Grisildis, for in certein he shal faille.  (*CT* IV(E) 1177–82)

In place of this paragon of female virtue now stands the Wife of Bath and 'al hire secte' (1170–2). Once good women existed, but we shall never (or, at best, rarely) see with our own eyes their like again. Indeed, Janet Cowen believes that such an 'antifeminist joke', albeit 'suppressed', actually 'runs through' the *Legend*: 'Simply the choice of the theme of good women continually invites transposition into its comic opposite. Lucrece is an exemplary figure, but, the question is, are there any to be found like her today?' (p. 433).

Moreover, the G Prologue contains the statement that the poet's 'entent' is 'to declare' the 'naked text in English'

Of many a story, or elles of many a geste,
As autours seyn; *leveth hem if yow leste.*

(87–8; italics mine)

The idea that one has the freedom to believe or disbelieve what 'story' has to say rather conflicts with the persona's earlier effusive protestation of trust in books—or is this to be dismissed as a throw-away phrase? If taken seriously, one possibility which it raises is that the figure of the bookish narrator (a construct we have encountered in the *Book of the Duchess* and *Parliament of Fowls*) is rather naïve to believe so totally in what he reads. His own readers, however, may be more discerning—a nice little compliment to them. Another implication is that the authorities he has followed may not be reliable in any case: the unreliability of written records was, of course, a central concern of the earlier *House of Fame*. One possible inference would be that the reader should approach the legends with a certain scepticism.

This inference appears to draw support from a stringent survey of the legends themselves. Some of Chaucer's choices seem rather odd, if we know the 'full story' of the lady in question rather than the heavily edited (censored?) version which he is offering us. Two women in particular could easily be (and often were) described as being indubitably bad, namely Medea and Philomela (cf. p. 361 above). Two other figures might be described as the best of a very bad lot. Hypsipyle was the only woman in her kingdom (of which she became queen) who failed to participate in a plot to kill all the menfolk—she spared her father's life. Hypermnestra was the only one of the fifty daughters of Danaus (in Chaucer, Aegyptus) who did not obey her father's command to kill her husband on their wedding night; the other forty-nine actually did the deed. Several of the other heroines could be described as morally dubious. Dido was indeed abandoned by Aeneas, but Virgil shows her raging and cursing her lover—who, it could be (and was) argued, had departed in obedience to a divine command, and not of his own volition. Phyllis was betrayed by Demophon, but in medieval exegesis of *Heroides* ii she was regarded as having been culpably foolish to have fallen in love with a seafarer (in moralistic medieval criticism, the nice girls do *not* love a sailor). Ariadne was treacherously abandoned by Theseus, but out of love for him she had betrayed her father and half-brother (the latter, the Minotaur, having been killed by Theseus).

In view of all this, it might seem reasonable to conclude that Chaucer deliberately planned his legends as a mere travesty on feminine virtue, to echo Goddard, whose radical study, published in 1908 and 1909, retains much of its original challenge, despite its belligerence and bluster. But the narratives raise many issues which were not dreamed of in Goddard's philosophy. First, it seems quite clear (at least to me) that one legend in particular, the story of Lucrece, is an irrefutably genuine tale of heathen heroics, her portrait being the closest Chaucer got to creating a female 'good pagan' who could genuinely compete with the female protagonists of, for example, Jacob of Voragine's *Legenda aurea* (on which, more later). And if this story is meant to be taken positively, is it not possible that that is how the others should be read also? Secondly, and more fundamentally, if one wishes to argue that some source-related joke or other is intended in the *Legend*, the first requirement is to prove that some people could have got the joke. Most, if not all, of the theories that postulate irony or satire in the poem, however much they may differ among themselves (and they can differ widely), depend on the premiss that the audience, or some part thereof, would have known the story which Chaucer is altering, the ironic or satiric effect being dependent on the recognition that a source is being altered. But if the audience does not have such privileged knowledge, the effect cannot occur and so the work fails in its objective.

Any reading of a medieval text which rests on a reconstruction of audience response and expectancy is on very shaky ground indeed, given, on the one hand, the paucity of our knowledge of what audiences actually *did* feel and think and, on the other, the understandable but reductive tendency of such speculation to make large assumptions concerning the homogeneity of the supposed audience and the monolithic nature of its response. In the case of the *Legend* the problem is further complicated by the possibility that the characteristic reaction of each sex (according to then current values) is being anticipated and exploited. Here Chaucer shows that he is acutely aware of his position as a man writing about women; it seems reasonable, therefore, to investigate the possibility that he might have envisaged the audience response as splitting down gender lines.

The underlying question is: who held the 'key of remembrance'? Educated males certainly had it, on account of their knowledge of Latin literature; but women, for the most part, were obliged to be content with the restricted and/or occasional loan of this privileged possession. Over and over again in his works, Chaucer reveals his awareness of the differences between what men read and what women read. Two of the Nun's Priest's jokes may serve to illustrate this. His tale of the cock and the fox, he declares, is as true as is

> the book of Launcelot de Lake,
> That wommen holde in ful greet reverence.     (*CT* VII. 3212–13)

—which can only be taken as implying that female readers of vernacular romance are a credulous lot. A little earlier, Chauntecleer, sexually excited by the beauty of Pertelote, quotes and translates a Latin saying as follows:

> For al so siker as *In principio*,                    *certain*
> *Mulier est hominis confusio,*—
> Madame, the sentence of this Latyn is,                    *meaning*
> 'Womman is mannes joye and al his blis.'          (VII. 3163–6)

The correct translation, of course, is that woman is the downfall of man. The specific target of this joke is a matter of debate: is the cock making the joke at the hen's expense, or is he himself ignorant of the real meaning? Or is this yet another instance of the jolly misogyny which permeates the tale of a figure who, one might be supposed to remember, earns his daily bread by administering to nuns? Anyway, Pertelote does not seem to get the joke, and it is tempting to speculate that many of the women readers/auditors of the poem would have been similarly excluded because of their ignorance of Latin—until, perhaps, the males condescended to explain it to them.

With this in mind, it would be possible to construct a reading model for the *Legend* based on the idea that Chaucer has produced a masterpiece of double-barrelled flattery, consonant with late medieval constructions of gender. The female ego is flattered by what, on the face of it, is a collection of stories of exceptional women who consistently outdo the male characters (who are, at best, their foils) in strength of character and singleness of purpose. If Alceste was indeed meant as some sort of idealizing portrait of Queen Anne, one need not doubt that she would have been well pleased with the likeness. Presumably Chaucer was as sensitive to such career considerations as the next courtly poet. On the other hand, the male ego is flattered in so far as the text is reserving an area of meaning for the entertainment and approval of men only. They are, as it were, being offered the interpretative equivalent of membership of some exclusive (and exclusively male) club. And what qualifies them for membership is, of course, their education and knowledge of Latin literature, particularly the Ovidian stories on which Chaucer based so many of his legends.

But this view of different textual communities (or of a division within a single textual community) is hard to sustain. In the case of the Ovidian heroines of the *Legend*, some basic knowledge of the original ventriloquizing of women's voices and the major narrative events can be assumed among both sexes, for some of the relevant material had appeared in vernacular works and hence could have been known to women readers (I am thinking of the *Roman d'Eneas*, the *Roman de Troie*, the *Roman de la Rose*, Machaut's *Navarre*, etc.). Therefore the theory that Chaucer meant the entire poem as a colossal joke against women which men only could enjoy, thanks to their superior education and knowledge of the classics, is simply untenable.

What, then, of the cases where detailed knowledge of a specific source appears to be necessary for the ironic effect? An excellent test case is afforded by Chaucer's depiction of someone whose fame had spread far and wide, namely Medea. As we have noted above, his main source was Guido delle Colonne's *Historia destructionis Troiae*, and it is apparent that here the poet systematically rewrote, and utterly changed the import of, a pervasively anti-feminist narrative. Did Chaucer expect his audience to laugh at the way in which he had turned his source inside out? To take one specific example, which constitutes his most striking piece of recasting, Guido had attacked the inconstant Medea through the metaphor of matter and form: just as matter proceeds from form to form, so the dissolute desire of women proceeds from man to man. In the Middle English version, however, the faithless Jason is the matter which always seeks form (1580–5; cf. pp. 376–7 above). Now, to recognize that Chaucer was doing something unusual here, one did not have to know Guido's Medea narrative. But, it could be argued, only those who had, and have, read Guido can enjoy the full savour of this joke. But *is* it a joke, something meant to provoke general laughter? For one can hardly postulate intimate knowledge of the details of Guido's account in the minds of auditors of the *Legend of Medea*. It could be argued, then, that evidence relating to the *makynge* of a legend should not be confused with evidence relating to its *intended effect*. That may come uncomfortably close to the proposition that the only person who would have been aware of some of the most amusing things in the *Legend* was Geoffrey Chaucer himself. But it appears preferable to the other extreme, wherein one is being asked to conceive of an audience earnestly consulting copies of the glossed *Heroides*, the *Speculum historiale*, Guido's *Historia*, and so forth as they read or heard Chaucer's poem—which would seem to be carrying scholarly self-reflexivity too far.

Then there is the possibility that the relationship of form and matter might have been too complicated a topic for women, who lacked knowledge of the Aristotelian philosophy which underpinned it. What happens in Castiglione's *Il Cortegiano* when the same distinction is introduced is illuminating. Having paused to reflect that 'this is not perhaps the right time to go into subtleties', the Magnifico Giuliano proceeds to do just that, arguing that 'as far as their formal essence is concerned, the male cannot be more perfect than the female, since both the one and the other are included under the species man, and they differ in their accidents and not their essence' (trans. Bull, p. 218). Gaspare, similarly prefacing his remarks with the protestation that he does 'not wish to go into such subtleties because these ladies would not understand them', counter-attacks with the theory of form and matter: 'it is the opinion of very learned men that man is as the form and woman as the matter, and therefore just as form is more perfect than matter, and indeed it gives it its being, so man is far more perfect than woman' (p. 220). Guiliano promptly replies that this is a false analogy, for woman does not receive her being from man in the same way as matter receives its being from form. But the ladies have had enough of this. 'In heaven's name', Signora Emilia exclaims, 'leave all this business of matter and form and male and female at once, and speak in a way that you can be understood . . . now we can't at all understand your way of defending us' (p. 221).

However, this elaborate exchange between Giuliano and Gaspare is light-years away from Chaucer's short (occupying a mere two lines) and relatively simple statement. And for anyone who might baulk at the business of matter and form, help is at hand. The first lines of the complete passage in question (1580–5) make it utterly clear that its objective is the presentation of Jason as a 'devourer and dragoun' in love. Moreover, the technical philosophical distinction is followed by an alternative—a homely image (not found in Guido) which is designed to dispel any vestige of doubt:

> Or as a welle that were botomles,
> Ryght so can false Jason have no pes.                    (1584–5)

Similarly, after the abstruse Boethian doctrine of *deus dator formarum* is invoked, its specific significance for the tale of Tereus is spelled out: why did God allow such a hideous creature to be born? And the narrator shows his audience the direction their emotional reaction should take by expressing his own disgust at the 'foule storye' (2228–43). Chaucer is speaking in a way that can be understood—by both men and women.

Of course, a medieval reader blessed with detailed knowledge of the sources and doctrines on which Chaucer was drawing would have approached and enjoyed the *Legend* in a way rather different from a person who lacked this information, and it should be freely acknowledged that the *Legend* can accommodate several different kinds of response. This, indeed, may be regarded as one of its great strengths. But in lines 1584–5, and in many other places, Chaucer seems to be doing his best to ensure that his most important gestures will not be lost on the greater part of his audience. At any rate, the *Legend* contains certain effects of a quite broad and general kind, and introduces tensions of a type which most readers would perceive, each according to his or her capacity; the extent to which Chaucer was deliberately doing this, as opposed to inscribing cultural discourses which have their own inherent contradictions, must remain a matter of debate.

For a start, there is the fact that Chaucer's narrator is portrayed as a somewhat frantic individual who, having been censured for writing about bad women, is now recording the martyrdoms of Cupid's saints with extraordinary zeal and determination. Sometimes he gets quite carried away, as when he describes Dido as a suitable mate even for God Almighty. Hyperbole can go no higher!

> if that God, that hevene and erthe made,
> Wolde han a love, for beaute and goodnesse,
> And womanhod, and trouthe, and semelynesse,
> Whom shulde he loven but this lady swete?
> Ther nys no woman to hym half so mete. *suitable*
>
> (1039–43)

Or, when he is overwhelmed by his own importance as Cupid's hagiographer and the only *praeceptor amoris* whom women can trust: 'trusteth, as in love, no man but me' (2561). Both these passages can be regarded as part of Chaucer's attempt to cultivate an Ovidian style, as suggested on p. 359 above. But Chaucer's audience(s), one may speculate, would have been more aware of their impact than their origin.

Secondly, there is the obvious tension between the graciously virtuous Alceste and the God of Love, whose pompous, blustering manner threatens to turn him into a tin-pot tyrant, a topic which will be considered in more detail below. Finally, it may be argued that Chaucer deliberately introduced some discrepancies into the narratives themselves, to bring the problems and paradoxes of the poem within the ken of less knowledgeable members of the audience, of either sex. A good example is afforded by the text's volte-face on the status of Dido's liaison with Aeneas. For most of the *Legend of Dido* it is assumed that Aeneas is Dido's husband in a sense which is legally specific and binding. Indeed, at one point we are assured that she

> tok hym for husbonde and becom his wyf
> For everemo, whil that hem laste lyf. (1238–9)

The echo of the Christian vow to remain faithful 'till death us do part' reinforces this sense of full marriage. Yet, at the end of the narrative, it is made clear that something is missing. 'Have ye nat sworn to wyve me to take'? Dido demands of Aeneas (1304), and goes on to ask that she should die 'as youre wif' (1322). Anyone who was aware of how Virgil had described Dido as seeking to hide the shame of her affair by honouring it with the mere name of marriage (*Aeneid*, iv. 227–8) would have recognized, quite early on in Chaucer's proceedings, that the narrator was acting as a spokesperson for Dido and seeing the situation entirely from her point of view. For other readers or auditors, the tension is made abundantly clear at a later stage.

These effects contribute to the success of the *Legend* as a highly entertaining poem, a work which, far from offering blandly indiscriminate panegyric, actually encourages debate—and as such is a fit poem to have been generated and enjoyed (one may imagine) by those groups of courtiers who demonstrated their wit and social graces by arguing for the respective merits of the flower and the leaf. To argue thus is to do no more than claim that the *Legend* was intended to please an audience similar to, if not identical with, the one addressed by the *Parliament of Fowls* (cf. the extended discussion of the 'implied audience' of that poem, pp. 290–307 above). Like the *Parliament*, the *Legend* combines doctrine and delight, the sublime and the ridiculous. Several of the passages quoted above are surely meant to amuse. Indeed, Chaucer (typically) sets himself up as a figure of fun: his I-persona's lifelong commission has obliged him to break ranks with his sex, as it were. And yet the text can also be deadly serious, as when that same narrator interrogates the 'yevere of the formes' who suffered Tereus to be born (2228–43; cf. p. 348 above). Those notes are as sombre as those struck near the beginning of the *Parliament*, when the Macrobian vision of the universe, with its values of heavenly harmony and retribution, unfolds with grace and reverence. And again like the *Parliament* (on the reading offered in my previous chapter), the *Legend* may well have been received as a relatively open-ended text (but certainly not wide open), which offers several possibilities for interpretation without holding out a single one as being definitive.

There is, then, no critical obligation to regard Chaucer's apparent scepticism regarding the written record and women's relationship to it as necessarily belonging within an argument which postulates irony or downright satire in Chaucer's construction of a series of heroines. Indeed, it can (far more justifiably and appropriately, in my view) be taken as the cornerstone of the hypothesis that he was pleasurably engaged in the exciting literary experiment of putting women on top for a change. The intimate nature of the relationship between the *House of Fame* and the *Legend of Good Women* has not received sufficient attention in most modern criticism of the later poem, but here may be found vital clues to its significance (cf. pp. 244–5 above). In the *House of Fame* it is made painfully clear that fame need not give people what they deserve. In the *Legend*, Chaucer seems to have pushed the speculations and suspicions presented in the earlier poem to a sort of logical conclusion as far as the regular victims of history were concerned. He would consistently be 'favorable' to women, adopting a deliberate and all-determining bias on their behalf.

After all, in *Troilus and Criseyde* Chaucer had sought to suck the poison from the misogynistic presentations of Criseyde (by Guido and Boccaccio) which were his sources; but there he was fighting a losing battle, because the final infidelity of the heroine could be obscured but not eliminated. In antiquity, however, could be found some women who did not require any special pleading. 'Penelopees truth and good Alceste', for instance, were unquestionably impressive, as was Lucrece's sacrifice, and in other cases 'creative editing' could yield positive results, revealing how very often hapless heroines had been 'betraised' by 'false' men (cf. *T&C* v. 1778–81). That Chaucer's scepticism concerning the total veracity of literary authorities should so totally permeate the *Legend* is, therefore, hardly surprising. It is at once writ small in the poem's detail, as when (yet again!) doubt is cast on something in the *Aeneid*—

> I can nat seyn if that it be possible,
> But Venus hadde hym [i.e. Aeneas] maked invysible—
> Thus seyth the bok, withouten any les.          *lies* (1020–2)

—and writ large in the overall strategy of the entire work, wherein such doubt is harnessed to generate a rereading and rewriting of anti-feminist literature.

The Chaucer persona is not telling lies himself, he assures us; we can believe him even though others who have written about love are to be mistrusted (cf. lines 2559–61). The written record is not being waived; literary authority is on his side. Jesus Christ praised feminine faith, 'and this is no lye' (1882). The *Legend of Cleopatra* is asserted to be 'storyal soth, it is no fable' (602). Here, then, is at work the same poet who had so daringly identified as the primary source for *Troilus and Criseyde* the grand-sounding but non-extant (and indeed non-existent) Latin 'auctour called Lollius' (*T&C* i. 394) and had suppressed and sometimes denied the damning things which his sources had said about Criseyde, even while proclaiming his deference to and dependence on them. He should be recognized as that poet. The ambitious project of compiling a legendary of Cupid's saints gave Chaucer the opportunity to indulge the tastes that had attracted him to the 'memorye' of Criseyde, a woman whose name was 'rolled . . . on many a tonge' and had 'No good word' written or sung about her (v. 1059–61), and to exploit the talents he had developed in reconstituting her subjectivity. The purpose of the *Legend*, according to this reading, is to 'draw to memorye' praising portraits of heroines who, in a characteristically feminine way (what is meant by that will be explored later), had made virtue of necessity. This would provide sophisticated (and supportive) entertainment for England's queen and noble ladies and, no doubt, earn the admiration of those among the *litterati* who could appreciate just how much of a *tour de force* the poem was. Here, then, is no small enterprise.

*Works*, ed. Skeat, iii, p. xviii, and v. 137–79; Kolve, 'From Cleopatra to Alceste'. Fyler, *Chaucer and Ovid*, p. 104, speaks interestingly of 'the hidden jokes of a translator'. Some of the 'problems of reading and narration' which the text's 'conflicting messages' raise are well described by Peter L. Allen, 'Reading Chaucer's Good Women', *ChR* 21 (1987), 419–34.

Cowen, 'Structure and Tone'. Goddard, 'Chaucer's *Legend*'.

Maybe lines 1039–43, Chaucer's praise of Dido as a suitable mate for God, was not meant to be as hyperbolical as it seems. For Chaucer could have had in mind the well-known womanizing proclivities of Jupiter, chief among the pagan gods (clearly, Dido would have been most attractive to *him*), which he mentally mingled with commonplace Christian notions regarding God Almighty. It may be added that the description of this god as a creator ('that hevene and erthe made') would not rule out my hypothesis, for similar remarks are to be found in other poems wherein Chaucer is endeavouring to create a pagan setting and in which non-Christian but vaguely monotheistic deities feature; see, for example, Dorigen's words in the *Franklin's Tale*, V(F) 865–72 (cf. Aurelius's oath 'by God that this world made', 967), and Troilus's prayer 'to God, that auctour is of kinde' (*T&C* iii. 1765). These accreditations of such insight to certain pagans is fully supported by late medieval scholastics, who often cite Augustine's praise of Plato for having conceived of a creative deity. See A. J. Minnis, 'From Medieval to Renaissance? Chaucer's Position on Past Gentility', *PBA* 72 (1986), 230–2.

The bibliography on the larger implications of the issues raised in this section is vast; good ways in are provided by Mary Jacobus (ed.), *Women Writing and Writing about Women* (London, 1979); and Toril Moi, *Sexual/Textual Politics* (London and New York, 1985). On the positions and problems of medieval women readers (and writers) see, for instance, Alexandra Barratt, '*The Flower and the Leaf* and *The Assembly of Ladies*: Is there a (Sexual) Difference?', *Philological Quarterly*, 66 (1987), 1–24; Peter Dronke, *Women Writers of the Middle Ages* (Cambridge, 1984); Karma Lochrie, '*The Book of Margery Kempe*: The Marginal Woman's Quest for Literary Authority', *JMRS* 16/1 (1986), 35–55; Angela Lucas, *Women in the Middle Ages* (Brighton, 1983), pp. 137–79; Susan Schibanoff, 'Early Women Writers: In-scribing, or, Reading the Fine Print', *Women's Studies International Forum*, 6/5 (1983), 475–89. Specially recommended is Meale's anthology *Women and Literature*; of particular relevance here are the essays by Bella Millett, Felicity Riddy, Carol Meale, and Julia Boffey. A useful analytical framework is offered by Alexandra Barratt's introduction to her anthology *Women's Writing in Middle English* (Harlow, 1992), pp. 1–23.

For discussion with specific reference to Chaucer, see especially Dinshaw, *Chaucer's Sexual Poetics*, *passim* but esp. pp. 28–64; Hansen, *Fictions of Gender*, pp. 163–4; Mann, *Chaucer*; Martin, *Chaucer's Women*; Meale, 'Legends of Good Women'. Meale makes the eminently plausible suggestion that 'Chaucer's primary concern with women was a literary one', by contrast with the more political aims of Christine de Pizan, 'and revolved around his freedom to experiment with female narrative voices' (pp. 69–70).

A QUESTION OF VALUE: TRUTH IN LOVE AND TRUTH-IN-LOVE

Cupid brings the following charges against the Chaucer persona:

| | |
|---|---|
| Thow art my mortal fo and me werreyest, | *war against me* |
| And of myn olde servauntes thow mysseyest, | *slander* |
| And hynderest hem with thy translacyoun, | |
| And lettest folk to han devocyoun | *prevent* |
| To serven me, and holdest it folye | |
| To truste on me. Thou mayst it nat denye, | |
| For in pleyn text, it nedeth nat to glose, | |
| Thou hast translated the Romauns of the Rose, | |
| That is an heresye ayeyns my lawe. | |
| And makest wise folk fro me withdrawe; | |
| And thynkest in thy wit, that is ful col, | |
| That he nys but a verray propre fol | |
| That loveth paramours to harde and hote. | |

(G Prol. 248–60; cf. shorter passage in F Prol. 322–31)

Then he criticizes Chaucer's account of Criseyde, on the grounds that it defames women in general—which is all the more reprehensible because the poet has 'sixty bokes olde and new' (273) in his personal possession from which he could learn that good women far outnumber the bad ('evere an hundred goode ageyn oon badde', 277). That there is a definite and important connection between the 'Romauns of the Rose' and the story of Criseyde seems clear from the way in which first Alceste and then the I-persona speak of them together in discussing Love's charges. A 'trewe man', responds the narrator, has no share in a thief's deed; likewise,

| | |
|---|---|
| a trewe lovere oghte me nat to blame | |
| Thogh that I speke a fals lovere som shame. | |
| They oughte rathere with me for to holde | *side with* |
| For that I of Criseyde wrot or tolde, | |
| Or of the Rose; what so myn auctour mente, | |
| Algate, God wot, it was myn entente | *At any rate* |
| To forthere trouthe in love and it cheryce, | *cherish* |
| And to be war fro falsnesse and fro vice | |
| By swich ensaumple; this was my menynge. | (G Prol. 456–64) |

How, then, may the charges be explained and interpreted? Here are some possibilities.

First, we may engage with the statement that the *Roman de la Rose* makes wise folk withdraw from Love. This could be a reference to what the character Reason has to say in Jean de Meun's part of the poem: she tries to turn the Lover away from his goal, but he is insistent and dismisses her. Or it could refer to the *remedium amoris* aspects of the *Roman* in general. For on many occasions, figures and incidents bring out in turn the painful, demeaning, and ridiculous aspects of the type of love here pursued so obsessively. Support for this view is afforded by the claim of Jean's supporters in the *querelle de la Rose* that he wrote in order to warn his readers against love. According to Pierre Col's response to the criticisms of Christine de Pizan and Jean Gerson (who had pointed out that the *Roman* draws on the work of a poet who had been exiled for inciting immorality), Jean de Meun's intention in showing the capture of the Castle of Jealousy, in which the Rose resides, is to teach the defenders to guard the Castle better. This, Col argues, is why Jean de Meun describes as many forms of attack as he can, drawing on Ovid's *Ars amatoria* 'and books by many others'. Col then gives a personal proof of the efficacy of the method: it made a friend of his withdraw from love. 'In fact, an acquaintance of mine, in his efforts to free himself from foolish love, borrowed the *Roman de la Rose* from me, and I have heard him swear by his faith that it was this book which helped him most to disentangle himself' (trans. Baird and Kane, p. 109). Little wonder, then, that Chaucer's Cupid should regard the book as containing heresy against his law.

Secondly, there are several interpretative problems presented by the statement that only a fool loves 'paramours' (261), which I presume means something like 'engages in a passionate love-affair'. Either this is simply a repetition, in slightly different terms, of what has already been said (in lines 56-8) as interpreted above, or it is a specific reference to Reason's attack on love for love's sake: 'A lover so burns and is so enraptured that he thinks of nothing else: he takes no account of bearing fruit [i.e. of engendering children], but strives only for delight' (*Roman de la Rose*, 4385-8; trans. Dahlberg, p. 96). The true doctrine, Reason declares, is that every man who sleeps with a woman should wish to reproduce himself: 'to continue his divine self and to maintain himself in his likeness in order that the succession of generations might never fail, since all such likenesses are subject to decay' (4403-10; p. 96). Nowhere in the Prologue does Chaucer clarify this matter.

What is perfectly clear is that, according to the reaction of the Chaucer persona, falsity in love in its widest aspect is what the God of Love is complaining about: false ideas about love were propounded in the *Roman*; a false lover (Criseyde) was portrayed in *Troilus*. His collection of legends of good women will put the record straight on all counts. That is to say, truth in love and good women are essentially linked, the presence of the one being essentially related to the existence of the other.

Indeed, there may be a hidden premiss in the argument here, to the effect that the *Rose*, as much as *Troilus*, was anti-feminist in that it

showed 'how that wemen han don mis' (G Prol. 266), and indeed implied
that the whole female sex was unreliable—that, certainly, was how
Christine de Pizan saw the *Rose*. 'Malicious slanderers who debase
women in this way', she declares,

still maintain that all women have been, are now, and always will be false, asserting that they have never been capable of loyalty. They say that lovers find all
women to be like this when they approach them amorously. At every turn,
women are put in the wrong: whatever wrong has been done is attributed to
them. This is a damnable lie, and one can easily see that the contrary is true.
For, in matters of love, far too many women have been, are now, and will be
faithful, in spite of deceit and falsehoods, deception and trickery, and the numerous lies which have been used against them. (pp. 36–7)

Certainly, this hypothesis would strengthen the link postulated between
the *Rose* and *Troilus*.

However, it is difficult to reconcile the rather subversive (of Love's
position) implication that is included in the God of Love's protest—that
is, that Jean makes wise folk withdraw from Love—with what the poet
has his persona say about his own intention of furthering truth in love.
If loving is unwise, why should anyone want to further its cause? Is there
a type of love which *is* consonant with wisdom? Interestingly, Cupid is
tacitly putting the Chaucer persona on the side of the supporters of de
Meun in the *querelle*, by attributing 'heretical' opinions to him: you
'thynkest in *thy wit*', Cupid complains to that construct, 'That he nys but
a verray propre fol / That loveth paramours to harde and hote' (258–60).
The claim that the narrator's wit is 'ful col' is significant, given the common belief that love required youthful heat (cf. pp. 142–3 above); this
insult is elaborated in G Prologue 261–3, where Cupid suggests that the
poet is beginning to dote. 'Olde foles', when their own spirits fail, 'blame
folk', the implication perhaps being that, being incapable of love themselves, they are grudging about hard and hot *young* folk, falling into the
trap of judging people in line with their own limitations. (If the usual dating of the G Prologue is accepted, Chaucer was over 50 when he wrote
it, definitely old by medieval standards.) The idea that with old age came
wisdom (despite the occasional *senex amans*) was part of a standard
medieval discourse relating to the ageing process: 'elde hath greet avan-
tage; / In elde is bothe wysdom and usage' (*CT* I(A) 2447–8). It is hardly
surprising, then, that the God of Love should see the poet's maturity as
potentially threatening. Indeed, in the *querelle de la Rose* one of the
defences offered in support of Jean de Meun was that he was not actually *in* love when he wrote the *Rose*, but rather composed it as someone
who had left behind his youthful concerns, and was well able to view
them with detachment and good judgement.

Alceste defends the Chaucer persona on the grounds that he didn't know what he was doing, which he himself supports with the protestation that he meant well. But there is more to it than that. The language of this figure's defence requires careful analysis. It was his 'entente', he declares, to reveal false love as shameful and to encourage the contrary, 'trouthe in love'; by such exemplification the reader is being warned against 'falsnesse' and 'vice'. The narrator seems to have appropriated the language of the standard medieval literary criticism of Ovid's *Heroides*, a major source of the *Legend*. In *accessus* (preface, introduction) after *accessus* to this poem, we are assured that Ovid's 'intention' (*intentio*) is to 'commend lawful marriage and love', and

in keeping with this end, he deals with love in three forms: lawful love, unlawful love, and foolish love. He uses the example of Penelope to discuss lawful love, the example of Canace to discuss unlawful love, and the example of Phyllis to discuss foolish love. He includes two of the forms, foolish and unlawful love, not for their own sake, but in order to commend the third. Thus, in commending lawful love he criticizes foolish and unlawful love. The work pertains to ethics, because he is teaching good morality and eradicating evil behaviour. The ultimate end of the work is this, that, having seen the advantage [*utilitas*, moral utility] gained from lawful love, and the misfortunes which arise from foolish and unlawful love, we may shun both of these [i.e. foolish love and unlawful love] and may adhere to chaste love. (trans. Minnis and Scott, p. 21)

Just as, on this analysis, Canace and Phyllis are contrary *exempla*, so, it would seem, Criseyde illustrates what must be avoided and condemned.

The Ovid cited in evidence here is 'the Moral Ovid', a rather different figure from the defamer of women attacked by Christine and Gerson, to be sure, but a figure generally recognized and respected in the Middle Ages (cf. pp. 360–1 above), the *auctor* on pagan myth and morality whose progress towards truth had culminated in his entry into the Christian Church (at least, according to the *De vetula*, actually a false attribution but perfectly indicative of the medieval need to secure the poet's respectability and ultimate conformity). Certainly, here we may locate John Gower's basic attitude to 'the clerk Ovid'. The project of the *Confessio Amantis* is to present the virtues of a good lover as being indistinguishable from those of a good man: good living makes possible good loving. Gower suceeds to a remarkable extent, but certain faultlines and fissures remain, and this is quite inevitable, given the cultural formation (cf. our similar remarks made in respect of the *Parliament of Fowls*, on pp. 309–14 above). Can a similar project be attributed to Chaucer? The problem is that we are still faced with that morally orthodox suggestion that wise men are rightly wary of love. Since this does not come from a morally orthodox speaker (by contrast with the similar statements made near the beginning of Gower's *Confessio*: Prologus, 76; i. 35–42) but rather from the lips of Cupid, it may be inferred that that figure, given the way in which he is constituted, could not wholly approve of a defence on the grounds of purely orthodox morality—for it would condemn him. (Gower has similar problems in using Genius, the priest of Venus, as an ethical spokesman.) Moreover, if love is a proper arena for women to demonstrate their moral prowess in (as the choice of stories by Cupid's exemplifier would seem to indicate), why should 'wise folk' want to withdraw from it?

There is, however, another way of interpreting the narrator's understanding of 'trouthe in love'. We could take it as truth-in-love in an *exclusive* sense, love being identified as a sphere of operation with its own value system, having an autonomy which to some extent distances it from the world of conventional morality. That is to say, love is not an arena in which one can implement and exercise one's *trouthe*; rather, love demarcates and constitutes its own particular brand of *trouthe*. Being true in love therefore need not mean the same as being true in the fullest and most comprehensive moral sense of that term; the doctrines and priorities of Venus and Cupid are often at variance, if not in total opposition, to those of Pallas, the goddess of wisdom.

That, the argument would run, is the kind of thing which the God of Love would want the I-persona to say (since he accepts that those who are ideologically sound in terms of orthodox morality are wary of him), and, since the I-persona wants to please the God of Love, perhaps that's what we should expect him to mean. This theory is given support by the fact that the vice to which the I-persona declares his opposition—falseness in love—is rather different from, and much more specific than, the butts of the moral attack in the medievalized *Heroides*, namely, foolish and unlawful types of love. And the way in which Chaucer has simplified the Ovidian pattern of positive and negative *exempla* by excluding the 'wikke ensample of Canacee' and similar material—the aspect of the *Legend* of most interest to the Man of Law (*CT* II. 77–81)—inevitably entails a loss of the moral categorization which the medieval commentators applied to Ovid. Likewise, Chaucer is not interested in contrasting Phyllis the foolish lover with Penelope the chaste and lawful lover, but rather in emphasizing what united them: in his legends exemplification is a great leveller. The classifications and interpretative codes of standard medieval *Heroides* commentary do not transfer easily to the *Legend* (not that they accommodate everything in the *Heroides* either, of course). To sum up, the production of Chaucer's legend of Cupid's saints may be perceived as a raid on the resources of hagiography by the inhabitants of an alien land rather than the colonization of that alien land by the dominant moral establishment. The land of love, to continue the metaphor, has its own laws, and they seek to govern the use to which the plunder is put.

And that is why one may harbour reservations about the part of Rita Copeland's challenging analysis of the *Legend* which presents Chaucer as having defined the terms of translation, through the use of medieval academic criticism, 'as an overt act of exegetical appropriation'. 'In so inserting his vernacular writings into this academic discourse', she continues, 'Chaucer also directs exegesis away from the *auctores* to his own texts. In applying these exegetical techniques to his own *Legend* he claims the status of *auctor*' (p. 186). I myself am more struck by the distance which Chaucer seems to be putting between traditional exegesis of Ovid and his own transformations of (mainly) Ovidian narratives. More generally, do the conditions necessary for a claim of *auctoritas* actually exist in the *Legend*? Consider the evidence. The laws of love refuse to be subordinated firmly to the dictates of conventional morality. An instability of meaning in matters relating to love is dramatized by the poem. Moreover, some of the *auctores* were in error when they wrote about love: that charge is levelled in the Prologue(s), and informs the pro-feminist (if I may use that term loosely for the moment) narratives which follow. Far from creating confidence in the proposition that other *auctores* got it right and that therefore the narrator, in following them, must be in line for canonization as an *auctor* himself, the *Legend* tacitly questions the assumption that it can ever be got absolutely right. Chaucer has not, I suspect, left the unauthorized world of the *House of Fame* (cf. pp. 245–51 above).

All that having been said, it must be acknowledged that in the *Legend* truth-in-love does not have the last word, that Venusian subversion is counterbalanced, and the poem is not fundamentally anarchic in respect of orthodox moral values. The God of Love's writ does not run that far. To suppose otherwise would mean that we would be questioning the 'goodness' in orthodox moral terms of the *Legend*'s 'good women'. But the behaviour of at least some of them (Alceste, Penelope, Lucrece) seems to be beyond reproach, according to then prevailing norms. Moreover, the entire text (as we have it) whole-heartedly subscribes to the institution and ideals of marriage—here is no advocacy of unbridled desire! Indeed, Chaucer's 'hethene pak' (cf. G Prol. 299) can be regarded as virtuous heathen who are in a state of 'shadowy perfection' (incomplete because non-Christian, but impressive nevertheless), an argument which will be pursued in my next section.

Moreover, Truth is served by a certain line of irony in the prologues, which is most highly developed in the G version. Directed against the

God of Love, it quietly connives at the 'heresy against love'. For instance, there appear to be some strange items on the God's supposedly pro-feminist 'reading list'. The 'Estoryal Myrour' of Vincent of Beauvais (G Prol. 307) is the source for the story of Cleopatra: while the account is brief (cf. pp. 354–5 above), it is certainly detrimental to the queen. Even more striking is the inclusion of 'Valerye' (280), presumably a reference to the *Epistola Valerii ad Rufinum*, and 'Jerome agayns Jovynyan' (281); for, while these texts do include praise of some virtuous women, their main tenor is misogynistic or at least misogamistic (the two often being intertwined in medieval thought). The *Epistola Valerii* declares that the 'very best woman' is 'rarer than the phoenix', while the 'swarm' of bad women is large. No woman, not even the most excellent, can be loved 'without the bitterness of fear, anxiety, and frequent misfortune' (trans. Blamires, p. 106). Believe the anti-feminist authorities, 'Valerius' advises 'Ruffinus', for 'they tell the truth': 'they know that the flower of Venus is a rose, for under its bright colour lie hidden many thorns' (p. 110). In the *Adversus Jovinianum*, the subordinate status which marriage occupies in relation to chastity and virginity is heavily emphasized. Its commendatory account of good pagan women, some of whom (like Lucretia) honourably committed suicide, was drawn on by Chaucer for the *exempla* in Dorigen's complaint (*CT* V(F) 1355–456); yet Jerome also cites numerous cases of wicked pagan wives. It seems reasonable to assume that these two works would have been best known for their attacks on marriage and women: certainly, the reader of the *Wife of Bath's Prologue* is expected to feel that they belong in the 'book of wikked wyves' with which Jankyn infuriates Dame Alice (*CT* III(D) 671, 673–5), and in composing her harangue, Chaucer drew on them both. It would seem, then, that Cupid has not read his authorities with sufficient care, although he has the confidence to ask the Chaucer persona,

> what eyeleth the to wryte        *is wrong with you*
> The draf of storyes, and forgete the corn?        *husks*
> (G Prol. 311–12)

However, there is much 'draf' (in Cupid's terms) in the 'storyes' which he has just recommended, written by 'heretics' who advised the wise to withdraw from him.

The God ends his lecture to the errant poet by swearing that he must repent, 'By Saint Venus, of whom that I was born' (G Prol. 313–16; cf. F Prol. 339–40). That is the same goddess who, in the *Legend of Dido*, we shall see telling a blatant lie (989, 998) and actively involving herself in Aeneas's deceit of the loving and giving queen (see esp. lines 1000 and 1021). Worse, she is identified as the mother (999, 1141) of that forsworn traitor in love. Clearly, the God of Love's family is not of the best. Neither is his *familia*, as is pointed out by the worthiest companion and counsellor he has, Alcestis of Thessaly. In his court, she claims, is many a flatterer and crafty slanderer, who drums into his ears dubious things, which are motivated by hate, jealousy, and the wish to be on good sociable terms with so high a lord. Envy, she adds, who is always the washer of a court's dirty linen, never leaves the house of Caesar, as Dante says. Doubtless these comments are applicable to any medieval court; one might expect more of a god's, however!

Alceste's own credentials are (in my view) impeccable, and show up the weaknesses in the God of Love's position. Her lore is profound and persuasive, as when she lectures Cupid on the proper regiment of princes, thereby demonstrating her own moral superiority, and establishing a pattern which will run through the actual narratives, whereby female character and conduct are revealed as being superior to those of the males who partner them. Her love is pure and selfless: when death came for her husband, Alcestis of Thessaly offered herself instead; this self-sacrificial model will be followed by most of the other heroines, in their different ways. Therefore, Love rightly describes her as the very 'calendar'

> Of goodnesse, for she taughte of fyn lovynge,
> And namely of wifhod the lyvynge,
> And alle the boundes that she oughte kepe.     (G Prol. 534–6)

As such she is the perfect counter-example to Criseyde, proof positive that 'fyn lovynge' may be reconciled with virtuous 'lyvynge'. In her *exemplum* the two value systems, of orthodox moral truth and truth-in-love, meet and mingle—and it should be noted that the meeting-point is found in virtuous marriage, 'wifhod'. Elsewhere in the *Legend* the overlap of value and generic systems is only partial; but Alceste is, as it were, always there, presiding over this anthology of frenetically pro-feminist poetry, to affirm that they are not, despite some appearances to the contrary, in fundamental opposition to each other. The tensions between the systems are real and obvious enough. They are constantly borne in upon us by the contrasts between Cupid and Alceste and by the questions raised in some of the legends. But they are not irresolvable in every case.

No wonder, then, that Alceste is universally praised: by Love, by the poet persona, and by the company of nineteen ladies who, in the G Prologue, sing the ballade in her honour. Some critics have found this queen of good women obdurate and surly, but I can find no evidence for this view. Her task is, surely, to moderate Cupid's fierceness. As Robert Payne says, she is 'the intercessor for a sinner whose case requires that justice be tempered with mercy' (p. 107). Here Chaucer may have envisaged her as playing a traditional feminine role: one may recall the way in which the (far less articulate) ladies in the *Knight's Tale* arouse the 'pite' of Duke Theseus.

Neither is there any compunction to believe that her untold but implicit legend is 'finally' to be understood as 'a myth concerning resurrection', as Kolve has argued (p. 177). It seems plausible enough, on the evidence of the G Prologue, to speculate that Chaucer's ultimate plan for the *Legend* envisaged it as ending with the story of Alceste; but the claim that the work would culminate in Christian transcendence ('she alone among this vast company points toward Christ', p. 174) cannot be substantiated and, indeed, seems out of keeping with the tone and tenor of the work as we have it. (That objection could be countered, however, with the hypothesis that the *Legend*, like *Troilus*, would have ended with a firm division being made between the Christian and pagan worlds. But that is not what Kolve has in mind.) John Gower's account of Alceste ends with the statement that the feminine truth and love which she illustrates is the greatest on this earth, save that of God himself:

> So mai a man be reson taste,
> Hou next after the god above
> The trouthe of wommen and the love,
> In whom that alle grace is founde,
> Is myhtiest upon this grounde
> And most behovely manyfold.
>
> (*Confessio Amantis*, vii. 1944–9)

This is reminiscent of Chaucer's attribution to Christ of the statement that, in the whole land of Israel, he did not find in anyone 'so gret feyth . . . / As in a woman' (1879–82). If Chaucer and Gower shared a vision of Alceste as superlative 'goode wif' (*Confessio*, vii. 1942), it seems reasonable to suggest that they may also have agreed that she was firmly of 'this grounde', and 'next after' the Christian God rather than being a fictional emanation of him.

Alceste's story, as postulated here, could have functioned powerfully within the priorities and polarities which are writ large in the *Legend* even in its present fragmentary state: as an *exemplum* of superlative 'lovynge' and 'lyvynge' in which, even more than in the *Legend of Lucrece*, moral truth and truth-in-love are in perfect harmony; as a celebration of *amor* rather than *caritas*; as a testament to human 'wifhod' rather than mystical marriage. For it is 'wifhod' which is the high argument of this legendary of secular saints. Moreover, Chaucer was very aware that Christians did not have a monopoly on virtue, and was sensitive to the historically justifiable differences between pagan and Christian ideologies which were being described by the 'classicizing' clerics of his day. The interpretative implications of this situation will emerge through an investigation of the poet's debts to, and deviations from, traditional hagiographic forms.

*Querelle de la Rose* materials, ed. Hicks, trans. Baird and Kane; *Roman de la Rose*, ed. Langlois, trans. Dahlberg; Minnis and Scott (eds.), *Medieval Literary Theory*. On Gower's inability to 'square the circle' see Minnis, *'De Vulgari Auctoritate'*, pp. 51–65. On the relationship between Ovid and Jean de Meun as postulated in the *querelle* see Minnis, 'Theorizing the Rose'.

Copeland, *Rhetoric, Hermeneutics*. Contrast Delany's application of her notion of 'skeptical fideism' (cf. pp. 214–5 above) to the *Legend*, in *Medieval Literary Politics: Shapes of Ideology* (Manchester and New York, 1990), pp. 83, 87.

Blamires (ed.), *Woman Defamed*. Payne, *Key of Remembrance*. Cf. Dinshaw, *Sexual Poetics*, who suggests that, in her intercession 'between two men at odds with one another', Alceste 'is at this moment in the paradigmatic position of woman in a patriarchal social structure' (p. 70). On the 'intercessory model' of queenly behaviour see especially Paul Strohm's article 'Queens as Intercessors' in his *Hochon's Arrow: The Social Imagination of Fourteenth-Century Texts* (Princeton, NJ, 1992), pp. 95–119, which includes discussion of Chaucer's Alceste and Anne of Bohemia's efforts as *mediatrix*. Kolve, 'From Cleopatra to Alceste'.

The tensions between Cupid and Alceste are well brought out by Delany, *Medieval Literary Politics*, pp. 78–80; Fyler, *Chaucer and Ovid*, pp. 96–123; Kiser, *Telling Classical Tales*; Rowe, *Nature to Eternity*. Cf. Kelly, *Love and Marriage*, who discusses the poem's 'two standards', pp. 109–13. Dinshaw, *Sexual Poetics*, speaks of the figure of Alceste as being 'a concentrated locus of the narrator's conflicting impulses' (p. 71).

It should be noted that the punctuation of G Prol. 261 is crucial. If a comma is inserted after 'paramours', to produce the line 'That loveth paramours, to harde and hote', then it could be taken as meaning that *all* love of the 'paramours' type, such love being identified as 'to harde and hote', is allegedly under attack by the Chaucer persona. On the other hand, if the comma is removed, as in the Shaner and Edwards edition, then the line could be read as attacking only the *excessive* pursuit of love. Though I have quoted the Shaner and Edwards edition above, my interpretation has presumed the existence of that comma.

## Hagiographic Form and Heathen Pack

### COMPILING PAGAN WOMEN

The title of Chaucer's poem as provided in the Introduction to the *Man of Law's Tale*, namely 'the Seintes Legende of Cupide' (II(B¹) 61), bespeaks a paradox. As Paul Strohm has pointed out, the generic term 'Legend' was quite rare, and was most often used with specific reference to Jacob of Voragine's *Legenda aurea* (composed between 1255 and 1266), a popular collection of saints' lives which Chaucer seems to have known in some form (witness *The Second Nun's Tale*). But Chaucer's legendary brings together lives not of Christian martyrs but of pagan women whose

virtue was, in some cases at least, disputable, the basic rationale seeming
to derive from the 'religion of love' conceit which was one of the trappings of 'fyn lovynge'. Just as John Gower penned an extensive account
of the lover's confession to a priest of Venus, Chaucer set about collect-
ing stories of women who had died for the God of Love rather than the
love of God (though of course the 'legends' of Lucrece and Philomela do
not fit that paradigm neatly, for various reasons). A specifically Christian
term, connoting a genre of Christian hagiography, is being transferred to
narratives which follow a very different agenda, set as they are within a
dark world of long ago in which heathen gods rule, and honour is a mere
word in the mouths of treacherous men.

   Did Chaucer wish to foreground some sort of comparison and contrast between Christian saints and pagan *sapientes*? Several critics have
thought so, though their arguments have taken different forms. V. A.
Kolve believed that the overall plan of the poem was signalled by the
contrast between an irredeemable Cleopatra (for whom earthly courage
and fame are all) and a salvific Alceste; Chaucer was trying to 'locate
within pagan history certain possibilities of human loving that Christian
history would later confirm and redeem' (pp. 177–8). Lisa Kiser's 1983
study claims that the narrator combines 'pagan erotic love and Christian
*caritas* in a facile union' which is meant to seem unsatisfactory.
'Chaucer's classical sources are cheapened by his forcing them into an
alien hagiographical pattern, and the spirit of hagiography is profoundly
violated by Chaucer's implicit suggestion in these stories that pagan
women who died for love are somehow morally comparable to saints
dying for the love of God' (pp. 102, 103). These views are reiterated in
her recent book, wherein it is claimed that the poem 'is a series of elaborate and very funny lies, stories so unfaithful to their classical sources
that we are forced to conclude that the poet intended them to be examples of a poor and unconvincing pagan/Christian synthesis' (pp. 101–2).
Among all those who have recently written on the *Legend*, however,
Donald W. Rowe is the most convinced that here Chaucer makes classical tales bear a *sentence* which is ultimately and essentially supportive
of Christian doctrine; his reading replicates the moralization of the
Orpheus myth (practised by Boethius, *De consolatione philosophiae*, III,
met. xii, and his medieval commentators) as a *descensus ad inferos*.
According to Rowe's 'subterranean view' of the poem, 'The soul's
descent into the constraints of history and desire, its fallen condition in
a fallen world, is assumed to begin a drama in which man is inevitably
misled by these constraints to experience the tragedy which is their
inevitable consequence; this experience in its turn enlightens man and
frees him to rediscover the good beyond history' (p. 136). There is,

therefore, hope for the Christian reader if not for the poem's pagan denizens, which is encouraged by Chaucer's dramatization of penance, 'that process which divine justice and mercy have ordained that the individual may attain to the good he or she is not' (p. 135).

The problem about these readings (Kolve's partly excepted) is that they tend to assume that pagan narrative must be ruled by Christian ideology, and in particular that Chaucer was unable to view pagan antiquity with a degree of detachment and a sense of cultural difference. I hope to show that he was eminently capable of doing just that, by relating his heathen pack of Cupid's saints to other late medieval attempts at constructing *vitae* of virtuous pre-Christian women. Of course, Chaucer's compilation represents an imposition of certain values of his 'present day' on antiquity; it is appropriate to recall that the verb *compilo* has connotations of snatching together and carrying off, of plundering and pillaging. But it is going too far, I believe, to claim that the *Legend* illustrates and tacitly critiques a sort of narrative 'rape' whereby poets 'steal what they want from the women's life stories and abandon what remains' (Kiser, *Truth and Textuality*, p. 102). For Chaucer was, to some extent at least, attempting to regard the famous women of pagan antiquity with what, by the standards of the time, passed for historical objectivity, and that is what should be emphasized, I feel, rather than the anachronism or the imperialism of his treatment.

The 'lives' of ancient heroines were a relatively late arrival on the literary scene, born from the rib of the 'lives' of the illustrious male philosophers and poets of the past, a genre with ancient precedents which had increased in popularity since the twelfth-century renaissance, and had established its own literary forms and conventions. Boccaccio, in the preface to his *De mulieribus claris*, firmly marks the transition. 'A long time ago some ancient authors wrote brief works on the lives of famous men,' and 'in our own times' the genre has been continued by 'my master Petrarch'. But astonishingly,

women have gained so little recognition in any work devoted especially to them, although it can be clearly seen in the more voluminous histories that some women have acted with as much strength as valour. . . . Lest, therefore, they be cheated of their just reward, the idea came to me to honour their glory by bringing together into one book those women whose memory is still alive, adding to them some of the many whom daring, intellectual power, perseverance, natural endowments, or Fortune's favour or enmity have made noteworthy. (trans. Guarino, p. xxxvii)

However, Chaucer did not have to go to the *De mulieribus claris* for the idea of a collection devoted exclusively to noteworthy women, any more than he had to go to the *Decameron* for the idea of the structure of his

*Canterbury Tales.* Given the number of *vitae philosophorum antiquorum* produced by the 'classicizing' clerics of his day, the development was inevitable.

The most important compilations of such *vitae* were the anonymous *Liber philosophorum moralium antiquorum*, the *Compendiloquium de vitis illustrium philosophorum* of John of Wales, and Walter Burley's *Liber de vita et moribus philosophorum*; in addition, brief lives were included in works which were more comprehensive in character, such as the *Speculum historiale* of Vincent of Beauvais. These biographies have in common a respect for the moral, scientific, and metaphysical achievements of the pagans, on the one hand, and a clear recognition of the limitations of heathen society, on the other.

That pagan virtue was a fit subject for qualified praise had been recognized by such Fathers of the Church as Saints Jerome, Augustine, and Gregory the Great, and the late medieval classicizers eagerly followed their lead, even to the extent of sometimes making their forebears sound more appreciative than they actually had been. A good example is afforded by the use which John of Wales (regent master at Oxford *c.*1260) made of a passage from the *Moralia in Job* of St Gregory, a commentary on the deeds of a 'good pagan' as recorded in the Old Testament, written by a great authority who was regarded as a champion of virtuous heathen (as is witnessed by his association with the Trajan legend). Gregory interpreted Isaiah 23: 4, 'Be thou ashamed, O Sidon: for the sea speaketh', as follows. 'Sidon' is 'a figure of the steadfastness of those settled upon the foundation of the [Christian] law', whereas 'the sea' signifies the life of the Gentiles. Well may Sidon be ashamed, for the life of virtuous pagans reproves life under the present dispensation, and the deeds of secular men confound the deeds of the religious. Christians promise but fail to practise what they receive as precepts, while the Gentiles in their lives kept those things to which they were by no means bound by legal obligation. And this explains why the book of Job appears in the Bible: 'a Gentile, one without the Law', is brought forward to shame those who, even though they have the best law of all, often fall short of the virtuous heathen in their achievements (*Moralia in Job*, Praefatio). John of Wales cites this exegesis in his *Compendiloquium*, to justify his anthology of 'the notable sayings of the philosophers and the imitable examples of virtuous men'. These will, among other things, 'encourage humility'; Christian men can hardly be 'puffed up' about their own achievements 'when they hear and read of the gentiles doing perfect things (in so far as these can be perfect without faith working through love) and bearing much for honour and human glory' (trans. in Pantin, p. 309). Thus John justifies his own

ardent classicism. Elsewhere in the same compilation he carefully
affirms that the perfection of even the best pagans can only be 'shadowy'. There can be no real perfection without divine grace; yet in many
pagans there was perfection of a kind, which 'consisted of the detesta-
tion of vice, so far as this was possible without the grace of the faith
which illuminates and purges'.

Similarly, in a chapter from *De civitate Dei* (v. 18) which was much
quoted by the classicizers, St Augustine had recounted numerous
instances of superlative pagan virtue in making the point that, faced with
what the Romans had done for their temporal city and for human glory,
Christians should be very far from boasting of their deeds for their eternal country, particularly since the one true God does not usually require
such excesses of valour (a point which modern readers of the *vitae
Sanctorum* might wish to dispute, however). For example, if Torquatus
killed his son for going against his command as general, why should
Christians feel pride when they give up things which are not as dear as
children—namely, earthly goods and possessions—for the laws of their
never-ending country? In sum, desire for human glory and (in the case
of public men) concern for the good of the state were at once the commendable objectives of much pagan endeavour and the boundary lines of
their aspirations and achievements. These arguments, quite clearly, are
double-edged swords. For, having been born in the wrong place at the
wrong time, the pagans could either be condemned (had they not fallen
far short of full enlightenment?) or commended (had they not done
exceptionally well, given all they had to go on?).

In the epistle which dedicates the *De mulieribus claris* to Andrea
Acciauoli (Countess of Altavilla) Boccaccio cleverly narrows the standard
discourse to apply specifically to women. Whenever the countess reads of
'a pagan woman having qualities which are worthy of those who profess
to be Christians',

if you feel that you do not have them, blush a little and reproach yourself that
although marked by the baptism of Christ you have let yourself be surpassed by
a pagan in integrity, chastity, or virtue. Call on the powers of your intellect, in
which you excel, and do not allow yourself to be surpassed but strive to outdo
all women in noble virtues. (trans. Guarino, p. xxxiv)

There is, of course, no doubt of the inherent inferiority of the pagans'
knowledge of deity and the moral values which motivated their virtuous
behaviour, as Boccaccio's preface makes clear.

In order to attain true and eternal glory Hebrew and Christian women did indeed
steel themselves to endure human adversities, imitating the sacred command-
ments and examples of their teachers. But these pagans through some natural

gift or instinct, or rather spurred by desire for this fleeting glory, reached their goal not without great strength of mind and often in spite of the assaults of Fortune, and they endured numerous troubles. (pp. xxxviii–ix)

It is this very sense of the historical and ideological distance between pagan and Christian world-views which enabled late medieval scholars to allow a degree of autonomy to heathen society.

For instance, for a Christian, suicide was a mortal sin (except in exceptional circumstances), but the heathen had no canon against self-slaughter. On the contrary, in pagan antiquity suicide could be the crown of a life of virtue. For pagan women *in extremis*, it was regarded as a perfectly honourable way out, as is made quite clear by the fact that Boccaccio had no compunction about commending Lucrece, who 'cleansed her shame harshly, and for this reason she should be exalted with worthy praise for her chastity, which can never be sufficiently lauded' (p. 103). He endorsed with even greater enthusiasm the demise of Dido (not the Virgilian fiction, but the historical Queen of Carthage who could not possibly have coincided chronologically with Aeneas).

O inviolate honour of chastity! O venerable and eternal example of constant widowhood! O Dido, I wish that widows would turn their eyes to you, and that especially those who are Christian would contemplate your strength. And if they can, let them consider with attentive mind you who shed your chaste blood, especially those who lightly go, I will not say to a second, but to a third wedding or more. And I ask, what will they say who are marked with the emblem of Christ, when they see this pagan to whom Christ was completely unknown, proceed with such a firm spirit to win fame and go with such firm determination towards a death given not by others, but by her own hand, rather than consent to a second marriage and allow her sacred wish to respect widowhood to be broken? (pp. 89–90)

This echoes Jerome (*Adversus Jovinianum*, i. 43, 46–7, etc.), who had praised pagan women, particularly Dido, for repudiating second marriages, and contrasted them with Christian women of his own acquaintance who were all too eager to rush into them. Quite clearly, for Boccaccio, as for Jerome, Dido's extreme and dated method of coping with her situation does not diminish the force which her example has for present-day women. (Boccaccio can assure Andrea Acciauoli that reading of the 'deeds of ancient women' may 'spur' her 'spirit to loftier things', p. xxxiv). 'By dying' Dido 'escaped 'in the only way she could' (p. 90), the implication being that she can hardly be blamed for that; modern women, by contrast, have Christ as their refuge, but since the purpose here is fulsome commendation of the Queen of Carthage, that point is not laboured.

The stance which Boccaccio adopted in the dedicatory epistle and prologue (as quoted above) is firmly reiterated in his account of Dido. 'That pagan woman, for the sake of vain glory, was able to master her ardour and curb it. Cannot a Christian woman master it in order to acquire eternal glory?' (p. 91) The Augustinian influence is obvious, but it can hardly be emphasized enough (given some recent criticism of the *Legend*) that late medieval readers of *De civitate Dei* regularly put its pagan lore to uses which would have surprised its author. Augustine had, after all, written with the polemical purpose of establishing the superiority of Christianity over paganism; his late medieval readers, taking that for granted, had different uses for his matter of antiquity. Hence Dante, in the *Convivio* (iv. 4–5), could transform Augustine's types of impressive but inadequate pagan virtue (Torquatus and the rest) into paragons of civic virtue who were inspired by a love of Rome which was divine rather than human.

Augustine's noble pagan women suffered similar sea-changes. In *De civitate Dei* (i. 18) the story of Lucrece is part and parcel of an affirmation of the supremacy of a religion which would not have required this woman to die for something which was someone else's fault.

Being a Roman, and covetous of glory, she feared, that if she lived still, that which she had endured by violence should be thought of to have been suffered with willingness. And therefore she thought good to show this punishment to the eyes of men, as a testimony of her mind unto whom she could not show her mind indeed: blushing to be held a partaker in the fact, which being by another committed so filthily, she had endured so unwillingly. Now this course the Christian women did not take; they live still, howsoever violated . . . For howsoever, they have the glory of their chastity still within them, it being the testimony of their conscience; this they have before the eyes of their God, and this is all they care for. (trans. Healey, i. 24)

But for many late medieval readers the commendable element in a case history like this could be more important than the caveat. After all, Jerome, concerned as he was to prove that his Christian misogamy was not an invented 'dogma against nature', had lavishly praised those Greek and Roman women who had preferred death to loss of virginity or remarriage.

This lead was followed by the English Dominican Robert Holcot, though the ideological context is radically different. Holcot espoused a nominalist brand of theology which held out the possibility of salvation for those virtuous heathen who had 'done what was in them' and lived by the best law available in their age (cf. p. 214 above). In his much read commentary on the Book of Wisdom, Lucrece appears in an adaptation of Jerome's catalogue of faithful pagan wives. By courtesy of Martial, Portia's story is fleshed out, and Arria is added to the list of fiercely monogamous women who, like Dido, died on account of their husbands. This remarkable excursus, in effect a commendation of the female sex with authorities drawn from both biblical and classical sources, emphasizes that feminine *gratitudo* ('grace', 'favour', 'goodwill') 'manifests itself not just in women of the [Christian] faith, but is sufficiently clear among the Gentiles also'. Holcot seems to have no trouble in accepting virtuous heathen women as forerunners of the Christian 'strong woman'.

Similarly, Chaucer regarded Lucrece as the closest approximation to a Christian saint which ancient Rome could produce:

> she was holden there
> A seynt, and ever hir day yhalwed dere    *worshipped*
> As in hir lawe                            (1870–2)

She belongs, therefore, in the pagan 'calendar', to use this term in the sense, current in the Christian Church, of a register of religious observances and commemorations of saints; for this was how the *Fasti*, Chaucer's main source for the *Legend of Lucrece* (cf. p. 362 above), was regarded in medieval literary criticism. Ovid had, according to the standard interpretation, composed the work in order to teach 'the usage of official sacrifices and how sacrifices ought to be presented on solemn feast days' (trans. Minnis and Scott, p. 30). (Chaucer's metaphor of Alceste as a 'kalender', G Prol. 542, is in similar vein.) Moreover, the goodness of Lucrece is vouched for not just by Roman history but by no less a Christian *auctor* than the great saint Augustine:

> Nat only that these payens hire comende,
> But he that cleped is in oure legende
> The grete Austyn hath gret compassioun
> Of this Lucresse                          (1688–91)

In the face of how Lucretia's story functions within Augustine's condemnation of suicide, it might be claimed (and has been) that Chaucer's use of the saint's good name is ironic if not an effrontery, but what Chaucer is doing is quite in line with the way in which late medieval classicizers and proto-humanists regularly drew on *De civitate Dei*. Besides, the idea that Lucrece has a place in Christian as well as in pagan doctrine was vouched for by no less an authority than St Jerome. Chaucer's declaration that her distress reflects the common virtue of good Roman wives—

> These Romeyn wyves lovede so here name
> At thilke tyme, and dredde so the shame   (1812–13)

—is reminiscent of the *Adversus Jovinianum*, as is the possible implication that Roman wives could teach Christian ones a thing or two. What, then, of the ending of the *Legend of Lucrece*, wherein Chaucer attributes to Christ a commendation of women which does not exist as such in the Bible?

> For wel I wot that Crist himselve telleth
> That in Israel, as wyd as is the lond,
> That so gret feyth in al that he ne fond
> As in a woman; and this is no lye.                        (1879–82)

The closest approximation is Matthew 15: 28, where Christ says to the woman of Canaan, 'O woman, great is thy faith', but there seems to have been added a touch of colouring from the story of the centurion to whom Christ said, 'I have not found so great faith in Israel' (Matthew 8: 10). Before it be suggested that Chaucer is being ironic here, or engaged in that technique of transferring male roles and categories to women which is well attested elsewhere in the *Legend* (cf. pp. 424–42 below), let us consider the analogous way in which Holcot set about commending good Christian women: 'Indeed Christ, while he still lived here on earth, found certain graceful men, but never discovered in Peter or John or Jacob such constant grace (*gratitudo*) as he found in the women who were devoted to him.' Such were those, Holcot continues, who when Christ was preaching ministered to him of their substance (Mark 15: 41, Luke 8: 3), and who, undeterred either by darkness or by the fierceness of armed soldiers, brought sweet spices to anoint his dead body in the tomb. Thus, Christ could advisedly use of them the words of Boethius:

> No terror could discourage them at least
> From coming with me on my way.
> (*De consolatione philosophiae*, I, met. i, 5–6; trans. Watts, p. 35)

And this was why the resurrected Christ chose to show himself to women first; he knew full well that 'a holy and shamefaced woman is grace upon grace' (Ecclesiasticus 26: 19).

Holcot may be cavalier with his quotations, but there is no need to doubt his sincerity—even when he appropriates lines from Boethius which in the *Consolatio* actually refer to those false friends of the wretched man's youth, the poetic Muses, who are described as 'hysterical sluts' and briskly banished by Dame Philosophy! Medieval citation and application of even the Bible could, by modern standards, be extraordinarily free, as anyone with experience of the scriptural exegesis of the age is aware. It is salutary to note that Holcot's commendation of the female sex is occasioned by a moralization of Wisdom 19: 18–20 ('The fire had power in water above its own virtue', etc.), wherein it is argued that woman's nature shares the six properties of water. Likewise, Chaucer may have been inaccurate in his textual detail, but there is no reason to doubt the sincerity of his commendation of women in the passage under discussion. After all, the two stories he assimilated were alike in one major particular: the woman of Canaan and the centurion were not Jews. It was easy enough to blend one instance of Gentile virtue with another. Homogenizing (if that is the right word here) of the kind which we have found in Holcot's account of the great faith of women regularly occurred in the *vitae Sanctorum* and the *vitae philosophorum antiquorum*; it is, indeed, part of the stock-in-trade of hagiography. And many scholars, even the most eminent, regularly used Bible concordances and collections of related quotations from Scripture and the Fathers, so that citations which were alike in one respect or another could be blended together, either in the reference book itself or in the recollection of its reader.

More fundamentally, a detailed examination of the *Legend of Lucrece* will reveal the considerable extent to which Chaucer (how consciously we shall never know) brought to bear on this tale of a pagan 'good woman' the conventions and clichés of Christian hagiography. The intent is, surely, to emphasize her virtue, not to make her into some kind of closet Christian. She and her 'sisters' remain essentially pagan figures who, as the God of Love assures us, maintain their situation (whether maidenhood, marriage, or widowhood) not on account of Christian holiness but in line with high moral standards of virtue and purity, and to put themselves beyond the moral censure of men (the significance of that 'of men' will be considered later).

> And this thing was nat kept for holynesse,
> But al for verray vertu and clennesse,
> And for men schulde sette on hem no lak;
> And yit they were hethene, al the pak,
> That were so sore adrad of alle shame.
>
> (G Prol. 296–300)

This praise of 'olde wemen' for the way in which, fearful of shame, they 'kepte . . . here name' (G Prol. 300–1) must be compared with the statement in the *Legend of Lucrece* about how 'Romeyn wyves lovede so here name / At thilke tyme, and dredde so the shame' (1812–13). All this is, of course, strongly reminiscent of the remarks of the Church Fathers, which were quoted with enthusiasm by the classicizers of late medieval England, concerning the extremes of virtue and sacrifice to which the heathen were prepared to go because of the respect in which they held the moral and civic virtues and on account of their love of glory.

In the other narratives as much as in the *Legend of Lucrece*, we are never allowed to forget that we have entered a pagan world. Just as the

Squire praised the Tartar king 'Cambyuskan' for living in accordance
with the best law available to him—

> As of the secte of which that he was born
> He kepte his lay, to which that he was sworn          *law*
>
> (*CT* V(F) 17–18)

—so the Chaucer persona in the *Legend* praises his heathen heroines for
their pagan faith and piety. Pyramus and Thisbe, we are assured,

> plyghten trouthe fully in here fey          *faith*
> That ilke same nyght to stele awey . . .
> This covenaunt was affermed wonder faste          (778 ff.)

and the place at which they arrange to meet is at once a pagan landmark
and a marker of an alien culture:

> here metynge sholde be
> There kyng Nynus was grave, under a tre,          *buried*
> For olde payens, that idoles heryed,          *worshipped*
> Useden tho in feldes to ben beryed          (784–7)

This is an expansion of *Metamorphoses*, iv. 88–9, the reference to worship
of 'idoles' being probably due to the traditional association of King Ninus
with the origin of idolatry. The piety of Queen Dido is emphasized by the
fact that we first meet her 'in hire devocyoun' in the 'mayster temple' of
Carthage (1016–18), this being a significant departure from the relevant
passage in the first book of the *Aeneid*, wherein she is shown performing
a political role, announcing new laws and statutes to her people from her
throne in the temple. Because Hypermnestra is aware of her wifely duty
and has her heathen 'feyth' (2700), she cannot murder her husband. (In
marked contrast to all this female religiosity, Theseus breaks a vow sworn
to Mars, the god who is 'the chef' of his 'bileve'; 2109.) The 'shadowy
perfection' of these women of the past is, therefore, quite apparent.
Lucrece prefers death to forgiveness; Hypsipyle and Phyllis die for men
who were false. The first case illustrates (according to Augustine) the inferiority of the pagan conception of purity; the others stand in sad contrast
to the security in love offered by Christ, who 'nyl falsen no wight . . . /
That wol his herte al holly on hym leye', to quote the *Troilus* epilogue (v.
1845–6). Yet, such extreme behaviour can be viewed quite positively, in
terms of the almost superhuman lengths to which certain pagans were prepared to go to serve their 'feyth' and to win praise. In their own female
sphere of endeavour, pagan women can perform feats of virtue which are
just as impressive as, say, the famous deeds of Torquatus.

Chaucer's 'hethene pak', then, suffer and sometimes die for principles
which are commendable even though they are not Christian, and shuffle

off this mortal coil in a manner which generally appears as a love-sacrifice and sometimes even as a heathen form of martyrdom (once again, we may observe the tension between the two value systems, of moral truth *simpliciter* and truth-in-love; cf. pp. 390–8 above). *Pace* Rowe, I cannot detect 'the stench of hell' (p. 96) anywhere in the *Legend*. There certainly is no need to suppose that Chaucer wished us to consistently and systematically weigh the pagan ethos of the *Legend* in the balance and find it sadly wanting. For he was fully prepared to accept that 'a Christian perspective is historically impossible' for his pagan heroines who lived under the natural law, as John McCall puts it in his excellent analysis. 'Because they cannot see with the eyes of faith', he continues, their beliefs and actions, 'even if mistaken, are more understandable and occasion more sympathy than would otherwise be the case' (p. 164 n. 1). This is perfectly in accord with the tenets of clerkly classicism, wherein a clear recognition of the limitations of the pagans was perfectly compatible with respect for their achievements. 'Ecch contree hath his lawes', to adopt an idiom from *Troilus and Criseyde* (ii. 42), and the past was recognized as a foreign country, even though some of its customs were familiar (or were made to seem familiar).

Indeed—and here we begin to scrutinize Chaucer's most original strokes—that very foreignness enabled the poet to set aside certain present-day Christian norms and imperatives, and to concentrate on the 'passions' (to use the term both in its psychological sense and in the religious sense of suffering) of women who were the exemplars of human love and/or the victims of human lust. This enquiry must involve a consideration of the relationship of the *Legend* with the *vitae Sanctorum*, and the extent to which, given its strong though not exclusive orientation towards marriage, the poem could be regarded as a riposte to two misogamistic works, the *Adversus Jovinianum* and the *Legenda aurea*, Chaucer's deployment of an antique setting enabling him to claim that poetic licence.

Paul Strohm, '*Passioun, Lyf, Miracle, Legende*: Some Generic Terms in Middle English Hagiographical Narrative', *ChR* 9 (1975–6), 62–75, 154–69. Cowen, 'Structure and Tone', p. 417, argues that it is quite likely that Chaucer's choice of the word 'legend' was 'intended to set his poem in relation to that well-known collection of saints' lives', the *Legenda aurea*, and her article explores several aspects of this relation.
The *Legenda* has been translated by Granger Ryan and Helmut Ripperger, *The Golden Legend of Jacobus de Voragine* (New York, 1969). However, this version omits and alters certain passages in the Latin text. The new, complete and accurate translation by Granger Ryan, *The Golden Legend. Readings on the Saints* (Princeton, NJ, 1993) appeared too late to be used here. For the original see the edition by T. Graesse, *Jacobi a Voragine Legenda Aurea* (repr. Osnabrück, 1969). See further Sherry L. Reames, *The Legenda Aurea: A Reexamination of its Paradoxical History* (Madison, Wis., 1985).

Kolve, 'From Cleopatra to Alceste'. Kiser, *Telling Classical Tales*; also her *Truth and Textuality*. Rowe, *Nature to Eternity*. In his review Dieter Mehl describes Rowe's approach as 'a kind of latter-day Robertsonianism': 'while continually paying lip-service to the text's openness, to the multiplicity of perspectives and teasing ironies, he comes down heavily on the side of a spiritual reading'. *Notes and Queries*, 234/3 (1989), 367.

On medieval ideas of *compilatio* see further M. B. Parkes, 'The Influence of the Concepts of *Ordinatio* and *Compilatio* on the Development of the Book', in J. J. G. Alexander and M. T. Gibson (eds.), *Medieval Learning and Literature: Essays Presented to R. W. Hunt* (Oxford, 1976), pp. 115–41; A. J. Minnis, 'Late-Medieval Discussions of *Compilatio* and the Role of the *Compilator*', *Beiträge zur Geschichte der deutschen Sprache und Literatur*, 101 (1979), 385–421.

Boccaccio, *Concerning Famous Women*, trans. Guarino; W. A. Pantin, 'John of Wales and Medieval Humanism', in *Medieval Studies Presented to Aubrey Gwynn* (Dublin, 1961), pp. 297–319. For the argument that Chaucer was influenced by one of John's works, the *Communiloquium*, see R. A. Pratt, 'Chaucer and the Hand that Fed Him', *Speculum*, 41 (1966), 619–42. On medieval notions of cultural relativism see Minnis, *Chaucer and Pagan Antiquity*, and 'From Medieval to Renaissance?'; also Nolan, *Chaucer and Roman Antique*. A different view is taken of the 'foreignness' of the *Legend*'s locations by Sheila Delany, 'Geographies of Desire: Orientalism in Chaucer's *Legend of Good Women*', *Chaucer Yearbook: A Journal of Late Medieval Studies*, 1 (1992), 1–32; reiterated in her monograph *Naked Text*. Partly inspired by Edward Said's *Orientalism* (New York, 1979), she offers a reading which has Chaucer appropriate a negative discourse concerning a 'sinister and insidious Orient'. Although the poet was able to deconstruct gender difference, she suggests, 'The same possibility did not exist for an alien ideology embodied in Orientals who, though exposed to Christian truth, rejected it. Woman isn't *eternally* Other; the infidel is' (p. 28). This seems to me to misjudge the thrust of the text's relativism. Specifically, there is no suggestion that the 'heathen pack' in this poem, or indeed in *Troilus*, the *Knight's Tale*, or the *Franklin's Tale*, was in any position to reject Christian truth; on the contrary, here Chaucer creates a sense of a distant and remote historical past, far removed from the age of the Christian dispensation. The *Legend*'s affinities are, I believe, with these three poems rather than with the *Second Nun's Tale*, where, as in conventional saints' lives, good Christians are opposed to bad pagans who *do* have a better law available to them but wilfully refuse it. Cf. the *Man of Law's Tale*, wherein Christian virtues triumph over the duplicity and ignorance of Muslims and pagans.

St Augustine, *The City of God*, trans. John Healey, ed. R. V. G. Tasker, with an introduction by Sir E. Barker (London and New York, 1945).

For the Holcot passage see Beryl Smalley, *English Friars*, pp. 155–6, 321–2; it was first related to Chaucer by Martha S. Waller, 'The Conclusion of Chaucer's *Legend of Lucrece*: Robert Holcot and the Great Faith of Women', *Chaucer Newsletter*, 2 (1980), 10–12. My own analysis involved consideration of Holcot's entire discussion, as printed in *Sapientiae Regis Salomonis praelectiones* (Basel, 1586), pp. 597–9.

Minnis and Scott (eds.), *Medieval Literary Theory*.

Boethius, *De consolatione philosophiae*, trans. Watts.

On pagan idolatry as depicted in the later Middle Ages see Minnis, *Chaucer and Pagan Antiquity*, pp. 32–40, 137–8; Camille, *Gothic Idol*.

McCall, *Chaucer among the Gods*. Chaucer, he argues, 'did not criticize his pagan women for being pagan rather than Christian—for that would have been truly anachronistic and beside the point' (p. 117).

FROM BRIDES OF CHRIST TO MARTYRS FOR MARRIAGE

The narrative features, not to say restrictions, which the *Legend* shares with the *vitae Sanctorum*, are striking. The saints' lives had, during their long history, developed firm editorial conventions and didactic strategies. Material which was merely circumstantial or of marginal relevance to the individual's devout self-realization tended to be excised, resulting in a 'flattening' and 'narrowing' of the narrative (one may compare the characteristics of exemplification, as described above); adventures and attributes which originally appeared in one *vita* could be transferred to another—indeed, some idioms seem to be virtually interchangeable, and on occasion one gains the distinct impression of indentikit paragons being made to stand in line. The same narrative 'deep structures' appear again and again, as is particularly clear in the case of the lives of women saints.

For women, a common route to martyrdom was the refusal to submit sexually to men (even if marriage was offered), love of Christ, the highest possible authority, justifying their refusal to bow to male superiority, a refusal which in the normal course of events would have been seen as gross insubordination. This happens in the cases of Saints Lucy, Agnes, Agatha, and Juliana, as described in the *Legenda aurea*. The usual reaction of the outraged males is the urge to have them physically defiled and humiliated, but God invariably intervenes to save their chastity. Thus, Lucy is put into the hands of panders, but 'the Holy Ghost made her so heavy that they were unable to move her' (trans. Ryan and Ripperger, p. 36). When the (unnamed) prefect locks up Agnes with prostitutes because she will not allow her virginity its proper heathen outlet, the worship of Vesta, she is protected with 'a tunic of dazzling whiteness' brought by an angel. (As is typical of the *vitae Sanctorum*, we are in a world of 'bad' rather than 'good' pagans, and so my reader should adjust accordingly. Here is yet another aspect of the paradoxical nature of a legendary of 'heathen saints'.) The prefect's son, whose offer of marriage Agnes had refused, encourages his friends to 'have their pleasure of the maiden', but her appearance terrifies them so much that they run away, and the young man himself, on rushing recklessly into her room, is promptly throttled by the Devil 'because he had not honoured God' (p. 111). When Agatha remains unshakable in her chastity, the consul Quintianus hands her over to a procuress (with the apt name of Aphrodisia) and her nine sinful daughters, but all their efforts to draw her away from the path of virtue are in vain. Enraged, the consul has her breasts torn off, her refusal to conform to what is expected of a woman leading to physical mutilation of her female form. However, they are miraculously restored by St Peter.

Agatha and her peers die only when God allows the natural to take its course. A variation on the theme is when the lady is actually married but strives to maintain her virginity or at least to live chastely, as in the cases of Elizabeth and Cecilia. The latter manages to convert her husband, who is martyred shortly before her own holy death, as is recounted in Chaucer's version of the story in the *Second Nun's Tale*. And, of course, there are occasions on which male desires are characterized as more obviously lustful, as in the accounts of Saints Margaret and Justina.

This structure might be dubbed the 'death before dishonour' type. It encodes the principle of equating virtue with victimization, which is why I feel Priscilla Martin's singling out of the *Legend* for criticism on this score (p. 203) is inappropriate. Chaucer follows the paradigm most obviously in the *Legend of Lucrece*. There his pagan heroine regards physical defilement with a horror worthy of, and reminiscent of, Saints Lucy, Agnes, Agatha, and Juliana, and it is obvious (to me at least) that in her case Chaucer worked hard to achieve an intensity of pathos of a kind which is characteristic of the *vitae Sanctorum*. Tarquinius takes advantage of the heroine whilst she is in a condition wherein she is not conscious of anything:

> And in a swogh she lay, and wex so ded,     *swoon, became*
> Men myghte smyten of hire arm or hed;            *strike off*
> She feleth no thyng, neyther foul ne fayr.        (1816–18)

Indeed, as Lisa J. Kiser notes, that reference to dismemberment calls to mind the horrific physical abuse regularly undergone by female saints, the pain of which is alleviated by the operation of divine grace. I cannot, however, accept Kiser's subsequent suggestion that 'Chaucer's attempt to equate Lucrece's life with that of a saint results in an obviously contrived piece of literary deception that violates the generic specifications of both hagiography and courtly narrative' (pp. 105–6). This seems to me to involve a reluctance to accept the medieval taste for grotesque displays of female sacrifice for what it was. The virtuous life and death of Chaucer's Lucrece seem quite straightforward if one approaches them after having experienced some of the virtuoso performances in the *Legenda aurea*.

Even more definitely than in Ovid's narrative, Lucrece is presented as blameless for her violation (cf. p. 364 above). In this respect one may compare the *vita* of Saint Theodora, a devout woman married to 'a god-fearing man', who is defiled by a man whom the Devil has aroused. Her responsibility for her violation is diminished, perhaps even denied, by the fact that her unwanted suitor sent a sorcerer to deceive her (with the highly dubious argument that God does not see deeds which are done by night!). But such reassurances are for the reader's benefit; defiled paragons of virtue are above such things. Their guilt, however involuntary, cannot be excused or assuaged by ordinary human rationalization or forgiveness. The only course of action open to them is to transform their supposed ignominy into triumph, through superhuman sacrifice. After her violation, St Theodora, disguised as a man and using the name of Theodore, enters a monastery, thereby seeking to do 'penance' for the 'wrong' she has done her husband (to use her own words). Yet all this is done without reference to him: he is quite unaware of what has happened, and at first even thinks that she may have gone off with another man (*Legenda aurea*, trans. Ryan and Ripperger, pp. 397–400).

Similarly, the defiled Lucrece is absolute for death. Ovid spoke only of her feelings of personal disgrace; in Chaucer it is the dishonour which she has, however involuntarily, inflicted on her husband that is emphasized:

> She seyde that, for her gylt ne for hir blame,
> Hir husbonde shulde nat have the foule name,
> That wolde she nat suffre by no wey. *allow*
>
> (1844–6)

—a fact which makes her refusal to accept the forgiveness of that same husband all the more impressive (to judge by the extreme standards of hagiography, having attuned our sensibilities with the case of St Theodora). Lucrece's husband and friends have, it would seem, no part to play in the outcome; she briskly and in a matter-of-fact way brushes their arguments aside. What she must do is clear, impersonal, inexorable:

> And they answerden alle, upon hir fey,
> That they forgave yt hyr, for yt was ryght;
> It was no gilt, it lay not in hir myght; *power*
> And seyden hir ensamples many oon.
> But al for noght; for thus she seyde anoon:
> 'Be as be may', quod she, 'of forgyvyng,
> I wol not have noo forgyft for nothing'. *forgiveness*
> But pryvely she kaughte forth a knyf,
> And therwithal she rafte hirself hir lyf . . . *deprived*
>
> (1847 ff.)

Of Augustine's criticism of her suicide there is no trace. Chaucer did not allow the categories and distinctions of Christian ethics to be applied by those who attempt to dissuade her, a device which we find in Jean de Meun's version of the story:

They urged her strongly to let go her sorrow; they gave her persuasive reasons; and her husband particularly comforted her with compassion and pardoned her with generous heart for the entire deed, and lectured her and studied to find lively arguments to prove to her that her body had not sinned when her heart did not wish the sin (for the body cannot be the sinner if the heart does not consent to it). But she, in her sorrow, held a knife hidden in her breast. (8617–31, trans. Dahlberg, p. 158)

In this respect at least Chaucer seems to have more in common with Jerome. 'Noble minds', declared the saint, 'care more for chastity than life'; his belief that 'the virtue of woman is, in a special sense, purity' underlies his praise of Lucretia for 'having blotted out the stain upon her person with her blood' (*Adversus Jovinianum*, i. 46). It would seem then, that (to adapt phrases from Goldsmith) the lovely lady on whom male folly has been imposed has only one 'art her guilt to cover'—to die. And this must be done with dignity and decorum, in a way which will move the immediate audience and edify posterity.

Chaucer brings his tale of Lucrece to a close by emphasizing that she was a superlative but by no means unrepresentative (for women are generally 'stable') example of a chaste and faithful wife:

> I telle hyt [i.e. this legend], for she was of love so trewe,
> Ne in hir wille she chaunged for no newe;
> And for the stable herte, sadde and kynde,
> That in these wymmen men may alday fynde.
> Ther as they kaste hir herte, there it dwelleth. (1874–8)

Robert Frank finds this 'somewhat curious', remarking: 'If the moral does not seem to do full justice to the story, let it pass. It will do as well as any sentiment, any moral. It springs from a rush of feeling, not a rational judgment' (p. 103). But Chaucer's *moralitas* is perfectly in keeping with certain alterations which he has made to his source throughout the *narratio*. His story of Lucrece is, after all, part and parcel of a legendary of Cupid's saints. Beside Alceste, who surpasses even Lucrece as a candidate for secular sainthood, stands the God of Love. Lucrece's passion, therefore, must be brought into line with the other legends. In Augustine, the heroine dies because, as a typical Roman, she was 'covetous of glory' (*De civitate Dei*, i. 18); in Jerome, because she seeks to blot out the stain upon her own person (*Adversus Jovinianum*, i. 46); in Jean de Meun, because of her personal sorrow (8578–620); in Boccaccio, because she wished to cleanse her shame and restore her good name (*De mulieribus claris*, trans. Guarino, p. 103). But in Chaucer, as has already been noted, she dies first and foremost because of her husband: 'Hir husbonde shulde nat have the foule name.' This devotion to her husband has been firmly established by the preceeding narrative; her 'wifly chastite' (1737) is the key to her character, the stress falling on the 'wifly'. Chaucer even omitted the Ovidian heroine's speculation about her husband's rashness in battle lest it would make her love for him seem somewhat less than perfect. St Augustine had, as an argument ploy, raised the possibility that Lucretia might have given a 'lustful consent, and after did so grieve at that, that she held it worthy to be punished with death' (trans. Healey, i. 23–4). But Chaucer's heroine, we are assured, was so true to her husband that her will did not consent to the attentions of any 'newe' man.

Noble 'wyfhod' is what Lucrece has in common with most of her companions in the *Legend*, though for some of them it is an ideal rather than an actuality. Like Lucrece, Hypsipyle is praised for her wifely fidelity and chastity:

> And trewe to Jason was she al hire lyf,
> And evere kepte her chast, as for his wif          (1576–7)

Furthermore, the 'death before dishonour' narrative paradigm is to some extent in evidence in the *Legend of Thisbe*, wherein the woman forsakes all her friends to be true to the solemn 'covenaunt' she has made to meet her beloved Piramus (790, 798–9), and then follows him into death, determined to prove that a woman can be as true in loving as a man (910–11). Like Lucrece, she is anxious to ensure that men will 'sette' on her 'no lak', to borrow an idiom from the God of Love (G Prol. 298).

But Chaucer was not content to follow this well-established hagiographic 'deep structure'. For the greater part of the poem, he invented and exploited a new one, at the very centre of which is a conception of marriage which is far broader than Lucrece's 'humblesse of wifhod, word and chere' (2269). (The same formulaic phrase is applied to Procne in the *Legend of Philomela*, 2269; no irony seems to be intended there, for Chaucer concentrates on the violation of the marriage bond by her hideous husband Tereus.) Cleopatra is referred to as Antony's 'wyf' on four occasions (594, 615, 632, 663); unreprovable in her 'wyfhod' (691), she follows her husband into death. Hypermnestra bravely refuses to obey her father's command because of her connubial obligations to the man she is supposed to murder; she prefers to die in 'wifly honeste' rather than live as a 'traytour' to what she believes to be right (2699–702). Indeed, Chaucer seems to have thrust marriage upon those whose claim to full and indisputable legality would be suspect to anyone who knew his sources, the most obvious example being the case of Dido (cf. pp. 386–7 above). Similarly, in the *Legend of Ariadne* we move from Ariadne's recommendation of marriage not only for herself but also for her sister— who, she declares, should marry the son of her lover Theseus—to the narrator's unselfconscious references to his 'wyves tresor', 'hys wif', and 'Adryane his wif' (2151–2, 2171). In the *Legend of Medea* the statement that Jason 'wedded yit the thridde wif' (1660) implies that he was fully and legally married to Medea as his second wife.

'Wif' could, of course, mean simply 'woman' in Chaucer's English (cf. the ambiguity of *mulier* in medieval Latin), but in these cases the implication of marriage is inescapable. Doubtless the fact that his heroines were, to a woman, heathen, meant that Chaucer was freer to blur the issue (the sanctity, not to mention the detail, of Christian marriage not being at issue). However, it should be noted that Chaucer alludes to the Christian couple's vow to remain true 'until death us do part' on two occasions: once, as already noted, in the *Legend of Dido*, and again, far more elaborately, in this arresting word-play from the *Legend of Thisbe*:

> 'And thogh that nothing, save the deth only,
> Mighte thee fro me departe trewely,
> Thow shalt no more departe now fro me
> Than fro the deth, for I wol go with thee!'          (896–9)

Here Thisbe goes beyond the call of marital duty in refusing to be parted from her lover by death. Similarly, Cleopatra's determination to keep her 'covenant' with her husband to the extent of sharing even death with him (691–4) might be seen as the supererogation of the liturgical injunction to take one's husband for better or worse, for richer or poorer. At any rate, it is clear that Cleopatra and Thisbe have been invested with emotions which are worthy of the superlative Alceste.

Where marriage is neither proclaimed nor implied through deliberate obfuscation, we are offered the next best thing: a firm plighting of troth, a solemn undertaking to marry in the future, what was technically known as *desponsatio* by *verba de futuro*. Dido, Medea, Ariadne, and Phyllis all seem to enter into such contracts with their men before they sleep with them. Demophon swears to marry Phyllis 'and hire his trouthe plyghte' (just as his father Theseus had promised Ariadne, 2459–69), and sails away on the pretext of arranging their 'weddynge', which presumably means a public solemnization (2472–4). Jason swears by both his knighthood and the heathen gods that he will become Medea's husband, and here *verba de futuro* are clearly implied:

> They been acorded ful bytwixe hem two
> That Jason shal hire wedde                          (1635–6)

However, Jason deserts her and in Thessaly 'wedded yit the thridde wyf anon' (1600). Was this legal? Yes, inasmuch as in medieval theory and practice a consummated match dependent on *verba de futuro* could be bested by a subsequent one which had been contracted by 'words of present consent' (*verba de presenti*), even if it were unconsummated. (H. A.

Kelly suggests that the line 'And doth his oth, and goth with hire to bedde' (1644) implies *verba de presenti*, which are followed by physical consummation—thus the marriage would become 'fully binding' (pp. 205–6). But this phrase may be too vague to support that reading: the 'oth' could simply be a reiteration of his promise to marry her in the future, or some other impressive but empty promise.) At any rate, the details of Jason's third alliance are not made clear, any more than is the form of Jason's first marriage, to Hypsipyle: in that case the text simply avoids the issue of degrees of legality. What is quite clear is that what Phyllis, Ariadne, and Medea (in the lines quoted above) have achieved is a relatively weak form of *desponsatio*; the firmest form of marriage possible, involving 'present consent' and public celebration, remains their ultimate goal in life.

There is no question of the utter legality of the marriages of Cleopatra, Hypsipyle, Lucrece, Procne, and Hypermnestra. The first of these may seem particularly strange to a modern audience which has received its image of Cleopatra mainly from Shakespeare, but Antony is described as having married Cleopatra ('matrimonio copulavit') in what was Chaucer's primary—and perhaps only—source for this narrative, the *Speculum historiale* of Vincent of Beauvais (cf. p. 354 above). But Chaucer goes further than Vincent, in depicting her as married in the fullest sense known to him; that is, her 'weddynge' and 'feste', so elaborate that he claims it would take too long to describe, may be read as the pagan equivalent of what in Chaucer's day was termed marriage *in facie ecclesiae*. (What he imagined such an ancient wedding to have been like is probably conveyed by lines 2610–17, where Hypermnestra's marriage is described.) Such a public celebration of marriage did not, technically speaking, make the marriage—'present consent' was what created an indissoluble bond. But it rendered the marriage fully licit.

Regarded in such legal terms, the status of Dido's alliance with Aeneas is problematic. The form of words originally used by the narrator—namely, that she took him 'for husbonde and becom his wyf' (1238)—seems to imply a contract by *verba de presenti*, but (as already noted) later in the tale it becomes clear that Dido lacks something which she passionately desires. Take me as your wife, she begs, 'as ye han sworn' (1319–20). It now seems that their contract was of the far weaker sort (*verba de futuro*, a pledge to marry in the future): clearly, Chaucer's narrator initially saw things from Dido's biased point of view (cf. pp. 386–7 above). It is not simply that she desperately wants to persuade Aeneas to stay with her—which is the obvious motivation for her plea that he should spare the life of their (putative) unborn child—for Dido is prepared to die on account of Aeneas's departure. The point is rather that she wants to die as his wife in the fullest sense of the term (1322–3). It may be added that the presence or absence of witnesses was often crucial in medieval marriage litigation; but, of course, according to literary tradition, the lovers' amatory encounter in the cave was a private affair. Chaucer coyly remarks: 'I not, with hem if there wente any mo' (1227): could he possibly be alluding to that vexed area of legal controversy?

By contrast, the course of Thisbe's love for Piramus is unable to run very far, and so in this case the 'covenaunt' which Chaucer emphasizes concerns only their solemn oath, made with impressive observance of the heathen pieties, to meet at an appointed place (778 ff.). Thisbe is the only woman to die a 'maide' (725, cf. 722) in the poem as we have it, and that is very much against her will, the only impediment to her marriage with Piramus being their fathers' refusal to agree to the match:

> certeyn, as by resoun of hire age,
> There myghte have ben bytwixe hem maryage,
> But that here fadres nolde it nat assente      (728–30)

The G Prologue speaks of women who kept their 'maydenhede', 'wedlok', and 'widewhede' (294–5), but the extant legends concentrate on those who are in 'wedlok' or at least totally committed to their mates.

In short, Chaucer's heroines are married, or are implied to be married, and/or are eager to be married. Cleopatra, Medea, Dido, and the rest cling to marriage with as much intensity as Saints Lucy, Agnes, Agatha, and Juliana sought to avoid it. (Procne is an exception, but it should be noted that in her case wifely virtue is explicitly related to sisterly love, thereby making clear the store she sets by family bonds and obligations (2260–9)). Indeed, the legend of Cupid's saints could well be seen as some sort of response to the *Legenda aurea*, which is replete with anti-matrimonial propaganda of a kind which sometimes verges on heterodoxy, as when certain legends 'flatly condemn sexual intercourse even within a lawful marriage', as Reames puts it (p. 206). Typically, when the prefect's son makes his (perfectly honourable) proposal of marriage to Agatha, she rejects the very idea of secular marriage in no uncertain terms: 'Begone from me, tinder of sin, nurse of evil, fodder of death! For I am already engaged to another lover . . . Him I love, who is far nobler than you and of much higher lineage' (trans. Ryan and Ripperger, p. 206). Reames instances this as one of the 'gratuitous insults that stand out in the *Legenda*' (p. 304 n. 24). Within the work's hyperbolic discourse, gratuitous insults give way to gratuitous violence, the most ingenious of tortures, and inflated marvels.

The contrast between the *vitae Sanctorum* and Chaucer's legendary is, therefore, quite diametric. In place of the mystical marriage of the female saint to Christ the Bridegroom (to adopt the conventional idiom deriving from the Song of Songs) stands human marriage. In Cupid's martyrology, this, rather than virginity or chastity, is the great legitimizing factor. Marriage, whether secured or desired, motivates and ennobles all the deaths for love, most notably Cleopatra's spectacular suicide in the snake-pit. It explains Thisbe's daring night-time expedition to a highly dangerous place, why Piramus, Thisbe, Medea, and Hypermnestra should reject the authority of their fathers, and why Dido first disregards and subsequently deceives the sensible sister who was apparently suspicious of Aeneas and only had her good at heart. Here, in sum, is the hagiographic rationale which justifies behaviour which would normally appear extreme, indecorous, or insubordinate (material which simply could not be justified in that way having quietly been omitted). Though the female figures in the *Legend* may appear as 'impulsive rebels against authority', as P. T. Overbeck puts it, that rebellion is brought about, and is validated, by their submission to a higher authority, in this case their menfolk—a principle which can take on quite abstract form, as in the *Legend of Lucrece* (1844–6, 1852).

Marriage, it may be added, provides a bridge between moral truth and truth-in-love. It is the acceptable face of the classical eroticism symbolized by Cupid. The firmly exclusive categories of the medievalized *Heroides* (e.g. legally loving Penelope versus infatuated Phyllis) having been set aside, Chaucer's text can invite the positive response which its audience would inevitably have to the state, acts, and fruit of marriage. Then again, pagan marriage—an exotic and (fortunately for Chaucer's project) unfamiliar institution—is an appropriate sphere in which pagan 'shadowy perfection' may reveal itself. Women living in ancient heathen cultures had to undergo many trials and tribulations, sometimes including death, on account of their menfolk; Christian women will have to do likewise for their God-become-man. One may respect the similarities—thereby respecting the heroines themselves—while being in no doubt concerning the essentially superior ends and means of the Christian 'feyth'.

Even more important, perhaps, marriage is an institution which must (almost inevitably) be commended in a work which sets out to commend women of secular estate. For medieval misogyny, as has already been noted, was often inextricably bound up with misogamy, a connection which is never more clear than in Jerome's *Adversus Jovinianum*. Therefore, to praise secular women is to praise marriage, and vice versa. Marriage may, after all, be identified as the most respectable of the natural outlets for the psychology and functions which were then held to be characteristic of the feminine gender. (Female sainthood involved some unsexing—a point to which we will return.) According to the Christian hierarchy of values, matrimony was inferior to chastity, which in turn was inferior to virginity. But in the pagan world of the extant legends of good women, it carries all before it, Chaucer's heathen heroines, unlike his Wife of Bath, not being obliged to defend their status against the superior orders of female existence (pagan virginity cults having conveniently been forgotten). *Matrimonia vincit omnia.*

The point that 'Saints' lives not only *seem* all the same to readers, they very frequently *are* the same' is well made by Dinshaw, *Sexual Poetics*, pp. 72–4.

Jacobus de Voragine, *Legenda aurea*, ed. Graesse, trans. Ryan and Ripperger. Martin, *Chaucer's Women*. Kiser, *Telling Classical Tales*. *Roman de la Rose*, ed. Langlois, trans. Dahlberg. St Jerome, *Adversus Jovinianum*, in *PL* xxiii, 221–352, trans. W. H. Freemantle, in *The Principal Works of St Jerome*, Select Library of Nicene and Post-Nicene Fathers, 6 (Oxford, 1893), 346–416. Frank, *Legend of Good Women*. Augustine, *City of God*, trans. Healey.

As D. S. Brewer notes, 'in every one of the legends . . . there is an explicit connection between love and marriage'; 'Love and Marriage in Chaucer's Poetry', *MLR* 43 (1954), 461–4. Similarly, Ruth Ames notes that 'the ladies in the legends love the very name of wife'; 'Feminist Connections', p. 65. For a fuller treatment see Kelly, *Love and Marriage*, pp. 101–20, 202–16.

On the legal vocabulary relating to present and future consent, etc., see especially K. H. Helmholz, *Marriage Litigation in Medieval England* (Cambridge, 1974), pp. 26–8; also Kelly, *Love and Marriage*, p. 176; Georges Duby, *Medieval marriage: Two Models from Twelfth-Century France* (Baltimore and London, 1978), pp. 2–4, 16–17, 42–3; Alan Macfarlane, *Marriage and Love in England: Modes of Reproduction 1300–1840* (Oxford and New York, 1986), pp. 309–13; and Christopher N. L. Brooke, *The Medieval Idea of Marriage* (Oxford, 1989), pp. 128–9, 137–8. See further Richard Firth Green, 'Chaucer's Victimized Women', *SAC* 9 (1988), 146–54; Minnis, 'Repainting the Lion'. I would wish also to emphasize the possibility that, among other things, Chaucer was seeking to compliment the noble 'wyfhod' of Anne of Bohemia (cf. p. 447 below).

The high value placed on family bonds and obligations in the *Legend of Philomela* is well brought out in the discussion by Kruger, 'Passion and Order', who lists (at p. 235 n. 16) the following references to various kinds of familial relation therein: 'wife' (2259, 2274, 2275, 2299, 2342, 2343); 'husband' (2263); 'father' (2272, 2285, 2329), 'son' (2296); 'daughter' (2247, 2281, 2297, 2299); 'brother' (2315, 2392); and 'sister' (2261, 2265, 2274, 2286, 2315, 2328, 2345, 2349, 2365, 2377, 2380).

Reames, *Legenda Aurea*. P. T. Overbeck, 'Chaucer's Good Woman', *ChR* 2 (1967), 75–94; she notes the ambition of Chaucer's quintessentially good woman 'to legitimate her "sensualitee" in the marriage relationship' (p. 85). Kruger, 'Passion and Order', argues that in the poem female passion is shown as breaking through social structures; his ultimate point, however, is that Chaucer reveals how 'passion and order, even as they do battle, remain inextricably dependent on each other' (p. 233).

To the hagiographic narrative paradigms described above may be added the 'Jephthah's daughter' (cf. Judges 11: 29–40) or 'sacrifice of beauty' type, a good example being afforded by the sad story of Petronella, whose father (supposedly St Peter, no less) keeps her, through his powers, in a state of permanent sickness so that her beauty does not attract the attention of pagan males, until she becomes mature spiritually: when this happens, and her beauty is duly restored, she chooses death rather than marriage (*Legenda aurea*, ed. Graesse, p. 343; trans. Ryan and Ripperger, pp. 300–1). Equally harrowing is the story of St Juliana, whose father, angry at her refusal to marry the prefect of Nicomedia, has her stripped and beaten, and then hands her over to that same prefect, who stretches her on a wheel and finally has her beheaded (ed. Graesse, pp. 177–8; trans. Ryan and Ripperger, pp. 166–7). Chaucer offers a secular version of this type of story in the *Physician's Tale*, wherein a questioning attitude to the father's sacrifice of his daughter is perhaps being encouraged: see Middleton, 'Love's Martyrs'.

## All Women's Friend?

Was Chaucer, then, a friend to all women? Gavin Douglas certainly thought so (cf. pp. 244–5), but some of his more recent readers have been less sure. There are, indeed, many grounds for modern unease regarding the *Legend*. Nowadays it seems quite absurd that women should have to die in order to preserve, or reclaim, their good name, and that they should conform so obsessively to male expectations: 'menne schulde sette on hem no lak' (298). By praising women for adhering so rigidly to a narrow and repressive ethos, the text (so the argument would run) is perpetuating the logistics of suttee, as summed up so well by the Man of Law's Constance:

> 'I, wrecche womman, no fors though I spille!       *matter, die*
> Wommen are born to thraldom and penance,
> And to been under mannes governance'.       (*CT* II(B¹) 285–7)

The *Legend*'s male narrator is very much one of 'us men' writing to 'ye wemen'. And men, it would seem, have written the rules of 'fyn lovynge' and wifely 'lyvynge' under which the female sex must operate. In Alceste's court room they are the lawgivers, the judges, and the jury. It's a man's world, a man's morality, even a man's posterity.

To think in that way, however, is to run the risk of engaging in an act of cultural imperialism wherein the complicated value system of the later Middle Ages is reduced to a set of predictable polemical points. Surely it is better to examine what the relevant possibilities for reversal, subversion, and dissent actually were in Chaucer's day, and gauge the room for manœuvre which the prevailing culture allowed to writers on the 'woman question'. We may begin with an exploration of the form which such a historicizing of difference might take, 'difference' being used here to designate the specific gender differences which were then believed to separate men and women.

These, it may be added, constitute features of medieval thought which make Chaucer's culture different from that of the likely readers of this book. Here, then, is another way in which 'difference' may be thought of, as indicating areas of cultural disjunction which separate certain historical periods and places. Such historicism is certainly not a matter of mere antiquarianism, or part of an authoritarian agenda which dictates that certain past 'facts' must be believed and accepted as non-negotiable as far as present culture is concerned. Rather, as Gillian Beer says, 'The encounter with the otherness of earlier literature can allow us to recognize and challenge our own assumptions, and those of the society in which we live. . . . This means engaging with the *difference* of the past in the present and so making us aware of the trajectory of arrival' (p. 67). The ambiguity of the following heading is, therefore, quite deliberate.

### HISTORICIZING DIFFERENCE

According to Hope Phyllis Weissman, the definition of literary anti-feminism must include *any* male-oriented presentation of women:

> The literary tradition of antifeminism may . . . be defined in a wider sense to include not simply satirical caricatures of women but any presentation of a woman's nature intended to conform her to male expectations of what she is or ought to be, not her own. By this wider definition, an image of woman need not be ostensibly unflattering to be antifeminist in fact or in potential; indeed, the most insidious of antifeminist images are those which celebrate, with a precision often subtle rather than apparent, the forms a woman's goodness is to take. (p. 94)

This 'wider definition' informs Elaine Tuttle Hansen's 1983 article on the *Legend*, wherein its narrator is seen as a

> personification of the subtle antifeminism of the courtly and clerical tradition he draws on. Presented by his overt limitations and inadequacies from identifying ourselves with or trusting this narrator very far, then, we see how this selection and treatment of good women ironically defines the double bind in which the female is caught: victimized if she follows the rules of Love and lives up to feminine ideals; unworthy, unloved, and unsung if she does not. (p. 28)

Chaucer, this argument runs, has directed his irony at Cupid, at the narrator, and at 'the antifeminist tradition to which both unwittingly perhaps but nevertheless certainly subscribe' (p. 12), with the intention of showing us 'how problems for real women arose from a literary tradition that theoretically idealizes their gender' (p. 28). It would seem, therefore, that medieval women could trust no man but Chaucer. But was he really such an exception? Looking back at this article in her *Chaucer and the Fictions of Gender*, Hansen admits that at least part of her motivation was the conviction that 'the blatant antifeminism of the Legends was unworthy of the subtle intelligence that is obviously Chaucer's', as is manifested by his 'treatment of women in other works' (p. 2; cf. p. 28 of her article). Now she seeks to challenge 'the attempt to recuperate a feminist

Chaucer who does not threaten the humanist Chaucer' which is based on assumptions such as the belief that 'Chaucer is sympathetic to woman's problems'. This is well said. And yet, in her book the working assumption is that what is 'antifeminist' in terms of the 1990s provides appropriate values for judgement of a poem of the 1380s (though much is done to locate Chaucer's works historically with reference to sociopolitical information, literary tradition, and so forth). Granted that postmodern thought has shaken our faith in 'the unity or knowability of any authorial position or any cultural stance' (p. 23), if certain late medieval cultural structures and faultlines which relate to gender are perceptible, it would be perverse to ignore them on the grounds that they cannot by definition be truly known.

The fundamental ideological structures are clear enough. Antifeminism, as understood nowadays (in terms of Weissman's 'wider definition'), had very deep roots in the intellectual culture of Chaucer's time. Medieval theology (following Genesis) and medieval science taught that women were inferior in body and in mind. Medieval biology often declared that women were incomplete males, and that sex was determined by the male seed—indeed, sometimes the strength of the male libido was deemed to be a contributory factor. Physically, a woman could be regarded as a man turned inside out: everything the male had outside, the female had inside. (It should be noted, however, that there was no single medical model for treating of masculine and feminine characteristics and types, as Cadden has emphasized.) Even virtue was often understood as something essentially male, this prejudice being embedded in the Latin language as understood by medieval grammarians. *Virtus* was held to derive from *vir*, 'man': 'Virtus a vir dicitur.' In its turn, *vir* came from *vireo*, meaning 'vigorous', 'because a man is vigorous in many things in comparison with a woman, or it is said to be from *vis* ["strength", "ability"], because a man is stronger than a woman'. Thus states a popular dictionary of the later Middle Ages, Giovanni de' Balbi's *Catholicon*. Under *mulier*, we read that 'a woman is pliant and feeble in comparison with a man. Therefore the virtue of the man is the greater and that of the woman the lesser.' In short, it would seem that Naomi Schor's generalization that 'in Western conceptual systems the feminine is always defined as a difference from a masculine norm' (p. 100) is abundantly supported by this evidence.

Consequently, for a woman to attain the heights of virtue often entailed a sort of gender alienation: she became a *virago*, a 'manly woman' in a sense which could be quite complimentary in medieval terms, as de' Balbi's definition illustrates: 'a strong woman who acts as a man, i.e. performs virile [or "manly"] deeds, and is of masculine strength'. On this definition, female heroism meant acting in man's image. For instance, Saint Theodora, to take but one figure from the *Legenda aurea*, reacts to her physical violation with what amounts to a denial of her own sex. Having cut off her hair and dressed as a man—the analogy with that other famous transvestite, Joan of Arc, is tantalizing—she enters a monastery (cf. p. 414 above). All this is done by way of 'penance' for the 'wrong' which, she assumes without the slightest hestiation, she has done her husband. Those same sexual attributes which lured the rapist must be negated in order that honour be satisfied; Theodora's manly appearance is the outward manifestation of the garb of spiritual virtue which she has assumed.

The contrary of this was that the 'womanly man' was often a negative figure, a moral and physical weakling who was the object of male ridicule and female rejection. A fairly mild version of this bias appears in that poem for which the *Legend* is offered by way of compensation, *Troilus and Criseyde*. In the love scene in the third book Pandarus demands of the swooning Troilus, 'Is this a mannes herte?' (1098), and promptly strips him of his clothes, that he may prove his virility with Criseyde. A few lines later, as Troilus recovers and Criseyde is faced with his self-torment, she expresses the same attitude in the remark 'Is this a mannes game?', and appeals to his sense of shame to make him snap out of it (1126–7).

There is, to be sure, in recent Chaucer criticism much talk of 'feminized men' (cf. pp. 60–1). This notion can have considerable purchase, as when Hansen argues that in the *Legend* men 'sometimes act as women are said to act and . . . are treated as women are often treated'; initially disadvantaged by 'circumstances, fate, or innate weakness' and dependent on the favour of powerful women, they weep, make false promises, and fall in lust, thus adopting behavioural patterns which usually are seen as feminine (*Fictions of Gender*, pp. 3, 6). Here, then, is no challenge to traditionally gendered subjectivities but rather a confirmation of them; the 'female' emotions which the males have imposed on them for the duration of the poem are clearly marked as debilitating ones.

However, 'feminization' has been taken in a more positive sense, as when Jill Mann claims that Troilus is feminized 'in his vulnerability and sensitivity of feeling' (p. 166). That sort of argument is problematic in terms of the sexual politics of our own day, for it reinforces essentializing gender distinctions rather than questioning them, by implying that boys don't cry and if they do they must be acting like girls. It is problematic in a different way for medieval sexual politics. For then, the male of the species was endowed with the best of everything: he was the stronger and the more intelligent, the determining force in every area of human endeavour, from the governance of Church and State to the engendering of children. Therefore his emotions could not fail to be of a high order. It may be recalled how, in the twelfth-century *Chanson de Roland*, a hundred thousand tough warriors—no sissies they—engage in communal weeping when they find the corpse of Roland. These figures are quite innocent of *fin' amors*, and it could hardly be said that they have been feminized by the poet, who clearly is concerned with the strength of the bonds between men, which take on their most intense form within the relationship between the warlord and his loyal retainers.

Similarly with Troilus: phrases like 'his manhod and his pyne', 'manly sorwe', and 'gentil herte and manhod' (ii. 676, iii. 113, iv. 1674) indicate that these admirable characteristics fall very much within the sphere of his gendered subjectivity, being an essential part of his 'manhod' as Chaucer's text regards it. Returning to Troilus's swoon, it may be argued that there is nothing particularly 'feminine' about that; such an action manifests a man's sensitivity—providing, of course, that he does not indulge in it too much or for too long. There is no risk of that here: soon Troilus is displaying his manly vigour by demanding of Criseyde, 'Now yeldeth yow!' (iii. 1208), which is slightly incongrous given that a few minutes ago she was the active one, working hard (with Pandarus) to help him recover his senses. Criseyde's famous reply is that if she did not want this, she would not be here (1211), and the entire passage has often been read, with good reason, as a beautiful expression of frankly mutual love. And yet, their love-making is seen very much through the male gaze. Criseyde's body is described in admiring (some would say voyeuristic) detail: 'armes smale', 'streghte bak and softe', 'sydes longe, flesshly, smoothe, and white', 'snowissh throte', 'brestes rounde and lite' (1247–50). By contrast, the realization of Troilus avoids his physicality whilst emphasizing the force of his male desire by likening him to a sparrow-hawk which has caught a lark in its claws (1191–2). For her part, Criseyde is all a-tremble—

> Right as an aspen leef she gan to quake,
> Whan she hym felte hire in his armes folde      (1200–1)

—as she accepts the ardour of her entrapping and enfolding lover. Earlier in the poem she had prominently displayed a timorousness and tendency to tremble (ii. 124, 302–3, 449–50), which Chaucer's text may well be proffering as attractively feminine qualities, by which I mean qualities supposed to make her highly attractive to men, who are thereby fired to protect and/or to possess her. Certainly, in this love scene the aggressive male is firmly on top. Which is why I find it impossible to accept Mann's suggestion that Troilus's supposedly 'feminized' emotions 'cleanse' his manhood 'of aggression' (p. 168).

'Facts' about gender difference like these were accepted by just about everyone. That exceptionally learned and articulate woman Christine de Pizan has been claimed as 'an important foremother of the feminist canon', as Lynne Huffer puts it (p. 71). Yet even she accepted traditional notions regarding the typical weaknesses of the female body, and her versions of modesty topoi comprised self-presentation as 'a little lonely woman' who wanted to stay that way (ballade 11). In the *Livre de la Mutacion de Fortune* she goes so far as to claim that Fortune transformed her into a man ('Homme suis'), because she was obliged to steer the ship of her life and family after its captain was thrown overboard in a storm; that is, she assumed qualities traditionally seen as 'manly' after the death of her husband.

Given the ubiquity of such données of medieval culture, it may be useful to view them as falling within the category of 'structural anti-feminism'—this term having been coined on the analogy of the economist's term 'structural unemployment'. The ideas in question are dictated and required by the structure; the structure itself must change before its characteristic ills can disappear. It would be improper to condemn a writer for structural anti-feminism (phobic anti-feminism being, of course, a different matter). If a medieval writer wished to commend the female sex, she or he inevitably engaged in the traditional gender politics. The male-oriented morality assumed in the *Legend* is, therefore, utterly typical. Chaucer did not invent it; neither did he exaggerate it. He was following traditions, participating in discourses of sexual difference which were to outlive him long into the future.

To accept this is not to take the line that history is to blame and there is nothing more to be done about it. For that would be an evasion, a refusal to come to terms with the past history of gender roles. It is perfectly possible to believe that within this area, as in so many others, history is a nightmare from which we are trying to awake (to adapt a sentence from Joyce's Stephen Dedalus), whilst reacting against criticisms of Chaucer's narrator—or, more daringly, Chaucer himself—for his failure to live up to the standards of the academic feminism current at the end of the twentieth century.

What, then, can be said about the possibilities for dissent? An excellent test case is afforded by what Christine de Pizan really did to *De mulieribus claris*. In her *Livre de la Cité des Dames* much of Boccaccio's material was recast in an ostentatiously pro-feminist mould. Christine had no problem in accepting the (quite standard) hierarchical subordination of pagan to Christian virtue: the grandest and most lofty parts of the City of Ladies are reserved for the Virgin Mary and the female Christian saints. What she almost certainly found objectionable was the way in which Boccaccio's placing of (most) virtuous women in the past served to isolate and distance them from modern women. The conclusion to *De mulieribus claris* begins with this revealing remark: 'As can be clearly seen, I have reached the women of our time, in which the number of illustrious ones is so small that I think it more suitable to come to an end here rather than proceed further with the women of today' (trans. Guarino, p. 251). Thus, Boccaccio's search for good women abruptly ceases. The vast majority of the women who were his subjects have one major thing in common: these exotic creatures are dead, and so are their outstanding qualities. We are very much in the world of the *Epistola Valerii ad Rufinum* and the ending of the *Clerk's Tale*, as quoted above (p. 380). Moreover, in Boccaccio there is the suggestion—which is not to be found anywhere in Chaucer's *Legend*—that superlative virtue in a woman is all the more precious because the natural odds are against it:

If men should be praised whenever they perform great deeds (with strength which nature has given them), how much more should women be extolled (almost all of whom are endowed with tenderness, frail bodies, and sluggish minds by Nature), if they have acquired a manly spirit and if with keen intelligence and remarkable fortitude they have dared undertake and have accomplished even the most difficult deeds? (Preface; trans. Guarino, p. xxxvii)

Hence the virtuous Hebrew and Christian women who are largely excluded from his anthology are in some sense disqualified as actual examples of womanhood, since by acting according to their religious precepts they 'behave almost contrary to human nature', by which Boccaccio means 'contrary to feminine nature'. To be virtuous is, on this familiar argument, to become unfeminine, to turn oneself into an honorary man. *Virtus a vir dicitur.*

Christine's prominent inclusion of Christian martyrs in her work may be seen as a response to such historical and psychological segregation. Her invitation is open-ended: ladies of all ages, whether past, present, or future, have a place in her city; female virtue is neither a thing of the past nor rarer than the phoenix. It was one thing to accept that ancient women who had behaved in accordance with the best law available to them had a code of conduct which was inherently inferior to the Mosaic and Christian systems; to swallow the notion that the virtuous Jewish and Christian females of bygone days were not as other women, was something else. And, indeed, it was quite contrary to other aspects of Boccaccio's work—not to mention the occasional exhortations by Church Fathers like Jerome and Gregory—that modern women should fail to learn from the experience of their predecessors. *Exempla* cannot function properly if their narratives seem irrelevant to present needs.

Boccaccio's bias is further revealed by the fact that, unlike Chaucer and Christine, he has not confined himself to case histories of good women. By 'famous' he means not necessarily 'virtuous' but rather 'renowned to the world through any sort of deed'; hence the chaste Penelope, Lucretia, and Sulpicia rub shoulders with women of 'very strong but destructive' character, like Medea, Flora, and Sempronia. And there are no prizes for guessing which characteristics are supposed to be the more 'normal' ones in womankind. In short, there was much in *De mulieribus claris* for Christine to react against. Her author Boccaccio, whose 'credibility', she affirms, 'is well-known and evident', could be cited as one who, for instance, 'praises and approves learning in women' and generally had warm words to say about female virtue (trans. Richards, pp. 78, 65). Yet he too, she must have recognized, often talked like one of the company of those phobic anti-feminists attacked in the polemical prologue to the *Cité des Dames* for having been, and being, 'so inclined to express . . . so many wicked insults about women and their behavior' (trans. Richards, pp. 3–4). What she actually made of Boccaccio is evident: in the *Cité des Dames* pro-feminist rosebuds are unobtrusively but firmly plucked from misogynistic thorns. (By 'pro-feminist' here, as elsewhere, I simply mean statements which *ostensibly* commend women, thereby functioning in accordance with the norms of the prevailing culture.) Christine's prologue, then, evinces a measure of dissent, whereas the work which follows covertly appropriates the best (in her terms) which the establishment has to offer.

The self-fashioning in this prologue provides us with the interpretative key to Christine's literary technique; a definite, clear, and unitary *raison d'être* has been provided. Chaucer's discourse of selfhood in the *Legend* is rather less stable, for the reasons explained above. It is harder to take this *sujet* at face value, even though at the level of literary technique what Chaucer did to his sources is virtually identical to what Christine did to hers. The strategy and the effect of the *Legend* bear strong resemblances to those of the *Cité des Dames*; the *entent* is harder to gauge. Chaucer does not theorize any dissent he may have felt; all one has to work on is his enigmatic literary artifice. He offers nothing to parallel the moving plea which Christine makes, in a letter written during the *querelle de la Rose*, for women to be treated as an integral part of the human race, rather than as creatures sharing no part of the nature of men, regarded as animals to be hunted and trapped. Here, so to speak, is the hunter being painted by the lion, to invert a phrase from the Wife of Bath (III(D) 688–91). Or, reverting to the idiom of *Troilus*, iii. 1191–2, the sparrow-hawk being viewed from the perspective of the lark.

Who are women? Who are they? Are they serpents, wolves, lions, dragons, monsters, or ravishing, devouring beasts and enemies to human nature that it is necessary to make an art of deceiving and capturing them? Read then the *Art* [i.e. Ovid's *Ars amatoria*]. Learn then how to make traps, capture the forts, deceive them, condemn them, attack this castle, take care that no woman escape from you men, and let everything be given over to shame! And, by God! these are your mothers, your sisters, your daughters, your wives, and your sweethearts: *they are you yourselves and you themselves are they*. (trans. Baird and Kane, p. 136; italics mine)

Christine is, of course, writing as one who has taken on the burden of defending her own sex. In another letter she assures Jean de Montreuil that in matters relating to female behaviour she can 'speak better . . . than one who has not had the experience' of being a woman (trans. Baird and Kane, p. 53), an incisive claim for the authority of experience, at least in this sphere. In the *Legend*, by contrast, Chaucer constructs his narrator very definitely as a male, a figure who is highly aware of his own gender. A lot could be made of this. 'In a long history men have been trained simply to read,' argues Stephen Heath; 'they have the acquired neutrality of domination, theirs is the security of indifference—it is women who are difficult, the special case' (p. 27). Recognition of this situation, the refusal to be complicit in this indifference, may mark the beginning of a new way of reading for men—and, for Chaucer, of a new way of writing. And yet: a major part of the I-persona's awareness of himself as male seems to be the feeling that he is playing an anomalous, perhaps even slightly ridiculous, role as scapegoat for those legions of male writers who have demeaned women: why should *he* be singled out? When a writer's self-reference is imbued with elaborate self-irony, interpretation is difficult indeed. But it may be emphasized yet again that there is no evidence that the 'good women' themselves are being set up as targets of male laughter; neither can it be argued that the I-persona is being constituted as a misogynist whose bias should be recognized and ridiculed. The poem's 'implied author'—if such a construct is perceptible from the overall literary strategy and form of the *Legend* (as discussed in previous sections), considered along with these self-presentational devices—may be accepted as a would-be friend to all women.

'He' can hardly be held as crucially responsible for the sins of the age, 'structural antifeminism' not being something which a person living in fourteenth-century England accepted only after much thought. Naturally, this 'implied author' invests his heroines with typical feminine traits: this reflects the consensus of medieval science and Scripture. That the *Legend* is drawing on traditional androcentric categories of female virtue (not to mention Christian-oriented categories of pagan virtue) is hardly surprising: what other valorizing techniques were available? What is significant is the specific form of the discourse of virtuous womankind which governs the *Legend*. Whatever else Cleopatra and her 'sisters' may be, they are certainly not mannish women, viragos who have been obliged to give up their gender in exchange for virtue. Intriguingly, Chaucer's only recorded use of the term 'virago' carries a wholly negative signification, the Sultan's Mother in the *Man of Law's Tale* being termed 'Virago, thou Semyarme the seconde!' (II(B¹) 358–9). Semiramis was an Assyrian warrior-queen who was sometimes condemned for her cross-dressing and insatiable lusts, as for instance in Boccaccio's *De mulieribus claris*. But not all medieval presentations of Semiramis were negative (or at least, not explicitly negative). For she figures as one of the *neuf preuses* or nine 'female worthies' of militant bent who make an early appearance in ballades by Deschamps. The full list is Semiramis, Teuta, Thamyris, Deipyle, and five Amazons, Hippolyta, Marpesia, Lampedo, Menalippe, and Antiope (or Sinope). Chaucer knew Queen Hippolyta and her sister Emilia from his reading of Boccaccio's *Teseida*, of course, but his versions of these figures in the *Knight's Tale* are paragons of traditional feminine virtues, who use woman's weapons such as tears and emotive pleas. The 'heathen pack' in the *Legend* have rather more to do, but their virtues remain traditionally feminine. Though Chaucer did include an account of the belligerent exploits and eventual downfall of Queen Zenobia in the Monk's collection of tragedies (his source may have been *De mulieribus claris*), in the *Legend* he was apparently uninterested in viragos or Amazons, female constructs who had 'fledde / Office of wommen' (*Monk's Tale*, VII. 2255–6). Here his concern is not with military prowess or atypical sexual behaviour but with marriage—and marriage was widely regarded in his day as the state in which woman's putative biological and psychological drives found their natural and respectable outlet in secular life. The *Legend*, then, wants its heroines to follow the 'Office of wommen', and this may be taken as a positive aspect of the text's constructions of good women, which should not be set at naught because the images of good womanliness presented therein are no longer acceptable.

In her essay, 'Chaucer's Women and Women's Chaucer', Arlyn Diamond suggests that the *Legend* may be too ambivalent for feminist analysis: 'It is of no help to look at the *Legend of Good Women*, the tone of which is so subtle that critics still can't decide whether the poet is making fun, or saints, of all those women' (p. 65). But this, in my view anyway, is a liberating rather than a devalorizing instability of meaning. Functioning as a whole, the poem interrogates gendered morality as maintained in Chaucer's day, and admits of several possible reactions, superior male laughter (whether medieval or modern) at the female figures and superior 'radical feminist' laughter at the narrator and his tale-telling techniques being only two of those possibilities, and very limited ones at that. Besides, it can hardly be stressed enough that the discourses present in the *Legend* are cultural as well as authorial; it is therefore inappropriate to reduce the issue to the matter of 'what Chaucer himself thought' or to the question, 'Was Chaucer himself a friend to women?' Cultural and linguistic systems, and complex textual configurations, often exceed the boundaries which they purport to delimit. And the tensions between and within the various discourses inscribed by Chaucer contribute hugely to the creation of space for readings of the text which are incorrigibly plural, and perhaps even contradictory.

'Playful pluralism' has been identified by Annette Kolodny as of the very essence of feminist literary theory; moreover, it is, she declares, 'the only critical stance consistent with the current state of the larger women's movement' (p. 187). And of course Roland Barthes has speculated that an insistence on the plural may be 'a way of denying sexual duality'; 'the confrontations and paradigms must be dissolved, both the meanings and the sexes must be pluralized' (p. 69). Those who sympathize with those positions (and some who do not) may find much to enjoy in the way in which the *Legend* offers gynocentric and gamocentric interpretations of 'olde appreved stories'. Of course, in the 1990s some readers will probably find it impossible to see beyond the 'structural antifeminism' which is certainly present in the poem. That, I would suggest, is to be more interested in the bricks than the building.

Gillian Beer, 'Representing Women: Re-presenting the Past', in Catherine Belsey and Jane Moore (eds.), *The Feminist Reader: Essays in Gender and the Politics of Literary Criticism* (Basingstoke and London, 1989), p. 67. Hope Phyllis Weissman, 'Antifeminism and Chaucer's Characterization of Women', in George D. Economou (ed.), *Geoffrey Chaucer. A Collection of Original Articles* (New York, 1975), pp. 93–110. Elaine Tuttle Hansen, 'Irony and the Antifeminist Narrator in Chaucer's *Legend of Good Women*', *JEGP* 82 (1983), 11–31; also her monograph *Fictions of Gender*. See further Bloch, *Medieval Misogyny*, as discussed on pp. 64–9 above.

On medieval biological, scientific, and theological views of women see especially the copious primary source materials translated in Blamires (ed.), *Woman Defamed*, along with Cadden, *Sex Difference*: Payer, *Bridling of Desire*; and Jacquart and Thomasset, *Sexuality and Medicine*. See further Vern L. Bullough, 'Medieval Medical and Scientific Views of Women', *Viator*, 4 (1973), 485–501, and Kari Elisabeth Børresen, *Subordination and Equivalence: The Nature and Role of Woman in Augustine and Thomas Aquinas*, trans. C. H. Talbot (Washington, DC, 1981).

Once again I cite the *Catholicon* of Giovanni de'Balbi from the Venice edition of 1495 (s.v. *vir, virtus, mulier, virago*).

Naomi Schor, 'Dreaming Dissymmetry: Barthes, Foucault, and Sexual Difference', in Jardine and Smith (eds.), *Men in Feminism*, pp. 98–115.

Jacobus de Voragine, *Legenda aurea*, ed. Graesse, trans. Ryan and Ripperger. With

Theodora may be compared Saints Marina and Margaret, since they all disguise themselves as men in order to enter monasteries. God inspires Margaret on her wedding-day to consider the implications of the loss of her virginity; she avoids her husband's attentions that night, and, cutting off her hair and dressing herself as a man (cf. the case of Theodora), runs away, and after a long journey is received into a monastery. Again like Theodora, she is falsely accused of fathering a child. On Joan of Arc as *virago* see especially Marina Warner, *Joan of Arc. The Image of Female Heroism* (New York, 1981), pp. 139–58. For a discussion of the wider cultural implications of transvestism see Marjorie Garber, *Vested Interests. Cross-Dressing and Cultural Anxiety* (New York and London, 1992). Materials relating to the 'effeminate man' are collected in Richard Firth Green, 'The Sexual Normality of Chaucer's Pardoner', *Mediaevalia*, 8 (1982), 351–8. Cadden, *Sex Difference*, offers extensive discussion of medical lore relating to 'masculine women' and 'feminine men'.

Mann, *Chaucer*. An interesting critique of this book is offered by Ruth Evans' review in *Textual Practice*, 7 (1993), 85–9, which suggests that 'Mann's Chaucer is a good old-fashioned liberal humanist'. Troilus's possession of Criseyde as imaged by the sparrow-hawk catching a lark in its claws may profitably be compared and contrasted with Chaucer's account of the rape of Lucrece, wherein the male is likened to a wolf which has caught an isolated lamb (1798). Similar images, it would seem, may be used to describe both acceptable and unacceptable forms of male sexual aggression. For an interesting treatment of the wider issues raised by such an analysis, see Myriam Miedzian, *Boys will be Boys. Breaking the Link between Masculinity and Violence* (London, 1992).

Lynne Huffer, 'Christine de Pisan: Speaking like a Woman/Speaking like a Man', in E. E. DuBruck (ed.), *New Images of Medieval Women: Essays towards a Cultural Anthropology* (Lewiston, Queenston and Lampeter, 1989), pp. 61–72. The opposite position is taken by Sheila Delany, who argues that Christine 'was not, even by the standards of her own day, a reformer or protofeminist' (*Medieval Literary Politics*, p. 91). Delany admits to having 'been angered' by what she sees as 'Christine's self-righteousness, her prudery, and the intensely self-serving narrowness of her views', and 'repulsed by the backwardness of her social attitudes'. This position is critiqued by Maureen Quilligan, *The Allegory of Female Authority: Christine de Pizan's 'Cité des Dames'* (Ithaca, NY, and London, 1991), pp. 8–9, 260–1, 264, 268, 273–4. It is anachronistic, she argues, 'to hold an author up to a litmus test of political purity few authors of any period could pass because the terms of comparison are incongruent'; in Delany's statements she finds a loss both of specific historical details and 'the necessary notion of the "alterity" of the Middle Ages, its difference from our own historical moment' (p. 8). The issues at stake here are also treated well by Susan Groag Bell, 'Christine de Pizan (1364–1430): Humanism and the Problem of a Studious Woman', *Feminist Studies* (1976), 173–84, and Beatrice Gottlieb, 'The Problem of Feminism in the Fifteenth Century', in Julius Kirshner and Suzanne F. Wemple (eds.), *Women of the Medieval World* (Oxford and New York, 1985), pp. 337–64. My own views substantially coincide with those of Gottlieb, who contrasts the 'feminist consciousness' she finds in Christine with 'a modern feminist program' (p. 346; cf. p. 360).

On Christine's self-construction see especially Quilligan's chapter 'The Name of the Author' in *Allegory of Female Authority*, pp. 11–68, and Kevin Brownlee, 'Discourses of the Self: Christine de Pizan and the *Roman de la Rose*', in *idem* and Sylvia Huot (eds.), *Rethinking the 'Romance of the Rose': Text, Image, Reception* (Philadelphia, 1992), pp. 234–61. On the *Cité des Dames* as approached above see Bell, 'Christine de Pizan', and E. Stecopoulos with Karl D. Utti, 'Christine de Pizan's *Livre de la Cité des Dames*: The Reconstruction of Myth', in Earl Jeffrey Richards et al. (eds.), *Reinterpreting Christine de Pizan* (Athens, Ga., and London, 1992), pp. 48–62.

Heath, 'Male Feminism'. For discussion of certain possibilities for seeing Christine writing as a woman *versus* Chaucer writing as man see Delany, *Medieval Literary Politics*, pp. 80–7, esp. p. 87.

On the *neuf preuses* see Ann McMillan, 'Men's Weapons, Women's War: The Nine Female Worthies, 1400–1640', *Mediaevalia*, 5 (1979), 113–39. For Semiramis see Boccaccio, *De mulieribus claris*, trans. Guarino, pp. 4–7, and also the discussions by Irene Samuel, 'Semiramis in the Middle Ages: The History of a Legend', *Mediaevalia et Humanistica*, 2 (1944), 32–44, and Johnstone Parr, 'Chaucer's Semiramis', *ChR* 5 (1970), 57–61. For Chaucer's Zenobia see Godman, 'Chaucer and Boccaccio's Latin Works'.

On the 'naturalness' of marriage see Payer, *Bridling of Desire*, pp. 66–8.

Arlyn Diamond, 'Chaucer's Women and Women's Chaucer', in *idem* and Lee R. Edwards (eds.), *The Authority of Experience: Essays in Feminist Criticism* (Amherst, Mass., 1977), pp. 60–83, 282–4.

Annette Kolodny, 'Dancing through the Minefield: Some Observations on the Theory, Practice and Politics of a Feminist Literary Criticism', repr. in Mary Eagleton (ed.), *Feminist Literary Theory: A Reader* (Oxford, 1986), pp. 184–8. Roland Barthes is quoted from *Roland Barthes by Roland Barthes*, trans. Richard Howard (London, 1977). A trenchant criticism of his position on pluralism is offered by Schor, 'Dreaming Dissymmetry'.

THE POETICS OF STEREOTYPE

There are several recent discussions of stereotyping in the *Legend*, of how Chaucer's text inscribes gender differences in very reductive terms. For example, Carolyn Dinshaw argues that the 'techniques of reading like a man', which she defines as 'imposing a single pattern, insisting on reducing complexity to produce a whole, monolithic structure, thus constraining the feminine' are 'reductive of *all* human experience'. In the *Legend*, she believes, 'reductiveness is, finally, shown to be profoundly narrow and unsatisfying' (p. 87).

One of the problems about such a reading is that it makes no distinction between the *kinds* of reductiveness in which the *Legend* is engaging. 'The female sex *en bloc* was a target of proverbial utterance', suggests Blamires, 'where the male sex was not' (p. 8). Of course, male subjectivities were often described in essentializing terms, but this tended to be a valorizing discourse, whereas the corresponding discourse about women was almost always disempowering. Even nowadays, according to the research of David H. J. Morgan, there is a tendency to believe that 'men are all different', and hence generalization about 'what men are' is impossible, whereas women are supposed to fall into distinctive types. Thus, 'In popular culture, male heroes tend to come in all shapes and sizes, ages and colours; the women (e.g. the "Bond girls") tend to be much more stereotyped and interchangeable' (p. 43).

It may therefore be suggested that Chaucer's construction of the figure of the faithless male is in fact an act of dissident reading of old

books wherein female figures regularly are stereotyped in a manner
which is highly derogatory and dismissive. In the *Legend* reduction is
being used to problematize reduction; an action of 'new' stereotyping
relating to men challenges the traditional stereotyping which relates to
women. Furthermore, Chaucer's 'new' process is reacting directly
against the 'old', in creating reverse, mirror images of great precision,
with a high recognition factor, by which I mean that their antecedents
(here their specific targets) in anti-feminist cliché would have been, and
are, very well known. Therefore, this process may also be described in
terms of 'feminization', providing that the negative sense of that term is
understood, men having been forced into a subject position, as traditionally occupied by women, which bespeaks inferiority and untrustworthiness.

  Where, asked the purveyors of anti-feminist clichés, is the virtuous
woman to be found; does the female who is at once fair and faithful actually exist? 'I have not yet found any,' declares the Lover's Friend in the
*Roman de la Rose*, 'however many I may have tested [!]. Not even
Solomon could find them' (9919–21; trans. Dahlberg, p. 177). Chaucer's
riposte is: where is the man who is true and stable? *He* is rarer than the
phoenix (to appropriate an image which Walter Map used to profess the
paucity of good women; cf. p. 396 above). Indeed, one will risk a
headache looking for such a prodigy; certainly no man could possibly
compete with Cleopatra's truth:

> Now, or I fynde a man thus trewe and stable,
> And wol for love his deth so frely take,
> I preye God let oure hedes never ake!                     (703–5)

In all his sources, the narrator declares, he has managed to find only one
faithful man:

> Of trewe men I fynde but fewe mo
> In alle my bokes, save this Piramus,
> And therfore have I spoken of hym thus.
> For it is deynte to us men to fynde          *pleasing*
> A man that can in love be trewe and kynde.                (917–21)

Antony does not, *pace* the arguments of some critics, die on account of
his beloved Cleopatra, but rather out of despair at having lost his 'wor-
shipe' at the battle of Actium: the flight of the queen is just one aspect
of the debacle, and not the direct cause of his suicide (651–2). Cleopatra,
therefore, gets all the credit in her *Legend* for dying for love, and Piramus
retains the unique distinction which the narrator claims for him.

  Moreover, according to Chaucer's poetics of stereotyping it is not simply that women can be as good as men—

> God forbede but a woman can
> Ben as trewe in lovynge as a man!　　　　　　　　　(910–11)

—but rather that they are much better. Chaucer's heroines excel in 'fyn lovynge' and good living. Legions of medieval misogynists had affirmed that women were not to be trusted. 'Deceive women before they deceive you!' is the advice which Ovid offers men in *Ars amatoria*, i. 645. 'All women are liars,' snarls Andreas Capellanus in the third book of *De amore*. 'There is not a living woman who does not make a pretence of what is untrue, and invent lies with reckless ingenuity' (trans. Walsh, p. 317). Indeed, Chaucer himself, in the *Troilus* epilogue, had seen Criseyde's infidelity as part and symptom of this 'false worldes brotelness' (v. 1832). But in the *Legend* it is shown that male fidelity is a 'brotel ground' on which to build (to borrow an idiom from the *Merchant's Tale*, IV(E) 1279). Thus, Phyllis learns to her cost just 'how brotel and how fals' Demophon really is (2556), and the *Legend of Lucrece* ends with the affirmation of this general rule:

> And as of men, loke ye which tirannye
> They doon alday; assay hem whose lyste,
> The trewest ys ful brotel for to triste.　　　　　　　(1883–5)

Chaucer has taken the fundamental strategy of the *Heroides*, wherein women's voices are raised in protest against their unworthy lovers, and augmented it with considerable skill and a degree of daring. In his poem women have in effect taken over the position of moral superiority traditionally enjoyed by men, the supposedly weaker sex being shown as the morally (though not, of course, physically) stronger and more constant. The world has been turned upside down; we are presented with a company of good women and (the inversion being total) a monstrous regiment of men.

The first man we encounter in the *Legend*, Mark Antony, is revealed in a most unflattering light. He 'falsly' deserts his wife, Caesar's sister, thereby initiating the pattern of male betrayal which will run through the entire poem. Aeneas is false to Dido, Jason to Hypsipyle and Medea, Theseus to Ariadne, and Demophon to Phyllis; Tereus rapes and savagely mutilates Philomela. Whatever virtues as a husband Colatyn may have, they are suppressed in order that the untrustworthiness of men should be manifested by the rapist Tarquinius (and it may be recalled that Lucrece dies for her high principles of wifely fidelity rather than for her actual husband). In the *Legend of Hypermnestra* Lyno, concerned to save his own skin, leaps out of a window with indecent (and almost farcical) haste, and runs off at great speed without looking to the weak and helpless woman who, because she cannot keep up with him, must sit down and await her fate.

> Allas! Lyno! whi art thow so unkynde?
> Why ne haddesst thow remembred in thy mynde
> To taken hire, and led hire forth with the?                    (2716–18)

Such character assassination is certainly not justified by Chaucer's source, where Hypermnestra simply makes the factual declaration, 'You fly, and I remain' (*Heroides*, xiv. 78). This is symptomatic of Chaucer's overall strategy. Where a source presents him with a false male (as in the very obvious case of Tereus), he channels that unfavourable construction; in other cases, he invents his hero's notoriety. It is little wonder, then, that some critics have designated the poem as the legendary of bad men. But Chaucer's goal was not the limited and specific one of blackening the characters of his male protagonists; the principle of inversion must be given the interpretative priority it deserves. Men are relegated to the bottom in order that women may be put on top for a change. This principle is an essential part of the *modus operandi* of the whole poem, manifested by its hagiographic structures (as examined above) and also in the delineation of its essentialized figures of male infidelity and female virtue.

Chaucer's male stereotype is often a 'traytour' (an epithet applied to Aeneas, Jason, and Tereus; 1328, 1656, 2324), a breaker of solemn covenants and bonds. He also counterfeits emotion, as when Aeneas, Jason, and Theseus pretend to be in (courtly) love (1264–76, 2114–22, 1376, 1548–56), or when Tereus feigns sorrow at the alleged death of Philomela (2342–5). Noblewomen were often shown in the grip of demeaning passions which robbed them of the respectability consonant with their social rank (an excellent example being the infatuated Queen Dido as portrayed in, say, the *Roman d'Eneas*); in the *Legend* we are shown how men demean themselves by wronging women. Though noble in status, men like Aeneas, Jason, Theseus, and Demophon are churlish in deed—hence class traitors as well as traitors in love. Thus, Phyllis demands that, when Demophon's 'olde ancestres peynted be, / In whiche men may here worthiness se', then her lover should be depicted in a way which will manifest his moral 'vilenye' to all (2536–42). By contrast, the women in the poem seem acutely aware of the demands and obligations of *gentilesse* (see especially *Legend of Ariadne*, 2089–94; *Legend of Hypsipyle*, 1504 ff.). Clearly, then, we are dealing with a legendary of good *gentle*women, whose behaviour lives up to their privileged birth and breeding.

The depths to which men will stoop are emphasized in several ways.

Sometimes the narrator openly declares his own sense of outrage. He wonders aloud how God, giver of forms and creator of the fair world, could allow such a blot as Tereus on his beautiful landscape (2228–37). The 'venym of so longe ago' is still active in that 'foule storye', he continues, and it has affected him deeply. Earlier the Chaucer persona had protested at the way in which Jason managed to deceive not one but two women with the same tricks (1377); later he will raise the grim possibility that male falsity runs in the family, passing from father (Theseus) to son (Demophon).

Sometimes the male stereotype behaves like a thief in the night. While Dido sleeps, Aeneas steals away from her bed (1333); while Lucrece sleeps, Tarquinius steals 'ful thefly' into her house and then her bed (1179 ff.). Jason is identified as a special kind of thief, the 'false fox' who 'wol have his part at nyght' (1393). Such animal imagery implies that a man may be no better than a beast or bird of prey. With the image of Jason as the fox devouring his two capons (Hypsipyle and Medea) may be compared the representation of Tarquinius as a wolf who has found a lamb alone (1798, cf. 1788), an image which is expanded in the *Legend of Philomela*:

> she wepte tenderly,
> And quok for fere, pale and pitously,                          *shook*
> Ryght as the lamb that of the wolf is biten;
> Or as the culver, that of the egle is smiten . . .             *dove*
>                                                             (2316 ff.)

Women, as Christine de Pizan complained, had traditionally been presented as animals to be caught, trapped, and possessed (cf. pp. 429–30); in the *Legend* Chaucer is seeing the hunter through the eyes of the prey.

Another recurrent variation is that of the romantic seafaring stranger with a girl in every port. Aeneas, Jason, Theseus and Demophon are all cast in that role, the psychology involved receiving most attention in the *Legend of Dido*. Whereas in the *House of Fame* it was stated that the Queen of Carthage did amiss in loving all too soon a 'gest' who was 'unknowen' to her (269–70, 287–8), here the emphasis is on the fact that some people—not just women—are impressed by novelty.

> And, for he was a stranger, somwhat she
> Likede hym the best, as, God do bote,                          *by God*
> To som folk ofte newe thyng is sote.                           *sweet*
>                                                             (1075–7)

Moreover, this point is carefully placed after we have been told that Dido 'hadde routhe and wo' for the sad condition to which a man of such high degree had been reduced. The essential nobility and virtue of this heroine must be preserved at all costs.

For Chaucer the thought that if certain women were bad then so were certain men, was something of a reflex action. That inference is made over and over again in his work, most notably in a rather curious passage near the end of *Troilus and Criseyde* which looks forward to the *Legend*. Boccaccio had concluded his *Filostrato* by advising men not to 'lightly place' their 'trust in any woman' (trans. Havely, p. 101); here Chaucer makes the counter-charge against deceptive men:

> N'y sey nat this al oonly for thise men,
> But moost for wommen that bitraised be
> Thorough false folk—God yeve hem sorwe, amen!—
> That with hire grete wit and subtilte
> Bytraise you. And this commeveth me     *moves emotionally*
> To speke, and in effect yow alle I preye,
> Beth war of men, and herkneth what I seye!     (v. 1779–85)

In the *Legend* the great wit and subtlety which men employ in deceiving women is illustrated in considerable detail, and the clear message is: 'Beware of men!'

> O sely wemen, ful of innocence,     *hapless*
> Ful of pite, of trouthe, and conscience,
> What maketh yow to men to truste so?
>     (*Legend of Dido*, 1254–6)

Albeit that men may not be as cruel to you as Tereus was to Philomela, the narrator declares at the end of that grisly tale, the sex should not be trusted, because their truth will not last; hence the blanket admonition, 'Ye may be war of men' (2387–91). Even in the unique case of the *Legend of Thisbe*, wherein we find a man who was worthy of the woman who loved him, women are advised not to put themselves at risk for men they hardly know:

> and that is routhe
> That evere woman wolde ben so trewe
> To truste man, but she the bet hym knewe!     (799–801)

Thus the exemplifier generalizes from individual cases, in accordance with the usual procedures of exemplification.

And indeed, the normatively didactic potential of the *exempla* in the *Legend* should not be ignored. One may recall how, in 1371, Geoffroy de la Tour-Landry became worried about what might befall his three daughters, especially in the light of his recollection of his own youth, when his companions were wont to try their luck with each and every lady they met. 'Thei had faire langage and wordes' at their disposal, and they swore many false oaths, thereby deceiving many a gentlewoman, who would give herself to 'a traitour fals churle': 'there ys mani of hem deceiued bi the foule and grete fals othes that the fals men vsen to swere to the women' (p. 2). Therefore, 'faire doughtres', the concerned parent warns, be careful of getting friendly too soon with smooth-talking men: 'it is not good to herkyn and take sodeyne aqueintaunce that hathe the herte of faire speche, for sum tyme her speche is deseyuable and venemous' (p. 55). Certain gentlemen are 'so fals and deceyuable' that they go to great lengths to feign love, swearing that they will be faithful and true, and will love them 'without falsed or deceyuaunce, and that rather they shold deye than to thynke ony vylonye or dyshonoure'. Furthermore, they will 'gyue oute of theyr brestes grete and fayned syghes, And make as they were thynkynge and Melancholyous'. Yet behind such 'semblaunt' they are nothing other than 'deceyuours or begylers' (p. 175). The last of those statements is put into the mouth of Geoffroy's wife, who is now dead; that fact adds weight to the words which are allegedly being reported, as maternal concern and worldly wisdom speak from beyond the grave. Geoffroy claims that his own marriage was a happy one—his wife delighted him so much, he says, that he 'made for her loue songges, balades, rondelles, viralles, and diuerse new thinges' as best he could (p. 1)—and seems anxious to do all in his power to maximize his daughters' chances of a similar experience. Yet it is perfectly obvious that for him a good marriage means a good match: Geoffroy's concern with position, power, and the secure continuity of the dynastic line are writ large in a text which seeks to control his daughters' behaviour through *exempla* of what to do and what to avoid (cf. p. 317 above). At any rate, the Knight of the Tower would probably have approved of the *Legend*. For Chaucer's *exempla* also function to make abundantly clear to women the many wiles of deceitful men, who can swear oaths and make high-sounding promises and professions of devotion, without compunction or sincerity.

But what of the mind of the exemplifier? Chaucer's purpose may have been rather less straightforward than that of Geoffroy of La Tour-Landry. The question must be posed, should the narrator of the *Legend* be trusted? It is hardly possible to read his appeal that women should 'trust no man but me' (2561) as being devoid of irony. Moreover, the zeal with which this construct systematically commends women and condemns men often comes across as extreme and hence amusing: can such blatant bias be taken with total seriousness? The poet, Alceste told the God of Love, didn't really know what he was doing when he wrote of Criseyde and of the Rose; one might draw the inference that he writes about good women with a comparable lack of awareness. Just as he followed his sources in the earlier works, here the tale-teller is following the directives of his patrons (so the argument would proceed), the reader being meant to laugh at his frantic pro-feminism. Against this, it may once again be pointed out that Alceste in some sense guarantees and validates that feminine goodness which is the poem's central belief. The ironic portrayal of the narrator's other director, the God of Love, is indeed unsettling, as has been suggested above. Yet it is perfectly possible to accept that Chaucer found his persona's position as a (uniquely trustworthy) man writing about (generally trustworthy) women somewhat comic, and also to enjoy the irony surrounding of God of Love, without leaping to the conclusion that irony or downright satire is the very taproot of the entire poem.

Although irony and satire can involve an element of inversion, the fact that Chaucer is turning the man's world upside down need not be taken as evidence that he intended his poem as a travesty against women. For inversion, as Mikhail Bakhtin has demonstrated so conclusively, can be an instrument of celebration and liberation. Surely we are now getting nearer to catching the curious tone of large tracts of Chaucer's text. And here the game is afoot. The pleasure which Cupid's hagiographer so palpably takes in his work may be taken as a festive delight: he enjoys officiating at a pro-feminist feast wherein the usual standards of life and literature have been suspended. The audience is asked to sympathize with the good women, awarding them its pity and praise, and to boo the bad men who are the villains of the piece. When the carnival is over, the values of patriarchal society will be reinstated, as everyone knew they would be. Yet, while it runs its course, we are caught up in its distinctive values and unconventional logic.

But a cautionary note must be struck. One should not be over-optimistic about the transformative purchase of inversion in general within late medieval culture, for quite clearly it did not always function in the way that we have just described. An inversive lyric of the early fifteenth century, entitled 'What Women are Not' by its modern editor, may be cited as a salutary warning, for here traditional prejudice is reinforced rather than challenged:

> Of all creatures women be best,
> *Cuius contrarium verum est.*
>
> In every place ye may well see
> That women be trewe as tirtill on tree . . .       turtle-dove
>
> The stedfastnes of women will never be don . . .
>
> Men be more cumbers a thousandfold,       troublesome
> And I mervail how they dare to be bold
> Against women for to hold

Thus 'the contrary' is said to be true of all the statements which are being made in praise of women. Everything, it would seem, depends on the uses to which the strategy is put.

On the other hand, certain forms of inversion were denounced as representing disorder and violation of proper hierarchy. In Jehan le Fèvre's French version of the *Liber lamentationum* of Matheolus the story is told of how 'a woman' (elsewhere identified as the courtesan Phyllis) rode the philosopher Aristotle, who was besotted with her, 'like a female ass'. 'The governor was governed and the roles of the sexes reversed, for she was active and he passive, willing to neigh under her. Thus the natural order of things was turned upside down. What was normally underneath was on top, and confusion reigned' (trans. Blamires, p. 180).

Such denunciation may be taken as an index of the subversive power of inversion, as harnessed in certain ways. Chaucer, I am convinced, was fully aware of that power, and sought to enlist it in the *Legend*, to create not chaos but an alternative world, which operates in accordance with the rules of its own poetic licence. Yet the question lingers: how *ultimately* transgressive is a story like the tale of Aristotle and Phyllis, as presented by Jehan le Fèvre? It may easily be read as confirming rather than challenging the traditional hierarchies, through its illustration of the ethical commonplaces that men in love act foolishly and women enjoy taking advantage of them, for such is their nature. The same question can be asked of Chaucer's problematizing of gender in the *Legend*. Here is an interpretative knot that requires careful untying. In order to present the issues more clearly we may now move to compare Chaucer's practice with some similar literary gender games as played in the early Renaissance. And once again, in Machaut's *Navarre* may be found a possible inspiration and model.

Dinshaw, *Sexual Poetics*. Blamires (ed.), *Woman Defamed*. Similarly, Fyler, *Chaucer and Ovid*, pp. 106–7, speaks of the 'comically indiscriminate' way in which the narrator characterizes all men as villains and divests the 'diversity and individuality' of the heroines in order that they may suffer martyrdom passively.

David H. J. Morgan, *Discovering Men*, Critical Studies on Men and Masculinities, 3 (London, 1992).

*Roman de la Rose*, ed. Langlois, trans. Dahlberg; Ovid, *Ars amatoria*, ed. and trans. Mozley; Andreas Capellanus, *De amore*, ed. and trans. Walsh. Ovid's view of 'deceptive women' is complicated by the fact that, in *Ars*, iii. 31 ff., when instructing women, he declares that 'often do men deceive' and alludes to Jason, Theseus, Demophon, and Aeneas to prove the point. Did Chaucer relish the reversal? Jean de Meun's Old Woman reprises this passage in *Roman de la Rose* 13,265–8, using the *exempla* as proof of her contention that women should deceive men in return for their deception of women.

On hunting imagery in love poetry see Thiébaux, *Stag of Love*, and Rooney, *Hunting* (cf. pp. 117–23, above). To the statement that Chaucer is viewing the hunter through the eyes of the prey may be added the observation that, in the eyes of the male poet, such a sight is in some measure aesthetically satisfying as well as morally outrageous.

Havely, *Chaucer's Boccaccio*.

*Book of the Knight of La Tour-Landry*, ed. Wright. On the later reception of this work, see Suzanne W. Hull, *Chaste, Silent and Obedient: English Books for Women, 1475–1640* (San Marino, Calif., 1982), who notes the Knight's concern with 'chastity, silence and obedience' (p. 31). I fully accept that my comparison of Geoffroy's book with Chaucer's puts at issue their shared 'patriarchal' opinions regarding the control and disposal of women.

Bakhtin, *Rabelais and his World*. I have benefited from the exegesis and elaboration of Bakhtin's views by Peter Stallybrass and Allon White, *The Politics and Poetics of Transgression* (London, 1986).

*Medieval English Lyrics: A Critical Anthology*, ed. R. T. Davies (London, 1963), p. 221.

## THE WORLD UPSIDE DOWN: GENDER GAME AS ALTERNATIVE ART

The subject of gender games in the Renaissance has received a lot of attention lately, one of the most recent manifestations being the collection of essays *Playing with Gender: A Renaissance Pursuit*, edited by Maryanne Horowitz, Jean R. Brink, and Allison P. Coudert. Horowitz notes in her introduction that gender games constitute a major renaissance *topos*, and draws attention to 'three personae that inhabit the Renaissance imagination'—the Other, the Amazon, and the hermaphrodite. Renaissance self-fashioning involves the refashioning of others, she suggests, and gender categories are questioned as authors and artists play with Amazons and other ancient figures who transcend gender stereotypes. Another type of Renaissance gender game, not discussed in this anthology, is found in the numerous formal treatises in praise of women. Many of these texts are concerned not so much with the transgression of traditional gender roles as with the challenge of providing an arsenal of counter-arguments to the anti-feminist beliefs which for centuries had circumscribed the status and limited the human dignity of women. Their procedure is therefore reactive and fundamentally inversive; male assumptions and pretensions are regularly humbled in order that women's roles and responsibilities may be revealed in the best possible light. This inversive strategy makes for a viable comparison with the *Legend*, as does the common factor that male authors, very much writing as males, have taken upon themselves the charge of writing on women's behalf.

The *laudatio mulierum* genre enjoyed a certain vogue in the fifteenth and sixteenth centuries; Conor Fahy has listed no less than forty-one examples published in Italy during that period. The flavour of such works may be caught from Bartolomeo Gogio's *De laudibus mulierum* of 1487. Gogio begins by arguing that woman is superior to man in terms of place of origin (Eve was created inside the Garden of Eden, whereas Adam was created outside it), in beauty and intellect, and in the qualities of constancy and strength, then declares that, in the process of procreation, the part played by the woman is just as active as that of the man. In the second book, it is proved that the discovery of letters, laws, and the arts was in each case due to women. After a fascinating digression on the origins of different languages (in book iii) Gogio asserts that in governance and military matters women are not inferior to men (book iv). The final books address the difficult subject of Eve's responsibility for the Fall, and here Gogio is at his most controversial: his argument minimizes the evil results of the Fall to such an extent that the post-lapsarian state of man is implied to be his natural condition. In particular, 'the knowledge of good and evil acquired by Adam and Eve on eating the forbidden fruit' is said to be 'beneficial to the human race in that it brought man into his proper intellectual kingdom'—an interestingly pro-feminist version of the theory of *felix culpa*.

The more usual practice in the treatises on praise of women is to place the responsibility for the Fall on the shoulders of Adam rather than those of Eve. This is what happens in the *Declamatio de nobilitate et praecellentia fœminei sexus* of Henricus Cornelius Agrippa (written in 1509; an English translation by David Clapam was published in 1542). Agrippa argues that 'the fruyte of the tree was forbidden to the man but not to the woman: which was not than created. For god wolde her to be fre from the begynning. Therfore the manne sinned in eatynge, not the woman. The man gaue vs deathe, not the woman. And all we synned in Adam, not in Eua. And we toke orygynalle synne of our father the man, not of our mother the woman.' That is why Christ the Redeemer was born a man: He 'toke vpon hym manhode, as the more humble and lower kynde, and not womankynde, the more hygher & noble' (trans. Clapam). And this is also why priests are male.

These examples must suffice by way of illustration of the strategies of praise which are characteristic of this genre. The old misogynistic clichés are found to have no basis in learning or logic; all the standard denigrations of women are overturned or bested. It seems that every proof that women are worse than men may be matched with a counter-proof that men are worse than women. Thanks to this creative casuistry, women come out on top. But how credible is all this? Is the rhetoric not rather strained, the argument too hyperbolic to be taken seriously? Can one ask of such texts, as so many readers of Chaucer have asked of the *Legend*, are we dealing with some sort of male joke at women's expense? In some cases anyway, the answer has to be in the negative; or at least it must be said that the issue is not as clear-cut as that. For some of the treatises under discussion seem to have been directed towards powerful women who were actual or potential patrons of the writer. Thus, Bartolomeo Gogio addressed his *De laudibus mulierum* to Eleonora da Aragonia, Duchess of Ferrara, and Agrippa's *Declaratio* was part of his attempt to win the favour of Margaret of Austria. So we can rule out the scenario of self-satisifed males sniggering into their beards at the naïvety of women who have taken fulsome flattery at face value, the joke being quite over their heads. One may assume that Eleonora da Aragonia and Margaret of Austria were not fools. And why would a suppliant for patronage risk offending the very person who could further his career? We can assume that Gogio and Agrippa were not fools either.

There is, however, another possibility, which I would like to support: the noble ladies in question may have been at once flattered and amused by such extravagant praise of their sex, this being the effect sought after by the text. For substantiation of this view we may turn to a work which usefully locates the formal praise of women in a social context (or, more accurately, a literary construction thereof) and allows commentary on its terms of reference which for our purposes would seem to be useful. This is *Il Cortegiano*, a text which we have already discussed with reference to the *Parliament of Fowls* (cf. pp. 298–9 above). Castiglione's treatise will help us to see how the *Legend*, like the *Parliament*, may be read within an anthropology of play.

*Il Cortegiano*, Castiglione declares, was written in order to commemorate Elisabetta Gonzaga (who died in 1526) and to testify to her 'rare virtues'. In the duchess, Fortune demonstrated that 'in the tender soul of a woman, and accompanied by singular beauty, there may also dwell prudence and a courageous spirit and all the virtues rarely found even in the staunchest of men' (trans. Bull, pp. 43–4). However, the text is largely a male affair inasmuch as the males do most of the debating, displaying their skills in debate and dialectic with studied effortlessness and controlled nonchalance. The men present at the gatherings invariably outnumber the women, Castiglione tells us, and the male voices certainly dominate, even when the nature and dignity of woman is being discussed.

At the beginning of the book the assembled company is in search of a new 'game' (*gioco*). Various alternatives having been suggested, the one which meets with general approval is the proposal that someone should be given the task of 'depicting in words a perfect courtier' (p. 51). This male self-fashioning produces as one of its effects the fashioning of the ideal courtly lady. Subsequently, in the third book, a series of stories of exemplary women is provided, including the sad tales of two modern Lucretias who die rather than live in dishonour (pp. 250–3); contemporary women are cited as well as the ancients, to prove the point that feminine virtue is not just a thing of the past. Anti-feminism is allowed space—but that space is carefully confined and controlled. Gaspare Pallavicino's complaints about women take the form of a licensed, perhaps even a buffoonish, misogyny, from which the sting has been taken. His first slighting remark provokes laughter of a kind which devalues anything he has said or will say in the future. Signora Emilia, the duchess's quick-witted companion, is laughing as she declares that 'Women have no need of a defender against a critic of so little authority. Lo, leave Signor Gaspare to his perverse opinion, which is caused more by the fact that he has never found a woman to look at him than by any frailty which exists in women themselves' (p. 176). And when Gaspare remarks that 'there are very few men of worth who have much respect for women by and large' (p. 199), encouraged by the duchess a large number of the ladies present make a mock-attack on him: 'laughing, they all ran towards signor Gaspare as if to rain blows on him and treat him as the Bacchantes treated Orpheus, saying at the same time: Now you shall see whether we care whether evil things are said about us' (p. 200). This is, of course, all in the game; Gaspare is never in the slightest danger of being torn apart, of replicating the fate of Orpheus at the hands of the women whose love he had spurned.

'Everything which provokes laughter exalts a man's spirit and gives him pleasure,' declares Bernardo Bibbiena on a later occasion in *Il Cortegiano*, 'and for a while enables him to forget the trials and tribulations of which life is full' (p. 155; cf. p. 298 above). Discussion of the dignity of woman seems to be undertaken very much in this spirit, as an escape from the trials and tribulations of life, rather than as a confrontation of the problems which women actually experience in their lives. On the one and only occasion on which a participant tries to raise the matter of the duchess's real-life tribulations with her old and impotent husband, she promptly tells him that they have better things to talk about. 'The source of the ridiculous', explains Bernardo Bibbiena, 'is to be found in a kind of deformity; for we laugh only at things that contain some elements of incongruity and seem disagreeable though they are not really so' (p. 155). Could exaggerated praise of women be seen thus? As a sophisticated gender game: primarily for recreational purposes and social display, a fashionable grace or licensed foolishness which contains more than a hint of the ridiculous, but never goes so far as to be displeasing and certainly not to be taken too seriously?

This view would seem to be supported by the passage in which Eve's sin in the Garden of Eden is mentioned, a deed said to have 'left to the human race a heritage of death, travails and sorrows and all the miseries and calamities suffered in the world today' (p. 223). The Magnifico Giuliano retorts that Eve's transgression was repaired by the Virgin

Mary, 'who won for us so much more than the other had lost that the fault for which her merits atoned is called a most happy one'. But he refuses to say 'how inferior are all other human creatures to Our Lady' on the grounds that 'this would be to confuse divine things with these *foolish discussions* of ours' (pp. 223–4). Apparently, religious profundities should be kept out of these recreational activities, the arguments of the holy men being out of bounds. And yet, games are often taken very seriously in *Il Cortegiano*. To take the most important instance, the fashioning of the ideal courtier is described as a game, yet it is very evident that the ideals thereby defined are meant to be sought after.

Now we may return to Chaucer. While one need not believe for a moment John Lydgate's statement that Chaucer composed the *Legend* at the request of Queen Anne of Bohemia, there seems no reason to doubt— to pitch the claim at its lowest—that Chaucer had considered the possibility of directing a 'presentation copy' to her:

> 'And whan this book ys maad, yive it the quene,
> On my byhalf, at Eltham or at Sheene.'          (F Prol. 496–7)

The fact that the superlative Alceste is willing to exert herself thus in Anne's service is, of course, quite a compliment to Richard II's queen: one good wife serves (and deserves) another. Therefore, Chaucer would hardly have allowed anything which was actually or potentially offensive to Anne into his poem any more than he would have dared to insult the memory of the Duchess Blanche in the *Book of the Duchess*. Like Bartolomeo Gogio and Henricus Cornelius Agrippa after him, he would have been fully aware of the career advantages of keeping the ladies sweet. This is not to suggest, of course, that the *Legend* is a bland panegyric, for its success is far more sophisticated than that, its level of entertainment possibly comparable with those elaborate affairs presided over by Duchess Elisabetta Gonzaga. The fact that it admits different interpretative possibilities can be taken as evidence that it was actually written to provoke debate—and as such is a fit poem to have been generated and enjoyed (one may imagine) by those groups of courtiers who demonstrated their wit and social graces by arguing for the respective merits of the flower and the leaf. Would that we had as much information about that aristocratic 'debating society' as Castiglione has provided us (in however idealized a form) about the gifted company who frequented the rooms of Elisabetta Gonzaga. But surely it is reasonable to assume some overlap of attitudes and tastes, including a liking for gender games.

This proposal may be supported further by a text which Chaucer knew very well indeed, and which may well have prompted him to think about compiling a number of stories of good women (cf. pp. 352–3 above). I am speaking, of course, of Machaut's *Navarre*. In the context of our chapter on the *Book of the Duchess* the significance of the hunting episode, coming as it does after the horrors of Machaut's account of the plague, was discussed in some detail, one of the main points being that the persona's enjoyment is described as that 'In which the heart willingly delights / Which has no concern for the pain / That is a part of trouble or strife' (cf. pp. 149–52). The subsequent debate with Bonneürte (Good Fortune, Happiness) may be regarded as a pleasure of the same kind, one type of honourable and edifying recreation having been exchanged for another. The tone is instantly established when Bonneürte describes Machaut as being knowledgeable

> About those sorts of merriment (*joileté*)
> Which accord with morality (*honesté*)
>
> (603–4, trans. Palmer, p. 29)

'I'll have some fun with him / That will keep him wondering a good time,' she continues (615–16). Thus her squire teases the Machaut persona regarding the distance he will have to travel in order to meet her, and warns him that his debating skills will be put to the test; he will have to play the advocate:

> 'And if you know something about debating.
> It'll be good for you in this situation,
> For you'll play the lawyer's role' (*vous devenez advocas*)
>
> (730–2; p. 33)

In this way the two male figures converse pleasantly, debating in these terms and with such game amusing themselves: 'De si fais mos nous debatiens, / Par gieu si nous en esbatiens' (735–6). When the nature of Bonneürte's interest is finally revealed, the I-persona welcomes the idea of a full debate and the judgement of some wise and discreet individual, as providing joyful entertainment:

> it will be a pleasant task (*biaus mestiers*)
> To hear the arguments rehearsed
> And the parties dispute
> With subtlety, with pretty distinctions (*biaus argumens*)
>
> (1084–7; p. 49)

Here the emphasis is on the 'biaus' nature of the discussion rather than on its weight—though, to be sure, weighty matters are indeed discussed in the subsequent debate, Machaut's reputation as a poet who offers *honesté* as well as *joileté* being amply confirmed. Henceforth, the persona declares, he will proceed in a manner which is wholly in accord with the lady's pleasure—'Einsi y sui acordans dès ci / A vostre plaisir' (1081–2).

Far from being a vague aside, this is a significant tone-marker, which helps to fix the parameters of what is to come (1084–5). And the lady laughingly agrees:

> At these words the lady began to laugh,
> And while laughing began at once to say
> 'Guillaume, I am very much in agreement
> With what you've just said;
> And I'll go ahead and debate, however it might turn out'
>
> (1089–93; p. 49)

In a very real sense, then, this is a debate which is controlled by Happiness, Bonneürte; filled with laughter and directed towards pleasure.

It is reasonable to assume that John of Gaunt's daughter Philippa of Lancaster, praised by Deschamps as a flower supporter, would have sought (and, one may hope, have got) a similar kind of pleasure from the *Legend*. Women like this probably would have accepted the flattery in the *Legend* inasmuch as it pleased them, and if it was perceived as extravagant, that would have been all part of the fun. There may have been another dimension to Chaucer's princess-pleasing. The female members of Anne of Bohemia's household, for example, might have felt somewhat superior to the Alcestes and Cleopatras of pagan antiquity, those members of a race of (now extinct) martyrs for marriage who were obsessed with self-sacrificial 'wyfhod' of a kind which Christian (and more sophisticated, they may have thought) women like themselves could admire, from a safe distance as it were, but had no compunction to emulate. Here are not just 'women on top' but 'women over the top'. For Ricardian courtly ladies had about as much in common with the heathen 'pak' of Cupid's martyrs as Elisabetta Gonzaga's ladies had with Ovid's Bacchantes. To say this is not in any way to diminish the didactic purchase of the work, several aspects of which I have canvassed earlier, including its warnings about deceitful men (of a kind similar to those in the *Book of the Knight of La Tour-Landry*) and its presentation of paragons of virtue who might well bring a blush of shame to the cheeks of a Christian lady (to adopt the idiom of Boccaccio's dedication of *De mulieribus claris* to Andrea Acciauoli). Yet, as with the *Parliament of Fowls* (cf. p. 304), so also with the *Legend*: the edification, though real, is in some measure optional. On the other hand, some of the males in that (hypothetical) first textual community of the *Legend* could well (whether in private or in public) have strutted their superior knowledge of the stories so narrowly 'exemplarized' in the poem. And if indeed men and women ever did meet to hear and discuss the poem—and Chaucer's tantalizing reference to the companies of the flower and the leaf allows us to entertain this possibility—their deliberations would probably have ended in laughter, everyone mindful that the world was being turned upside down for a limited period only, and that the party would soon come to an end. Thus literature would perform the recreational purpose which Glending Olson has described so well, enabling its audience 'to forget' for a while 'the trials and tribulations' of which their life was certainly full (cf. pp. 296–301 above) as they set about the pleasant task of debating with subtlety and *biaus argumens* the various issues raised by the *Legend*.

But this can hardly be regarded as simple or naïve escapism. For many earnest things are said in gender games, as is made very clear by Machaut's *Navarre* and the early Renaissance treatises in praise of women, not to mention *Il Cortegiano*. While some of their writers may have felt that they were engaged in a rhetorical and logical exercise of the type wherein the traditionally weaker case is put in the best possible light, the force and sophistication of much of the writing is none the less impressive for that. The fact that they were often trying to secure the patronage of powerful noblewomen does not alter the great eloquence and considerable rigour of argument with which they affirmed the dignity of woman. To borrow some phrases from Natalie Zemon Davis's essay on 'Women on Top' in early modern France, 'by showing the good that could be done by the woman out of her place', their writings had the 'potential to inspire a few females to exceptional action and feminists to reflection about the capacities of women', whether or not that potential was often realized; but of course they presented 'unlikely symbols for moving masses of people to resistance' (p. 133). Taking a more broadly ludic view, in the manner of such cultural analysts as Berne, Caillois, Ehrmann, and Huizinga, it could be said that the texts we have been discussing are *not* culturally marginal but microcosmic of many of society's vital concerns. In respect of the *Legend* in particular, the possibility that Chaucer was playing elaborate gender games need not diminish the poem's challenge in our minds, On the contrary, it shows what can be done by 'the woman out of her place', for in the *Legend* the female of the species is more virtuous than the male, while the menfolk display weaknesses which were held to be characteristic of women.

And yet, the women constructed by Chaucer are often shown as knowing their place to a remarkable (many would say excessive) extent; hence their obsession with the achievement of marriage in the fullest possible form. Men's fates are in the hands of such figures as Dido, Medea, and Phyllis—and to that extent they are empowered, but they certainly are not immasculated, given their preparedness to stand by their men (a sentiment unfortunately not reciprocated) and their quite naïve conviction that man is woman's joy and all her bliss. (And Dido even tries to appeal to Aeneas's fatherly instinct at one point.) Thus, they—and indeed most of Chaucer's heroines in the *Legend*, Philomela and Procne being the exceptions—could be seen as fulfilling Zemon Davis's paradigm of inversive figures who ultimately function 'as sources of order and stability in a hierarchical society. They can clarify the structure of the process by reversing it. They can provide an expression of, and a safety valve for, conflicts within the system.' It could then be concluded that 'they do not question the basic order of the society itself. They can renew the system, but they cannot change it' (p. 130). (Zemon Davis distinguishes this paradigm from that of inversive figures whom she regards as genuinely transgressive, on which more in a moment.) In similar vein, Ivan Illich notes that 'the gender line is kept *intact* through' the 'ritual mockery' of travesty; 'Putting women occasionally, publicly, and festively on top was a way of ridiculing men without seriously undermining their dominance' (p. 146). Perhaps, then, the *Legend* ridicules without undermining.

However, it is perfectly possible to push the argument beyond this point, by claiming that the overall inversive strategy of the poem may be seen as functioning to make readers aware of different interpretative possibilities for literature, and perhaps for life. Once we have returned from our journey through the looking-glass of Chaucer's alternative art, things may never seem quite the same again. If this approach is accepted, at least some of what Zemon Davis says about her radically inversive and 'unruly' female figures can, with due alteration, be applied to Chaucer's superlatively ruly and morally righteous martyrs for marriage. These case histories could have encouraged men and women alike to push at the hierarchical limits of what was possible, thus providing a site for actual dissent. The logistics of traditional gender stereotyping are certainly being challenged. What Linda Woodbridge says of Agrippa's *De nobilitate et praecellentia fœminei sexus* applies with equal validity to the *Legend*: the text's 'hyperbolic praise of women is not an ironic vehicle for laying bare the sex's unworthiness but a graphic demonstration of the absurdities one must resort to if one claims superiority for either sex' (p. 42). More obviously, perhaps, Chaucer's text offers a rhetoric which connives at the enhancement of female self-esteem. Aristocratic women from all over the ancient world—Egypt, Babylon, Carthage, Thessaly, Rome, Crete, Thrace, Greece—are revealed to be eminently capable of actions which are *gentil*, generous, unselfish, courageous, and expressive of great faith, piety, and trust. (The fact that that trust is often misplaced or manipulated serves to accentuate rather than undermine it, male misdemeanour serving as an effective foil.) Fire will be fire, even though it should appear in the Caucasus mountains, as the Wife of Bath's wise old woman maintains (III(D) 1139–45). Similarly, female virtue will out, no matter where or when women live, and the fact that it is found among pagans, who have less reliable doctrine to guide them than is available to Christians, demonstrates that it really must exist. The test in this literary laboratory, so to speak, turns out to be positive. Modern women may take some pride in, and perhaps feel vindicated by, the supreme examples of Chaucer's good women, though God forbid that they should be placed in such extreme situations in their own lives. Though to some extent distant, that heathen pack may make some difference.

Here I have self-consciously made the strongest possible case. But to talk in terms of dissidence in this context may be at once simplistic and sensationalistic. Cultures, as Edward Said has recently emphasized, should not be regarded as totalistic and enclosed things; people—at least some people—are not condemned endlessly to repeat all the same old gestures. Far from being fixed in every significant detail, orthodoxy can take many forms and be followed in different ways and to different extents. Conversely, dissent (or what passes for it) lacks demarcation lines, and is not obliged to be monolithic.

It may be hoped—for it is impossible to tell—that the more responsive members of the *Legend*'s early audiences came away wishing to question the social norms and to interrogate the established boundaries of gender. Whether such a quarrel should be seen as having been pursued within or against the culture must remain a matter of personal judgement.

Jean R. Brink, Maryanne C. Horowitz, and Allison P. Coudert (eds.), *Playing with Gender: A Renaissance Pursuit* (Urbana, Ill., and Chicago, 1991).

Conor Fahy, 'Three Early Renaissance Treatises on Women', *Italian Studies*, 11 (1956), 47–55. Gogio's treatise is summarized on pp. 34–6. The other two texts discussed here are Mario Equicola's *De mulieribus* and Agostino Strozzi's *Defensio mulierum*, both written in the first few years of the fifteenth century for Margherita Cantelma. Agrippa's treatise is summarized in Charles G. Nauert, *Agrippa and the Crisis of Renaissance Thought*, Illinois Studies in the Social Sciences, 4 (Urbana, Ill., 1965), p. 26. But see especially the excellent discussion of this work in the most extensive study of the *commendatio mulierum* genre, Linda Woodbridge's *Women and the English Renaissance: Literature and the Nature of Womankind, 1540–1620* (Brighton, 1984), pp. 38–45. For the English translation of Agrippa, as quoted above, see Henricus Cornelius Agrippa, *A Treatise of the Nobilitie and exellencye of woman kynde, translated out of Latine into englysshe by Dauid Clapam*, Thomas Bertheleti typis impress. (London, 1542), unfol. The significance of the treatises of Agrippa and Castiglione in Tudor England is well brought out by Woodbridge, *Nature of Womankind*, pp. 18–48. See further Minnis, 'From Medieval to Renaissance?', pp. 242–4, which includes a brief summary of the discussion of the nobility of women included in William of Aragon's *Liber de nobilitate animi* (late thirteenth century). Boccaccio's *De mulieribus claris*, which is dedicated to the Countess of Altavilla (cf. p. 403 above), includes accounts of women who were quite vicious, but of course they are accompanied by stories of women who were superlatively virtuous; the countess is being offered *exempla* of both good and bad behaviour, a strategy different from that followed in many of the later treatises. The interpretative problems of Boccaccio's text are discussed by Pamela

J. Benson, *The Invention of the Renaissance Woman* (University Park, Pa., 1992), pp. 9–31.

The argument, as quoted above from Gogio, that woman is superior to man in terms of place of origin (Eve having been created inside the Garden of Eden) is anticipated in Peter Abelard's Letter 6, 'De auctoritate vel dignitate ordinis sanctimonialium', in which he claims that 'a certain dignity' enhances 'woman's creation, since she was made in paradise, but man outside it' (Blamires (ed.), *Woman Defamed*, pp. 235–6). Abelard may be twisting an argument by Ambrose, who had said that the Genesis account demonstrates that 'every individual acquires grace through virtue, not location or family stock. Indeed, although created outside Paradise, that is in an inferior place, man is found to be superior, whereas woman was created in a better place, that is in Paradise, yet is found to be inferior' (Blamires (ed.), p. 61). See further the relevant passages in Christine de Pizan's *Epistre au dieu d'amours* and *Cité des Dames* (in Blamires (ed.), pp. 284, 292), where the argument is turned to woman's advantage. Aspects of Agrippa's *Declamatio* are interestingly presaged by the Middle English *Dives and Pauper* (1405–10), which claims that Adam's sin was the greater, and since humankind was lost through man, it had to be saved through man (Blamires, (ed.), pp. 265–6). For the original passage see *Dives and Pauper*, I.2, ed. P. H. Barnum, EETS OS 280 (Oxford, 1980), p. 82. In marked contrast is the use to which Thomas Hoccleve put such arguments in his *Regement of Princes*, 5104–94 (ed. F. J. Furnivall, EETS ES 72 (London, 1897), pp. 184–7). The rib from which woman was made, he says, was a material superior to the slime from which man came; moreover, all the supreme things—heaven, the sun, and the moon—are rounded just like that rib, and thereby its superiority is indicated. Then again, man was made outside Paradise, whereas woman was made inside it. But Hoccleve concludes this excursus with a *reductio ad absurdum*, in declaring that all this proves that husbands should be ruled by their wives.

See further Ian Maclean, *The Renaissance Notion of Woman* (Cambridge, 1980), pp. 47–67, which includes discussion of Torquato Tasso's *Discorso della virtù feminile e donnesca* (1582), wherein it is argued that a princess is, as it were, a man by virtue of her birth, and hence masculine standards of morality apply to her. Also Constance Jordan, 'Feminism and the Humanists: The Case of Sir Thomas Elyot's Defence of Good Women', in M. W. Ferguson, M. Quilligan, and N. J. Vickers (eds.), *Rewriting the Renaissance: The Discourses of Sexual Difference in Early Modern Europe* (Chicago and London, 1986), pp. 242–58. She suggests that Elyot's Zenobia, his principal example of a good woman, may have been meant to refer to Catherine of Aragon. For an interesting case of *a woman* employing the *commendatio mulierum* discourse—and the little good that it did her—see the account of Isotta Nogarola (1418–66) in Margaret L. King and Albert Rabil (eds.), *Her Immaculate Hand: Selected Works by and about the Women Humanists of Quattrocento Italy* (Binghampton, NY, 1983), pp. 57–69.

Castiglione, *Il Cortegiano*, ed. Cordié, trans. Bull. P. J. Benson, *Invention*, writes well on how 'women's willingness to cooperate and play a fostering and nondisruptive role is exemplified by the Duchess' (p. 75). 'She offers the women of the court an example of womanhood cooperative with the needs of the larger society rather than dedicated to her own pleasures and power' (p. 77). On the ludic aspects of this work (and an earlier text which influenced it, Boccaccio's *Decameron*) see the references on p. 306 above. For the serious political agenda underlying the third book (which concentrates on female virtue), see Dain A. Trafton, 'Politics and the Praise of Women: Political Doctrine in the *Courtier*'s Third Book', in Hanning and Rosand (eds.), *Ideal and the Real*, pp. 29–44.

Machaut, *Navarre*, ed. and trans. Palmer. On Philippa of Lancaster see above, pp. 25, 296.

Natalie Zemon Davis, 'Women on Top', in her *Society and Culture in Early Modern France* (Stanford, Calif., 1975), pp. 124–51, 310–15; Ivan Illich, *Gender* (London and

New York, 1983). An interesting (if highly problematic) test case for the extent to which medieval ideas of the carnivalesque may be deemed to relate to events of quite exceptional historical significance is provided by the Peasants' Revolt of 1381; Strohm, *Hochon's Arrow*, pp. 33–56. I fully endorse these general remarks: 'Ideas of "carnival" per se remain relatively unprescriptive of social consequences, except as they are articulated or fail to be articulated with other ideas in a more comprehensively oppositional ideology, except as they are either embraced or rejected by actual centers of social power. The failure of the carnivalesque to eventuate in social change must finally be sought in these areas, rather than in the temporary or inherently conservative nature of "carnival" itself' (p. 54).

Many of the manœuvres in Woodbridge's splendid analysis of Agrippa's *De nobilitate* will seem all too familiar to readers of *LGW*. For Woodbridge finds the text highly attractive, but worries lest it was not meant to be taken seriously. The arguments which Agrippa marshalls are, she believes, often 'ingenious if not outrageous'; 'many have that bright casuistical flair that characterizes the work of Neoplatonists'; a few are almost certainly tongue in cheek. On the other hand, she finds in the *De nobilitate* straightforward and very powerful arguments for the equality of women. Moreover, Woodbridge relates the work to the Renaissance genre of 'paradox literature', which exhibits 'serious intent': 'the need for . . . outlandish arguments to maintain an extreme opinion is meant to reflect on the outlandishness of argument that would be necessary to maintain the opposite extreme. The rhetorical paradox is an over-correction, pointing up the untenable nature of one extreme position by demonstrating the feasibility of arguing its opposite.' Paradox is therefore to be contrasted with 'the mock-heroic mode, where the inadequacies of the subject are exposed by the inflated terms in which it is celebrated' (pp. 39–42). Similar arguments can be offered regarding *LGW*. Woodbridge goes on to claim that, despite the lack of guarantees of true authorial concern about the woman question, the formal controversy, 'for all its preoccupation with stylistic finesse, could occasionally produce a thinker capable of laying philosophic foundations for modern feminism' (p. 44).

Edward Said, *Culture and Imperialism* (London, 1993).

# The Short Poems
## (by V. J. Scattergood)

*Canon and Context*

Chaucer's references to his short poems are both helpful and frustratingly inexact: they create as many problems as they solve. In the Prologue to the *Legend of Good Women* Alceste assures the God of Love that Chaucer has made:

> 'many an ympne for your halydayes          *hymn*
> That highten balades, roundels, virelayes'          *are called*
> (F Prol. 422–3; cf. G Prol. 410–11)

And in the Retractions to the *Canterbury Tales* the author mentions among his 'translacions and enditynges of worldly vanitees' 'many a song and many a leccherous lay, that Crist for his grete mercy foryeve me the synne' (X(I) 1085–7). His contemporaries and early followers add more evidence of the same sort: Gower refers to the 'Ditees' and 'songes glade' which Chaucer made in his youth for Venus's sake and with which 'The lond fulfild is overal' (*Confessio Amantis*, viii. 2941\*–57\*); and Lydgate includes in a much longer list of works the evidence that Chaucer:

> Made and compiled ful many a fresh dite
> Complaintes, ballades, roundles, virelaies.
> (*Fall of Princes*, I. 352–3)

But to take these statements with absolute literalness may be ill-advised, because lists so similar as to suggest a well-known formula appear in the writings of Machaut, Froissart, and Deschamps, and Chaucer attributes a similar repertoire of poetry to the love-sick squire Aurelius in the *Franklin's Tale*, where it is asserted that he made 'manye layes, / Songes, compleintes, roundels, virelayes' (V(F) 747–8). If these lists are genuine attempts at description, they are not very exact in relation to what has survived. The implication that Chaucer's short poems are all about love ignores the fact that a number treat religious and moral subjects. And, on a formal level, there is no surviving *virelai* (unless parts of *Anelida and Arcite*, 211–380, can be counted as such). Most of all, however, scholars have been puzzled by the impression that Chaucer is said to have written 'many' short poems, whereas only twenty-two are now usually accepted as canonical.

To many scholars the implication of all this is that the short poems now attributed to Chaucer form but a part of what was a more considerable output. A number may have disappeared, or are now unidentifiable among the undifferentiated mass of later medieval courtly poetry which has come down in an anonymous state in fifteenth-century manuscripts. These views have something to commend them. The textual tradition of Chaucer's short poems is not particularly well defined. A number of manuscripts certainly contain groups of authentic poems—Oxford, Bodleian Library, MS Fairfax 16, MS Bodley 638, MS Tanner 346; Cambridge University Library MS Gg. 4. 27; Cambridge, Trinity College MS R. 3. 20; Coventry, City Record Office, MS Accession 325—all of which suggests that there may been some sense among fifteenth-century collectors of what constituted Chaucer's *œuvre*. But equally, it has to be recognized that there are poems which survive in one manuscript only (such as *Rosemounde* in Oxford, Bodleian Library MS Rawlinson poet. 163, or *Womanly Noblesse* in London, British Library Additional MS 34360), poems where the text is problematic (the envoy to *Truth* survives in only one among twenty-three manuscripts), and poems which are never attributed to Chaucer in the manuscripts (such as *Against Women Unconstant*, *Complaynt d'Amours*, *Merciles Beaute*, and *A Balade of Complaint*) but are sometimes considered to be his on grounds of general stylistic plausibility or by association with authentic poems in manuscript collections. In such a situation losses may have occurred. And fifteenth-century copyists (like John Shirley) and sixteenth-century editors were not slow to attribute to Chaucer poems they felt might reasonably be his—often wrongly. Chaucer scholars have for many years worked with a canon which has been relatively stable. But that does not mean that it is secure.

A number of scholars have argued that the surviving body of Chaucer's short poems should be augmented by the addition of various lyrics set into his longer works (cf. pp. 82–4 above). This is a feature of his poems to which Chaucer sometimes draws attention by elaborate introductory signalling to tell the audience that a 'song' (*BD* 471–2) or a 'balade' (*LGW*, F Prol. 199–202) is about to appear, or by using a stanza form for the lyric which is different from that of the narrative in which it appears (*PF* 680–92). Lyrics of this sort, which differ in certain formal features from the narrative which incorporates them, are relatively easy to isolate. More often, though, as with the many intercalated lyrics in *Troilus and Criseyde*, they share the same stanza form as the narrative, and have to be recognized by the use of a different set of literary conventions, by changed stylistic features, or by an alteration in the manner of discourse. Chaucer's longer poems are full of lyrics or lyric moments. Thus, to take a few examples, one encounters love songs (*T&C* i. 400–20, ii. 827–75; *BD* 1175–80; *LGW*, F Prol. 249–69), epistles (*T&C* v. 1317–421, 1590–631), aubes both serious and comic (*T&C* iii. 1422–518, 1702–8; *CT* I(A) 4234–9, IV(E) 1831–57), two serenades (*CT* I(A) 3352–63, 3687–707), two reverdies (*PF* 380–92, *CT* IV(E) 2138–48), an *ubi sunt* complaint (*T&C* v. 218–45), many other complaints on various subjects, and even a brief lament for the dead (*BD* 475–86).

The relationships between these lyrics and the texts in which they occur are complex and differ from instance to instance. Some of the lyrics are more firmly integrated than others, and each contributes in a different way to the general sense of the work in which it is found. But all, to some degree, 'reify' the text: by referring to objects (lyrics, letters) with which the text deals, the author is the better able to authenticate it in fictional terms. They are also part of the *amplificatio* of the subject-matter: they enable the author to point up the significance of various areas, and allow him to interpret and clarify his narrative. But as important as all this, especially to the original listening audience, these episodes no doubt provided 'refreshment' by diversifying the nature of the discourse, allowing rests from concentration on the plot, and providing some variety in tone and occasionally in stanza pattern. These lyric interludes are part of the polyphony and multi-levelledness of Chaucer's habitual narrative process. They contribute to his complex dialectic by providing an elaborate commentary which is at once part of the text and different from it. Only one of these lyrics, however, achieved anything like a separate status in early manuscripts—Troilus's song beginning 'If no love is' (i. 400), which is a fairly close rendering of the Petrarchan sonnet 'S'amor no e' (*Canzoniere*, no. 132).

Though the intercalated lyrics are important, this chapter will concentrate on those twenty-two shorter poems of Chaucer which had a separate existence. They appear to derive from a courtly context and to have been written for a courtly audience: some are addressed to kings, Richard II and Henry IV, others to aristocrats, and the more personal and philosophical of them to Chaucer's own circle of friends, who were, like him, career diplomats, royal servants, officials, and administrators attached to the court and the government. Short poems such as these appear to have served the recreative intellectual needs of courtly society, providing materials and topics for diversion and discussion: they articulate, often in highly elaborate artistic form, those shared assumptions which separated off the court from what was outside it, refining ideas, feelings, and language, and playing with forms, genres, and modes. Like most coterie poems, they operate indirectly, and are full of buried allusions and private references. The evidence suggests that Chaucer wrote this sort of poetry throughout his creative life. Occasionally it is possible to establish dates for particular poems, but not very often. However, it looks as though the complaints are generally early, and the philosophical and political ballades and begging poems later. So the treatment here will be roughly chronological.

Lydgate, *Fall of Princes*, ed. Bergen, p. 124.

On the canon with particular reference to the lyrics intercalated in the longer poems see Arthur K. Moore, 'Chaucer's Lost Songs', *JEGP* 48 (1949), 196–208; and for their use see his 'Chaucer's Use of Lyric as an Ornament of Style', *Comparative Literature*, 3 (1951), 32–46. See more recently Julia Boffey, 'The Lyrics in Chaucer's Longer Poems', *Poetica*, 37 (1993), 15–37. For the lyrics in *Troilus and Criseyde* see Windeatt, *OGC: T&C*, pp. 163–9.

On the audience for Chaucer's short poems see Scattergood, 'Literary Culture at the Court of Richard II'; and Paul Strohm, 'Chaucer's Audience', *Literature and History*, 5 (1977), 26–41. For the social function of courtly lyrics see G. Olson, *Literature as Recreation*, esp. pp. 147–9, and cf. pp. 147, 294, 296–8, above.

For an exhaustive bibliography of studies on Chaucer's short poems see Russell A. Peck, *Chaucer's Lyrics and 'Anelida and Arcite': An Annotated Bibliography 1900–1980*, The Chaucer Bibliographies (Toronto, 1983). For a book-length study of the lyrics see Jay Ruud, *'Many a Song and Many a Lecherous Lay': Tradition and Individuality in Chaucer's Lyric Poetry*, Garland Studies in Medieval Literature, 6 (New York and London, 1992). For brief general treatments see Clemen, *Early Poetry*, pp. 170–207; Kean, *Making of English Poetry*, i. 31–66; Arthur K. Moore, *The Secular Lyric in Middle English* (Lexington, Ky., 1951), pp. 101–54; and Rossell Hope Robbins, 'The Lyrics', in Rowland (ed.), *Companion to Chaucer Studies*, pp. 313–31. For an invaluable study of all aspects of about half the short poems see *A Variorum Edition of the Works of Geoffrey Chaucer*, vol. v: *The Minor Poems*, pt. 1, ed. George B. Pace and Alfred David (Norman, Okla., 1982). All references and quotations are from the *Riverside Chaucer*.

## Literary Traditions

Of the literary languages available to the learned author in fourteenth-century England, Chaucer preferred English to either French or Latin, though the choice may not have been an automatic one: Gower wrote ballades in French, and the chronicler Creton says that Sir John Montagu wrote good 'balades et chancons / Rondeaulx et lais', which may have been in French. It has been suggested that Chaucer, early in his career, wrote lyrics in French which are now lost or unidentifiable as his, and James Wimsatt has recently drawn attention to fifteen French poems with the letters 'Ch' between the rubric and the text in University of Pennsylvania MS French 15 (cf. p. 15 above). But though Chaucer chose to write in English, the sources of his lyric inspiration were almost always French, occasionally Italian, and, in certain particular instances, Latin. He appears to have detached himself almost completely from the rich and complex English tradition that was available to him. This is not because he was unaware of what existed already in English. In the *Nun's Priest's Tale* Chauntecleer sings, in the morning sun, a song referred to as 'My lief is faren in londe' (VII (B²) 2877–9) which seems to be the brief lyric preserved in Cambridge, Trinity College MS 599, fol. 154ʳ, where it is also said to be a 'song':

> My lefe ys faren in a lond.
> Allas, why ys she so?
> And I am so sore bound
> I may not com her to.
> She hath my hert in hold
> Where ever she ryde or go,
> With trew love a thousand fold!

What is more, in the *Miller's Tale* Chaucer appears to use English lyric poetry of the previous generation for comic effect: his lovesick Oxford wooers use the sort of sentiments and language characteristic of the kind of love-poetry preserved in London, British Library MS Harley 2253, a collection made about half a century earlier in the West Midlands. For Chaucer this sort of idiom had apparently become *déclassé*, and was associated in his mind with provincial matters and characters and with uncourtly (though would-be courtly) behaviour. The refinement of his own lyrics is asserted through continental forms and by means of a very different vocabulary.

The influence of French lyric poetry on Chaucer is pervasive: he used French sources, and adopted and developed French forms. Both Jean Froissart and Oton de Graunson (whose poems were used and translated by Chaucer) were at the English court for long periods at the same time as Chaucer, and may have been known personally to him. It is clear also from his ballade 285, addressed to Chaucer, that Eustache Deschamps both admired his work and sent him his own poems, using the diplomat and friend of Chaucer Sir Lewis Clifford as an intermediary (cf. pp. 15, 20, above). But Chaucer and his French contemporaries all derived much from the example of a poet of the previous generation, Guillaume de Machaut: it was Machaut who established the *formes fixes*, particularly the ballade and the roundel, which were to dominate courtly writing for more than a century. He also, in two of his *dits amoreux*, *Le Remede de Fortune* and *Le Voir Dit*, provided a powerful impetus for the inclusion of lyrics in longer narratives, though Chaucer was very familiar with other texts, such as Boethius's *De consolatione philosophiae* and Boccaccio's *Filostrato*, which also did this (cf. pp. 82, 84 above).

In the thirteenth century the ballade was principally a musical form, but in the fourteenth it became an established literary pattern for lyric utterance—three through-rhymed stanzas, usually of seven or eight lines, but sometimes more, with a refrain. Later, an envoy was often·added, usually but not always following the stanza pattern of the body of the poem. Chaucer wrote ballades with and without envoys, but restricted himself, in the body of his poems, to two stanza patterns, both imitations of the French, the seven-line rhyme-royal stanza (*ababbcc*), and the eight-line 'Monk's Tale' form *ababbcbc*)—though in his envoys he uses other patterns. The form of his roundels is also less varied than that of his French contemporaries: three French models were available to him, eight-line, eleven-line, and thirteen-line types. But Chaucer used the thirteen-line form exclusively, with a rhyme scheme *ABBabABabbABB*. Chaucer's ballades and roundels are the first of their type in English, and he is aware both of his originality and of the difficulties involved. The technical demands of these strict forms are considerable in any language, but they are much easier to write in French than English, as he recognizes in a rueful envoy appended to his translation of a set of Graunson's ballades:

| | |
|---|---|
| Princes, receyveth this compleynt in gre, | *favourably* |
| Unto your excelent benignite | |
| Direct after my litel suffisaunce. | *Dedicated* |
| For elde, that in my spirit dulleth me, | *old age* |
| Hath of endyting al the subtilte | |
| Wel nygh bereft out of my remembraunce, | *taken away* |
| And eke to me it ys a gret penaunce, | |
| Syth rym in Englissh hath such skarsete, | |
| To folowe word by word the curiosite | *intricate workmanship* |
| Of Graunson, flour of hem that make in Fraunce. | |

(*The Complaint of Venus*, 73–82)

One way out of the problem, of course, was to use words with Latin or French suffixes in rhyming positions, which is what Chaucer does here: of the rhyme-words only 'me' is native English. He also appears to have experimented with the possibilities of using the Italian *terza rima* form in some twenty-five lines of *A Complaint to his Lady*, but the text of this poem is problematic, and it may be unfinished. For the most part he was content to use the French *formes fixes*, or some variation thereof.

Whether Chaucer's short poems were originally set to music is a difficult question. The roundel, like the ballade, was originally a musical form, and in some French examples the music is preserved. But exactly what the status of the musical accompaniment was is difficult to be sure about. Machaut, as accomplished musically as he was poetically, provided settings for his intercalated lyrics in both *Le Remede de Fortune* and *Le Voir Dit*, but only one manuscript of the latter work (Paris, Bibliothèque Nationale MS français 9221) preserves the music. Music was certainly much practised and was highly prized at the English court. According to Edward IV's *Household Book*, piping, harping, and singing were some of the accomplishments expected of an esquire of the king's household such as Chaucer had become in 1368: his own fictional squire could sing, play the flute, and 'songes make and wel endite' (*CT* I (A) 91, 95). And there is much about music and musical instruments and the effects of music in Chaucer's writings. But he is never referred to as a musician, and no settings of his lyrics by his contemporaries or successors in the fourteenth and fifteenth centuries are known, though it is possible to sing them to French settings. But whether original settings existed for most of them is uncertain: Chaucer's references to the intercalated lyrics in his longer works seem to leave their status as song and text ambiguous, perhaps deliberately. The narrator twice describes the first *canticus Troili* as a 'song', but equally insists that he will 'seyn' all that Troilus 'Seyde' (*Troilus and Cryseyde*, i. 386–99), and later in the same poem the narrator tells us that Antigone 'Gan on a Troian song to singen clere', but introduces it as 'She seyde' (ii. 824–7). Even more strikingly, in the *Book of the Duchess* the black knight's two songs are 'sayd' and 'told' to the narrator (471, 1181), not sung, though both are referred to as 'songs', and though musical settings are extant for the French poems which have been identified as their sources—but whether Chaucer had access to these settings cannot be determined for sure. The only one of Chaucer's lyrics which fairly certainly had music is the birds' roundel at the end of the *Parliament of Fowls* (see 677–9)—and here, clearly, the setting ('note') was an already existing French one (cf. p. 256 above). Perhaps Chaucer generally accepted Deschamps' view that the music of poetry should be 'naturele'—that is, spoken rather than sung (*Œuvres*, vii. 270) but was prepared to be flexible on the matter. Or perhaps the use of a musical setting was optional, depending on the ability of the performer, as seems to have been the case with the songs in the English mystery plays.

For the information about Sir John Montagu see Jean Creton, *Metrical History of the Deposition of King Richard II*, ed. J. Webb, *Archaeologia*, 20 (1824), 320. For Deschamps' poems see *Œuvres*, ed. Marquis de Queux de Saint-Hilaire and Raynaud, in which the ballades are referred to by number. For the information about Edward IV's esquires see *The Household Book of Edward IV*, ed. A. R. Myers (Manchester, 1959), p. 129.

For Chaucer's use of English lyric poetry of the previous generation see Donaldson, 'Idiom of Popular Poetry'. For Chaucer's much more extensive debt to the French lyric see generally Robbins, 'Geoffroi Chaucier'. On more specific relations see Braddy, *Chaucer and Graunson*; G. Olson, 'Deschamps' *Art de dictier* and Chaucer's Literary Environment', *Speculum*, 48 (1973), 714–23; and James I. Wimsatt, 'Guillaume de Machaut and Chaucer's Love Lyrics', *MÆ* 47 (1978), 66–87. For the French poems possibly by Chaucer, see Wimsatt, *Poems of 'Ch'*.

For the musical aspects of Chaucer's lyrics see Nigel Wilkins, *Music*, pp. 111–24; and *idem*, *Chaucer Songs*.


## An ABC

'Chaucers ABC called La Priere de nostre Dame; made as some say, at the request of Blanche Duchesse of Lancaster, as a praier for her priuat vse, being a woman in her religion very deuout'. Thus Speght in his 1602 edition of Chaucer's works describes what may be Chaucer's earliest poem, for Blanche died in 1368 or 1369 (see pp. 73, 78 above). But this testimony comes two centuries after Chaucer's death, and two formal features of the poem, the decasyllabic line and the eight-line ('Monk's Tale') stanza form, might suggest that it was written later, since most of Chaucer's known early poetry is in octosyllabic couplets.

*An ABC* is a translation, preserving the same alphabetical form, of a poem from Guillaume de Deguileville's *Pélerinage de la Vie Humaine*, a widely influential book which exists in two recensions from the early 1330s. Chaucer's poem was evidently quite well known and highly regarded: in most of the sixteen manuscript copies of it which survive the text is elaborately ornamented. And the English translators of Deguileville, rather than translate the poem for themselves, prefer to use Chaucer's version. It is incorporated in five manuscripts of the prose version, and the English verse translator, usually thought to be Lydgate, also defers to Chaucer's version and says he will include it,

> ffor memorye of that poete,
> Wyth al hys rethorykes swete,
> That was the ffyrste in any age
> That amendede our langage. (19,773–6)

Space is left for inclusion of Chaucer's poem in the text, but no copy of it was made.

According to this writer, Chaucer's translation is made 'word by word, as in substaunce' (19,757), but this is not so. Not only does Chaucer omit Deguileville's final two stanzas (on *et* and *cetera*), but in each individual stanza there is a mixture of literal translation, paraphrase, and original composition. The B stanza is in some ways typical:

> Bountee so fix hath in thin herte his tente
> That wel I wot thou wolt my socour be;
> Thou canst not warne him that with good entente      *refuse*
> Axeth thin helpe, thin herte is ay so free.
> Thou art largesse of pleyn felicitee,
> Haven of refut, of quiete, and of reste.      *refuge*

Loo, how that theeves sevene chasen mee.
Helpe, lady bright, er that my ship tobreste.　　*burst apart*
(9–16)

This stanza is about the comfort and succour provided for the fallible Christian by Mary, and Chaucer follows his source in expressing confidence in her. But Chaucer's images are generally more energetic and graphic: the 'larrons' (= rascals), glossed as the seven deadly sins, who lead the pilgrim astray in Deguileville, become the more threatening 'theeves sevene' who hunt their prey in Chaucer; and the conventional phrase 'salu porte', which Chaucer renders as 'Haven of refut' generates the idea of shipwreck, not in Deguileville, in his memorable and urgent last line. Chaucer omits a good deal of his source, but also augments Deguileville's poem with ideas from elsewhere, mainly the Bible and the liturgy.

The poem is a petitionary prayer: it asks for Mary's help as mediatrix. But it is also a meditative assemblage of ways of seeing Mary. Chaucer thinks about the etymology of her name, the epithet 'bitter' (50) reflecting the play on 'Maria' and Hebrew *marah* (= bitterness). He also uses typology in the M stanza where he speaks 'in figure':

Moises, that saugh the bush with flawmes rede
Brenninge, of which ther never a stikke brende,　　*twig burned*
Was signe of thin unwemmed maidenhede　　*unblemished*
(89–91)

But both these ideas are from Deguileville, and neither way of thinking seems to have been particularly important to Chaucer—though he uses both elsewhere. For the most part, the poem attempts to define the relationship between Mary and the petitioner through a series of images which recur from time to time in the poem: he is a troubled child to her serene and patient motherhood, a hunted fugitive seeking the safety of her refuge, a stained traveller hoping to be received in the 'hye tour / Of Paradys' (154–5), a storm-tossed sailor looking for the harbour of her grace, a wounded patient awaiting her healing, and (most emphatic and pervasive of all) a guilty criminal hoping for God's justice to be mitigated by her intercession.

But though the poem is full of potential story-lines, it is not a narrative, and though it suggests various ways of seeing Mary, it is not a description. It is an invocation, an apostrophe, as well as a prayer, and, if Speght is to be believed, a prayer made for someone else: though it is Chaucer's, it is intended to be said by Blanche. There is a fluctuation in the poem between the singular and plural uses of the first-person pronoun: Chaucer uses twenty-four plurals as against Deguileville's three.

Clearly the writer or speaker, though testifying to personal sinfulness, is meant in some way to be representative of all erring Christians. What Chaucer's personal involvement in the poem might have been is difficult to know. It can be read as marking a religious crisis in Chaucer's life, if one closely identifies the 'I' of the poem with the poet; or, alternatively, if one does not, it can be regarded simply as an exercise of some technical difficulty against which he could test and refine his poetical capacities. But whatever his commitment to what he says, Chaucer appears to have taken some pride in the workmanship of his *ABC*. He responds to the sense of completeness and perfection implied by the alphabetical form (A to Z, first to last) by imposing a circularity on his sequential material through a ring closure. The initial invocation 'Almighty and al merciable quene' (1) is picked up in the last request:

> Now, ladi bryghte, sith thou canst and wilt      *since*
> Ben to the seed of Adam merciable,
> Bring us to that palais that is bilt
> To penitentes that ben to merci able.     (181–4)

It is Mary's ability to obtain mercy, with which it begins and ends, that is very much at the centre of the poem's petitioning.

Two other Marian prayers are intercalated into Chaucerian narratives: both the Prioress and the Second Nun (both women, both religious) ask for assistance in formal invocations. They use ideas and terminology which are to be found also in the *ABC*, and manifest the same serious, rapt, high-style piety. In both cases also, Mary becomes something of a Muse, since her help is requested in fashioning a poem. The Prioress declares her abilities ('konnyng') to be slight, and compares herself to a 'child of twelf month old or lesse' who can hardly utter a word, before asking Mary, 'Gydeth my song that I shal of yow seye' (VII(B) 481–7). Similarly, the Second Nun ends her prologue with:

> O havene of refut, O salvacioun      *refuge*
> Of hem that been in sorwe and in distresse,
> Now help, for to my werk I wol me dresse.   (VIII(G) 75–7)

In both examples the prayer is shaped to fit a particular context. In the Prioress's case the unknowing piety of an unlearned child, here prefigured in a simile, is at the heart of the tale she tells, and the Second Nun's stress on 'werk' is very much part of her admirable determination to eschew 'the norice unto vices / Which that men clepe in Englissh Ydelnesse' (VIII(G) 1–2). In these instances the prayers are used in prefaces to tales; they precede a literary performance. Moreover, when Chaucer, in his own person, invokes divine assistance for poetry, it is

Apollo and the Muses he calls on (e.g. *HF* 520–2, 1091–109) or other classical gods and goddesses, not Mary. But Jonathan Culler would argue that apostrophes and invocations more generally have reference to the poetical process. 'Thus, invocation is a figure of vocation,' he says; 'it is the pure embodiment of poetic pretension: of the subject's claim that in his verse he is not merely an empirical poet, a writer of verse, but the embodiment of poetic tradition and of the spirit of poesy. Apostrophe is perhaps always an indirect invocation of the muse. Devoid of semantic reference, the *O* of apostrophe refers to other apostrophes and thus to the lineage and conventions of sublime poetry.' If this is true, the *ABC*, for all its implied humility as beginner's work, may paradoxically be Chaucer's announcement of himself as a poet, his early claim to a vocation and to a place in the tradition.

For Jonathan Culler on 'apostrophe' see the *The Pursuit of Signs: Semiotics, Literature, Deconstruction* (London, 1981), pp. 142–3.

For the French text of Chaucer's source see Guillaume de Deguileville, *Le Pèlerinage de la Vie Humaine*, ed. J. J. Sturzinger (London, 1893). W. W. Skeat prints the relevant stanzas in *Chaucer: The Minor Poems* (Oxford, 1888), pp. xlvii–lvi. For the English verse translation see *The Pilgrimage of the Life of Man, translated by John Lydgate*, ed. F. J. Furnivall, with an introduction by Katherine B. Locock, EETS ES 77, 83, 92 (London, 1899–1904). For the prose version see *The Pilgrimage of the Lyfe of Manhode*, ed. Avril Henry, EETS 288 and 292 (Oxford, 1985–8); for the editor's comments on the *ABC* see ii. 485.

The often ornate presentation of the text of Chaucer's prayer is discussed by George B. Pace, 'The Adorned Initials of Chaucer's *ABC*', *Manuscripta*, 23 (1979), 88–98. See Clemen, *Early Poetry*, pp. 175–9; and for a detailed recent literary study see Georgia Ronan Crampton, 'Chaucer's Singular Prayer', *MÆ* 59 (1990), 191–213.

## The Complaints

*The Complaint of Venus; The Complaint unto Pity; Anelida and Arcite; The Complaint of Mars; A Complaint to his Lady; Compleynt d'Amours; A Balade of Complaint*

Similar in tone and style to these prayers are the many complaints which Chaucer wrote, though these are secular rather than religious. Whether as a separate poem or as a passage intercalated in a longer work, the complaint (though often included among lists of poetic forms by French poets) in Chaucer is not a form, perhaps not even a genre, but a type of expression. It is a lament for some loss incurred or injustice suffered or grief experienced. The function of the poem, as is made clear in the *Complaint of Mars*, is to enunciate the reason for the complaint:

The ordre of compleynt requireth skylfully
That yf a wight shal pleyne pitously
Ther mot be cause wherfore that men pleyne          (155–7)

To complain without good reason is to complain 'folily', and the intention of the complaint, in this exposition, is not 'redresse' but to explain
the reason for the speaker's sadness. This is sometimes the case elsewhere, but not always: some complaints, particularly 'begging' poems, of
which Chaucer wrote several, have a practical end—the acquisition of
favour, position, or money.

The origins of the complaint are complex, and various strands of
influence are discernible in Chaucer. W. A. Davenport cites complaints
based on the Latin *planctus*, moral complaints deriving indirectly from
Roman satire, complaints against Fortune on Boethian lines, laments for
the dead which take ideas from the tradition of elegy, and laments by
those facing death. Various brief complaints made by the betrayed heroines of the *Legend of Good Women* derive from the lamenting letters
attributed to the tragic figures of Ovid's *Heroides* (cf. pp. 348, 359–60
above) Chaucer's preferred type, however, appears to have been the
amorous complaint (with which this section will principally deal). This
type of complaint had been made fashionable by Machaut and Froissart,
who intercalated examples in their longer works, and by Deschamps,
some of whose ballades are subtitled 'complaincte'. Chaucer is not the
first to write this type of poem in English. The London, British Library
MS Harley 2253 carole 'Blow Northern Wind' begins with a lengthy
head-to-foot itemizing *descriptio* of a 'lussum ledy lasteles' whom the poet
loves, and then moves into an amorous complaint made to a personified
Love about the persecution of the poet 'Ayeyn the poer of Pees' by three
of the lady's allegorical knights. Perhaps some courtroom scene is envisaged, since Love leans forward over a table ('over bord') as he advises the
poet to ask the lady for a remedy ('bote'). But Chaucer, though he uses
legal terminology in some of his own amorous complaints, either did not
know this poem or chose to ignore it.

The most prolific contemporary exponent of the complaint in French
was Oton de Graunson, and it is likely that he and Chaucer developed
an interest in this type of poem together, though Chaucer's *Complaint of
Venus*, which includes a tribute to Graunson, is translated not from the
latter's complaints but from a sequence of five ballades. In this poem
Chaucer does not follow the intricacy ('curiosite') of Graunson 'word by
word' as he suggests, in his envoy, that he tried to: he does not translate
all of ballades 2 and 3, though he uses material from both, and he alters
the speaker from a man to a woman (which may be the reason for the

modern editorial title of the poem). In Chaucer's version the poem becomes a triple ballade with envoy, and some have seen it as a triptych. But this is misleading, for the tendency of the poem is linear: there is a development in the speaker's position which is communicated not by anything which could be as crudely described as an argument, but by something which is more a modification of feeling and perception, an emotional adjustment. The poems are held together by particular words and images which recur and are recalled.

The opening stanza (1–8) of the first ballade introduces many of the concerns of the sequence. The speaker admits to grief and to comfort in this grief by remembrance of a lover whose nobility ('gentilesse') is praised by everybody and to whose person the speaker is everlastingly devoted: nobody ought to blame her for her lifelong commitment. The basic elements of the poem—a private mutual joy shared by the lovers, vitiated by some intrusion from the outside world, the present seen in relation to past and future—are all here. But as this first ballade develops, those things which diminish the joy of the speaker are suppressed by a rapt description of the virtues of the object of her love—'In him is bounte, wysdom, governaunce' (9), and so on. But, as the second ballade makes clear, the fortunate wealth of love (its 'worthynesse', 'richesse', and 'aventure') has to be paid for: 'Thus dere abought is Love in yevyng' (37), and Love's 'yift' lasts only 'A lytel tyme' (41). The prying, inquisitive 'Jelosie' of others disturbs the lovers' joy, and causes fear, grief, and suffering: 'In nouncerteyn [i.e. uncertainty] we languisshe in penaunce' (46). The idea of penance is picked up and developed in the final ballade, in which the speaker sees herself as someone constrained by the snare and fetters of love ('las' 50), who is being tortured ('turmente', 53) by jealousy, who is being tested ('putte in assay', 62) in terms of her belief, but who refuses to yield to the pressures to recant:

> for no peyne wol I not sey nay;
> To love him best ne shal I never repente. (63–4)

Though the first fine careless rapture of her earlier contemplation of the virtues of her lover has been modified by the pressures of jealousy, the speaker asserts that the love that remains is enough:

> Sufficeth me to sen hym when I may (54)
> Herte, to the hit oughte ynogh suffise (65)
> Sith I have suffisaunce unto my pay (70)

But this is not quite the same as the all-inclusive 'suffisaunce' (17) of the object of her love as described in the first ballade. Time and the pressures of the outside world have not destroyed that which has lasted 'longe' and will last until her 'endyng day' (51, 55), but it has modified her expectations. She is at once haunted and consoled by 'remembraunce' (3).

The shifts of feeling, the compromises, charted in this sequence of ballades are finely observed. Chaucer reveals an impressive imaginative empathy with the woman's predicament. These ballades are not 'conventional praises' as R. H. Robbins describes them (p. 322), and they do constitute a complaint, despite his doubts: the speaker describes the poem as 'this compleynt or this lay', and the 'cause' of it is subtly conveyed. Chaucer echoes this description in his envoy, 'receyveth this compleynt in gre' (93), just as he echoes, with great tact and taste, some of the themes of the poem. The envoy itself is a kind of complaint (and, indeed, Chaucer's phrase 'this compleynt' could refer back to his triple ballade or forward to his envoy) not about love, but about the failing of his poetic power, about age, about the inadequacies of the English language, about the difficulties of translation. But he uses words and concepts which have been important in the three ballades: his poems are the best his 'litel suffisaunce' can achieve (75); age has taken the skill of writing almost completely out of his 'remembraunce' (78); translating French ballades is his 'penaunce' (78). The *Complaint of Venus* does not replicate all of Graunson's five ballades; it is a diminished version of them, an *abbreviatio*, and a rewriting. Chaucer appears to be saying that just as the memory of a fulfilling love-affair represents a diminished version of the original experience but at the same time can be sufficiently consoling, so a translation, though it may be less than the original which it recalls, can suffice for what it seeks to do. He keeps in touch with the woman's complaint, but does not encroach upon it. His own dissatisfactions, his own compromises, are those not of a lover, but of a poet making versions of other people's love-poems. He also seems to recognize that it is difficult for a man to speak for a woman.

The complaint in this poem implies a narrative, a sequence of events with causes and effects which account for the changes in the speaker's moods. In other short poems of this type the complaints are introduced by, or framed by, brief overt narratives which provide contexts. Scholars usually consider that the earliest of these is the *Complaint unto Pity*, though there are no specific indications of date. Nothing much happens in the poem, but in a curious way this is the point, and the reason why nothing happens is made plain: this is a poem about frustration, an emotional dead end.

The speaker appears before the lady he loves, intending to utter his complaint, evidently a prepared discourse, but he becomes convinced that she will be unresponsive and remains, in the fiction of the poem, silent.

Probably the most interesting aspect of the poem is the distinctive social dimension which fashions part of its meaning: in a hierarchically organized society, social frustrations and the frustrations of love could sometimes amount to more or less the same thing. As the speaker approaches the figurative household of the lady, he finds that Pity, whom he had hoped would intercede on his behalf against Cruelty, is dead 'and buried in an herte' (14). Around the coffin he finds the lady's virtues, which are construed as household retainers, but feels they are his enemies, because none is likely to be helpful in interceding for him (50–3). He withholds his complaint: 'to my foes my bille I dar not shewe' (54–5), but nevertheless reveals its contents to the reader. The 'Bill of Complaint' has some of the characteristics of a legal bill, a tripartite division of address ('Humblest of herte . . .', 57 ff.), a statement of grievance ('Hit stondeth thus . . .', 64 ff.), and a petition for remedy ('Have mercy on me . . .', 92). It is also full of legal terminology: in the lady's household, warns the speaker, Cruelty intends to displace the 'regalye' of Pity (65), deprive her of her 'heritage', and occupy her 'place' (= position) (89–90). And this has a bearing on the speaker, because without Pity he can make no progress in his love-affair (99–101). He feels like a petitioner whose friend at court is no longer available to be called upon, who cannot get his case properly heard, who has no access to justice because the forces ranged against him are too formidable. He is silenced before he can speak: 'I suffre and yet I dar not to yow pleyne' (108). So the eloquence of the prepared discourse is fruitless, because the complaint is never uttered to the lady, only revealed to the reader of the poem. Fittingly, the poem turns back on itself with another ring closure. The final line, 'With herte sore and ful of besy peyne' (119), exactly replicates line 2, and in three of the nine surviving manuscripts line 117 reads, 'Now pite that I have soughte so yore agoo' which almost repeats line 1. This fashions an elegant completeness for the lyric, but it also figures the trapped mind of the speaker, enclosed in its own powerlessness.

The structure of this poem—narrative followed by complaint—is repeated in *Anelida and Arcite*, though this is a much more ambitious and elaborate performance. It is almost certainly unfinished, and is textually so unsatisfactory that it has been argued that parts of it may not be by Chaucer at all: after Anelida's complaint, a continuation is promised which the audience will 'after here' (357), but nothing follows. Perhaps because of its incompleteness, it has attracted the attention of those scholars who like to seek references to contemporary events (particularly court scandals) in Chaucer's lyrics. It has been suggested that it relates to the infidelity of Robert de Vere, Earl of Oxford, who repudiated his wife, Philippa de Courcy, in 1387; or that it relates to the Butler earls of

Ormonde. But these suggestions are unconvincing and, indeed, unnecessary; for Chaucer's motives appear, as often, to be artistic and experimental. The poem is set in ancient Thebes, and the material comes largely from Statius and Boccaccio's *Teseida*: it looks as though Chaucer is trying to give the complaint back to its original classical setting.

Critics have not been kind to this poem. It has been seen as an early attempt to do something with the same materials as were used later for the *Knight's Tale*, because there Chaucer reuses several lines first used here. It has also been seen as a vehicle for virtuoso metrical experiments and structuring in Anelida's complaint (211–350). But many have agreed with Wolfgang Clemen that the epic dimensions of the opening are not sustained in the more personal and private sections of the poem, that the first three stanzas 'are full of promises that are not kept and statements that are not true' (p. 199). The opening is certainly ambitious with its invocation to Mars and Bellona; its plea for help from Polyhymnia, the Muse of sacred song, who sings with her sisters under the everlasting laurel tree (15–19); its allusion to the memorializing capacity of poetry, which can preserve stories otherwise destroyed by time 'that al can frete and byte' (12); and its use of the traditional but powerfully evocative comparison between the enterprise of poetry and the riskiness of sea journeys ('do that I my ship to haven wynne', 20). But this is not a detached or detachable prologue. There is an attempt to integrate these invocations with the body of the poem: in the introductory narrative section, which covers the war between the Greeks and the Thebans, Theseus is 'laurer crowned' (24, 43), and on his banner is the image of Mars (31), the deity responsible for the war 'through his furious cours of ire' (50). It is also to Mars that Anelida sacrifices in the final stanza, though it never emerges why.

Yet the scope of the poem redeems its ambitious prologue, and is worthy of it. Chaucer here tries to write, on a smaller scale, about the same subject-matter as the epic poets of antiquity, love in time of war, personal relationships in the context of national politics. The love-story takes place in a city wrecked by armed conflict ('desolat . . . bare', 62) under the tyranny of Creon (64–70), and the brutal, essentially male-dominated ethos invades its conduct. In this martial poem women are objects to be acquired, by conquest either actual or metaphorical, and the relationship between the sexes is defined in terms of contests: one either dominates or is dominated. Theseus takes back to Athens as wife Hippolyta, the 'hardy' queen of the Amazons 'that he conquered hadde' (37), with Emily, her sister, in his triumphal chariot, as if they were spoils of war. And this leads indirectly, by the 'slye way' (48), to the acquisition of 'fair Anelida the quene' by 'fals Arcite': he had to do a great deal 'er that he myghte his lady winne' (100), but at last he 'with his kunnyng wan this lady bright' (89). The development of the relationship is not elaborated, but its main characteristics are clear—on her side a sweet and generous caringness, on his unreasonable demands, deceit, and a feigned jealousy (126). When to the distress of Anelida he seeks, albeit unsuccessfully, someone else, images of domination and violence are again used to define the relationship:

> His newe lady holdeth him so narowe      *tightly*
> Up by the bridil, at the staves ende,
> That every word he dredeth as an arowe      (183–5)

And from this story, Chaucer, disabused and knowing, elicits a general universalizing moral truth about the perverseness of men, whose acquisitiveness alternates with dissatisfaction and produces unhappiness:

> Ensample of this, ye thrifty wymmen alle,      *worthy*
> Take her of Anelida and Arcite,
> That for hir liste him 'dere herte' calle      *was pleased*
> And was so meke, therfor he loved her lyte.
> The kynde of mannes herte is to delyte      *nature*
> In thing that straunge is, also God me save!
> For what he may not gete, that wolde he have.
>
>          (197–203)

The rest of the poem represents Anelida's reaction to these events, and consists largely of her 'compleynynge' to Arcite.

The shift from narrative to complaint is marked metrically: the decasyllabic rhyme royal gives way to more complicated stanzas, and a carefully shaped, self-enclosed structure. The complaint is something of a literary *tour de force* in its metrical ingenuity and intricacy. Opening and closing nine-line stanzas of decasyllabics enclose two sets of six stanzas. In each set the first four stanzas are in nine-line decasyllabics each using only two rhymes. The fifth is of sixteen lines mixing octosyllabics and decasyllabics, again using two rhymes, and the sixth returns to the nine-line form but with heavy internal rhyming. This elaborate artifice, this controlled patterning, contains the often conflicting and unruly emotions of Anelida. Her sense of injury is framed in martial language, again drawing attention to the context of aggression and violence in which the love-story is set: Arcite is the 'foo that yaf my herte a wounde' (239); his cruelty caused the 'swerd of sorwe' to pierce her unhappy heart (270–1); she is 'sleen . . . with the peyne' (288) of love. But her complaint is also general and inclusive. She testifies to her lovesickness (292–7), suspects that she is going mad and is about to die (322), blames her destiny (243, 339, 348), uses images of the reversal of Fortune (214–15), and *ubi sunt* formulae (247–52). She has to choose between extremes of excess and deficiency, either a relationship based on constraint or parting; there is no Aristotelian mean of virtue: 'Ther ben non other mene weyes newe' (286). She imagines what it might be like to have him back, but dismisses the idea as an impossibility:

> For thogh I hadde yow to-morowe ageyn
> I myghte as wel holde Aperill fro reyn
> As holde yow, to make yow be stidfast.                    (308–10)

The complaint ends with the familiar ring closure: Anelida has been 'thirled with the poynt of remembraunce' (350), recalling the opening line (211). The image is from *Purgatorio*, xii. 20, where 'la puntura della rimembranza' provokes tears from those who are moved by pity at the contemplation of the fallen proud. It provides an apt frame for Anelida's bitter regret at her former joys and present desolation: there is no way out of her circle of torment.

In complaints, sentiments such as those uttered by Anelida are commonplace. But that is perhaps the point. Chaucer wishes her to be the representative betrayed heroine in an archetypal story. She asks questions about 'the trouth of man' (312) and is conscious of her own role as a woman: 'And shal I preye, and weyve womanhede?' (299). Chaucer also generalizes and broadens the scope of his Theban material by alluding to other stories, setting this story in the context of unchronological history. Behind this text are other texts. He compares Anelida's constancy to that of Penelope and Lucretia (82–4) and Arcite's behaviour to that of Lamech (Genesis 4: 19), the first bigamist. Various aspects of the story also suggest comparison with Dido's betrayal by Aeneas. Perhaps that is why differences in rank are insisted upon: Anelida, like Dido, is a 'quene'; Arcite, though she 'did him honour as he were a kyng' (130), is but a knight. She similarly rejects other suitors (113 ff.). And certainly the image of the swan which sings before its death, used by Anelida in the final stanza of her complaint, recalls it, for she refers to it as part of an old story:

> as the swan, I have herd seyd ful yore,
> Ayeins his deth shal singen his penaunce,
> So singe I here my destinee or chaunce                    (346–8)

In Ovid, Dido begins her letter with this image (*Heroides*, vii. 1–2), and Chaucer uses it again, as here, to close off her story in the *Legend of Good Women*, significantly in the context of complaint:

> 'Ryght so,' quod she, 'as that the white swan
> Ayens his deth begynnyth for to synge,
> Right so to yow make I my compleynynge'                    (1355–7)

Perhaps this is a clue as to how Chaucer meant to end the story—assuming he knew. W. A. Davenport speculates: 'Anelida is to sacrifice to Mars within the temple and to pray, possibly for revenge in the shape of Theseus's destruction of Creon's regime' (p. 32). This would make a neat outcome, but she never talks of revenge. On the other hand, the kinds of death depicted on the walls of the temple of Mars in the *Knight's Tale* include suicide: 'The sleere of hymself yet saugh I ther' (I(A) 2005). And Anelida's words, like Dido's, have a desolating air of finality: 'I yeve hit up for now and evermore' (343). The authenticity of the final stanza of this poem has seriously been questioned however; in many manuscripts it does not appear. It may be that Chaucer meant to end the poem with Anelida's complaint, and to leave the story suspended. Perhaps, as has recently been argued by Lee Patterson, he wished to leave the lovers trapped in history, doomed, like others to whom he alludes, to play out their roles in an endlessly repeated cycle of eroticism and violence: 'The Theban legend harshly argues that the natural self is by definition ill-behaved and self-defeating, an unconstrained appetitiveness that bespeaks not a transcendent origin but one that is primordial and earthbound' (p. 78).

The *Complaint of Mars* is even more complex and ambitious, though it has the same basic structure as the previous two poems discussed—narration followed by complaint. The events to which it refers can be precisely dated from the many astronomical references, which, as has been authoritatively shown, fit the planetary situation of Mars, Venus, the Sun, and Mercury as it was in late March and early April 1385: Mars dates his discomfiture as 12 April (139). Whether it has a precise human application, however, is doubtful. John Shirley's heading and colophon in Cambridge, Trinity College MS R. 3. 20 suggest a topicality in terms of a court scandal, and have encouraged allegorical readings in relation to Isabella of York and John Holland, Duke of Exeter (cf. p. 30 above). Shirley himself appears unsure about the status of his evidence ('some men sayne') and, in any case, the poem makes perfectly good sense in other terms.

A four-stanza introduction establishes a temporal setting for the poem, a narrator, and a tone: it is St Valentine's Day, and early morning, and the poem is sung by a bird (13–15), who undertakes to give advice both to birds and others in a cheerfully coercive manner:

> Gladeth, ye foules, of the morowe gray *Rejoice*
> Lo, Venus rysen among yon rowes rede, *red streaks*
> And floures fressh, honoureth ye this day;
> For when the sunne uprist then wol ye sprede.
> But ye lovers, that lye in any drede,

Fleeth, lest wikked tonges yow espye.
Lo, yond the sunne, the candel of jelosye!                    (1–7)

One of the oldest, most traditional themes of the love lyric, the springtime joy of nature contrasted with the misery of unhappy lovers, is set
out in a jaunty and uncomplicated manner. Again, the standard setting
for the aube, the lament of illicit lovers forced to part by the breaking of
day, is called up—but this does not apply to birds. The narrator recommends to his avian fellows that they awake, choose their mates or renew
their service, dedicate themselves to constancy and endure what tran-
spires with patience. Natural love is set against the complications of 'fyn
lovynge', where love may produce on the one hand high moral refinement
and joyousness, but on the other wretchedness, jealousy, despair, and so
on. The bird has pragmatic advice for lovers forced apart by the approach
of dawn:

Tyme cometh oft that cese shal your sorowe;
The glade nyght ys worth an hevy morowe.                    (11–12)

But this argument, though a traditional feature of the aube, is never seen
as a consolatory possibility in the story of Mars and Venus which follows.
    Chaucer's source, the Ovidian fable in *Metamorphoses*, iv. 167–89, is
altered interestingly. In Ovid, jealousy is a factor, as it is here (7, 140);
but much more powerful is revenge. Informed by the all-seeing Phoebus
of his wife's infidelity with Mars, Vulcan fashions intricate chains, nets,
and snares with which he imprisons the lovers in the act of embracing,
and exposes them in their shame to the ridicule of the other gods. Venus,
in revenge, punishes Phoebus by making him fall uncontrollably and mis-
erably in love with Leucothoe. Chaucer is not interested in this aspect of
the story, though Vulcan's revenge is alluded to in the 'broche of Thebes'
section of the complaint; nor is he interested in the exposure of the
lovers—rather the reverse, for he makes them take steps to avoid detec-
tion by parting as soon as Phoebus approaches. The narrative, like the
introductory section, uses the conventions of the aube, but on a grand
scale. Again, though the story as told here stops short of the ridicule
which is part of the Ovidian account, something of the narrator's comic
view of lovers' problems comes through.
    The narrative, though it deals with gods and goddesses, operates on at
least two other levels—the astronomical and the human—and the reader
is encouraged to look at them at the same time: Mars, we are told at the
outset, won Venus to his love, 'As wel by hevenysh revolucioun / As by
desert' (30–1). Planetary movements define the course of the relationship,
but human emotions emerge from it. Mars and Venus are initially in

aspect, 'Thus be they knyt and regnen as in hevene / Be lokyng most' (50–1). They fix an assignation in Venus's 'nexte paleys' (54)—that is, the sign of Taurus, indicated by the 'white boles grete' (86) with which it is decorated. Mars, with a wider and therefore seemingly slower orbit, arrives first, and Venus catches him up: 'she sped her as faste in her weye / Almost in oo day as he dyde in tweye' (69–70). Briefly in conjunction in Taurus they are 'in joy and blysse' (74), but with the approach of Phoebus within the palace gates comes 'drede' (80–2), and the lovers lament (89–91, 112) and part as quickly as possible, which in Mars's case is not very quickly since, comically trapped in his traditional iconography, he has to clothe himself in full armour before escaping (97–102). Accoutred thus heavily, he cannot keep pace with Venus, who flees to 'Cilenios tour' where she is joined and comforted by the even speedier Mercury (144–7). There is a reductive irony in the fact that the planetary gods and goddesses, whatever their intentions and their wills, are helplessly confined to predestined configurations. Mars is left 'compleynyng ever' at Venus's departure, and the cheerfully uninvolved voice of the narrator breaks in to assure the reader that he will 'seyn and synge' Mars's complaint, wishing everyone 'joy of his make' on this 'lusty morning' (148–54)—rather incongruously in view of the material with which he has just dealt and with which he promises to deal.

The complaint offers a different perspective on the affair, and is divided off formally from the narrative—nine-line stanzas replace the rhyme royal of the preceding material. It also has a particular structure: after an introductory stanza, five three-stanza poems follow. Each treats a separate subject, but cumulatively they add up to a puzzled exploration of a variety of topics emerging from the narrative, and are set out in an eloquent and serious manner, with none of the comedy or the ironic reservations of the narrative. Nowhere is the disjunction between the two parts of an amatory complaint more marked, though two of the traditional subjects of the aube—love and time, especially love in relation to time— are confronted. In the first poem Mars testifies to his 'trewe servise' of his lady, who is the 'verrey sours and welle' of all desirable female qualities (174), and in the second he speaks of the 'perilous aventure' (199) that lovers endure—his lady's refusal to have pity, jealousy, envy. The third shifts to a metaphysical level:

> To what fyn made the God, that sit so hye,
> Benethen him love other company
> And streyneth folk to love, malgre her hed?    *despite all they could do*
> And then her joy, for oght I can espye,
> Ne lasteth not the twynkelyng of an ye,
> And somme han never joy til they be ded.

> What meneth this? What is this mistihed?          *mysteriousness*
> Wherto constreyneth he his folk so faste
> Thing to desyre, but it shulde laste?                    (218–26)

There are no answers to this uncomfortable questioning. But the fourth poem seeks to explore these issues further by means of the conceit of the brooch of Thebes—a jewel made by the vengeful cuckold Vulcan for Harmonia, daughter of Mars and Venus—which was coveted by all, but which brought misfortune to all who possessed it. Using this analogy, Mars explores the causation of suffering because of love:

> She was not cause of myn adversite
> But he that wroghte her, also mot I the,         *as I may prosper*
> That putte such a beaute in her face,
> That made me coveyten and purchace
> Myn oune deth—him wyte I that I dye,                      *blame*
> And myn unwit that ever I clamb so hye.             (266–71)

To blame are the maker of the object of his desire and himself for desiring her. Love is not sin but folly, though difficult to avoid. The poem, true to its pagan setting, offers no Christian moral or transcendent resolution. In a direct address to knights, ladies, and lovers in the fifth poem, Mars asks only for 'some compassion', 'pite', and 'kyndenesse' (276, 283, 298)—that is, some understanding and sympathy for those grieved by love. In this harsh and deterministic scheme of things, suffering cannot be explained away or accommodated, only mitigated by some human generosity of feeling.

The multi-levelled story, the contrasts in attitude and manner of discourse, the mixture of comedy and seriousness, the irony, the unanswered questions, the compelling sense of bafflement of its central figure—all make this the most philosophically daring and complex of Chaucer's amorous complaints. The *Complaint of Mars* transcends its own genre. It is more than a social poem, more even than a love-poem.

By comparison, the remaining complaints are disappointing, and may not be by Chaucer. *A Complaint to his Lady* is attributed to Chaucer by Shirley in two manuscripts, but doubts have been expressed about its authenticity. Even if genuine, the poem was either not properly completed or has come down in a ruined textual state. As it stands, it is a first-person complaint in four sections about unrequited love. The first section, two stanzas of rhyme royal, introduces a sleepless and despairing poet. The second and third, which are both partly in *terza rima*, reveal the cause of the poet's grief—an unresponsive lady whose 'surname is Faire Rewthelees' with whom, not surprisingly, he can make no progress:

> Love hath me taught no more of his art
> But serve alwey and stinte for no wo.                              *cease*
>                                                                    (38–9)

The final section, in ten-line stanzas (one of which appears to have lost two lines) is the most completely articulated part of the poem. As in other complaints, there seems to be an attempt at ring closure: the 'trouble careful herte' of the last line recalls the 'trew and careful herte' of line 40. And the familiar conditions of the trapped mind which can envisage no way out of its predicament are set out in fairly traditional terms. There is no perspective beyond the love-affair, and the poet can hope for no resolution except through the lady's pity:

> And therfor, swete, rewe on my peynes smerte,
> And of your grace graunteth me som drope.          (124–5)

Several passages in this poem are used, with minor changes, elsewhere by Chaucer in other complaints, so it may be that he came to regard this rather unsatisfactory (though it has a recognizable narrative line) and perhaps abandoned piece as source material, rather than as a finished work of art.

The *Complaynt d'Amours*, an 'amerowse compleynte made at Wyndesore', is nowhere actually attributed to Chaucer, though it is found in Chaucer manuscripts. It has a Chaucerian feel: in individual lines and in some longer passages it recalls genuine poems. Like the *Complaint of Mars* it is set on St Valentine's Day, 'Whan every foughel chesen shal his make' (86; cf. *Parliament of Fowls*, 419), but no contrast between natural affection and the complications of human love is made explicit. Briefly, the poem promises to go beyond the standard configuration of the unhappy lover and the unresponsive mistress, and to explore suffering at a more philosophical level. Perhaps, the poet suggests, the lady is not morally responsible for her deficiency of pity:

> Yit is al this no lak in her, pardee,                              *indeed*
> But God or Nature sore wolde I blame.                              (57–8)

But the idea is not developed in any particularly interesting way. Since she behaves in the same way towards everybody, the poet resigns himself to her instinctual cruelty and abjectly makes excuses for her: 'It is her play to laughen whan men syketh' (62). This may be a fifteenth-century imitation of Chaucer, as *A Balade of Complaint* almost certainly is. In three gracefully written rhyme-royal stanzas the poet dedicates himself to his lady, 'My worldes joye, whom I wil serve and sewe', and asks her to accept 'in my most humble wyse . . . this litel pore dyte' (12–16). A modesty formula is given a dual function, amorous and literary. To write and present a poem is to take part in the game of love; the poetic gesture itself has meaning.

On complaints in general see the comprehensive study by W. A. Davenport, *Chaucer: Complaint and Narrative* (Cambridge, 1988). For briefer treatments see Norton Smith, *Chaucer*, pp. 16–34; and Nancy Dean, 'Chaucer's Complaint: A Genre Descended from the *Heroides*', *Comparative Literature*, 19 (1967), 1–27.

On the *Complaint of Venus* see Braddy, *Chaucer and Graunson*, pp. 77–83; Davenport, *Complaint*, pp. 15–18; Norton Smith, *Chaucer*, pp. 17–21; Robbins, 'The Lyrics', pp. 321–2. For attempts to link the poem to the *Complaint of Mars* see G. H. Cowling, 'Chaucer's *Complaintes of Mars and Venus*', *RES* 2 (1926), 405–10; and Rodney Merrill, 'Chaucer's *Broche of Thebes*: The Unity of *The Complaint of Mars* and *The Complaint of Venus*', *Literary Monographs*, 5 (1973), 3–61.

On the *Complaint unto Pity* see Clemen, *Early Poetry*, pp. 179–85; Davenport, *Complaint*, pp. 18–20; Norton Smith, *Chaucer*, pp. 21–3; and especially Charles J. Nolan, 'Structural Sophistication in "The Complaint unto Pity"', *ChR* 13 (1979), 363–72.

For a study of the text of *Anelida and Arcite* which questions its authenticity see A. S. G. Edwards, 'The Unity and Authenticity of *Anelida and Arcite*: The Evidence of the Manuscripts', *Studies in Bibliography*, 41 (1988), 177–88. For an analysis of the metrical patterning of this complaint see Baum, *Chaucer's Verse*, pp. 99–101. James I. Wimsatt points out that the rhyme scheme for Chaucer's sixteen-line stanza is also to be found in Machaut's and Froissart's complaints; see *French Love Poets*, p. 173. For Clemen's harsh assessment see *Early Poetry*, pp. 197–209, and for a more sympathetic reading, Davenport, *Complaint*, pp. 24–33. For a generous and searching essay which reads the poem off in relation to Chaucer's sense of the pattern of history see Patterson, *Subject of History*, pp. 47–83.

For the astronomical and astrological background to *Complaint of Mars* see the authoritative account of North, *Chaucer's Universe*, pp. 304–25. On the poem's relation to literary types and traditions see Gardiner Stillwell, 'Convention and Individuality in Chaucer's *Complaint of Mars*', *Philological Quarterly*, 35 (1956), 69–89. For interpretations see Clemen, *Early Poetry*, pp. 188–97; Davenport, *Complaint*, pp. 33–40; Norton Smith, *Chaucer*, pp. 23–34; and on the implications of the 'broche of Thebes' see Patterson, *Subject of History*, pp. 75–8.

On *A Complaint to his Lady* see Clemen, *Early Poetry*, pp. 185–8.

## Love Lyrics

### *Womanly Noblesse*; *To Rosemounde*; *Merciles Beaute*; *Against Women Unconstant*

The amorous complaint was the type of love-poem which most appealed to Chaucer, but he experimented with a number of other genres, both separately and within longer poems, and for both serious and comic effect. His love lyrics, in which he addresses a lady directly, are in general shorter and less elaborate than the complaints, and are all in either ballade or roundel form. From the comparatively few that have survived one may perhaps deduce that he was not particularly interested in this type of poem.

Of the separate ballades *Womanly Noblesse* is perhaps the most affirmatory and unequivocal about love, but it looks simpler than it is. As in most of these poems the author's relation to his lady, to himself, and to the process of writing about love is problematic. The poet persona asserts that he has in his 'remembraunce' the beauty, 'stidefast governaunce', virtues, and 'hie noblesse' of the lady, that he will serve her and never change, 'for no maner distresse' (1–9). All this is fairly standard and routine, recognizable gestures in a conventional literary form. But it emerges that the speaker is no abject lover (though he has a proper humility), but someone who has expectations of reciprocity. He feels he can ask the lady to remember him: 'have me somewhat in your souvenaunce' (13). His expectation of even-handed treatment is figured in the image of the balance in which he hangs, for he sees the lady as both Fortune, suggested by 'chaunce' (19), and Justice, suggested by 'alleggeaunce' (= alleviation), 'rebatyng' (= abatement), and 'outrance' (21–5). In either case he feels he has a right to receive grace and pity in return for his service. The envoy treats this reciprocity from a slightly different angle, exposing an aspect of the relationship between the subject of a poem and the poet:

> Auctor of norture, lady of plesaunce,         *good manners*
> Soveraigne of beautee, floure of wommanhede,
> Take ye non hede unto myn ignoraunce,
> But this receyveth of your goodlihede,
> Thynkyng that I have caught in remembraunce,
> Your beaute hole, your stidefast governaunce.       (27–32)

The lady may be the 'auctor' of refinement and good manners in the sense of originator, but the poet, despite his formulaic apology for his deficiencies, is an 'auctor' too: he is the creator or the efficient cause of his own poem, which he offers to the lady ('this receyveth'). And, as he closes the circle of his poem by repeating 'remembraunce', he appears to be alluding to his ability to perpetuate in memory the fame of an individual, a traditional source of pride in poets, and a traditional reminder, in relation to the poetry of praise, that the subjects owe something to the poets who celebrate them.

Nor is the lover in *To Rosemounde* at all abject, though he has even less to hope for. Both the identity of the addressee and the mood of the poem have puzzled commentators. Some have doubted its authenticity, like Brusendorff, who maintained that 'its rather dry and caustic irony reminds one not so much of Chaucer's ripe comic power as of the more primitive forms of humour employed by lesser men' (pp. 439–40). The tone, however, seems to me lighter: the poet mocks himself and the poetic which he uses and abuses. Many of the expected gestures of the courtly tradition of love-poetry are to be found in this poem: the lady is 'mery' and 'jocounde' (5), and is compared to jewels in her beauty; the lover has an almost religious devotion to her ('shryne', 1; 'penaunce', 14); he sees himself as the romance hero 'trewe Tristram' (20); he is wounded by his love for the lady, he burns and is her slave (7, 22–3). There is no reciprocal gesture from the lady, but that does not matter, says Chaucer, as he juggles the personal pronouns to emphasize the point:

> 'Suffyseth me to love you, Rosemounde,
> Thogh ye to me ne do no daliaunce.' (15–16)

He appears to propose that being in love in this way and writing love-poetry of this sort are essentially self-indulgent and self-regarding enterprises, and that really the lady's response or lack of it may be irrelevant. But the possibility that such a posture may be absurd is suggested by the two controversial images from the buttery or the pantry, the barrel of tears and the pike in jellied aspic sauce, which are excessive and indecorous:

> For thogh I wepe of teres ful a tyne,         *barrel*
> Yet many that wo myn herte nat confounde.    (9–10)

> Nas never pyk walwed in galauntyne   *pike steeped in galantine sauce*
> As I in love am walwed and ywounde.    (17–18)

Commentators often treat these images separately, but it may be that they should be read together. The word 'tyne' is unusual in Middle English, but it has been pointed out that, in French sources, a 'tyne' often held fish in galantine sauce. In one instance, from Gautier de Coinci, the fish in question is pike:

> une grant tine
> plaine de luz en galentine.

So there may be a distinct literary reference in the humour here. A way of feeling as expressed in a particular way of writing is being questioned, as a variety of discordant voices expose the poem's contradictions.

The triple roundel *Merciles Beaute* also deals with unreturned affection in a comic way. The progress of an unsuccessful love-affair is impressionistically conveyed in three linked poems. The first sets out the poet's suffering in terms of the familiar dying-for-love manner: his heart is pierced with the beauty of the lady's eyes, and unless a word or promise from her heals it 'while that it is grene' (5), it will mean his death. The second effectively erases all hope, using simple personification allegory: Beauty has chased Pity from the lady's heart, and 'Daunger halt your mercy in his cheyne' (14–16); the poet appears to be destined for a

'Giltles' (17) death. The third section turns the poem round, and makes it an emphatic farewell to love. The poet shakes off the servitude and bondage of love, and talks down the high style of the previous roundels with common sense and proverbs:

> Sin I fro Love escaped am so fat,
> I never thenk to ben in his prison lene;
> Sin I am free, I counte him not a bene.  (27–9)

The concept of escaping 'fat' is interesting here for several reasons. This poem is nowhere attributed specifically to Chaucer, but is almost always taken to be his, partly because of the tone and partly because, if the portraits of him can be trusted, he appears to have been rather short and fat in physique something he alludes to elsewhere. But the expression has a distinct literariness too. The opening line of the third roundel corresponds exactly to the first line of a ballade by the Duke of Berry, dated 1389, replying to the authors of the *Cent Ballades*, 'Puis qu'a Amours suis si gras eschape'. If Chaucer is the debtor, its appropriateness might have amused the ageing poet and his audience, especially since it fitted in well with the wry self-image of the unsuccessful lover which he cultivated. But behind both poems is another layer of allusion, to the *Roman de la Rose*, 2545–50, where it is said that lovers should be lean, not fat. The end of the poem brings its literariness to the fore: since Love strikes the poet's name 'out of his sclat', the poet will strike Love 'out of my bokes clene' (34–5). A poet can always choose not to write about love.

*Against Women Unconstant* is not certainly by Chaucer, but it is another farewell to love. The title is not very appropriate, because the poem is not a general anti-feminist attack, but a leave-taking from one particular woman, because of her 'newefangelnesse', 'unstedfastnesse', and 'brutelnesse' (1, 3, 15). Part of the condemnation involves biblical and classical comparisons: she is more fickle than Delilah, Cressida, or Candace (16). At one point, it touches, albeit lightly, on weighty philosophical matters, where the impermanence of the lady's love is compared to the transitory image one may see in a mirror:

> Right as a mirour nothing may impresse,
> But, lightly as it cometh, so mot it pace,
> So fareth your love, youre werkes bereth witnesse.  (8–10)

The linking of the ideas of the mind as a mirror and the mind as a waxen tablet which may (unlike a mirror) receive and retain permanent 'impressions' appears in Chaucer's *Boece*, V, met. iv, 6–29, a lengthy discussion of Stoic epistemological ideas and an account of the lower and higher forms of cognition. In Jay Ruud's words, 'When he compares the lady's mental facilities to a "mirour nothing may impresse", the speaker implies that the woman is a slave of her passions, of her sensitive soul, and is unable or unwilling to think rationally about the images her mind receives.' She is therefore incapable of 'permanent love', follows her appetites, and 'changes with her every whim' (p. 202). But the tone generally is familiar and colloquial. A number of common proverbs are used (in lines 9, 12, 19), and another provides the refrain 'In stede of blew, thus may ye were al grene' (7 etc.), alluding to the notion that blue was the colour of constancy, green of inconstancy—though it is possible, again, that the reference is literary, for one of Machaut's ballades in *Le Voir Dit* has a French version, 'Qu'en lieu de bleu, Dame, vour vestez vert'. The poem is not heavily censorious or moralistic, partly because it suggests, and not only in the refrain, that, for the lady, changing lovers exists on something of the same plane as changing dresses in response to fashion, which gives relevance to the 'mirour' image on quite another level. The phrase 'Al light for somer' (20), which has puzzled commentators, refers almost certainly to clothes. John Skelton's Ryotte, a disreputable would-be courtier who is dressed in short garments which were both fashionable and disapproved of by moralists, 'wente so all for somer lyghte' (*The Bowge of Courte*, 355), and Chaucer's Canon rode 'Al light for somer' (*CT* VIII(G) 568). The poet expects the lady, and the audience, to understand that the phrase connoted disreputableness and volatility ('ye woot wel what I mene', 20), like the colour green an outward manifestation of an inner quality. And, if the poet is Chaucer, there may be a reference to his own, presumably earlier, use of the phrase.

For Gautier de Coinci's lyrics see A. Langfors, 'Mélanges de Poésie lyrique française, II, Gautier de Coinci', *Romania*, 53 (1927), 474–538; III, *Romania*, 54 (1930), 33–48.

For an interesting attempt to define the tone of Chaucer's love lyrics (and other early poems) see Earle Birney, 'The Beginnings of Chaucer's Irony', *PMLA* 54 (1939), 637–55; and also Edmund Reiss, 'Dusting off the Cobwebs: A Look at Chaucer's Lyrics', *ChR* 1 (1966), 55–65.

On *Womanly Noblesse* see Pace and David (eds.), *Minor Poems*, pp. 179–86; and especially Ruud, *Many a Song*, pp. 154–72.

On *To Rosemounde* see generally Pace and David (eds.), *Minor Poems*, pp. 161–70, for a survey of the scholarship. For an attempt to relate the poem specifically to Queen Isabella, Richard II's child bride, who came to London in 1396, see Rossell Hope Robbins, 'Chaucer's "To Rosemounde"', *Studies in the Literary Imagination*, 4 (1971), 73–81. For Aage Brusendorff's sceptical comments on the poem's authenticity see *The Chaucer Tradition* (Oxford, 1905), pp. 439–40, where he also questions the authenticity of *Merciles Beaute*.

On *Merciles Beaute* see generally Pace and David (eds.), *Minor Poems*, pp. 171–8. On possible echoes of French poems see J. L. Lowes, 'The Chaucerian "Merciles Beaute" and Three Poems by Deschamps', *MLR* 5 (1910), 33–9; and W. L. Renwick, 'Chaucer's Triple Roundel, "Merciles Beaute"', *MLR* 16 (1921) 322–3.

For *Against Women Unconstant* see Pace and David (eds.), *Minor Poems*, pp. 187–93; see especially the fine reading by Ruud, *Many a Song*, pp. 198–208. For poems of the 'farewell to love' type see generally Louis B. Salomon, *The Devil Take Her: A Study of the Rebellious Lover in English Poetry* (Philadelphia, 1931); for his comments on Chaucer see pp. 67–9, and for some remarks on this poem see p. 117.

## Philosophical and Political Lyrics

*Gentilesse; The Former Age; Lak of Stedfastnesse; Truth; Proverbs; Lenvoy de Chaucer a Bukton; Chaucer's Wordes unto Adam, His Owne Scriveyn*

A number of Chaucer's most personal lyrics deal with philosophical or moral questions, or questions where the philosophical or moral shades into the political. In the Middle Ages generally it is not always easy to separate the philosophical or moral from the political, and Chaucer's characteristic manner of handling political issues and events is often highly individualistic. For example, the Rising of 1381, when the peasants of Kent and Essex took over the capital and threatened the monarchy, is mentioned directly only in the *Nun's Priest's Tale* (VII(B²) 3393–7) as a way of indicating the noise made by those chasing the fox. Again, the most serious heterodox movement of the later fourteenth century, Lollardy, which numbered among its sympathizers some of Chaucer's closest friends, is mentioned only in the context of an argument about swearing in the epilogue to the *Man of Law's Tale* (II(B¹) 1170–83). Neither of these passages constitutes a serious political statement. Nor does Chaucer usually write poems for the occasions normally covered by official poets—royal marriages, coronations, victories in battle, deaths of important people, and the like—and when he does, the works produced treat these situations in unusual and oblique ways. Chaucer and the friends to whom several of his lyrics are addressed were often directly involved in, and affected by, policies and decisions made at court and by the government, so it may have been difficult for them to treat issues openly. Political discretion, and perhaps good manners, demanded that literary expression should be indirect. Meaning emerges from the choice of particular types of poem or genres, and from the different ways in which these are handled.

Among Chaucer's philosophical and moral ballades are a group which scholars have traditionally termed 'Boethian' because the topics which make up their subject-matter are all treated in *De consolatione philosophiae*, which Chaucer translated probably in the late 1370s or early 1380s. However, Chaucer's response to texts, even to *auctores* such as Boethius, is not simple. He often uses more than one source, sometimes in a rather scholarly and pernickity way, comparing and contrasting his materials.

A case in point is the ballade *Gentilesse*, which, in three through-rhymed rhyme-royal stanzas with refrain, advances the proposition that true nobility depends on virtuous behaviour rather than ancestry or birth. He begins:

| | |
|---|---|
| The firste stok, fader of gentilesse— | *stock/ancestor* |
| What man that desireth gentil for to be | |
| Must folowe his trace, and alle his wittes dresse | *tracks, prepare* |
| Vertu to love and vyces for to flee. | |
| For unto vertu longeth dignitee | |
| And noght the revers, saufly dar I deme, | *safely, judge* |
| Al were he mytre, croune, or diademe. | *he may wear* |
| | (1–7) |

And he develops this in a logical and unsurprising way by saying that 'This firste stok' was virtuous in all things and that if his heir does not love virtue he cannot claim to be 'gentil' (8–13), and that though a vicious man may inherit 'old richesse', nobody can bequeath 'vertuous noblesse' (15–17). The idea of 'generositas virtus, non sanguis' was a commonplace of classical and medieval literature. But Chaucer appears to have taken the line 'For unto vertu longeth dignite' from Boethius's 'Inest enim dignitas propria virtute' (III, pr. 4), the phrase 'Olde richesse' from Dante's 'antica richezza' (used six times in the *Convivio*) or from Jean de Meun's 'richeces ancienes' (*Roman de la Rose*, 20,313), and the refrain listing the symbols of temporal and ecclesiastical power from Boccaccio's *Il Filostrato*, vii. 94 ff.: 'Corona o scettre o vesta imperiale'. As he deliberated on this subject, which was one of immense contemporary importance and interest, Chaucer seems to have consulted several of his most frequently used sources.

The phrase 'firste stok' has caused some difficulty, and commentators have read it off in different ways: some take it to mean God or Christ, whereas others think that it indicates Adam, the earliest race of men, or worthy human ancestors. This difficulty is not a modern invention. Chaucer's poem is homiletic in manner and hortatory: it does not treat the question of true nobility (as its sources had done) in discursive argument, and it seems that its rather lapidary phrasing left it open to various interpretations by Chaucer's contemporaries and followers. Henry Scogan, who incorporates the whole of *Gentilesse* in his *Moral Balade* addressed in about 1407 to the sons of Henry IV, referring to Chaucer's poem, says: 'Than is god stocke of vertuous noblesse' (100). This is consistent with Chaucer's line about 'the firste fader in magestee' (19). But Lydgate, in *A Thoroughfare of Woe*, obviously understood the phrase differently:

> Oure fader Adam bygan with sore travaile,
> When he was flemed out of Paradice.                    *driven*
> Lord! what myght than gentillesse availe,
> The firste stokke of labour toke his price              (33–6)

To read Chaucer's phrase in this way makes sense, particularly of the second stanza and its commendation of 'besinesse' which refers to God's injunction to Adam that, on his expulsion from Eden, he should eat his bread in the sweat of his face (Genesis 3: 19). Both readings seem to be valid. Chaucer appears to be talking about inheritance in general—in terms of spiritual and moral virtue, and in terms of name and wealth— for the word 'gentilesse' could comprehend all these meanings.

But though the poem is in some sense polyvocal, it is important to appreciate what it does not say. According to Alfred David, 'no tinge of democratic sentiment adheres to the short poem' (Pace and David, p. 67), and this seems to me valid. It is possible, in the context of the 'generositas virtus, non sanguis' topos, to argue that virtue conferred, or ought to confer, nobility. This is one of the arguments that the hag in the *Wife of Bath's Tale* puts to her knightly husband, with references to Seneca and Boethius, and after citing the example of Tullius Hostilius (III(D) 1172–6). And this is a possibility to which Scogan draws the attention of the royal princes:

> Taketh hede also, how men of povre degree
> Through vertue have be set in greet honour,
> And ever have lived in greet prosperitee
> Through cherisshing of vertuous labour.                 (89–92)

But he reminds them also that things could go in the opposite direction: 'many a governour' had been brought down 'through missing of right and for errour' (93–4). He gives examples from classical and biblical sources, including Tullius Hostilius (167–8). But the sons of Henry IV would not have needed much reminding of what had happened to Richard II a few years earlier. And those who, like Chaucer and Scogan, had lived through the summer of 1381 would have been aware of the revolutionary potential of egalitarian ideas about 'gentilesse'. John Ball had helped fashion a revolt using the implications of the laconic sermon couplet,

> Whan Adam dalf and Eve span                           *dug the earth*
> Wo was thanne a gentilman?

But these ideas, of which Chaucer was certainly aware, are not in this poem. Presumably he felt them to be inappropriate to the audience he was addressing.

*Gentilesse* has no envoy, and does not refer formally to a particular

audience. But since it is largely concerned with those who have the lin-
eaments of ancestral nobility and wealth, it seems likely that he is
addressing the aristocracy. He is not threatening them, or even issuing a
stern warning, but merely reminding them what their obligations are:
they should seek to make themselves worthy of the positions in which
God and their virtuous ancestors have placed them; they should cherish
their nobility with virtuous action and not let it degenerate through vice.
It enunciates its truth in abstract and generalizing language, but it may
be rather more specific than it at first seems. The word 'stok' in this poem
is obviously being used in the metaphorical sense of 'the source of a line
of descent', and Chaucer has clearly in mind the idea of a family tree, for
the primary meaning of 'stok' is the trunk of a tree or tree stump. In
addition, the word 'stok' was connected with heraldry in later medieval
England: it was the term used for the tree trunks which appeared (in both
couped and eradicated forms) in some armorials and on badges—including the royal badges of Edward III, Richard II, and Henry IV. Thomas
of Woodstock, Duke of Gloucester, son of Edward III and uncle to
Richard II, wore a rebus which featured a dead tree, a stock of wood
which punned on Woodstock (Oxfordshire), the place of his birth. So it
may be that Chaucer's moral reminder about true nobility and its responsibilities had a particular reference to the English royal house—if it were
meant to apply specifically to one person, its natural target would have
been Richard II.

In *The Former Age* criticism of contemporary England is more direct,
and also fiercer. Again, the background of the poem is Boethian: it draws
heavily on the famous description of the 'golden age' which appears in
*De consolatione philosophiae*, II, met. v, and perhaps Nicholas Trevet's
commentary on this metre. But Chaucer again uses other materials on the
same subject: Boethius's source, Ovid's *Metamorphoses*, i. 89–112; Jean de
Meun's treatment of the topic in the *Roman de la Rose*, especially lines
8325 ff.; perhaps Virgil's *Eclogue* iv and Tibullus's *Elegies*, i. iii; and
other texts also. Descriptions of the golden age evoke the perfect state of
natural man—before the development of agriculture and commerce, arts
and sciences, crafts, war, or any kind of social organization. They are
regretful laments for the lost innocence of mankind. But nostalgia for a
forfeited paradise usually involves a criticism of the less than perfect present, as Boethius makes plain:

> Utinam modo nostra redirent
> In mores tempora priscos                    (II, met. v, 23–4)

Or, as Chaucer's English version has it: 'I wolde that our tymes sholde
torne ayen to the oolde maneris' (*Boece*, II, met. v, 30). In three of his

ballades (nos. 181, 375, 972) Deschamps sets the degeneracy of late four-teenth-century life against this ideal: 'L'aage dore estoit bien autrement' (no. 375), and it is very much in this spirit that Chaucer uses the myth.

In part, the 'blisful lyf', peaceful and sweet (1) enjoyed by the people of the 'golden age' is evoked in its pastoral simplicity using the terms of Chaucer's sources, but largely it is suggested by describing what it lacks (for the poem is full of negatives); and what it lacks are the benefits of late fourteenth-century civilization, questionable benefits as far as the argument of this poem is concerned. The processes of civilization are sometimes presented as injurious to the earth: 'Yit nas the ground nat wounded with the plough' (9), 'Uncorven [i.e. unpruned] and ungrobbed [i.e. untilled] lay the vine' (14). Sometimes they appear as a perversion of the natural:

> No madder, welde, or wood* no litestere           *dyer*
> Ne knew; the flees was of his former hewe.   *fleece, original colour*
> (17–18)

And sometimes simply as redundant: 'No marchaunt yit ne fette out-landish [i.e. foreign] ware [wares]' (22). None of this need be taken to mean that Chaucer disapproved of wine or coloured woollen cloth or overseas trade (his family were vintners, and he was Controller of Customs in the port of London for twelve years). Nor, when he mentions 'doun of fetheres' and the 'bleched shete' (45) later, does it mean that he repudiates a comfortable life-style. But the basic sufficiencies enjoyed in the 'golden age' are used as ways of criticizing the excesses of a high-life civilization 'forpampred with outrage [overindulged with excess]' (5), which gave itself over to luxuries such as 'clarre' (a spiced and sweetened wine, sometimes apparently used as an aphrodisiac) or 'sause of galan-tyne' (16). Moreover, so runs the argument, one of the fruits of civiliza-tion is the creation of wealth (expecially from gold and gems, 27–30), and from wealth comes 'the cursednesse / Of coveytyse' (31–2), war for gain, and tyranny. In the fifth stanza Chaucer gathers together and sharpens his criticism, giving it a firm political emphasis: he temporarily abandons his sources which dealt with the 'golden age', and uses an instance from John of Salisbury's *Policraticus*, viii. 6 (or Jerome's *Epistola adversus Jovinianum*, ii. 11):

> Thise tyraunts putte hem gladly nat in pres
> No wildnesse ne no busshes for to winne,
> Ther poverte is, as seith Diogenes,
> Ther as vitaille is ek so skars and thinne
> That noght but mast or apples is therinne;

* Plants used for making red, yellow, and blue dyes.

> But, ther as bagges ben and fat vitaille,
> Ther wol they gon, and spare for no sinne
> With al hir ost the cite for to asayle.                    (33–40)

[These tyrants will not cheerfully make an effort to gain any wild place or bushes, where there is poverty, as Diogenes says, where food is scarce and meagre, so that there is nothing but nuts and apples; but where there are bags (of goods or money) and rich foodstuffs, there will they go, and they will not hold back out of any sense of sin from attacking the city with all their army.]

The targets of Chaucer's criticism are plain—greed, acquisitiveness, materialism, aggression, but in a context which associates these vices with dominion and the ruthless desire for rule.

   This stanza decisively shifts the focus of the poem. Though the last three stanzas again take up ideas to do with the 'golden age', they are directed emphatically and narrowly at courts and kings: a line such as 'Yit was no paleis-chaumbres ne non halles' (41) makes explicit what was implicit earlier in the poem. And the parallelism of the following

> No pryde, non envye, non avaryce,
> No lord, no taylage by no tyrannye              *taxation*
>                                                    (53–4)

leaves no room for doubt that Chaucer equates these vices with rule and the ability of rulers to impose their wills on others. In the final stanza, two rulers, one from classical myth and the other from the Bible, are instanced as the originators of the destruction of the 'golden age' paradise:

> Yit was not Jupiter the likerous,
> That first was fader of delicacye,              *voluptuousness*
> Come in this world, ne Nembrot, desirous
> To reyne, had nat maad his toures hye.              (56–9)

Jupiter here stands for all that is luxurious and over-indulgent in courtly living, and Nimrod is seen as the first tyrant, or perhaps more generally as the first ruler. In ballade 961, Deschamps wrote:

> Nembroth le grant fut seigneur premerain
> Grant et corsu, de toute fierte plain,
> Villes ferma, de son peuple fut maistre,
> Lors commenca guerre et envie a plain

Here, much like the rulers in Chaucer, Nimrod is associated with lordship and dominion, pride and envy, the enclosure of towns and cities, and war.

   In the last three stanzas, however, the contrast between an idealized past and an imperfect present is not discarded. In the 'golden age' people slept securely (46); they had no wish to quarrel (51); they lived with each other in humility, peace, and good faith (55). But the poem closes with a list of contemporary vices and crimes:

> Allas, allas, now may men wepe and crye!
> For in our dayes nis but covetyse,
> Doublenesse, and tresoun, and envye,
> Poyson, manslawhtre, and mordre in sondry wyse.     (60–3)

John Norton Smith believes that the poem may date from 1397–9, the period of Richard II's 'tyranny', and this may be so. But Richard II's court was criticized from within, particularly for its extravagance and factionalism, at other times too. Sir John Clanvowe, a chamber knight and a long-time friend of Chaucer, in 1391 wrote forthrightly against the 'greet werreyours and fighteres' of his society who 'distroyen and wynnen manye loondis' and who 'dispenden outrageously in mete, in drynke, in cloothing, in buyldyng, and in lyvyng in eese, slouthe, and manye oothere synnes' and who 'woln bee venged proudly and dispitously of every wrong that is seid or doon of hem' (*The Two Ways*, 485–501). But though Clanvowe's indictment of the aggression, acquisitiveness, self-indulgence, and vengefulness of the contemporary world is very similar to Chaucer's here, his secular piety is sustained by Lollard sympathies, and he argues for the virtues of a modest life-style and quietist simplicities, based on biblical precepts. Chaucer sets out no positive moral position, but is negative, depressed, and pessimistic. This is the bleakest poem he ever wrote.

Like this poem, *Lak of Stedfastnesse* uses Boethius as a starting-point—the famous lines from *De consolatione philosophiae*, II, met. viii, on the bond of love which holds together in stability the contrarious elements of the world. There are also echoes of II, pr. v, and III, pr. xii. The refrain 'That al is lost for lak of stedfastnesse' (7 etc.) may, however, be taken from Deschamps' ballade 234, 'Tout se destruit et par default de garde'. But both in what it complains about and in its generalized way of stating it, it owes much to the traditional 'abuses of the age' or 'evils of the times' genre of poetry. The third stanza, for example, opens as follows:

> Trouthe is put doun, resoun is holden fable,
> Vertu hath now no dominacioun;
> Pite exyled, no man is merciable     *exiled*
> Through covetyse is blent discrecioun.     *blinded*
> The world hath mad a permutacioun
> Fro right to wrong     (15–20)

With it one may compare a thirteenth-century Latin complaint:

> Verus amor expiravit,
> Pax in terris exsulavit,
> Patri proles imperat;
> Legem dolus impugnavit,
> Totus mundus se mutavit,
> Nova lex exsuperat.

[True love has expired, peace on earth has gone into exile, children rule their father; trickery has assailed law, all the world has altered itself, a new law has taken over.]

In both sentiment and manner of expression Chaucer echoes this sort of writing, and, what is more, at least one of his followers appreciated this aspect of the poem—the author of the spurious fourth stanza in the Bannantyne MS:

> Falsheid, that sould bene abhominable,
> Now is regeing, but reformatioun,       *raging, without reform*
> Quha now gifis largly ar maist dissavable,       *deceivable*
> For vycis ar the grund of sustentatioun;       *basis of support*
> Al wit is turnit to cavillatioun,       *trifling objection*
> Lawtie expellit, and all gentilnes,
> That all is loist for laik of steidfastnes.

This may not be very good, but it is entirely in keeping with the genre of the poem: the Scottish author added his own 'evils of the times' material which is entirely compatible with what he found.

In their generalized ways, poems of this sort pillory the vices of the present by reference to the past: they lament the erosion of old moral certainties, and deplore the corruption of current institutions and the instability which has turned the world upside down. But though essentially non-specific, poems of this sort were sometimes used in specific contexts which served to release their political potential: a version of the 'evils of the times' poem was used by John Ball in 1381 to encourage his fellow rebels that 'now is tyme' to act. Chaucer's poem becomes specific in its envoy, which is addressed, according to the Cambridge, Trinity College MS R. 3. 20 version, to 'Kyng Richarde'. The heading to the poem in this manuscript also says that Chaucer wrote it in 'in hees laste yeeres', and this has encouraged some scholars to assign it to the period 1397–9. It seems to me, however, to date from somewhat earlier.

The envoy addresses itself to a 'prince' and deals with the rights and responsibilities of kingship: in fact line 27, 'Dred God, do law', looks like an echo of the English coronation oath, the four parts of which concentrate on precisely these matters. During his reign, Richard II was several

times reminded of his duty as king, and on occasions his coronation oath
was brought to his attention. But two other lines may allude to something
even more precise:

> Suffre nothing that may be reprevable
> To thyn estat don in thy regioun. (24–5)

If 'estat' means 'royal rank or authority, sovereignty' (*MED*, 'estat', n.
11b), as it must in the context of an address to a 'prince', what Chaucer
is urging is that Richard II maintain the prerogatives belonging to the
crown. This was an issue on several occasions during Richard II's reign,
but particularly in 1386–7. At the Wonderful Parliament of October 1386,
which Chaucer attended as Knight of the Shire for Kent, a great many
of the king's powers were effectively taken away and delegated to a 'great
and continuous council'. At the end of the parliament Richard II made a
personal statement in an attempt to salvage something of his position:

> pur riens q'estoit fait en le dit Parlement il ne vorroit qe
> prejudice avendroit a luy ne a sa corone; einz qe sa Prerogatif,
> et les Libertees de sa dite Corone feussent sauvez et gardez

[in spite of anything that was done at the said parliament he did not wish that
prejudice should come to him or his crown; so that his prerogative, and the liberties of the said crown might be saved and preserved.] (*Rotuli Parliamentorum*,
iii. 224)

The matter of the royal prerogative was something which concerned
Richard II deeply, and he asked in the summer and autumn of 1387 for
a formal legal verdict on the proceedings of the Wonderful Parliament in
his 'questions to the judges'.

When the judges pronounced, they said that the Westminster parliament of 1386 had passed legislation which derogated from the king's prerogatives, and that those who brought forward the legislation should be
punished by death as traitors (*proditores*). These answers may have provoked Chaucer's suggestion that the king use his 'swerd of castigacioun'
(26)—for sometimes traitors of high rank were beheaded with the sword,
rather than the axe. It would make some sense of the envoy, therefore, if
the poem were to be dated 1387, perhaps in late October or early
November when Richard II was actually, in the words of the London,
British Library MS Harley 7333 copyist, 'thane . . . in his Castell of
Windesore'. Or alternatively, one might argue for a date right at the end
of December when the king was, albeit temporarily, deposed: as Thomas
of Woodstock, Duke of Gloucester, said in his confession of 1397, he and
his fellow appellants consented to the 1387 deposition 'for two dayes or
thre and than we for to have done our homage and oure oothes and putt

hym as hely in his estate as ever he was'. Some of these problems reappeared in 1397–9. In the parliament of September 1397 there was much talk of the 'Regalies', 'Prerogatives', and 'Droits' attaching to the crown and the need to respect them. But by this time Richard II was powerfully in charge of events and set on vengeance for the earlier slights done to his prerogative. He would hardly have needed Chaucer's encouragement to impose himself.

Like other poems in this group, *Truth*, which is sometimes referred to as a 'balade de bon conseyl', offers advice of a gnomic sort. It is generally agreed to be Boethian in tone, though Chaucer does not appear to have used specific passages therefrom in its composition. And it is clear that he also used ideas from a number of other areas, particularly the Bible. But the resulting mix proved popular, for this poem is extant in twenty-four manuscript copies, more than any other of his lyrics. It usually appears as three through-rhymed rhyme-royal stanzas with refrain, but in London, British Library MS Additional 10,340 an envoy appears addressed to 'thou Vache'. Some scholars have doubted the authenticity of this stanza, but most agree with the proposal first offered by Edith Rickert that it does come from Chaucer and that it refers to Sir Philip de la Vache (1346–1408), a fellow courtier and son-in-law of Chaucer's friend Sir Lewis Clifford. De la Vache is associated with Chaucer in a number of records and with men whom Chaucer evidently knew. As Edith Rickert pointed out, in one respect his career was very like Chaucer's, for during the years 1386–9 the smooth course of his prosperity and promotion was interrupted. He was evidently out of favour, because the Lords Appellant, who either influenced or controlled the government of the country during those years, identified him as one of those close to Richard II who needed to be removed from office for the public good. When Richard II resumed power, de la Vache's career picked up again: he recovered some of the positions he had vacated, and eventually achieved sufficient eminence to be made a Knight of the Garter in 1399. It looks as though the good counsel Chaucer offered to de la Vache was to console him in a witty and sympathetic way during the period of his disfavour and to persuade him to act prudently—necessarily so, for men lost their lives for resisting this particular baronial *coup d'état*. If the envoy is authentic, the poem also takes one closer to Chaucer, for he lost or resigned posts during the supremacy of the Lords Appellant just as de la Vache did; so what he advises him to do might reasonably be supposed to be the course of action he had devised for himself, and the consolation offered, though perhaps not entirely serious, may be the way Chaucer came to terms with his own misfortunes in the years 1386–9.

Chaucer's poem addresses de la Vache directly, and names him as if in a letter; and, indeed, its important literary relationships are with epistles, particularly those pieces which criticize the court and its values. Curial satires often take the form of letters written by literary men engaged with, but alienated from, the court. They seek to persuade the reader (who is usually specifically named) to eschew the court by cataloguing its evils, and they often recommend a different life-style sustained by a different set of values. In origin the form is classical: both Horace and Seneca, amongst others, in letters to friends, advise the avoidance of fashionable cities for the slower, more peaceful and virtuous life-style of the country. And the tradition continues into the Middle Ages in works such as Walter Map's *De nugis curialium* or Alain Chartier's *Curial* (dating from 1428). In the fiction of this last epistle Chartier seeks to persuade his brother not to come to court, but to remain in his quiet, private mode of existence. In Caxton's version of 1484, this reads:

> And yf thou wylt use my counseyl / Take none
> example by me for to poursewe the courtes / Ne
> the publycque murmures of hye palaysis / But
> alleway late my perylle be example to the for
> to fle and eschewe them. (3)

> Flee, ye men, and holde and kepe you ferre fro
> suche an assemblee. (14)

In William Dunbar's briefer verse curial beginning 'To dwell in court, my friend, gife that thow list' there are two injunctions to 'Fle' from perils. And in Thomas Wyatt's *Epistolary Satire I* the poet seeks to explain to John Poyntz 'the cause why that homeward' he goes to 'flee the press of courts' (2–3), a phrase he may well have taken from Chaucer. *Truth* does not have all the characteristics of the epistolary curial satire by any means; but the opening injunction, 'Fle fro the prees' (1) and the suggestion that the recipient of the poem not regard the court as his 'hoom' (17) but leave in order the better to know his 'contree' (19) mark it off as something in what is recognizably the same tradition (though 'hoom' and 'contree' both bear meanings in addition to their literal ones). To this tradition also belong such quietist precepts as 'Gret rest stant in litel besinesse' (10). The notion of withdrawal from the turmoil of the court into the peace of the country, which provides the dynamic of the curial satire tradition, also gives shape and momentum to Chaucer's poem.

'Virtus est vitium fugere' (To flee vice is virtue), writes Horace to Maecenas (*Epistulae familiares*, I. i. 42), and curial satires specify, in general terms, what are the vices of the court. They mostly have to do with ambition for the power associated with high office, avarice for material wealth, and also with envy, either one's own because of the success of the others or theirs towards one's own success. In Caxton's version of Chartier:

> Thou shalt be enuyous of theyr power / yf thou
> be in mene estate / of whyche thou hast not
> suffysaunce / thou shalt stryue for to mounte
> and ryse hyer / and yf thou mayst come unto
> the hyge secrets whych ben strongly for to
> doubte and drede / in the doubtous courtlynes
> of the most hye prynces. (5)

And this compulsion for success, this desire to rise, makes the would-be courtier a prey to Fortune, which brings worry and feelings of insecurity: 'There knoweth noman in certayn yf hyys estate be sure or not / But who someuer it be, alwey he is in doubt of hys fortune' (12). Dunbar warns his friend against any seeking after the 'gift of fortoun' (2), and Wyatt, though he does not 'scorn or mock' them, makes it plain that his esteem for those powerful courtiers 'to whom Fortune hath lent / Charge over us' (8–9) is heavily qualified. Chaucer is using traditional ideas from the anti-court complaint genre when he says in two terse, monitory lines:

> hord hath hate, and climbing tikelnesse,          *avarice, instability*
> Prees hath envye, and wele blent overal.    *The* (ambitious) *crowd, prosperity*
> [*deceives everywhere*
> (3–4)

Here are the vices of avarice and envy, and the insecurity of 'climbing' suggests the whole concept of the rise and fall of Fortune's wheel, so it is no surprise to find that elsewhere de la Vache is advised not to put his trust in her 'that turneth as a bal' (9).

The type of virtue to be sought has to do with moderation, restraint, and self-sufficiency. And it is to Stoicism, which is predominantly the philosophy of happiness in the face of adversity, that Chaucer goes for his precepts. Seneca frequently counsels Lucilius against the acquisition of wealth and seeks to persuade him to be satisfied with little, but *Epistulae morales* XVII deals centrally with this question, and is full of aphoristic advice such as 'natura minimum petit, naturae autem se sapiens accommodat' (nature demands but little, and the wise man suits his needs to nature) (9). Chartier's advice to his brother is more discursive, but in the same vein: 'thou art and shal be puyssaunt as longe as thou hast, and shal haue of thy self, suffysaunce' (15). Dunbar repeats the same advice in a single line: 'Be thow content, of mair thow hes no neid' (19). Chaucer advises de la Vache to 'stryve not', and on three occasions makes the point that he should be content with what he has:

Suffyce unto they thing, though it be smal.                                    (2)
Savour no more than thee bihove shal.                                          (5)
That thee is sent, receyue in buxumnesse.                                     (15)

The first of these lines is very similar to the Latin maxim 'Si res tuae tibi non sufficiant, fac ut rebus tuis sufficiant', which is quoted by Gower in *Confessio Amantis*, v. 7735–9, and attributed in a marginal gloss to Seneca. It is not from Seneca, however, but from the *De nugis philosophorum* of Caecilius Balbus, even if the sentiment is thoroughly Senecan in tone.

From these virtues comes self-control. Dunbar makes an aphorism on this subject the refrain of his anti-court satire: 'He rewlis weill that weill him self can gyd [guide]' (8 etc.). This may be a reminiscence of Chaucer's line 'Reule wel thyself, that other folk canst rede' (6). But whether it is or not, it is clear that both poets are using precepts commonly associated with the curial satire tradition. And Chaucer's line 'Daunte thyself, that dauntest otheres dede' (13) appears to be another version of the same idea. Chaucer appears to be saying that exemplary restraint is necessary for those with any sort of authority, but the principal object of the man who sought to achieve self-sufficiency and self-control was liberty—a freedom from dependence on the vicissitudes of Fortune or the values of the world. If he goes to court, Chartier tells his brother, 'thou shalt nomore enioye the droytes and ryghtes of thy franchyse and liberte' (13–14), and he urges him to reconsider remaining in 'the liberte and franchyse' that his present life-style allows him. Chaucer, in the manner of the epistolary curial satirist, urges de la Vache, 'Unto this world leve now to be thrall' (23), and has a refrain which maintains that 'trouthe thee shal delivere, it is no drede' (7 etc.), where 'delivere' means 'set free'.

Chaucer, with great tact and sensitivity, seeks to console a friend, whose hopes at court have been disappointed, in the appropriate way by means of the type of poem which measures the value system of courts against ethical and moral precepts which diminish its importance. He tries to cheer de la Vache up by reminding him of the existence of a greater good. For the most part the poem is sombre, but towards the end Chaucer, with a sort of high clowning, deepens its seriousness and lightens its tone: he puns on de la Vache's name (the French word meaning 'cow') and perhaps on 'mede' meaning both 'reward' and 'meadow'. The idea of wittily encouraging a friend with a beast-like name to assert his manly capacity for making moral choices and lifting his mind from a contemplation of worldly matters may have been suggested by a text from Boethius (or from *Metamorphoses*, i. 84–6, its source): 'Only the lynage of man heveth [*raises*] heyest his heie heved, and stondith light with his

ypryght body and byholdeth the erthes under hym' (*Boece*, V, met. v).
This may lie behind lines 18–19, though other suggestions have been
offered:

> Forth, pilgrim, forth! Forth, beste, out of thy stal!
> Know thy contree, look up, thank God of al.

But the consolation proposed at the end of the poem (fittingly since
Chaucer advises de la Vache to pray to God for himself and for others)
is based predominantly on biblical texts. The refrain appears to derive
from 'veritas liberavit vos' (John 8: 32); the idea that man is engaged in
a pilgrimage towards God comes from Hebrews 11: 13; and 'lat thy gost
thee lede' (20) is perhaps based loosely on Romans 8: 4. But a Christian
solution to the vicissitudes of courtly life is not unusual. Dunbar
advises,

> Hald God thy friend, evir stabill be him stand;
> He will the confort in all misaventur. (43–4)

Similarly, though Chaucer's advice to de la Vache is largely Stoic, it is
Stoicism decisively modified by transcendental Christian values.

   The sententiousness of Chaucer's writing in his poems which give
advice, such as the last two studied, appears to have favourably impressed
some of his followers, who valued him for, amongst other things, his
proverbial wisdom. Lydgate makes the point that Chaucer embellished
his work 'with many proverbe, divers and unkouth', and John Metham
says that 'proffoundely / With many proverbys, hys bokys he rymed
naturelly'. There survive two cross-rhymed quatrains, attributed to
Chaucer in London, British Library MS Harley 7578, which encapsulate
proverbial wisdom: the first two lines of each quatrain supply a question,
and the last two an aphoristic answer. The form is emphasized in the
rubrics to the poem in London, British Library Additional MS 10,392,
which preserves only the second quatrain: before the question comes
'Interrogacio Juvenis', and before the answer, 'Responsio sapientis'. Some
collections of proverbs take this dialogic form in which an older and wiser
man replies to a youth's questions, and it has been suggested that these
may be fugitive stanzas from some longer collection, now lost. The first
quatrain of *Proverbs* is a warning against negligence:

> What shul these clothes thus manyfold,
>   Lo this hote somers day?
> After grete hete cometh cold;
>   No man cast his pilche away.   *fur outer garment*

The second is a wry observation on acquisitiveness:

> Of al this world the large compas
> > Yt wil not in myn armes tweyne;                    *two*
> Who so mochel wol embrace,
> > Litel therof he shal distreyne.                      *retain*

Both sayings, which are known in slightly different forms from other sources (see Whiting C365, M774), have to do with human limitations and with the way in which men have to negotiate their way with care through a difficult world—a cautionary note, typical both of the genre and of Chaucer's response to moral problems.

But the use of proverbs is more generally a feature of Chaucer's writing, and it is clear that some subjects appear to have attracted a treatment involving this sort of material more than others. When Chaucer thought controversially but not very seriously about marriage, for example, he often made use of proverbs. The Wife of Bath's fifth husband, Jankin, was fond of lecturing her in gnomic terms about the way in which husbands and wives should relate, though she disparages his sayings using a proverb of her own (Whiting H192): 'I sette nought a hawe / Of his proverbes n'of his olde sawe' (III(D) 644–60). So when Chaucer came to write his *Lenvoy a Bukton*, which is probably addressed to Sir Peter Bukton of Holderness (Yorkshire) rather than Sir Robert Bukton of Goosewold (Essex), advising him against remarrying, it was natural that his mind turned to proverbial wisdom on the subject. In the final stanza, with more than usual helpfulness, he tells the recipient (and the larger audience) how to read the poem:

> > This lytel writ, proverbes, or figure,
> > I sende yw; take kepe of yt, I rede.                    (25–6)

Here 'writ' probably means 'missive, letter', and 'figure' is more likely to mean 'a parable, a comparison, or metaphor' rather than 'a poetic composition, a poem' which is how the *MED* ( *figure*, n. 4c and 4a) defines this occurrence. This is a letter of advice which makes use of the wisdom of commonplaces: it is largely built around proverbs and sayings, though it takes in biblical texts and quotations from Chaucer's own poems also.

It is not difficult to appreciate the main direction of Chaucer's advice to Bukton, comic though it is. But he makes a show of being even-handed and intellectually impartial, of exploring the subject fully, and taking into account a variety of authoritative statements. He sets text against text.

> > My maister Bukton, whan of Crist our kyng
> > Was axed what is trouthe or sothfastnesse,
> > He nat a word answerde to that axing,
> > As who saith, 'No man is al trewe,' I gesse.
> > And therefore, though I highte to expresse                    *promised*

> The sorwe and wo that is in mariage,
> I dar not writen of it no wikkednesse,
> Lest I myself falle eft in swich dotage.          (1–8)

Fittingly, he begins with a famous biblical passage which poses a difficult, unanswered question: 'Pilate saith unto him, what is truth?' (John 18: 38). In the account of the examination before Pilate in St John's Gospel, Christ has already claimed that he has come into the world to 'bear witness unto truth' and that 'Every one that is of the truth' hears his voice (18: 37), and though he does not answer Pilate's question, it appears to be because Pilate broke off the conversation: 'And when he said this, he went out again unto the Jews.' This is, at any event, Francis Bacon's interpretation: 'What is truth? said jesting Pilate; and would not stay for an answer.' Chaucer, however, is more interested in what he sees as Christ's reticence: his line 'He nat a word answerde to that axing' (3) is based, though commentators do not point this out, not on the account in St John, but on the questioning before Pilate and Herod in the other Gospels, where the specific question on truth is not posed: 'And he answered him to never a word' (Matthew 27: 14); 'but he answered nothing', 'But Jesus yet answered nothing' (Mark 15: 3, 5); 'but he answered him nothing' (Luke 23: 9). Chaucer is interested here, for his own humorous purposes, in the difficulty of truth, and interprets what he supposes to be Christ's reticence in terms of a proverb: 'No man is al trewe' (4), though it is difficult to be precise about its exact meaning. It appears to correspond to some proverb such as 'No man is without fault (sin)' (Whiting M235, Tilley M116), or perhaps 'All men are not true' (Whiting M31, Tilley M503), or perhaps 'Not all is sooth nor all lies that men say' (Whiting S485, Tilley T594). Chaucer is interested in the problems of being 'al trewe', because his own position on Bukton's marriage is an ambiguous one: he has promised to express 'The sorwe and wo that is in mariage', but does not wish to risk writing 'wikkednesse', lest he himself 'falle eft in swich dotage' (5–8)—that is to say, lest he himself foolishly remarries. It is interesting that Chaucer here recalls a phrase from the Wife of Bath, the first of several in the poem: 'To speke of who that is in marriage' (III(D) 3).

He opens his second stanza with a contrast between what he 'wil nat seyn' and what he 'dar seyn' (9–10), and he uses commonplaces, things that others have said, to exemplify both positions. However, what he will not say and what he dare say are similar, and concern marriage as a denial of freedom—a frequent Chaucerian topic. The 'cheyne / Of Sathanas, on which he gnaweth evere' (9–10) is of biblical origin, as found in Revelation 20: 2 or 2 Peter 2: 4 or Jude 6. But lines 11–12 appear to be based on some such proverb as 'He is a fool that goes at large and makes himself thrall' (Whiting F429), and lines 13–14, on the folly of preferring prison to freedom, may be paralleled elsewhere in Chaucer in connection with second marriages:

> Were I unbounden, also moot I thee,      *as I may prosper*
> I wolde nevere eft comen in the snare.   (*CT* IV(E) 1226–7)

It is a common enough concept, but the wording of these lines makes it likely that a sentence of John of Salisbury's on marriage in general and second marriages in particular may be the source: 'Quis enim ei compatiretur qui, semel solutus a vinculis, revolat ad cathenas?' [Who, truly, can have pity on that man who, once released from fetters, flies back to his chains?] (*Policraticus*, viii. 11).

In the third stanza the argument, briefly, turns back upon itself as Chaucer adduces St Paul's words in 1 Corinthians 7: 9: 'But if they cannot contain, let them marry: for it is better to marry than to burn.' But, in the comic fiction of his advice to Bukton, he sees marriage (as does St Paul in earnest) as simply the lesser of two evils, and he quickly turns the subject back to the servitude of marriage. The sentiments

> thou shal have sorwe on thy flessh, thy lyf,
> And ben thy wyves thral, as seyn these wise      *wise men*
>                                                  (19–20)

had been used earlier by the Wife of Bath, who determines to have a husband 'which shal be bothe my dettour and my thral' (III(D) 155–7), and she continues by elaborating on her 'power . . . Upon his propre body'. The idea of a husband as a 'wyves thral' is based on part of a Pauline verse dealing with reciprocity in marriage—'likewise also the husband hath not power of his own body, but the wife' (1 Corinthians 7: 4)—and the idea of marriage as a sorrow or tribulation to the flesh is from a little later in the same chapter, 'Nevertheless such shall have trouble in the flesh' (7: 28). The phrase 'as seyn these wise' suggests that Chaucer may think he is dealing with proverbial or sententious material, but since in the next line he refers to 'hooly writ' (21) it may be that St Paul is his only source here. The main point of this and the next line, however, is the contrast between 'hooly writ' and 'Experience': if Bukton cannot be persuaded by one, perhaps he will respond to the other. Chaucer appears to have in mind the Wife of Bath's opening words: 'Experience though noon auctoritee / Were in this world' (III(D) 1–2), based on the *Roman de la Rose*, 12,803–5. So being a prisoner 'in Frise' (22) comes within the category of experience, and it may be that Chaucer had in mind the expedition of August 1396—dangerous for those who went on it because of the Frieslanders' reputation for refusing to ransom their own soldiers if they were captured and of putting enemy prisoners to death. Friesland was a byword as a place of danger and discomfort. Deschamps, in ballade 977, has a speaker who says he has been a captive in Syria among the Saracens and implies that marriage is a worse bondage than that:

> J'ay demoure entre les Sarrasins,
> Esclave este en pays de Surie.

Perhaps Chaucer, if he knew Deschamps' ballade, simply substituted Friesland for Syria because of its contemporary relevance.

In the final stanza of this poem Chaucer advises Bukton that he should 'rede' the Wife of Bath on the subject of marriage, 'this matere that we have on honde' (28–30). In view of the number of ideas and actual phrases from that source which Chaucer reuses here, such a statement is unsurprising. It even suggests that Chaucer, in the fiction of the poem at least, had come to regard the *Wife of Bath's Prologue and Tale* as a repository of sententious wisdom, like proverbs or the Bible, on the subject of marriage. But most of the advice in this stanza, in a way which is consistent with the rest of the poem, is based on proverbs. Line 27, 'Unwys is he that kan no wel endure', is, in B. J. Whiting's view, proverbial (Whiting W134): this is the only instance given, but there are enough other proverbs close to it in sentiment to make the assumption reasonable—'Let well alone' (Tilley W260), 'Who finds himself well let him not stir' (Tilley W223), 'He is wise that when he is well can hold him so' (Tilley H512). Line 28 can be paralleled in a collection of proverbs dated about 1450, 'If thou be sykyr [secure] kepe thi place' (Whiting S297). And line 32 appears to be a version of 'Woe is a man that is bound' (Whiting W433), though the general shape of the sentiment is similar to what Chaucer had written in line 12 earlier. What Bukton made of all this advice is unknown; the equivocal, ironic tone of the poem leads us to believe that he was not expected to accept it uncritically. Whether the rather cynical misogyny which characterizes Chaucer's views on marriage as expressed here represents what he really felt is again something about which it is difficult to be confident, but it is worth remembering that after the death of his wife in 1387 Chaucer did not remarry.

It is fairly clear from the way in which the Wife of Bath is cited in this poem that Chaucer thought his work was of some contemporary importance, and the approving tributes from writers such as Deschamps, Usk, and Gower would, no doubt, have helped to persuade him of this. It is also clear that the preservation and transmission of his work was something that concerned him. In the final stanzas of *Troilus and Criseyde* he worries about the 'gret diversite / In Englissh and in writyng of our tonge', and prays to God that nobody should 'myswrite' or 'mysmetre' his book (v. 1793–8). It is this same concern for the accurate transmission of his text which lies behind the *Wordes Unto Adam*, a single rhyme-royal stanza extant in only one authoritative manuscript, Cambridge, Trinity College MS R. 3. 20, which belonged to John Shirley, who perhaps preserved the poem because he was himself a professional copyist:

> Adam scriveyn, if evere it thee befalle
> Boece or Troylus for to wryten newe,
> Under thy long lokkes thou most have the scalle,\*
> But after my makyng thow wryte more trewe;
> So ofte adaye I mot thy werk renewe,
> It to correcte and eke to rubbe and scrape,
> And al is thorugh thy negligence and rape.                    *haste*

A number of attempts have been made to identify 'Adam' among late fourteenth-century copyists—Adam Stedeman, Adam Acton, and Adam Pinckhurst have all been proposed—but none has been conclusive. Some scholars have interpreted the poem as alluding to the biblical Adam, who ruined God's creation, much as this copyist is accused of ruining what Chaucer had made. But the cues for this sort of reading do not seem to me to be present in the poem.

At its most important level the poem is a recognizable type of complaint—that of a creative literary artist about the transmitter of his art. That is why Chaucer insists so firmly on the distinction between his 'makyng'—that is, his status as the composer of original works—and Adam's function as 'scriveyn', whose duty it is to 'wryte' correctly, in the sense of copy accurately. Complaints of this sort are traditional in Western culture. In twelfth- and thirteenth-century Provence the *trobador* poets, in the *sirventes joglaresc*, criticize the *joglars* who perform their works. And, from the fifteenth century onwards, authors complain about the mistakes of printers. From classical times onwards copyists have been the subjects of outraged diatribes, and these continued into the Middle Ages. The Anglo-Norman Philippe de Thaon expresses fears for his works once they get into the hands of the incompetent, 'because often through the hands of bad copyists books are corrupted and therefore lost' (*Li Cumpoz*, 157–60). And Petrarch, in a famous letter to Boccaccio, complains about the difficulty of getting books copied quickly and accurately and about the general failings of scribes; 'tantum vel ignorantiae est vel inertiae vel contemptus' (such is their ignorance, their idleness and their arrogance) (*Epistulae de rebus senilium*, V. i). Chaucer is not quite as denunciatory as this. The slightly exaggerated irritation, the comically

---

\* *scalle*: a scaly skin-disease

inappropriate physical ill-will towards the copyist, common enough in many of these complaints, tend to mitigate the displeasure of the author. Perhaps part of the joke is that Adam might be called upon to copy words that are derogatory to him, just as a Provençal *joglar* might be asked to perform a *sirventes joglaresc* which insults him. But despite the hint of comedy, this is basically a manifestation of Chaucer's seriousness about his art: his 'makyng', he says, is to be respected in exact detail, and is important enough to warrant care and accuracy of a high order in its transmission.

On Chaucer's general debt to Boethius see B. L. Jefferson, *Chaucer and the Consolation of Philosophy* (Princeton, NJ, 1917). More specifically on these poems see Jane Chance, 'Chaucerian Irony in the Boethian Short Poems: The Dramatic Tension between Classical and Christian', *ChR* 20 (1986), 235–45.

For Scogan's use of *Gentilesse* in his *Moral Balade* see *Chaucerian and Other Pieces*, in Skeat (ed.), *Works*, vii. 237–44; and for Lydgate's see his *Minor Poems*, ed. MacCracken, ii. 822–8. On the intellectual background to its ideas see G. McGill Vogt, 'Gleanings for the History of a Sentiment: Generositas Virtus, Non Sanguis', *JEGP* 24 (1925), 102–25. For differing interpretations of the poem see Brusendorff, *Chaucer Tradition*, pp. 254–8; Howard H. Schless, 'Chaucer and Dante', in Dorothy Bethurum (ed.), *Critical Approaches to Medieval Literature* (New York, 1960), pp. 134–54, esp. 150–3; Pace and David (eds.), *Minor Poems*, pp. 67–76. On the heraldic dimension of 'stok' see Valerie Allen, 'The "Firste Stok" in Chaucer's *Gentilesse*: Barking up the Right Tree', *RES* 40 (1989), 531–7.

For *The Two Ways* see Clanvowe, *Works*, ed. Scattergood, pp. 57–80. For Trevet's commentary on Boethius's book ii, met. v see Minnis and Scott (eds.), *Medieval Literary Theory*, pp. 336–8. On the background to the ideas in *The Former Age* see Harry Levin, *The Myth of the Golden Age in the Renaissance* (Bloomington, Ind., 1969), esp. pp. 3–31. See also Pace and David (eds.), *Minor Poems*, pp. 91–101; John Norton Smith, 'Chaucer's *Etas Prima*', *MÆ* 32 (1963), 117–24; and A. V. C. Schmidt, 'Chaucer and the Golden Age', *Essays in Criticism*, 26 (1976), 99–115.

On *Lak of Stedfastnesse* see Pace and David (eds.), *Minor Poems*, pp. 73–89, for a survey of the scholarship. For the commonplace nature of the sentiments see J. E. Cross, 'The Old Swedish *Trohetsvisan* and Chaucer's *Lak of Stedfastnesse*—a Study in Mediaeval Genre', *Saga-Book of the Viking Society*, 16 (1965), 283–314, especially appendix B. For 'Verus Amor Expiravit' see *Analecta Hymnica*, ed. G. M. Dreves (Leipzig, 1886), p. 456 (the translation is mine). For the stanza from the Bannantyne MS see Skeat (ed.), *Minor Poems*, p. 367, where it is described as 'very poor stuff'. For John Ball's verses see Rossell Hope Robbins (ed.), *Historical Poems of the XIVth and XVth Centuries* (New York, 1959), pp. xlii and 54. For a more detailed version of the argument relating this poem to Richard II's prerogatives see V. J. Scattergood, 'Social and Political Issues in Chaucer: An Approach to *Lak of Stedfastnesse*', *ChR* 21 (1987), 469–75. For arguments for a later date see Haldeen Braddy, 'The Date of Chaucer's *Lak of Stedfastnesse*', *JEGP* 36 (1937), 481–90; and Norton Smith, 'Chaucer's *Etas Prima*', pp. 123–4. Recently Paul Strohm has argued for a period from September 1388 to May 1390 as an appropriate moment when Chaucer may have addressed the poem to Richard II; see *Hochon's Arrow*, pp. 57–74.

For a general survey of the scholarship on *Truth* see Pace and David (eds.), *Minor Poems*, pp. 49–65. For Horace see *Satires, Epistles, and Ars Poetica*, ed. and trans. H. R. Fairclough, Loeb Classical Library (Cambridge, Mass., 1926); and for Seneca see *Ad*

*Lucilium epistulae morales*, ed. and trans. R. M. Gummere, Loeb Classical Library (Cambridge, Mass., 1917). For Caxton's version of Chartier see *The Curial Made by Maystere Alain Chartier*, trans. William Caxton (1484), ed. F. J. Furnivall, EETS ES 54 (London, 1888). For Dunbar's anti-court satire see William Dunbar, *Poems*, ed. James Kinsley (Oxford, 1979), pp. 204–5; and for Wyatt's see *Collected Poems*, ed. Joost Daalder (London, 1975), pp. 100–4. For Edith Rickert's identification of the subject of the poem see 'Thou Vache', *MP* 11 (1914), 209–25. The present account of the poem is based on V. J. Scattergood, 'Chaucer's Curial Satire: The *Balade de Bon Conseyl*', *Hermathena*, 133 (1982), 29–45. For an attempt to relate the poem to iconographic and bestiary traditions see D. E. Lampe, 'The Truth of a "Vache": The Homely Homily of Chaucer's *Truth*', *Papers in Language and Literature*, 9 (1973), 211–14; and for arguments against this view see Alfred David, 'The Truth about Vache', *ChR* 11 (1977), 334–7.

On *Proverbs* generally see Pace and David (eds.), *Minor Poems*, pp. 195–8. For the Lydgate quotation see *The Siege of Thebes*, ed. A. Erdmann and E. Ekwall, EETS ES 108 and 125 (London, 1911–1930), i. 3 (lines 51–2); and for Metham see *Political, Religious and Love Poems*, ed. F. J. Furnivall, EETS OS 15 (London, 1903), p. 307. For an authoritative collection of Middle English proverbs see B. J. and H. W. Whiting, *Proverbs, Sentences, and Proverbial Phrases, From English Writings Mainly before 1500* (Cambridge, Mass., 1968).

On *Lenvoy de Chaucer a Bukton* generally see Pace and David (eds.), *Minor Poems*, pp. 139–48. The account of the poem here is based on V. J. Scattergood, '*Chaucer a Bukton* and Proverbs', *Nottingham Medieval Studies*, 31 (1987), 98–107. For the proverbs see Whiting and also Morris Palmer Tilley, *A Dictionary of the Proverbs in England in the Sixteenth and Seventeenth Centuries* (Ann Arbor, Mich., 1950). For the quotation from Bacon see *Essays* (Oxford, 1937), p. 5. On the quotation from John of Salisbury see J. S. P. Tatlock, 'Notes on Chaucer: Earlier or Minor Poems', *MLN* 29 (1914), 95–101; and on the habits of the Frieslanders see J. L. Lowes, 'The Date of the Envoy to Bukton', *MLN* 27 (1912), 45–8. For an analysis of the epistolary tone and the form of the poem see Norton Smith, *Chaucer*, pp. 221–5. For an interesting recent reading see Ruud, *Many a Song*, pp. 107–20.

On Chaucer's *Wordes Unto Adam* see Pace and David (eds.), *Minor Poems*, pp. 133–7. This account of the poem is based on V. J. Scattergood, 'The Jongleur, the Copyist, and the Printer: The Tradition of Chaucer's *Wordes Unto Adam, His Own Scriveyn*', in Keith Busby and Erik Kooper (eds.), *Courtly Literature: Culture and Context* (Amsterdam, 1990), pp. 499–508. For the quotation from Philipe de Thaon see his *Li Cumpoz*, ed. Eduard Mall (Strasbourg, 1873); Petrarch's *Epistulae de rebus senilium* can be found in *Opera* (Basel, 1581). For attempts to identify the subject of the poem see the correspondence in the (London) *TLS*, 3 May 1929, p. 383 (Ramona Bressie); 16 May 1929, p. 403 (J. M. Manly); and 13 June 1929, p. 474 (Bernard M. Wagner). For an attempt to identify 'Adam' with the biblical Adam see Russell A. Peck, 'Public Dreams and Private Myths: Perspective in Middle English Literature', *PMLA* 90 (1975), 461–8.

## Begging Poems

*Fortune; Lenvoy de Chaucer a Scogan; The Complaint of Chaucer to his Purse*

Though he came from a fairly wealthy family, Chaucer never seems to have possessed much property or to have enjoyed income from a landed estate. Instead, he depended on grants and annuities, which were, nevertheless, quite large, though sometimes, as in 1388, 1392, and 1399, he found himself in debt for relatively small amounts or found he needed to borrow money. So, though he held positions of responsibility and influence, like most royal servants he depended to some degree on the goodwill and favour of men better placed than he was. And, like other poets in the service of kings, such as Hoccleve and Dunbar, he sometimes used verse as a medium for requests for preferment or money.

Of his three begging poems *Fortune* is the most problematical: textually, it is very complicated, and was perhaps never properly finished or may be partially revised. It is a triple ballade with envoy, and is, like most of Chaucer's poems about adversity at court, heavily based on Boethius. The subtitle, 'ballades de visage sanz peinture', echoes the *Consolatio*, II, pr. i, where Philosophy tells Boethius, 'Thou hast now knowen and ateynt the doutous or double visage of thilke blynde goddesse Fortune. She, that yit covereth and wympleth hir to other folk, hath schewyd hir every del to the.' Fortune appears to the complainant ('pleyntef') in her true colours, and confronts him directly. Many of the ideas discussed in the poem derive from book II, especially pr. ii and iv; so too does the dialogic form. In pr. ii Philosophy undertakes to respond to Boethius's complaints 'usynge the wordes of Fortune', and here Fortune speaks on her own behalf. The argument of the poem is not particularly tidy. In places it twists back upon itself and becomes repetitive. But the three ballades are held together by a common theme which weaves in and out of the argument—true as opposed to false friendship—and the concluding envoy, though surprising, becomes on reflection logical and just.

The poem is quasi-legal in its process and in some of its language. The complainant opens with a statement of grievance: the 'wrecched worldes transmutacioun', the variability of earthly things, is governed by the 'errour' (= fickleness) of Fortune; but though he is injured because he lacks her favour, he vows to 'defye' her (1–8). His consolation takes a variety of forms. There are the essentially Stoic virtues of self-control and self-sufficiency (14–15), the example of the steadfastness of Socrates (17–22), cited by Reason in the *Roman de la Rose*, 5845–50 and 6887–90 as a man indifferent to good or bad fortune, and the knowledge of Fortune's true nature as a 'fals dissimular' (23), which serves to arm the complainant against her. He has also acquired the ability to distinguish who his friends are:

> Yit is me left the light of my resoun
> To knowen friend fro fo in thy mirour.　　　　　(9–10)

Fortune's reply is casuistical and self-justifying, but not entirely dismissive of the complainant's case. She points out that if he claims self-sufficiency and self-control, he really has only himself to blame if he feels miserable at her disfavour towards him (25–8). She says that he ought to be grateful for benefits received rather than grieving about their loss (29–30). She also adverts to the subject of friendship, reminding him that through adversity she has made clear to him the difference between true and false friends (33–4). And she consoles him in the second refrain that his 'beste frend' is still living (32 etc.). All these points are responses to his opening speech. Her main addition to the argument is that she has not behaved differently towards the complainant than towards the rest of humanity who live under her 'regne of variaunce' (45). She generalizes the argument in a way that will be important in the final ballade, pointing out in consolatory fashion that the logic of Fortune's mutability is not only that bad fortune may follow good but equally that good may follow bad (38–9). He needs both to understand the universality of the process in which he is involved and also to cultivate the virtues of steadfastness and patience, and wait for prosperity again.

That the complainant has not acquired these virtues and that he has difficulty thinking beyond his own personal case is clear from his opening words in the third ballade, where he speaks angrily and dismissively about false friends and about Fortune's ability to instruct (49–52). He consoles himself with the thought that the miserliness of his false friends may be a sign that Fortune means to destroy them, because it is a general rule that 'Wikke appetyt cometh ay before sykness' (55)—again a proverbial truth (cf. Whiting A154, G167). But she replies by defining the more important general rule by which she exists, that she has to be consistent in her 'brutelnesse' (63), and that she acts simply as an agent of God (65–7). In heaven there is 'sikerness', but on earth, until death, there is only 'resteles travayle' (69–71). This is the definitive late medieval answer, in transcendental Christian terms, to the complaint's grief. But having argued him down, Fortune then intercedes for him in the envoy:

> Princes, I prey you of your gentilesse
> Lat nat this man on me thus crye and pleyne,
> And I shal quyte you of your bisinesse      *requite*
> At my requeste, as three of you or tweyne,      *two*
> And but you list releve him of his peyne,
> Preyeth his beste frend of his noblesse
> That to som better estat he may atteyne.      (73–9)

The change of mind to asking that the complainant be given good fortune is not problematic, since its possibility had been signalled earlier;

but precisely what she asks on his behalf is puzzling. At issue appears to be money, suggested by words used earlier such as 'povre' (2), 'haboundaunce' (29), 'negardye' (53), and 'richesse' (53, 58), so behind the poem, perhaps, lurks the request for payment of some annuity or grant. The oddness of the wording 'as three of you or tweyne' in line 76 (which appears in only one manuscript) may be elucidated by reference to a Privy Council ordinance of 8 March 1390 which, in order to curb Richard II's extravagances, said that the king should not make gifts or grants without the consent of the dukes of Lancaster, Gloucester, and York (the king's uncles) and the chancellor, or any two of them. Fortune, therefore, appears to be asking on behalf of Chaucer, that the 'princes' on the Privy Council should either look after him themselves ('releve him of his peyne') or ask Richard II, his 'beste frend', to put him in some better position.

If this is what is meant, it has to be said that this is not a particularly direct begging poem. But *Lenvoy de Chaucer a Scogan* is even less so, though it shares many of *Fortune*'s ideas, particularly on friendship. The form of the poem—six stanzas of rhyme royal followed by an envoy— suggests that a double ballade might have been in Chaucer's mind, but the rhyming does not bear this out. And in structure and argument the poem is loose and digressive—perhaps deliberately so. It looks as though Chaucer is imitating the manner of the familiar letter. 'Envoy' of the title evidently means 'missive' or 'letter': the Cambridge, University Library MS Gg. 4. 27 version is actually headed 'Litera directa de Scogon per G.C.', and some of the more obvious gestures of the epistolary style are to be found—the naming of the recipient, and the 'Far-wel' formula at the end. There are those, however, who have suggested more precise relations. John Norton Smith holds that in this and the poem to Bukton Chaucer attempted to imitate the conversational style of the Horatian epistle (pp. 213–35), and supports this by arguing that Horace's *Satires*, II. i. 39–44, is the source of Chaucer's image of the unused pen rusting like a sword in its sheath—though it has to be remembered that some pen-holders could be worn on the belt and that the comparison may have been suggested because of that:

> Nay, Scogan, say not so, for I m'excuse—
> God helpe me so!—in no rym, douteles
> Ne thynke I never of slep to wake my muse,
> That rusteth in my shethe stille in pees (36–9)

But there are alternative suggestions for sources in Alan of Lille's *Anticlaudianus*, Prologue 3, and Ovid's *Tristia*, V. xii. 31 ff. And a number of French poems by Machaut and Deschamps have been suggested as possible models for the poem. However, none of these ideas has commanded general acceptance. This appears to be one of Chaucer's most inventive and original lyrics.

It begins in a vein of high irony as Chaucer explains the onset of a 'diluge of pestilence' (14)—evidently heavy rainstorms which coincided with a visitation of the plague as in 1391—as being the fault of Scogan because he had blasphemed against the gods on the subject of love and caused Venus to weep. He warns Scogan that the 'rebel word' (23) he had spoken may cause Cupid to lose interest in him and all those like him, including Chaucer, who are 'hoor and rounde of shap' (31), another allusion to his portliness, causing all their efforts in love to come to nothing. However, he hastens to assure Scogan that he is not personally interested in love any more: he does not wish to 'ryme and pleye' (35), as he did when he was young. He appears to be saying what he said in the envoy to the *Complaint of Venus*, that he is too old for love and for writing love-poetry. The envoy here, however, appears to shift the ground of the poem, though it does return to Scogan's defiance of Love in the final line:

> Scogan, that knelest at the stremes hed
> Of grace, of alle honour and worthynesse,
> In th'ende of which strem I am dul as ded,
> Forgete in solytarie wildernesse—
> Yet, Scogan, thenke on Tullius kyndenesse,              
> Mynne thy frend, there it may fructyfye!     *Remember*
> Far-wel, and loke thow never eft Love dyffye      *defy*
>                                    (43–9)

It is not immediately obvious how this relates to what has gone before, and scholars have puzzled as to what the threads might be which connect the disparate topics of this subtle and intriguing poem.

One way into the problem is provided by the allusion in the envoy to 'Tullius kyndenesse' (47), to which Chaucer draws Scogan's attention. Though some have suggested that it may be a reference to Tullius Hostilius, the legendary king of Rome, mentioned by the Wife of Bath (III(D) 1166–7), most have taken it to indicate Cicero's *De amicitia*. This was a well-known and widely available text: Dante speaks movingly of its importance to him in *Convivio*, ii. 13. But the circumstances in which it was read in the Middle Ages also provide grounds for thinking that the connection with Chaucer's poem may be closer and more complex than has commonly been supposed. The *De amicitia* was written in the summer of 44 BC shortly after the treatise on old age, the *De senectute*, to which it refers in i. 4. Both are dedicated to Cicero's friend Atticus, and both are in dialogue form: in each, the main speaker, respectively Laelius and Cato, is rather older than his listeners, who are asked to profit from his experience. So close was the connection between them thought to be that they were frequently copied together in the same manuscripts. Laurent de Premierfait translated both for Louis de Bourbon in about 1405, and Caxton translated and printed them together in 1481. And writers drawing on the authority of Cicero often quote them in close proximity. They were natural companion pieces: if a person read one, it is likely that he would also read the other.

Both of Cicero's treatises praise the subjects they treat—old age and friendship—but because both were written at a time of deep personal and political disappointment, both are in some sense consolatory: in true Stoic manner Cicero seeks through a contemplation of virtue to make the best of a situation which is by no means ideal. In both treatises, amongst other things, he speaks about the cooling of sexual passion in relation to old age and friendship. In one passage of the *De senectute* he refers to the complaint, frequently made by the old, about losing material pleasures and being neglected; but this, he says, is not invariably the case, particularly if they have good friends (iii. 7). And towards the end of the *De amicitia* he raises similar questions: the speaker talks of the friendships he had formed in his youth with older men, and in his old age with younger ones, but affirms that friends of the same age are best. And, he continues, friends kept over many years are to be preferred. He maintains that virtue or goodness of character is the basis of friendship, and seeks to define it in relation to love and the pursuing of material advantage:

> ex quo exardescit sive amor sive amicitia; utrumque
> enim ductum est ab amando; amare autem nihil est
> aliud nisi eum ipsum diligere, quem ames, nulla
> indigentia, nulla utilitate quaesita, quae tamen
> ipsa efflorescit ex amicitia, etiamsi tu eam
> minus secutus sis. (xxvii. 100)

[. . . from which virtue is kindled love or friendship; and each is derived from loving, and loving is nothing else but the feeling of esteem you have towards the person you love, without the requirement that any need should be satisfied or usefulness served. But usefulness does grow out of friendship, although you may not have sought it]

So a strain of idealism underlies the practical advice that the treatises give.

The themes raised here—the decline of sexuality, the value of old friendships, the possibility of advantage arising from friendship—are all close to the matter of Chaucer's poem. Chaucer talks of his and Scogan's age: they are both old and fat (31, 35). Neither of them are 'lykly folk in love to spede' (32): Scogan has given up his mistress because she did not respond to his 'dystresse' (18), and Chaucer feels that both he and his friend will, because of this, be divorced from the pains and the pleasures of love (28). Yet, in the midst of this discontinuity, the seriousness of which Chaucer mocks with his exaggerated cataclysmic opening about the breaking of heavenly statutes 'That creat were eternally to dure' (1–2), he stresses the continuity of the friendship between Scogan and himself: he addresses Scogan as 'frend' (29) before asking him to do something useful for him which will turn to advantage: 'Mynne thy frend, there it may fructyfye' (48). It has been suggested by R. T. Lenaghan that Chaucer is urging Scogan after his disappointment in love to concentrate on friendship, because 'love and friendship were antithetical terms of an old commonplace of school rhetoric, so the dialectical relationship of the two subjects must have been familiar' (p. 55). But this is not what Cicero said. He maintained that friendship derives from love: 'Amor, enim, ex quo amicitia nominata est' (viii. 26), he says, using etymology as a way of sustaining his argument, and that appears here to be the way Chaucer understood the relationship. So Scogan can quite logically be urged to continue his friendship with Chaucer and not to separate himself from love: 'loke thow never eft Love deffye' (49). Whether Chaucer's wording in this final stanza is taken from Cicero's Latin or from the *Roman de la Rose*, 4693 ff., is difficult to say. What is clear, however, is that the nexus of ideas is Ciceronian: the reference to 'Tullius kyndenesse' belatedly gives a coherence to the poem.

It also seems clear to me that *Lenvoy a Scogan* is a begging poem. As the glosses to all three manuscripts testify, Scogan is 'at the stremes hed / Of grace', which indicates Windsor and the royal court, while Chaucer is forgotten 'in solytarie wildernesse' at the end of the Thames in Greenwich (43–6). The well-connected Henry Scogan is Chaucer's friend at court, who is asked, in the name of their friendship, to remember him ('mynne') in such a way that it will materially benefit him. And a particular urgency is given to the request by the mention to 'Michelmesse' (19)—which is another of the threads which hold the poem together.

The feast of St Michael and All Angels, or Michaelmas, occurs on 29 September, one of the 'quarter days', and was an important date in the medieval calendar. After 1362 the Quarter Sessions Courts met on each of the quarter days and the eight days following. At Michaelmas, guild expenses fell due, rents had to be paid, and accounts settled. Most importantly for courtiers and civil servants such as Chaucer and Scogan, Michaelmas was the time when annuities were renewed, and the first instalment (usually of two) was paid. In the autumn of 1407, the indigent Thomas Hoccleve, like Chaucer and Scogan a royal servant, wrote a poem on behalf of himself and his fellow clerks at the Office of the Privy Seal to the sub-treasurer Sir Henry Somer, punning on Somer's name and asking for the 'hervest' of their Michaelmas pay, without which they would fear 'stormes'—which on one level refers to the equinoctial gales associated with this time of the year, and on another to adversity associated with a lack of money, trouble with creditors, and a generally impoverished life-style (*Minor Poems*, p. xiii). In Chaucer's poem, the autumnal storms, 'this diluge of pestilence' (14), are the result of Scogan's proud and rash action at Michaelmas, when he not only ended a relationship with a mistress but incurred the wrath of a superior—the God of Love. And, much as in Alceste's speech in the *Legend of Good Women*, F Prol. 341–408, the language Chaucer uses to express the power of the God of Love has a broad relevance to the political relationship between medieval secular lords and their servants:

> he wol no longer be thy lord (24)
> Than shal we for oure labour have no mede. *reward*
> (33)

Chaucer appears to be saying, through the metaphors associated with love, that Michaelmas is a particularly sensitive date for people like Scogan and himself, and not a time to be altering relationships or provoking the displeasure of those on whom one depends.

It was the non-payment, because the government had changed with the deposition of Richard II, of the Michaelmas instalment of his annuity, which fell due on 29 September 1399, that apparently provoked Chaucer's last poem. Although Henry IV confirmed the grant of £20 for life which had been given to Chaucer by Richard II, and though he awarded Chaucer an additional grant of 40 marks 'because of good service', the records reveal that Chaucer received only part of this money: a partial back payment of £10 in February 1400 and another £5 the following June. Chaucer did not live to benefit from Henry IV's generosity, and died with money owing to him from the previous reign. So in the autumn of 1399 and in early 1400 he may well have been short of money.

The opening lines of the *Complaint of Chaucer to his Purse* define its methodology:

> To yow, my purse, and to noon other wight *creature*
> Complyne I, for ye be my lady dere. (1–2)

This appears to be based on the first two lines of a perfectly orthodox amorous complaint attributed to the Chatelain de Courcy:

> A vos, amant, plus qu'a nule altre gent
> Est bien raisons que ma dolor complaigne.

[To you, love, rather than to any other person, it is right that my sorrow should complain.]

And Chaucer continues to travesty a genre he had taken seriously earlier in his career. The language of the amorous complaint is applied to money: he comments on the 'blisful soun' and the colour of gold 'lyke the sonne bryght' (9–10); he affirms that money can guide his heart (12), become the light of his life (15), and, through mercy, save him from death (5–6). Partly, of course, this is a joke against himself: the love poet succumbs to avarice, the vice of old age. And in seven of the thirteen extant manuscripts the medieval reader would have been encouraged to see the poem as a witty non-specific complaint about impecuniousness, a typical piece of Chaucerian self-mockery, since these manuscripts have only the through-rhymed rhyme-royal stanzas, and lack the envoy. But the five-line envoy, present in the other copies, makes it clear that this is a begging poem, or, at least, that it has been made into one:

> O conquerour of Brutes Albyon,
> Which that by lyne and free eleccion
> Been verray kyng, this song to yow I sende,          *true*
> And ye, that mowen alle oure harmes amende,          *may*
> Have mynde upon my supplicacion.                     (22–6)

This flatters Henry IV by referring to some of the claims to the throne of England made by him or on his behalf—conquest, lineage, and parliamentary election (*collaudatio*); it reminds him of his promise to right the wrongs of the country ('oure harmes'), and makes it clear that Chaucer regards his own petition ('my supplicacion') as part of what is wrong and something to be attended to. This is a sad end to a career spent in the service of kings, but not an unspirited one.

On the problematic textual and literary background to *Fortune* see Pace and David (eds.), *Minor Poems*, pp. 103–9, for a summary of the scholarship; and particularly John Norton Smith, 'Chaucer's Boethius and *Fortune*', *Reading Medieval Studies*, 2 (1976), 63–76. The date was first suggested by J. B. Bilderbeck, 'Chaucer's "Fortune"'. *Athenaeum*, pt. 1 (18, Jan. 1902), 82–3.

On *Lenvoy de Chaucer a Scogan* see Pace and David (eds.), *Minor Poems*, pp. 149–60, for a survey of the scholarship. For Cicero see *Cato Maior de senectute, Laelius de amicitia*, ed. P. Venini (Torino, 1958); the translations are mine. For Hoccleve see *The Minor Poems*, ed. F. J. Furnivall and I. Gollancz, rev. by Jerome Mitchell and A. I. Doyle, EETS ES 61 and 73 (Oxford, rev. reprint 1970). This account of the poem is based on V. J. Scattergood, 'Old Age, Love, and Friendship in Chaucer's *Envoy to Scogan*', *Nottingham Medieval Studies*, 35 (1991), 92–101. For Norton Smith's sensitive reading see *Chaucer*, pp. 213–35; and for R. T. Lenaghan's valuable comments see 'Chaucer's *Envoy to Scogan*: The Uses of Literary Convention', *ChR* 10 (1975), 46–61. For the argument that the reference in the poem is to Tullius Hostilius see T. M. Phipps, 'Chaucer's Tullius', *MLN* 58 (1943), 108–9.

For a survey of the scholarship on *The Complaint of Chaucer to his Purse* see Pace and David (eds.), *Minor Poems*, pp. 121–32. For Chaucer's tedious and only partially successful attempts to obtain the money due to him see Sumner J. Ferris, 'The Date of Chaucer's Final Annuity and "The Complaint to his Empty Purse"', *MP* 65 (1967), 45–52; and also Andrew J. Finnel, 'The Poet as Sunday Man: "The Complaint of Chaucer to his Purse"', *ChR* 8 (1973), 147–58. For the political background to the envoy see Paul Strohm, 'Saving the Appearances: Chaucer's *Purse* and the Fabrication of the Lancastrian Claim', in Hanawalt (ed.), *Chaucer's England*, pp. 21–40; repr. in Strohm, *Hochon's Arrow*, pp. 75–94.

# Appendix: Chaucer's Language
## (by Jeremy J. Smith)

The problem faced by the student of Chaucer's language is a historical one. Chaucer wrote and spoke in a variety of English far removed from those of the present day; and, since language is above all a social practice, the poet's lexis, syntax, pronunciation, and spelling can be understood only within the historical context in which he lived. Furthermore, an understanding of the linguistic choices available to Chaucer is a prerequisite for appreciation of the choices the poet actually made and in which his style consists. These insights from stylistics and from what has been called 'socio-historical linguistics' are central to what follows.

With the possible—if still controversial—exception of the *Equatorie of the Planetis*, we have, as far as is known, no piece of connected writing in the hand of Geoffrey Chaucer. Chaucer's language has been mediated to us by scribes, whose activities need further interpretation if we wish readily to comprehend the poet's intended message. The linguistic intervention of scribes is largely at the level of orthography, so it is perhaps logical, in a study of this kind, to begin with a brief history of English spelling in the medieval period.

At the time Chaucer was writing, the history of written English had reached a fascinating transitional stage. How it had reached this position is well known, and has to do with the social standing of the English language at the time. During the late Anglo-Saxon period, before the Norman Conquest of 1066, the English language was seen as appropriate for most governmental and literary purposes, and one variety—Late West Saxon—appears to have achieved the status of a standardized written language. Latin was the only rival in prestige to English in Anglo-Saxon England, and appears to have been comparatively restricted in use. After the Norman Conquest, this situation changed. Latin seems to have become more widespread as the language of record and of literature, and the native language of the new rulers was Norman French (which later developed into Anglo-Norman). English became a debased vernacular, not suited for discourse on matters of fundamental importance. As a result, no variety of English possessed any special prestige, and when English *was* written, it reflected the natural variation of the spoken mode more closely than it ever has since. This state of affairs gradually changed during the course of the Middle Ages, but it was not until *c*.1450 that a new written standard, this time based upon contemporary London English, began to emerge. In short, between the Norman Conquest and that time, Middle English (as the language during this period is known) was, in Barbara Strang's words, '*par excellence*, the dialectal phase of English' (p. 224).

This variation manifests itself in the spelling systems adopted by medieval scribes. Middle English (ME), unlike present-day English (PDE), had no model orthography, and the scribal spellings of this period are extremely various, conditioned and constrained by a whole range of factors. It is, for instance, quite common to find variant spellings for the same word written by the same scribe. Thus in these lines from London, British Library MS Harley 7334 of the *Canterbury Tales* it will be observed that the scribe has two spellings for 'first':

> And at a knight than wol I first bygynne
> A Knight þer was and þat a worþy man
> That from þe tyme þat he ferst bigan
> To ryden out he louede Chyualrye
> (MS reading: cf. 1(A)42–5)

To many readers, such confusions are merely a nuisance. However, it is in the study of the varied orthographies of Chaucerian manuscripts that some of the most important recent work on the poet's language has been done. In 1983 M. L. Samuels re-examined the spelling systems of two early copies of the *Canterbury Tales*, the well-known 'Hengwrt' and 'Ellesmere' manuscripts, in the light of recent paleographical studies by A. I. Doyle and M. B. Parkes. Doyle and Parkes had shown that both manuscripts were copied by one scribe, who had also copied a fragment of *Troilus and Criseyde* and a portion of a manuscript of Gower's *Confessio Amantis*. Samuels showed that this scribe, in general, 'translated' the forms of his exemplars into those of his own spelling system, but that, for some items, he displayed what has been called 'constrained' behaviour; that is, the influence of his exemplar caused him to choose one from a whole range of orthographic variables available to him in his repertoire of spellings. Through analysis of the constrained forms in the Chaucer manuscripts by this scribe, Samuels established that the copyist's exemplar must have been written in a language very like that found in the *Equatorie of the Planetis* and in 'layers' of language appearing in important manuscripts of the *Boece* and the *Treatise on the Astrolabe*. The suggestion is that this spelling system is that of Chaucer himself.

Whatever the precise details of Chaucer's orthographic system, however, in its essentials his written language must have been very like that found not only in the Hengwrt and Ellesmere manuscripts but also in a number of other manuscripts produced in the London area towards the end of the fourteenth century. Although there is no evidence that this kind of language was written outside London in Chaucer's time, it can nevertheless be seen as one of the initial stages in the movement towards a written standard, based upon London English, which was finally established in the late fifteenth century. The evidence for this is plain: although this form of English often employs forms which are unfamiliar to us—such as *nat* for PDE 'not', *swich(e)* for PDE 'such', *hir(e)* for PDE 'their', *thise* for PDE 'these', etc.—it is certainly much easier for a modern student to read than, say, the language of a Middle English text from the North-west Midlands such as *Sir Gawain and the Green Knight*. A comparison will make the difference clear. Here are descriptions of two knights. The first is Chaucer's, from the General Prologue to the *Canterbury Tales*:

> A Knyght ther was, and that a worthy man,
> That fro the tyme that he first began
> To riden out, he loved chivalrie,
> Trouthe and honour, fredom and curteisie.
> Ful worthy was he in his lordes werre,
> And therto hade he riden, no man ferre,      *further*
> As wel in cristendom as in hethenesse,
> And evere honoured for his worthynesse.    (I(A) 43–50)

The spelling is a little odd to us; some of the courtly connotations of *trouthe* and *curteisie* for the medieval audience are perhaps lost on an untutored modern student; and the word order presents certain problems of translation. But, in general, this text offers few difficulties for the present-day reader. Here, for comparative purposes, is the *Gawain* poet's description of the Green Knight:

> Þer hales in at þe halle dor an aghlich mayster;    *rushed: terrible man*
> On þe most on þe molde on mesure hyghe:    *the very biggest on earth*
> Fro þe swyre to þe swange so sware and so þik,    *neck: waist: squarely built*
> And his lyndes and his lymes so longe and so grete,    *loins*
> Half etayn in erde I hope þat he were,    *half-giant; earth; believe*
> Bot mon most I algate mynn hym to bene,    *biggest of men: declare*
> And þat þe myriest in his muckel þat my3t ride:    *handsomest for his size*
> For of bak and of brest
> al were his bodi sturne,    *although his body was strong*
> Both his wombe and his wast were worthily smale.    *belly*
> And alle his fetures fol3ande, in forme þat he hade, ful clene.    *in keeping*
>         (Fitt I, 136–46)

Such language may fairly be characterized as difficult for the modern reader; and the reason for its being more difficult than that of Chaucer is simple. The dialect of *Sir Gawain and the Green Knight* is an example of those linguistic systems which had no *written* successors in the history of English, and it is thus visually unfamiliar to us. By contrast, as has already been indicated, Chaucer's language is within the tradition which ultimately produced the standard written English we use today. In such circumstances, it is not surprising that Chaucer's works were widely read in the century after his death, during which standardization of the written mode took place. The only hint of a posthumous audience before the nineteenth century for the author of *Sir Gawain*—other than a possible cryptic reference in John Paston I's list of books—is an orally transmitted ballad.

Even so, although Chaucerian English lies within the tradition which ultimately produced standard written English, it is plain that full standardization had not yet been achieved. The English which Chaucer used was much more heterogeneous than would be acceptable in modern written language. Like other varieties of Middle English, Chaucer's written language reflects the variousness of the spoken mode—specifically the variousness of London English, the dialect in which he spoke and wrote. Mainly because of large-scale immigration to the capital during the fourteenth century, London was a linguistic melting-pot at this time.

The variation which was available to Chaucer is perhaps best demonstrated initially through an examination of his rhyming practice, for it is in rhymes that subsequent scribal intervention is most limited. Chaucer was certainly interested in rhymes, and complains of their scarcity in English:

> And eke to me it ys a gret penaunce,
> Syth rym in Englissh hath such skarsete,
> To folowe word by word the curiosite        *fine workmanship*
> Of Graunson, flour of hem that make in Fraunce.   *compose poetry*
> (*Complaint of Venus*, 79–82)

Although some of Chaucer's rhymes are undoubtedly imperfect, the indications are that most are true rhymes and are, therefore, an important piece of evidence for establishing Chaucerian pronunciation. Most notably, the rhymes clearly show that the 'long vowels' of Chaucer's language had not yet undergone the process of raising and diphthongization known as the 'Great Vowel Shift', which took place in the late fifteenth and early sixteenth centuries, and which resulted in the system of spelling English long vowels becoming separated from the corresponding systems in other European languages. Thus Chaucer rhymes *pris* 'price' and *flour-de-lys* 'fleur-de-lis' in the General Prologue to the *Canterbury Tales* (I(A) 237–8), where the latter word still retains in present-day English its older pronunciation because of its obvious French connections, but the former, although also a loan-word from French, has undergone the processes of the Shift.

Rhymes also show that Chaucer admitted a degree of variation into his spoken repertoire. A good example of such variation is to be found in the range of forms he has for words containing vowels corresponding to an Old English (= West Saxon) *y* (pronounced, in Anglo-Saxon times, /y(:)/, like the *u* in present-day French *tu*). Old English (OE) *y*-words appear with *i/y* (which, confusingly, are interchangeable in Middle English), *e*, and *u* in Chaucer's rhymes. For instance, in the following lines from the *Miller's Tale*, Chaucer rhymes *kisse* (from OE *cyssan*) with *misse* (from OE *missan*):

> My love-longynge, for yet I shal nat mysse
> That at the leeste wey I shal hire kisse.
>
> (I(A) 3679–80)

But in the *Squire's Tale* the following lines appear:

> That muchel drynke and labour wolde han reste:
> And with a galpyng mouth hem alle he keste . . .     *yawning*
> (V(F) 349–50)

where *keste* (OE *cyste*, 3rd pret. sing. of *cyssan*) rhymes with *reste* (from OE *rest*). The usual form in Chaucer's rhymes for PDE 'merry' is, as the modern pronunciation may suggest, *merye* with *e* (from OE *myrige*); but it is noticeable that Chaucer allows a form with *u*, *murie*, occasionally in rhyme: for example, with *Mercurie* in the *Merchant's Tale*, IV(E) 1733. Such variables were available to Chaucer because, in late fourteenth-century London, many OE *y*-words had alternative reflexes in *i*, *e*, and *u*, reflecting the close relationship which London English had with Midland, South-eastern, and South-western dialects respectively. In standard written English today, most OE *y*-words have *i*, but *merry*, *busy*, and *bury*, the latter two with their lack of correlation between spelling and pronunciation, are relics of the confused situation in medieval London.

Of course, this variation had its limits, and J. D. Burnley has indicated that Chaucer selects variables which are rarer—if not unknown—in contemporary London English in circumstances where rhymes must have been hard to find: 'It is more noticeable . . . that Chaucer is compelled to seek unusual rhyming variants more often in poems like the *Parliament of Fowls* or *Troilus and Criseyde*, where the stanza form requires more than a pair of rhyming words' (p. 128). Most famously, these limits are demonstrated by Chaucer's well-known perceptiveness about

Northerners' speech in his linguistic characterization of the two students in the *Reeve's Tale*.

Even so, it may be taken as established that Chaucer's pronunciation admits into literary usage a degree of variation that would not be acceptable in many quarters today. When we turn to the poet's morphology and syntax, we find a similar willingness to allow a wide range of variation. In this context, knowledge of Chaucer's metrical practices enables us to determine his usage, rather than that of the manuscripts in which his poetry survives.

Chaucer's prosody depends on a steady alternation between unstressed and stressed syllables; it is for this reason that it is referred to as 'stress-syllabic' poetry (as distinct from the 'pure-stress' tradition of Old English and Middle English alliterative verse). His metrical norm, against which deviations are foregrounded for stylistic reasons, may be illustrated by lines such as

$$x \quad / \quad x \quad / \quad x \quad / \quad x \quad / \quad x$$
That brak her mast and made it falle
(*Book of the Duchess*, 71)

with four stresses, or, with five

$$x \quad / x \quad / \quad x \quad / x \quad / \quad x \quad / x$$
Thy litel wit was thilke tyme aslepe
(*Legend of Good Women*, F Prol. 547)

At the beginning of his poetic career, Chaucer used the four-stress line, as in the example above from the *Book of the Duchess*; this metrical type is usual in earlier Middle English poetry (as, in, for example, the late twelfth-century poem the *Owl and the Nightingale*). Its origins lie in a blend of the Old English pure-stress alliterative tradition, which demanded four stresses in each line, and the octosyllabic line (depending on quantitative distinctions) of much medieval French verse. Many linguists have observed that the four-stress metrical unit, often with a medial pause (or 'caesura'), is the most common underlying rhythm in English popular verse, and that it seems to correspond to a pattern of psychologically salient sense units in universal grammar (as revealed, for instance, in children's word-games). There is a tendency in such metrical structures for clause or phrase boundaries to occur at the ends of lines; in combination with end-rhyme, the effect (called 'end-stopping') can be somewhat soporific for the reader, and it is hard for the poet to avoid.

In his maturer poetry, however, Chaucer used the five-stress line, derived from the decasyllabic lines of contemporary Italian and French verse. He seems to have been the first English poet to use such a line, which subsequently became the metrical unit favoured by authors as diverse as Shakespeare, Milton, Pope, Wordsworth, and Keats. A major reason for the adoption of this line is that it offers the poet an easy way of overcoming end-stopping by accommodating the four-stress sense unit within a five-stress measure. The difference between the two metrical forms may be illustrated by two passages from Chaucer's poetry, the first showing the earlier, four-stress measure with end-stopping; the second, the later, five-stress form where end-stopping is avoided. It will be observed that in the latter phrase and clause boundaries do not generally correspond with the ends of lines, whereas in the former the correlation is much more common.

> But at my gynnynge, trusteth wel,
> I wol make invocacion,
> With special devocion,
> Unto the god of slep anoon,
> That duelleth in a cave of stoon . . .
>
> (*House of Fame*, 66–70)

> Glorye and honour, Virgil Mantoan,
> Be to thy name! and I shal, as I can,
> Folwe thy lanterne, as thow gost byforn,
> How Eneas to Dido was forsworn.
> In thyn Eneyde and Naso wol I take
> The tenor, and the grete effectes make.
>
> (*Legend of Good Women*, 924–9)

Just as Chaucer could exploit phonological variables for the sake of rhyme, so he could exploit morphological variables for the sake of metre. We might exemplify this variation by examining his use of the infinitive of the verb. Basically, Chaucer's forms for the infinitive can occur either with or without a final -*n*—for example, *speke* or *speken*. The opportunities for metrical variation which this gave the poet are obvious. We might compare the following lines from *Troilus and Criseyde*:

(1) And for to speke of her in special     (i. 981)
(2) But for to speken of her yen clere     (v. 815)

Both lines are regular metrically, but the regularity depends on the variant forms of the infinitive being available. In the first example the final -*e* in *speke* is elided; if *speken* had been used, an extra unstressed syllable would have interrupted the regular stress pattern. If Chaucer had used *speke* in the second instance, then elision with *of* would have taken place, an unstressed syllable would have been lost, and the line would have become irregular. Similar metrical considerations seem to have affected Chaucer's choice of other variables—for example, *comth/cometh* (3rd pers. sing.):

(3) Whan maistrie comth, the God of Love, anon

> (*Franklin's Tale*, V(F) 765)

(4) Of which ther cometh muchel harm and wo

> (*Manciple's Tale*, IX(H) 202)

—or *bounden/ybounden* (past participle)

(5) For which thou art ybounden as a knyght

> (*Knight's Tale*, I(A) 1149)

(6) That man is bounden to his observaunce

> (*Knight's Tale*, I(A) 1316)

*Ybounden*, a compromise between Southern Middle English *ybounde* and Midland *bounden*, is particularly interesting, because it shows Chaucer exploiting the dialect resources available to him. Metrically, only the compromise form could work in (5) above.

Detecting such possibilities for exploitation of variables in syntax is a more problematic matter, given the close relationship between syntax and individual style. However, it does seem probable that metrical constraints are, for instance, behind Chaucer's employment of the *gan* periphrasis, beside simple preterite forms, to express past tense. This is a controversial matter, since Chaucer seems to have used *gan* for a variety of purposes, 'extending [reports J. Kerkhof] from that of a verb meaning *to begin* to the function of a mere stop-gap, only used for metrical reasons' (p. 30). Nevertheless, it is fairly plain that in, for instance, the following line:

> This Palamon gan knytte his browes tweye
>
> (*Knight's Tale*, I(A) 1128)

*gan knytte* is selected instead of *knytted* on metrical grounds, to maintain stress on the lexical element in the verb phrase.

When we turn to Chaucer's lexis, we can perceive a similar pattern of exploitation of linguistic resource. The position here is complicated by the multilingual atmosphere in which Chaucer lived, where his friend Gower could write poetry in Latin and French as well as in English. In this context, the relationship between English and French in the Middle Ages is important. By the end of the fourteenth century, it appears that French had ceased to be the usual language of the governing classes of the country, but that it still retained cultural prestige. As a result, those wishing to reinforce the importance of their social origins or wishing to be included among such people appear to have taken over a large number of French words into their English, with the aim of emphasizing their social difference from those not privileged with French culture. Chaucer himself seems to have been no exception—at least according to the

'Chaucerians' of the fifteenth century who, among other things, praised him for augmenting and (in Caxton's phrase) 'ornating' a language which, until his appearance, was 'rude speche and incongrue'. As Chaucer's Scots disciple William Dunbar put it.

> O reverend Chaucere, rose of rethoris all,
> As in oure tong ane flour imperiall
> That raise in Britane, evir quho redis rycht,
> Thou beris of makaris the tryumph riall;                  *poets*
> Thy fresch anamalit termes celicall
> This mater coud illumynit have full brycht:
> Was thou noucht of oure Inglisch all the lycht,
> Surmounting eviry tong terrestriall
> Alls fer as Mayes morow dois mydnycht?
> (*Golden Targe*, 253–61)

*Fresch anamalit termes celicall* ('freshly enamelled, heavenly diction') suggests that Chaucer's diction was 'new' to the fifteenth century; and the evidence from Scots writers like Dunbar and from their English contemporaries such as John Lydgate is that Chaucer was seen as drawing these 'fresch' words from prestigious languages like French and Latin.

The study of Chaucer's vocabulary, however, is not simply a matter of statistical assessment of the proportion of French words in the poet's lexis. Understanding why Chaucer chose particular words depends more on the connotations of those words in their various contexts than on their individual etymologies.

Establishing these contexts can be comparatively straightforward. For instance, the following lines show Chaucer's vocabulary at its grandest:

> O sonnes lief, O Joves doughter deere,
> Plesance of love, O goodly debonaire,
> In gentil hertes ay redy to repaire!                  *find a home*
> O veray cause of heele and of gladnesse,
> Iheryed be thy myght and this goodnesse!
> (*Troilus and Criseyde*, iii. 3–7)

Some of the vocabulary of this passage (*plesance, debonaire, gentil, repaire, veray cause*) is derived from French; but other elements (*lief, goodly, hertes, heele, gladnesse, iheryed, myght, goodnesse*) are native. The important thing here is not so much the diverse etymologies, but the associations of the words, established here by the solemn context—formal, polite, abstract. As N. Davis has pointed out, *iheryed* seems to have been archaic in Chaucer's time; such archaism may be seen as appropriate in the context of heightened language, just as nowadays we may address God in prayer with the archaic 'Thou'. On the other hand, Alisoun in the *Miller's Tale* is plainly informal, impolite, and concrete in her intentions, even if she uses a French loan-word like *blame*:

> 'Go from the wyndow, Jakke fool,' she sayde:
> 'As help me God, it wol nat be "com pa me,"
> I love another—and elles I were to blame—
> Wel bet than thee, by Jhesu, Absolon,
> Go forth thy wey, or I wol caste a ston,
> And lat me slepe, a twenty devel wey!'
>
> (*Miller's Tale*, I(A) 3708–13)

The contrast between a decorated, polysyllabic, and rhetorical 'high' style and a plain, monosyllabic, 'low' style could not be made more clearly.

The difficulty with Chaucer's vocabulary for the modern reader does not lie so much in these obvious cases, but in more subtle situations where the connotations can be more easily missed. Comparison with modern French and German practice may enable us to perceive the Chaucerian distinction between *thou* (informal, familiar) and *ye* (formal, polite), and thus make it possible for us to enjoy one of the contrasts between Alisoun's speech to Absolon just quoted and Absolon's earlier request to his beloved:

> 'What do ye, hony-comb, sweete Alisoun,
> My faire bryd, my sweete cynamome?
> Awaketh, lemman myn, and speketh to me!
> Wel litel thynken ye upon my wo,
> That for youre love I swete ther I go.'
>
> (*Miller's Tale*, I(A) 3698–702)

However, the Middle English semantic distinction between *shal* and *wol* is probably lost on a modern audience. In present-day English, both *will* and *shall* are used to express prediction and volition, *shall* being used rather rarely and largely interchangeably with *will* and almost always with first-person subjects. In Chaucerian English, *shal* and *wol* could both be used for prediction, but also had distinctive modal uses, *shal* implying obligation, *wol* volition. J. D. Burnley has drawn attention to lines such as these:

> Werk al by conseil and thou shalt nat rewe,
> And if thou werken wolt by good conseil,
> I undertake, withouten mast or seyl
> Yet shal I saven hire and thee and me.
>
> (*Miller's Tale*, I(A) 3530–3)

In Nicholas's words here Burnley finds 'an instructive variation between *shal* and *wol*, in which the distinction between inevitability and volitional colouring is very clear' (p. 45). In other words, the carpenter, if he *will* act according to the dictates of Nicholas, *is obliged* not to regret it; and if he *will* act thus, Nicholas *must* save them all from 'Nowelis flood'.

Knowledge of the meaning of *shal* and *wol* in Chaucerian English has come about through historical and contextual study, and some of Chaucer's most important lexical effects become clear only after comparison with other contemporary texts, both within and outside the poet's own works. The former is demonstrated by the poet's creation of a particular set of associations for words, peculiar to himself, through his use of them in different contexts. Examples include his repeated use of variations on the theme of 'pitee renneth soone in gentil herte', apparently unironic in the *Knight's Tale* but heavily loaded in the *Merchant's Tale*. Such devices of 'textual coherence' may even include repeated rhyme-words in different contexts; for instance, the lines

> But sodeynly she saugh a sighte queynte,
> For right anon oon of the fires queynte
>
> (*Knight's Tale*, I(A) 2333–4)

and

> As clerkes ben ful subtile and ful queynte;
> And prively he caughte hire by the queynte
>
> (*Miller's Tale*, I(A) 3275–6)

which use the device of rhyming words with different meaning and the same form, taken in the context of Chaucer's fondness for puns and word-play, help establish a network of connections—it would be too crude to call them 'ironic'—forward and backward within the text. Comparison with non-Chaucerian texts can be equally illuminating. In this context, a useful study remains E. T. Donaldson's 'The Idiom of Popular Poetry in the *Miller's Tale*'. Through comparison of the vocabulary of the *Miller's Tale* (and *Sir Thopas*) with that of a number of pre-Chaucerian Middle English lyrics and romances, Donaldson was able to show that, in using hackneyed expressions like *hende*, *gent*, etc., Chaucer parodied what Donaldson called 'popular' poetry. *Hende* ('noble') is recorded in the *Middle English Dictionary* as appearing in such unironic texts asserting courtly virtues as *Floris and Blancheflour*, *William of Palerne*, and the Alliterative *Morte Arthure*; thus, to assign to the libidinous scholar Nicholas the repeated epithet *hende*, as Chaucer does, is to make him the mock-hero of a mock-romance. Donaldson's term 'popular', though, begs questions as to the audiences of Middle English romances which are hard to answer. It is perhaps safer to follow Burnley, who indicates that words like *hende* were 'once used in courtly contexts, but [had in Chaucer's time and circle] . . . declined into socially-ironic use' (p. 142; see also pp. 139–40). It is therefore unsurprising that, elsewhere in the Chaucer canon, it appears unironically only in the English translation of the *Roman de la Rose*, a work whose authorship has been disputed, but, if in part by Chaucer, was probably composed at the beginning of his poetic career.

Such mockery of an older tradition of English poetry reaches its height in Chaucer's parody of romance, *Sir Thopas*. It is important, however, in gauging the force of Chaucer's attack on 'popular' poetry, to be aware of how much he drew upon English traditions. D. S. Brewer has drawn attention to how much the language of the earlier Middle English romances has left its mark on Chaucer's poetry. For instance, in the following lines at the beginning of the *Book of the Duchess*, Chaucer uses a series of set formulas, all of which are common in the rhyming romances of an earlier generation (e.g. those which survive in the Auchinleck manuscript, such as *Sir Orfeo*):

> I have gret wonder, be this lyght,
> How that I lyve, for day ne nyght
> I may nat slepe wel nygh noght;
> I have so many an ydel thoght,
> Purely for defaute of slep,
> That, by my trouthe, I take no kep
> Of nothing, how hyt cometh or gooth,
> Ne me nys nothing leef nor looth.
>
> (*Book of the Duchess*, 1–8)

Phrases like *be this lyght, for day ne nyght, wel nygh noght* carry little or no lexical meaning; they are remnants of an oral tradition in which built-in redundancy, time to assimilate information that had just been recited, was necessary for an audience's understanding. These lines from the beginning of the *Book of the Duchess* may, in subject-matter, be derived from the beginning of Jean Froissart's *Paradys d'Amours* (cf. pp. 104–5), but they look back to an English heritage which Chaucer never overtly rejected, even if he may have mocked it. Moreover, such phraseology seems to have had an additional, pragmatic function. Since it would have been familiar to its contemporary readership, its appearance emphasized the intimacy between author and audience characteristic of Chaucer's time, whereby the poet sought to include, in a collective act of poetic creation, those who first encountered his work.

It can be argued that Chaucer's use of English in general has to be seen in the light of this close relationship between author and audience. Literary students, perhaps influenced by Shelley's opinion of poets as 'unacknowledged legislators' for the world, often have a rather high opinion of the influence of authors on society; but it does not seem appropriate in the light of our present-day knowledge of Middle English to refer to Chaucer, as some older critics used to do, as in some sense the 'father' of the English language. Despite Caxton's opinion as cited above (p. 521), what Chaucer did—as we have seen—was to exploit to the full the possibilities of linguistic variation available to him, which he must have come across through social intercourse with his contemporaries—no more, and no less, than any other great poet. Chaucer's English is the English of contemporary London; and London English, after his death, gave him a continuing audience.

On Middle English in general see A. C. Baugh and T. Cable, *A History of the English Language*, 3rd edn. (London, 1978), ch. 7 (a good basic account); G. Bourcier, *An Introduction to the History of the English Language* trans. C. Clark (Cheltenham, 1981), pt. 2 (includes excellent bibliographies): J. A. Burrow and T. Turville-Petre, *A Book of Middle English* (Oxford, 1992) (an outstanding introduction); C. Millward, *A Biography of the English Language* (Fort Worth, Tex., 1989), ch. 6 (an up-to-date historical survey); B. M. H. Strang, *A History of English* (London, 1970), ch. 3 and 4 (rather advanced).

On Chaucer's English, J. D. Burnley, *A Guide to Chaucer's Language* (London, 1983), is an important and valuable study. Norman Davis, 'Chaucer and Fourteenth-Century English', in D. S. Brewer (ed.), *Writers and their Background: Geoffrey Chaucer* (London, 1974), pp. 58–84, is a useful introduction, as is his section on 'Language and Versification' in *Riverside Chaucer*, pp. xxv–xli. N. Davis *et al.*, *A Chaucer Glossary* (Oxford, 1979), is an essential reference work. R. W. V. Elliott, *Chaucer's English* (London, 1974) is especially good on Chaucer's vocabulary. H. Kökeritz, *A Guide to Chaucer's Pronunciation* (New York, 1961; repr. Toronto, 1978), is a useful pamphlet-sized account, although the reader used to the symbolic conventions of the International Phonetic Association will find Kökeritz's notation rather unsatisfactory. A. O. Sandved, *Introduction to Chaucerian English* (Cambridge, 1985), is a good description of Chaucer's phonology and morphology, with valuable introductory comments, but is avowedly more for the philologist than the literary student. D. G. Scragg, *A History of English Spelling* (Manchester, 1974), is a useful outline history of the development of orthography.

On the status of English during the Middle English period and its relationship to the other languages of Britain see M. T. Clanchy, *From Memory to Written Record* (London, 1979), esp. ch. 6. A short account of the situation of Middle English, with full references, appears in the introduction to M. L. Samuels and J. J. Smith, *The English of Chaucer* (Aberdeen, 1988), pp. 1–6; see also J. J. Smith, 'The Use of English: Language Contact, Dialect Variation and Written Standardisation during the Middle English Period', in T. W. Machan and C. T. Scott (eds.), *English in its Social Contexts* (Oxford, 1992), pp. 47–68. For the role of French vocabulary in signalling social class see Burnley, *Guide*, esp. pp. 178–9.

Good general accounts of the development of standard written English are to be found in Strang, *History*, pp. 161–5, and Bourcier, *Introduction*, ch. 14. Both accounts are derived from the seminal article by M. L. Samuels, 'Some Applications of Middle English Dialectology', *English Studies*, 44 (1963), 81–94; repr. with corrections in M. Laing (ed.), *Middle English Dialectology* (Aberdeen, 1989), pp. 64–80. See also A. O. Sandved, 'Prolegomena to a Renewed Study of the Rise of Standard English', in M. Benskin and M. L. Samuels (eds.), *So meny people longages and tonges: Philological*

*Essays in Scots and Mediaeval English presented to Angus McIntosh* (Edinburgh, 1981), pp. 31–42. Samuels, 'Chaucer's Spelling', appears in D. Gray and E. Stanley (eds.), *Middle English Studies Presented to Norman Davis* (Oxford, 1983), pp. 17–37; repr. in Samuels and Smith, *English of Chaucer*, pp. 23–37. The work of A. I. Doyle and M. B. Parkes is to be found in their 'The Production of Copies of the *Canterbury Tales* and *Confessio Amantis* in the Early Fifteenth Century', in M. B. Parkes and A. G. Watson (eds.), *Medieval Scribes, Manuscripts and Libraries: Essays Presented to N. R. Ker* (London, 1978), pp. 163–210. On the language of the Ellesmere manuscript in its fifteenth-century context see J. J. Smith, 'The Language of the Ellesmere Manuscript', in D. Woodward (ed.), *Essays on the Ellesmere Manuscript of the 'Canterbury Tales'* (San Marino, Calif., forthcoming).

On the question of the linguistic relationship between scribes and their exemplars, see M. Benskin and M. Laing, 'Translations and *Mischsprachen* in Middle English Manuscripts', in Benskin and Samuels (eds.), *So meny people*, pp. 55–106.

The passage from *Sir Gawain and the Green Knight* is cited from the edition of J. R. R. Tolkien and E. V. Gordon, rev. N. Davis (Oxford, 1967).

On the attitude of Middle English poets to rhyme see E. J. Dobson, *English Pronunciation 1500–1700*, 2nd edn. (Oxford, 1968), p. 613. For Chaucer's awareness of contemporary varieties of Middle English see J. R. R. Tolkien, 'Chaucer as a Philologist', *Transactions of the Philological Society* (1934), 1–70; see also N. F. Blake, 'The Northernisms in *The Reeve's Tale*', *Lore and Language*, 3 (1979), 1–8; C. Clark, 'Another Late-Fourteenth-Century Case of Dialect Awareness', *English Studies*, 62 (1981), 504–5, and J. J. Smith, 'The Great Vowel Shift in the North of England, and Some Forms in Chaucer's *Reeve's Tale*', *NM* (forthcoming). Burnley's work on variation in London English appears in his *Guide*: the quotation is from p. 128. On the Great Vowel Shift see J. J. Smith, 'Dialectal Variation in Late Middle English and the Actuation of the Great Vowel Shift', *NM*, 94 (1993), 259–77 and references cited therein.

The most sensible account of the debate about Chaucer's metre is T. F. Mustanoja, 'Chaucer's Prosody', in Rowland (ed.), *Companion to Chaucer Studies*, pp. 58–84. Special points are dealt with by M. L. Samuels, 'Chaucerian Final -*e*', *Notes and Queries*, 217 (1972), 445–8; repr. in Samuels and Smith, *English of Chaucer*, pp. 7–12, and by J. D. Burnley, 'Inflexion in Chaucer's Adjectives', *NM* 83 (1982), 169–77. On metrical theory in general see D. Attridge, *The Rhythms of English Poetry* (London, 1982). Chaucer's use of the *gan* construction is discussed by J. Kerkhof, *Studies in the Language of Geoffrey Chaucer* (Leiden, 1966). See also H. M. Smyser, 'Chaucer's Use of *Gin* and *Do*', *Speculum*, 42 (1967), 68–83, and Burnley, *Guide*, p. 53. On Chaucerian syntax and its relationship to style see Burnley, *Guide, passim*; ch. 4 is especially important. I have not covered Chaucer's prose usage here: for this see I. A. Gordon, *The Movement of English Prose* (London, 1966), esp. pp. 53–4.

Caxton's words are to be found in the Proem to his second edition of *The Canterbury Tales* (1484). The quotation from Dunbar's *Golden Targe* is taken from Dunbar, *Poems*, ed. Kinsley.

On Chaucer's vocabulary in general see Davis, 'Chaucer and Fourteenth-Century English', and Elliott, *Chaucer's English*. On the three levels of rhetoric as described by Geoffrey of Vinsauf see Burnley, *Guide*, esp. pp. 199–200.

On 'shall' and 'will' in Chaucer's language see Burnley, *Guide*, p. 45. PDE usage seems to have emerged from an older pragmatic distinction; the sense of obligation connoted by 'shall' made it peremptory for second- and third-person use, and thus potentially impolite, whereas this problem did not arise in the first person. This point is made by a number of eighteenth-century prescriptive grammarians. On the use of 'shall' and 'will' in PDE, see R. Quirk *et al.*, *A Comprehensive Grammar of the English Language* (London, 1985), pp. 229–31.

For variations on the theme of 'pitee renneth soone in gentil herte' see *Knight's Tale*, I(A) 1761; *Man of Law's Tale*, II(B) 660; *Merchant's Tale*, IV(E) 1986; *Squire's Tale* V(F) 479; and *LGW* 503. See also E. T. Donaldson, 'The Effect of *The Merchant's Tale*', in *Speaking of Chaucer* (London, 1970), pp. 30–45. For 'textual coherence' in Chaucer see Burnley, *Guide*, ch. 4 and *passim*. For Chaucer's word-play see Burnley, *Guide, passim*; see also P. F. Baum, 'Chaucer's Puns', *PMLA* 71 (1956), 225–46, and J. A. Burrow, 'Four Notes on Chaucer's *Sir Thopas*', in his *Essays on Medieval Literature* (Oxford, 1984), pp. 60–78. General and detailed comment on the literary effect of Chaucer's style is found in Cooper, *OGC: CT*, *passim*, and Windeatt, *OGC: T&C*, esp. pp. 314–59 and references cited therein.

Donaldson's article 'The Idiom of Popular Poetry in the *Miller's Tale*', appears in *Speaking of Chaucer*, pp. 13–29. Epithets are also applied to the carpenter (*sely*) and Absolon (*joly*), though the latter, significantly, takes over the former's epithet at I(A) 3744. See also G. Cooper, '"Sely John" in the "legende" of *The Miller's Tale*', *JEGP* 79 (1980), 1–12. See also Helen Cooper's discussion of the *Miller's Tale* in *OGC: CT*.

On the context in which Middle English romances were read see J. D. Hirsh, '*Havelok* 2933: A Problem in Medieval Literary History', *NM* 78 (1977), 339–49.

Burnley's reference to *hende* appears in his *Guide*, p. 142.

D. S. Brewer's discussion of Chaucer's use of English vernacular traditions appears in 'Chaucer's Poetic Style', in Boitani and Mann (eds.), *Chaucer Companion*, pp. 227–42.

# BIBLIOGRAPHY

This Bibliography excludes editions of Chaucer's poems and of facsimiles of manuscripts containing the Shorter Poems, which are listed on pp. 6–7 above.

ACART, JEAN, *La Prise Amoureuse*, ed. E. Hoepffner, Gesellschaft für romanische Literatur, 22 (Dresden, 1910).

ADAMS, ROBERT, *Strains of Discord: Studies in Literary Openness* (Ithaca, NY, 1958).

AERS, DAVID, *Chaucer*, New Readings Series (Brighton, 1986).

—— 'Chaucer's *Book of the Duchess*: An Art to Consume Art', *Durham University Journal*, 69 (1976–7), 201–5.

—— *Community, Gender and Individual Identity. English Writing 1360–1430*, (London and New York, 1988).

—— 'Masculine Identity in the Courtly Community: The Self Loving in *Troilus and Criseyde*', in idem, *Community, Gender*, pp. 117–52.

—— 'The *Parliament of Fowls*: Authority, the Knower and the Known', *ChR* 16 (1981), 1–17.

AGRIPPA, HENRICUS CORNELIUS, *A Treatise of the Nobilitie and exellencye of woman kynde, translated out of Latine into englysshe by Dauid Clapam*, Thomas Bertheleti typis impress. (London, 1542).

AIKEN, PAULINE, 'Chaucer's *Legend of Cleopatra* and the *Speculum Historiale*', *Speculum*, 13 (1938), 232–6.

AELRED OF RIEVAULX, *Spiritual Friendship*, trans. Mary Eugenia Laker, Cistercian Fathers Series, 5 (Kalamazoo, Mich., 1974).

ALAN OF LILLE, *Complaint of Nature*, trans. Douglas M. Moffat (New Haven, Conn., 1908; repr. Hamden, Conn., 1972).

—— *De planctu naturae*, ed. N. M. Häring, in *Studi Medievali*, 3rd ser. 19/2 (1978), 797–879.

—— *Plaint of Nature*, trans. J. J. Sheridan, Pontifical Institute of Mediaeval Studies: Mediaeval Sources in Translation, 26 (Toronto, 1980).

ALLEN, JUDSON B., *The Ethical Poetic of the Later Middle Ages* (Toronto, 1982).

—— and MORITZ, T. A., *A Distinction of Stories: The Medieval Unity of Chaucer's Fair Chain of Narratives for Canterbury* (Columbus, Oh., 1981).

ALLEN, PETER L., 'Reading Chaucer's Good Women', *ChR* 21 (1987), 419–34.

ALLEN, ROBERT J., 'A Recurring Motif in Chaucer's *House of Fame*', *JEGP* 55 (1956), 393–405.

ALLEN, VALERIE, 'The "Firste Stok" in Chaucer's *Gentilesse*: Barking up the Right Tree', *RES* 40 (1989), 531–7.

AMES, RUTH M., 'The Feminist Connections of Chaucer's *Legend of Good Women*', in J. N. Wasserman and R. J. Blanch (eds.), *Chaucer in the Eighties* (Syracuse, NY, 1986), pp. 57–74.

*Analecta Hymnica*, ed. G. M. Dreves (Leipzig, 1886).

ANDERSON, DAVID, *Before the 'Knight's Tale': Imitation of Classical Epic in Boccaccio's 'Teseida'* (Philadelphia, 1988).

ANDERSON, W. S., 'The "Heroides"', in J. W. Binns (ed.), *Ovid* (London and Boston, 1973), pp. 49–83.

ANDREAS CAPELLANUS, *De Amore*, ed. and trans. P. G. Walsh, *Andreas Capellanus on Love* (London, 1982).

—— *The Art of Courtly Love by Andreas Capellanus*, trans. J. J. Parry (New York, 1941; repr. 1959).

AQUINAS, ST THOMAS, *Disputed Questions on Truth*, trans. J. V. McGlynn (Chicago, 1963).

—— *Opera omnia* (Parma, 1852–72).

—— *Summa theologiae*, Blackfriars edn. (London and New York, 1964–76).

ARIÈS, PHILIPPE, *The Hour of our Death*, trans. Helen Weaver (1981; repr. Harmondsworth, 1983).

ARISTOTLE, *Basic Works*, trans. R. McKeon (New York, 1941).

ARMITAGE-SMITH, SYDNEY, *John of Gaunt* (London, 1905).

—— (ed.), *John of Gaunt's Register*, Camden Third Series, 20–1 (London, 1911).

ATTRIDGE, D., *The Rhythms of English Poetry* (London, 1982).

AUGUSTINE, ST, *The City of God*, trans. John Healey, ed. R. V. G. Tasker, with an introduction by Sir E. Barker (London and New York, 1945).

—— *Confessions*, trans. R. S. Pine-Coffin (Harmondsworth, 1961).

AVERROES, *Middle Commentary on Aristotle's 'Poetics'*, trans. C. E. Butterworth (Princeton, NJ, 1986).

BACON, FRANCIS, *Essays* (Oxford, 1937).

BADEL, P.-Y., *Le Roman de la Rose au XIVe siècle* (Geneva, 1980).

BAIRD, JOSEPH L., and KANE, JOHN R. (trans.), *La Querelle de la Rose: Letters and Documents*, North Carolina Studies in the Romance Languages and Literatures (Chapel Hill, NC, 1978).

BAKER, DONALD, 'Recent Interpretations of the *House of Fame*: A New Suggestion', *Studies in English* (University of Mississippi), 1 (1960), 97–104.

BAKHTIN, MIKHAIL, *The Dialogic Imagination: Four Essays*, ed. Michael Holquist, trans. C. Emerson and M. Holquist (Austin, Tex., 1981).

—— *Rabelais and his World*, trans. Hélène Iswolsky (Bloomington, Ind., 1984).

BARNEY, STEPHEN A., 'Chaucer's Lists', in Benson and Wenzel (eds.), *Wisdom of Poetry*, pp. 189–223.

BARRATT, ALEXANDRA, '*The Flower and the Leaf* and *The Assembly of Ladies*: Is there a (Sexual) Difference?', *Philological Quarterly*, 66 (1987), 1–24.

—— (ed.), *Women's Writing in Middle English* (Harlow, 1992).

BARRY, PETER (ed.), *Issues in Contemporary Critical Theory* (London, 1987).

BARTHES, ROLAND, 'The Death of the Author', in *The Rustle of Language*, trans. Richard Howard (Oxford, 1986), pp. 49–55.

—— *The Pleasure of the Text* (London, 1976).

—— *Roland Barthes by Roland Barthes*, trans. Richard Howard (London, 1977).

BARTHOLOMEW THE ENGLISHMAN, *On the Properties of Things*, trans. John Trevisa, ed. M. C. Seymour *et al.* (Oxford, 1975).

BASWELL, CHRISTOPHER, 'The Medieval Allegorization of the *Aeneid*: MS Cambridge, Peterhouse 158', *Traditio*, 41 (1985), 181–237.

BATES, CATHERINE, *The Rhetoric of Courtship in Elizabethan Language and Literature* (Cambridge, 1992).

BATESON, F. W., Editorial Appendix, *Essays in Criticism*, 11 (1962), 255–63.

—— *Essays in Critical Dissent* (London, 1972).

BAUGH, A. C., and CABLE, T., *A History of the English Language*, 3rd edn. (London, 1978).

BAUM, PAULL F., 'Chaucer's "Glorious Legende"', *MLN* 60 (1945), 377–81.

—— 'Chaucer's Puns', *PMLA* 71 (1956), 225–46.

—— *Chaucer's Verse* (Durham, NC, 1961).

BEER, GILLIAN, 'Representing Women: Re-presenting the Past', in Catherine Belsey and Jane Moore (eds.), *The Feminist Reader: Essays in Gender and the Politics of Literary Criticism* (Basingstoke and London, 1989), pp. 63–80.

BEICHNER, PAUL E., 'Non Alleluia Ructare', *MS* 18 (1956), 135–44.

BELL, SUSAN GROAG, 'Christine de Pizan (1364–1430): Humanism and the Problem of a Studious Woman', *Feminist Studies* (1976), 173–84.

BENNETT, J. A. W., 'Chaucer, Dante and Boccaccio', in Boitani (ed.), *Italian Trecento*, pp. 89–113.

—— *Chaucer's Book of Fame* (Oxford, 1986).

—— 'Gower's "Honeste Love"', in John Lawlor (ed.), *Patterns of Love and Courtesy* (London, 1966), pp. 107–21; revised reprint in *The Humane Medievalist*, ed. Boitani, pp. 49–66.

—— *The Humane Medievalist and Other Essays*, ed. P. Boitani (Rome, 1982).

—— *The 'Parliament of Foules': An Interpretation* (Oxford, 1957).

—— 'Some Second Thoughts on *The Parlement of Foules*', in E. Vasta and A. P. Thundy (eds.), *Chaucerian Problems and Perspectives. Essays Presented to Paul E. Beichner* (Notre Dame, Ind., and London, 1979), pp. 132–46.

BENNETT, MICHAEL, 'The Court of Richard II and the Promotion of Literature', in Hanawalt (ed.), *Chaucer's England*, pp. 3–20.

BENOÎT DE SAINTE-MAURE, *Roman de Troie*, ed. Léopold Constans (Paris, 1904–12).

BENSKIN, M., AND LAING, M., 'Transactions and *Mischsprachen* in Middle English Manuscripts', in M. Benskin and M. L. Samuels (eds.), *So meny people longages and tonges: Philological Essays in Scots and Medieval English presented to Angus McIntosh* (Edinburgh, 1981), pp. 55–106.

BENSON, LARRY D., 'The "Love Tydynges" in Chaucer's *House of Fame*', in J. N. Wasserman and R. J. Blanch (eds.), *Chaucer in the Eighties* (Syracuse, NY, 1986), pp. 3–22.

—— 'The Occasion of *The Parliament of Fowls*', in Benson and Wenzel (eds.), *Wisdom of Poetry*, pp. 123–44.

—— and WENZEL, SIEGFRIED (eds.), *The Wisdom of Poetry* (Kalamazoo, Mich., 1982).

BENSON, PAMELA J., *The Invention of the Renaissance Woman* (University Park, Pa., 1992).

BENTON, JOHN F., *Culture, Power and Personality in Medieval France*, ed. Thomas N. Bisson (London and Rio Grande, Oh., 1991).

BERNARD SILVESTER, *Cosmographia*, trans. Winthrop Wetherbee (New York and London, 1973).

BERNARD SILVESTER (?), *The Commentary on the First Six Books of the 'Aeneid' of Vergil commonly attributed to Bernardus Silvestris*, ed. J. W. Jones and E. F. Jones (Lincoln, Nebr., and London, 1977); trans. E. G. Schreiber and T. E. Maresca (Lincoln, Nebr., and London, 1979).

BERNE, ERIC, *Games People Play: The Psychology of Human Relationships* (London, 1968).

BERRY, REGINALD, 'Chaucer's Eagle and the Element Air', *UTQ* 43 (1974), 285–6.

BERSUIRE, PIERRE, *Reductorium morale, liber xv: Ovidius moralizatus, cap. i, De formis figurisque deorum*, ed. J. Engels, Werkmateriaal 3 (Utrecht, 1966).

BETHEL, J. P., 'The Influence of Dante on Chaucer's Thought and Expression' (Ph.D. diss., Harvard University, 1927).

BEVINGTON, DAVID, 'The Obtuse Narrator in Chaucer's *House of Fame*', *Speculum*, 36 (1961), 288–98.

BILDERBECK, J. B., 'Chaucer's "Fortune"', *Athenaeum*, pt. 1 (18 Jan. 1902), 82–3.

BILLER, PETER, 'Marriage Patterns and Women's Lives: A Sketch of a Pastoral Geography', in P. J. P. Goldberg (ed.), *Woman is a Worthy Wight: Women in English Society c.1200–1500* (Stroud, Gloucestershire, 1992), pp. 60–107.

BIRNEY, EARLE, 'The Beginnings of Chaucer's Irony', *PMLA* 54 (1939), 637–55.

BLAKE, N. F., 'Geoffrey Chaucer: The Critics and the Canon', *Archiv*, 221 (1984), 65–79.

—— 'The Northernisms in *The Reeve's Tale*', *Lore and Language*, 3 (1979), 1–8.

—— 'The Textual Tradition of *The Book of the Duchess*', *English Studies*, 62 (1981), 237–48.

—— (ed.), *The Cambridge History of the English Language*, vol. 2: 1066–1476 (Cambridge, 1992).

BLAMIRES, ALCUIN (ed.), *Woman Defamed and Woman Defended: An Anthology of Medieval Texts* (Oxford, 1992).

BLAND, C. R., *The Teaching of Grammar in Late Medieval England: An Edition, with Commentary, of Oxford, Lincoln College MS Lat. 130* (East Lansing, Mich., 1992).

BLOCH, R. HOWARD, *Medieval Misogyny and the Invention of Western Romantic Love* (Chicago and London, 1991).

BLOOMFIELD, MORTON W., 'Chaucer's Sense of History', repr. in *idem. Essays and Explorations* (Cambridge, Mass., 1970), pp. 12–26.

—— (ed.), *Allegory, Myth and Symbol* (Cambridge, Mass., 1981).

BOASE, ROGER, *The Origin and Meaning of Courtly Love* (Manchester, 1977).

BOCCACCIO, GIOVANNI, *Concerning Famous Women*, trans. Guido A. Guarino (London, 1964).

—— *Decameron*, trans. G. H. McWilliam (Harmondsworth, 1972).

—— *Teseida*, trans. Bernadette Marie McCoy (New York, 1974).

—— *Tutte le Opere*, gen. ed. V. Branca (Milan, 1964– ).

BOETHIUS, ANICIUS MANLIUS SEVERINUS, *The Consolation of Philosophy*, trans. V. E. Watts (Harmondsworth, 1969).

—— *The Theological Tractates and 'The Consolation of Philosophy'*, ed. and trans. H. F. Stewart, E. K. Rand, and S. J. Tester (Cambridge, Mass., and London, 1973).

BOETHIUS OF DACIA, *On the Supreme Good, On the Eternity of the World, On Dreams*, trans. John F. Wippel, Medieval Sources in Translation, 30 (Toronto, 1987).

—— *Opera. Opuscula De aeternitate mundi, De summo bono, De somniis*, ed. N. M. G. Green-Pedersen, Corpus Philosophorum Danicorum Medii Aevi, 6/2 (Copenhagen, 1976).

BOFFEY, JULIA, 'The Lyrics in Chaucer's Longer Poems', *Poetica*, 37 (1993), 15–37.

—— 'Women Authors and Women's Literacy', in Meale (ed.), *Women and Literature*, pp. 158–82.

BOITANI, PIERO, *Chaucer and Boccaccio*, Medium Ævum Monographs, NS 8 (Oxford, 1977).

—— *Chaucer and the Imaginary World of Fame* (Cambridge, 1984).

—— 'Chaucer's Labyrinth: Fourteenth-Century Literature and Language', *ChR* 17 (1982), 197–220.

—— *English Medieval Narrative in the Thirteenth and Fourteenth Centuries*, trans. J. K. Hall (Cambridge, 1982).

—— 'Old Books Brought to Life in Dreams: The *Book of the Duchess*, the *House of Fame*, the *Parliament of Fowls*', in Boitani and Mann (eds.), *Cambridge Chaucer Companion*, pp. 39–57.

—— 'Style, Iconography and Narrative: The Lesson of the *Teseida*', in Boitani (ed.), *Italian Trecento*, pp. 185–99.

—— 'What Dante Meant to Chaucer', in Boitani (ed.), *Italian Trecento*, pp. 115–39.

—— (ed.), *Chaucer and the Italian Trecento* (Cambridge, 1983).

—— and MANN, JILL (eds.), *The Cambridge Chaucer Companion* (Cambridge, 1986).

BONAVENTURE, ST, *Itinerarium mentis*, in *Opera omnia* (Quaracchi, 1882–1902), v. 293–313.

*The Book of Margery Kempe*, ed. S. B. Meech, EETS OS 212 (London, 1940).

*The Book of the Knight of La Tour-Landry, translated from the Original French into English in the Reign of Henry VI*, rev. edn. by Thomas Wright, EETS OS 33 (London, 1906).

BOOSE, LYNDA E., 'The Family in Shakespeare Studies; or—Studies in the Family of Shakespeareans; or—The Politics of Politics', *Renaissance Quarterly*, 40 (1987), 707–42.

BORGES, JORGE LUIS, 'The Library of Babel', in *idem*, *Labyrinths*, ed. D. A. Yates and J. E. Irby (Harmondsworth; repr. 1981), pp. 78–86.

BORNSTEIN, DIANE, 'Courtly Love', in Joseph R. Strayer (ed.), *The Dictionary of the Middle Ages* (New York, 1983), iii. 668–74.

BØRRESEN, KARI ELISABETH, *Subordination and Equivalence: The Nature and Role of Woman in Augustine and Thomas Aquinas*, trans. C. H. Talbot (Washington, DC, 1981).

BOSWELL, JOHN, *Christianity, Social Tolerance, and Homosexuality: Gay People in Western Europe from the Beginning of the Christian Era to the Fourteenth Century* (Chicago, 1980).

BOTTERILL, STEVEN, ' "Quae non licet homini loqui": The Ineffability of Mystical Experience in *Paradiso I* and the *Epistle to Can Grande*', *MLR* 83 (1988), 332–41.

BOURCIER, G., *An Introduction to the History of the English Language*, trans. C. Clark (Cheltenham, 1981).

BOWDEN, BETSY, 'The Art of Courtly Copulation', *Medievalia et Humanistica*, 9 (1979), 67–85.

BRADDY, HALDEEN, *Chaucer and the French Poet Graunson* (Port Washington, NY, 1968).

—— 'The Date of Chaucer's *Lak of Steadfastnesse*', *JEGP* 36 (1937), 481–90.

BRASWELL, M. F., 'Architectural Portraiture in Chaucer's *House of Fame*', *JMRS* 11 (1981), 101–12.

BREWER, DEREK S., *Chaucer*, 3rd edn. (London, 1973).

—— *Chaucer and his World* (London, 1978).

—— *Chaucer: The Poet as Storyteller* (London, 1984).

—— 'Chaucer's Poetic Style', in Boitani and Mann (eds.), *Chaucer Companion*, pp. 227–42.

—— 'Chaucer's Venuses', in Juliette Dor (ed.), *A Wyf Ther Was: Proceedings of the Conference in Honour of Paule Mertens-Fonck* (Liège, 1992), pp. 30–40.

—— 'The Genre of *The Parliament of Fowls*', in *idem*, *Poet as Storyteller*, pp. 1–7.

—— 'The Ideal of Feminine Beauty in Medieval Literature, Especially the Harley Lyrics, Chaucer,. and some Elizabethans', in *idem*, *Tradition and Innovation*, pp. 30–45.

—— 'Love and Marriage in Chaucer's Poetry', *MLR* 43 (1954), 461–4.

—— 'Orality and Literacy in Chaucer', in Willi Erzgräber and Sabine Volk (eds.), *Mündlichkeit und Schriftlichkeit im englischen Mittelalter* (Tübingen, 1988), pp. 85–119.

—— 'The Relationship of Chaucer to the English and European Traditions', in *idem*, *Poet as Storyteller*, pp. 8–36.

—— *Tradition and Innovation in Chaucer* (Basingstoke and London, 1982).

BREWER, DEREK S., (ed.) *Chaucer: The Critical Heritage* (London, 1978).

BRINK, JEAN R., HOROWITZ, MARYANNE C., and COUDERT, ALLISON P. (eds.), *Playing with Gender: A Renaissance Pursuit* (Urbana, Ill., and Chicago, 1991).

BRONSON, BERTRAND H., '*The Book of the Duchess* Re-opened', *PMLA* 67 (1952), 863–81; repr. in Edward Wagenknecht (ed.), *Chaucer: Modern Essays in Criticism* (New York, 1959), pp. 271–94.

—— 'Chaucer's *Hous of Fame*: Another Hypothesis', *University of California Publications in English*, 3 (1934), 171–92.

BROOKE, CHRISTOPHER N. L., *The Medieval Idea of Marriage* (Oxford, 1989).

BROWN, EMERSON, 'Priapus and the *Parlement of Foulys*', *SP* 72 (1975), 258–74.

BROWNLEE, KEVIN, 'Discourses of the Self: Christine de Pizan and the *Roman de la Rose*', in *idem* and Sylvia Huot (eds.), *Rethinking the 'Romance of the Rose': Text, Image, Reception* (Philadelphia, 1992), pp. 234–61.

—— *Poetic Identity in Guillaume de Machaut* (Madison, Wis., 1984).

BRUSENDORFF, AAGE, *The Chaucer Tradition* (Oxford, 1905).

BULLOUGH, VERN L., 'Medieval Medical and Scientific Views of Women', *Viator*, 4 (1973), 485–501.

BUNDY, M. W., *The Theory of Imagination in Classical and Medieval Thought* (Urbana, Ill., 1927).

BURGH, BENET, *see Paruus Cato.*

BURLIN, ROBERT B., *Chaucerian Fiction* (Princeton, NJ, 1977).

BURNLEY, J. D., *A Guide to Chaucer's Language* (London, 1983).

—— '*Fine Amor*: Its Meaning and Context', *RES* NS 3 (1980), 129–49.

—— 'Inflexion in Chaucer's Adjectives', *NM* 83 (1982), 169–77.

BURNS, E. JANE, *Bodytalk: When Women Speak in Old French Literature* (Philadelphia, 1993).

—— and Krueger, Roberta L. (eds.), 'Courtly Ideology and Woman's Place in Medieval French Literature', special issue of *Romance Notes*, 25/3 (Spring 1985).

BURROW, JOHN A., *The Ages of Man: A Study in Medieval Writing and Thought* (Oxford, 1986).

—— 'Four Notes on Chaucer's *Sir Thopas*', in *idem*, *Essays on Medieval Literature* (Oxford, 1984), pp. 60–78.

—— *Medieval Writers and their Work* (Oxford, 1982).

—— *Ricardian Poetry* (London, 1971).

—— 'The Sinking Island and the Dying Author: R. W. Chambers Fifty Years On', *Essays in Criticism*, 40 (1990), 1–23.

—— (ed.), *Geoffrey Chaucer: A Critical Anthology* (Harmondsworth, 1969).

—— and Turville-Petre, T., *A Book of Middle English* (Oxford, 1992).

BURTON, ROBERT, *Anatomy of Melancholy*, ed. H. Jackson (New York, 1977).

BUTLER, JUDITH, *Gender Trouble* (New York and London, 1991).

BUTTERFIELD, ARDIS, 'Froissart, Machaut, Chaucer and the Genres of

Imagination', in André Crépin (ed.), *L'Imagination médiévale: Chaucer et ses contemporains: Actes du Colloque en Sorbonne*, Publications de l'Association des Médiévistes Anglicistes de l'Enseignement Supérieur, 16 (Paris, 1991), pp. 53–69.

—— 'Interpolated Lyric in Medieval Narrative Poetry' (Ph.D. diss., University of Cambridge, 1988).

—— 'Lyric and Elegy in the *Book of the Duchess*', *MÆ* 60 (1991), 33–60.

—— 'Medieval Genres and Modern Genre-Theory', *Paragraph*, 13/2 (1990), 184–201.

CADDEN, JOAN, *Meanings of Sex Difference in the Middle Ages* (Cambridge, 1993).

CAILLOIS, ROGER, *Man, Play, and Games*, trans. M. Barash (New York, 1961).

CALIN, WILLIAM, *A Poet at the Fountain* (Lexington, Ky., 1974).

CAMILLE, MICHAEL, *The Gothic Idol: Ideology and Image-Making in Medieval Art* (Cambridge, 1989).

CAMPROUX, CHARLES, *Le Joy d'amour des troubadours* (Montpellier, 1965).

CANNON, CHRISTOPHER, '*Raptus* in the Chaumpaigne Release and a Newly Discovered Document concerning the Life of Geoffrey Chaucer', *Speculum*, 68 (1993), 74–94.

CARRUTHERS, MARY, *The Book of Memory. A Study of Memory in Medieval Culture* (Cambridge, 1990).

CARSON, MOTHER ANGELA, 'The Sovereignty of Octovyen in *The Book of the Duchess*', *AnM* 8 (1967), 46–57.

CARTIER, N. R., 'Froissart, Chaucer and Enclimpostair', *Revue de littérature comparée*, 38 (1964), 18–34.

—— '*Le Bleu Chevalier* de Froissart et le *Livre de la duchesse* de Chaucer', *Romania*, 88 (1967), 232–52.

CASTIGLIONE, BALDASSARE, *Il Cortegiano*, ed. Carlo Cordié, in *Opere di Baldassare Castiglione, Giovanni della Casa, Benvenuto Cellini* (Milan and Naples, 1960), pp. 5–361; trans. George Bull (Harmondsworth, 1967).

CATO, MARCUS PORCIUS, *Cato Maior 'De Senectute', Laelius 'De Amicitia'*, ed. P. Venini (Torino, 1958).

CATO, Pseudo-, see *Disticha Catonis* and *Paruus Cato*.

CAXTON, WILLIAM, *The Curial Made by Maystere Alain Chartier*, ed. F. J. Furnivall, EETS ES 54 (London, 1888).

—— *Eneydos*, ed. W. T. Culley and F. J. Furnivall, EETS ES 57 (London, 1890; repr. 1962).

—— *The Game and Playe of the Chesse* (1474), repr. with an introduction by William H. A. Axon (1883; repr. St Leonards-on-sea, Sussex, n.d.).

CHAMBERLAIN, DAVID, 'The Music of the Spheres and *The Parlement of Foules*', *ChR* 5 (1970), 32–56.

CHANCE, JANE, 'Chaucerian Irony in the Boethian Short Poems: The Dramatic Tension between Classical and Christian', *ChR* 20 (1986), 235–45.

CHARLES D'ORLÉANS, *French Chansons*, ed. Sarah Spence (New York and London, 1986).

CHAUCER, GEOFFREY, *Troilus and Criseyde, A Facsimile of Corpus Christi College Cambridge MS 61* with introductions by M. B. Parkes and E. Salter (Cambridge, 1978).

CHAYTOR, H. J., *From Script to Print* (London, 1945).

CHRISTINE DE PIZAN, *La Livre de la Cité des dames*, ed. Maureen Cheney Curnow (diss., Vanderbilt University, 1975); trans. Earl Jeffrey Richards, *The Book of the City of Ladies* (London, 1983).

—— *The Epistle of Othea, translated from the French by S. Scrope*, ed. C. F. Bühler, EETS OS 264 (London, 1970).

CICERO, MARCUS TULLIUS, *Cato Maior de senectute, Laelius de amicitia*, ed. P. Venini (Tornio, 1958).

CLANCHY, M. T., *From Memory to Written Record* (London, 1979).

CLANVOWE, SIR JOHN, *Works*, ed. V. J. Scattergood (Cambridge, 1975).

CLARK, C., 'Another Late-Fourteenth-Century Case of Dialect Awareness', *English Studies*, 62 (1981), 504–5.

CLARK, ELAINE, 'The Decision to Marry in Thirteenth- and Early Fourteenth-Century Norfolk', *MS* 49 (1987), 496–516.

CLEMEN, WOLFGANG, *Chaucer's Early Poetry*, trans. C. A. M. Sym (London, 1963).

COHEN, WALTER, 'Political Criticism of Shakespeare', in Jean E. Howard and Marion F. O'Connor (eds.), *Shakespeare Reproduced: The Text in History and Ideology* (New York and London, 1987), pp. 18–46.

COLEMAN, JANET, *Ancient and Medieval Memories: Studies in the Reconstruction of the Past* (Cambridge, 1992).

COLEMAN, WILLIAM E., 'Chaucer, the *Teseida*, and the Visconti Library at Pavia: A New Hypothesis', *MÆ* 51 (1982), 92–101.

—— 'Chaucer's Manuscript and Boccaccio's Commentaries on *Il Teseida*', *Chaucer Newsletter*, 9/2 (Fall 1987), 1–6.

CONDREN, EDWARD, 'The Historical Context of the *Book of the Duchess:* A New Hypothesis', *ChR* 7 (1971), 195–212.

CONNELY, W., 'Imprints of the *Heroides* of Ovid on Chaucer, *The Legend of Good Women*', *Classical Weekly*, 18/2 (1924), 9–13.

COOK, A. S., *Chaucerian Papers* (New Haven, Conn., 1919; repr. New York, 1973).

COOLEY, F. D., 'Two Notes on the Chess Terms in *The Book of the Duchess*', *MLN* 63 (1948), 30–5.

COOPER, G., '"Sely John" in the "legende" of *The Miller's Tale*', *JEGP* 79 (1980), 1–12.

COOPER, HELEN, 'Chaucer and Ovid: A Question of Authority', in Charles Martindale (ed.), *Ovid Renewed* (Cambridge, 1988), pp. 71–81.

COOPLAND, G. W., *Nicole Oresme and the Astrologers. A Study of his 'Livre de Divinacions'* (Liverpool, 1952).

COPELAND, RITA, *Rhetoric, Hermeneutics and Translation in the Middle Ages: Academic Traditions and Vernacular Texts* (Cambridge, 1991).

CORMIER, R. J., *One Heart, One Mind: The Rebirth of Virgil's Hero in Medieval French Romance*, Romance Monographs (University, Miss., 1973).

COULSON, FRANK T., 'Hitherto Unedited Medieval and Renaissance Lives of Ovid (I)', *MS* 49 (1987), 152–207.

COULTON, G. G., *Chaucer and his England*, 8th edn. (London and New York, 1950).

COWEN, JANET M., 'Chaucer's *Legend of Good Women:* Structure and Tone', *SP* 82 (1985), 416–36.

—— 'Women as Exempla in Fifteenth-Century Verse of the Chaucerian Tradition', in Julia Boffey and Janet Cowen (eds.), *Chaucer and Fifteenth-Century Poetry* (London, 1991), pp. 51–65.

COWGILL, B. K., 'The *Parlement of Foules* and the Body Politic', *JEGP* 74 (1975), 315–35.

COWLING, G. H., 'Chaucer's *Complaintes of Mars and Venus*', *RES* 2 (1926), 405–10.

CRAMPTON, GEORGIA RONAN, 'Chaucer's Singular Prayer', *MÆ* 59 (1990), 191–213.

CRANE, SUSAN, 'Froissart's *Dit dou Bleu Chevalier* as a Source for Chaucer's *Book of the Duchess*', *MÆ* 61 (1992), 59–74.

CRETON, JEAN, *Metrical History of the Deposition of King Richard II*, ed. J. Webb, *Archaeologia*, 20 (1824), 1–423.

CROMPTON, LOUIS, 'The Myth of Lesbian Impunity: Capital Laws from 1270–1791', *Journal of Homosexuality*, 6 (1980/1), 11–25.

CROSS, J. E., 'The Old Swedish *Trohetsvisan* and Chaucer's *Lak of Stedfastnesse*— a Study in Mediaeval Genre', *Saga-Book of the Viking Society*, 16 (1965), 283–314.

CROW, M. M., and OLSON, C. C., *Chaucer Life-Records* (Oxford, 1966).

CULLER, JONATHAN, *The Pursuit of Signs: Semiotics, Literature, Deconstruction* (London, 1981).

CURRY, W. C., *Chaucer and the Medieval Sciences*, rev. edn. (London, 1960).

CURTIUS, E. R., *European Literature and the Latin Middle Ages*, trans. W. R. Trask (London, 1953).

DANTE ALIGHIERI, *The Divine Comedy*, ed. and trans. Charles S. Singleton (Princeton, NJ, 1970–5); *Inferno*, 2nd printing, with corrections (1977).

—— *Il Convivio*, ed. Bruna Cordati (Turin, 1968); trans. P. Wicksteed, *The Il Convivio of Dante Alighieri* (London, 1931).

—— *Opere*, ed. E. Moore and P. Toynbee, 4th edn. (London, 1963).

—— *Vita nuova*, in E. Moore and P. Toynbee (eds.), *Opere di Dante Alighieri* (Oxford, 1924), pp. 205–33; trans. B. Reynolds (Harmondsworth, 1969).

DAVENPORT, W. A., *Chaucer: Complaint and Narrative* (Cambridge, 1988).

DAVID, ALFRED, 'How Marcia Lost Her Skin: A Note on Chaucer's Mythology', in Larry D. Benson (ed.), *The Learned and the Lewed* (Cambridge, Mass., 1974), pp. 19–29.

—— 'Literary Satire in the *House of Fame*', *PMLA* 75 (1960), 333–9.

DAVID, ALFRED, 'The Truth about Vache', *ChR* 11 (1977), 334–7.

DAVIS, NATALIE ZEMON, 'Women on Top', in *idem, Society and Culture in Early Modern France* (Stanford, Calif., 1975), pp. 124–51, 310–15.

DAVIS, NORMAN, 'Chaucer and Fourteenth-Century English', in D. S. Brewer (ed.), *Writers and their Background: Geoffrey Chaucer* (London, 1974), pp. 58–84.

—— *et al., A Chaucer Glossary* (Oxford, 1979).

DEAN, JAMES, 'Artistic Conclusiveness in Chaucer's *Parliament of Fowls*', *ChR* 21 (1986), 16–25.

DEAN, NANCY, 'Chaucer's Complaint: A Genre Descended from the *Heroides*', *Comparative Literature*, 19 (1967), 1–27.

DE BOER, C., 'Guillaume de Machaut and l'*Ovide moralisé*', *Romania*, 43 (1914), 335–52.

DELANY, SHEILA, *Chaucer's 'House of Fame': The Poetics of Skeptical Fideism* (Chicago and London, 1972).

——·'Chaucer's *Legend of Good Women:* The Relevance of Wyclif' (forthcoming).

—— 'Geographies of Desire: Orientalism in Chaucer's *Legend of Good Women*', *Chaucer Yearbook: A Journal of Late Medieval Studies*, 1 (1992), 1–32.

—— 'The Logic of Obscenity in Chaucer's *Legend of Good Women*', *Florilegium*, 7 (1985), 189–205.

—— *Medieval Literary Politics: Shapes of Ideology* (Manchester and New York, 1990).

—— *The Naked Text: Chaucer's 'Legend of Good Women'* (Berkeley and Los Angeles, 1994).

—— 'The Naked Text, Chaucer's "Thisbe", the *Ovide moralisé*, and the Problem of *Translatio Studii* in the *Legend of Good Women*', *Mediaevalia*, 13 (1987), 275–94.

DEMATS, PAUL, *Fabula*, Publications romanes et françaises, 122 (Geneva, 1973).

DENOMY, A. J., 'The *De amore* of Andreas Capellanus and the Condemnation of 1277', *MS* 8 (1946), 107–49.

DESCHAMPS, EUSTACHE, *Œuvres complètes*, ed. Marquis de Queux de Saint-Hilaire and G. Raynaud, SATF (Paris, 1878–1903).

DESMOND, MARILYNN, *Reading Dido: Gender, Textuality and the Medieval 'Aeneid'* (Minneapolis, 1994).

DIAMOND, ARLYN, 'Chaucer's Women and Women's Chaucer', in *idem* and Lee R. Edwards (eds.), *The Authority of Experience: Essays in Feminist Criticism* (Amherst, Mass., 1977), pp. 60–83, 282–4.

DIEKSTRA, F. N. M., 'The Poetic Exchange between Philippe de Vitry and Jean de la Mote: A New Edition', *Neophilologus*, 70 (1986), 504–19.

DINSHAW, CAROLYN, *Chaucer's Sexual Poetics* (Madison, Wis., 1989).

*Disticha Catonis*, ed. Marcus Boas (Amsterdam, 1952); ed. and trans. W. J. Chase, *The Distichs of Cato: A Famous Medieval Textbook*, University of Wisconsin Studies in the Social Sciences and History, 8 (Madison, Wis., 1922).

DIVERRES, A. H., 'Froissart's *Meliador* and Edward III's Policy towards Scotland', in *Mélanges offerts à Rita Lejeune* (Gembloux, 1969), ii. 1399–409.

*Dives and Pauper*, pt. 1, ed. P. H. Barnum, EETS OS 280 (Oxford, 1980).

DOBSON, E. J., *English Pronunciation 1500–1700*, 2nd edn. (Oxford, 1968).

DONALDSON, E. TALBOT, 'The Effect of the *Merchant's Tale*', in idem, *Speaking of Chaucer*, pp. 30–45.

—— 'The Idiom of Popular Poetry in the *Miller's Tale*', in idem, *Speaking of Chaucer*, pp. 13–29.

—— *Speaking of Chaucer* (London, 1970).

DONALDSON, IAN, *The Rapes of Lucretia: A Myth and its Transformations* (Oxford, 1982).

DONNER, MORTON, 'Chaucer and his Narrators: The Poet's Place in his Poems', *Western Humanities Review*, 27 (1973), 185–95.

DONOGHUE, DENIS, *Ferocious Alphabets* (London and Boston, 1981).

DOOB, PENELOPE REED, *The Idea of the Labyrinth from Classical Antiquity through the Middle Ages* (Ithaca, NY, 1990).

DOUGLAS, GAVIN, *Virgil's 'Aeneid' translated into Scottish Verse*, ed. David F. C. Coldwell, STS (Edinburgh, 1960).

DOVE, MARY, *The Perfect Age of Man's Life* (Cambridge, 1986).

DOYLE, A. I., and PARKES, M. B., 'The Production of Copies of the *Canterbury Tales* and *Confessio Amantis* in the Early Fifteenth Century', in M. B. Parkes and A. G. Watson (eds.), *Medieval Scribes, Manuscripts and Libraries: Essays Presented to N. R. Ker* (London, 1978), pp. 163–210.

DRONKE, PETER, *Fabula: Explorations into the Uses of Myth in Medieval Platonism* (Leiden, 1974).

—— *Women Writers of the Middle Ages* (Cambridge, 1984).

—— (ed.), *A History of Twelfth-Century Western Philosophy* (Cambridge, 1988).

DUBY, GEORGES, *Medieval Marriage: Two Models from Twelfth-Century France* (Baltimore and London, 1978).

DUGGAN, ALFRED, *Thomas Beckett of Canterbury* (London, 1952).

DUNBAR, WILLIAM, *Poems*, ed. J. Kinsley (Oxford, 1979).

EAGLETON, TERRY, *Literary Theory: An Introduction* (Oxford, 1983).

ECKHARDT, C. D., 'The Art of Translation in *The Romaunt of the Rose*', *SAC* 6 (1984), 41–63.

ECONOMOU, GEORGE D., *The Goddess Natura in Medieval Literature* (Cambridge, Mass., 1972).

—— 'The Two Venuses and Courtly Love', in Joan M. Ferrante and George D. Economou (eds.), *In Pursuit of Perfection: Courtly Love in Medieval Literature* (Port Washington, Wis., 1975), pp. 17–50.

EDWARD, SECOND DUKE OF YORK, *The Master of Game*, ed. W. A. and F. Baillie-Grohman (London, 1909).

EDWARDS, A. S. G., 'The Text of Chaucer's *House of Fame*: Editing and Authority', *Poetica*, 29–30 (1989), 80–92.

EDWARDS, A. S. G., 'The Unity and Authenticity of *Anelida and Arcite*: The Evidence of the Manuscripts', *Studies in Bibliography*, 41 (1988), 177–88.

EDWARDS, ROBERT R., *The Dream of Chaucer. Representation and Reflection in the Early Narratives* (Durham, NC, and London, 1989).

—— and SPECTOR, STEPHEN (eds.), *The Olde Daunce: Love, Friendship, Sex and Marriage in the Medieval World* (Albany, NY, 1991).

EHRMANN, JACQUES (ed.), *Games, Play, Literature* (Boston, 1968).

ELLIOTT, R. W. V., *Chaucer's English* (London, 1974).

—— 'Chaucer's Reading', in A. C. Cawley (ed.), *Chaucer's Mind and Art* (London, 1969), pp. 46–68.

ELLIS, R., (ed.), *Appendix Vergiliana* (Oxford, 1957).

ELLIS, STEVE, 'Chaucer, Dante, and Damnation', *ChR* 22 (1988), 282–94.

ELLMANN, MAUD, 'Blanche', in Jeremy Hawthorn (ed.), *Criticism and Critical Theory* (London, 1984), pp. 99–110.

*Eneas: A Twelfth-Century French Romance*, ed. J.-J. Salverda de Grave (Paris, 1925–9); trans. John A. Yunck (New York and London, 1974).

ENRIGHT, D. J. (ed.), *The Oxford Book of Death* (Oxford, 1983).

ERICKSON, CAROLLY, *The Medieval Vision: Essays in History and Perception* (New York, 1976).

ESTRICH, R. M., 'Chaucer's Prologue to the *Legend of Good Women* and Machaut's *Le Jugement dou Roy de Navarre*', *SP* 36 (1939), 20–39.

EVANS, RUTH, review of Mann, *Chaucer*, in *Textual Practice*, 7 (1993), 85–9.

EVERETT, DOROTHY, 'Chaucer's Love Visions, with Particular Reference to the *Parliament of Foules*', in *idem*, *Essays*, pp. 97–114.

—— *Essays on Middle English Literature*, ed. Patricia Kean (Oxford, 1955).

—— 'Some Reflections on Chaucer's "Art Poetical"', in *idem*, *Essays*, pp. 149–74.

EVRART DE CONTY, *Le Livre des Eschez amoureux moralisés. Edition critique*, ed. G. Tesson and Bruno Roy (Montreal and Paris, 1994).

FAHY, CONOR, 'Three Early Renaissance Treatises on Women', *Italian Studies*, 11 (1956), 47–55.

FARAL, EDMOND (ed.), *Les Arts poétiques du XIIe et du XIIIe siècle* (Paris, 1924).

FEIMER, JOEL NICHOLAS, 'The Figure of Medea in Medieval Literature: A Thematic Metamorphosis' (Ph.D. diss., City University of New York, 1983).

FERRANTE, JOAN, 'Public Postures and Private Maneuvers: Roles Medieval Women Play', in Mary Erler and Maryanne Kowaleski (eds.), *Women and Power in the Middle Ages* (Athens, Ga., and London, 1988), pp. 213–29.

FERRIS, SUMNER J., 'The Date of Chaucer's Final Annuity and "The Complaint to his Empty Purse"', *MP* 65 (1967), 45–52.

FINNEL, ANDREW J., 'The Poet as Sunday Man: "The Complaint of Chaucer to his Purse"', *ChR* 8 (1973), 147–58.

FISCHER, STEVEN R., *The Complete Medieval Dreambook: A Multilingual, Alphabetical 'Somnia Danielis' Collation* (Bern and Frankfurt, 1982).

FISHER, SHEILA, and HALLEY, JANET E. (eds.), *Seeking the Woman in Late Medieval and Renaissance Writings: Essays in Feminist Contextual Criticism* (Knoxville, Tenn., 1989).

*'Floure and the Leafe' and 'The Assembly of Ladies'*, ed. Derek Pearsall (Manchester, 1962).

FONTENROSE, JOSEPH, *The Delphic Oracle: Its Responses and Operations, with a Catalogue of Responses* (Berkeley and Los Angeles, 1978).

FOWLER, DAVID C., *The Bible in Middle English Literature* (Seattle and London, 1984).

FOX, JOHN, *The Lyric Poetry of Charles d'Orléans* (Oxford, 1969).

FRADENBERG, LOUISE, 'The Manciple's Servant Tongue: Politics and Poetry in *The Canterbury Tales*', *ELH* 52 (1985), 85–118.

FRANK, R. W., 'The *Canterbury Tales* III: Pathos', in Boitani and Mann (eds.), *Chaucer Companion*, pp. 143–58.

—— *Chaucer and 'The Legend of Good Women'* (Cambridge, Mass., 1972).

—— 'The *Legend of Good Women*: Some Implications', in R. H. Robbins (ed.), *Chaucer at Albany* (New York, 1975), pp. 63–76.

FRENCH, W. H., 'Medieval Chess and the *Book of the Duchess*', *MLN* 64 (1949), 261–4.

FRIEDMAN, J. B., *Orpheus in the Middle Ages* (Cambridge, Mass., 1971).

FROISSART, JEAN, *Chroniques*, ed. S. Luce and G. Raynaud (Paris, 1869–99).

—— *Chroniques*, trans. Sir John Bourchier, with an introduction by W. P. Ker, Tudor Translations (London, 1901–3).

—— *Chroniques*, trans. G. Brereton (Harmondsworth, rev. edn., 1978).

—— *Chroniques*, ed. G. T. Diller (Geneva, 1972).

—— *Dits et débats*, ed. A. Fourrier (Geneva, 1979).

—— *Le Joli Buisson de Jonece*, ed. A. Fourrier (Geneva, 1975).

—— *Œuvres*, ed. A. Scheler (Brussels, 1870–2).

FRY, DONALD K., 'The Ending of the *House of Fame*', in R. H. Robbins (ed.), *Chaucer at Albany* (New York, 1975), pp. 27–40.

FURNIVALL, JOHN, *Trial Forewords* (London, 1871).

FYLER, JOHN, *Chaucer and Ovid* (New Haven, Conn., 1979).

—— 'Chaucer, Pope, and the *House of Fame*', in J. M. Dean and C. K. Zacker (eds.), *The Idea of Medieval Literature: New Essays on Chaucer and Medieval Culture in Honour of D. R. Howard* (Newark, Del., London, and Toronto, 1992), pp. 149–59.

GALLOP, DAVID, *Aristotle on Sleep and Dreams* (Peterborough, Canada, 1990).

GARBER, MARJORIE, *Vested Interests. Cross-Dressing and Cultural Anxiety* (New York and London, 1992).

GARDNER, JOHN, *The Life and Times of Chaucer* (New York, 1977).

GARRETT, R. (ed.), 'De arte lacrimandi', *Anglia Zeitschrift*, 32 (1909), 269–94.

GAUNT, SIMON, 'From Epic to Romance: Gender and Sexuality in the *Roman d'Enéas*', *Romanic Review*, 83 (1992), 1–27.

GAUNT, SIMON, *Troubadours and Irony* (Cambridge, 1989).

GAYLORD, ALAN T., 'Scanning the Prosodists: An Essay in Metacriticism', *ChR* 11 (1976), 22–82.

GELLRICH, JESSE M., *The Idea of the Book in the Middle Ages* (Ithaca, NY, and London, 1985).

GENET, JEAN-PHILIPPE (ed.), *Four English Political Tracts of the Later Middle Ages*, Camden Fourth Series, 18 (London, 1977).

GEOFFREY OF VINSAUF, *Documentum de modo et arte dictandi et versificandi*, trans. Roger P. Parr (Milwaukee, 1968).

—— *Poetria nova*, trans. J. B. Kopp, in Murphy (ed.), *Medieval Rhetorical Arts*, pp. 29–108.

*Gest Hystoriale*, ed. G. A. Panton and D. Donaldson, EETS OS 39, 56, repr. as 1 vol. (New York, 1969).

GHISALBERTI, F., 'Medieval Lives of Ovid', *Journal of the Warburg and Courtauld Institutes*, 9 (1946), 10–59.

GILLESPIE, VINCENT, review of Boitani, *Imaginary World*, in *Notes and Queries*, 232 (1987), 253–5.

GILLMEISTER, HEINER, *Chaucer's Conversion. Allegorical Thought in Medieval Literature*, Aspekte der englischen Geistes- und Kulturgeschichte, 2 (Frankfurt-on-Main, 1984).

GIOVANNI DE' BALBI OF GENOA, *Catholicon* (Venice, 1495).

GIVEN-WILSON, CHRISTOPHER, *The Royal Household and the King's Affinity. Service, Politics and Finance in England, 1360–1413* (New Haven, Conn., and London, 1986).

—— and CURTEIS, ALICE, *The Royal Bastards of Medieval England* (London and Boston, 1984).

GODDARD, H. C., 'Chaucer's *Legend of Good Women*', *JEGP* 7 (1908), 87–129; 8 (1909), 47–112.

GODMAN, PETER, 'Chaucer and Boccaccio's Latin Works', in Boitani (ed.), *Italian Trecento*, pp. 269–95.

GOFFIN, R. C., 'Quiting by Tidings in the *Hous of Fame*', *MÆ* 12 (1943), 40–4.

GOODMAN, ANTHONY, *John of Gaunt* (London, 1992).

GORDON, I. A., *The Movement of English Prose* (London, 1966).

GOTTLIEB, BEATRICE, *The Family in the Western World from the Black Death to the Industrial Age* (New York and Oxford, 1993).

—— 'The Problem of Feminism in the Fifteenth Century', in Julius Kirshiner and Suzanne F. Wemple (eds.), *Women of the Medieval World* (Oxford and New York, 1985), pp. 337–64.

GOWER, JOHN, *Complete Works*, ed. G. C. Macaulay (Oxford, 1899–1902).

—— *The English Works*, ed. G. C. Macaulay, EETS ES 81–2 (Oxford, 1900–1).

GRANDSEN, ANTONIA, *Historical Writing in England*, ii: *c.1307* to the Early Sixteenth Century (London and Henley, 1982).

GRAY, DOUGLAS, *Robert Henryson* (Leiden, 1979).

GREEN, RICHARD FIRTH, 'Chaucer's Victimized Women', *SAC* 9 (1988), 146–54.

—— 'The *Familia Regis* and the *Familia Cupidinis*', in Scattergood and Sherborne (eds.), *English Court Culture*, pp. 87–108.

—— *Poets and Princepleasers: Literature and the English Court in the Late Middle Ages* (Toronto, 1980).

—— 'The Sexual Normality of Chaucer's Pardoner', *Mediaevalia*, 8 (1982), 351–8.

—— 'Women in Chaucer's Audience', *ChR* 18 (1983), 146–54.

GREENBLATT, STEPHEN, *Renaissance Self-Fashioning. From More to Shakespeare* (Chicago and London, 1980).

GREENE, THOMAS M., '*Il Cortegiano* and the Choice of a Game', in Hanning and Rosand (eds.), *Ideal and the Real*, pp. 1–15.

GUIDO DELLE COLONNE, *Historia destructionis Troiae*, ed. N. E. Griffin (Cambridge, Mass., 1936); trans. M. E. Meek (Bloomington, Ind., and London, 1974).

GUILLAUME DE DEGUILEVILLE, *Le Pélerinage de Vie Humaine*, ed. J. J. Sturzinger (London, 1893).

—— *The Pilgrimage of the Life of Man, translated by John Lydgate*, ed. F. J. Furnivall, with an introduction by Katherine B. Locock, EETS ES 77, 83, 92 (London, 1899–1904).

—— *The Pilgrimage of the Lyfe of Manhode*, ed. Avril Henry, EETS 288 and 292 (Oxford, 1985–8).

GUILLORY, JOHN, *Poetic Authority: Spenser, Milton and Literary History* (New York, 1983).

GUTHRIE, STEVEN R., 'Prosody and the Study of Chaucer', *ChR* 23 (1988), 30–49.

HAAS, RENATE, 'Chaucer's Use of the Lament for the Dead', in J. N. Wasserman and R. J. Blanch (eds.), *Chaucer in the Eighties* (Syracuse, NY, 1986), pp. 23–37.

HALL, LOUIS BREWER, 'Chaucer and the Dido-and-Aeneas Story', *MS* 25 (1963), 148–59.

HANAWALT, BARBARA A. (ed.), *Chaucer's England. Literature in Historical Context*, Medieval Studies at Minnesota, 4 (Minneapolis, 1992).

HANNING, R. W., and ROSAND, DAVID (eds.), *Castiglione. The Ideal and the Real in Renaissance Culture* (New Haven, Conn., and London, 1983).

HANSEN, ELAINE TUTTLE, *Chaucer and the Fictions of Gender* (Berkeley and Los Angeles, 1992).

—— 'Irony and the Antifeminist Narrator in Chaucer's *Legend of Good Women*', *JEGP* 82 (1983), 11–31.

HANSON-SMITH, ELIZABETH, 'A Woman's View of Courtly Love: The Findern Anthology, CUL Ff.1.6', *Journal of Women's Studies in Literature*, 1 (1979), 179–94.

HARDMAN, P., 'Chaucer's Muses and his Art Poetical', *RES* 37 (1986), 478–94.

HARRISON, R. P., 'Approaching the *Vita nuova*', in Rachel Jacoff (ed.), *The Cambridge Companion to Dante* (Cambridge, 1993), pp. 34–44.

HARRISON, TONY, *The Gaze of the Gorgon* (Newcastle, 1992).

HARVEY, E. RUTH, *The Inward Wits: Psychological Theory in the Middle Ages and the Renaissance*, Warburg Institute Surveys, 6 (London, 1975).

HARVEY, JOHN, *English Medieval Architects* (London, 1954).

HAVELY, N. R., *Chaucer's Boccaccio* (Cambridge, 1980).

HAWTHORN, JEREMY, *A Concise Glossary of Contemporary Literary Theory* (London and New York, 1992).

HEATH, STEPHEN, 'Male Feminism', in Jardine and Smith (eds.), *Men in Feminism*, pp. 1–32.

HELMHOLZ, R. H., *Marriage Litigation in Medieval England* (Cambridge, 1974).

HENRIQUES, J., HOLLWAY, W., URWIN, C., VENN, C., and WALKERDIKE, V., *Changing the Subject: Psychology, Social Regulation and Subjectivity* (London and New York, 1984).

HENRY OF LANCASTER, *Livre des Seyntz Medicines*, ed. E. J. Arnould (Oxford, 1940).

HENRYSON, ROBERT, *Poems*, ed. Denton Fox (Oxford, 1981).

HEXTER, RALPH J., *Ovid and Medieval Schooling. Studies in Medieval School Commentaries on Ovid's 'Ars amatoria', 'Epistulae ex Ponto', and 'Epistulae Heroidum'*, Münchener Beiträge zur Mediävistik und Renaissance-Forschung, 38 (Munich, 1986).

HIEATT, CONSTANCE B., *The Realism of Dream-Visions: The Poetic Exploitation of the Dream-Experience in Chaucer and his Contemporaries* (The Hague and Paris, 1967).

—— '*Un autre fourme*: Guillaume de Machaut and the Dream Vision Form', *ChR* 14 (1979–80), 79–115.

HIGDEN, RALPH, *Polychronicon*, ed. C. Babington and J. R. Lumby (London, 1865–86).

HILL, JOHN M., 'The *Book of the Duchess*, Melancholy, and that Eight-Year Sickness', *ChR* 9 (1974), 35–50.

HILLMAN, RICHARD, 'Gower's Lucrece: A New Old Source for *The Rape of Lucrece*', *ChR* 24 (1990), 263–70.

HIRSH, J. D., '*Havelok* 2933: A Problem in Medieval Literary History', *NM* 78 (1977), 339–49.

HISSETTE, R., *Enquête sur les 219 articles condamnés à Paris le 7 mars 1277* (Louvain and Paris, 1977).

—— 'Étienne Tempier et ses condemnations', *RTAM* 47 (1980), 213–70.

*Historia Anglicana*, ed. H. T. Riley (London, 1863–4).

HOCCLEVE, THOMAS, *Minor Poems*, ed. F. J. Furnivall and I. Gollancz, rev. Jerome Mitchell and A. I. Doyle, EETS ES 61 and 73 (rev. repr., Oxford, 1970).

—— *Regement of Princes*, ed. F. J. Furnivall, EETS ES 72 (London, 1897).

HOLCOT, ROBERT, *Sapientiae Regis Salomonis praelectiones* (Basel, 1586).

HOLLANDER, ROBERT, 'The Validity of Boccaccio's Self-Exegesis in his *Teseida*', *Medievalia et Humanistica*, 8 (1977), 163–83.

HORACE (QUINTUS HORATIUS FLACCUS), *Satires, Epistles and Ars Poetica*, ed. and trans. H. R. Fairclough, Loeb Classical Library (Cambridge, Mass., 1926).

*The Household Book of Edward IV*, ed. A. R. Myers (Manchester, 1959).

HOWARD, DONALD R., *Chaucer and the Medieval World* (London, 1987).

—— 'Chaucer the Man', *PMLA* 80 (1965), 337–43.

—— 'Flying through Space: Chaucer and Milton', in J. A. Wittreich (ed.), *Milton and the Line of Vision* (Madison, Wis., 1975), pp. 3–23.

—— *The Idea of the 'Canterbury Tales'* (Berkeley, Calif., 1976).

HUDSON, ANNE, *The Premature Reformation: Wycliffite Texts and Lollard History* (Oxford, 1988).

HUFFER, LYNNE, 'Christine de Pisan: Speaking like a Woman/Speaking like a Man', in E. E. DuBruck (ed.), *New Images of Medieval Women: Essays towards a Cultural Anthropology* (Lewiston, Queenston, and Lampeter, 1989), pp. 61–72.

HUGHES-HALLETT, LUCY, *Cleopatra: Histories, Dreams and Distortions* (London, 1990).

HUIZINGA, J., *Homo Ludens: A Study of the Play-Element in Culture* (Boston, 1950).

HULL, SUZANNE W., *Chaste, Silent and Obedient: English Books for Women, 1475–1640* (San Marino, Calif., 1982).

HULT, DAVID F., *Self-Fulfilling Prophecies: Readership and Authority in the First Roman de la Rose* (Cambridge, 1986).

HUNT, TONY, *Teaching and Learning Latin in Thirteenth-Century England* (Cambridge, 1991).

HUOT, SYLVIA, *The 'Romance of the Rose' and its Medieval Readers* (Cambridge, 1993).

HUPPÉ, B. F., and ROBERTSON, D. W., *Fruyt and Chaf: Studies in Chaucer's Allegories* (Princeton, NJ, 1963).

ILLICH, IVAN, *Gender* (London, and New York, 1983).

IRVINE, MARTIN, 'Medieval Grammatical Theory and Chaucer's *House of Fame*', *Speculum*, 60 (1985), 850–76.

ISIDORE OF SEVILLE, *Etymologiae*, ed. W. M. Lindsay (Oxford, 1911).

JACOBSON, HOWARD, *Ovid's 'Heroides'* (Princeton, NJ, 1985).

JACOBUS DE VORAGINE, *Legenda Aurea*, ed. T. Graesse (repr. Osnabrück, 1969); trans. Granger Ryan and Helmut Ripperger (New York, 1969).

—— *The Golden Legend. Readings on the Saints*, trans. G. Ryan (Princeton, NJ, 1993).

JACOBUS, MARY (ed.), *Women Writing and Writing about Women* (London, 1979).

JACOFF, RACHEL, 'Transgression and Transcendence: Figures of Female Desire in Dante's *Commedia*', in Marina S. Brownlee, Kevin Brownlee, and Stephen G. Nichols, (eds.), *The New Medievalism* (Baltimore, 1991), pp. 183–200.

—— (ed.), *The Cambridge Companion to Dante* (Cambridge, 1993).

JACQUART, DANIELLE, and THOMASSET, CLAUDE, *Sexuality and Medicine in the Middle Ages*, trans. M. Adamson (Cambridge and Oxford, 1988).

JARDINE, ALICE, and SMITH, PAUL (eds.), *Men in Feminism* (London, 1987).

JEAN DE CONDÉ, *Messe des Oisiaus*, ed. J. Ribard (Geneva, 1970).

JEFFERSON, B. L., *Chaucer and the Consolation of Philosophy* (Princeton, NJ, 1917).

JEFFREY, DAVID LYLE, 'Sacred and Secular Scripture: Authority and Interpretation in *The House of Fame*', in *idem* (ed.), *Chaucer and Scriptural Tradition* (Ottawa, 1984), pp. 207–28.

JEROME, ST, *Adversus Jovinianum*, in *PL* 23, 221–352, trans. W. H. Freemantle, in *The Principal Works of St Jerome*, Select Library of Nicene and Post-Nicene Fathers, 6 (Oxford, 1893), pp. 346–416.

JOHN OF SALISBURY, *Frivolities of Courtiers and Footprints of the Philosophers. Being a translation of the First, Second and Third Books of the 'Policraticus' of John of Salisbury*, trans. Joseph B. Pike (Minneapolis and London, 1938).

—— *Policraticus*, ed. C. C. J. Webb (Oxford, 1909).

—— *Policraticus. On the Frivolities of Courtiers and the Footprints of Philosophers*, trans. Cary J. Nederman (Cambridge, 1990).

JONES, JOAN MORTON, 'The Chess of Love [Old French Text with Translation and Commentary]' (Ph.D. diss., University of Nebraska, 1968).

JORDAN, CONSTANCE, 'Feminism and the Humanists: The Case of Sir Thomas Elyot's Defence of Good Women', in M. W. Ferguson, M. Quilligan, and N. J. Vickers (eds.), *Rewriting the Renaissance: The Discourses of Sexual Difference in Early Modern Europe* (Chicago and London, 1986), pp. 242–58.

JORDAN, ROBERT, *Chaucer's Poetics and the Modern Reader* (Berkeley and Los Angeles, 1987).

JOSEPH OF EXETER, *The Iliad of Dares Phrygius*, trans. Gildas Roberts (Cape Town, 1970).

—— *Werke und Briefe*, ed. L. Gompf, Mittellateinischen Studien und Texte, 4 (Leiden and Cologne, 1970).

KALLENDORF, CRAIG, *In Praise of Aeneas. Virgil and Epideictic Rhetoric in the Early Italian Renaissance* (Hanover, NH, and London, 1977).

KANE, GEORGE, *Chaucer* (Oxford, 1984).

KARNEIN, ALFRED, '*Amor est passio*—A Definition of Courtly Love?', in G. S. Burges (ed.), *Court and Poet: Selected Proceedings of the Third Congress of the International Courtly Literature Society* (Liverpool, 1981), pp. 215–21.

—— '*De amore' in volkssprachlicher Literatur: Untersuchungen zur Andreas-Capellanus-Rezeption in Mittelalter und Renaissance* (Heidelberg, 1985).

KAULBACH, ERNEST, *Imaginative Prophecy in the B-Text of 'Piers Plowman'*, Piers Plowman Studies, 8 (Cambridge, 1993).

KEAN, P. M., *Chaucer and the Making of English Poetry* (Oxford, 1972).

KELLEY, MICHAEL R., 'Antithesis as the Principle of Design in the *Parlement of Foules*', *ChR* 14 (1979), 61–73.

KELLY, DOUGLAS, *Medieval Imagination. Rhetoric and the Poetry of Courtly Love* (Madison, Wis., 1978).

KELLY, H. A., *Chaucer and the Cult of Saint Valentine* (Leiden, 1986).

—— *Ideas and Forms of Tragedy, from Aristotle to the Middle Ages* (Cambridge, 1993).

—— *Love and Marriage in the Age of Chaucer* (Ithaca, NY, and London, 1975).

KELLY-GADOL, JOAN, 'Did Women Have a Renaissance?', in Renate Bridenthal and Claudia Koonz (eds.), *Becoming Visible: Women in European History* (Boston, 1977), pp. 137–64.

KENDRICK, LAURA, 'Chaucer's House of Fame and the French Palais de Justice', *SAC* 6 (1984), 121–33.

—— 'Rhetoric and the Rise of Public Poetry: The Career of Eustache Deschamps', *SP* 80 (1983), 1–13.

KERKHOF, J., *Studies in the Language of Geoffrey Chaucer* (Leiden, 1966).

KERMODE, FRANK, *The Sense of an Ending: Studies in the Theory of Fiction* (Oxford, 1966).

KERRIGAN, JOHN (ed.), *Motives of Woe: Shakespeare and 'Female Complaint'. A Critical Anthology* (Oxford, 1991).

KING, MARGARET L., and RABIL, ALBERT (eds.), *Her Immaculate Hand: Selected Works by and about the Women Humanists of Quattrocento Italy* (Binghampton, NY, 1983).

KINGHORN, A. M. (ed.), *The Middle Scots Poets* (London, 1970).

KISER, LISA J., *Telling Classical Tales: Chaucer and the 'Legend of Good Women'* (Ithaca, NY, and London, 1983).

—— *Truth and Textuality in Chaucer's Poetry* (Hanover, NH, and London, 1991).

KITCHEL, A. T., 'Chaucer and Machaut's *Dit de la Fonteinne Amoureuse*', in C. F. Fiske (ed.), *Vassar Medieval Studies* (New Haven, Conn., 1923), pp. 217–31.

KITTREDGE, G. L., *Chaucer and his Poetry* (Cambridge, Mass., 1915).

—— 'Chaucer and Some of his Friends', *MP* 1 (1903), 1–18.

—— 'Guillaume de Machaut and *The Book of the Duchess*', *PMLA* 30 (1915), 1–24.

KLIBANSKY, R., PANOFSKI, E., and SAXL, F., *Saturn and Melancholy. Studies in the History of Natural Philosophy, Religion and Art* (London, 1964).

KÖKERITZ, H., *A Guide to Chaucer's Pronunciation* (New York, 1961; repr. Toronto, 1978).

KOLODNY, ANNETTE, 'Dancing through the Minefield: Some Observations on the Theory, Practice and Politics of a Feminist Literary Criticism', repr. in Mary Eagleton (ed.), *Feminist Literary Theory: A Reader* (Oxford, 1986), pp. 184–8.

KOLVE, V. A., *Chaucer and the Imagery of Narrative* (London, 1984).

—— 'From Cleopatra to Alceste: An Iconographic Study of *The Legend of Good Women*', in John P. Hermann and John P. Burke (eds.), *Signs and Symbols in Chaucer's Poetry* (University, Ala., 1981), pp. 130–78.

KOONCE, B. G., *Chaucer and the Tradition of Fame* (Princeton, NJ, 1966).

KOOPER, E. S., *Love, Marriage and Salvation in Chucer's 'Book of the Duchess' and 'Parliament of Foules'* (Utrecht, 1985).

KRANS, RUSSELL, *Chaucerian Problems: Especially the Petherton Friendship and the Question of Thomas Chaucer* (1932; repr. New York, 1973).

KRETZMANN, N., KENNY, A., and PINBORG, J. (eds.), *The Cambridge History of Later Medieval Philosophy* (Cambridge, 1982).

KRUEGER, ROBERTA L., *Women Readers and the Ideology of Gender in Old French Verse Romance* (Cambridge, 1993).

KRUGER, STEVEN F., *Dreaming in the Middle Ages* (Cambridge, 1992).

—— 'Passion and Order in Chaucer's *Legend of Good Women*', *ChR* 23 (1989), 219–35.

LAING, M. (ed.), *Middle English Dialectology* (Aberdeen, 1989).

LAMPE, D. E., 'The Truth of a "Vache": The Homely Homily of Chaucer's *Truth*', *Papers in Language and Literature*, 9 (1973), 211–14.

LANGFORS, A., 'Mélanges de Poésie lyrique française, II, Gautier de Coinci', *Romania*, 53 (1927), 474–538; 54 (1930), 33–48.

LANGHANS, V., 'Chaucer's Book of the Leoun', *Anglia*, 52 (1928), 113–22.

LANGLAND, WILLIAM, *The Vision of Piers Plowman: A Complete Edition of the B-Text*, ed. A. V. C. Schmidt (London and New York, 1978).

LAQUEUR, THOMAS, *Making Sex: Body and Gender from the Greeks to Freud* (Cambridge, Mass., 1990).

LARKIN, PHILIP, *The Whitsun Weddings* (London, 1964).

LAWLOR, JOHN, 'The Earlier Poems', in D. S. Brewer (ed.), *Chaucer and Chaucerians* (London, 1966), pp. 39–64.

—— 'The Pattern of Consolation in *The Book of the Duchess*', in R. J. Schoeck and J. Taylor (eds.), *Chaucer Criticism* (Notre Dame, Ind., 1961), ii. 232–60; originally printed in *Speculum*, 31 (1956), 626–48.

LAWTON, DAVID, *Chaucer's Narrators* (Cambridge, 1985).

LEICESTER, H. MARSHALL, *The Disenchanted Self. Representing the Subject in the 'Canterbury Tales'* (Berkeley and Los Angeles, 1990).

—— 'The Harmony of Chaucer's *Parlement*: A Dissonant Voice', *ChR* 9 (1974), 15–34.

LENAGHAN, R. T., 'Chaucer's *Envoy to Scogan*: The Uses of Literary Convention', *ChR* 10 (1975), 46–61.

LEUPIN, ALEXANDRE, 'Alan of Lille's Grammar of Sex', *Diagraphe*, 9 (1975), 119–30.

LEVIATHAN, ALAN, 'The Parody of Pentecost in Chaucer's *Summoner's Tale*', *UTQ* 40 (1970/1), 236–46.

LEVIN, HARRY, *The Myth of the Golden Age in the Renaissance* (Bloomington, Ind., 1969).

LEVY, BERNARD, 'Biblical Parody in the *Summoner's Tale*', *Tennessee Studies in Literature*, 11 (1966), 45–60.

LEWIS, C. S., *The Allegory of Love* (Oxford, 1936).

LEYERLE, JOHN, 'Chaucer's Windy Eagle', *UTQ* 40 (1971), 247–65.

LOCHRIE, KARMA, '*The Book of Margery Kempe*: The Marginal Woman's Quest for Literary Authority', *JMRS* 16/1 (1986), 33–55.

—— *Margery Kempe and Translations of the Flesh* (Philadelphia, 1990).

LOMBARD, PETER, *Sententiae in IV Libris Distinctae*, 3rd edn. (Grottaferrata, 1971–81).

LOMPERIS, LINDA, and STANBURY, SARAH (eds.), *Feminist Approaches to the Body in Medieval Literature* (Philadelphia, 1993).

LORD, MARY LOUISE, 'Dido as an Example of Chastity: The Influence of Example Literature', *Harvard Library Bulletin*, 17 (1969), 22–44, 216–32.

LORRIS, GUILLAUME DE: *see Roman de la Rose*.

LOWES, JOHN L., 'Chaucer and Dante's *Convivio*', *MP* 13 (1915–16), 19–33.

—— 'The Chaucerian "Merciles Beaute" and Three Poems by Deschamps', *MLR* 5 (1910), 33–9.

—— 'The Date of the Envoy to Bukton', *MLN* 27 (1912), 45–8.

—— 'Is Chaucer's *Legend of Good Women* a Travesty?', *JEGP* 8 (1909), 513–69.

—— 'The Loveres Maladye of Hereos', *MP* 11 (1913–14), 491–546.

—— 'The Prologue to the *Legend of Good Women* as Related to the French *Marguerite* Poems, and the *Filostrato*', *PMLA* 19 (1904), 593–683.

LUCAS, ANGELA, *Women in the Middle Ages* (Brighton, 1983).

LUMIANSKY, R. M., 'Chaucer's *Parliament of Foules*: A Philosophical Interpretation', *RES* 29 (1948), 82–9.

LYDGATE, JOHN, *Fall of Princes*, ed. H. Bergen, EETS ES 121 (London, 1924).

—— *Minor Poems*, ed. H. N. MacCracken, EETS ES 107 and OS 192 (London, 1910, 1934, repr. 1961–2).

—— *Poems*, ed. John Norton Smith (Oxford, 1966).

—— *The Siege of Thebes*, ed. A. Erdmann and E. Ekwall, EETS ES 108 and 125 (London, 1911, 1930).

—— *Troy Book*, ed. Henry Bergen, pt. 1, EETS ES 97 (London, 1906).

LYNCH, KATHRYN L., *The High Medieval Dream Vision: Poetry, Philosophy and Literary Form* (Stanford, Calif., 1988).

MACDONELL, DIANE, *Theories of Discourse: An Introduction* (Oxford, 1986).

MACFARLANE, ALAN, *Marriage and Love in England: Modes of Reproduction 1300–1840* (Oxford and New York, 1986).

MACHAUT, GUILLAUME DE, *The Judgment of the King of Navarre*, ed. and trans. R. Barton Palmer (New York and London, 1988).

—— '*Le Jugement du roy de Behaigne*' and '*Remede de Fortune*', ed. James I. Wimsatt and William W. Kibler (Athens, Ga., and London, 1988).

—— *Œuvres*, ed. E. Hoepffner, SATF (Paris, 1808–21).

MACLEAN, IAN, *The Renaissance Notion of Woman* (Cambridge, 1980).

MACROBIUS, *Commentarium in Somnium Scipionis*, trans. William Stahl (New York, 1952: repr. 1990).

—— *Opera*, ed. J. Willis, Bibliotheca scriptorum Graecorum et Romanorum Teubneriana (Leipzig, 1963).

MACROBIUS, *The Saturnalia*, trans. P. V. Davies (New York and London, 1969).

MCCALL, JOHN P., *Chaucer among the Gods: The Poetics of Classical Myth* (University Park, Pa., and London, 1979).

—— 'The Harmony of Chaucer's *Parliament*', *ChR* 5 (1970), 22–31.

MCDONALD, CHARLES O., 'An Interpretation of Chaucer's *Parliament of Foules*', *Speculum*, 30 (1955), 444–57; repr. in *Chaucer Criticism*, ed. R. J. Schoeck and J. Taylor (Notre Dame, Ind., 1961), ii. 275–93.

McFarlane, K. B., *Lancastrian Kings and Lollard Knights* (Oxford, 1972).

—— *The Nobility of Later Medieval England* (Oxford, 1973).

MCGERR, ROSEMARIE P., 'Medieval Conceptions of Literary Closure: Theory and Practice', *Exemplaria*, 1 (1989), 149–79.

MCKINNON, WILLIAM, *Apollo's Blended Dream: The Poetry of Louis MacNeice* (Oxford, 1971).

MCLUHAN, MARSHALL, *The Gutenberg Galaxy* (Toronto, 1962).

MCMILLAN, ANN, 'Men's Weapons, Women's War: The Nine Female Worthies, 1400–1640', *Mediaevalia*, 5 (1979), 113–39.

MCNAMER, SARAH, 'Female Authors, Provincial Setting. The Re-Versing of Courtly Love in the Findern Manuscript', *Viator*, 22 (1991), 279–310.

MALONE, KEMP, *Chapters on Chaucer* (Baltimore, 1951).

MANLY, J. M., 'Chaucer and the Rhetoricians', *PBA* 12 (1926), 95–113.

—— 'What is *The Parlement of Foules?*', *Studien zur englischen Philologie*, 50 (1913), 279–90.

MANN, JILL, *Geoffrey Chaucer*, Harvester Feminist Readings (New York and London, 1991).

MANNING, STEPHEN, 'Chaucer's Good Fair White: Woman and Symbol', *Comparative Literature*, 10 (1958), 97–105.

MANZALAOUI, M., 'Ars Longa, Vita Brevis', *Essays in Criticism*, 12 (1962), 221–4.

MARGOLIS, NADIA, '*Flamma, Furor*, and *Fol'Amors*: Fire and Feminine Madness from the *Aeneid* to the *Roman d'Enéas*', *Romanic Review*, 78 (1987), 131–47.

MARTIN, PRISCILLA, *Chaucer's Women: Nuns, Wives and Amazons* (London, 1990).

*The Marvels of Rome (Mirabilia Urbis Romae)*, ed. Roberto Valentini and Giuseppe Zuchetti, *Codice topografico della Città di Roma*, Fonti per la Storia d'Italiano per il medio evo (Rome, 1940–53), iii. 17–65; trans. (with numerous additions) by F. M. Nichols, 2nd edn. by Eileen Gardiner (New York, 1986).

MASUI, MICHIO, *The Structure of Chaucer's Rime Words* (Tokyo, 1964).

MATHESON, LISTER M., 'Chaucer's Ancestry: Historical and Philological Reassessments', *ChR* 25 (1991), 171–89.

MATHEW, GERVASE, *The Court of Richard II* (London, 1968).

MATTHEW OF VENDÔME, *Ars versificatoria*, trans. Roger P. Parr (Milwaukee, 1981).

MAZZOTTA, GIUSEPPE, *The World at Play in Boccaccio's 'Decameron'* (Princeton, NJ, 1986).

MEALE, CAROL M., '"... alle the bokes that I haue of latyn, englisch, and frensch": Laywomen and their Books in Late-Medieval England', in Meale (ed.), *Women and Literature*, pp. 128–58.

—— 'Legends of Good Women in the European Middle Ages', *Archiv*, 144 (1992), 55–70.

—— (ed.), *Women and Literature in Britain 1150–1500* (Cambridge, 1993).

*Medieval English Lyrics: A Critical Anthology*, ed. R. T. Davies (London, 1963).

MEECH, S. B., 'Chaucer and an Italian Translation of the *Heroides*', *PMLA* 45 (1930), 110–28.

—— 'Chaucer and the *Ovide moralisé*', *PMLA* 33 (1918), 302–25.

—— 'Chaucer and the *Ovide moralisé*: A Further Study', *PMLA* 46 (1931), 182–204.

MEHL, DIETER, 'Chaucer's Audience', *Leeds Studies in English*, NS 10 (1978), 58–73.

—— *Geoffrey Chaucer: An Introduction to his Narrative Poetry* (Cambridge 1986).

—— Review of Rowe, *Through Nature to Eternity*, in *Notes and Queries*, 234/3 (1989), 367.

MERRILL, RODNEY, 'Chaucer's *Broche of Thebes*: The Unity of *The Complaint of Mars* and *The Complaint of Venus*', *Literary Monographs*, 5 (1973), 3–61.

MEUN, JEAN DE: *see Roman de la Rose*.

MIDDLETON, ANNE, 'Chaucer's "New Men" and the Good of Literature in the *Canterbury Tales*', in Edward W. Said (ed.), *Literature and Society*, Selected Papers from the English Institute, NS 3 (Baltimore and London, 1980), pp. 15–56.

—— 'The Idea of Public Poetry in the Reign of Richard II', *Speculum*, 53 (1978), 94–114.

—— 'The *Physician's Tale* and Love's Martyrs: "Ensamples mo than ten" as a method in the *Canterbury Tales*', *ChR* 8 (1973), 9–32.

MIEDZIAN, MYRIAM, *Boys will be Boys. Breaking the Link between Masculinity and Violence* (London, 1992).

MILLER, JACQUELINE T., *Poetic License: Authority and Authorship in Medieval and Renaissance Contexts* (New York and Oxford, 1986).

—— 'The Writing on the Wall: Authority and Authorship in Chaucer's *House of Fame*', *ChR* 17 (1982), 95–115.

MILLER, PAUL, 'John Gower, Satiric Poet', in A. J. Minnis (ed.), *Gower's 'Confessio Amantis': Responses and Reassessments* (Cambridge, 1983), pp. 79–105.

—— 'The Mediaeval Literary Theory of Satire and its Relevance to the Works of Gower, Langland and Chaucer' (Ph.D. thesis, The Queen's University of Belfast, 1982).

MILLER, ROBERT P. 'The Wounded Heart: Courtly Love and the Medieval Antifeminist Tradition', *Women's Studies*, 2 (1974), 335–50.

—— (ed.), *Chaucer: Sources and Backgrounds* (New York, 1977).

MILLWARD, C., *A Biography of the English Language* (Fort Worth, Tex., 1989).

MINNIS, A. J., 'The *Accessus* Extended: Henry of Ghent on the Transmission and Reception of Theology', in Mark D. Jordan and Kent Emery (eds.), *Ad Litteram: Authoritative Texts and their Medieval Readers* (Notre Dame, Ind., and London, 1992), pp. 275–326.

—— '*Amor* and *Auctoritas* in the Self-Commentary of Dante and Francesco da Barberino', *Poetica*, 32 (1990), 25–42.

—— 'A Note on Chaucer and the *Ovide moralisé*', *MÆ* 48 (1979), 254–7.

—— *Chaucer and Pagan Antiquity* (Cambridge, 1982).

—— '*De Vulgari Auctoritate*: Chaucer, Gower, and the Men of Great Authority', in R. F. Yeager (ed.), *Chaucer and Gower: Difference, Mutuality, Exchange* (Victoria, B.C., 1991), pp. 36–74.

—— 'From Medieval to Renaissance? Chaucer's Position on Past Gentility', *PBA* 72 (1986), 205–46.

—— 'Langland's Ymaginatif and Late-Medieval Theories of Imagination', *Comparative Criticism*, 3 (1981), 71–103.

—— 'Late-Medieval Discussions of *Compilatio* and the Role of the *Compilator*', *Beiträge zur Geschichte der deutschen Sprache und Literatur*, 101 (1979), 385–421.

—— 'Late-Medieval Vernacular Literature and Latin Exegetical Traditions', in J. Assmann and B. Gladiglow (eds.), *Text und Kommentar. Archäologie der literarischen Kommunikation IV* (Munich, 1994), pp. 309–29.

—— *Medieval Theory of Authorship: Scholastic Literary Attitudes in the Later Middle Ages*, 2nd edn. (Aldershot, 1988).

—— '"Moral Gower" and Medieval Literary Theory', in Minnis (ed.), *Gower's 'Confessio Amantis'*, pp. 50–78.

—— 'Repainting the Lion: Chaucer's Profeminist Narratives', in Roy P. Eriksen (ed.), *Contexts of Pre-Novel Narrative* (Berlin, 1994), pp. 1–23.

—— 'Theorizing the Rose: Commentary Tradition in the *Querelle de la Rose*', in Piero Boitani and Anna Torti (eds.), *Poetics: Theory and Practice in Medieval English Literature* (Cambridge, 1991), pp. 13–36.

—— (ed.), *Chaucer's 'Boece' and the Medieval Tradition of Boethius* (Cambridge, 1993).

—— (ed.), *Gower's 'Confessio Amantis': Responses and Reassessments* (Cambridge, 1983).

—— and SCOTT, A. B. (eds.), *Medieval Literary Theory and Criticism, c.1100–c.1375: The Commentary Tradition*, rev. edn. (Oxford, 1988).

MOI, TORIL, 'Desire in Language: Andreas Capellanus and the Controversy of Courtly Love', in David Aers (ed.), *Medieval Literature: Criticism, Ideology and History* (Brighton, 1986), pp. 11–33.

—— *Sexual/Textual Politics* (London and New York, 1985).

MONSON, DON A., 'Andreas Capellanus and the Problem of Irony', *Speculum*, 63 (1988), 539–72.

MOORE, ARTHUR K., 'Chaucer's Lost Songs', *JEGP* 48 (1949), 196–208.

—— 'Chaucer's Use of Lyric as an Ornament of Style', *Comparative Literature*, 3 (1951), 32–46.

—— *The Secular Lyric in Middle English* (Lexington, Ky. 1951).

MORGAN, DAVID H. J., *Discovering Men*, Critical Studies on Men and Masculinities, 3 (London, 1992).

MORGAN, GERALD, 'A Defence of Dorigen's Complaint', *MÆ* 46 (1977), 77–97.

MORGAN, J. J., 'Chaucer and the *Bona Matrimonii*', *ChR* 4 (1970), 123–41.

MURPHY, J. J., 'A New Look at Chaucer and the Rhetoricians', *RES* 15 (1964), 1–20.

—— (ed.), *Three Medieval Rhetorical Arts* (Berkeley, Calif., 1971).

MURRAY, H. J. R., *A History of Chess* (Oxford, 1913).

MUSCATINE, CHARLES, *Chaucer and the French Tradition* (Berkeley, Calif., 1957).

—— *Poetry and Crisis in the Age of Chaucer* (Notre Dame, Ind., and London, 1972).

MUSTANOJA, T. F., 'Chaucer's Prosody', in B. Rowland (ed.), *Companion to Chaucer Studies* (Toronto, 1968), pp. 58–84.

*The Myroure of oure Ladye*, ed. J. H. Blunt, EETS ES 19 (London, 1873).

NAUERT, CHARLES G., *Agrippa and the Crisis of Renaissance Thought*, Illinois Studies in the Social Sciences, 4 (Urbana, Ill., 1965).

NEWTON, K. M. (ed.), *Twentieth-Century Literary Theory. A Reader* (Basingstoke and London, 1988).

NICOLE DE MARGIVAL, *Dit de la Panthère d'Amours*, ed. H. A. Todd, SATF (Paris, 1883).

NOLAN, BARBARA, 'The Art of Expropriation: Chaucer's Narrator in *The Book of the Duchess*', in Donald W. Rose (ed.), *New Perspectives in Chaucer Criticism* (Norman, Okla., 1981), pp. 203–22.

—— *Chaucer and the Tradition of the 'Roman Antique'* (Cambridge, 1991).

NOLAN, CHARLES J., Jun., 'Structural Sophistication in "The Complaint unto Pity"', *ChR* 13 (1979), 363–72.

NOONAN, JOHN T., 'Marital Affection in the Canonists', *Studia Gratiana*, 12 (1967), 481–509.

—— 'Power to Choose', *Viator*, 4 (1973), 419–34.

NORTH, JOHN D., *Chaucer's Universe* (Oxford, 1988).

OBERMAN, H. A., and WEISHEIPL, J. A., 'The *Sermo Epinicius* ascribed to Thomas Bradwardine (1346)', *AHDLMA* 25 (1958), 295–329.

O'CONNOR, M. C., *The Art of Dying Well: The Development of the Ars Moriendi* (New York, 1942).

OLSON, GLENDING, 'Deschamps' *Art de dictier* and Chaucer's Literary Environment', *Speculum*, 48 (1973), 714–23.

—— *Literature as Recreation in the Middle Ages* (Ithaca, NY, and London, 1982).

—— 'Making and Poetry in the Age of Chaucer', *Comparative Literature*, 31 (1979), 272–90.

OLSON, PAUL A., 'The *Parliament of Foules*: Aristotle's *Politics* and the Foundations of Human Society', *SAC* 2 (1980), 53–69.

ONG, WALTER, *Orality and Literacy: The Technologizing of the Word* (London, 1982).

ORUCH, JACK B., 'St Valentine, Chaucer, and Spring in February', *Speculum*, 56 (1981), 534–65.

OTIS, BROOKS, 'Ovid and the Augustans', *Transactions and Proceedings of the American Philological Association*, 69 (1938), 188–229.

OTTO, BISHOP OF FREISING, *The Two Cities*, trans. Charles C. Mierow (New York, 1928).

OULMONT, C. (ed.), *Les Débats du Clerc et du Chevalier* (Paris, 1911).

OVERBECK, P. T., 'Chaucer's Good Woman', *ChR* 2 (1967), 75–94.

OVID (Publius Ovidius Naso), *'The Art of Love' and Other Poems*, ed. and trans. J. H. Mozley, 2nd edn. (Cambridge, Mass., and London, 1939).

—— *The Erotic Poems*, trans. Peter Green (Harmondsworth, 1982).

—— *Fasti*, ed. and trans. J. G. Frazer, Loeb Classical Library (London and Cambridge, Mass., 1931).

—— *Heroides*, ed. and trans. Grant Showerman, 2nd edn. by G. P. Goold, *Ovid: 'Heroides' and 'Amores'*, Loeb Classical Library (Cambridge, Mass., 1986).

—— *Metamorphoses*, ed. and trans. F. J. Miller, Loeb Classical Library (London and Cambridge, Mass., 1921).

—— *Metamorphoses*, trans. Mary M. Innes, Loeb Classical Library (Harmondsworth, 1955).

*Ovide moralisé*, ed. C. de Boer (Amsterdam, 1915–38).

*The Owl and the Nightingale*, ed. E. G. Stanley (Manchester and New York, 1960).

*Oxford Latin Dictionary*, ed. P. G. W. Glare (Oxford, 1982).

PACE, GEORGE B., 'The Adorned Initials of Chaucer's *ABC*', *Manuscripta*, 23 (1979), 88–98.

PAGET, VIOLET, *Euphorion, being Studies of the Antique and the Mediaeval in the Renaissance* (London, 1884).

PALMER, J. J. N., 'The Historical Context of the *Book of the Duchess*: A Revision', *ChR* 8 (1974), 253–61.

PANTIN, W. A., 'John of Wales and Medieval Humanism', in *Medieval Studies Presented to Aubrey Gwynn* (Dublin, 1961), pp. 297–319.

PARIS, GASTON, 'Lancelot du Lac: Le Conte de la Charrette', *Romania*, 12 (1883), 459–534.

PARKES, M. B., 'The Influence of the Concepts of *Ordinatio* and *Compilatio* on the Development of the Book', in J. J. G. Alexander and M. T. Gibson (eds.), *Medieval Learning and Literature: Essays Presented to R. W. Hunt* (Oxford, 1976), pp. 115–41.

PARR, JOHNSTONE, 'Chaucer's Semiramis', *ChR* 5 (1970), 57–61.

PARTNER, N. F., 'No Sex, No Gender', *Speculum*, 68 (1993), 419–43.

*Paruus Cato, Magnus Cato*, trans. Benet Burgh, ed. Fumio Kuriyagawa, Seijo English Monographs, 13 (Tokyo, 1974).

PATCH, H. R., *On Rereading Chaucer* (Cambridge, Mass., 1939).

PATTERSON, LEE, *Chaucer and the Subject of History* (London, 1991).

—— (ed.), *Literary Practice and Social Change in Britain, 1380–1530* (Berkeley and Los Angeles, 1990).

PAYER, PIERRE J., *The Bridling of Desire: Views of Sex in the Later Middle Ages* (Toronto and London, 1993).

PAYNE, ROBERT O., *The Key of Remembrance: A Study of Chaucer's Poetics* (New Haven, Conn., 1963).

PEARSALL, DEREK, *The Life of Geoffrey Chaucer* (Oxford and Cambridge, Mass., 1992).

—— 'The *Troilus* Frontispiece and Chaucer's Audience', *YES* 7 (1977), 68–74.

PECK, RUSSELL A., *Chaucer's Lyrics and 'Anelida and Arcite': An Annotated Bibliography 1900–1980*, The Chaucer Bibliographies (Toronto, 1983).

—— 'John Gower and the Book of Daniel', in R. F. Yeager (ed.), *John Gower: Recent Readings* (Kalamazoo, Mich., 1989), pp. 159–87.

—— 'Love, Politics and Plot in the *Parlement of Foules*', *ChR* 24 (1990), 290–305.

—— 'Public Dreams and Private Myths: Perspective in Middle English Literature', *PMLA* 90 (1975), 461–8.

PECOCK, REGINALD, *The Reule of Crysten Religioun*, ed. W. C. Greet, EETS OS 171 (London, 1927).

PEDEN, ALISON M., 'Macrobius and Medieval Dream Literature', *MÆ* 54 (1985), 59–73.

PELEN, M. M., 'Machaut's Court of Love Narratives and Chaucer's *Book of the Duchess*', *ChR* 11 (1976–7), 128–55.

PERCIVAL, FLORENCE M., 'Contextual Studies in Chaucer's *Legend of Good Women*' (Ph.D. diss. University of Sydney, 1988).

PETRARCH, FRANCIS, *Opera* (Basel, 1581).

PHILIPE DE THAON, *Li Cumpoz*, ed. Eduard Mall (Strasbourg, 1873).

PHILLIPPY, PATRICIA A., 'Establishing Authority: Boccaccio's *De Claris Mulieribus* and Christine de Pizan's *Le Livre de la Cité des Dames*', *Romanic Review*, 77 (1986), 167–93.

PHIPPS, T. M., 'Chaucer's Tullius', *MLN* 58 (1943), 108–9.

PIAGET, A., 'La Cour Amoureuse, Dite de Charles VI', *Romania*, 20 (1891), 417–54.

—— *Oton de Grandson, sa vie et ses poésies* (Lausanne, 1941).

—— 'Un manuscrit de la *Cour Amoureuse de Charles VI*', *Romania*, 31 (1902), 597–603.

PLATO, *Dialogues*, trans. B. Jowett, 4th edn. (Oxford, 1953).

POIRION, DANIEL, *Le Poète et le prince* (Paris, 1965).

*Political, Religious and Love Poems*, ed. F. J. Furnivall, EETS OS 15 (London, 1903).

PRATT, R. A., 'Chaucer and the Hand that Fed Him', *Speculum*, 41 (1966), 619–42.

—— 'Chaucer's Use of the *Teseida*', *PMLA* 62 (1947), 598–621.

—— 'Conjectures Regarding Chaucer's Manuscript of the *Teseida*', *SP* 42 (1945), 745–63.

—— 'Some Latin Sources of the Nonnes Preest on Dreams', *Speculum*, 52 (1977), 538–70.

PSEUDO-CATO, *see Disticha Catonis*.

*Querelle de la Rose, see* Baird and Kane, and Hicks, Eric (ed.), *Le Débat sur le 'Roman de la Rose'* (Paris, 1977).

QUILLIGAN, MAUREEN, 'Allegory, Allegoresis, and the Deallegorization of Language: The *Roman de la Rose, De Planctu Naturae*, and the *Parlement of Foules'*, in Bloomfield (ed.), *Allegory, Myth and Symbol*, pp. 164–86.

—— *The Allegory of Female Authority: Christine de Pizan's 'Cité des Dames'* (Ithaca, NY, and London, 1991).

QUIRK, R., *et al.*, *A Comprehensive Grammar of the English Language* (London, 1985).

REAMES, SHERRY L., *The Legenda Aurea: A Reexamination of its Paradoxical History* (Madison, Wis., 1985).

REBHORN, WAYNE A., *Courtly Performances: Masking and Festivity in Castiglione's Book of the Courtier* (Detroit, 1978).

REED, THOMAS L., Jun., 'Chaucer's *Parliament of Foules*: The Debate Tradition and the Aesthetics of Irresolution', *Revue de l'Université d'Ottawa*, 50 (1980), 215–22.

REISS, EDMUND, 'Dusting off the Cobwebs: A Look at Chaucer's Lyrics', *ChR* 1 (1966), 55–65.

RENWICK, W. L., 'Chaucer's Triple Roundel, "Merciles Beaute"', *MLR* 16 (1921), 322–3.

RICE, P., and WAUGH, P., *Modern Literary Theory. A Reader* (London and New York, 1989).

RICHARD DE FOURNIVAL, *Li Bestiaires d'Amours*, ed. C. Segré (Milan, 1957).

—— *Master Richard's Bestiary of Love and Response*, trans. J. Beer (Berkeley and Los Angeles, 1986).

RICHARD OF MIDDLETON, *Quodlibeta . . . quaestiones octuaginta continentia* (Brussels, 1591).

RICHARD OF ST VICTOR, *Benjamin Minor*, in *PL* 196, 1–64.

—— *'The Twelve Patriarchs', 'The Mystical Ark', Book Three of 'The Trinity'*, trans. Grover A. Zinn, Classics of Western Spirituality (New York and London, 1979).

RICKERT, EDITH, 'Thou Vache', *MP* 11 (1914), 209–25.

RIGG, A. G., *A History of Anglo-Latin Literature, 1066–1422* (Cambridge, 1992).

ROBBINS, ROSSELL HOPE, 'Chaucer's "To Rosemounde"', *Studies in the Literary Imagination*, 4 (1971), 73–81.

—— 'Geoffroi Chaucier, Poète Français, Father of English Poetry', *ChR* 13 (1978), 93–115.

—— 'The Lyrics', in Rowland (ed.), *Companion to Chaucer Studies*, pp. 313–31.

—— (ed.), *Historical Poems of the XIVth and XVth Centuries* (New York, 1959).

ROBERTSON, D. W., *A Preface to Chaucer. Studies in Medieval Perspectives* (Princeton, NJ, 1962).

—— 'The Concept of Courtly Love as an Impediment to the Understanding of Medieval Texts', in F. X. Newman (ed.), *The Meaning of Courtly Love* (New York, 1972), pp. 1–18.

—— *Essays in Medieval Culture* (Princeton, NJ, 1980).

—— 'The Historical Setting of the *Book of the Duchess*'; originally published in 1965, repr. in *idem*, *Essays in Medieval Culture*, pp. 235–56.

ROBINSON, JAMES H. (ed. and trans.), *Petrarch. The First Modern Man of Letters* (1898; repr. New York, 1970).

*Roman de la Rose*, ed. Ernest Langlois (Paris, 1914–24); trans. Harry W. Robbins (New York, 1962) and Charles Dahlberg (Princeton, NJ, 1971).

ROONEY, ANNE, *Hunting in Middle English Literature* (Cambridge, 1993).

ROOT, R. K., 'Chaucer's *Legend of Medea*', *PMLA* 24 (1909), 124–53.

—— *The Poetry of Chaucer*, 2nd edn. (Boston, 1922).

ROSENTHAL, C. L., 'A Possible Source of Chaucer's *Book of the Duchess*—Li *Regret de Guillaume* by Jehan de la Mote', *MLN* 48 (1933), 511–14.

ROSSI, ALBERT POGUE, 'The Unfinished Author: Dante's Rhetoric of Authority in *Convivio* and *De Vulgari Eloquentia*', in Jacoff (ed.), *Cambridge Companion to Dante*, pp. 45–66.

ROUSE, R. H., and ROUSE, M. A., *Preachers, Florilegia and Sermons: Studies on the 'Manipulus florum' of Thomas of Ireland* (Toronto, 1979).

ROWE, DONALD W., *Through Nature to Eternity: Chaucer's 'Legend of Good Women'* (Lincoln, Nebr., and London, 1988).

ROWLAND, BERYL, *Blind Beasts* (Kent, Oh., 1971).

—— 'The Chess Problem in Chaucer's *Book of the Duchess*', *Anglia*, 80 (1962), 384–9.

—— (ed.), *Animals with Human Faces* (Knoxville, Tenn., 1973).

—— (ed.), *Companion to Chaucer Studies* (Toronto, New York, and London, 1968).

ROY, BRUNO, 'A la recherche des lecteurs médiévaux de *De amore* d'André le Chapelain', *Revue de l'Université d'Ottawa*, 55 (1985), 45–73.

RUBIN, GAYLE, 'The Traffic in Women: Notes on the "Political Economy" of Sex', in Rayna R. Reiter (ed.), *Toward an Anthropology of Women* (New York and London, 1975), pp. 157–210.

RUDOLF, R., *Ars Moriendi* (Cologne, 1959).

RUGGIERS, PAUL, 'The Unity of Chaucer's *House of Fame*', *SP* 50 (1953), 16–29.

RUUD, JAY, *'Many a Song and Many a Lecherous Lay': Tradition and Individuality in Chaucer's Lyric Poetry*, Garland Studies in Medieval Literature, 6 (New York and London, 1992).

SADLER, LYNN V., 'Chaucer's *Book of the Duchess* and the "Law of Kynde"', *AnM* 11 (1970), 51–64.

SAID, EDWARD, *Culture and Imperialism* (London, 1993).

—— *Orientalism* (New York, 1979).

SALOMON, LOUIS B., *The Devil Take Her: A Study of the Rebellious Lover in English Poetry* (Philadelphia, 1931).

SALTER, ELIZABETH, 'Chaucer and Internationalism', *SAC* 2 (1980), 71–9.

—— 'Chaucer and Medieval English Tradition', in *idem, English Poetry*, pp. 117–40.

—— *Fourteenth-Century English Poetry: Contexts and Readings* (Oxford, 1983).

SAMUEL, IRENE, 'Semiramis in the Middle Ages: The History of a Legend', *Mediaevalia et Humanistica*, 2 (1944), 32–44.

SAMUELS, M. L., 'Chaucerian Final -*e*', *Notes and Queries*, 217 (1972), 445–8; repr. in Samuels and Smith, *English of Chaucer*, pp. 7–12.

—— 'Chaucer's Spelling', in D. Gray and E. Stanley (eds.), *Middle English Studies Presented to Norman Davis* (Oxford, 1983), pp. 17–37; repr. in Samuels and Smith, *English of Chaucer*, pp. 23–37.

—— 'Some Applications of Middle English Dialectology', *English Studies*, 44 (1963), 81–94; repr. with corrections in A. McIntosh, M. L. Samuels, and M. Laing, *Middle English Dialectology* (Aberdeen, 1989), pp. 64–80.

—— and SMITH, J. J., *The English of Chaucer* (Aberdeen, 1988).

SANDVED, A. O., *Introduction to Chaucerian English* (Cambridge, 1985).

—— 'Prolegomena to a Renewed Study of the Rise of Standard English', in Benskin and Samuels (eds.), *So meny people*, pp. 31–42.

SCATTERGOOD, V. J., 'The Authorship of *The Boke of Cupide*', *Anglia*, 82 (1964), 37–49.

—— '*Chaucer a Bukton* and Proverbs', *Nottingham Medieval Studies*, 31 (1987), 98–107.

—— 'Chaucer's Curial Satire: The *Balade de Bon Conseyl*', *Hermathena*, 133 (1982), 29–45.

—— 'The Jongleur, the Copyist, and the Printer: The Tradition of Chaucer's *Wordes unto Adam, His own Scriveyn*', in Keith Busby and Erik Kooper (eds.), *Courtly Literature: Culture and Context* (Amsterdam, 1990), pp. 499–508.

—— 'Literary Culture at the Court of Richard II', in Scattergood and Sherborne (eds.), *English Court Culture*, pp. 29–43.

—— 'Old Age, Love, and Friendship in Chaucer's *Envoy to Scogan*', *Nottingham Medieval Studies*, 35 (1991), 92–101.

—— '*Sir Gawain and the Green Knight* and the Sins of the Flesh', *Traditio*, 37 (1981), 347–71.

—— 'Social and Political Issues in Chaucer: An Approach to *Lak of Steadfastnesse*', *ChR* 21 (1987), 469–75.

—— and SHERBORNE, J. W. (eds.), *English Court Culture in the Later Middle Ages* (London, 1983).

SCHIBANOFF, SUSAN, 'Early Women Writers: In-scribing, or, Reading the Fine Print', *Women's Studies International Forum*, 6/5 (1983), 475–89.

SCHLEICH, G., *Die mittelenglische Umdichtung von Boccaccios 'De claris mulieribus'*, Palaestra, 144 (Leipzig, 1924).

SCHLESS, HOWARD H., 'Chaucer and Dante', in Dorothy Bethurum (ed.), *Critical Approaches to Medieval Literature* (New York, 1960), pp. 134–54.

—— *Chaucer and Dante: A Revaluation* (Norman, Okla., 1984).

SCHMIDT, A. V. C., 'Chaucer and the Golden Age', *Essays in Criticism*, 26 (1976), 99–115.

SCHMITZ, GÖTZ, *The Fall of Women in Early English Narrative Verse* (Cambridge, 1990).

—— 'Gower, Chaucer and the Classics: Back to the Textual Evidence', in R. F. Yeager (ed.), *John Gower: Recent Readings* (Kalamazoo, Mich., 1989), pp. 95–111.

SCHOECK, R. J., 'A Legal Reading of Chaucer's *House of Fame*', *UTQ* 23 (1954), 185–92.

SCHOR, NAOMI, 'Dreaming Dissymmetry: Barthes, Foucault, and Sexual Difference', in Jardine and Smith (eds.), *Men in Feminism*, pp. 98–115.

SCHREIBER, EARL G., 'Venus in Medieval Mythographic Tradition', *JEGP* 74 (1975), 519–35.

SCRAGG, D. G., *A History of English Spelling* (Manchester, 1974).

SEATON, ETHEL, 'Le *Songe Vert*: Its Occasion of Writing and its Author', *MÆ* 19 (1950), 1–16.

*Secretum secretorum. Nine English Versions*, ed. M. A. Manzalaoui, EETS OS 276 (Oxford, 1977).

SEDGWICK, EVE KOSOFSKY, *Between Men: English Literature and Male Homosocial Desire* (New York and Oxford, 1985).

SENECA, LUCIUS ANNAEUS, *Ad Lucilium Epistulae Morales*, ed. and trans. R. M. Gummere, Loeb Classical Library (Cambridge, Mass., 1917).

SEVERS, J. B., 'The Sources of *The Book of the Duchess*', *MS* 25 (1963), 355–62.

SEYMOUR, M. C., 'Chaucer's *Legend of Good Women*: Two Fallacies', *RES* NS 37 (1986), 528–34.

SHANER (née Edwards), MARY, 'A Study of Six Characters in Chaucer's "Legend of Good Women" with reference to Medieval Scholia on Ovid's "Heroides"' (B.Litt. diss., University of Oxford, 1970).

SHANNON, EDGAR F., 'Chaucer's Use of the Octosyllabic Verse in the *Book of the Duchess* and the *House of Fame*', *JEGP* 12 (1913), 277–94.

SHERBORNE, JAMES, 'Aspects of English Court Culture in the Later Fourteenth Century', in Scattergood and Sherborne (eds.), *English Court Culture*, pp. 1–27.

SHOWALTER, ELAINE, 'Towards a Feminist Poetics', in Newton (ed.), *Twentieth-Century Literary Theory*, pp. 268–72.

SIDNEY, SIR PHILIP, *An Apology for Poetry*, ed. Geoffrey Shepherd (London, 1965).

SINFIELD, ALAN, *Faultlines. Cultural Materialism and the Politics of Dissident Reading* (Oxford, 1992).

SINGLETON, C. S., *An Essay on the 'Vita nuova'* (1949; repr. Baltimore, 1977).

*Sir Gawain and the Green Knight*, ed. J. R. R. Tolkien and E. V. Gordon, rev. N. Davis (Oxford, 1967).

SKLUTE, LARRY M., 'The Inconclusive Form of the *Parliament of Fowls*', *ChR* 16 (1981), 119–28.

SKLUTE, LARRY M., *Virture of Necessity: Inconclusiveness and Narrative Form in Chaucer's Poetry* (Columbus, Oh., 1984).

SLEDD, JAMES, 'Dorigen's Complaint', *MP* 45 (1947), 36–45.

SMALLEY, BERYL, *English Friars and Antiquity in the Early Fourteenth Century* (Oxford, 1960).

SMITH, G. GREGORY (ed.), *Elizabethan Critical Essays* (London, 1904).

SMITH, J. J., 'Dialectal Variation in Late Middle English and the Actuation of the Great Vowel Shift', *NM* (forthcoming).

—— 'The Language of the Ellesmere Manuscript', in D. Woodward (ed.), *Essays on the Ellesmere Manuscript of the 'Canterbury Tales'* (San Marino, Calif., 1994).

—— 'The Use of English: Language Contact, Dialect Variation and Written Standardisation during the Middle English Period', in T. W. Machan and C. T. Scott (eds.), *English in its Social Contexts* (Oxford, 1992), pp. 47–68.

SMITH, JOHN NORTON, 'Chaucer's Boethius and *Fortune*', *Reading Medieval Studies*, 2 (1976), 63–76.

—— 'Chaucer's *Etas Prima*', *MÆ* 32 (1963), 117–24.

—— *Geoffrey Chaucer* (London, 1974).

SMYSER, H. M., 'Chaucer's Use of *Gin* and *Do*', *Speculum*, 42 (1967), 68–83.

*Somniale Danielis*, ed. L. T. Martin (Frankfurt, 1981). See also: Fischer, Stephen R.

SPEARING, A. C., *Medieval Dream-Poetry* (Cambridge, 1976).

—— *The Medieval Poet as Voyeur: Secrecy, Watching and Listening in Medieval Love-Narratives* (Cambridge, 1993).

—— *Medieval to Renaissance in English Poetry* (Cambridge, 1985).

—— *Readings in Medieval Poetry* (Cambridge, 1987).

*The Spectator*, ed. Donald F. Bond (Oxford, 1965).

STALLYBRASS, PETER, and WHITE, ALLON, *The Politics and Poetics of Transgression* (London, 1986).

STEADMAN, JOHN M., 'Chaucer's Eagle: A Contemplative Symbol', *PMLA* 75 (1960), 153–9.

—— *Disembodied Laughter: 'Troilus' and the Apotheosis Tradition* (Berkeley and Los Angeles, 1972).

—— '"Goddess Boteler" and "Stellifye" (*The Hous of Fame*, 581, 592)', *Archiv für das Studium der neuren Sprachen*, 197 (1960), 16–18.

STECOPOULOS, E., with UTTI, KARL D., 'Christine de Pizan's *Livre de la Cité des Dames*: The Reconstruction of Myth', in Earl Jeffrey Richards *et al.* (eds.), *Reinterpreting Christine de Pizan* (Athens, Ga., and London, 1992), pp. 48–62.

STEVENS, JOHN, *Music and Poetry in the Early Tudor Court* (London, 1961; repr. Cambridge, 1979).

STEVENSON, K., 'The Endings of Chaucer's *House of Fame*', *English Studies*, 59 (1978), 10–26.

STEVENSON, S. W., 'Chaucer's Ferses Twelve', *ELH* 7 (1940), 215–22.

STILLWELL, GARDINER, 'Convention and Individuality in Chaucer's *Complaint of Mars*', *Philological Quarterly*, 35 (1956), 69–89.

—— 'Unity and Comedy in the *Parliament of Foules*', *JEGP* 49 (1950), 470–95.

STOCK, BRIAN, *The Implications of Literacy* (Princeton, NJ, 1982).

STONE, BRIAN, *Chaucer: A Critical Study* (Harmondsworth, 1978).

STRANG, B. M. H., *A History of English* (London, 1970).

STROHM, PAUL, 'Chaucer's Audience', *Literature and History*, 5 (1977), 26–41.

—— *Hochon's Arrow: The Social Imagination of Fourteenth-Century Texts* (Princeton, NJ, 1992).

—— '*Passioun, Lyf, Miracle, Legende*: Some Generic Terms in Middle English Hagiographical Narrative', *ChR* 9 (1975–6), 62–75, 154–69.

—— 'Politics and Poetics: Usk and Chaucer in the 1380s', in Patterson (ed.), *Literary Practice and Social Change*, pp. 83–112.

—— 'Saving the Appearances: Chaucer's *Purse* and the Fabrication of the Lancastrian Claim', in Hanawalt (ed.), *Chaucer's England*, pp. 21–40; repr. in Strohm, *Hochon's Arrow*, pp. 75–94.

—— *Social Chaucer* (Cambridge, Mass., and London, 1989).

SUTTON, JONATHAN, 'A Reading of Chaucer's *Legend of Good Women*' (diss., University of Indiana, 1979).

SYPHERD, W. O., '*Le Songe Vert* and Chaucer's Dream-Poems', *MLN* 24 (1909), 46–7.

—— *Studies in Chaucer's 'Hous of Fame'*, Chaucer Society, 2nd ser., 39 (London, 1908).

SZITTYA, PENN R., *The Antifraternal Tradition in Medieval Literature* (Princeton, NJ, 1986).

—— 'The Friar as False Apostle: Antifraternal Exegesis and the *Summoner's Tale*', *SP* 71 (1974), 19–46.

TATLOCK, J. S. P., *The Mind and Art of Chaucer* (Syracuse, NY, 1950).

—— 'Notes on Chaucer: Earlier or Minor Poems', *MLN* 29 (1914), 95–101.

TAYLOR, BEVERLY, 'The Medieval Cleopatra', *JMRS* 7 (1977), 249–69.

TAYLOR, JOHN, *English Historical Literature in the Fourteenth Century* (Oxford, 1987).

TAYLOR, J. H. M. (ed.), *Dies Illa. Death in the Middle Ages*, Proceedings of the 1983 Manchester Colloquium (Liverpool, 1984).

TAYLOR, KARLA, *Chaucer Reads 'The Divine Comedy'* (Stanford, Calif., 1989).

TAYLOR, PAUL BEEKMAN, with BORDIER, SOPHIE, 'Chaucer and the Latin Muses', *Traditio*, 47 (1992), 215–32.

TEAGER, F. E., 'Chaucer's Eagle and the Rhetorical Colors', *PMLA* 47 (1932), 410–18.

TESSON, F. GUICHARD, 'Evrart de Conty, auteur de la "Glose des Eschecs amoureux"', *Le Moyen français*, 8–9 (1981), 111–48.

THIÉBAUX, MARCELLE, 'An Unpublished Allegory of the Hunt of Love: *Le dis dou cerf amoreus*', *SP* 62 (1965), 531–45.

THIÉBAUX, MARCELLE, '*Sir Gawain*, the Fox Hunt and Henry of Lancaster', *NM* 71 (1970), 469–79.

—— *The Stag of Love. The Chase in Medieval Literature* (Ithaca, NY, and London, 1974).

THOMSON, DAVID (ed.), *An Edition of the Middle English Grammatical Texts* (New York and London, 1984).

*Three Medieval Views of Women*, trans. and ed. G. K. Fiero, W. Pfeffer, and M. Allain (New Haven, Conn., and London, 1989).

TILLEY, MORRIS PALMER, *A Dictionary of the Proverbs in England in the Sixteenth and Seventeenth Centuries* (Ann Arbor, Mich., 1950).

TISDALE, C. P. R., 'The *House of Fame*: Virgilian Reason and Boethian Wisdom', *Comparative Literature*, 25 (1973), 247–61.

TOLKIEN, J. R. R., 'Chaucer as a Philologist', *Transactions of the Philological Society* (1934), 1–70.

TRAFTON, DAIN A., 'Politics and the Praise of Women: Political Doctrine in the *Courtier*'s Third Book, in Hanning and Rosand (eds.), *Ideal and the Real*, pp. 29–44.

TRISTRAM, PHILIPPA, *Figures of Life and Death in Medieval Literature* (London, 1976).

TUCK, J. A., 'The Baronial Opposition to Richard II, 1377–89' (Ph.D. diss., University of Cambridge, 1966).

—— 'Carthusian Monks and Lollard Knights: Religious Attitudes at the Court of Richard II', *SAC*, *Proceedings*, 1 (1984), 149–61.

—— *Richard II and the English Nobility* (London, 1973).

TURVILLE-PETRE, THORLAC, review of Vale, *Edward III and Chivalry*, and Scattergood and Sherborne (eds.), *English Court Culture*, in *Nottingham Medieval Studies*, 27 (1983), 92–101.

TWYCROSS, M., *the Medieval Anadyomene: A Study in Chaucer's Mythography*, Medium Ævum Monographs, NS 1 (Oxford, 1972).

—— 'The Representation of the Major Classical Divinities in the Works of Chaucer, Gower, Lydgate and Henryson' (B.Litt. diss., University of Oxford, 1961).

VALE, JULIET, *Edward III and Chivalry. Chivalric Society and its Context, 1270–1350* (Woodbridge, 1983).

VANCE, EUGENE, 'The Modernity of the Middle Ages in the Future', *Romanic Review*, 64 (1973), 140–51.

VEESER, H. ARAM (ed.), *The New Historicism* (New York and London, 1988).

VERDUCCI, FLORENCE, *Ovid's Toyshop of the Heart. 'Epistulae Heroidum'* (Princeton, NJ, 1985).

*The Vidas of the Troubadours*, trans. Margarita Egan (New York and London, 1984).

VINCENT OF BEAUVAIS, *Speculum Maius*, Apologia totius operis, ed. A.-D. v. den Bricken, 'Geschichtsbetrachtung bei Vincenz von Beauvais', *Deutsches Archiv für Erforschung des Mittelalters*, 34 (1978), 410–99.

—— *Speculum Quadruplex* (Douai, 1624; repr. Graz, Austria, 1964).

VIRGIL (PUBLIUS VERGILIUS MARO), *Aeneid*, trans. W. F. Jackson Knight (Harmondsworth, 1958).

—— *Aeneid*, ed. and trans. H. R. Fairclough, rev. edn., Loeb Classical Library (Cambridge, Mass., 1934).

VOGT, G. MCGILL, 'Gleanings for the History of a Sentiment: Generositas Virtus, Non Sanguis', *JEGP* 24 (1925), 102–25.

VOSSLER, KARL, *Medieval Culture. An Introduction to Dante and his Times*, trans. W. C. Lawton (London, 1929).

WACK, MARY W., *Lovesickness in the Middle Ages: The 'Viaticum' and its Commentaries* (Philadelphia, 1990).

WAGENKNECHT, EDWARD (ed.), *Chaucer: Modern Essays in Criticism* (New York, 1959).

WALKER, SIMON, *The Lancastrian Affinity, 1361–1399* (Oxford, 1990).

WALKER, SUE SHERIDAN, 'Free Consent and Marriage of Feudal Wards in Medieval England', *Journal of Medieval History*, 8 (1982), 123–34.

WALLACE, DAVID, 'Chaucer and Boccaccio's Early Writings', in Boitani (ed.), *Italian Trecento*, pp. 141–62.

—— *Chaucer and the Early Writings of Boccaccio* (Cambridge, 1985).

—— 'Chaucer's Continental Inheritance', in Boitani and Mann (eds.), *Chaucer Companion*, pp. 19–37.

WALLER, MARGUERITE, 'The Empire's New Clothes: Refashioning the Renaissance', in Fisher and Halley (eds.), *Seeking the Woman*, pp. 160–83.

WALLER, MARTHA S., 'The Conclusion of Chaucer's *Legend of Lucrece*: Robert Holcot and the Great Faith of Women', *Chaucer Newsletter*, 2 (1980), 10–12.

WALTHER, HANS, *Proverbia sententiaeque latinitatis medii aevi: Lateinische Spichwörter und Sentenzen des Mittelalters in alphabetischer Anordnung*, 5 (Göttingen, 1967).

WARNER, MARINA, *Joan of Arc. The Image of Female Heroism* (New York, 1981).

WEISSMAN, HOPE PHYLLIS, 'Antifeminism and Chaucer's Characterization of Women', in George D. Economou (ed.), *Geoffrey Chaucer. A Collection of Original Articles* (New York, 1975), pp. 93–110.

WELTER, J. T., *L'Exemplum dans la littérature religieuse et didactique du moyen âge* (Paris, 1927).

WETHERBEE, WINTHROP, *Platonism and Poetry in the Twelfth Century: The Literary Influence of the School of Chartres* (Princeton, NJ, 1972).

WHITE, HAYDEN, 'New Historicism: A Comment', in Veeser (ed.), *New Historicism*, pp. 293–302.

WHITE, HUGH, *Nature and Salvation in 'Piers Plowman'* (Cambridge, 1988).

WHITING, B. W., and WHITING, H. W., *Proverbs, Sentences, and Proverbial Phrases, From English Writings Mainly before 1500* (Cambridge, Mass., 1968).

WILKINS, NIGEL, *Chaucer Songs* (Cambridge, 1980).

WILKENS, NIGEL, '*En Regardant Vers le Païs de France*: The Ballade and the Rondeau, a Cross-Channel History', in W. M. Ormrod (ed.), *England in the Fourteenth Century: Proceedings of the 1985 Harlaxton Symposium* (Woodbridge, 1986), pp. 298–323.

—— 'Music and Poetry at Court: England and France in the Late Middle Ages', in Scattergood and Sherborne (eds.), *English Court Culture*, pp. 183–204.

—— *Music in the Age of Chaucer* (Cambridge, 1979).

WILLIAMS, SARAH JANE, 'Machaut's Self-Awareness as Author and Producer', in M. P. Cosman and B. Chandler (eds.), *Machaut's World: Science and Art in the Fourteenth Century* (New York, 1978), pp. 189–97.

WIMSATT, JAMES I., *Chaucer and his French Contemporaries* (Toronto, 1991).

—— *Chaucer and the French Love Poets* (Chapel Hill, NC, 1968).

—— *Chaucer and the Poems of 'Ch'* (Cambridge, 1982).

—— 'Guillaume de Machaut and Chaucer's Love Lyrics', *MÆ* 47 (1978), 66–87.

—— 'Machaut's *Lay de confort* and Chaucer's *Book of the Duchess*', in R. H., Robbins (ed.), *Chaucer at Albany* (New York, 1975), pp. 11–26.

—— 'The Apotheosis of Blanche in *The Book of the Duchess*', *JEGP* 66 (1967), 26–44.

—— *The Marguerite Poetry of Guillaume de Machaut* (Chapel Hill, NC, 1970).

—— 'The Sources of Chaucer's "Seys and Alcyone"', *MÆ* 36 (1967), 231–41.

—— 'Vincent and Beauvais and Chaucer's Cleopatra and Croesus', *Speculum*, 12 (1937), 375–81.

WINDEATT, B. A., *Chaucer's Dream Poetry: Sources and Analogues* (Cambridge, 1982).

WIPPEL, J., 'The Condemnations of 1270 and 1277 at Paris', *JMRS* 7 (1977), 169–201.

WOODBRIDGE, LINDA, *Women and the English Renaissance: Literature and the Nature of Womankind, 1540–1620* (Brighton, 1984).

WOODS, M. C. (ed. and trans.), *An Early Commentary on the 'Poetria nova' of Geoffrey of Vinsauf* (New York and London, 1985).

WOOLF, ROSEMARY, *The English Religious Lyric in the Middle Ages* (Oxford, 1968).

WRIGHT, H. G., *Boccaccio in England from Chaucer to Tennyson* (London, 1957).

WYATT, SIR THOMAS, *Collected Poems*, ed. Joost Daalder (London, 1975).

YATES, FRANCES A., *The Art of Memory* (London, 1966; repr. Harmondsworth, 1969).

YOUNG, KARL, 'Chaucer's Appeal to the Platonic Deity', *Speculum*, 19 (1944), 1–13.

ZIOLKOWSKI, JAN, *Alan of Lille's Grammar of Sex: The Meaning of Grammar to a Twelfth-Century Intellectual*, Speculum Anniversary Monographs, 10 (Cambridge, Mass., 1985).

# INDEX

Abelard, Peter 237, 239, 453
Absolon 339
Acart, Jean 121, 123
*accessus* 348, 393
Acciauoli, Andrea, Countess of Altavilla 403–4, 449, 452
Achilles 180, 202
Adam scriveyn 501–2
Adams, Robert 255
Aelred of Rievaulx 58–9
Aeneas 120, 161, 162, 164, 165, 168, 173, 186, 187, 188, 192, 193, 194, 208, 210, 228–39 *passim*, 240–5 *passim*, 336, 381, 386–7, 404, 418–9, 420, 436, 437, 438, 442, 472
Aers, David 71, 78, 239, 255, 260, 270–1, 301–2, 318, 319
Aesop 229, 277–8, 300, 320
affectivity 232–5, 238, 344–6, 347, 363–4, 356–6, 466–78 *passim*
Agamemnon 182
Agatha, St 412, 413, 419
ages of man 142–4, 146, 200, 291, 392, 507–9, 511
Agnes, St 412, 413, 419
Agrippa, Henricus Cornelius 444, 445, 447, 451, 452, 453, 454
Aiken, Pauline 357
Aimeric de Peguilhan 132
Alan of Lille 4, 164, 183, 271, 311, 342, 506; *De planctu naturae* 254, 255, 264, 265, 266, 271–4, 276, 277, 279–80, 287, 304, 307, 309–10
Albertano of Brescia 323
Alceste 38, 39, 51, 57, 326, 327, 328, 331, 335, 341, 348, 351, 357, 378–9, 383, 386, 388, 393, 395, 397–9, 400, 406, 417, 422, 440, 447, 449, 510
Alcibiades 136, 145
Alcyone 51, 70, 79, 84, 91–100 *passim*, 112, 115–16, 120, 122, 130, 138, 147, 160, 193, 265, 266
Alexander the Great 105, 145, 186, 205, 347
Alexander, Jonathan 12
allegory and allegorical interpretation 95–6, 98, 123, 137–41, 145, 192–5, 229, 232–3, 235, 248, 255, 276, 282, 283–5, 286, 288, 292, 297, 313, 320, 331, 332, 333–4, 350, 361, 400–1, 410, 411, 501
Allen, Judson B. 229, 231, 349
Allen, Peter L. 389
Allen, Robert J. 207
Allen, Valerie 502

Althusser, Louis 7, 304
Amazons 303, 431, 443, 470
Ambrose, St. 311, 453
Ames, Ruth M. 325, 421
*Analecta Hymnica* 502
Anderson, David 289
Anderson, W. S. 345, 347
Andreas Capellanus: *De amore* 56–7, 67, 72, 295, 305–6, 315, 316–17, 319, 343–4, 358, 361, 436
Anelida 469, 470, 471–2, 473
Anne (Dido's sister) 235
Anne of Bohemia, Queen of England 17, 18, 25, 29, 30, 32, 76, 168, 172, 257, 260, 275, 291, 296, 312, 327–9, 343, 383, 399, 421, 447, 449
Antony 337, 354–5, 356, 357, 416, 418, 435, 436
Apollo 51, 91, 92, 173, 174, 177–81 *passim*, 182, 250, 465
Apollonius of Tyre 313
Aquinas, St Thomas 41–2, 48, 54, 200
Ariadne 208, 224, 348, 352, 359, 361, 362, 381, 416, 417, 418, 436, 437
Arion, Philippe 160
Aristotle 39–40, 42, 44, 52–3, 54, 136, 143, 215, 216, 228, 229, 278, 279, 384, 442, 472
Armitage-Smith, Sydney 76, 78
Arnold, Matthew 165
Arnulf of Orléans 320
*ars moriendi* 160
*artes poetriae* 85, 86, 181, 190, 338
Ascanius 210
astrology and astronomy 28, 50, 55, 149–50, 170–1, 183, 201, 257, 261, 267–8, 272–3, 279, 280, 474–5
Attridge, D. 526
Auden, W. H. 66, 116
Augustine, St. 41, 45, 49, 176, 200, 268, 389; *Confessions* 233–4, 237, 238; *De civitate Dei* 200, 210–11, 212, 274, 403, 405, 406, 409, 414, 415, 416; *De Genesi ad Litteram* 40–1, 54
Augustus, Roman Emperor 119, 123, 237, 239, 359
authority 7, 43, 45, 166, 170, 200, 218–19, 220, 221–2, 227–51 *passim*, 271, 280, 301, 341, 360, 379, 381, 395, 412, 479, 495, 497, 499; men of authority 38, 167, 169–70, 214, 225, 226, 236–7, 239–40, 251, 270, 318
Averroës 216
*Awntyrs off Arthure* 118